B2C Arbitration:
Consumer Protection in Arbitration

Alexander J. Bělohlávek

JURIS

Questions About This Publication

For assistance with shipments, billing or other customer service matters,
please call our Customer Services Department at:
1-631-350-2100

To obtain a copy of this book, call our Sales Department:
1-631-351-5430
Fax: 1-631-351-5712

Toll Free Order Line:
1-800-887-4064 (United States & Canada)
See our web page about this book:
www.arbitrationlaw.com

Printed in the United States of America.
ISBN 978-1-937518-12-7

Juris Net, LLC
71 New Street
Huntington, New York 11743
USA
www.arbitrationlaw.com

The first edition of this book was published in the Czech language in 2012
by C.H. Beck, Prague, (Czech Republic).

"Arbitration is a justice.

Justice is not a business."

Prof. Dr. Hab. Jerzy Rajski
Sopot (Poland), 29 September 2011
Forum of New Ideas

CONTENTS

Contents

Contents

Contents

GRATIARUM – ACKNOWLEDGMENTS

The author would like to express his gratitude to his colleagues for their effective help and support in drafting this publication, especially (without limitation) Prof. Pierre Lalive and Matthias Scherer (both of Geneva, Switzerland), Mgr. Petr Kalla, JUDr. Filip Černý, Mgr. Lukáš Havel, Mgr. Tereza Profeldová, Mgr. Tomáš Řezníček, Mgr. Eliška Šrotová, and Mariana Jungwirthová.

He would also like to thank PhDr. Světluška Sobolová, PaeDr. Milena Frydrychová, Jan Halfar, František Halfar, Naděžda Motyčková, Lenka Němečková, and dipl. Ing. Karel Nohava for their linguistic and technical assistance in drafting this book.

ABOUT THE AUTHOR

Prof. Dr. et Mgr., Ing. (oec) Alexander J. Bělohlávek, Dr. h. c. studied at the Law Faculty, Jan Evangelista Purkyně University in Brno [today Masaryk University in Brno], and graduated from the Faculty of Law, Charles University in Prague. He earned his first degree (Civil Law I.) at the Law Faculty, Charles University in Prague (CZ) in early December 1993. In 1991–1996 he lectured at the Law Faculty, Charles University in Prague (CZ), the Institute of Copyright, Industrial Property Rights, and Competition Law and subsequently at the Department of Commercial and Economic Law – Private International Law Division at the same university. He has been a member of the Department of Law, Faculty of Economics, VŠB – Technical University of Ostrava (CZ) since 1992. He is a member of the department council for postgraduate doctoral studies at the Faculty of Economics, VŠB – Technical University (CZ), at the Faculty of Law, Masaryk University in Brno (CZ). He was awarded the title of *Associate Professor* (*Docent*) in 1996. He has been a commercial lawyer since 1993; in 1994 he was admitted to the bar in Prague, with a licensed branch of his law firm in the *U.S.* (New Jersey). On 1 April 2001 the author was pronounced a *full professor*. In 2002 he was also awarded the honorary title of *doctor honoris causa* at Kiev University in Ukraine, Faculty of Law and Economics.

Apart from his legal practice and lecturing, the author has held many offices and has become a member of several major foreign institutions, associations, and commissions. Since 2011 the author has served as President of the *WJA - The World Jurist Association* (established in Washington, D. C. / *USA*).

He has worked as an arbitrator with: the Arbitration Court attached to the Economic Chamber of the Czech Republic and the Agricultural Chamber of the Czech Republic for domestic and international disputes, the International Arbitration Court with the Austrian Economic Chamber, the International Arbitration Court with the Ukrainian Chamber of Commerce and Industry in Kiev, as well as with arbitral institutions in Almaty (Kazakhstan), Chisinau (Moldova), Moscow (Russia), and Vilnius (Lithuania); he resolves disputes under the auspices of the *ICC* (International Chamber of Commerce) International Court of Arbitration in Paris and under the UNCITRAL rules. He is also a member of: the *ICC* (International Chamber of Commerce) International Court of Arbitration, the Swiss Arbitration Association (*ASA*), the Austrian Arbitration Association, the German Institution of Arbitration (*DIS*), the London Court of International Arbitration (LCIA), the International Chamber of Commerce (*ICC*). In addition, he is also Chairman of the Commission on Arbitration – *ICC* (National Committee Czech Republic), a member of ASIL (American Society of International Law), an Associated Member of the Law Society of England and Wales, a member of the ILA (International Law Association, *Headquarters branch*, London), and a member of the IBA (International Bar Association) as well as of other international organizations.

He has also authored almost 40 monographs (in Czech, German, English, Russian, Ukrainian, Polish, and Romanian), more than 320 academic articles especially on private international law, procedural law, commercial and financial law, as well as certain topics concerning public international law and international finance. In the Czech Republic, the author is a member of the editorial board of: *Časopis pro právní vědu a praxi* [Legal Science and Practice Magazine] published by the Faculty of Law, Masaryk University in Brno, Bulletin advokacie [the Advocacy Bulletin] published by the Czech Bar Association in Prague, and *The Lawyer Quarterly* published by the Institute of State and Law of the Academy of Sciences of the Czech Republic (AV ČR, v.v.i.); he is also one of the principal editors of *Česká ročenka mezinárodního práva*® (*The Czech Yearbook of International Law*®) and Česká (& Středoevropská) ročenka pro rozhodčí řízení® (The Czech /& Central European / Yearbook of Arbitration®) published in New York and the Rome Case Law periodical (*Rome Convention – Rome I and II Regulation Case Law*). In addition, he is a member of the editorial board of the Law and Technology periodical published in Washington, D. C., a member of both the academic and publishing councils of the institute for international law, private international law, EU law, and constitutional law, *Lex Lata*, in the Hague (the Netherlands), etc. The author regularly lectures in the Czech Republic and abroad (his lectures abroad were held, for instance, in Germany, the Netherlands, Austria, Switzerland, Poland, Ukraine, Ireland, South Africa, Qatar, India, Mauritius, Australia, the U.S. and other countries).

INDEX COMPENDIORUM – LIST OF ABBREVIATIONS

AA [GBR-ENG]	Arbitration Act (England and Wales) 1996.
AAA [USA]	American Arbitration Association.[1]
ABGB [AUT]	Allgemeines Bürgerliches Gesetzbuch (General Civil Code) – Act No. 946/1811, as subsequently amended.
ADR	Alternative Dispute Resolution (other than through courts).
ADR Directive	Proposal for a Directive of the European Parliament and of the Council on Alternative Dispute Resolution for Consumer Disputes and Amending Regulation (EC) No. 2006/2004 and Directive 2009/22/EC, 29 November 2011.[2]
AFA [USA]	Arbitration Fairness Act.
AG	Advocate-General.
AGBG [DEU]	Act on General Business Terms and Conditions.[3]
Amendment to the ArbAct [CZE]	Act amending Act No. 216/1994 Coll., on Arbitration and Enforcement of Arbitral Awards, as subsequently amended, and other related legislation.
APR(C)	Annual percentage rate of charge (in consumer credit agreements).
ArbAct [CZE]	Act No. 216/1994 Coll., on Arbitration and Enforcement of Arbitral Awards, as subsequently amended.[4]
ArbAct [SVK]	Act No. 244/2002 Coll. [SVK], on Arbitration, as subsequently amended.
ArbAut [AUT]	Austrian Arbitration Association.
Arb. Int.	Arbitration International. Periodical.
ASA	Swiss Arbitration Association (*Association suisse de l'arbitrage / Schweizerische Vereinigung für Schiedsgerichtsbarkeit / Associazione svizzera per l'arbitrato*).

---

[1] See also http://www.adr.org.
[2] Available online at: http://ec.europa.eu/consumers/redress_cons/docs/directive_adr_en.pdf [last access 5 December 2011].
[3] The Act was repealed in connection with the last major reform of the law of obligations, and a significant number of the provisions were incorporated directly into the BGB [DEU].
[4] See also "Amendment to the ArbAct [CZE]".

ASA bull.	Bulletin of the ASA.
AUT	Austria (Republic of Austria).
BB [DEU]	Betriebs-Berater. Periodical.
BEL	Belgium (Kingdom of Belgium).
BGB [DEU]	Federal Law Gazette [DEU] (*Bundesgesetzblatt*). Official authority for the publication of laws.
BGR	Bulgaria (Republic of Bulgaria).
BOE [ESP]	State Gazette [ESP] (*Boletín Oficial del Estado*).[5] Official authority for the publication of laws and selected announcements.
Brussels I Regulation	[EU] Council Regulation (EC) No. 44/2001 of 22 December 2000 on jurisdiction and the recognition and enforcement of judgments in civil and commercial matters.[6]
Bull. [FRA]	Bulletin officiel des arrêts de la Cour de cassation / Title in translation – Official Law Reports of the [French] Court of Cassation's [Supreme Court's] Decisions. Periodical with the case law of the Supreme Court (*Cour de cassation* [FRA]).
BW	[NDL] Civil Code.
Cass. [FRA]	Cour d' cassation. Supreme Court of Cassation.[7]
CC [CZE]	Act No. 40/1964 Coll., as subsequently amended, Civil Code.[8]
CC [SVK]	Act No. 40/1964 Coll., as subsequently amended, Civil Code.
CCP [CZE]	Act No. 99/1963 Coll., as subsequently amended, Code of Civil Procedure.
CCP [SVK]	Act No. 99/1963 Coll., as subsequently amended, Code of Civil Procedure.
Charter [CZE]	Charter of Rights and Freedoms of the Czech Republic. Resolution of the Presidium of the Czech National Council No. 2/1993 of 16 December 1992 on the promulgation of the Charter of Fundamental

---

[5] See also http://www.boe.es.
[6] OJ 2001, L 12, p. 1.
[7] All cases mentioned in this book were adjudicated in the Civil Chamber.
[8] To be replaced with a new Code – see the NCC. The new Civil Code is supposed to replace, inter alia, the current CC [CZE].

	Rights and Freedoms as a part of the constitutional order of the Czech Republic, as amended by the Constitutional Act of the Czech Republic No. 162/1998 Coll.
CHE	Switzerland (Swiss Confederation).
CISG	United Nations Convention on Contracts for the International Sale of Goods. Promulgated as an Annex to the Communication of the Federal Ministry of Foreign Affairs No. 160/1991 Coll.
CoCiv [FRA]	Civil Code [FRA] (*Code Civil*) of 1804, as subsequently amended.
CoE	Council of Europe.
Coll.	Collection of Laws [CZE].
Coll. [SVK]	Collection of Laws.
Coll. Int. Tr.	Collection of International Treaties [CZE].
ComC [CZE]	Act No. 513/1991 Coll., as subsequently amended, Commercial Code.[9]
Commission	European Commission.
Community	European Community.
ConCourt CR [CZE]	Constitutional Court of the Czech Republic.
Council	European Council.
CUP	Cambridge University Press.
CYP	Cyprus (Republic of Cyprus).
CZE	Czech Republic.
CZK [CZE]	Czech crown (unit of currency).[10]
DEU	Germany (Federal Republic of Germany).
Directive	Council Directive 93/13/EEC of 5 April 1993 on unfair terms in consumer contracts.[11]
DNK	Denmark (Kingdom of Denmark).
DNotZ [DEU]	Deutsche NotarZeitschrift. Periodical.

[9] To be replaced with a new Code – see the NCC. The new Civil Code is supposed to replace, inter alia, the current ComC [CZE].
[10] "CZK" is an abbreviation according to the ISO-4217 standard.
[11] OJ L 95 of 21 April 1993, pp. 29–34. CELEX: 31993L0013.

DVBl. [DEU]	Deutsches Verwaltungsblatt / Title in translation – German State Administration Magazine. German-language periodical.
Dz.U. [POL]	Law Gazette [POL] (*Dzienik Ustaw*). Official authority for the publication of Polish laws.
EC	European Community.
ECHR	European Convention on Human Rights.
ECHR Rep.	Report of the European Commission of Human Rights.
ECJ	Court of Justice of the European Union (formerly the Court of Justice of the European Communities). Unless the context suggests otherwise, the ECJ shall comprise the Court of Justice, the Tribunal, and the Civil Service Tribunal. Where the case law of the ECJ is cited, the ECJ shall be interpreted as comprising the Court of Justice (Court).
ECtHR	European Court of Human Rights.
EEA	European Economic Area.
EGBGB [DEU]	Einführungsgesetz zum Bürgerlichen Gesetzbuch. Statute to the German Civil Code.[12]
EP	European Parliament.
EP Resolution	[EU] European Parliament resolution of 8 June 2011 on policy options for progress towards a European Contract Law for consumers and businesses (2011/2013 (INI)).[13]
ESP	Spain (Kingdom of Spain).
EST	Estonia (Republic of Estonia).
EU	European Union.
EuR [DEU]	Europarecht. Periodical.[14]
European Convention	European Convention on International Commercial Arbitration, prepared in Geneva on 21 April 1961.

[12] Introductory statute to the Civil Code, as amended by Decree of 21 September 1994 (published in: BGBl. [DEU] 1994 I p. 2494 et seq. and BGBl. [DEU] 1997 I p. 1061 et seq.), last amended by Act of 10 December 2008 (published in: BGBl. [DEU] I p. 2401 et seq.
[13] Available online at the EP website at: http://www.europarl.europa.eu/sides/getDoc.do?pubRef=-//EP//TEXT+TA+P7-TA-2011-0262+0+DOC+XML+V0//CS&language=EN [last access 19 August 2011].
[14] ISSN: 0531-2485.

EuZW	Europäische Zeitschrift für wirtschatsrecht. Periodical.[15]
EWS [DEU]	Europäisches Wirtschafts- und Steuerrecht / Title in translation – European Economic and Tax Law. German-language periodical. Issued since 1990.
FAA [USA]	Federal Arbitration Act.
FIN	Finland (Republic of Finland).
FRA	France (French Republic).
Gaz. Pal. [FRA]	Gazette du Palais.
GBR	United Kingdom of Great Britain and Northern Ireland.
GBR-ENG	United Kingdom of Great Britain and Northern Ireland, here: England and Wales (especially as the law of England and Wales).
GRE	Greece (Hellenic Republic).
Green Paper	Green Paper from the *Commission* of 1 July 2010 on policy options for progress towards a European Contract Law for consumers and businesses.[16]
HC in [...] [CZE]	High Court. In the given case either: (i) the High Court in Prague, or (ii) the High Court in Olomouc.
HGB [DEU]	Commercial Code (*Handelsgesetzbuch*).[17]
HUN	Hungary.
IA	Ignotus auctor – unknown author.
IBLJ/RDAI [FRA]	Revue de droit des affaires internationales.
ICC	International Chamber of Commerce.
ICC Court	ICC International Court of Arbitration.
ICC Rules	Rules of the International Court of Arbitration (International Chamber of Commerce).
ILA	International Law Association.
ILM	International Law Materials. Periodical.

---

[15] ISSN: 0937-7204.
[16] CELEX 52010DC0348.
[17] Commercial Code, as amended and promulgated (with all amendments incorporated) in the Federal Law Gazette, Part III, Ref. No. 4100-I, and as amended by Article 2(39) of Act of 22 December 2011 (BGBl. I S. 3044).

ILO	International Law Office. Website (for non-periodical publication of academic work on various current topics, according to individual areas of interest).
ILR	International Law Reports.
Int. Arb.	International Arbitration. Periodical.
IPrax	Praxis des internationalen Privat- und Verfahrens-Rechts. Periodical.[18]
IPRG [CHE]	Swiss Act on Private International Law of 18 December 1987.[19]
ITA	Italy (Italian Republic).
ITA Arb.	ITA Arbitration Report.[20]
J. Int. Arb.	See *JIA*.
JIA	Journal of International Arbitration.
JORF [FRA]	Journal Officiel de la République Française. Official authority for the publication of laws and selected announcements.
K.c. [POL]	Civil Code (*Kodeks cywilny*).
K.p.c. [POL]	Kodeks Postępowania Cywilnego / Polish Code of Civil Procedure. Act of 17 November 1964.
KSchG [AUT]	Consumer Protection Act (*Konsumentenschutzgesetz*).[21]
LCIA	London Court of International Arbitration.
LCIA Rules	Rules of the London Court of International Arbitration.
LG [DEU]	District Court (*Landesgericht*).[22]
LTU	Lithuania (Republic of Lithuania).
LVA	Latvia (Republic of Latvia).
MLT	Malta (Republic of Malta).
MU	Masaryk University, Brno, Czech Republic.
NCC [CZE]	Proposal for a new Civil Code.[23]

[18] ISSN: 0720-6585.
[19] Published in: RS 291.
[20] Wolters Kluwer Law & Business, website; http://www.kluwerlaw.com; Alford, R., Maleh, S. (eds.).
[21] Published in: BGBl. [AUT] No. 140/1979 (as subsequently amended).
[22] Plus, the place (venue) of the LG.

NDL   Netherlands (Kingdom of the Netherlands).

New York Convention   Convention on the Recognition and Enforcement of Foreign Arbitral Awards, the New York Convention.[24]

NJW   Neue Juristische Wochenschrift. Periodical.[25]

NJW-RR [DEU]   Neue Juristische Wochenschrift – Rechtsprechungsreport. Periodical.

NOR   Norway (Kingdom of Norway).

NZG [DEU]   Neue Zeitschrift für Gesellschaftsrecht.

ODR   Online Dispute Resolution.

ODR Regulation   [EU] Proposal for a Regulation of the European Parliament and of the Council on online dispute resolution for consumer disputes, 29 November 2011.[26]

OFT [GBR]   Office of Fair Trading. Office for the protection of competition in the United Kingdom.

OGH [AUT]   Oberstes Gerichtshof / Supreme Court of the Republic of Austria with its seat in Vienna.

OJ   Official Journal (EU) Official Journal of the European Union / European Union periodical.[27]

OLG [DEU]   Higher Regional Court (*Oberlandesgericht*).[28]

OUP   Oxford University Press.

PECL   Principles of European Contract Law.

PEICL   Principles of European Insurance Contract Law.

Period.   Periodical.

---

[23] Situation as of the closing date of this manuscript: The proposal was passed by the Chamber of Deputies of the Parliament of the Czech Republic on 9 November 2011, and subsequently by the Senate of the Parliament of the Czech Republic on 25 January 2012. The anticipated effective date is 1 January 2014.

[24] See Ministry of Foreign Affairs Decree No. 74/1959 Coll., http://www.uncitral.org/uncitral/en/uncitral_texts/arbitration/NYConvention.html.

[25] ISSN: 0341-1915.

[26] Available online at: http://ec.europa.eu/consumers/redress_cons/docs/odr_regulation_en.pdf [last access 5 December 2011].

[27] The versions published in the Official Journal, including the pre-1998 versions, are also available (as .tif, .pdf and/or .html files, as applicable) and can be found using the search engines available at the website. Official EU publication authority.

[28] Plus, the place (venue) of the OLG.

POL	Poland (Republic of Poland).
PRT	Portugal (Portuguese Republic).
Recommendation	[EU] Commission (EC) Recommendation No. 98/257/EC.
Regulation 1346/2000	[EU] Council Regulation (EC) No. 1346/2000 of 29 May 2000 on insolvency proceedings.
Rev. arb. [FRA]	Revue de l'arbitrage. Periodical.
Rome Convention	Rome Convention on the Law Applicable to Contractual Obligations, opened for signature in Rome on 19 June 1980, EEC Document No. 80/934/EEC.
Rome I Regulation	[EU] Regulation (EC) No. 593/2008 of the European Parliament and of the Council of 17 June 2008 on the law applicable to contractual obligations.
Rome II Regulation	[EU] Regulation (EC) No. 864/2007 of the European Parliament and of the Council of 11 January 2009 on the law applicable to non-contractual obligations.
RUS	Russia (Russian Federation).
SBA	Communication from the Commission to the Council, the European Parliament, the European Economic and Social Committee and the Committee of the Regions, "Think Small First", A "Small Business Act" for Europe, COM(2008) 394 final (25 June 2008).[29]
SC CR [CZE]	Supreme Court of the Czech Republic.
SchiedsVZ [DEU]	Zeitschrift für Schiedsverfahren (German Arbitration Journal).
SN [POL]	Supreme Court (Sąd Najwyższy).
StGB [AUT]	Strafgesetzbuch / Criminal Code. Federal Act of 23 January 1974.
StGB [DEU]	Strafgesetzbuch / Criminal Code of the Federal Republic of Germany. Federal Act of 15 May 1871, as subsequently amended.
SVK	Slovakia (Slovak Republic).

---

[29] Communication from the Commission to the Council, the European Parliament, the European Economic and Social Committee, and the Committee of the Regions – "Think Small First". COM/2008/0394.

SVN	Slovenia (Republic of Slovenia).
SWE	Sweden (Kingdom of Sweden).
SZ	Entscheidungen des österreichischen Obersten Gerichtshofes in Zivil- und Justizverwaltungssachen / Title in translation – Decisions of the Austrian Supreme Court in Civil and Judicial Administration Matters. Authority for the publication of the decisions rendered by the court. German-language publication.
TEC	Treaties establishing the European Community. Also referred to as "Treaty" in some original documents quoted in this book.
TFEU	Treaty on the Functioning of the European Union.[30]
TILA [USA]	Truth in Lending Act (1968).
UKR	Ukraine.
UNCITRAL	United Nations Commission on International Trade Law.
UNCITRAL Model Law	UNCITRAL Model Law on International Commercial Arbitration of 21 June 1985.
UNCITRAL Rules	UNCITRAL Arbitration Rules (1976).
UNIDROIT	International Institute for the Unification of Private Law.
U.S.	United States of America.
USA	United States of America.
USA-CAL	USA, California.
Vand. J. Transnat'l L.	Vanderbilt Journal of Transnational Law.
VIAC	Vienna International Arbitral Centre, International Arbitral Centre of the Austrian Federal Economic Chamber.
WM [DEU]	Wertpapier-Mitteilungen. Periodical.
ZPO [AUT][31]	Code of Civil Procedure (*Zivilprozessordnung* [AUT]).

---

[30] See OJ C 115, 9 May 2008, p. 1 et seq., or the version incorporating the amendments, corrections, protocols, and all annexes – see OJ C 83, 30 March 2010.

ZPO [DEU][32]   Code of Civil Procedure (*Zivilprozessordnung* [DEU]).

ZvglRWiss [DEU]   Zeitschrift für vergleichende Rechtswissenschaft. Periodical.[33]

---

[31] Arbitration rules in German and translated into English, Czech (the author of the translation is the author of this book), and Russian are available at the website of VIAC [AUT] at: www.wko.at/arbitration.

[32] RGBl. Nr. 113/1895 as subsequently amended, here the version applicable since 1 July 2006.

[33] ISSN: 0044-3638.

I. Introduction

I.1. Subject of this publication

1.   This book analyzes the interaction between the power exercised by public authorities (primarily in court proceedings) and the power of arbitration in the resolution of consumer disputes. It also focuses on the different arbitration regimes in consumer cases and analyzes certain issues related to their harmonization and the importance of their unification. It is necessary to emphasize that there are fundamental, albeit only apparently latent differences between the individual national laws.

2.   The primary concentration is on the generalization of the country specific or regional models and, thus conversely, the importance of national laws, or even the rules adopted by certain permanent or other arbitral institutions was suppressed. No differences were made between domestic and international arbitration.

3.   The mutual relationship between arbitration and consumer protection laws is also discussed with respect to the conflict between the perspective of the courts and the perspective of arbitrators and arbitration.

I.2. Different national approaches and experience in the resolution of consumer disputes

4.   Arbitration is usually classified as one of several alternative dispute resolution methods (ADR),[1] i.e. as different from litigation in courts. The other alternatives, apart from arbitration, may include mediation or mediation connected with arbitration, expert proceedings,[2] assisted conciliation, and procedures which could be labeled as arbitration but lack some of its features, such as voluntariness, the right to appoint an arbitrator, etc. Some of these procedures include online dispute resolution similar to mediation or government-promoted consumer dispute resolution regimes, such as those in Spain [ESP] or Portugal [PRT]. The United Kingdom [GBR] has adopted a specific consumer

---

[1] Several passages will analyze the difference between common law and civil law; common law (as opposed to continental schools) classifies arbitration as one of the ADR methods. Conversely, civil law is closer to the jurisdictional (but mostly hybrid) approach, and it therefore separates arbitration from ADR as a special method of finding the law and resolving disputes.

[2] Cf. *Bělohlávek, A. et Hótová, R.* Znalci v mezinárodním prostředí (v soudním řízení civilním a trestním, v rozhodčím řízení a v investičních sporech). [Title in translation: Experts in the International Environment (in Civil and Criminal Court Proceedings, Arbitration and Investment Disputes)]. Prague: C. H. Beck, 2011 (also available in Polish – Warsaw: C. H. Beck, 2011, in Russian – Kiev: Taxon, 2011 and in Romanian – Bucharest: C. H. Beck, 2012).

dispute resolution system according to which all disputes from consumer credits are obligatorily resolved by the Financial Ombudsman in compliance with the Consumer Credit Act [GBR] (1974).[3] The formal aspects of these proceedings are significantly different from arbitration. The outcomes of these procedures (however authoritative the decision) cannot be enforced in international relations even under the *New York Convention*.

I.3. Positive and negative aspects of litigation and arbitration in consumer disputes, fair trial, and efficiency of dispute resolution

5.   Arbitration is not a cure-all and is definitely not a method suitable for the resolution of every dispute. It has its proponents as well as opponents. Indeed, one would be hard put to claim that a particular type (class) of disputes is *a priori* fit to be resolved in arbitration, rather than through litigation, or vice versa. The same could be said of consumer disputes (disputes arising from consumer contracts). That consumers deserve some specific protection in cases where they are forced to enter into a particular contract and have no other option but to accept the conditions stipulated by the other party (the professional) is fairly indisputable. But neither can one principally claim that the resolution of these disputes in court would be more suitable than arbitration or any other alternative dispute resolution (ADR) method. The individual states, as well as the entire international community, realize with an ever increasing awareness that litigation is often unable to offer effective legal protection. Take as an example Germany [DEU]. The ECtHR has repeatedly held that the unreasonable length and procedural complexity of judicial proceedings have breached the right to a fair trial in a number of countries. Germany was the usual culprit, but on more than one occasion, similar complaints have been filed against other countries, too. Indeed, it was a series of complaints against Germany [DEU] which actually resulted in a resolution delivered by the Grand Chamber of the ECtHR—in which *Sümerli v. Germany* [DEU][4] was used as a model

---

[3] Consumer Credit Act (1974), as amended in 2006 – Consumer Credit Act (2006). The current version of the Consumer Credit Act (1974) is available at: http://www.legislation.gov.uk/ukpga/1974/39/contents#485933 [last access 14 January 2012]. Amendments implemented in 2006 are also analyzed at the website of the Office of Fair Trading at: http://www.oft.gov.uk/about-the-oft/legal-powers/legal/cca/CCA2006/ [last access 14 January 2012].

[4] Decision of the ECtHR, Case No. 75.529/01 of 8 June 2006 (*Sümerli v. Germany*). Indeed, German constitutional law fully adheres to the principle of the right to a speedy trial before an independent and impartial tribunal; this right is even explicitly incorporated in the constitutions of some of the federal states (for instance, Article 51(4) of the Brandenburg Constitution [DEU], etc.). Cf. the Council of Europe, the Venice Commission. Can Excessive Length of Proceedings be Remedied? (Science and Technique of Democracy), 2007, p. 164. This publication issued by the CoE contains a detailed analysis with national reports filed by the Member States of the ECHR. It is easy to see that most countries suffer from excessive length of proceedings, procedural obstacles, and other problems

case—and which even ruled that contemporary German procedural law does not safeguard effective instruments[5] for the protection of rights enshrined in the *European Convention* on Human Rights (ECHR). *Sümerli v. Germany* [DEU] (and other similar complaints filed with the ECtHR against various states) is notorious in many countries for the relationship between the factual and legal findings, but also for the procedural complications and delays, the repeated remanding of cases for a new trial in a lower court, delays in the drafting of expert appraisals and their discussion in court—all of which contributed to the fact that a basically simple dispute took many years to settle. The promotion of arbitration and alternative dispute resolution (ADR)[6] is therefore a logical solution.[7] On the other hand, as a method for finding the law and resolving disputes it entails many risks. Despite the existing role of the court (support and supervision), the decisions are rendered by private-law entities, i.e. outside the absolute control exercised by public authorities. The potential risks are therefore obvious. However, the just protection of the weaker parties in contractual relationships is not the only criterion; it is also in the *public interest* that such protection be effective, efficient, and expeditious. The present work focuses, inter alia, on the mutual contradictions [between these public and the private interests] from the perspective of consumer protection and arbitration. Naturally, it would be impossible to analyze their every aspect, but the attempt is here made to define and examine some of the most important.

---

with the enforcement of rights in courts. These excesses are often repeated and extreme; what is even worse, these problems occur more and more frequently and the proceedings in developed countries with traditional democracy and a mature judiciary and infrastructure are taking longer and longer.

[5] As concerns this issue, see an interesting article by *Hájek, O.* Winning your case is good, effective remedy is better! Recognition of Foreign Judgments and Arbitral Awards in the Czech Republic. Common Law Review, 2008, No. 8.

[6] It is necessary to emphasize that the conceptual approach to ADR differs depending on the individual legal culture. While most jurisdictions based on common law principles classify arbitration among alternative dispute resolution methods (ADR), most civil law countries perceive arbitration as separate from ADR. This highlights the fact that arbitration is an alternative to litigation, as concerns both the nature, and especially the outcome of the proceedings. Arbitral awards are mostly equaled with court judgments. This is not to say that common law would not often arrive at the same conclusion. But the doctrinal reasons behind the solution are different. The reason is that the common law regime (depending on the individual country) is based on the presumption that even the judiciary (the exercise of judicial authority by courts as public authorities) has a contractual basis, similar to the exercise of any other public authority. Conversely, most civil law countries are more inclined towards the assumption that the power exercised by public authorities is derived from state sovereignty as an immanent component of the "state," both under international law and from the perspective of national (domestic) law.

[7] *Bělohlávek, A.* Arbitration from the Perspective of the Right to Legal Protection and the Right to Court Proceedings (the Right to have One's Case Dealt with by a Court): Significance of Autonomy and Scope of the Right to a Fair Trial. In: *Bělohlávek, A. et Rozehnalová, N.* CYArb - Czech (& Central European) Yearbook of Arbitration: The Relationship between Constitutional Values, Human Rights and Arbitration, Huntington (New York): JurisNet, 2011, Vol. I, pp. 47–70, here p. 47–49.

6. It is also necessary to point out that arbitration and ADR have developed over the years and differ significantly from arbitration and ADR as it was known until the late 1980s. In the era of the politically bipolar, the militarily and economically strictly-divided global system beset by political problems, the main purpose of arbitration and ADR was to overcome problems with the recognition and enforcement of foreign decisions. Logically, political reasons prevented the states from eagerly recognizing the decisions rendered by courts in other countries for that would de facto imply acceptance of a foreign state power within a state's own territory. However, this phenomenon is being gradually eliminated, and arbitration (or ADR) has developed to fulfill a completely different function. It has begun replacing the power exercised by state authorities, wherever they may be, and for many reasons, including systemic dysfunctionality or ineffectiveness. Naturally, the emergence of this new function should not imply that any method of dispute resolution employed by state authorities would necessarily be less effective or that arbitration would always be more effective. In commercial disputes, especially complicated international disputes or with respect to certain classes of disputes, arbitration in many countries has become a very specific and specialized instrument, which may often entail increasingly extreme costs. All in all, arbitration is definitely not the conceptual panacea, and it is necessary to carefully consider whether the replacement of litigation by other methods is suitable and effective.

I.4. Importance of consumer protection against the background of the dispute resolution mechanism

7. Despite the basically undisputed importance of and the need for special consumer protection (whether provided by special laws, typically in Europe, or on the basis of general legal principles and the application of general contract law, as in the United States), the degree of such protection can be considered somewhat problematic. Whereas the weaker party does deserve special protection under the regime that assumes the equal status of the contracting parties, the increase in this protection often results in the potential abuse of this standard by the consumer; and thus naturally consumer abuse of those rights should void any right to their protection. Consumers typically have proven themselves prone to exercise their right to rescind or cancel contracts by the statutory deadline, despite having actively made use, all the while, of the goods that fulfilled the purpose of the purchase (this is specifically the case with seasonal goods). Moreover, even a consumer should be required to exhibit a reasonable and usual degree of responsibility for his or her legal (juridical) acts, including the conclusion of contracts and an assumption of obligations. For instance, the experience in the Czech Republic [CZE] demonstrates that the overwhelming majority of consumer disputes are lawsuits filed by professionals against consumers

for the consumers' unwillingness or inability to meet their financial obligations. Only a negligible number of cases are initiated by consumers' petitions against professionals for defective performance (defective goods or services). Fairly slow litigation has proven unable to afford sufficient protection to professionals who often become hostage to consumers. Consequently, should the consumer fail to properly estimate his or her financial capabilities and fail to meet his or her financial obligations as a result thereof, then arguably, any special protection afforded to the consumer, despite the consumer's receipt of all information at the conclusion of the contract, should constitute, as a matter of course, an abuse of right. In these cases, the absence of expeditious and efficient dispute resolution and the denial of an otherwise available and speedy means of finding the law with a guarantee of a fair trial both contradict the principles of the rule of law. Indeed, they go further and result in the law approving the abuse of rights by consumers who can now rely on the fact that litigation can very well last several years. On the other hand, it is hardly imaginable that litigation could waive some of the traditional and essential elements of civil procedure. As a result, arbitration is in many states one of the suitable options for resolving this situation, provided that the agreement on arbitration is beyond any doubt the outcome of the parties' genuine expression of their will.

8.   In addition, it is unfortunate that the special consumer protection and especially its amplification (for instance, in the EU) focuses only on the elimination of the consequences and not on the root causes.[8] The reason for this situation is that the special protection concerns the invalidity of certain terms in consumer contracts. But no rules (let alone any mandatory rules) apply, for example, to banks which launch huge and well-designed advertising campaigns before the summer holidays or usually before Christmas holidays accompanied with slogans such as, *"You can afford it with us."* No state authority has imposed: any obligation on the providers of consumer credit[9] to present a specific warning to consumers that they might not be able to meet their obligations, nor any obligation that they perform a detailed analysis of the creditworthiness of the consumer to whom the loan or credit is being extended, nor any obligation to refuse to provide the consumer

---

[8] Under EU law, Directive 2008/48/EC, which repeals the preceding rules incorporated in Directive 87/102/EEC regarding consumer credits, stipulates in Article 20 that *"Member States shall ensure that creditors are supervised by a body or authority independent from financial institutions, or regulated."* But the scope of such supervision is defined in very loose terms. As concerns unfair practices adopted by the providers of consumer credits in advertising, supervision in the individual states is exercised only very randomly.

[9] Concerning the issue of consumer credits and arbitration, see *Nový, Z.* Spotřebitelské úvěry a rozhodčí řízení. [Title in translation: Consumer Credits and Arbitration]. Jurisprudence, 2010, No. 8, p. 22 et seq. et al.

credit unless clearly defined criteria are met. Such preventative mechanisms would probably help remove the underlying causes of disputes, thus eliminating the eventual need for resolving their consequences. Resolution is often brought about in a rather forceful manner that necessarily interferes with the principles of protection of civil-law autonomy. Nonetheless, even those consumers who assume very risky obligations are afforded a high degree of protection. These circumstances should also be considered by the legislators before they lay down consumer protection rules, which are frequently very rigorous ones, as well as by the forum when assessing the proportion of the application of special consumer protection over and against the protection of contractual autonomy. It is virtually indisputable that a consumer, when confronted with the prospect of an expected and often *luxurious* performance, will enter into any contract irrespective of the information provided to him or her by the professional, and irrespective of the form in which such information is given (in a separate / separately signed documents, with certain terms visually highlighted, etc.). Moreover, the volume of information which must be provided to the consumer often exceeds the quantity that an *ordinary consumer* is able to process or, in particular, to realize what the actual basis of that information may be. Any solution which only increases the volume of mandatory information provided to the consumer or any solution consisting in a crusade against any and all methods of an alternative exercise of rights by the professional is more of a political excuse which – as already noted above – does not solve the underlying causes, but merely addresses in a somewhat populist manner, a vain resolution of the consequences. Such a solution, unfortunately and by no means accidentally, resembles the solutions often adopted by past authorities, who advanced popular but useless measures, such as a general postponement of the due date of debts in crises (for instance, the postponement of the maturity of bills of exchange and promissory notes during the Paris Commune or, even earlier in history, the pogroms targeted at groups of persons extending credit accruing at higher rates of interest). The attempts to maximize measures at a stage which requires the exercise of rights in an authoritative manner arising from a contract concluded by the consumer are, just as unsuitable as an attempt to have a naughty child *finally touch the hot oven* and experience the painful consequences of his or her thoughtlessness. Indeed, such an approach could also be applied to the broad area of other civil-law relationships. It is not unlike such well-known axioms as: *The bankers most skilled in the evaluation of credit risks are those businessmen who have experienced their own bankruptcy at least once*, etc. Again, it should be recalled that arbitration is not being touted here as the *cure-all* as it is generally suitable only for a rather small class of civil disputes. But arbitration *can* be one of the methods which facilitate a proportional satisfaction of protected interests even in consumer disputes, but only on the condition

– that the arbitration in such cases guarantees high quality and safeguards its inherent principles which cannot be waived in any contradictory proceedings. The maximum level of arbitration expertise which, thanks to the quality of the decision-making in the merits and the possibility of influencing the composition of the *arbitral forum* by the parties, would represent the counter pole of the procedural deviations of such proceedings (arbitration) from litigation.

I.5. Risk of abuse of the special protection by the consumer

9.   To return to the initial premise – that a certain regime of protection for the *weaker party* is indispensable – is a fact borne out by experience; but so too is it a fact that this *weaker party* is prone to abuse these standards. National legal systems should find protective mechanisms to prevent such unfair practices by these consumers. In the EU Member States, the individual countries should employ their procedural autonomy to the fullest extent.

10. Many examples could be easily provided of how consumers have managed to find ways to abuse the special protection afforded them. Under the special regime introduced by the EU, it is by no means an exception today that the consumer intentionally avails himself or herself of the defense of invalidity of the arbitration clause and reserves the right of such arguments during the proceedings on annulment of the arbitral award, should his or her arguments in the merits fail. The fact that this or any other abuse of the respective protection is not the purpose of EU law (or of the national regimes outside the EU) is hardly ever mentioned, let alone discussed in any cogent manner. Nonetheless, the national regimes (perhaps within their procedural autonomy) must find a way to prevent such situations.[10] Moreover, even the ECJ ruled in the *Asturcom* case that **certain limitations comply with *Community law (EU law)*.** In other words, while the courts may substitute for the consumer's omission to plead unfairness of the arbitration clause in arbitration, they may do so only to a certain extent. They may not substitute for an entirely passive consumer, such as a consumer who fails to take part in any manner in the arbitral proceedings and who, on top of that, fails to sue for annulment of the arbitral award.[11] This list must be perceived only as an indicative list, mainly if the specification of the rules and, especially, all the procedural rules are within the autonomous

---

[10] For a more specific analysis and an idea of the possible concept of such measures, see below in a detailed annotation of ECJ judgment C-168/05 of 26 October 2006 in *Elisa María Mostaza Claro* v. *Centro Móvil Milenium SL.*

[11] ECJ Judgment, Case C-40/08 of 6 October 2009 in *Asturcom Telecomunicaciones SL* v. *Cristina Rodríguez Nogueira* (*Asturcom*), published in: ECR 2009, p. I–09579. CELEX 62008CA0040. A separate detailed annotation of this ECJ judgment is provided elsewhere in this publication.

legislative competence of the EU Member States. Nonetheless, this conclusion alone cannot serve as the basis for the concept of a balanced procedural status (considering all the specifics of a consumer contractual relationship). But the complete passivity of the consumer in arbitration is not the only problem; the issue also encompasses situations in which the consumer intentionally does not plead the invalidity of the arbitration clause. Furthermore, an omission to claim the clause in arbitration and a failure to sue for annulment of the arbitral award constitute, procedurally, two different categories.

II. Terminological and Conceptual Delimitation of Consumer Disputes with respect to Arbitration

II.1. Consumer protection laws

11.   The word "consumer" is not uniformly defined. A consumer is generally described as a person who is economically active other than in connection with his or her profession. Persons trading with consumers who are doing so in performance of their profession, are designated as "professionals" (businesspeople).

12.   The concept of "consumer legislation" has no uniform definition either. It differs with each individual jurisdiction. For the purposes of this publication, consumer legislation shall be interpreted in the broader sense, i.e. as rules (including interpretation in practice and case law) regulating the relationship between consumer and professional.

13.   Consumer disputes at the level of the EU (formerly the EC) have already been briefly defined as follows: "*The concept of what constitutes a consumer will determine the concept of what constitutes a consumer dispute [...].*"[1] This is the reason why "arbitration in consumer matters/disputes" or, if you wish, "*consumer arbitration*" has no uniform definition. This book focuses, inter alia, on the analysis of the fundamental hypotheses of consumer legislation and its juncture with arbitration. Consequently, arbitration in consumer matters will in most cases include any arbitration (for an attempted definition see below) between a consumer and a person other than a consumer (business-to-consumer arbitration). In those jurisdictions studied herein, arbitration between two consumers (consumer-to-consumer arbitration) is specifically excluded from the scope of consumer legislation. These proceedings would be conducted between two natural persons and as such would be governed by the applicable rules incorporated in the given legal system. Specific sources of consumer protection laws (specific provisions), whether national or supranational (especially EU laws), will be analyzed later in the following parts of this publication.

II.2. Arbitration

14.   Arbitration is usually perceived as a means of resolving disputes where the given dispute is submitted to one or more private individuals – arbitrators – for the purpose of its authoritative resolution. Arbitration has the following characteristic features: **(i)** vestment of jurisdiction over

---

[1] Opinion of the Economic and Social Committee on the Green Paper on Access of Consumers to Justice and the Settlement of Consumer Disputes in the Single Market (94/C 295/01), OJ C 295, 22/10/1994, Ps. 0001.

the dispute in an arbitral tribunal to the exclusion of courts, **(ii)** independence and impartiality of arbitrators,[2] and **(iii)** power (authority) of the arbitral tribunal (arbitral institution) to render a final decision on the merits of the dispute (arbitral award).

15. Judges or state employees can also serve as arbitrators in certain countries. Arbitration is confidential to the extent these individuals do not exercise their public offices. These private arbitral tribunals composed of one or more "judges" acting outside their public offices must be distinguished from the jurisdiction and the acts of courts as public-law institutions which can possess the status of "arbitral tribunals" but in reality are state authorities. The procedure is usually an obligatory arbitration or mediation (conciliation).

16. The arbitral tribunal commonly consists of one or more (usually three) arbitrators. The parties may agree on the application of procedural rules issued and approved by specialized arbitral institutions (*permanent arbitral institutions*), such as the ICC Rules of Arbitration (ICC Rules), the Swiss Rules of International Arbitration of the Swiss Chambers of Commerce, or the Rules adopted by the London Court of International Arbitration (LCIA, LCIA Rules). Arbitration which is not governed by the rules of any particular institution is usually referred to as *ad hoc* arbitration. For the purposes of these non-institutional arbitrations, the United Nations Commission on International Trade Law (UNCITRAL) has drawn up arbitration rules for parties who do not wish to conduct institutional arbitral proceedings (UNCITRAL Rules).

17. Some countries distinguish between domestic and international arbitration. The definitions of a domestic and international dispute often differ, to some extent, from one jurisdiction to another. Domestic arbitration is very often subject to more rigorous supervision by the state than international arbitration. Domestic arbitration also offers more remedial measures whereby arbitral awards can be challenged.

II.3. *Public policy* and *public interest*

II.3.1. Inconsistent application of two materially different categories

18. The terms *public policy (ordre public)* and *public interest* are very frequently used categories. But their application and their substance are not clearly defined and, unfortunately, even the authorities which

---

[2] Regarding the material difference as concerns the protected interests vis-à-vis the independence of arbitrators in consumer disputes compared to arbitration in commercial matters, as illustrated by transactions in the capital market, see *Wiebecke, M.* ... und es gibt sie doch – Schiedsgerichtsbarkeit in Finanz- und Kapitalmarkttransaktionen. SchiedsVZ, 2008, pp. 34–39, see especially p. 37.

employ them in their reasoning either do not distinguish between them at all or often use them rather inconsistently. At the international (supranational) level, one of the causes of this frequent inconsistent application of these terms is the different scope of *public policy* (*ordre public*) under *civil law* versus *common law*. Whereas *civil law* perceives [the principles of] *ordre public* as the pillars of the legal system and social order which should represent a long-term constant on which especially (though not exclusively) the constitutional and legal order rest, *public policy* under *common law* is a significantly broader category. The reason is that *public policy* in *common law* is also an expression of a certain degree of the prevalent (current) political opinion of the social priorities in the given period. *Public interest* and *public policy* in *common law* are therefore much closer to each other than under *civil law*. In any case, however, these two categories are not identical in any legal system, and it is necessary to distinguish between them. This distinction is all the more important in international law, in private international law, as well as in any *supranational normative systems*, such as EU law. At the same time, it is necessary to ensure that the linguistic similarity, which especially in multilingual / international environments can easily lead to errors in terminology, does not result in an inaccurate expression. Inaccurate language is in many cases the key causative factor which leads to references being made to *public policy* when the reality of the case [*only*] concerns *public interest*, and when conversely, [mere] *public interest* is, as a result of the inaccurate linguistic expression, promoted to a qualitatively higher category, for example, in being referred to as *public policy* (*ordre public*). Hence, it should come as no surprise that the erroneous use of these terms is very frequent, especially in EU law, as most general and many individual normative acts are translated into all the official languages of the European Union. It is important to realize that many proceedings are conducted in languages which differ from the language in which the resultant decisions are subsequently interpreted (at least as concerns their interpretation in literature and references to them in later rulings). Diligent differentiation between *public policy* and *public interest* is therefore an issue of special importance.

II.3.2. *Public policy* (*ordre public*)

(a) *Domestic and international public policy (ordre public)* in legal cultures

19.   Although, according to the continental (*civil law*) approach, *ordre public* is certainly subject to changes, its delimitation is narrower and more stable. Consequently, it comes as no surprise that especially after World War II, when the wording of the multilateral international treaties from said period shifted from customary use of French towards either

bilingual (English and French), or exclusively English transcriptions, the English term *"public policy"* is found accompanied with the alternative expression (usually in *brackets*) *"ordre public"* in order to emphasize that all High Contracting Parties interpret the concept in the same manner. But this international practice does not *eo ipso* mean that it is one and the same concept. The concept of *public policy* (*ordre public*) is usually used in the context of a *reservation regarding public policy*, i.e. as a correction to the undesired effect of an international treaty for a particular High Contracting Party which would be unacceptable for the given state in a particular case. But the reservation regarding *public policy* is intended to serve as an exception to the general rule, i.e. an expression of an exceptional situation which even an international treaty is not able to duly take into account. The fact that the terms, i.e. *public policy* and *ordre public*, both appear in international treaties as synonyms does not of itself signify that their essence is the same. On the one hand, the joint use of both terms (*public policy* and *ordre public*) in international treaties represents a *technical* expression which is supposed to express the common purpose of the said concept. On the other hand, it is a manifestation of the desire to find a compromise in applicable practice. This *compromise* is usually reflected in the concept of *international public policy* which is supposed to both augment the exceptionality of the reservation regarding *public policy* (*ordre public*) in international practice and persuade the parties to apply the respective *corrective* of the effects of the treaty only to those cases (effects of treaties) which can be considered an isolated *excess* even compared to the standard in international practice. However, some international treaties explicitly refer to *public policy* (in terms of the reservation regarding *public policy*) of the country in which the particular effect of the treaty is to occur. This is identical to the practice employed by a number of national conflict-of-laws rules; others do not use such an adjective. Thus, it appears that wherever the international treaty does not contain any limitation of *public policy*, one must presume that the treaty refers to *international public policy*.[3]

20. It is possible that the varying approach of the legal cultures to the differences between *public policy* and *ordre public*, which even sophisticated international practice does not always realize in its everyday usage, as well as the domination (in a positive sense) of English in international practice after World War II, have both contributed to the fact that lawyers are often unaware of the true essence of both expressions. Thanks to its broad scope, *public policy* as perceived in the Anglo-American legal tradition is often significantly intertwined with the concept of *public interest*, although the two concepts are not and

---

[3] But this interpretation does not enjoy universal acceptance, and there are opinions claiming that it is always a reservation in terms of *national public policy*. The author does not share this opinion.

must not be regarded as one and the same, not even under *common law*. Conversely, *ordre public* must be clearly distinguished from *public interest*, indicating that these terms are two fundamentally different concepts. Unfortunately, due to the universal and global importance of English in modern international practice, all of these terms and categories are frequently referred to as *public policy*. We can witness such an approach in a number of important acts at the international level. It is a conceptual mistake, and, in consequence thereof, we can see an explosion of arguments referring to *public policy* and to the application of the reservation regarding *public policy*, although it ought to be something very exceptional. Conversely, the international community (whether in the global or in the regional sense) should be interested in minimizing the consequences of *public policy* (*ordre public*), primarily (though not exclusively) the consequences which the application of the *reservation regarding public policy* entails.

(b) *Public policy* in arbitration

21. *Public policy* (or *ordre public* in the continental *civil law* approach) is an important concept in international arbitration and often touches on consumer protection laws. It is significantly reflected in many stages of the arbitral proceedings, beginning with the validity (or enforceability, i.e. effectiveness) of the arbitration agreement and ending with the enforceability of the arbitral award rendered in the proceedings conducted on the basis of this arbitration agreement. Most countries allow annulment of arbitral awards which are contrary to *public policy*; such arbitral awards are not enforceable (cannot be subject to forced enforcement and/or could be dismissed upon motion). According to Article V Par. 2(b) of the [New York] Convention on the Recognition and Enforcement of Foreign Arbitral Awards ("*New York Convention*"), the recognition and enforcement of an award may be refused if the recognition or enforcement of the award in any country would be contrary to the *public policy* of that country. However, "*public policy*" is not defined. Consequently, each state has its own definition of its "*public policy.*" The general rule is that this expression refers to the *international public policy*[4] of the host country and that the scope of the *international public policy* is narrower than domestic (national) public policy.[5]

---

[4] See *Mantilla-Serrano, F.* Towards a Transnational Procedural Public Policy. In: *Degos, L., Pinsolle, P. et Schläpfer, A. -V. (ed.)* Towards a Uniform International Arbitration Law, New York: Juris Publishing Inc., 2005, p. 186.

[5] For instance, the absence of reasons for which an award could be set aside in domestic arbitral proceedings was held not sufficient to set aside an international award: French Act No. 81–500 of 12 May 1981, Sections 1471 and 1495.

22.   In its "Interim Report on Public Policy as a Bar to Enforcement of International Arbitral Awards," the Committee on International Arbitration of the International Law Association (ILA) concluded that apart from purely *domestic (national) public policy*, there exists a narrower category of *international public policy* limited only to breaches of really fundamental principles of the respective country's legal system. Also, the Swiss Federal Tribunal (or the Swiss Supreme Court) in *W* v. *F. et V.* (1994) was in favor of taking into account a *"universal conception of public policy, under which an award will be incompatible with public policy if it is contrary to the fundamental moral or legal principles recognized in all civilized countries."*

II.3.3.   *Public interest*

(a)   National basis for the historical delimitation of *public interest*

23.   The concept of *public interest* has developed mainly at the national level. It is the interest of the entire group, transcending the interest of an individual or a mere fraction of the group. Although *public interest* belongs to the category of important concepts, our valid and applicable laws, logically, lack any definition thereof. It is referred to as a vague concept. However, it is not a vague legal concept; it is an abstract institution (abstract category) which is endowed with clearly defined content only in connection with a particular legal rule, primarily in connection with the purpose of a particular rule. *Public interest* is interpreted as a contradiction to private interests[6] from which it differs by benefiting a group of persons which is never specifically delimited. It can be an interest of the entire society (environment), a local interest (construction of local infrastructure), or a group interest (protection of the weaker contracting party, for instance, consumers). A democratic legal system forbids, however, speaking of a state interest to which citizens must be subjected. Nevertheless, not even *public interest* may prevail over the interest protected by the category of *public policy (ordre public)*, i.e. over categories which represent fundamental values (pillars) of the constitutional and social order[7] in those situations where *public interest* is not identical to the interest protected by *public policy*.

---

[6] See *Mates, P. et Barton, M.* Public versus Private Interest – Can the Boundaries Be Legally Defined? In: *Bělohlávek, A. et Rozehnalová, N.* (eds.): CYIL – Czech Yearbook of International Law, Huntington (New York, USA): Juris Publishing Inc., 2011, Vol. II, pp. 171–190.

[7] See the Judgment of the Constitutional Court of the Czech Republic, Case No. IV ÚS 557/09 of 18 August 2009 (referring to a preceding Judgment of the Constitutional Court of the Czech Republic, Case No. IV. ÚS 412/04 of 7 December 2005) (cit.): "[... in proceedings on the limitation of legal capacity] *the legislator treated persons as "objects" of the law; the underlying opinion was that a strong public interest was involved in these matters. Nonetheless, this public interest cannot always and completely, i.e. automatically, outweigh the interest of the individual and deprive him or her of the above-mentioned fundamental rights."*

24. The fact that our valid and applicable laws do not define *public interest* poses problems especially in those cases where state power, referring to the existence of an alleged *public interest*, interferes in the sphere of the private rights of natural and legal persons. This especially appears in connection with measures targeted at expropriation, both direct[8] and indirect.[9] Expropriation is not principally unlawful, provided fundamental standards are observed which are strongly supported not only by national legal systems, but also by a number of international treaties.[10] But the ever increasing scope and reach of *public interest* is alarming, in particular the attempts to violate what should remain inviolable, i.e. the protection of fundamental values covered by *public policy*. This category obviously also includes the protection of ownership and certain rights which form part of ownership. Violation of these fundamental imperatives, components of *public policy*, is often justified by *public interest*. The attempt to shift the limits of *public interest* through its ever widening semantic scope must give great cause for concern.[11]

---

[8] Direct expropriation is rather rare these days. Nonetheless, international practice has documented cases in which direct expropriation was held legal in connection with a specific *public interest*; these precedents generally accepted the opinion that the policy of nationalization meets the requirements of legality. See the following rulings:

➤ *Amoco International Finance Corp.* v. *Iran*, Award, published in: US-Iran Claim Tribunal Reports ("US-Iran CTR," 1987, Vol. 15, marg. (145) through (146) (The implementation of basic economic and political objectives of the new regime was a valid *public interest*. Financial considerations are not sufficient grounds for depriving such conduct of its legitimacy unless they are the sole motive.), the cited Award in: para. (146);

➤ *The American Independent Oil Co.* v. *The Government of the State of Kuwait*, Award of 24 May 1982, published in: ILM, 1982, Vol. 21, p. 976 et seq., Paras. (85) through (86), as well as para. (109) (National policy directed at the takeover of full title to the oil resources of the country was held a valid *public interest*, and the stabilization clause did not eliminate the state's right to nationalize.), the cited Award in para. (95);

➤ *Libyan American Oil Co.* v. *The Government of the Libyan Arab Republic*, Award of 12 April 1977, 62 ILR, 1982, Vol. 62, p. 141 et seq., para. (194) (This award concluded that the principle of public benefit is not a precondition for the legality of expropriation.).

[9] In general cf. *Heiskanen, V.* The Doctrine of Indirect Expropriation in Light of the Practice of the Iran-United States Claims Tribunal. Journal of World Investment & Trade, 2007, Vol. 8, No. 2, p. 215 et seq.; *Heiskanen, V.* The Contribution of the Iran-United States Claims Tribunal to the Development of the Doctrine of Indirect Expropriation. International Law FORUM du droit international, 2003, Vol. 5, No. 3, p. 176 et seq.

[10] Cf. *Bělohlávek, A. J.* Hmotněprávní standardy ochrany přímých zahraničních investic. [Title in translation: Substantive Standards of the Protection of Direct Foreign Investment]. Právník, 2012, Vol. 151, No. 1, pp. 1–51 et al.

[11] For a typical example, see the statement regarding excessive profits (luxuryprofits) in the Award ICSID, Case No. ARB/07/22 of 23 September 2010 (*AES Summit Generation Limited AES-Tisza Erömü Kft* v. *The Republic of Hungary*), para. (10.3.34). This paragraph, although rather as an obiter dictum, demonstrates the negative expansion of *public interest*. In this regard, the arbitral award went too far, and although it was rendered by a highly renowned tribunal, such excesses must not be approved. Not because one might agree (or disagree) with the conclusion voiced in the respective paragraph, but because the statement went beyond the subject matter of the dispute and the tribunal was not obliged to comment on that issue. It is an example of an expansion of *public interest* which is harmful for the international environment and jeopardizes the functioning of its basic mechanisms.

(b) Genesis and the constitution of *public interest*

25. According to *Rochdi Goulli*,[12] various forms of *public interest* already appeared in the first communities of people. For example, *Hippodamus of Miletus* used *public interest* when he summarized his experience in the construction of the public area and defined the role of private and public buildings in the development of cities and villages. *Plato* used *public interest* especially in his *Politeia* and *Nomoi* in which he generalized his knowledge of cities, their structure and government. The concept of *public interest* was only settled, however, during the Roman Republic when public law developed alongside private law, which was defined by *Ulpianus* using his already notorious interest theory.[13] However, the original *Law of the Twelve Tables* already contained the principles of *public interest*, "*Utilitas Publica*," which were used to define private (civil) interest; this Law also contained provisions regulating punishment for breaching the general interest. At that time, cities and collegia (associations) of inhabitants became holders of *public interest*.[14] Nonetheless, the individual groups were not in agreement, frequent conflicts devalued the essence and the original objectives of this institution.[15] This ultimately resulted in the creation of a new category of *domestic (national) interest*, which came into existence thanks to the transition from city to state governance.[16]

26. The historical changes which necessitated the transformation of the Roman Republic into an imperium and subsequently into medieval

---

[12] *Rochdi Goulli*. Problémy definování a prosazování veřejného zájmu. [Title in translation: Problems with the Definition and Enforcement of Public Interest]. In: *Ivan MALÝ* (ed.) Sborník referátů z teoretického semináře pořádaného Katedrou veřejné ekonomie ESF MU v Brně ve spolupráci s Asociací veřejné ekonomie. [Collection of Papers from the Theoretical Seminar Organized by the Department of Public Economics, Faculty of Economics and Administration, Masaryk University in Brno, in cooperation with the Public Economics Association]. Brno: MU, 1999. p. 10.

[13] "*Publicum ius est, quod ad statum rei romanae spectat; privatum, quod ad singulorum utilitatem pertinet.*" (Public law benefits the state, private law benefits the individual.) *Ulpianus*, Digesta 1, 1, 1, 2. In this connection, *public interest* means the interest of the state.

[14] For a historical excursus, see also *Müller, R.* Orgány ochrany veřejného zájmu (Nejvyšší kontrolní úřad a Úřad pro zastupování státu ve věcech majetkových). [Title in translation: Authorities for the Protection of the Public Interest (Supreme Audit Office and the Office for Government Representation in Property Affairs)]. Thesis (master's degree) successfully defended at the Department of Administrative Studies, Administrative Law and Financial Law, Faculty of Law, Masaryk University, 2009/2010, available in the electronic information system of the Faculty of Law, MU [last access 14 January 2011].

[15] We have been witnessing a similar disproportionate expansion of the *public interest* in the international environment.

[16] *Goulli, R.* Problémy definování a prosazování veřejného zájmu. [Title in translation: Problems with the Definition and Enforcement of Public Interest]. In: *Malý, I.* (ed.) Sborník referátů z teoretického semináře pořádaného Katedrou veřejné ekonomie ESF MU v Brně ve spolupráci s Asociací veřejné ekonomie. [Collection of Papers from the Theoretical Seminar Organized by the Department of Public Economics, Faculty of Economics and Administration, Masaryk University in Brno, in cooperation with the Public Economics Association]. Brno: MU, 1999. p. 10.

monarchies were also inevitably reflected in the interpretation of *public interest*. Due to the position of the ruler in these state units who became the representative of the state, i.e. the enforcer and exponent of the *public interest*, the original content of the term was twisted, and the ruler determined the *public interest* himself. There arose the origin of royal law, and *public interest* became a component of the royals (courts, fiscal measures, etc.).[17]

27. Further developments in the 19th Century led to the fall of absolutism and brought about liberal ideas. These ideas also influenced the concept of *public interest* which was, at least to some extent, cleared of absolutist influence, reformed, and gradually took on a new structure. Nonetheless, it did not revert to its original essence. That was not even possible. *Rektořík* defines *public interest* as an interactive concept; it must therefore always be perceived in its historical context.[18] Other authors are more inclined to conceive of it as a "vague legal concept.[19]" However, careful analysis shows *public interest* is not a vague (ambiguous) legal concept. It is an abstract category, and its abstract nature is its indispensable feature. Without this nature, it would lose its meaning.

28. After the economic crisis in the 1930s and after World War II, the importance of the public sector rapidly increased, especially in the communist countries. This went hand-in-hand with the increasing importance of the concept of the *public interest*. At the same time, however, it was acquiring new content which only masked the individual interest of the ruling party. This was supported by the concept that a single entity (the state) could be the holder of the *public interest*. This theory was abandoned after the fall of communism in those countries, and the new holders of *public interest* became individual decision-making centers and associations of citizens.[20]

---

[17] *Goulli, R.* Problémy definování a prosazování veřejného zájmu. [Title in translation: Problems with the Definition and Enforcement of Public Interest]. In: *Malý, I.* (ed.) Sborník referátů z teoretického semináře pořádaného Katedrou veřejné ekonomie ESF MU v Brně ve spolupráci s Asociací veřejné ekonomie. [Collection of Papers from the Theoretical Seminar Organized by the Department of Public Economics, Faculty of Economics and Administration, Masaryk University in Brno, in cooperation with the Public Economics Association]. Brno: MU, 1999. p. 10.

[18] *Rektořík, J.* Problémy definování a prosazování veřejného zájmu. [Title in translation: Problems with the Definition and Enforcement of Public Interest]. In: *Malý, I.* (ed.) Sborník referátů z teoretického semináře pořádaného Katedrou veřejné ekonomie ESF MU v Brně ve spolupráci s Asociací veřejné ekonomie. [Collection of Papers from the Theoretical Seminar Organized by the Department of Public Economics, Faculty of Economics and Administration, Masaryk University in Brno, in cooperation with the Public Economics Association]. Brno: MU, 1999. p. 29.

[19] *Průcha, P.* Základní pojmy a instituty správního práva. [Title in translation: Basic Terms and Institutions of Administrative Law]. Brno: MU, 1998, p. 355.

[20] *Goulli, R.* Problémy definování a prosazování veřejného zájmu. [Title in translation: Problems with the Definition and Enforcement of Public Interest]. In: *Malý, I.* (ed.) Sborník referátů z teoretického semináře pořádaného Katedrou veřejné ekonomie ESF MU v Brně ve spolupráci s Asociací veřejné ekonomie. [Collection of Papers from the Theoretical Seminar Organized by the Department of

29.   In other words, the term *public interest* has manifested itself throughout the documented history of mankind. Academic literature also mentions one interesting aspect,[21] i.e. that the growing density of population and the increasing technical possibilities which, inter alia, enable the realization of new personal needs, go hand-in-hand with the need to enforce the *public interest*; fears that this trend will continue are fully justified. In the international arena, though, such developments are not positive. The reason is that the aim of the international community is to achieve a broad compromise over a number of important issues.[22] It is irrelevant whether the purpose of a particular international treaty, or any other instrument, manifests itself in the particular case only in the territory of a single state or in a small number of states and perhaps only temporarily, or – conversely – whether it manifests itself in the entire international milieu. It is also irrelevant whether the objective is enshrined in a bilateral or a multilateral (regional or universal, closed or opened) international treaty. Whatever the case, *public interest* should not be incorporated into the glossary of international law and, above all, should not be confused with *public policy* (*ordre public*).

(c)   Delimitation of *public interest*

30.   As alluded to earlier, some authors have suggested that *public interest* is a vague (ambiguous) legal notion,[23] but, on the contrary, the term proves itself to be a concept which can be accurately defined. Although its contents may vary depending on the time or place; and although as a consequence, it is a concept that appears to be left to the discretion of

---

Public Economics, Faculty of Economics and Administration, Masaryk University in Brno, in cooperation with the Public Economics Association]. Brno: MU, 1999. pp. 10–11.

[21] *Dostálková, D. et Křivková, K.* Problémy definování a prosazování veřejného zájmu. [Title in translation: Problems with the Definition and Enforcement of Public Interest]. In: Malý, I. (ed.) Sborník referátů z teoretického semináře pořádaného Katedrou veřejné ekonomie ESF MU v Brně ve spolupráci s Asociací veřejné ekonomie. [Collection of Papers from the Theoretical Seminar Organized by the Department of Public Economics, Faculty of Economics and Administration, Masaryk University in Brno, in cooperation with the Public Economics Association]. Brno: MU, 1999. p. 28.

[22] See *Müller, R.* Orgány ochrany veřejného zájmu (Nejvyšší kontrolní úřad a Úřad pro zastupování státu ve věceh majetkových). [Title in translation: Authorities for the Protection of the Public Interest (Supreme Audit Office and the Office for Government Representation in Property Affairs)]. Thesis (master's degree) successfully defended at the Department of Administrative Studies, Administrative Law and Financial Law, Faculty of Law, Masaryk University, 2009/2010, available in the electronic information system of the Faculty of Law, MU [last access 14 January 2011].

[23] *Hendrych, D.* Správní právo, obecná část. [Title in translation: Administrative Law, General Part]. 7th ed. Prague: C. H. Beck, 2009. p. 86. This opinion has also been adopted by various sources, see for instance Müller, R. Orgány ochrany veřejného zájmu (Nejvyšší kontrolní úřad a Úřad pro zastupování státu ve věcech majetkových). [Title in translation: Authorities for the Protection of the Public Interest (Supreme Audit Office and the Office for Government Representation in Property Affairs)]. Thesis (master's degree) successfully defended at the Department of Administrative Studies, Administrative Law and Financial Law, Faculty of Law, Masaryk University, 2009/2010, available in the electronic information system of the Faculty of Law, MU [last access 14 January 2011].

the entity vested with the authority to enforce *public interest* to determine whether a particular case falls within the scope of said notion or not, its very abstract category resides in the fact that if deprived of its high degree of abstraction, the concept would fail to fulfill its purpose. The best way to explain this category is perhaps to put it in contrast to private,[24] i.e. individual, interest.

31. *Public interest* means an interest where the holder of said interest is a group of persons, undefined but yet capable of definition by its fundamental features, which could be designated as *"the public."*[25] The group need not represent an aggregate of individual interests.[26] Any attempt at such a simple conjunction of individual interests is grossly misleading. This is because the quality of the *public interest* is arguably best viewed as substantially different from the *individual interests* of those persons representing the public, i.e. as the addressees of the acts contingent on or influenced by the *public interest*. This should not be taken to mean, however, that the *public interest* could never evolve from individual interests. An interest becomes public if it benefits a bigger group of [at least potential] individuals. Its quality significantly changes during the transition from individual interest to *public interest*. Only the change in this qualitative dimension causes that the *public interest*, as opposed to individual interests, is determined by the absolutely binding (overriding mandatory) nature of general normative acts.

32. Furthermore, despite the obvious relationship between the *public interest* and public law, it is not possible to limit the *public interest* exclusively to public law. This is all the more important in the international arena, because, for example, *civil law* and *common law* perceive the differences between public and private law differently. Also, the distinction is substantially less clear-cut under *common law* and some legal systems do not distinguish these categories at all. Furthermore, the international environment hardly allows us to speak of private and public law at all. While it is true that we do employ the concepts of *public international law* and *private international law*, the comparison is not suitable, because the distinctions specific to them are completely different from the distinction between private law and public

---

[24] For an analogous conclusion, see also the ECJ (Tribunal) Judgment, Joined Cases T-109/05 and T-444/05 of 24 May 2011 (*Navigazione Libera del Golfo Srl.* /formerly *Navigazione Libera del Golfo SpA/* v. *Commission of the EU*) (unpublished).

[25] Cf. *Průcha, P.* Správní právo. Obecná část. [Title in translation: Administrative Law. General Part]. 7th ed. Brno: Doplněk, 2007, p. 54.

[26] *Hyánek, V.* Problémy definování a prosazování veřejného zájmu. [Title in translation: Problems with the Definition and Enforcement of Public Interest]. In: *Malý, I.* (ed.) Sborník referátů z teoretického semináře pořádaného Katedrou veřejné ekonomie ESF MU v Brně ve spolupráci s Asociací veřejné ekonomie. [Collection of Papers from the Theoretical Seminar Organized by the Department of Public Economics, Faculty of Economics and Administration, Masaryk University in Brno, in cooperation with the Public Economics Association]. Brno: MU, 1999. p.60.

law at the national level (perhaps with the exception of the qualities vested in public-law entities or the holders of rights in private international law, as the case may be).[27] Some authors maintain that *public interest* at the national level denotes a concept which also has its meaning in private law[28] and is reflected, for instance, in the observance of fundamental private-law principles. This may well be correct, because the observance of these principles increases legal certainty and the enhancement of legal certainty is surely in the *public interest*. After all, some opinions from administrative law support this conclusion and there are opinions suggesting, for example,[29] that each legal rule is in the *public interest*; in other words, the *public interest* is an interest safeguarded by both private-law rules and public-law rules.

33. Others claim[30] that the problem with the definition of *public interest* inheres in the fact that if something is in the *public interest*, it is presumed that it concerns an issue generally beneficial, favorable, and good for society. The problem therefore consists in the identification of "*welfare*," which has other practical implications as well. We can ask whether this or that is more in the *public interest*. Or more precisely, the problem inheres in the determination of whether the former is better than the latter or vice versa. A conflict may arise between economic interests on the one hand (such as a new highway) and an interest in the protection of the environment on the other.

34. The currently applicable laws employ the concept of *public interest* more as an argument supporting the regulation of particular specific conduct. Definition of this notion is seldom attempted, or when it is what is usually offered is only an indicative list which is further limited by the scope of the given statute or regulation.

---

[27] Nonetheless, this is also not a rule without exceptions; modern international law does, in specific cases, grant certain rights to private entities. This is typically the case with investment protection, and it is irrelevant whether the rights of private investors guaranteed by international mechanisms are the original rights of these entities or rights derived from the rights of the investor's state. However, direct claims benefiting private entities under international law can be found in other areas as well, for instance in certain cases relating to consular protection, but also in connection with international mechanisms of human rights protection, etc.

[28] *Bejček, J.* Veřejný zájem v obchodním právu. [Title in translation: Public Interest in Commercial Law]. In: *Bejček, J.* (ed.) Sborník příspěvků z VI. Mezinárodní vědecké konference pořádané katedrou obchodního práva. [Collection of Papers from the 6th International Scientific Conference Organized by the Department of Commercial Law]. Brno: MU, 2008, p. 6.

[29] *Havlan, P.* Veřejné vlastnictví v právu a společnosti. [Title in translation: Public Ownership in Law and Society]. Prague: C. H. Beck, 2008, p. 48 and p. 54.

[30] *Malý, I.* Problémy definování a prosazování veřejného zájmu. [Title in translation: Problems with the Definition and Enforcement of Public Interest]. In: *Malý, I.* (ed.) Sborník referátů z teoretického semináře pořádaného Katedrou veřejné ekonomie ESF MU v Brně ve spolupráci s Asociací veřejné ekonomie. [Collection of Papers from the Theoretical Seminar Organized by the Department of Public Economics, Faculty of Economics and Administration, Masaryk University in Brno, in cooperation with the Public Economics Association]. Brno: MU, 1999. pp. 21–22.

II.3.4. *Public policy* and *public interest* in EU law

(a) Autonomous interpretation of *public policy* and *public interest*; an exception to the freedoms guaranteed by primary EU law

35. *"Public policy"* is an individual term employed in *Community* law (EU law) which co-determines the scope of fundamental freedoms; as such, it must be defined autonomously and not, for instance, on the basis of one or more national legal systems.[31] The term is subject to interpretation by the ECJ. Consequently, the Member States cannot define the scope of the term unilaterally and without any supervision by EU authorities.[32] This does not preclude, however, the possibility of the Member States invoking *"public policy"* in special situations; the Member States are endowed, under certain circumstances, with a margin of discretion, within the limits stipulated (exclusively) by the TEC.[33] However, this limitation only applies with respect to *public policy* used in terms of EU law, not in terms of international law. Such limits as to the margin of discretion do not exist outside the EU Member States when applying EU law, despite the fact that EU primary law is a part of international law albeit only with a regional impact. In spite of these common principles, however, the term *"public policy"* is associated with different meanings depending on the position and the role of the respective rule within the

---

[31] See the following ECJ rulings:
> ECJ Judgment, Case C-296/95 of 2 April 1998 *(The Queen* v. *Commissioners of Customs and Excise, ex parte EMU Tabac SARL, The Man in Black Ltd, John Cunningham)*, CELEX: 61995J0296, published in: ECR 1995, p. I–1605, marg. (30);
> ECJ Judgment, Case 53/81 of 23 March 1982 *(D. M. Levin* v. *Staatssecretaris van Justitie)*, CELEX: 61981CJ0053, ECR 1982, p. 01035, marg. (10) through (12).

[32] According to settled case law, the invocation of the concept of *"public policy"* by the national authority is in any case contingent on, apart from the social disturbance caused by any violation of the law, the existence of a genuine and sufficiently serious threat to a fundamental interest of society. See the following ECJ rulings:
> ECJ Judgment, Case 36-75 of 28 October 1975 *(Roland Rutili* v. *Ministre de l'intérieur)*, CELEX: 61975J0036, marg. (35);
> ECJ Judgment, Case 30/77 of 27 October 1977 *(Regina* v. *P. Bouchereau)*, published in: ECR 1977, p. 1999, marg. (33);
> ECJ Judgment, joined cases C-482/01 and C-493/01 of 29 April 2004 *(Georgios Orfanopoulos et al. et Raffaele Oliveri* v. *Land Baden Württemberg)*, CELEX: 62001J0482, ECR 2004, p. I–5257, marg. (64) and (66);
> ECJ Judgment, Case C-503/03 of 31 January 2006 *(Commission of the EC* v. *Spain)*, CELEX: 62003CJ0503, ECR 2006, p. I–1097, marg. (46);
> ECJ Judgment, Case C-441/02 of 27 April 2006 *(Commission of the EC* v. *Germany, ECR 2006, p. I–3449, para. (35);
> ECJ Judgment, Case C-50/06 of 7 June 2007 *(Commission of the EC* v. *the Netherlands)*, published in: ECR 2007, p. I–4383, para. (43).

[33] ECJ Judgment, Case 41-74 of 4 December 1974 *(Yvonne van Duyn* v. *Home Office)*, CELEX: 61974CJ0041, published in: ECR 1974, p. 1337, marg. (18) and (19).

system of EU law.[34] As already mentioned elsewhere, it is a concept used somewhat indiscriminately, especially when combined with the term *"public interest."* But these two expressions are not identical.

(b) Free movement of persons and protection of security

36.   *Public policy* and/or *public interest* are probably most frequently referred to in connection with the **free movement of persons**. The restrictions of the right to residence in exercising the right to the free movement of persons, workers, services, and the freedom to settle, based on *public policy* or security, have comparable contents. Consequently, the principles derived from the ECJ rulings concerning the restriction of said right are probably applicable to all freedoms.[35] It is necessary to point out, though, that in this case we are referring to *public policy* within the meaning of *security* and protection against security risks. Nonetheless this is a dimension of the term *public policy* that is somewhat different from *international public policy (ordre public)*. Although this category is sometimes also subsumed under the concept of *public policy*, it is more advisable to use expressions like *public security* and *security policy*. Undoubtedly, the interests associated with security issues are influenced by *public interest*. The association may be attributed to a conceptual terminological inconsistency which results in the frequent use of *public policy* in international practice.[36] That is to say, also the term *public policy* understood within the meaning of international law, if we are speaking about exceptions to primary EU law which is the subject of international law. Nevertheless, EU law (primarily its application practice) especially employs the term *public policy* in a very broad sense, even in those situations which do not concern the

---

[34] Classified in the category of EU rules out of which especially the following primary law provisions have become significant as "restrictions of fundamental freedoms" allowing, under certain circumstances, the limitation of the free movement of goods, persons, services, and capital guaranteed under primary law: Article 30 TEC, Article 39(3) TEC, Article 46 TEC, Article 55 TEC, and Article 58(1)(b) TEC. To a limited extent, however, the term *"public policy"* is also used in secondary EU law, either as a rule providing for an exception, or as a secondary law (rule) the function of which is to provide for interpretation and specification (in that connection, see *Schneider, H.* Die öffentliche Ordnung als Schranke der Grundfreiheiten im EG-Vertrag, Baden-Baden 1998, p. 53).

[35] *Karlová, H.* Omezení a ukončení práva na vstup a pobyt občanů Unie z důvodu veřejného pořádku a bezpečnosti. [Title in translation: Limitation and Termination of the EU Citizens' Right to Enter and Reside in a Country for Public Policy and Security Reasons]. Právník, Vol. 1946, 2007, No. 8, pp. 923–924.

[36] Cf. Directive 2004/38/EC of the European Parliament and of the Council of 29 April 2004 on the right of citizens of the Union and their family members to move and reside freely within the territory of the Member States amending Regulation (EEC) No. 1612/68 and repealing Directives 64/221/EEC, 68/360/EEC, 72/194/EEC, 73/148/EEC, 75/34/EEC, 75/35/EEC, 90/364/EEC, 90/365/EEC and 93/96/EEC.

Security policy can be the subject of *public policy (ordre public)*, but this connection has to be established in each particular case.

reservation regarding *public policy* within the meaning of a refusal to apply primary EU law as a source of international law. As concerns the limitation of the movement of persons, the terms *public policy* and security are most often used together. Still it is not a typical conjunction, however; in most cases, it is rather a manifestation of the fact that "security" is an "adjective" to (a qualification of) *public policy*. The ECJ entrusts the authority of defining the term in greater detail to the Member States in connection with their **substantial interests** and **the interests of their citizens**, although this possibility of free interpretation by the Member States is not unlimited either, with a restrictive approach being the more common.[37] As opposed to *"public policy,"* the ECJ has attempted, however, to define the terms "**external security**"[38] and "**internal security.**"[39] The prerequisites for the application of the reservation regarding *public policy* (here in connection with fundamental freedoms) are a breach of the law by the perpetrator. Further, the personal interest of the perpetrator must represent a **genuine**[40] **and sufficiently serious threat to a fundamental interest of society.**[41] We must always ensure no less rigorous measures

---

[37] See the following rulings of the ECJ:

➢ ECJ Judgment, Case 36-75 of 28 October 1975 (*Roland Rutili* v. *Ministre de l'intérieur*), CELEX: 61975J0036 (The EU Member States may determine the strength of the reservation regarding *public policy* according to their national laws, providing they observe the limits stipulated by EU authorities);

➢ ECJ Judgment, Case 41-74 of 4 December 1974 (*Yvonne van Duyn* v. *Home Office*), CELEX: 61974CJ0041 (It is an exception to the fundamental freedom of the free movement of workers which must be interpreted narrowly so that the importance cannot be unilaterally determined by each individual Member State without any control being exercised by EU authorities);

➢ ECJ Judgment, Case C-268/99 of 20 November 2001 (*Aldona Malgorzata Jany and Others* v. *Staatssecretaris van Justitie et al.*), CELEX: 61999J0268 (EU law does not prescribe a uniform scale of values the endangerment of which would simultaneously constitute a danger to *public policy*).

[38] ECJ Judgment, Case C-83/94 of 17 October 1995 (*criminal prosecution of Peter Leifer, Reinhold Otto Krauskopf et Otto Holzer*), CELEX: 61994CJ0083 (This case involved danger to the country presented by foreign armies as well as the threat of serious disturbance to foreign relations of the state and the peaceful existence of the nation).

[39] ECJ Judgment, Case 222/86 of 15 October 1987 (*Union nationale des entraîneurs et cadres techniques professionnels du football (Unectef)* v. *Georges Heylens et al.*), CELEX: 61986J0222 (This case involved preserving the existence of the state, its institutions and important functions, as well as securing the further existence of the population).

[40] See *ADC Affiliate Limited and ADC & ADMC Management Limited* v. *Republic of Hungary*, ICSID Case No.ARB/03/16, Award of 2 October 2006. As concerns the requirement of *public interest*, the arbitral tribunal reached the following conclusion (in connection with expropriation) (cit.:) "[...] *requirement* [...] *of public interest requires some genuine interest of the public. If mere reference to "public interest" can magically put such interest into existence and therefore satisfy this requirement, then this requirement would be rendered meaningless, since the Tribunal can imagine no situation where this requirement would not have been met."* Consequently, despite the respect paid to expropriating states, current case law suggests that expropriation must meet some genuine interest of the public in order to be considered justified from a legal perspective.

[41] See Article 27(2) of Directive 2004/38/EC of the European Parliament and of the Council of 29 April 2004.

to sufficiently protect the fundamental interest of society.[42] The application of exceptions to fundamental freedoms (within the meaning of a reservation regarding *public policy*) always exclusively depends on the specific conduct of the obligee; the application of the reservation on the basis of general prevention is prohibited.[43] At the same time, the Member States must honor the general principles of EU law, primarily the prohibition of discrimination on grounds of nationality.[44] However, intentionally fabricating and then abusing a certain situation in order to apply the freedom of movement (within the meaning of EU law) is forbidden,[45] as is also required maintaining a sense of proportion between the threat and the decision, especially with regard to the inability of diverting the threat by any other means.[46]

See ECJ Judgment, Case C-100/01 of 26 November 2002 (*Ministre de l'Intérieur* v. *Aitor Oteiza Olazabal*), CELEX: 62001J0100 (tax fraud and terrorism).

[42] The frequently quoted examples are, for instance, situations where the breach of the right to freedom of movement is precluded by a delict committed while driving a motor vehicle (a penalty such as a driving prohibition is sufficient) or failure to submit an identity card or a foreigner's failure to register. It is not necessary, however, that the foreigner's conduct be classifiable as a criminal offence.
Concerning these issues in greater detail, see also *Bělohlávek, A. J.* Rozhodčí řízení, ordre public a trestní právo: Interakce mezinárodního a tuzemského práva soukromého a veřejného [Title in translation: Arbitration, Ordre Public and Criminal Law: The Interaction of International and Domestic Private and Public Law], Prague: C. H. Beck, 2008, Part I and II (in Czech) and Kiev [UKR]: Taxon, 2009, Part I, II and III (bilingual in English and in Russian).
[43] See the following rulings of the ECJ:
➢ ECJ Judgment, Case 36-75 of 28 October 1975 (*Roland Rutili* v. *Ministre de l'intérieur*), CELEX: 61975J0036;
➢ ECJ Judgment, Case 67/74 of 26 February 1975 (*Carmelo Angelo Bonsignore* v. *Oberstadtdirektor der Stadt Köln*), CELEX: 61974CJ0067.
➢ ECJ Judgment, Case 41-74 of 4 December 1974 (*Yvonne van Duyn* v. *Home Office*), CELEX: 61974CJ0041. This decision is exceptional. A Dutch citizen accepted an offer of employment in Great Britain, with the Church of Scientology. This is an organization which was officially considered socially harmful by the British government, but its activities were not legally restricted. The ECJ ruled that the employment of the state's own citizens cannot be restricted in such a case; but as concerns a foreigner, this situation represents a certain demonstration of the current thinking and the receiving state's public security could be jeopardized.
➢ ECJ Judgment Joined Cases 115/81 and 116/81 of 18 May 1982 (*Rezguia Adoui* v. *The Belgian State and the City of Liege; Dominique Cornuaille* v. *The Belgian State*), CELEX: 61981CJ0115: this decision modifies the judgment rendered in the *Yvonne van Duyn* case; the ECJ ruled that the extradition of two French citizens from Belgium [BEL] for prostitution, which is not prohibited in Belgium, does not comply with EU law. Behavior, which is perhaps immoral, but falls short of being illegal, is not a reason justifying the restriction of the freedom of movement. Cf. also Svoboda, P. Úvod do evropského práva. [Title in translation: Introduction to European Law]. 3rd ed. Prague: C. H. Beck, 2010. p. 194 et seq.
[44] Article 18 TFEU.
[45] See the ECJ rulings:
➢ ECJ Judgment, Case C-19/92 of 31 March 1993 (*Dieter Kraus* v. *Land Baden-Württemberg*), CELEX: 61992CJ0019;
➢ ECJ Judgment, Case C-109/01 of 23 September 2003 (*Secretary of State for the Home Department* v. *Hacene Akrich*), 62001J0109.
[46] See the ECJ rulings:
➢ ECJ Judgment, Case 157/79 (*Piech*), published in: ECR, p. 2171, No. 10;

37. The exceptions relating to the *free movement of workers in the provision of services* form another area of interest with respect to public policy. This primarily involves the case law concerning the Member States which requires that the enterprises posting their workers in the territory of said state automatically adjust wages, other than the adjustment of the minimum wages, to comply with changes in the costs of living,[47] although a restrictive interpretation is still mandatory.[48] Despite the fact that a precise specification is always up to the relevant Member State, these situations constitute exceptions to fundamental EU rules, the scope of which cannot be unilaterally determined by the Member States.[49] These *other conditions* must be justified by a *public interest* pursuant to the state's national needs, although a restrictive approach is mandatory in this case as well. Such exceptional conditions do not include, for instance, requirements resulting from generally

---

> ECJ Judgment, Case 41-74 of 4 December 1974 (*Yvonne van Duyn* v. *Home Office*), CELEX: 61974CJ0041;

> ECJ Judgment, Case C-348/96 of 19 January 1999 (*criminal proceedings against Donatella Calfa*), CELEX: 61996CJ0348, published in: ECR 1999, p. I–11, para. (23).

[47] In that connection, this is primarily true in the sense of the obligations specified in the first subparagraph of Article 3(10) of Directive (EC) 96/71 concerning the posting of workers in the framework of the provision of services. A Member State may apply to activities in posting workers on the territory of said Member State the terms and conditions of employment relating to matters other than those referred to in the first subparagraph of Article 3(1) of Directive 96/71, with a reservation stipulating that the terms and conditions represent *public policy* provisions.

[48] *Georgiadis, N.* Derogation clauses: The protection of national interests in EC law, Bruxelles, 2006, p. 72; This work points out that all provisions regulating exceptions, primarily the reservation concerning *public policy*, are subject to the principle of narrow interpretation. According to *J. Wichmann* in: Dienstleistungsfreiheit und grenzüberschreitende Entsendung von Arbeitnehmern, Frankfurt a. M., 1998, p. 104 and p. 105, it is possible to adduce systematic considerations against extensive interpretation. Their very status of contractual terms regulating exceptions implies that the reservation regarding *public policy* must be interpreted narrowly. Successful invocation of *public policy* therefore requires that the interests concerned are the sovereign interests of the Member States.

[49] See the following ECJ rulings:

> ECJ Judgment, Case 67/74 of 26 February 1975 (*Carmelo Angelo Bonsignore* v. *Oberstadtdirektor der Stadt Köln*), para. (6). Published in: ECR, p. 297;

> ECJ Judgment, Case 36-75 of 28 October 1975 (*Roland Rutili* v. *Ministre de l'intérieur*), para. (27). Published in: ECR, p. 1219. CELEX: 61975J0036;

> ECJ Judgment, Case 30/77 of 27 October 1977 (*Regina* v. *P. Bouchereau*), published in: ECR 1977, p.1999, marg. (33), cf. also *Blanpain, R.* European Labour Law, 9th ed., Kluwer, 2003, p. 314 et al.;

> ECJ Judgment, Case C-348/96 of 19 January 1999 (*criminal proceedings against Donatella Calfa*), CELEX: 61996CJ0348, published in: ECR 1999, p. I–11, para. (23);

> ECJ Judgment, Joined Cases C-482/01 and C-493/01 of 29 April 2004 (*Georgios Orfanopoulos et al. et Raffaele Oliveri* v. *Land Baden Württemberg*), CELEX: 62001J0482, ECR 2004, p. I-5257, marg. (64) and (65);

> ECJ Judgment, Case C-503/03 of 31 January 2006 (*Commission of the EC* v. *Spain*), CELEX: 62003CJ0503, ECR 2006, I-1097, marg. (45);

> ECJ Judgment, Case C-441/02 of 27 April 2006 (*Commission of the EC* v. *Germany*, ECR 2006, p. I–3449), para. (34);

> ECJ Judgment, Case C-50/06 of 7 June 2007 (*Commission of the EC* v. *the Netherlands*), published in: ECR 2007, p. I–4383, para. (42);

binding collective labor agreements, as the ECJ held for example in *The Commission* v. *Luxembourg* (C-319/06).[50] This decision demonstrates, however, how inadequately the terms *"public policy"* and *"public interest"* are handled; the original wording employs the term *"public policy,"* whereas some translations refer to *"public interest."*[51] *Public policy* must represent a threat to fundamental legal and social principles.[52] As concerns the terms and conditions of employment, *public policy* must represent a fundamental principle, as defined by the receiving state, the breach of which jeopardizes the integrity of the state's labor market and labor and social conditions. The delimitation of the relationship between *public policy* and *public interest* was attempted by the Advocate-General in the above-mentioned case, *The Commission* v. *Luxembourg* (C-319/06);[53] the AG stated that the expression *public policy* was to be construed as covering those *"mandatory rules from which there can be no derogation and which, by their nature and objective, meet the imperative requirements of public interest."* The present study does not fully concur with this opinion, because such a definition shifts the contents of *public policy* to the level of mere mandatory rules or, viewed within the framework of private international law (conflict-of-laws rules), to *overriding mandatory rules*. However, without doubt *public policy* must simultaneously constitute *public interest.* Whereas *public interest* must be targeted at a specific group of addressees of the legal imperative (a specific norm), *public policy* represents the framework of the normative system. In other words, the two categories are not completely identical, and *public interest* can only represent one component of *public policy*, though not the only one and probably not even an indispensable one, considering the essential role that *public policy* fulfills in the law. However, the AG's opinion, voiced in the same case (here as concerns the conditions for posted workers), is accurate when it maintains that *"public policy can encompass only those terms and conditions of employment stipulated by law which are indispensable for the legal system of the Member States."* In that connection, one must always examine, in each individual case,

---

[50] ECJ Judgment, Case C-319/06 of 19 June 2008 (*Commission of the EC* v. *Luxembourg*), CELEX: 62006J0319.

[51] See the inaccurate translation to Czech.

[52] Cf. *Fuchs, M. et Marhold, M.* Europäisches Arbeitsrecht, Wien, 2006, p. 322; *Görres, S.* Grenzüberschreitende Arbeitnehmerentsendung in der EU, Wien/Graz, 2003, p. 122 et al. The authors thereby admit that the application of Article 3(10) of Directive 96/71 must observe certain criteria, necessarily including both the free movement of services, which is being realized, and the precise objectives of the *Communities'* [EU] legislator. According to the opinion maintained by *AG Mengozzi* in para. (212) of his opinion presented on 23 May 2007 in *Laval un Partneri* (ECJ Case C-341/05, ECR I-11767), the fact that the national rules belong to the category of *public policy* laws or mandatory rules does not absolve the Member States of the obligation to observe the provisions of the TEC – see Article 3(10) of Directive 96/71/EC.

[53] ECJ Judgment, Case C-319/06 of 19 June 2008 (*Commission of the EC* v. *Luxembourg*), CELEX: 62006J0319.

whether the required conditions meet that requirement. Indeed, this was quite fittingly expressed by the ECJ in C-36/02 (*"Omega"*[54]), where the Court ruled that measures restricting the free movement of services can be justified by *public policy* only if such measures are necessary for the protection of interests they are supposed to safeguard and only if these objectives cannot be achieved by less restrictive measures. At the same time, the need for and the proportionality of the provisions are not excluded simply because one Member State has chosen a system of protection different from that adopted by another Member State.[55] Measures restricting the free movement of services can be justified by *public policy* only if such measures are necessary for the protection of interests they are supposed to safeguard and only if these objectives cannot be achieved by less restrictive measures; in that connection, it is not required that the restrictive measures imposed by the authorities of one Member State correspond to a concept shared by all Member States as regards the methods of protecting the fundamental right or legitimate interest in question. This means, that the need for and the proportionality of the measures are not excluded simply because one Member State has chosen a system of protection different from that adopted by another Member State. *Public policy* can be invoked **only in a situation of a genuine and sufficiently serious threat to a fundamental interest of society.**[56] Special circumstances justifying the application of *public policy* may, however, differ from one jurisdiction to another as well as in time; similarly, it is not important whether the Member States share the same approach to a particular issue. In that connection, it is thus necessary to allow the competent national authorities some margin of discretion within the limits stipulated by the EC Treaty.[57] The threat to a fundamental interest can be eliminated, especially if the reasons – separated from their original function – are

---

[54] ECJ Judgment, Case C-36/02 of 14 October 2004 (*Omega Spielhallen- und Automatenaufstellungs-GmbH* v. *Oberbürgermeisterin der Bundesstadt Bonn*), CELEX: 62002J0036, paras. (36) through (38) (This case involved the restriction of a certain version of a computer game which simulated the acts of killing and therefore interfered with human dignity).

[55] It is a certain margin of discretion granted to the Member States in terms of their value criteria. See the following ECJ rulings:

➢ ECJ Judgment, Case C-124/97 of 21 September 1999 (*Markku Juhani Läärä, Cotswold Microsystems Ltd et Oy Transatlantic Software Ltd* v. *Kihlakunnansyyttäjä (Jyväskylä) et Suomen valtio*), CELEX: 61997J0124, ECR 1999, p. I–06067;

➢ ECJ Judgment, Case C-67/98 of 21 October 1999 (*Questore di Verona* v. *Diego Zenatti*), CELEX: 61998J0067, ECR 1998, p. I–7289, marg. (33).

[56] See ECJ Judgment, Case C-54/99 of 14 March 2000 (*Association Eglise de scientologie de Paris and Scientology International Reserves Trust* v. *The Prime Minister*), CELEX: 61999J0054, published in: ECR 2000, p. I–1335, marg. (17).

[57] See the following ECJ rulings:

➢ ECJ Judgment, Case 41-74 of 4 December 1974 (*Yvonne van Duyn* v. *The Home Office*), CELEX: 61974CJ0041, marg. (18);

➢ ECJ Judgment, Case 30/77 of 27 October 1977 (*Regina* v. *P. Bouchereau*), published in: ECR 1977, p. 1999, marg. (34).

actually applied in the interest of purely economic objectives.[58] Similarly, a Member State cannot adopt any measures against a national of another Member State *"by reason of conduct which, when engaged in by nationals of the first Member State, does not give rise to punitive measures or other genuine and effective measures intended to combat that conduct."*[59] In the above-mentioned *Omega* case, the ECJ ruled that (cit.) *"[a] measure adopted by an individual state targeted against the commercial activity held by a national court as offending the fundamental values enshrined in the constitution, must be regarded as compatible with the provisions of the EC Treaty regarding the free movement of services, providing the measure is indeed justified on public policy grounds targeted at a public interest and it is guaranteed that this objective cannot be attained by measures restricting the free movement of services to a lesser extent.* The ECJ, again, does not sufficiently distinguish between *public policy* and *public interest*; nonetheless, the ratio of the ECJ's ruling can be construed as admitting that *public policy* can serve as grounds justifying the restriction of the fundamental freedoms guaranteed by primary EU law provided it fulfills the requirement of *public interest*. In other words, if the principle involved in the *public policy* simultaneously incorporates another element, namely *public interest*, such element being possible but by no means necessary and certainly not exclusive. On the contrary, the *public interest* must in such cases be considerable in order to be thought identical to *public policy*. Nonetheless, the cited opinion of the ECJ confirms that these are two different categories which represent a different level of normative order and have (though not necessarily) a common intersection; where such an intersection exists, though, there is a qualified opportunity to exclude in an individual case the effects of the freedoms guaranteed by primary EU law. It is necessary to emphasize, however, that such expression is easily imaginable at the level of EU law but not under international law. *Public policy* which allows the reservation concerning *public policy* is, herein understood to be a specifically classified category, as opposed to EU law, and must be

---

[58] See the following ECJ rulings:
- ECJ Judgment, Case 36-75 of 28 October 1975 (*Roland Rutili* v. *Ministre de l´intérieur*), para. (27). Published in: ECR, p. 1219. CELEX: 61975J0036, marg. (30);
- ECJ Judgment, Case C-54/99 of 14 March 2000 (*Association Eglise de scientologie de Paris and Scientology International Reserves Trust* v. *The Prime Minister*), CELEX: 61999J0054, published in: ECR 2000, p. I–1335.

[59] See the following ECJ rulings:
- ECJ Judgment, Case C-100/01 of 26 November 2002 (*Ministre de l'Intérieur* v. *Aitor Oteiza Olazabal*). CELEX: 62001J0100, marg. (42) ;
- ECJ Judgment Joined Cases 115/81 and 116/81 of 18 May 1982 (*Rezguia Adoui* v. *The Belgian State and the City of Liège*; *Dominique Cornuaille* v. *The Belgian State*). CELEX: 61981CJ0115, marg. (9);
- ECJ Judgment, Case C-243/01 of 6 November 2003 (*criminal proceedings against Piergiorgio Gambelli et al*), CELEX: 62001J0243, marg. (69);
- ECJ Judgment, Case C-42/02 (*Diana Elisabeth Lindman*), CELEX: 62002J0042, marg. (114).

interpreted without regard to the existence of *public interest*, although the reservation concerning *public policy* in international law may (and actually does and very frequently) simultaneously express the *public interest* of a particular state. But, it is not an essential precondition which international law would necessarily (save for certain exceptions) have to examine. The difference between *public policy* and *public interest* is even more distinct in private international law than in public international law, especially in the **difference between the reservation regarding *public policy (ordre public)* and the overriding mandatory rules** – for a brief analysis see the end of this chapter.

(c)   Access to information

38.   As concerns access to documents, the ECJ (Tribunal) held in 2011[60] that the authorities of the relevant Member State enjoy a wide margin of discretion and may themselves determine whether the disclosure of documents from the areas falling within the exceptions[61] may endanger a *public interest*. The ECJ has ruled that this margin of discretion is justified by the fact that the decision on the denial of access is in those cases a comprehensive and sensitive decision and requires an exceptional degree of cautiousness and that the criteria specified in legal rules[62] are very general.[63] The relevant rule (the interpretation of which was the subject of the proceedings) stipulates that access to documents can be denied in the case of a (justified and specified[64]) *public interest* providing the matter concerns (i) public security, (ii) military and defense matters, (iii) international relations, or (iv) the financial, monetary or economic politics of the *Community* or a Member State. The cited legal opinion therefore indicates that these areas are not a *public interest* in itself but a *public interest* may manifest itself in them. It is clear that the list in the provision cited above is only indicative, and *public interest* may manifest itself in a number of other areas, too. It is interesting that the law cited above (Regulation No. 1049/2001) and the 2011 ruling consistently refer to *public interest* and do not

---

[60] See ECJ Judgment (Tribunal), Case T-362/08 of 13 January 2011 (*IFAW Internationaler Tierschutz-Fonds* v. *Commission*), CELEX: 62008TJ0362.

[61] This involves the disclosure of documents and exceptions pursuant to Article 4(1)(a) of Regulation (EC) No. 1049/2001 of the European Parliament and of the Council regarding public access to EP, Council and *Commission* documents.

[62] Here in Article 4(1)(a) of Regulation No. 1049/2001.

[63] See ECJ Judgment (Tribunal), Case T-341/07 of 23 November 2011 (*Jose Maria Sison* v. *The Council of the EU*), CELEX: 62007TJ0341(01), paras. (34) through (36).

[64] See the following rulings of the ECJ:
  ➢ ECJ Judgment Joined Cases C-39/05 and C-52/05 of 1 July 2008 (*Sweden et Maurizio Turco* v. *The Council of the EU*), CELEX: CELEX:62005J0039, published in: ECR, p. I-4723, marg. (49);
  ➢ ECJ Judgment (Tribunal / First Instance), Case T-166/05 of 11 March 2009 (*Borax Europe Ltd.* v. *The Commission of the EC*), This case, however, concerned an exception pursuant to Article 4(1)(b), i.e. an exception consisting in the protection of privacy.

mention *public policy*, although there is specialized case law concerning the restriction of certain freedoms under primary EU law. This indicates that, for instance, *public security* could in specific cases also represent a component of *public policy*. Nonetheless, these are two different categories. *Public policy* could (but does not necessarily) encompass a *public interest*. *Public policy* represents the fundaments of the legal environment in which both public and private interests are involved and can be found in both substantive and procedural law. Conversely, *public interest* is an exclusively substantive-law category, which also manifests itself otherwise than through the medium of *public policy*, depending on the intensity of the *public interest*. Indeed, it was the above-mentioned 2011 decision of the ECJ (Tribunal) in which *public interest* was, inter alia, explained by being contrasted with private interest.

39.   In another 2011 ruling, the ECJ explains *public interest* by using the example of interest in a discussion concerning legislation (general normative acts) as opposed to individual (administrative) normative acts. It is true that in the latter case there could also exist an interest in a *public discussion* (*public interest*), but such an interest lacks the intensity associated with the legislative process.[65] In another case, the ECJ highlighted a *public interest* in EU law issues, for instance in competition issues; the ECJ concluded, however, that this interest does not prevail over the interest in the protection of pending court proceedings.[66] In that decision, though, the ECJ referred to a *political interest* rather than to a *public interest*. This example clearly indicates that whereas *public policy* ought to be (at least in the continental *civil law* tradition) principally separated from politics, a *public interest* could be to a great extent identified with a *political interest*; after all, politics ought to be the *management of public affairs*. It is important to point out, though (as has already been mentioned above), especially that the *common law* tradition often associates *public policy* with an important *political interest* and the boundary between *public policy* and *public* (*political*) interest is becoming hazy, as opposed to the *continental* (*civil law*) *tradition* where the boundary between *public policy* and *public interest* must be strictly defined.

---

[65] See ECJ Judgment, Case C-506/08P of 21 July 2011 (*Sweden* v. *My Travel et Commission*); In this case, the Court also highlighted the claimant's obligation to prove a *public interest*; the Court did not, however, offer any definition thereof although in this particular case it could have legitimately been expected, because the case required the proof of a *prevailing* or *exceptional public interest*.

[66] See ECJ Judgment Joined Cases C-514/07 P, C-528/07 P and C-532/07 P of 21 September 2010 (*Sweden* v. *Association de la presse international ASBL /API/* et al.), CELEX: 62007CJ0514, para. (157) et seq.

(d) Consumer protection

40.   The difference between *public policy* and *public interest* is specifically remarkable in EU law when it comes to **consumer protection**. Although consumer law is a branch of the law where both terms are often used interchangeably, it is one of the areas typically subject to *public interest*, not *public policy*. For instance, Article 4 of Directive 85/577 to protect the consumer in respect to contracts negotiated away from business premises does not preclude a national court from declaring, of its own motion, that a contract falling within the scope of that directive is void on the ground that the consumer was not informed of his right of cancellation, even though the consumer at no stage pleaded that the contract was void before the competent national courts.[67] This situation is typically classifiable under *public interest* with the use of the positive effect of a mandatory rule of special importance; such rules can be classified under the category of *overriding mandatory rules* in private international law which, however, do not have to, and very often do not, form part of *public policy*.

41.   It is possible, though, that the required level of protection will be secured by other measures, for instance the time limits for the cancellation of the contract will run anew which will allow the consumer to exercise his or her rights under Article 5(1) of Directive 85/577. Furthermore, the national court could, under certain circumstances, be bound by the obligation to take account of the consumer's will not to have the contract held invalid. The possibility of using alternative legal mechanisms which permit the achievement of the same purpose, as well as a broad margin of discretion and the necessity of examining the factual and legal circumstances in the case of imperatives justified by a *public interest*, distinguish these rules from *public policy*, which is, conversely, endowed with such fundamental legal significance that the intensity of the effects of the rule representing a component of *public policy* allows only one solution, namely to deny the effects of a certain legal fact.

42.   Consumer protection is an example which very clearly demonstrates the difference between both categories, because national courts are not obliged to apply the consequences of a breach of EU law if the review of the grounds by the courts entailed transgressing the limits of the dispute as defined by the parties to the proceedings and the necessity of relying on facts and circumstances other than those on which the party interested in the application of said rules based his or her claim.[68] Only

---

[67] See ECJ Judgment, Case C-227/08 of 17 December 2009 (*Eva Martín Martín* v. *EDP Editores SL*), CELEX: 62008P0227C(01).
[68] In that connection, see especially the following ECJ rulings:

an imperative supported by *public interest*, not *public policy*, allows the courts such discretion. The limitation of the national court's jurisdiction is justified by the principle stipulating that the initiative in the proceedings rests in the hands of the parties themselves, and the court can act of its own motion only in exceptional cases when the *public interest* requires its intervention.[69] **It is clear, then, that consumer protection is associated with** *public interest***; it is not the subject of** *public policy***.**

43.   Consumer protection therefore requires that we identify the main obligations stipulated by a particular source of law. For instance, going back to Directive 85/577, the key obligation is the obligation to provide instructions pursuant to Article 4 of Directive 85/577 as the necessary guarantee of an effective exercise of the right to cancel the contract, i.e. of the useful effect of consumer protection intended by the Communities' legislator. Consequently, such a provision can be classified under *public interest* in terms of the case law mentioned above, which can justify the positive intervention of a national court aimed at eliminating the imbalance between consumer and professional in respect to contracts negotiated away from business premises. Under these circumstances, it is necessary to presume that if the consumer was not sufficiently informed of his or her right to cancel the contract, then the national court has the right to apply in the proceedings on the merits, of its own motion, the consequences of a breach of the requirements stipulated in Article 4 of Directive 85/577.[70] However, for instance the words "*appropriate consumer protection measures*" in the third subparagraph of Article 4, Directive 85/577, award to national authorities a margin of discretion as concerns the determination of the consequences of an absence of instructions. This is providing that the discretion is exercised in compliance with the objective of this directive,

---

> ECJ Judgment, Case C-430/93 of 14 December 1995 (*Jeroen van Schijndel et Johannes Nicolaas Cornelis van Veen* v. *Stichting Pensioenfonds voor Fysiotherapeuten*), published in: ECR I-4705, marg. (22), CELEX: 61993J0430;

> ECJ Judgment, Joined Cases C-222/05 through C-225/05 of 7 June 2007 (joined cases *J. van der Weerd et al.* /C-222/05/, *H. de Rooy Sr. et H. de Rooy Jr.* /C-223/05/, *Maatschap H. et J. van 't Oever et al.* /C-224/05/ et *B. J. van Middendorp* /C-225/05/ v. *Minister van Landbouw, Natuur en Voedselkwaliteit*), published in: ECR, p. I–4233, para. (36), CELEX: 62005CJ0222.

[69] In that connection, see especially the following ECJ rulings:

> ECJ Judgment, Case C-430/93 of 14 December 1995 (*Jeroen van Schijndel et Johannes Nicolaas Cornelis van Veen* v. *Stichting Pensioenfonds voor Fysiotherapeuten*), published in: ECR, p. I–4705, marg. (21), CELEX: 61993J0430;

> ECJ Judgment, Joined Cases C-222/05 through C-225/05 of 7 June 2007 (*J. van der Weerd et al.* /C-222/05/, *H. de Rooy Sr. et H. de Rooy Jr.* /C-223/05/, *Maatschap H. et J. van 't Oever et al.* /C-224/05/ et *B. J. van Middendorp* /C-225/05/ v. *Minister van Landbouw, Natuur en Voedselkwaliteit*), published in: ECR, p. I–4233, para. (35), CELEX: 62005CJ0222.

[70] See ECJ Judgment, Case C-227/08 of 17 December 2009 (*Eva Martín Martín* v. *EDP Editores SL*), CELEX: 62008P0227C(01).

so that the protection afforded to consumers is preserved under reasonable circumstances, considering the facts of the given case. In that connection, it is necessary to emphasize that a number of directives relating to consumer protection stipulate only the minimum standard (cf. Article 8 of Directive 85/577).[71]

44.   The inconsistency with which the ECJ uses the terms *public policy* and *public interest* in consumer protection cases, is rather controversial. The landmark decision in the ***Mostaza Claro*** case is a typical example of this approach.[72] The ECJ ruled that a national court has the right to set aside the arbitral award for a breach of *public policy*. However, what is clear is that the ECJ did not mean *public policy* but *[only]* a specific *public interest* expressed through *[absolute]* mandatory rules (internationally binding rules, i.e. *overriding mandatory rules* from the perspective of private international law), which is not a component of *public policy*. Furthermore, it is hardly possible to speak of *public policy* in those matters which are regulated by secondary EU law and with respect to which EU law usually only stipulates the minimum standard (such as Directive 85/577) or the minimum standard with general guidelines (such as the *Directive* and the indicative list of unfair terms in the Annex to the *Directive*). One may also barely speak of *public policy* where the methods of safeguarding that protection are exclusively within the discretion of national law and national mechanisms of finding and protecting the law. Nonetheless, it is certainly a *qualified public interest* which, however, cannot be elevated to the level of *public policy (ordre public)*.

II.3.5. *Public interest*, overriding mandatory rules and comparison with *public policy*

45.   The importance of overriding mandatory rules has been growing, primarily in private international law; these rules are becoming a significant part of the modern conflict of laws. Article 9 of the *Rome I Regulation* is a typical example of this trend.[73] An overriding mandatory

---

[71] See ECJ Judgment, Case C-412/06 of 10 April 2008 (*Annelore Hamilton v. Volksbank Filder eG.*), CELEX: 62006CJ0412, published in: ECR, p. I–2383, para. (33).

[72] ECJ Judgment, Case C-168/05 of 26 October 2006 in *Elisa María Mostaza Claro v. Centro Móvil Milenium SL*), CELEX: 62005CJ0168, published in: ECR 2006, p. I–1421. For a detailed annotation of this decision, see below; see also a separate comparative analysis in the context of other ECJ rulings in the opening part of Chapter III.9.

[73] Rome I Regulation (cit.): Article 9 – "*1. Overriding mandatory provisions are provisions the respect for which is regarded as crucial by a country for safeguarding its public interests, such as its political, social or economic organisation, to such an extent that they are applicable to any situation falling within their scope, irrespective of the law otherwise applicable to the contract under this Regulation. 2. Nothing in this Regulation shall restrict the application of the overriding mandatory provisions of the law of the forum. 3. Effect may be given to the overriding mandatory provisions of the law of the country where the obligations arising out of the contract have to be or have been performed, in so far as*

rule exhibits, to a great extent, a number of common denominators with *public policy* enforced in the substantive-law area through the conflict-of-laws substantive reservation regarding *public policy*. Both alternatives concern the protection of an important interest of the particular country which could be classified as a *public interest*.

46. *Public policy* is a general category of value whereas an overriding mandatory rule is a normative mechanism employed to enforce the *public interest*. *Public interest* is protected by an overriding mandatory rule which may, however, pursue many other objectives as well.

47. *Public policy* is a category much narrower than *public interest*. *Public policy* is aimed at basic, fundamental values on which the life of the state is based, the violation of which may disrupt these value indicators. This is not necessarily the case (nor is it usually) with overriding mandatory rules. *Public policy* is subject to historical changes, but these changes are rather evolutionary in nature. For instance, the cohabitation of same-sex

---

those overriding mandatory provisions render the performance of the contract unlawful. In considering whether to give effect to those provisions, regard shall be had to their nature and purpose and to the consequences of their application or non-application."

The *Rome I Regulation* contains special conflict-of-law rules regarding contracts of carriage (Article 5), consumer contracts (Article 6), insurance contracts (Article 7), and individual employment contracts (Article 8).

Article 6 of the *Rome I Regulation* incorporates special conflict-of-law rules regulating consumer contracts which correlate with Article 9 of the *Rome I Regulation* and which are often considered as lex specialis to the lex generalis contained in Article 9 of the *Rome I Regulation* (cit.). Article 6 [Rome I Regulation] – [Consumer contracts] "1. *Without prejudice to Articles 5 and 7, a contract concluded by a natural person for a purpose which can be regarded as being outside his trade or profession (the consumer) with another person acting in the exercise of his trade or profession (the professional) shall be governed by the law of the country where the consumer has his habitual residence, provided that the professional: (a) pursues his commercial or professional activities in the country where the consumer has his habitual residence, or (b) by any means, directs such activities to that country or to several countries including that country, and the contract falls within the scope of such activities. 2. Notwithstanding paragraph 1, the parties may choose the law applicable to a contract which fulfils the requirements of paragraph 1, in accordance with Article 3. Such a choice may not, however, have the result of depriving the consumer of the protection afforded to him by provisions that cannot be derogated from by agreement by virtue of the law which, in the absence of choice, would have been applicable on the basis of paragraph 1. 3. If the requirements in points (a) or (b) of paragraph 1 are not fulfilled, the law applicable to a contract between a consumer and a professional shall be determined pursuant to Articles 3 and 4. 4. Paragraphs 1 and 2 shall not apply to: (a) a contract for the supply of services where the services are to be supplied to the consumer exclusively in a country other than that in which he has his habitual residence; (b) a contract of carriage other than a contract relating to package travel within the meaning of Council Directive 90/314/EEC of 13 June 1990 on package travel, package holidays and package tours [...]; (c) a contract relating to a right in rem in immovable property or a tenancy of immovable property other than a contract relating to the right to use immovable properties on a timeshare basis within the meaning of Directive 94/47/EC; (d) rights and obligations which constitute a financial instrument and rights and obligations constituting the terms and conditions governing the issuance or offer to the public and public take-over bids of transferable securities, and the subscription and redemption of units in collective investment undertakings in so far as these activities do not constitute provision of a financial service;(e) a contract concluded within the type of system falling within the scope of Article 4(1)(h).*

couples was once entirely unacceptable in society (and under the law), and any approbation thereof would have constituted an unsustainable interference with general societal norms, an interference ultimately thought to threaten the potential complete *disintegration of society*. Today, this is a category currently perceived by a significant part of society as a natural element. The purpose of *public policy* is to safeguard protection by identifying and prohibiting phenomena conflicting with fundamental value categories, which are subject to very limited and very gradual developments. Conversely, the purpose of overriding mandatory rules is the interest in actively influencing a specific behavior in a given area; they are also capable of having consequences in the future by influencing development in a certain direction in order to secure a *public interest*. This includes, for instance, situations in which developments in the capital markets necessitate the adjustment of behavior of individual investors by subjecting them to certain restrictions. This is the reason why overriding mandatory rules are very frequently administrative and financial rules. However, such rules could also include provisions stipulating certain limitations of the parties' autonomy in negotiating their contracts. This often includes rules restricting contracts on the administration of deposit accounts, current accounts, asset management of securities, and recently also the increasingly frequently discussed consumer contracts (B2C contracts). The rules thereby influence the behavior of the market participants and the parties to such relationships and regulate developments in society. These rules often strive to eliminate a specific negative phenomenon. The purpose of an overriding mandatory rule can manifest itself only in the territory of a single country, because, for example, the negative circumstances occur (to any significant extent) or have harmful social consequences only in the territory of the given state. This does not mean that, for instance, the same interest, at a general level, would not be pursued by other Member States, too. The social situation in the other Member States might not force the legislator to stipulate any strict rules for the behavior of the parties but affords the parties no, or almost no, freedom of contract with respect to the particular issue. Consequently, a particular area may be regulated identically (or almost identically) in several states, but the particular rule does not always have to be an overriding mandatory rule. When examining the purpose of a particular law, it is often necessary to thoroughly analyze the purpose of the rule in order to establish that the law has to be classified as normative. As opposed to *public policy* which guarantees protection that can be manifested as the purpose of a particular law, the interest protected by an overriding mandatory rule may sometimes respond to rapid changes in the current trends in society or in the territory of a particular Member State.

48. Contrary to *public policy* which could be classified as a more general and a significantly more intense value, the value (i.e. the interest) protected by an overriding mandatory rule must be much more specific, clearly defined, and definable. Consequently, a *public interest* protected by an overriding mandatory rule must always be precisely *identified (labeled)*, both as concerns the object of the protection and as concerns the reasons which caused the legislator to articulate and adopt the rule. On the other hand, the relevant law must be capable of protecting the interest. This does not mean that the same purpose could not be served by more overriding mandatory rules; each of them, however, must have a sufficiently effective influence on a particular protected (public) interest. As opposed to standards covered by *public policy*, a *public interest* in overriding mandatory rules must be clearly articulated, specified, and identified with a particular group of persons. *Public interest* is expressed by a specific rule or rules which find their place in valid and applicable laws and in applied legal practice. Conversely, the protection of *public policy* can be pursued by a whole set of laws, and only the mutual interaction of these laws may be able to secure the protection of this (specifically important) interest. *Public policy* does not require that the addressees of the specific interest be identified; its effects are often spread evenly and across several branches of law. The important difference between overriding mandatory rules and *public policy* is that the former have positive effects achieved by positive rules prescribing a particular behavior, whereas the latter has negative (prohibitive) effects. This is especially true as the reservation regarding *public policy* has negative (prohibitive) effects and prevents the occurrence or the consequences of a specific, principally undesirable effect. Consequently, an overriding mandatory rule positively shapes the relationship between the parties (in contractual relationships) or directs the behavior of a party (a party to a contractual or a non-contractual relationship, private-law or public-law relationship). Consumer protection is a typical example; it is the subject of *public interest*; it is manifested in the form of mandatory rules (in the national arena) and overriding mandatory rules (in the international arena, i.e. within the regime of private international law). Its intensity, however, falls below the level of *public policy*; the reservation regarding *public policy* is consequently not applicable. For a typical example, see the decision of the Austrian Supreme Court (OGH [AUT]), Case No. 3 Ob 144/09m of 22 July 2009, concerning the application of the New York Convention on the Recognition and Enforcement of Foreign Arbitral Awards (1958); the court held that a breach of the consumer protection laws in arbitral proceedings conducted in the seat of arbitration does not constitute grounds for a refusal to recognize and enforce the arbitral award in Austria [AUT] based on the reservation regarding *public policy* under Article VI(2)(b) of the *New York Convention*. Although Austria [AUT] opted for a restrictive model as concerns the admissibility (or

inadmissibility) of arbitration clauses in consumer contracts and does not allow arbitration clauses in contracts (i.e. pre-dispute arbitration clauses, for instance clauses incorporated in the business terms and conditions), it allowed the enforcement of the arbitral award in *Denmark* and concluded that it was not the subject of *public policy*. This conclusion was made despite the fact that the arbitration clause was probably contrary to Danish law as well; however, the respondents failed to raise the defense in arbitration, failed to file a motion in Denmark for annulment of the arbitral award, and raised their defense only at the stage of enforcement of the arbitral award in Austria [AUT] subject to the *New York Convention*.

II.4. Issues common to consumer protection and arbitration

49. It might appear unnecessary, but it indeed must be mentioned in this part of the book that any considerations regarding the resolution of consumer disputes, i.e. any study focused on such disputes and the resolution thereof by any method other than litigation, require that we first understand the usual laws regarding contractual consumer relationships. These laws are supposed to guarantee specific protection to the consumer and their application in a situation where no amicable resolution of the dispute appears possible or where an authoritative resolution of the dispute arising from the consumer contract is necessary. On the one hand, problems arise in common transactions between consumers and professionals and are connected with the often presumed vulnerability of the consumer in his or her relations with professionals. These problems exhibit certain common features in most countries. On the other hand, the alternatives whereby these problems can be solved are diverse. They include, in particular, various forms of conciliation (mediation) or dispute resolution methods other than adversarial trials aimed at finding the law – such as arbitration or litigation. Such methods of resolving consumer disputes, i.e. other than by an authoritative finding of the law, which are also heavily supported, for instance, at the *Community* level, differ under the individual legal systems. It is necessary to point out that these alternative dispute resolution (ADR – Alternative Dispute Resolution)[74] methods are treated in this publication only marginally.[75] The aim of this book is to

---

[74] It has to be emphasized that many countries, especially those with the Anglo-American tradition, classify arbitration under the category of *ADR*. The continental approach separates arbitration from *ADR* and finds it much closer to litigation. In any case, however, the continental approach views arbitration as adversarial proceedings aimed at finding the law, which results in an authoritative decision subject to enforcement supported by the enforcement power of public authorities, despite the fact that the arbitral proceedings as such exhibit a private-law nature.

[75] This book is therefore based on the traditional continental approach, i.e. that arbitration is not a part of ADR. It is necessary to point out, though, that the EU conception published on 29 November

focus exclusively on the issue of the resolution of consumer disputes in adversarial proceedings, specifically those in arbitration.

II.5. Scope of consumer protection issues

II.5.1. Weaker contracting party and the average consumer

50.   The vulnerability of consumers results from their relationships with professionals who have a strong negotiating position and broader access to information. The conclusion of a contract with a consumer is an ordinary task for the professional, repeatedly and regularly performed in the course of his or her business. It is justified to presume that the professional can manage the task better than the consumer who has little experience and, frequently, limited possibilities of active and efficient legal support. It is often highlighted, and this is particularly significant in the context of arbitration, that the consumer often has only a limited possibility of implementing any changes in the business terms and conditions. The circumstances attending the conclusion of consumer contracts are also frequently characterized by the somewhat laconic but nonetheless very fitting *"take it or leave it."*[76] On the other hand, it is always necessary – and probably fundamental even in proceedings regarding consumer contracts – to properly estimate the limits of this protection which ought to be (simply speaking) a protection within the standard afforded to the **average consumer.**[77] The reason is that although consumer protection is regarded as one of the crucial perspectives even in EU legislation, it is not acceptable to impose all the risks of the contractual relationship on the professional and de facto absolve the consumer of all responsibility. Such an approach would constitute an abuse of rights and conflict with the fundamental principles of a law-abiding society. These principles require, inter alia, that each individual assume an adequate measure of responsibility for his or her own legally binding acts. Principally this entails an estimate of the degree of knowledge, skills, and possibilities of the average or rather common consumer,[78] and application of this estimate to the specific

---

2011 does include arbitration under ADR, which is somewhat surprising considering the prevailing doctrinal trends in the EU. The proposals of 29 November 2011 are analyzed below.

[76] See also below, the footnote regarding *adhesion contracts.*

[77] See also para. (18) of the Preamble to Directive 2005/29/EC according to which the degree of prudence possessed by today's *average consumer* must be subject to a stricter test than before (not only cursory or perfunctory diligence but a reasonable degree of circumspection and carefulness). For an analogous example, see also Supreme Court (CZ) Judgment, Case No. 32 Cdo 4661/2007 of 23 October 2008, available online at: http://www.nsoud.cz/rozhod.php?action=read&id=45311 &searchstr=32+Cdo+4661%2F2007 [last access 24 May 2009]. Concerning the term *"average consumer"*, see also Judgment of the SC CR [CZE], Case No. 23 Cdo 1201/2009 of 29 June 2010; this judgment is annotated in detail elsewhere in this book – see the excursus into Czech law.

[78] Concerning said issue see also the Judgment of the SC CR [CZE], Case No. 32 Odo 229/2006 of 30 May 2007, which reads as follows (cit.): "(1) *The criterion of 'average consumer' is based on a sufficiently informed consumer who is reasonably circumspect and diligent, considering the social,*

factual and legal situation and ultimately to the individual dispute and its resolution. Indeed, even EU standards do not go so far as to afford absolute protection to the consumer who fails to protect his or her interests or, indeed, abuses the consumer protection laws.[79]

51. A typical example of a situation in which the safeguarding of a reasonable special protection to the consumer is justified and desirable are **adhesion contracts,** i.e. contracts with respect to which **the consumer may either accept or decline the offer as a whole;** he or she can hardly influence the contents of the offer by any negotiation nor modify the offer on the basis of the process of establishing the contractual consensus of the parties. If a particular consumer enters into legal transactions with bigger professional entities, modifications (changes) of the contract or of the general terms and conditions compared to the standard forms used by the professional are often out of the question. Consequently, professionals find themselves able to exert substantial pressure and introduce provisions in their contracts which put consumers at a major advantage. Combined with the consumer's lack of information, this situation results in significantly imbalanced contracts.

52. In the international arena, i.e. in an environment crossing state borders (i.e. in relationships with an international dimension), this problem is further multiplied. Consumer contracts were once mostly national. Consumers were expected to leave their domestic environment and the exclusive jurisdiction of [their] national law much less frequently than professionals were. Consequently, the resolution of any conflicts which have arisen has been traditionally the domain of national laws (laws of national origin). Even tourists who enter into consumer contracts outside their home country cannot be distinguished from domestic consumers (simply because they are not entering into the contract "*from*" another country). The recent unusual expansion of private-law

---

cultural and linguistic factors. (2) *Almost every consumer expects that advertisements promoting goods or services of daily consumption necessarily entail a certain degree of exaggeration and hyperbole which the consumer does not believe."* Adopted from an annotation in: *Ondrejová, D.* Generální klauzule nekalé soutěže v aktuální rozhodovací praxi Nejvyššího soudu ČR. [Title in translation: The General Unfair Competition Clause in the Contemporary Case Law of the Supreme Court of the Czech Republic]. Soudní rozhledy, 2009, Vol. 15, No. 4, pp. 121–126, here p. 126. The judgment is also available online at: http://www.nsoud.cz/rozhod.php?action=read&id= 36076&searchstr=32+Odo+229%2F2006 [last access 23 May 2009].

[79] These conclusions can be reached, for instance, on the basis of the following rulings: the ECJ judgment in *Pannon GSM* which is annotated in detail in the excursus into EU law, the ECJ's case law, the Judgment of the Madrid Appeals Court [ESP], Case No. 28079370102010100498 of 12 November 2010 (*Juan Pedro v. Metrovacesa S.A.*), which is annotated in detail in the excursus into Spanish law included in this book, as well as other decisions. Moreover, these rulings and other circumstances indicate that the violation of consumer protection rules in the conclusion of arbitration agreements does not have the consequences referred to in some legal systems as "*absolute invalidity*" (for instance, in [CZE], [AUT], et al.), "*ineffectiveness*" (for instance, [DEU]), etc.

relationships with an international or transnational, cross-border, dimension at the European level has been, naturally, strongly influenced by migration within the single (free) market. The application of the fundamental freedoms of the single market means that any legal relationship, and primarily any contractual relationship, must be basically *a priori* viewed from the perspective of the [potential] existence of a specific international dimension.[80] This dimension can significantly influence the legal (conflict-of-laws) status of the relationship. In that connection, the focus is primarily on the governing (applicable) substantive law, including the applicable mechanisms employed to protect and enforce rights. Consequently, it comes as no surprise that this particular issue has attracted exceptional attention within the EU in the form of a fairly extensive and wide-reaching harmonizing legislation.

53.   In addition, active electronic communication has significantly facilitated and helped to expand the practice of concluding consumer contracts between parties from different countries. Nonetheless, the presumption is that when dealing with professionals outside their home country, consumers are even less acquainted with the potentially applicable laws of another country. The same, however, holds true for certain groups of professionals. It especially applies to small enterprises which may be capable of doing business with the use of electronic media, but they are presumed to have more limited knowledge with respect to consumer legislation in the markets of those countries where they succeed thanks to their electronic communication.

II.5.2. Claims made in consumer disputes

54.   These and many other specific considerations influence consumer legislation at the national as well as the international level. National consumer protection laws in turn influence the resolution of disputes to which the consumer is a party. Nonetheless, **litigation involving consumer claims**, despite the existence of many national specifics, **exhibits a number of common features.** For instance: **(i)** The quantification of consumer claims indicates that such claims are often small (petty), and frequently almost negligible.[81] **(ii)** It is unlikely that consumers could afford extensive and often very demanding, i.e. expensive, legal consultancy or be able to pay high court fees, albeit only in the form of down payments. This contrasts with the fact that most

---

[80] Cf. for instance *Bělohlávek, A.* Význam mezinárodního prvku v závazkových vztazích. [Title in translation: Significance of the International Dimension in Obligations]. Právník, 2006, Vol. 145, No. 5, pp. 568–578 et al.

[81] See *Favre-Bulle, X.* Arbitrage et Règlement alternative des litiges (ADR): une autre justice pour les consommateurs? In: *Théovenoz, L. et Reich, N.* (eds.) Droit de la consommation, Liber Amicorum Bernd Stauder, Genève: Schulthess, 2006, p. 97 et seq., here p. 182 and IA. European Citizens and Access to Justice, Eurobarometer Special 195/ Edition 60.0, October 2004.

legal systems (at least in consumer disputes) broadly apply the principle which stipulates that the obligation to pay the costs of proceedings is imposed on the parties depending on their success in the dispute. We could similarly analyze many other typical features exhibited by consumer disputes in various proceedings. In consequence thereof, disputes with consumers are characteristic for the **disproportion between the contested economic value and the costs of its settlement in court.**[82] It is therefore unlikely that consumers would sue if the anticipated costs compared to the likely outcome were not in their favor or if the financing of such costs, albeit only in the form of down payments, placed an unreasonable or even an unbearable burden on consumers. This could ultimately result in the *denial of justice for consumers' claims.*

II.5.3. Consumer contract

(a) Consumer contract (contract concluded by a consumer)

55.   It is necessary to emphasize that basically all legal systems are based on the premise that the *consumer contract* is not a special type of contract. Indeed, consumer contracts only demarcate the nature of the particular contract, for instance a purchase contract, a contract for the manufacture or production of goods, etc., as well as any other associated legal effects explicitly provided for by the law.[83] Any contract (contractual relationship) can be a consumer contract if characterized by, primarily, **(i)** special contracting parties. The important thing is that one of the parties usually acts in connection with a business or a particular profession, or in the pursuit of the purpose for which it was established (this applies to legal persons), while the other party, conversely, acts exclusively in connection with satisfying his or her personal needs.[84] Consequently, the emphasis is not on the type of

---

[82] Commission [EC] Recommendation 98/257/EC of 30 March 1998, *OJ* L 115, 17 April 1998, pp. 31–34.
[83] Cf. *Wright, I.* Spotřebitelské smlouvy. [Title in translation: Consumer Contracts]. Juristic.cz. Available online at: http://obcanskepravo.juristic.cz/69897/ (last access 2 May 2009).
[84] An example of how the consumer is defined under certain EU directives:
➢ Directive 85/577/EEC (Article 2) according to which consumer means a natural person who is acting for purposes which can be regarded as outside his trade or profession;
➢ Directive 87/102/EEC (Article 1(2)(a)) defines consumer as a natural person who is acting for purposes which can be regarded as outside his trade or profession;
➢ Directive 90/314/EEC (Article 2(4)) defines consumer as a person who orders a package (travel service), or any person on whose behalf a package is ordered (differentiation of the principal contractor and other beneficiaries) or even any person to whom a package is transferred;
➢ Directive 90/13/EEC (Article 2(b)) defines consumer as any natural person who is acting for purposes which are outside his trade, business or profession (outside its purpose);
➢ Directive 94/47/EC (Article 2) mentions purchaser as a natural person to whom a right is being transferred and who acts outside his or her profession or job;
➢ Directive 97/7/EC (Article 2(2)) according to which consumer means a natural person who is acting for purposes which can be regarded as outside his trade or profession;

contract. The legislation in certain countries therefore attempts to enhance the transparency of the concept by abandoning the usual term *consumer contract* and using a more verbose expression such as a *"contract concluded by a consumer."*[85] However, a *"consumer contract"* has another qualifying feature, namely **(ii)** the purpose of the contract and, as a secondary though not negligible element, **(iii)** the method whereby the contract was entered into. In any case, in order for the contract to be classified as a consumer contract **it must meet both the first and the second above-mentioned criteria,**[86] i.e. one or more parties to the contract must be in the position of a consumer (most often a natural person although despite the ECJ's attempt to limit the concept of *consumer* to individuals or rather, natural persons),[87] the proper interpretation of consumer is not quite clear and a more extensive

---

➢ Directive 98/6/EC (Article 2(e)) defines consumer as any natural person who buys a product for purposes that do not fall within the sphere of his commercial or professional activity;
➢ Directive 1999/44/EC (Article 2(e)) according to which consumer means a natural person who is acting for purposes which can be regarded as outside his trade or profession;
➢ Directive 2000/31/EC (Article 2(e)) which subjects the consumer's acts to the same conditions, although it only refers to distance contracts;
➢ Directive 2002/65/EC (Article 2(d)) which defines the consumer as any natural person who is acting for purposes which are outside his trade, business, or profession;
➢ Directive 2005/29/EC (Article 2(a)) defines the consumer as any natural person who, in commercial practices, is acting for purposes which are outside his trade, business, craft, or profession.
The differences between the definitions in the individual directives are rather negligible although the individual language versions feature more or less significant variations. Nevertheless, there are two basic denominators common to these definitions, i.e. (i) a natural person (ii) who is acting for purposes which cannot be attributed to his or her professional, business, or commercial activity. Cf. *Ebers, M.* Strukturelle Gemeinsamkeiten der Richtlinien: Der Begriff des Verbrauchers. Verbraucherrechtskompendium – Rechtsvergleichende Studie. Available online at: www.eu-consumer-law.org/consumerstudy_part3a_de.pdf (last access 31 May 2009).
[85] For example:
➢ Czech terminology which is to be introduced by the new Civil Code (NCC [CZE]) *"smlouvy uzavírané spotřebitelem"* [*contracts concluded by a consumer*];
➢ French terminology: *"contracts conclus avec les consommateurs"*;
➢ Italian terminology: *"contratti stipulati con i consumatori"*;
➢ Spanish terminology: *"contratos celebrados con consumidores"*;
and others. The author does not, however, consider the circumlocutory expression necessary and uses the widely accepted and well-understood *"consumer contract."*
[86] Cf. also *Schmitz, P.* Schiedsvereinbarungen in der notariellen Praxis. Rheinische Notar-Zeitschrift, 2003, No. 12, pp. 591–612, here p. 601. Schmitz analyzes the definition of consumer disputes and points out that the determination of whether a given dispute is a consumer dispute or not depends both on the nature of the parties and on the nature of the dispute (probably primarily as concerns the subject of the dispute, although Schmitz does not elaborate on this point any further). The author of this book fully supports this opinion and emphasizes that in defining a dispute as a *potential* consumer dispute the nature of the dispute (subject) is often unreasonably suppressed and only the classification of the parties is emphasized, which is certainly not correct.
[87] See also:
➢ ECJ Judgment, Case C-541/99 of 22 November 2001 (*Sté Cape Snc* v. *Idealservice Srl.*) or
➢ ECJ Judgment, Case C-542/99 of 22 November 2001 (*Idealservice*) in which the ECJ ruled that only a natural person could be a consumer.

interpretation of *consumer*[88] is sometimes accepted in legislation[89] and in practical application, including case law,[90] of the individual Member

---

[88] Cf. Judgment of the BGH [DEU], Case No. XI ZR 63/01 of 23 October 2001 (decision annotated in: NJW, 2002, p. 368 et seq.), according to which a *civil-law corporation* (*Gesellschaft des bürgerlichen Rechts*) can also be a consumer if all members of the corporation are natural persons who have thereby joined forces in order to protect their interests. The case law of the Member States contains many similar examples, because the limits of interpretation in the Member States are rather liberal in this regard. However, it is necessary to emphasize the traditional general rules of German law which affords broad protection to the *weaker contracting party*, irrespective of the status of the party (formerly in the AGBG [DEU], after the amendment of the civil law of obligations incorporated in the BGB [DEU]).

[89] After all, each country has its own national rules and attempts to define the consumer; see:

- ➤ [AUT] [Austria] Consumer Protection Act (*Konsumentenschutzgesetz*): definition in Subparagraph 2 of Section 1(1) and in Section (1)(2) implementing Directives 85/577/EEC, 93/13/EEC, 94/47/EC, 97/7/EC, and 1999/44/EC.
- ➤ [BEL] [Belgium] Act of 14 July 1991 on Business Practices, Consumer Information and Consumer Protection: Definition in Article 1(7). The Act implements Directives 85/577/EEC, 93/13/EEC, 97/7/EC, 98/6/EC, and Act of 2 August 2002 on Misleading and Comparative Advertising and Unfair Terms in Contracts and on Doorstep Selling through Independent Salesmen, definition in Article 2(2); these rules are implemented by Directives 93/13/EEC, and 97/7/EC. It combines the rules concerning distance contracts with the rules concerning contracts concluded away from the professional's business premises. The same approach is also taken in Estonia, [EST], Latvia [LVA], and Portugal [PRT].
- ➤ [BGR] [Bulgaria] Consumer Protection Act of 9 December 2005 which defines the consumer in Section 13(1) and which implements Directives 85/577/EEC, 93/13/EEC, 94/47/EC, 97/7/EC, and 1999/44/EC.
- ➤ [CZE] [Czech Republic] In the Czech Republic, the definition of consumer, *collectively* encompassing several sources of *Community* law, is incorporated in Section 52(3) of the CC [CZE]; the CC [CZE] especially introduces the following into the Czech legal system: Directives 85/577/EEC, 93/13/EEC, 94/47/EC, 97/7/EC, and 1999/44/EC (at least as concerns the definition of consumer). Regarding the approach adopted by the new Civil Code (NCC [CZE]), see the excursus into Czech law.
- ➤ [DEU] [Germany] As the author has already mentioned above, the German definition of consumer is incorporated in Section 13 of the BGB [DEU]; the German Civil Code thereby especially implements Directives 85/577/EEC, 93/13/EEC, 94/47/EC, 97/7/EC, 98/6/EC, and 1999/44/EC.
- ➤ [DNK] [Denmark] Act No. 451 of 9 June 2004 on Certain Consumer Contracts, which defines consumer in Section 3(1) and which implements Directives 85/577/EEC and 97/7/EC. Act No. 26/1984 on Consumer Protection: Articles 1(2) and (3). The Act implements Directives 85/577/EEC, 93/13/EEC, 97/7/EC, and 1999/44/EC.
- ➤ [EST] [Estonia] Consumer Protection Act: Article 2(1). This Act implements in the Estonian legal system Directives 93/13/EEC, 97/7/EC, 98/6/EC, and 1999/44/EC. The Act on Obligations contains the definition of consumer in Article 34; the Act primarily implements Directives 85/577/EEC, 93/13/EEC, 94/47/EC, 97/7/EC, and 1999/44/EC. Estonia logically combines the rules concerning distance contracts with the rules concerning contracts entered into in the form of door-to-door selling, or sales made away from the professional's business premises. The laws of Belgium [BEL], Latvia [LVA], and Portugal [PRT] have adopted a similar approach.
- ➤ [FIN] [Finland] The respective rules are primarily incorporated in Consumer Protection Act No. 38/1978 of 20 January 1978, as amended by Act No. 29/2005, Chapter 1, Section 4; the Act implements Directives 85/577/EEC, 93/13/EEC, 94/47/EC, 97/7/EC, 98/6/EC, and 1999/44/EC. An unofficial translation is available at the website of the Finnish Ministry of Justice at: http://www.finlex.fi/pdf/saadkaan/E9780038.PDF [last access 14 January 2012].
- ➤ [GRE] Act No. 2251/94 on Consumer Protection. Consumer is defined in Section 1(4)(α). This Act also implements Directives 85/577/EEC, 93/13/EEC, 97/7/EC, and 1999/44/EC.

States) in relation to whom the performance under the contract is supposed to meet his or her private (i.e. other than employment) or professional needs and **(ii)** one or more parties (individuals or legal entities) conclude the contract and provide performance under the contract within the scope of and in performance of their entrepreneurial, professional, or other similar activity, this being of other than a dependent nature, and in relation to whom the conclusion of the contract is supposed to fulfill the purpose of their business in the broadest sense. Indeed, the ECJ itself admits that even a professional could be considered a consumer, providing the professional concluded the contract for a purpose which is not related to his or her business.[91]

- ➢ [ITA] [Italy] The definition of consumer in Italy, implementing several directives collectively, is incorporated in Article 3(1)(a) and (b) of the Consumer Protection Act which implements Directives 85/577/EEC, 93/13/EEC, 97/7/EC, 98/6/EC, and 1999/44/EC.
- ➢ [LTU] [Lithuania] Consumer Protection Act: Article 2(1) implementing Directives 85/577/EEC, 93/13/EEC, 94/47/EC, 97/7/EC, 98/6/EC, and 1999/44/EC.
- ➢ Civil Act: Article 6.350 para. 1. The Act implements Directives 85/577/EEC, 93/13/EEC, 94/47/EC, 97/7/EC, 98/6/EC, and 1999/44/EC.
- ➢ [LVA] [Latvia] Consumer Rights Protection Act: Article 1(1) sub-par. (3). The Act implements Directives 85/577/EEC, 93/13/EEC, 94/47/EC, 97/7/EC, 98/6/EC and 1999/44/EC.
- ➢ [MLT] [Malta] Act Regulating Certain Consumer Issues: Article 2. The Act implements Directives 85/577/EEC, 93/13/EEC, 94/47/EC, 97/7/EC, 98/6/EC, and 1999/44/EC.
- ➢ [NDL] The Dutch Civil Code (BW [NDL] contains the definition of consumer in Article 7:5(1) and implements Directives 97/7/EC and 1999/44/EC.
- ➢ [PRT] Consumer Protection Act No. 94/96: Article 2(1). Implements Directives 93/13/EEC, 98/6/EC, 1999/44/EC and Regulation No. 143/2001 of 26 April 2001, in which the consumer is defined in Article 1(3)(a) and which implements in the Portuguese legal system the obligations arising from Directives 85/577/EEC and 98/7/EC. Portugal [PRT] combines the rules concerning distance contracts with the rules concerning contracts entered into in the form of door-to-door selling, or sales made away from the professional's business premises, similarly see Belgium [BEL], Estonia [EST], and Latvia [LVA]).
- ➢ [POL] Article 22 k. c. [POL] in connection with Directives 85/577/EEC, 98/6/EC, and 97/7/EC.
- ➢ [SVK] Act No. 108/2000 on Consumer Protection in Doorstep Selling and Distance Contracts: Section 1 which implements Directives 85/577/EEC, 97/7/EC, and the Slovak Civil Code which defines the consumer in Section 52 and implements Directives 93/13/EEC and 94/47/EC.
- ➢ [SVN] Act on Consumer Protection in Distance Contracts and Doorstep Selling: Article 2. The Act implements both Directive 85/577/EEC and Directive 97/7/EC.
- ➢ [SWE] Act on Consumer Protection in Distance Contracts and Doorstep Selling. Joint definition of consumer is incorporated in Article 2. The Act implements Directives 85/577/EEC and 97/7/EC.

[90] See Judgment of the BGH [DEU], Case No. X ZR 17/01 of 16 April 2002, available online at: http://www.eu-consumer-law.org/caselaw14.pdf [last access 21 December 2010]; This case is in connection with Directive 90/314/EEC of 13 June 1990 on package travel, package holidays and package tours, published in: Official Journal L 158, 23 June 1990, pp. 59–64, CELEX: 31990LO324 et al.

[91] See ECJ Judgment, Case C 361/89 of 14 March 1991 (*criminal proceedings against Patrice Di Pinto*), CELEX: 61989CJ0361, published in: ECR 1991, p. I–01189.

The same conclusion was reached by the national (domestic) courts in Hungary [HUN] and in France [FRA]:

- ➢ Judgment of the Supreme Court of Hungary [HUN], Case No. EBH2004.1093, available in: Legf. Bír. Kfv., 2003, under the Ref. No. III. 38.675/2003;
- ➢ Decision of the Cass. [FRA] (civ. I), Case No. 02-13285 of 15 March 2005 (*Syndicat départemental de contrôle laitier de la Mayenne*).

The purpose of the performance agreed in the contract is in this regard closely connected with the personality of the party to the contract and can therefore be regarded as a part of the subjective requirement characterizing the consumer contract rather than the requirement itself. The purpose therefore determines the **status** of the party as the *professional* or the *consumer*, as they assume such positions within the regime of *consumer contractual relationships*.

(b) Consumer and professional

56. The **subjective requirement of consumer contracts** especially means (without limitation) the **person of the consumer** as a *natural person*, or exceptionally and in special cases in certain countries, though not in the Czech Republic, also a legal person, as evidenced by the interpretation adopted in certain EU Member States and their courts. In practice, including international practice, however, the term *consumer contract* (or *consumer relationship*) is employed in various contexts. It is true that the first attempts at the definition of this concept, (at least more intensive attempts pursuing a certain uniform approach) using the legal and legislative rules of diverse legal force and origin, have appeared only in the last 25 years, but the history of the concept of consumer protection in contractual obligations as part of a broader concept of protection afforded to the *weaker party* to a legal relationship is much older, and its consequences are much broader in the international and even in the global context. Consequently, the definition of *consumer* or *consumer contract* (or *consumer relationship*) as well as the definitions of many other concepts employed by various legal mechanisms of consumer protection and within the broader category of the protection of *weaker parties* to contractual [obligations] relationships, differ in various international situations. This enables us to define the consumer by a negative delimitation, from the perspective of the activities carried out by the consumer.

57. After all, the **concept of professional** is not subject to any uniform definition at the national level either, let alone at the international level; sometimes it is not defined at all. We can nevertheless agree that the professional is **perceived as a person whose economic activity is characterized as follows: (i)** the activity is performed by the professional in his or her own name, **(ii)** for the purpose of generating profit or other revenues which represent the professional's income necessary to cover his or her vital needs, **(iii)** the activity is performed

Other countries, however, define the consumer strictly as a natural person. These states guarantee protection against the abuse of the stronger position enjoyed by a contracting party in cases other than contracts concluded by a consumer as a *natural person* in certain specifically enumerated cases, usually on the basis of the general rules of the law of obligations or on the basis of the general principles of law, avoiding the application of special consumer protection laws.

with a certain element of stability suggesting that the person intends to carry out such activity continuously, and it is irrelevant how long the activity has actually been carried out, and **(iv)** it is an activity for which the particular person is liable, and the liability is usually characterized as strict liability.

(c) The average consumer (connection with the essential and other terms of the contract and with arbitration agreements)

58. The assessment of (un)fairness of the terms of a contract is particularly contingent on the definition of the so-called *"average consumer"* (*"common consumer"*), the evaluation criteria of which certainly change over time, just as the volume of information available to the consumer logically increases. The degree of cautiousness required of the consumer is therefore gradually increasing, too. An interesting definition of the *average* (*common*) *consumer* was offered by the German Federal Court of Justice (Supreme Court, GBH [DEU]) in 1999.[92] The court was dealing with the degree of cautiousness required of an *average consumer* which depends on the importance of the text for the particular individual.[93] Similar assessments appear from time to time in the case law of other countries, too. The Supreme Court of the Czech Republic [CZE][94] defined the *average consumer* as a sufficiently informed consumer who is reasonably diligent and careful.

59. In said case the claimant, a funeral services provider, demanded that the respondent (a healthcare facility operator) refrain from using the leaflet "Funeral Information for the Survivors," which the respondent presented to the relatives of deceased patients or other survivors in connection with the affairs that needed to be arranged after death. The leaflet recommended the services of a funeral company that was the claimant's competitor. The claimant demanded financial compensation and an apology published in three daily papers. The trial court granted the claimant's claim as concerns the obligation to refrain from the respective conduct and the published apology, but refused to award her

---

[92] Judgment of the BGH [DEU], Case No. I ZR 167/97 of 20 October 1999 (*"Orient-Teppich Muster"*). This decision belongs to the most frequently cited German decisions on unfair competition. Although the decision is based on rules which have since been repealed, the principles of the decision are still valid.

[93] This case concerned the attention paid by the reader to the individual parts of the offer of goods in advertisements.

[94] Judgment of the SC CR [CZE], Case No. 32 Odo 229/2006 of 30 May 2007. The following rulings were rendered in the preceding stages of the proceedings:
➤ Judgment of the High Court in Olomouc [CZE] (as the court of appeals), Case No. 4 Cmo 88/2003-130 of 16 December 2004 which partially reversed the
➤ Judgment of the Regional Court in Brno (as the trial court), Case No. 17 Cm 8/2001-66 of 14 March 2002.

any financial compensation. The appellate court, conversely, cancelled the obligation to publish an apology but awarded financial compensation. In the cassation appeal proceedings, the Supreme Court, however, reversed the judgment of the court of appeals and remanded the case for a new trial, holding that an *average consumer* is in this case aware of the option not to use the services of the company offered by the respondent. The Supreme Court also held that almost every consumer expects that an advertisement for goods or services of daily consumption will involve exaggeration and hyperbole which the consumer will not believe; in a situation where the consumer needs funeral services, the reasoning of a contemporary *"average customer"* will be similar, although the consumer is in a somewhat more sensitive situation.

60.   It must be emphasized, though, that **most attempts at the definition of an *average* (*common*) consumer,** as they are presented in published case law, **are not fully applicable to those terms in a consumer contract which constitute what could be referred to as the abstract *infrastructure of the contract*,** i.e. the terms which do not represent the determination of the **main subject of the contract** – the contents of mutual performance.[95] It is something that certainly attracts less attention from the consumer. It is reasonable to expect that the consumer will approach such terms with a higher degree of perceptiveness, and it is also necessary to place more rigorous demands on the clarity of the text for the consumer. Such terms obviously include **terms regarding the method whereby the parties may enforce their rights** (including arbitration agreements). On the other hand, **it is necessary to take into consideration what attention (over a longer period of time) is paid to the general amount of information possessed by the consumer.** For instance, the Ministry of Justice of the Czech Republic [CZE] estimates that the total number of disputes resolved in arbitration annually has been 150,000, most of them in connection with consumer contracts, and the Czech Republic therefore certainly belongs to those countries in which arbitration agreements have recently become the subject of heated discussions and in which the media cover this topic especially extensively. In these countries (such as the Czech Republic [CZE]), where the media pay so much attention to the topic, arbitration and arbitration agreements cannot be considered a concept unfamiliar to the [common/average] consumer; at least the term "arbitration agreement" ("arbitration," "arbitrator") ought to draw the consumer's attention. Apart from this, it is necessary to start with

---

[95] Indeed, the application of EU law in various EU Member States also indicates that special consumer protection laws [explicit special laws] can be fully applicable primarily to the main subject of the contract, or to such terms and provisions which are related to the main subject of the contracts (rescission/cancellation of the contract, information on performance, etc.) and that the general terms of the contract must often be subjected to special criteria; the factual and legal findings must also be subjected to diligent scrutiny with special care for the individual specifics of the case.

the general presumption (a rebuttable presumption) that the requirements of *transparency* for an *average consumer* are satisfied if the arbitration agreement entered into by the consumer meets the applicable special rules, providing there are any (see, for instance, Section 1031 of the ZPO [DEU], Section 3 of the ArbAct [CZE] as amended by the Amendment to the ArbAct [CZE], effective date 1 April 2012 et al.).

(d) Multilateral criteria defining a consumer contract

61.   Consumer contracts basically **only define the nature of the particular contract**, for instance, a purchase contract, a contract for the manufacture or production of goods, etc. as well as any other associated legal effects explicitly provided for by the law.[96] In other words, basically any contract (with certain exceptions) can be a consumer contract providing it meets the special requirements concerning primarily **(i)** the parties to these legal relationships, **(ii)** the purpose of the contract and, as a subsidiary but a very frequent criterion, also **(iii)** the method of conclusion of these contracts.

62.   In connection with the effects of consumer contracts on the conclusion, terms, and enforcement of these contracts, i.e. both the substantive-law and the procedural aspects, we need to employ a yet more detailed classification of *consumer contracts* characterized mainly (though not exclusively) by the method whereby they were concluded, etc. For example, we must distinguish **distance contracts, contracts concluded away from business premises (door-to-door sales), adhesion contracts,** etc.

63.   From the perspective of their effects, we must especially highlight **distance contracts** which are characterized by the lack of any personal contact between the contracting parties at the conclusion of the contract and by the fact that the expressions of will (*offer*) meet and acceptance is realized by means of distance communication all of which enable the contract to be entered into without the simultaneous physical presence of the contracting parties. These *means of communication* are also extensively elaborated on in legislation and interpretation practice (primarily including in case law as well as in explicit legal rules). For example, Czech provisions in the CC [CZE] stipulate that the means of distance communication include any and all means with the exception of written communication[97] operated by the professional whose line of

---

[96] Cf. *Wright, I.* Spotřebitelské smlouvy. [Title in translation: Consumer Contracts]. Juristic.cz. Available online at: http://obcanskepravo.juristic.cz/69897/ [last access 2 May 2009].

[97] In other words, the reference to a "communication in writing" must be construed as an exchange of messages with the use of *traditional* postal consignments (which can be delivered by postal license holders or by other entities). The reason for this exclusion of the respective method of communication, although it is also a method of distance communication, is understandable. The

business includes the provision of one or more means of distance communication, primarily anonymous (unaddressed) and addressed communication means (addressed papers, typed letters, advertisements in the press with an order form, catalogs, telephone with or without a human operator, radio, videotelephone, videotext, e-mail, fax, and television). According to the wording of the respective provision, this list is only indicative.

64.   "Consumer contract" therefore denotes a special qualifying feature of any type of contract, or any contract as such, which especially meets (without limitation) the subjective requirements (relating to the parties to these relationships); it would probably be more appropriate to speak about contracts concluded within the scope of consumer relationships or about contracts concluded with a consumer(s). In certain legal systems and subject to certain circumstances (although exceptionally) the category of consumer contracts includes employment contracts[98] through the rules generally afforded to the *weaker contracting party*; the decisive criterion is the method whereby the contract was concluded.[99] However, if the protection afforded under consumer legislation conflicts with the protection afforded under applicable labor laws (or any other special protection), the latter usually prevails, i.e. the protection which is incorporated in the labor laws or which constitutes the special protection that pursues a similar purpose as consumer protection legislation, i.e. protection of the *weaker party*. With respect to the definition of *consumer contracts* as a rather *technical* designation of

purpose of the consumer protection laws is to guarantee protection, especially in a situation where the consumer (*person*) is, by various marketing practices employed by the professionals, drawn into a situation which he or she was not prepared for. This is a situation where the consumer did not have a chance to consider in advance and thoroughly whether he or she wanted to enter into a particular contract for the purpose of receiving a particular performance or type of performance. This situation also includes when the consumer often responds to an offer which he or she is not ready for, in a situation when the consumer acts subconsciously as a result of these, usually highly sophisticated, marketing practices. However, distance communication via traditional letters is, considering the historical traditions of this means of communication, the slowest one, and both the processing of the offer and, especially, acceptance are usually realized in a situation when the party to the contract (future contract) is not under pressure and/or is at least able to consider more carefully the consequences of his or her conduct and, at the same, the party has a real opportunity to compare this offer with other offers presented by other professionals. Conversely, other means of distance communication, *faster* and often *interactive*, either do not allow such possibility or employ marketing practices (due to their direct and often *live* influence on the consumer) which *force the consumer* (again, often subconsciously) to respond automatically (for instance, advertising like "[...] *and if you call in the next ten minutes, you will get [...] completely free of charge*").

[98] Cf. Judgment of the BGH (D), Case No. XI ZR 34/05 of 8 November 2005, annotated in the final part of this commentary on Article 6 of the *Regulation*. The judgment is available online at: http://lexetius.com/2005,2955 (last access on 6 September 2008).

[99] Application of consumer protection laws to employment relationships is allowed under Section 13 of the BGB [DEU] defining the consumer; the provision refers to an *independent* business or professional activity. Employment relationships are specifically characteristic for the dependent relationship between the professional and the consumer.

contracts that are concluded within the scope of relationships of a particular type, this method of classification does not cause major problems in practice. Consequently, there is no reason to abandon the simple term *consumer contract*, whether in practice or in academic literature. It is a simplification of an expression acceptable in professional terminology. Whereas the term *consumer contract* ipso facto as a legal *institution* does not cause major problems, the definition of *consumer* and *professional*, the contents and interpretation of which determine the definition of a particular contract as a *consumer-type* contract, is the subject of heated discussions. Considering it is not a completely *new* topic, but which has only appeared in *Community* (EU) legislation in recent years, we can refer to the sufficiently rich case law of the ECJ as well as of the national courts. After all, the center of gravity inheres in the substantive laws of national origin, notwithstanding the fact that the national laws of the EU Member States are, due to wide-reaching unification, principally and in almost all regards influenced by EU law, and primarily by a number of directives and other sources.

II.6.   Resolution of consumer issues

65.   Due to the significant number of consumers – more than 360 million in the EU[100] – and their associated political influence – the legal systems of many countries have recently devoted more attention and more space to consumer disputes. The purpose of the corresponding special regulation is to safeguard an effective goods and services market for the consumer. Apart from that, the special regulation is also supposed to perform functions beneficial for professionals doing business in the consumers' markets despite the fact that in certain situations the professionals will have to waive the opportunity of applying their negotiating power to the full extent.

66.   The basis of consumer legislation (consumer protection rules) can be summarized by the following quotation (in translation) "[...] *between the strong and the poor* [...] *freedom limits and the law liberates.*"[101] Consumer legislation attempts to balance the unequal relationship.

67.   The extent to which the ability and the legal potential of professionals to apply their negotiating power can be restricted is very diverse in the international environment, especially in the non-harmonized area (as opposed to, for instance, the EU single market). For instance, whereas American law is more concentrated on the freedom of the parties to commercial transactions to resolve their disputes in compliance with

---

[100] *Rutherford, M.* Documents-Only Arbitration in Consumer Disputes. In: *Bernsteina, R. et al.* Handbook of Arbitration Practice, London, 1998, marg. 8-06.
[101] The original wording (cit.): *"Entre le fort et le faible* [...] *c'est la liberté qui opprime et la loi qui affranchit."* Lacordaire, R., P., H. -D. 52ème Conférence de Notre-Dame. Œuvres, Vol. IV, p. 494.

their needs, European law attempts to protect the party to the transaction that it considers weaker. Simply speaking (and this is perhaps the most misleading aspect), the American approach subordinates the protection of the weaker party to the concept and the principle of greater autonomy of will, whereas the European approach prefers to limit this autonomy by the *public interest* in consumer protection which could, in certain countries, be perceived as part of *public policy*.[102]

68.   There are principally two basic models that provide specific solutions to consumer disputes. The first model allows consumers to organize in associations aimed at the collective protection of their interests and at attaining a certain critical number, which will give them the opportunity to enforce their rights under standard conditions with a reasonable ratio between the costs and the results of a dispute. In consequence thereof, the association of a greater number of consumers will result in a certain equilibrium among the interest in legal protection, the actual possibilities of enforcing their rights, and the costs of exercising their rights by legal means. Many legal systems call such procedure a **class action**.

69.   The second model of resolution for consumer disputes focuses on the establishment of special fora (special mechanisms) for dispute resolution. From the very beginning the intent of the proceedings is to minimize the costs of the proceedings and to employ simple procedures.[103] For example, many legal systems have courts for minor claims which are inexpensive and easily accessible. Similar mechanisms and procedural instruments are often employed as a special method of resolution of consumer disputes. Some of these legal systems have introduced corresponding judicial (procedural) mechanisms with simplified procedures, others use various forms of out-of-court dispute resolution, including both arbitration, which is principally an authoritative process of finding the law, and other forms of alternative dispute resolution (ADR). Lawyers as legal counsel for the parties are usually unnecessary. In certain countries, the applicable laws even prescribe that a verbal pronouncement of the decision suffices and drafting detailed judgments or awards is not necessary, because the final order and a brief reasoning are usually recorded in the simplified minutes from the hearing of the case. This method of dispute resolution is not always successful. In Switzerland [CHE], for instance, federal laws

---

[102] *Drahozal, C. et Friel, R. A.* A Comparative View of Consumer Arbitration. Arbitration, 2005, Vol. 2, p. 135. Concerning the issues of *public policy* and *public interest* (especially from the EU law perspective), see separate chapter above.
[103] This is advocated by the OECD Guidelines for Consumer Protection in the Context of Electronic Commerce (E-commerce), 2000, pp. 18–19.

stipulate that the individual cantons are obliged to secure mechanisms for the resolution of minor (small) claims, but the results are described as very negative.[104] Conversely, the system of the institutional resolution of consumer disputes in Spain [ESP] or Portugal [PRT] is considered successful.

70.   The selected method then determines whether arbitration is perceived as a problem or, conversely, as a suitable, or alternative, solution. The crucial problem which is frequently (albeit not always competently) voiced in the media is that the commentators – whether the proponents or the opponents of this or that solution – usually defend one or the other of the contravening standpoints and hardly ever attempt to, or are able to, find an unbiased opinion and a neutral assessment. The practical experience of the individual countries is diverse, and the resolution of consumer disputes is precisely the arena where any simplistic conclusions are more than harmful and often ultimately detrimental to one or the other form of resolution of consumer disputes, as well as to both groups of parties to the legal (contractual) relationships of a consumer type. Unfortunately, the opinions presented in various judicial decisions are a typical example of a simplification, an a priori refusal. Such decisions can be considered an aberration, see for instance the opinion articulated in a judgment of the Regional Court in Ostrava [CZE] of 2010[105] in which the judge held, inter alia: *"The arbitral award is not a document which could serve as the basis for enforcement; it is merely a legally null and ineffective piece of scribbled paper."* Whether or not the judge in said case concluded that the arbitration agreement had suffered from defects which had rendered the agreement null and void, the words used by the judge clearly indicate his general view of arbitration as such. Such excessive statements are basically nonsensical, and only a sober view of the matter can help find suitable instruments for the resolution of consumer disputes and the corresponding legal framework. It is quite logical that the framework will often be significantly influenced by national specifics. Similarly, we frequently encounter a somewhat simplified argument used by the radical opponents of arbitration in consumer disputes, according to which EU law prohibits arbitration agreements in consumer disputes. It is not possible to draw such a conclusion after a thorough analysis of EU standards; EU law does not prohibit arbitration clauses (i.e. pre-dispute arbitration agreements) and does not principally condemn the practice of incorporating arbitration

---

[104] Favre-Bulle, X. *Arbitrage et Règlement alternative des litiges (ADR): une autre* justice pour les consommateurs? In: *Théovenoz, L. et Reich, N.* (eds.) Droit de la consommation, Liber Amicorum Bernd Stauder, Genève: Schulthess, 2006, p. 97 et seq., here p. 98.

[105] Judgment of the Regional Court in Ostrava, Case No. 33 Cm 13/2009 of 8 March 2010. The author of this book has at his disposal the full text of the respective decision. Nonetheless, it has already been cited in various sources. See *Babjáková, G.* Smlouvy uzavírané se spotřebitelem. [Title in translation: Consumer Contracts]. Právní fórum, 2011, Vol. 8, No. 7, pp. 334–339, here p. 337.

clauses in the general terms and conditions of contracts.[106] Similarly, it is not possible to argue that any and every limitation of the arbitrability of consumer disputes is a part of *public policy*.[107] EU law merely stipulates certain fundamental and, principally, very general standards for the protection of certain contracting parties (i.e. weaker contracting parties). The mechanism whereby the protection will be safeguarded is, to a great extent, a task entrusted to the national legislators in the individual Member States. Indeed, the simplification of these issues and the use of the above-mentioned arguments shielded behind EU law, without any substantial analysis, are also harmful to the search for the most effective means of protecting legal relationships as such.

II.7. Consumer arbitration

71. A global assessment necessarily requires an evaluation of the degree of success and the prevailing opinions regarding arbitration in consumer disputes. This is probably the most difficult task. The analysis of the problem must principally start with its empirical assessment. How common is arbitration in consumer disputes? How prevalent (or unavoidable) is it in the markets for basic goods and services, such as medical care, banking and employment? Were the results of arbitration indeed unfavorable to the consumer when compared to the results achievable by other dispute resolution methods, i.e. if we did not employ arbitration or if the application of arbitration or some other ADR method in these relationships were not mandatory as prescribed by some of the national legal systems?[108]

72. For example, surveys conducted in the United States reveal very conflicting results. It is sometimes argued that a survey of arbitration regarding consumer disputes does not suffice as a basis for the evaluation and application of special consumer protection procedures. The approach adopted in the U.S. is, in this regard, very reserved and very moderate as concerns the provision of different protection to the parties in consumer disputes resolved by arbitrators, compared to arbitration in regular commercial disputes (i.e. other than consumer disputes). Some surveys with reasonably specific results are sufficiently valid to support the conclusion that arbitration in consumer disputes is favorable both to the

---

[106] See Judgment of the BGH [DEU], Case No. III ZR 256/03 of 13 January 2005 annotated in detail in this book (in the part concerning arbitration in consumer disputes in Germany [DEU]).
[107] Decision of the OGH [AUT], Case No. 3 Ob 144/09m of 22 July 2009; this decision will be annotated in detail elsewhere in this book.
[108] However, this information is usually not available, save in various court reports which often do not hesitate to present absurd and extreme cases. See *Dauer, E.* Judicial Policing of Consumer Arbitration. Pepperdine Disp. Res. L. J., 2000, Vol. 91, No. 1, p. 2.

consumer[109] and to the professional. As concerns the success ratio of the parties, the results of certain studies are more in favor of the consumers[110] whereas others indicate that the professionals are almost certain to win.[111]

73. But the very fact that the professional, i.e. principally the author of the contract offer, includes an arbitration clause in the consumer contract, is a major indication of his or her conviction that it will be advantageous for him/her. From this perspective, many arbitration agreements incorporated in consumer contracts in the U.S. support the opinions voiced by the proponents of special protection for the consumers' interests. The most that could be said is that both the professional and the consumer try to benefit from arbitration. Such (available) benefits include the costs of proceedings in particular countries and for particular types of arbitration, for instance the elimination of complicated court proceedings, special simplified procedures for admitting evidence,[112] proceedings based only on written briefs or, conversely, only on oral hearings without any protracted exchange of sophisticated and, unfortunately, increasingly voluminous submissions (not only as a result of the possibility of using electronic communication and data processing).

74. One cannot, however, dismiss that arbitration in consumer disputes generally entails a number of problems, especially as concerns the access of consumers to information; there are also many issues concerning fair trial[113] and the extent to which the principles of fair trial in arbitration are (or could be) transformed, to an acceptable extent, into a form (and give rise to manifestations) different from litigation.

75. Opinions from certain countries argue that arbitration deprives the consumers of their fundamental rights in proceedings and in the protection of their rights. These rights include a jury trial in those countries where the jury is a mechanism incorporated in the legal system, or the right to court proceedings guaranteed in each and every case. The legal counsel for the parties may also argue that professionals are unduly benefiting from the process of admitting

---

[109] There are even opinions claiming that the speed of the proceedings is ultimately always an asset for the consumer. Cf. *Casey, K. R.* Hot Issues Alerts – Law Firms. Mandatory Consumer Arbitration. The Metropolitan Corporate Counsel, 5 August 2009. Available online at: http://www.metrocorpcounsel.com/current.php?artType=view&artMonth=August&artYear=2009&EntryNo=10019 [last access 7 August 2011].

[110] See *Rutledge, P.* Testimony before the U.S. House of Representatives Committee on the Judiciary (The topic of the session was "The Arbitration Fairness Act of 2007"), 25 October 2007, p. 5.

[111] See *Rutledge, P.* Testimony before the U.S. House of Representatives Committee on the Judiciary (The topic of the session was "The Arbitration Fairness Act of 2007"), 25 October 2007, p. 6.

[112] See *Amerasinghe, Ch. F.* Evidence in International Litigation, Brill Martinus Nijhoff Publishers, 2005, p. 43 et al.

[113] See *Kurkella, M.* Due Process in International Commercial Arbitration, New York: Oceana Publishing, 2005, regarding the principles of fair trial see p. 47 et al.

evidence which is, considering its complexity and systematics, insufficiently or only partially regulated in a number of the applicable arbitration rules.[114] Although an essentially identical procedural system applies to both parties to the same extent, the insufficient legal regulation of the process of admitting evidence de facto constitutes the heaviest burden for the consumer, because the consumer is more likely to be interested in getting evidence from the professionals, so that the evidence could be used against them, than vice versa.[115]

76.   Another point of criticism is targeted at the professionals who are considered to be **frequent parties to arbitration.** As concerns dispute resolution, professionals are said to have an advantage over consumers due to the fact that they are repeatedly involved in arbitration over these types of disputes. By being a party to arbitration more frequently than the individual consumer, professionals gain experience in dispute resolution which gives them an advantage over consumers; conversely, consumers have no or very limited experience. Apart from the advantage gained by experience, the issue can be complicated by a conflict of interests. Some dispute resolution centers (arbitral centers, *permanent arbitral institutions*)[116] can consider professionals who repeatedly appear as parties to disputes as permanent clients. Consequently, it is more likely that they will establish a system benefiting these "permanent clients," because the usages of large enterprises are important for strictly commercial entities providing arbitration services and facilities.[117] The same could be said about arbitrators (especially in *ad hoc* proceedings) who could realize that

---

[114] See *Kaufmann-Kohler, G.* Globalization of Arbitral Procedure, Vand. J. Transnat'l L., 2003, Vol. 36, p. 1313 et seq.

[115] See *Bělohlávek, A.* Právo použitelné na řízení před rozhodci. [Title in translation: The Law Applicable to Arbitration]. Právo a podnikání, 2005, No. 11, pp. 2 9, *Bělohlávek, A.* Procesní předpisy a rozhodčí řízení. [Title in translation: Procedural Laws and Arbitration]. Právní fórum, 2007, Vol. III, No. 12, pp. 431–444, *Bělohlávek, A. et Pezl, T.* Aplikace procesních předpisů na rozhodčí řízení. [Title in translation: The Application of Procedural Laws to Arbitration]. Právní rádce, 2008, Vol. 16, No. 2, pp. 16–24; *Degos, L., Pinsolle, P., Schläpfer, A. -V.* (ed.) Towards a Uniform International Arbitration Law, New York: Juris Publishing, 2005; *Goode, R.* The Role of the Lex Loci Arbitri in International Commercial Arbitration. Arbitration International, 2001, Vol. 17, No. 1, pp. 25–27 and in many other publications.

[116] The author is intentionally silent on *permanent arbitral institutions*. An attentive reader certainly will not miss the very sensitive context of this issue, especially in the Czech Republic. However, the focus of and the room reserved for this article do not allow even a sufficient identification of the problem, which has been labeled in our country as the status problem of arbitration centers v. *permanent arbitral institutions* in terms of Section 13 of Act No. 216/1994 Coll., as subsequently amended, on the Arbitration and Enforcement of Arbitral Awards. A diligent and serious analysis of the issue is therefore entirely out of the question. This is the reason why the author intentionally hinted at the issue and associated problems, without following this train of thought any further.

[117] See the 2010 International Arbitration Survey: Choices in International Arbitration, Queen Mary University of London / School of International Arbitration (supported by many international corporations and law firms). It follows preceding studies conducted in 2006 and 2008. Available at: http://www.arbitrationonline.org/research/2010/index.html [last access 5 August 2011] and elsewhere.

their regular appointment (and their associated remuneration) is a remuneration for awards favoring a frequent party, i.e. the party which often resorts to arbitration.

77. The factor of a frequent party [to the proceedings] is also significant with regard to the absent, or only limited, permissible review of the awards in the merits rendered in arbitration. Although Czech law, namely Section 27 of the ArbAct [CZE], and some other similar national arbitration laws, principally permit the review of arbitral awards by other arbitrators based on the parties' agreement, this possibility is employed only exceptionally, whether in national or international practice. Despite the fact that the absence of appeal in arbitration principally reduces the costs and the length of the dispute, we cannot rule out reputedly unfair decisions irremediable *au fond*.[118] For a professional involved in a number of disputes, the risk of an incidental unfavorable decision is acceptable compared to the costs saved as a result of waiver of appeal. For the unsuccessful natural person, the results could be calamitous.[119]

78. Arbitration in consumer disputes is also criticized for its lack of transparency. As opposed to most national court proceedings, arbitration is principally confidential.[120] However, this criticism is usually countered by the fact that the other recognized dispute resolution methods, which could be considered an alternative to the finding of law outside the general judicial system, such as out-of-court settlements, are confidential, too.[121] On the other hand, although

---

[118] Cf. *Bělohlávek, A. et Pezl, T.* Mezinárodní a tuzemské rozhodčí řízení z pohledu čl. 36 listiny základních práv a svobod a pravomocí soudů a ústavou garantovaných práv (Institut zrušení rozhodčího nálezu v souvislosti se zákazem revision au fond). [Title in translation: International and Domestic Arbitration from the Perspective of Article 36 of the Charter of Fundamental Rights and Freedoms and the Powers of the Courts and the Rights Guaranteed under the Constitution (Annulment of Arbitral Awards in Connection with the Prohibition of *Revision au Fond*)]. Právník, 2006, Vol. 146, No. 7, pp. 768–802.

[119] *Dauer, E.* Judicial Policing of Consumer Arbitration. Pepperdine Dispute Resolution Law Journal, 2000, Vol. 91, No. 1, p. 3.

[120] *Bělohlávek, A.* Confidentiality and Publicity in Investment Arbitration, Public Interest and the Scope of Powers Vested in Arbitral Tribunals. In: *Bělohlávek, A. et Rozehnalová, N.* CYArb – Czech (& Central European) Yearbook of Arbitration, 2011, Vol. 1, pp. 23–47 (in the cited source see also the comparison to arbitrations in other than consumer disputes).

[121] Indeed, the ECtHR has repeatedly concluded that a waiver of the right to public proceedings (public trial / public hearing) is legitimate if based on a voluntary expression of will. In connection with arbitration, see the ECtHR in *Osmo Suovaniemi* et al. v. *Finland* (dec.), Case No. N. 31.737, 23 February 1999. The issue of fair trial within the meaning of oral hearings and public proceedings was addressed by the ECtHR generally with respect to litigation in:
➢ *Allan Jacobsson* v. *Sweden*, ECHR Rep., 19 February 1998 (an unpublished decision);
➢ *Håkansson* v. *Sweden*, 13 EHRR 1 (1990), ECHR Rep.;
➢ *Pauger* v. *Austria*, 25 EHRR 105 (1997), ECHR Rep.;
➢ *Bryan* v. *The United Kingdom*, 21 EHRR 342 (1995), ECHR Rep.
The issues of public court proceedings were specifically addressed by the ECtHR in:
➢ *Diennet* v. *France*, 21 EHRR 554 (1995), ECHR Rep.;

litigation is public (with certain exceptions)[122] the course of the proceedings is hardly interesting to any third party. After all, the same holds true for the publicity of case law. General case law is not well-known either, with the exception of certain decisions of the lower courts which deserve being published or annotated, but this is usually only incidental. For example, in the Czech Republic the only decisions which are systematically published are usually only the rulings of the Supreme Court and the Supreme Administrative Court, as the results of frequently long-term proceedings; the decisions of the lower courts are published only exceptionally. The same holds true for most countries. In connection with lengthy litigation involving more instances, it is necessary to emphasize the qualities of arbitration as cheaper and simpler proceedings – the minimization of costs, the expeditiousness, and the less rigorous formal requirements are the general criteria which consumer dispute resolution methods ought to fulfill. Besides, litigation in many countries is presently a very formal procedure, which often jeopardizes its ability to serve as a general guarantee of efficient protection of the law. For instance, one may find that the Czech procedural system often makes the very informal substantive law difficult to enforce. But the problem is not just limited to the Czech Republic, it greatly affects many other countries.[123] Also, important not to dismiss is the significant psychological factor which hypothetically disqualifies litigation compared to arbitration in consumer disputes. Whether admitted or not, it is true that receiving even a simple service notification document from the court is frequently stressful for regular people. The rules regulating behavior and hearings in courts (gowns,

---

➤ *Sutter* v. *Switzerland*, 6 EHRR 272 /1984), ECHR Rep.;
➤ *Ruiz-Mateo* v. *Spain* 16 EHRR 505 /1993), ECHR Rep.;
➤ *X* v. *Austria* (Dec. Commission), No. 5362/72, 42 CD 145 (1972), EComHR, (ix) *Kamasinski* v. *Austria*, 13 EHRR 36 (1989), ECHR Rep.
At the same time, however, it is required that the waiver of a particular right (as a component of a fair trial) must be unequivocal. For more details see, Bělohlávek, A. Arbitration from the Perspective of the Right to Legal Protection and the Right to Court Proceedings (the Right to Have One's Case Dealt with by a Court): Significance of Autonomy and the Scope of Right to a Fair Trial. In: Bělohlávek, A. et Rozehnalová, N. Czech (& Central European) Yearbook of Arbitration. The Relationship between Constitutional Values, Human Rights and Arbitration, Huntington (New York): JurisNet, 2011, Vol. I, pp. 47-70.
[122] See the ECtHR in *Osmo Suovaniemi et al.* v. *Finland* (dec.), Case No. N. 31.737, 23 February 1999 et al. However, some sources are based on the presumption that the arbitration agreement automatically implies an intention to exclude the public. This is typical primarily for common law countries. See *Joseph, D.* Jurisdiction and Arbitration Agreements and Their Enforcement. London: Sweet & Maxwell, 2005, p. 97, marg. 4.22. *Joseph* refers to the case [GBR] *Dept. of Economic Policy and Development of the City of Moscow* v. *Bankers Trust Co. International Bank*, [2004] 2 Lloyd's Rep. 1, 17. It is evident that the key point is voluntariness in a genuine consensus regarding the arbitration agreement. After all, this is the crucial issue especially as concerns consumer contracts and arbitration agreements concluded between a consumer and a professional.
[123] As a matter of fact, the proceedings in the Czech Republic are faster than in many other European countries.

oral presentations done in standing positions, etc.), which are undoubtedly necessary, correct, and justified among public authorities, could in consumer disputes favor the entities regularly appearing in these proceedings, i.e. the professionals. This very simple and often rather simplified list of certain factors, many of which are criticized by this or that system, indicates how easy it is to criticize one or the other system and how difficult it is to come up with an impartial and objective evaluation. Unfortunately, most of the various evaluations of the individual systems are limited to the same list and to the same extent attempted above in the listing of their most important aspects. A thorough and objective analysis is usually absent, and many commentators and persons evaluating the dispute resolution methods voice their opinions before the analysis itself and rather look for and emphasize arguments favoring their own views. Obviously, the procedure should be reversed, i.e. the opinion should be articulated only after a thorough and objective analysis.

II.8. Right to legal protection versus right to judicial protection and the importance of autonomy

79.   The European Court of Human Rights (ECtHR) is regularly confronted with issues and decisions dealing with arbitration. Logically, arbitral issues are discussed in connection with applications complaining of the violation of Article 6(1) of the ECHR.[124] However, one may argue that the application of the ECHR and, generally, the constitutional principles relating to arbitration cannot be limited to the issue of a *fair trial*. These matters are also important from the view of the protection (inviolability) of ownership and other fundamental rights, although this particular perspective has been somewhat neglected by the case law of the ECtHR.[125]

80.   The ECtHR commonly deals with issues such as whether and to what extent Article 6(1) of the ECHR is applicable to arbitration and whether and to what extent it is possible to *waive* these standards or modify the arbitral proceedings by contract, meaning the right to agree upon an arbitration agreement and, as the case may be, the case management of the arbitral proceedings. In that connection, the ECtHR distinguishes between *ad hoc* arbitral proceedings and institutionalized proceedings[126] and also deals with a number of other issues.

---

[124] Cf. in general *Mikule, V.* Ještě ke správnímu soudnictví a jeho organizaci. [Title in translation: A Few More Comments on the Administrative Judiciary and its Organization]. Právní praxe, 1994, No. 4, p. 185.

[125] But it is not an *omission* on the part of the ECtHR. The ECtHR is bound by the wording of the complaint (application) addressed to the Court. It is usually the fault of the parties who fail to see a number of potential connections under constitutional law in conjunction with other fundamental rights. This problem is, however, by no means limited to arbitration.

[126] Cf. *Bělohlávek, A.* Rozhodčí řízení ad hoc vs. řízení před stálými rozhodčími soudy a postavení tzv. rozhodčích center. [Title in translation: Ad Hoc Arbitration v. Proceedings before Permanent

81.   The right to enter into an arbitration agreement, i.e. waive judicial protection in terms of the protection afforded by public authorities (the judiciary), must be looked for primarily in another fundamental freedom, namely the freedom to express one's will.[127] Freedom of will is guaranteed by national constitutional codes of fundamental rights and by rules of international origin, especially the ECHR.[128] The freedom to express one's will must be interpreted as included in the principles of the rule of law;[129] at the same time, the case law of the supreme and constitutional courts of many countries also indicates that this doctrine must be perceived as principally defining the limits of the exercise of state power vis-à-vis the individual's autonomous will. Autonomy of will and the free individual conduct of individuals must be interpreted both as a restriction on the state's power to limit the conduct of individuals by means other than an explicit statutory prohibition or an explicit statutory order and as full respect observed by the state in the exercise of free will, or a respect for the acts of individuals which are not explicitly prohibited or ordered (subject to mandatory or even overriding mandatory rules).[130]

Arbitral Institutions and the Status of Arbitral Centers]. Bulletin advokacie, 2005, No. 10, p. 54; *Lisse, L.* K právnímu postavení arbitrážních center. [Title in translation: Regarding the Legal Status of Arbitral Centers]. Bulletin advokacie, 2006, No. 1, p. 40; *Pavelka, M.* Rozhodčí řízení před tzv. rozhodčími centry. [Title in translation: Arbitration before Arbitral Centers]. Bulletin advokacie, 2005, Nos. 7–8, p. 58; *Schütze, R. A. et al.* Institutionelle Schiedsgerichtsbarkeit, Köln/R.: Carl Heymanns, 2006; *Trapl, V.* K otázce zřizování stálých rozhodčích soudů [Title in translation: Regarding the Issue of Forming Permanent Arbitral Institutions], Právní praxe v podnikání, 1999, Vol. 8, No. 7, p. 19; *Lachnit, P.* Statut rozhodčího soudu při HK ČR a AK ČR. [Title in translation: The Statute of the Arbitration Court Attached to the Economic Chamber of the Czech Republic and the Agricultural Chamber of the Czech Republic]. Daně a finance, 1998, No. 24, p. 5 (1998) et al.

[127] For more details, see *Bělohlávek, A. et Pezl, T.* Mezinárodní a tuzemské rozhodčí řízení z pohledu čl. 36 Listiny základních práv a svobod a pravomocí soudů a ústavou garantovaných práv (Institut zrušení rozhodčího nálezu v souvislosti se zákazem *revision au fond*). [Title in translation: International and Domestic Arbitration from the Perspective of Article 36 of the Charter of Fundamental Rights and Freedoms and the Powers of the Courts and the Rights Guaranteed by the Constitution (Annulment of Arbitral Awards in Connection with the Prohibition of *Revision au Fond*)]. Právník, 2007, Vol. 146, No. 7, p. 768. Regarding certain partial issues cf. *Slováček, D.* Ochrana spotřebitele a rozhodčí doložky. [Title in translation: Consumer Protection and Arbitration Clauses]. Bulletin advokacie, 2009, Vol. 20, Nos. 7–8, p. 46; *Slováček, D.* Rozhodčí řízení a směrnice o nepřiměřených podmínkách ve spotřebitelských smlouvách. [Title in translation: Arbitration and the Directive on Unfair Terms in Consumer Contracts]. Právní rozhledy, 2010, Vol. 18, p. 331 et seq., here p. 332 et al.

[128] For instance, this can be observed from the perspective of Article 2(4) of the Constitution [CZE] which is identical to Article 3 of the Charter [CZE]. For instance, in Article 2(3) of the Charter [CZE] which reads as follows (cit.) *"Everyone may do that which is not prohibited by law; and no one may be compelled to do that which is not imposed upon him or her by law."* Similar provisions also occur in national constitutional regimes.

[129] See *Hendrych, D., Svoboda, C.* et al. Ústava České republiky. Komentář. [Title in translation: Constitution of the Czech Republic. Commentary]. Prague: C. H. Beck, 1997, p. 613.

[130] Cf. the Decision of the Constitutional Court [CZE], I ÚS 546/03, published in Sbírka nálezů a usnesení Ústavního soudu [CZE] [Constitutional Court Reports], Vol. 32 under the Ref. No. 12. The possibility of excluding the jurisdiction of courts as public authorities within the framework of the given legal system, in terms of the requirements of objective and subjective arbitrability, in connection with Article 36(1) of the Charter [CZE], was confirmed by the ConCourt CR [CZE] in its

82. Consequently, where the two above-mentioned doctrines of the constitutional system intersect, the conflict (albeit only illusory) must always result in a conclusion which will not suppress either of the two doctrines. If we apply the above said to the conflict of free will and inalienability of right, we must presume that the individual's expression of will was performed freely and with full knowledge of the consequences of such an expression of will for the individual. If, and only if, there is any reasonable doubt regarding the freedom of the expression of will or its very purpose, one must examine whether the free expression of will resulted in a waiver of rights to such an extent that the waiver is made constitutionally unacceptable. The legislative incorporation of the freedom of will also implies the right to make free decisions as to whether and how the relevant individual does or does not exercise his or her right.[131] No such step adopted by the individual could generally be labeled as violating the principle of inalienability of rights. By defining these fundamental rights and freedoms and the doctrines of their application, the state undertakes to honor these rights. The primary issue is to define the vertical effect of the fundamental rights, i.e. in the *state* v. *citizen* relationship.[132] The delimitation of the relationship between citizens (the horizontal effect) is generally perceived as secondary. In other words, it is not possible to apply the general constitutional doctrine to the relationship between private entities unless one of them breaches a subjective right of the other and the breach is the subject of proceedings before the competent state authority safeguarding the protection of rights.[133]

Decision Case No. I. ÚS 16/02, which reads as follows (cit.) "[...]*The procedural guarantee in Article 36(1)* [of the Charter], *when combined with the constitutional principle in Article 2(2) of the Charter, acquires its material substance because a transgression of the competence vested in the state authority by the law would result in a failure to protect rights* [...]," id est conversely, failure to honor the expression of will of the parties incorporated in the arbitration agreement and a permission of *revision au fond* in the case of an arbitral award if the award was issued within the limits of objective and subjective arbitrability, would violate Article 36(1) of the Charter [CZE] in conjunction with Article 2(2) of the Charter [CZE] and Article 2(3) of the Charter [CZE], as well as other constitutional imperatives and principles. Cf. also *Šamalík, F.* Lidská práva – základ demokratické legitimity. [Title in translation: Human Rights – The Basis of the Democratic Legitimacy]. Právník, 1994, No. 1. Concerning the meaning of overriding mandatory rules, see *Bělohlávek, A.* Rome Convention / Rome I Regulation. Commentary. New EU Conflict-of-Laws Rules for Contractual Obligations. Vol I & II, JurisPublishing, 2010, commentary on Article 9 of the Rome I Regulation, *Pauknerová, M.* Overriding Mandatory Rules and Czech Law. In: *Bělohlávek, A. et Rozehnalová, N.* CYIL – Czech Yearbook of International Law, 2010, Vol. 1, pp. 81–94.

[131] Cf. *Telec, I.* Přirozené právo osobnosti a jeho státní ochrana. [Title in translation: Natural Privacy Law and its Protection by the State]. Právní rozhledy, 2007, Vol. 15, No. 1, pp. 1–10.

[132] For instance, Article 1(3) of the Fundamental Law of the Federal Republic of Germany ("*Grundgesetz*") states (cit.): "*The following fundamental rights are binding on the legislature, the executive and the judiciary as directly applicable law.*" In: *Klokočka, V. et Wagnerová, E.* Ústavy států Evropské unie [Title in translation: Constitutions of the EU Member States], Prague: Linde, 1997, p. 236.

[133] Cf. *Bartoň, M.* Horizontální působení základních práv jako způsob pronikání ústavního práva do práva obyčejného (podústavního). [Title in translation: The Horizontal Effect of Fundamental Rights

83.   Once the inalienability of rights has been clarified, the analysis of what constitutes the generally recognized right to submit one's dispute to an independent and unbiased court must follow.[134] It is a guarantee afforded to individual persons (both natural and legal persons), i.e. the right to address an unbiased and independent court through the legally prescribed proccdure, in order to protect and/or enforce one's rights. Nevertheless, the possibility of protecting one's rights by submitting them to court is a right, not an obligation. At the same time, the *forum* which is to rule on the person's rights must be independent and unbiased. Last but not least, the exercise of the right by the individual as well as the fulfillment of the right by the court are subject to adherence to the prescribed procedure.

84.   Article 6(1) of the ECHR guarantees the right to a fair and public hearing by an impartial and independent tribunal established by law. The wording of Article 6(1) of the ECHR clearly indicates that it only applies to those institutions which are established by law and for which the state can therefore assume liability. Obviously, the assessment of the relationship of the rights set forth in Article 6(1) of the ECHR depends on whether the decisions made by arbitrators in arbitration can be considered, under *lex arbitri* and other national rules, as decisions rendered by public authorities, i.e. authorities established by law and deemed to be tribunals for the purposes of the ECHR. One may contend however, that such an interpretation can only be accepted with respect to the scope of application of the mechanisms designated by the ECHR as international instruments for the protection of fundamental rights (especially the right to address the ECtHR after the instruments of protection at the national level are exhausted). The right to legal protection as such, however, is much more extensive and broader. It cannot be limited to the mechanisms anticipated by the ECHR (here in terms of the ECHR) or other legal (juridical) acts, whether at the international level or at the national levels. The right to legal protection is inherent to the essence of power exercised by public authorities, in whatever manner, over every individual depending on his or her personal status (usually nationality) and/or depending on the place of

---

as a Method Whereby Constitutional Law Penetrates Ordinary (Sub-Constitutional) Law]. In: *Klíma, K.* (ed) Interpretace práva Ústavními soudy (teoretické reflexe), Sborník teoretického semináře [Title in translation: Interpretation of the Law by Constitutional Courts (Theoretical Essays), Theoretical Seminar Collection], Plzeň: Aleš Čeněk, 2006.

[134] In the Czech Republic [CZE], see Article 36 of the Charter [CZE] (and similarly other constitutional systems). The relevant provision reads as follows (cit.): *"Everyone may assert, through the legally prescribed procedure, his or her rights before an independent and impartial court or, in specified cases, before a different authority [...] Unless the law provides otherwise, a person who claims that his or her rights were curtailed by a decision of a public administrative authority may turn to a court for review of the legality of that decision. However, judicial review of decisions affecting the fundamental rights and basic freedoms listed in this Charter may not be removed from the jurisdiction of courts."*

his/her residence or temporary stay. Public authorities are not only endowed with rights, they are also bound by obligations owed to individuals, such as offering potential legal protection. State power is not only the bearer of authority, it has also assumed obligations towards those persons who are subject to this authority. It is irrelevant whether we view state power as a contract between the citizen and the state or as something implied by the essence of the state and a fundamental quality thereof.

85.   Drawing strict distinctions between the right to judicial protection and the right to legal protection is necessary. The former represents the right to submit one's case to a court or another public authority. It can be *waived* on the basis and to the extent of the autonomy of will and freedom of contract enjoyed by the particular entity. Conversely, the latter cannot be waived. The possibility of such waiver would imply a waiver of one's own personhood, unacceptable in a modern society. Any right guaranteed by substantive law loses its meaning when deprived of the procedural instruments safeguarding the protection thereof, i.e. protection *by way of law*. It is clear that the conclusion of an arbitration agreement means that the person (the party to the agreement) waives the right to judicial protection, i.e. protection afforded by public [procedural] mechanisms. It is not a waiver of legal protection, though. Due to, and in consequence of, his or her autonomy of will, the person – when he or she concluded the arbitration agreement – only opted for an alternative which is, nonetheless, also offered by law, i.e. the same fundamental law which allows him or her to invoke judicial protection. Consequently, the state (state power) does not restrict the right to legal protection and only offers various alternatives. If the person exercises his or her autonomy and chooses arbitration, he or she waives the right to judicial protection. Nonetheless, judicial protection as a public-law mechanism applies whenever the person fails to exercise his or her autonomy and freedom of contract or the exercise is contra legem (usually to an extent which is not permitted by law or in a manner which is null and void or without effect for other reasons). This means that arbitration is the finding and application of the law, not a mere process of searching for an agreement or the terms of an agreement between the parties. Naturally, however, the state cannot assume liability for how legal protection is administered by private-law mechanisms (in the present case through arbitration). Although arbitrators and arbitral tribunals are not public authorities, they represent instruments of legal protection. Their decision-making therefore constitutes a mechanism for finding the law, establishing the contents of the law, and applying the law to the facts of the case, all in a manner approved by law.

86.   Finally, it is necessary to emphasize that some national *leges arbitri* explicitly accept the possibility of an agreed waiver of the right to demand annulment of an arbitral award in court. Such an alternative is

not unique at the level of national legal systems. This only demonstrates the respect paid to the individual's autonomy of will. It does not constitute a waiver of the right to legal protection. It is merely an accentuation of contractual autonomy as a component of the autonomy of will, with a more explicit emphasis on the responsibility of the individual for his or her legal (juridical) acts (his or her conduct). This possibility is usually contingent on the requirement that the respective proceedings are international proceedings, i.e. one of the parties is an entity foreign to the state in which the proceedings are conducted. This is logical, because the state (state power) assumes much less responsibility for the performance of its commitments owed to individuals where such an international dimension is present.

87. Undoubtedly, the right to legal protection as well as the right to judicial protection assume a different dimension with respect to consumer protection. Autonomy of will enjoyed by the parties may be seen as colliding with the protection of the supposed weaker party. For example, the ConCourt CR [CZE][135] commented on the conflict as follows (cit.): *"The respect for and the protection of the autonomy of will are the elementary prerequisites for the functioning of the material rule of law; it is a matrix of the relationship between an individual and the state power, in the sense of a constant which encompasses individual fundamental rights articulated by positive law in response to their massive violation by authoritarian or totalitarian regimes. Consequently, the principle of autonomy allows the parties to an arbitration agreement to waive, freely and intentionally, their right to submit their dispute to an independent and unbiased court.[136] The consumer protection laws aim primarily at the protection of the weaker contracting party (the consumer); this is a distinct trend in our modern private law. However, protection of the autonomy of will cannot be absolute in a situation which involves another fundamental right of the individual or a constitutional principle or another constitutionally approved public interest which is capable of proportionately restricting the autonomy of will."[137]* This conclusion can basically be accepted. It is necessary to emphasize and require, however, that the expression of the will of the parties and their true interest be examined in each individual case. Any attempts at generalization must be rejected. It is also necessary to refuse any attempt at presuming the absence of the expression of will, which should be a manifestation of the right to legal protection (whether judicial

---

[135] Judgment of the ConCourt CR [CZE], Case No. II. ÚS 2164/10 of November 2011.
[136] The Constitutional Court of the Czech Republic [CZE] invoked its prior rulings:
➤ Resolution of the ConCourt CR [CZE], Case No. I. ÚS 2619/08 of 18 November 2008;
➤ Resolution of the ConCourt CR [CZE], Case No. II. ÚS 805/06 of 8 January 2007.
[137] The Constitutional Court of the Czech Republic [CZE] invoked its prior ruling, namely the Judgment of the ConCourt CR [CZE], Case No. II. ÚS 3/06 of 6 November 2007.

protection or protection in arbitration). A contrary principle would result in an undue suppression of the rights of the other contracting party, namely the professional. This conflict can be resolved through the mechanism of the burden of proof. Indeed, this approach has largely been implemented by courts in the United States (including, and especially by, the courts of the individual U.S. states), and it is by no means exceptional that the contract negotiation process between the professional and the consumer (or wherever the specific protection of the *weaker party* is required) is recorded audiovisually. Therefore the balance between contractual autonomy and the protection of the weaker party must be found in the procedural mechanisms which should apply both in arbitration and in litigation. The key issues are: **(i)** an individual detailed examination of the factual and legal circumstances of each particular case and **(ii)** shifting the burden of proof (as opposed to the regular finding of the law in which consumer protection does not apply) to the detriment of the professional who is required to prove that the arbitration clause (just like the other terms of the contract negotiated between the professional and the consumer) is a genuine, serious, and unambiguous expression of will of both parties.[138] The same criteria must be applied to the approach of the parties to the performance of the contract after it was concluded. For instance, if the consumer failed to challenge the arbitration clause during arbitration and raised the defense only in proceedings on the annulment of the arbitral award, or only in the proceedings on the (recognition and) enforcement of the arbitral award, such approach can in individual cases be interpreted as proof that the arbitration clause was negotiated as a genuine expression of will and the consumer invoked the consumer protection mechanisms only after he or she did not succeed in the proceedings on the merits. Naturally, such an approach constitutes an abuse of the consumer's rights. This is the reason why the approach of the parties to the performance of the contract and the exercise of their rights under the contract is also a significant indicator for a conclusion as to whether the arbitration clause and the other terms of the contract concluded by the consumer are (were at the conclusion of the contract) contrary to the legal standards for the protection of the weaker party, and whether they are consequently subject to the corresponding consequences (nullity or invalidity, etc., depending on the doctrine adopted by the respective national legal system), or whether,

---

[138] See ECJ Judgment, Case C-243/08 of 4 June 2009 (*Pannon GSM Zrt v. Sustikné Győrfi Erzsébet* [*Pannon GSM*]). This decision is analyzed in great detail in Chapter III.9.6 of this book and cited in various contexts elsewhere. In this particular context, the decision in the *Pannon GSM* case is sometimes neglected, and the relevant conclusions are somewhat *suppressed*. This decision is also less often cited in connection with arbitration, because the case concerned a choice-of-court clause, not an arbitration clause. In terms of consumer protection, however, the conclusions (such as in the *Pannon GSM* case) regarding choice-of-court agreements must under usual circumstances be applied to arbitration agreements as well.

conversely, the arbitration agreement (and, as the case may be, the other contract terms) is an expression of the genuine will of the parties.

88.   One must carefully distinguish between a situation where the consumer acts in compliance with the contract or a provision of the contract and thereby demonstrates that the contract reflected his or her [genuine] will, and a situation where the consumer *merely* fails to challenge the validity of the contract, usually as a result of his or her lesser knowledge of the law, which must be assessed according to the benchmark of *lay knowledge of the law* attributable to the usual (average) consumer. The latter case requires that we allow more room for the application of the law in other stages of the proceedings, not only at the main stage of finding the law. After all, this is closely related to the court's obligation to examine the nature of the terms in a consumer contract *sua sponte* (of its own motion), as well as to the determination of what information was provided to the consumer at the negotiation of the contract and in what form.[139] Besides, the ECJ's case law also highlights the obligation to have regard for the will of the consumer when deciding on the validity (or nullity) of the contract or an individual term thereof.[140] Such an expression can be assessed not only in view of the circumstances attending the conclusion of the contract but also with respect to the parties' approach to the performance under the contract[141] (including the period after the claim or lawsuit was filed, irrespective of the *forum*).

II.9.   Role of courts with respect to consumer arbitration

89.   Generally speaking, there are several situations in which both courts and arbitral tribunals can be employed in the resolution of consumer disputes. This interaction can either be in parallel, or in sequence, following the individual stages of arbitration and litigation.

II.9.1.   Appeals (review)

90.   Laws on arbitration (*lex arbitri*) in most countries stipulate that arbitral awards can be, to some extent, challenged in courts in the seat of

---

[139] Cf. ECJ Judgment, Case C-227/08 of 17 December 2009 (*Eva Martín Martín* v. *EDP Editores SL*), CELEX: 62008P0227C(01). According to the ECJ ruling (cit.): "*Article 4 of Directive 85/577 to protect the consumer in respect of contracts negotiated away from business premises does not preclude a national court from declaring, of its own motion, that a contract falling within the scope of that directive is void on the ground that the consumer was not informed of his right of cancellation, even though the consumer at no stage pleaded that the contract was void before the competent national courts.*"

[140] See ECJ Judgment, Case C-227/08 of 17 December 2009 (*Eva Martín Martín* v. *EDP Editores SL*), CELEX: 62008P0227C(01). Although the ECJ rendered its decision in connection with Article 5(1) of Directive 85/577 to protect the consumer in respect of contracts negotiated away from business premises, there is no reason not to apply the conclusion in a more general context. In other words, the ECJ does not limit its opinion to the quoted provision.

[141] See ECJ Judgment, Case C-243/08 of 4 June 2009 (*Pannon GSM Zrt* v. *Sustikné Győrfi Erzsébet* [*Pannon GSM*]).

arbitration (or in the place where the arbitral award was rendered). This right is usually contingent on a breach of several fundamental procedural principles or the absence of the essential procedural prerequisites of arbitration. Some legal systems have systematic provisions, even with the option of reviewing arbitral awards (including a more or less extensive review *au fond*) specifically in consumer disputes; or at least the consumer is granted the option of having the arbitral award set aside upon the consumer's motion – because it is a consumer dispute.

91. The requirement of an appellate review (i.e. de facto a *revisio au fond*) in consumer disputes was also voiced by the ConCourt CR [CZE] in its Decision Case No. II. ÚS 2164/10 rendered in November 2011.[142] This opinion, however, appears rather excessive considering that Czech law generally allows arbitration in consumer disputes and, at the same time, recognizes the principle of no appeal in arbitration, which can be eliminated only by an explicit agreement of the parties. It is indeed rather obvious that many decisions concerning arbitration agreements and arbitral awards (especially in consumer disputes) are influenced by a more or less subjective evaluation made by the judges whose approach to arbitration is sometimes positive and sometimes (personally) negative. Such excesses and, possibly, certain *turmoil* can be found in many countries; for a comparison between the approaches adopted by individual countries, see especially Chapter IV of this book. Germany, for example, has experienced some interesting developments – in the 1990s it belonged to a group of countries with a more or less negative approach to arbitration; its current approach is, conversely, one of the most liberal. The same applies to consumer disputes, too, despite the fact that the German legal system is otherwise, generally and traditionally, almost unusually protective of the supposed weaker contracting party.

II.9.2. Court intervention at the stage of enforcement of arbitral awards

92. Arbitration in consumer disputes can become a problem when the courts are petitioned to rule on the enforcement of arbitral awards. This applies to domestic as well as foreign arbitral awards. The enforcement of foreign arbitral awards is significantly influenced by sources of international origin (international agreements/treaties), the most important of which is undoubtedly the *New York Convention*.[143] None of

---

[142] This ruling is annotated in great detail in the excursus into Czech law – see the "*Case Law*" section; the conclusion of the Constitutional Court that it is necessary in consumer disputes to adhere to the prescribed procedure and go through the individual instances, in terms of the cited decision, is criticized in the respective chapter.

[143] Another important source of international origin which concerns arbitration is, for instance, the European Convention on Commercial Arbitration of 1961 (the "*European Convention*"), the very scope of which excludes the possibility of its application to consumer disputes.

the international instruments (save certain exceptions, especially in the application of the reservation concerning *ordre public* in unique extreme cases) offers the option of refusing the recognition and/or enforcement of a foreign arbitral award only because one of the parties is a consumer. Neither do international sources allow review of the merits. Simply speaking, international mechanisms for the recognition and enforcement of foreign arbitral awards do not explicitly count on consumer protection qualifying as grounds for refusal. Apart from a conflict with *public policy*, which is one of the exceptions, the enforcement of an arbitral award could also be refused if consumer disputes were generally non-arbitrable in the country where the recognition/enforcement is sought.

II.9.3. Control and support exercised by the courts (*juge d'appui*)

93. Most *leges arbitri* stipulate that the courts in the seat of arbitration have the power (authority) and even the obligation to support the parties and the arbitrators in order to secure smooth arbitral proceedings, for example by assisting the parties in the appointment and replacement of arbitrators[144] and by issuing interim measures.[145]

---

[144] Cf. Sections 7–9, Section 12 of the ArbAct [CZE].
[145] Cf. Section 23 of the ArbAct [CZE].

III. Consumer Protection and Consumer Disputes under EU Law

III.1. Restrictive model under EU law

94. Based on the above-defined fundamental questions relating to consumer relations and consumer arbitration, we distinguish two basic approaches. The first model is common in most European countries and is based on consumer protection laws – special rules regulating consumer contracts limit the freedom of contract. On the other hand, the second, American model is based on a complete freedom of contract, and the protection of consumers is left to the courts and to the application of standard legal instruments and institutions of substantive and procedural law; in other words, the American model attempts to avoid any special consumer protection rules.

95. When examining the European model, it is necessary to concentrate primarily on the special EU approach and the concepts adopted by the EU Member States. The reasons are twofold: first, the extension of European legislation to cover the EEA means that most European countries fall within the scope of the legislation, and second, European law is now the only example of international (harmonizing) consumer protection laws. Whereas the domestic (national) nature of consumer contracts significantly limits the efforts of consumer legislation down to the protection of the individual countries, the EU's objective was to create favorable conditions in its Member States.

96. Secondary EU law is broad and has a fairly significant impact on consumer arbitration, despite the fact that arbitration itself is beyond the scope of EU law. The impact on arbitration is therefore mediated through consumer protection laws. Consequently, EU law does not regulate arbitration as a procedural instrument, but as a special instrument, and intervenes subjectively by way of a strong protectionist policy favorable to consumers.

97. Consumer protection is the subject matter of many EU laws governed by the **"cumulation of consumer protection" principle.** The application of one consumer protection directive does not exclude the application of another.[1] National (domestic) laws which transpose directives in the legal systems of the EU Member States must be interpreted in compliance with the text and the purpose of the directive, in order to achieve the result (objective) stipulated in the directive(s).[2] The

---

[1] ECJ Judgment, Case C-423/97 of 22 April 1999 (*Travel Vac SL* v. *Manuel José Antelm Sanchis*, published in: ECR [1999], p. I–02195), CELEX: 61997CJ0423.

[2] ECJ Judgment Joined Cases C-240/98 through C-244/98 *Océano Grupo Editorial SA et Rocío Murciano Quintero and between Salvat Editores SA et José M. Sánchez Alcón Prades et al*, published

directives themselves are autonomous. They must be interpreted in the context of EU law, not national (domestic) law.[3]

111.2. Fundamental consumer rights

98.   Consumer protection in the European Union rests on the following **five categories of fundamental rights: (i)** right to the protection of health and safety, **(ii)** right to the protection of economic interests, **(iii)** right to information and education, **(iv)** right to compensation for loss and damage sustained, and **(v)** right to fair trial.[4] The normative basis in the EU is supplied by Article 169 TFEU[5] (ex Article 153 TEC[6]). The European Communities started to pass consumer protection laws in 1984, specifically Council Directive 84/450/EEC on misleading advertising,[7] followed by Council Directive 85/577/EEC to protect the

---

in: ECR [2000], p. I–4941. This decision is annotated in greater detail below, in the ECJ's case law section.

Generally as concerns the interpretation according to the wording and the purpose of directives, see ECJ Judgment C-350/03 of 25 October 2005 (*Elisabeth Schulte et Wolfgang Schulte* v. *Deutsche Bausparkasse Badenia AG*), CELEX: 62003CJ0350, published in: ECR, p. I– 9215, paras. (69), (71) and (102) and many other decisions.

[3] ECJ Judgment, Case C-29/76 of 14 October 1976 (*LTU Lufttransportunternehmen GmbH & Co. KG v. Eurocontrol*), published in: ECR [1976] 01541.

[4] Cf. Tichý, L., Arnold, R., Svoboda, P., Zemánek, J. et Král, R. Evropské právo [Title in translation: European Law], 3rd ed., Prague: C. H. Beck, 2006, p. 742 et al.

[5] TFEU (cit.): Title XV – Consumer Protection – Article 169 – "(1) *In order to promote the interests of consumers and to ensure a high level of consumer protection, the Union shall contribute to protecting the health, safety and economic interests of consumers, as well as to promoting their right to information, education and to organise themselves in order to safeguard their interests.* (2) *The Union shall contribute to the attainment of the objectives referred to in paragraph 1 through: (a) measures adopted pursuant to Article 114 in the context of the completion of the internal market; (b) measures which support, supplement and monitor the policy pursued by the Member States.* (3) *The European Parliament and the Council, acting in accordance with the ordinary legislative procedure and after consulting the Economic and Social Committee, shall adopt the measures referred to in paragraph 2(b).* (4) *Measures adopted pursuant to paragraph 3 shall not prevent any Member State from maintaining or introducing more stringent protective measures. Such measures must be compatible with the Treaties. The Commission shall be notified of them.*"

[6] TEC (cit.): Title XIV – Consumer Protection – Article 153 – "(1) *In order to promote the interests of consumers and to ensure a high level of consumer protection, the Community shall contribute to protecting the health, safety and economic interests of consumers, as well as to promoting their right to information, education and to organise themselves in order to safeguard their interests.* (2) *Consumer protection requirements shall be taken into account in defining and implementing other Community policies and activities.* (3) *The Community shall contribute to the attainment of the objectives referred to in paragraph 1 through: (a) measures adopted pursuant to Article 95 in the context of the completion of the internal market; (b) measures which support, supplement and monitor the policy pursued by the Member States.* (4) *The Council, acting in accordance with the procedure referred to in Article 251 and after consulting the Economic and Social Committee, shall adopt the measures referred to in paragraph 3(b).* (5) *Measures adopted pursuant to paragraph 4 shall not prevent any Member State from maintaining or introducing more stringent protective measures. Such measures must be compatible with this Treaty. The Commission shall be notified of them.*"

[7] Council Directive 84/450/EEC of 10 September 1984 relating to the approximation of the laws, regulations, and administrative provisions of the Member States concerning misleading advertising, (CELEX: 31984L0450; published in: OJ L 250, 19 September 1984, pp. 17–20) as amended by

consumer in respect of contracts negotiated away from business premises.[8] But the first directive with a significant impact on consumer legislation was Council Directive 93/13/EEC (the *"Directive"*) followed by Commission Recommendation 98/257/EC (the *"Recommendation"*). Furthermore, the ECJ's case law has only recently (see especially the ECJ rulings of 2006–2010) started to shape consumer protection with respect to arbitration and its limits, in connection with consumer disputes (i.e. from the perspective of consumer protection, not from the view of the arbitration itself).

III.3. Directive 93/13/EEC on unfair terms in consumer contracts (the *"Directive"*)

99.   Council Directive 93/13/EEC (referred to as the *"Directive"* in this book) stipulates that the standard terms of consumer contracts (except the price and the subject matter[9]) can be challenged by consumers as **unfair**. According to the *Directive*, unfair terms cause a significant imbalance to the detriment of the consumer and are contrary to the requirement of fairness. The court is supposed to rule on whether these conditions are fulfilled or not.

III.3.1. Identification of unfair terms in court rulings

100.   According to the *Directive*, the courts should examine **four aspects:** **(i) the strength of the bargaining positions of the parties, (ii)** whether the consumer had an **inducement to enter into the contract, (iii)** whether the contract was negotiated based on any **special (individual, targeted) order of the consumer,** and **(iv)** the extent to

---

97/55/EEC (in the Czech Republic implemented by Act No. 40/1995 Coll., on the Regulation of Advertising and Amending and Supplementing Act No. 468/1991 Coll. on Radio and Television Broadcasting, as subsequently amended).

[8] Directive of 25 July 1985 (CELEX: 31985L0577; published in: OJ L 372, 31. 12. 1985, pp. 31–33). In the Czech Republic [CZE], this was implemented primarily through Section 57 of the CC; this was taken into consideration in the entire context of Sections 52–57 of the CC [CZE].

[9] In ECJ Judgment, Case C-484/08 of 3 June 2010 (*Caja de Ahorros y Monte de Piedad de Madrid* v. *Asociación de Usuarios de Servicios Bancarios [Ausbanc]*) the Court concluded that neither the *Directive* nor the TEC preclude the national law (law of national origin) from setting up a judicial mechanism for the review of (un)fairness of the contractual terms even if they concern the main subject of the contract and/(or) the unfairness of the price (remuneration). This also applies if such provisions are articulated clearly and comprehensibly. This particular case concerned a provision on rounding. According to the Spanish Supreme Court (Tribunal Supremo [ESP]), a provision on rounding can constitute an essential term of a bank loan contract (here a loan contract for the purchase of an apartment). However, Article 4(2) of the *Directive* rules out the possibility that a term mainly concerning the subject of the contract can be considered abusive; the abusive nature of such a term cannot, in principle, be subject to adjudication (in terms of the *Directive*). At the same time, however, the Court ruled that Spain [ESP] had failed to implement Article 4(2) of the *Directive* in its national law and that the entire contract was subject to such adjudication (assessment) under Spanish law. The judgment is published in: OJ C 209/6, 31 July 2010. CELEX: 62008CJ0484. Language of the case: Spanish.

which the seller has dealt **fairly and equitably** with the consumer. However, these criteria cannot be applied to the full extent on terms regulating dispute resolution. The primary considerations are the *incentives* to enter into the contract. This last criterion can only be applied to the main performance, i.e. only to the main contract, not to the arbitration agreement. Dispute resolution agreements are only the **means of enforcement of rights,** and it would be illogical to examine any incentive to enter into an arbitration agreement from the perspective of consumer protection.[10]

III.3.2. Annex to the *Directive*

101. The *Directive* includes an **annex which contains an overview of contract terms which can be prima facie considered as unfair (rebuttable presumption).** The terms listed in the Annex (Annex to the *Directive*) need not always be (automatically) considered unfair; similarly, terms which are not included in the list need not always and under any and all circumstances be automatically fair. The list is therefore based on a certain degree of high probability founded on long-term observations. The individual language versions employ different words to express the nature of the list. But all language versions indicate that the individual items are only examples, i.e. the list is a *tool*, not a binding norm. The clearest wording is used in the German version which describes the nature of the Annex *"as als Hinweis dienende [...] Liste"*, i.e. (approximate translation – cit.:) *"a list which serves as a 'reference', i.e. as a 'guideline.'"* It may thus be considered erroneous and somewhat artificially construed if such terms are *prima facie* considered unfair. There is a significant difference in quality between the indicative nature of a *guideline* and a *prima facie* presumption (albeit a rebuttable presumption).

102. These **indicative** [potentially] **unfair terms** include:
   ▶ Excluding or limiting the legal liability of a seller or supplier in the event of the death of a consumer or personal injury to the latter resulting from an act or omission of that seller or supplier;
   ▶ Inappropriately excluding or limiting the legal rights of the consumer vis-à-vis the seller or supplier or another party in the event of total or partial non-performance or inadequate performance by the seller or supplier of any of the contractual obligations, including the option of offsetting a debt owed to the seller or supplier against any claim which the consumer may have against him [i.e. the exclusion of unilateral offsets];

[10] Cf. Judgment of the BGH [DEU], Case No. III ZR 265/03 of 13 January 2005 which reads as follows (approximate translation, cit.): *"It is not necessary that the consumer have any special reason for submitting the given dispute (type of dispute) to arbitration."* The judgment is annotated and analyzed in greater detail in the excursus into German law.

- ▶ Making an agreement binding on the consumer whereas provision of services by the seller or supplier is subject to a condition whose realization depends on his own will alone;
- ▶ Permitting the seller or supplier to retain sums paid by the consumer where the latter decides not to conclude or perform the contract, without providing for the consumer to receive compensation of an equivalent amount from the seller or supplier where the latter is the party cancelling the contract;
- ▶ Requiring any consumer who fails to fulfill his obligation to pay a disproportionately high sum in compensation;
- ▶ Authorizing the seller or supplier to dissolve the contract on a discretionary basis [unilateral act dependent exclusively on the will of the seller or supplier] where the same facility is not granted to the consumer, or permitting the seller or supplier to retain the sums paid for services not yet supplied by him where it is the seller or supplier himself who dissolves the contract;
- ▶ Enabling the seller or supplier to terminate a contract of indeterminate duration without reasonable notice except where there are serious grounds for doing so;[11]
- ▶ Automatically extending a contract of fixed duration where the consumer does not indicate otherwise, when the deadline fixed for the consumer to express this desire not to extend the contract is unreasonably early;
- ▶ Irrevocably binding the consumer to terms with which he had no real opportunity of becoming acquainted before the conclusion of the contract;
- ▶ Enabling the seller or supplier to alter the terms of the contract unilaterally without a valid reason which is specified in the contract;[12]
- ▶ Enabling the seller or supplier to unilaterally alter without a valid reason any characteristics of the product or service to be provided;
- ▶ Providing for the **price of goods to be determined at the time of delivery or allowing a seller of goods or supplier of services to**

---

[11] Point 2/ of the Annex to the *Directive* stipulates that it is not possible to consider *a priori* as unfair such contract terms whereby a supplier of financial services reserves the right to unilaterally terminate a contract of indeterminate duration without notice to the consumer where there is a valid reason, provided that the supplier is required to inform the other contracting party or parties thereof immediately.

[12] Point 2/ of the Annex to the *Directive* stipulates, however, that the *Directive* is without hindrance to terms under which a supplier of financial services reserves the right to alter the rate of interest payable by the consumer or due to the latter, or the amount of other charges for financial services without notice where there is a valid reason, provided that the supplier is required to inform the other contracting party or parties thereof at the earliest opportunity and that the latter (consumer(s)) are free to dissolve the contract immediately.

Terms under which a seller or supplier reserves the right to unilaterally alter the conditions of a contract of indeterminate duration, provided that he is required to inform the consumer with reasonable notice and that the consumer is free to dissolve the contract, can neither be considered as *a priori* unfair.

increase their price without in both cases giving the consumer the corresponding right to cancel the contract if the final price [for the consumer] is too high in relation to the price agreed when the contract was concluded;[13]

▶ **Giving the seller or supplier the right** to determine whether the goods or services supplied **are in conformity with the contract,** or giving him the exclusive right to interpret any term of the contract (contract term or condition);

▶ Limiting the seller's or supplier's obligation to respect commitments undertaken by his agents or making his commitments subject to compliance with a particular formality;

▶ Obliging the consumer to fulfill all his obligations where the seller or supplier does not perform his;

▶ Giving the seller or supplier the possibility of **transferring his rights and obligations** under the contract, where this may serve to reduce the guarantees for the consumer (or where the intended purpose is such an impairment of the consumer's position), **without the latter's agreement;**

▶ Excluding or hindering the consumer's right to take legal action or exercise any other legal remedy, particularly by requiring the consumer to take disputes exclusively to arbitration **not covered by legal provisions,** unduly restricting the evidence available to him, or imposing on him a burden of proof which, according to applicable law, should lie with another party to the contract.

103.   The ECJ's case law indicates that the list of unfair terms specified in the Annex to the *Directive* need not be implemented in the national legislation (national law of the EU Member States) at all. However, the Member States must, for the purpose of achieving the objectives of the *Directive*, choose such form and means which sufficiently guarantee that the public has an opportunity to get acquainted with the list.[14]

104.   Consequently, these terms and/or terms concerning these issues can be considered unfair. Whether the term is indeed unfair and, ultimately, invalid must be considered individually with respect to each contract and in each dispute. One cannot even presume that the terms listed in the Annex are based on a rebuttable presumption that these particular

---

[13] According to Point 2/ of the Annex to the *Directive*, the examples of unfair (unreasonable) terms listed under Subparagraphs (g), (j) and (l) do not apply to: (•) transactions in transferable securities, financial instruments and other products or services where the price is linked to fluctuations in a stock exchange quotation or index or a financial market rate that the seller or supplier does not control; (•) contracts for the purchase or sale of foreign currency, traveller's cheques or international money orders denominated in foreign currency.
The same applies to price-indexation clauses, where lawful, provided that the method by which prices vary is explicitly described.
[14] ECJ Judgment, Case C-478/99 of 7 May 2002 (*The Commission of the EC* v. *Sweden*), published in: ECR [2002], p. I–04147, CELEX: 61999CJ0478.

terms are unfair, unless it is proven otherwise. The nature of the Annex to the *Directive* is only indicative. It is undeniable, however, that in reality such terms are often formulated to the detriment of the consumer. The professional therefore assumes a significant burden of proof in a dispute obliging him to prove that the term is not unfair in the particular case. The opponents of arbitration as a method of resolving consumer disputes often interpret the Annex as stipulating that these terms are *prima facie* unfair and invalid, or at least subject to a rebuttable presumption. They invoke the *Directive* and the quoted list and, without any detailed reasoning, label arbitration clauses in consumer contracts as unfair terms, i.e. invalid under European law. Such a conclusion, however, is incorrect, and this view has also been confirmed by the ECJ's case law (for a detailed analysis of the case law, see below). At the same time, though, a provision which is not included in the list need not necessarily be fair. The list is based on probability.

III.3.3. Application of the Annex to the *Directive* to consumer arbitration

105.   Two of the terms which are considered unfair specifically concern arbitration, namely:

▶ **Point (i)** [of the Annex to the *Directive*] regarding terms irrevocably binding the consumer to conditions with which he had no real opportunity of becoming acquainted with before the conclusion of the contract. This can be applied if the party – consumer – entered into the arbitration agreement in the form of an adhesion contract.

▶ And **Point (q)** [of the Annex to the *Directive*] which concerns terms *"excluding or hindering the consumer's right to take legal action or exercise any other legal remedy, particularly by requiring the consumer to take disputes exclusively to arbitration not covered by legal provisions, unduly restricting the evidence available to him or imposing on him a burden of proof which, according to the applicable [procedural] law, should lie with another party to the contract."*

106.   One may legitimately ask whether **Points (i) and (q) of the Annex to the *Directive*** ought to be interpreted **individually (separately) or cumulatively.**[15]

107.   If the latter alternative were correct (cumulative application), the nature of any notice of termination of a contract (or a cancellation of a contract) or any plea of invalidity of any provision in a consumer contract raised by a consumer with respect to an arbitration agreement or, from a broader perspective, any agreement with procedural

---

[15] See *Schiavetta, S.* Does the Internet Occasion New Directions in Consumer Arbitration in the EU? Journal of Information, Law and Technology, University of Warwick, 2004, No. 3, p. 3.

consequences, would have to be examined in each individual case irrespective of the type of the particular proceedings, irrespective of the powers entrusted to the arbitrators (or the *forum* as such), irrespective of the governing law and of the manner of applying the governing law, and irrespective of the position of the parties in the particular proceedings or the procedure to be adopted in the respective case. The cumulative approach would require us to examine any and all terms, i.e. even all procedural terms, from the perspective of Point (i) of the Annex to the *Directive* even if the term could not otherwise be considered an unfair term from the perspective of Point (q) of the Annex to the *Directive*.

108.   In the case of separate interpretation, we can assume that a term which is not contrary to the principles enshrined in Point (q) of the Annex to the *Directive* would not have to be examined strictly pursuant to Point **(i)** of the Annex to the *Directive*. In the case of such interpretation, Point **(i)** of the Annex to the *Directive* would be devoid of any logic and would undermine the entire concept (purpose and objective) of the *Directive*.

III.3.4. Obligation of the [arbitral] tribunal to decide according to the applicable laws and regulations

109.   Point (q) **of the Annex to the *Directive*** concerns terms excluding or hindering the consumer's right to take legal action or exercise any other legal remedy, particularly by requiring the consumer to submit disputes **exclusively to an arbitral tribunal which would not be obliged to apply valid and applicable law**, or unduly restricting the evidence available to the consumer, in terms of the evidence which the consumer may invoke or the submission of which would be necessary under applicable laws and which should, under applicable law, lie with the other party to the contract (professional).

110.   Some commentaries argue that the words in Point (q) of the Annex to the *Directive*, i.e. "[...] *arbitration not covered by legal provisions* [...]," is unclear.[16] In any case, it is an inaccurate expression causing problems in interpretation. It is probably the consequence of the fact that it was included in the legislative process at a late stage.[17] Until recently, the interpretation at the EC level often suggested that EU (EC) law does not allow arbitration. This interpretation was supported by certain national (domestic) arbitration laws which indeed allow wide discretion to arbitrators in the *finding of the law*, i.e. when determining the

---

[16] See *Drahozal, C. et Friel, R. A.* A Comparative View of Consumer Arbitration. Arbitration, 2005, Vol. 2, p. 132.

[17] See *Favre-Bulle, X.* Arbitrage et Règlement alternative des litiges (ADR): une autre justice pour les consommateurs? In: *Thévenoz, L. et Reich, N.* (eds.) Droit de la consommation, Liber Amicorum Bernd Stauder, Genève: Schulthess, 2006, p. 97 et seq., here p. 109.

substantive law applicable to the merits of the dispute – typical, for instance, for the legal systems influenced by French law. Some authors argue that this is supposed to prevent: decision-making following the principles of equity, unfair terms in settlements, or means of uncontrolled freedom of action.[18] Other theories hold that the principle prevents *ad hoc* arbitrations, i.e. resolving disputes by a person or entity other than a *permanent arbitral institution*.[19]

111. Such interpretation, however, is by no means shared by all Member States (their courts and authorities), although they do agree that the *Directive* is not well-drafted in this particular point.[20] Several language versions[21] and an analysis of the *travaux préparatoires* indicate that the *Directive* provides for mechanisms similar to arbitration which have been introduced in certain states to resolve consumer disputes.[22] From the formal point of view, these mechanisms[23] are not arbitration (see

---

[18] See *Schiavetta, S.* Does the Internet Occasion New Directions in Consumer Arbitration in the EU? Journal of Information, Law and Technology, University of Warwick, 2004, No. 3, p. 3. and *Odams de Zylva, M.* Effective Means of Resolving Distance Selling Disputes. European Workshop on Business Process Models and Technical Requirements for Online Dispute Resolution, 2001, p. 10.

[19] *Schiavetta, S.* Does the Internet Occasion New Directions in Consumer Arbitration in the EU? Journal of Information, Law and Technology, University of Warwick, 2004, No. 3, p. 3.

[20] See *Favre-Bulle, X.* Arbitrage et Règlement alternative des litiges (ADR): une autre justice pour les consommateurs? In: *Théovenoz, L. et Reich, N.* (eds.) Droit de la consommation, Liber Amicorum Bernd Stauder, Genève: Schulthess, 2006, pp. 9–7 et seq., here p. 109.

[21] For instance, in the French version it reads as: *"une juridiction d'arbitrage non couverte par des dispositions légales."*

[22] See *Favre-Bulle, X.* Arbitrage et Règlement alternative des litiges (ADR): une autre justice pour les consommateurs? In: *Théovenoz, L. et Reich, N.* (eds.) Droit de la consommation, Liber Amicorum Bernd Stauder, Genève: Schulthess, 2006, p. 97 et seq., here p. 97 et seq., here p. 109 and Fouchard, Ph. Clause abusives en matière d'arbitrage. Rev. arb., 1995, p. 149.

[23] Some work as *ex aequo et bono*, which is contrary to the possible interpretation of the wording of the applicable legal rules.

Nevertheless, national laws on arbitration (*lex arbitri*) have also adopted a fairly narrow approach to the possibility of decision-making according to the principles of *ex aequo et bono* and/or as *amiable compositeur*. By way of illustration only:

AUT: Only if the arbitrator is authorized by the parties.

BEL: Only if agreed by the parties.

BGR: No provisions.

CYP: Only if the parties grant an express authorization to the arbitrator(s).

CZE: Only if the parties grant an express authorization to the arbitrator(s).

DEU: Only if the parties grant an express authorization to the arbitrator(s).

ESP: Unless the parties expressly chose arbitration pursuant to the law, the arbitrators may decide *ex aequo et bono*; this shall not apply if the administration of the proceedings is entrusted to a corporation or association.

FIN: Only if the parties grant an express authorization to the arbitrator(s).

GBR-ENG : Choice of other laws on the basis of an agreement of the parties or determination thereof by the arbitral tribunal. English law (AA [GBR-ENG]) is probably most liberal in this regard and explicitly provides the arbitrators with the highest degree of flexibility.

GRE: Arbitrators apply substantive law unless the parties agree otherwise. At the same time, however, the law stipulates that the agreement cannot exclude the application of *public policy* rules (*"ordre public"*).

also above). Indeed, this conclusion has been supported by the case law of several Member States. For instance, the German Federal Court of Justice (Supreme Court, BGH [DEU]) held that the very fact that arbitration is in a particular case governed by the national laws on arbitration suffices to classify the procedure as compliant with EU law.[24]

112. A landmark decision significantly supporting arbitration agreements in consumer contracts was delivered by the ECJ as late as 2006, in Judgment C-168/05 of 26 October 2006 (*Mostaza-Claro* v. *Centro Móvil*),[25] which is discussed in detail in the Chapter on the ECJ's case law.[26] Neither the *Directive*, nor any other EU law a priori prohibits arbitration agreements in consumer contracts, as the ECJ's rulings confirm.

113. An arbitration agreement in a consumer contract must not, inter alia, limit the application of applicable law. Consequently, the resolution of consumer disputes following the principles of equity (*ex aequo et bono*) and/or other procedures which would tolerate that the arbitrators do not strictly adhere to applicable law, including conflict-of-law rules, are out of the question. This applies irrespective of whether the procedure could be employed in the particular proceedings only on the basis of an

---

HUN: Only if the parties grant an express authorization to the arbitrator(s).

ITA: An agreement concerning disputes under Article 409 of the Code of Civil Procedure [ITA] (collective agreements) is null and void if it authorizes decisions under the *ex aequo et bono* principle. Other disputes require the explicit agreement of the parties.

NDL: As *amiable compositeur* only if the parties grant an authorization to the arbitrator(s).

NOR: Explicit authorization by the parties.

PRT: Authorization by the parties required. The authorization must be incorporated in the arbitration agreement or in a subsequent agreement entered into before the statement of defense. However, if the parties authorize the arbitrators to adopt decisions according to the rules of equity, the arbitrators can case manage the proceedings as they see fit. If the arbitrators are authorized to decide according to the rules of equity, they can resolve the dispute as they consider fair.

SUI: In international proceedings only upon agreement of the parties.

SWE: No rules.

UKR: Only if the parties grant an express authorization to the arbitrator(s).

etc.

For more details see also Table IV as an annex to the commentary on Article 1(2)(e)) of the *Rome I Regulation* and Article 1(2)(d) of the *Rome Convention* in: Bělohlávek, A. Římská úmluva / Nařízení Řím I. Komentář. [Title in translation: Rome Convention / Rome I Regulation. Commentary]. Part I. Prague: C. H. Beck, 2009.

[24] See Judgment of the BGH [DEU], Case No. III ZR 256/03 of 13 January 2005 annotated in detail in this book (in the part concerning arbitration in consumer disputes in Germany [DEU]). In that decision, the German Federal Supreme Court ruled that it sufficed if the arbitration met the requirements of a state-approved arbitration system regulated by law. In the case decided by the BGH [DEU] regarding the dispute over the validity of an arbitration agreement (inter alia), the court considered it sufficient that the proceedings were governed by German arbitration laws (Book X of the ZPO [DEU]), to which arbitration agreement even ("on top of that") generally and explicitly referred.

[25] The decision is published in: ECR 2006, p. I–10421 et seq.

[26] *Kirry, A.* Arbitrability: Current Trends in Europe. Arb. Int., 1996, p. 377 et seq.

explicit agreement of the parties (which would be invalid in a consumer contract) or without such an agreement, for instance based on the procedural rules applicable to the arbitral proceedings.

114. The mutual interaction of the law applicable to the merits of the dispute and the jurisdiction of the forum must also be viewed from another significant perspective, i.e. that many countries presume that arbitrators are significantly less (to say the least) bound by applicable substantive law, including the conflict-of-law rules of private international law, than the standards to which courts are bound to apply. Many published opinions maintain that the words *"arbitration not covered by legal provisions"* are unclear.[27] Some authors propose that the definition is supposed to prevent decision-making following the rules of *equity*, i.e. amicable settlements, or the means of unrestrained freedom in determining the merits of a dispute.[28] Other theories suggest that the rule prevents *ad hoc* arbitrations, i.e. arbitral proceedings which are not formally conducted under the auspices of any permanent entity organizing arbitral proceedings.[29] The words employed in Point (q) of the Annex to the *Directive* should by no means be taken to prohibit the possibility of also resolving consumer disputes in *ad hoc* arbitrations, i.e. outside the jurisdiction of *permanent arbitral institutions*. The definition clearly covers any type of arbitration, providing, however, the arbitrators are strictly bound by applicable [substantive] law. The reason is that most legal systems do not distinguish between institutionalized or *ad hoc* proceedings, i.e. outside the jurisdiction of a *permanent arbitral institution*, and some national (domestic) arbitration laws do not even provide for any such distinction.

115. Considering the consequences of the *non-reviewability* of a decision, one may doubt that an agreement of the parties complies with EU law if it stipulates that an **arbitration agreement need not specify any reasons** for the decision, as anticipated by several legal systems.[30] Such an agreement could probably be considered as an agreement which could ultimately impair the consumer's position when enforcing his or her rights. Arbitration principally does not allow an appeal unless a particular legal system provides for the possibility of review of the

---

[27] See *Drahozal, C. et Friel, R. A.* A Comparative View of Consumer Arbitration. Arbitration, 2005, Vol. 2, p. 132. et seq.

[28] See *Schiavetta, S.* Does the Internet Occasion New Directions in Consumer Arbitration in the EU? Journal of Information, Law and Technology, University of Warwick, 2004-2005, p. 3 et seq. (here p. 3), as well as *Odams de Zylva, M.* Effective Means of Resolving Distance Selling Disputes. European Workshop on Business Process Models and Technical Requirements for Online Dispute Resolution, 2001, p. 10.

[29] *Schiavetta, S.* Does the Internet Occasion New Directions in Consumer Arbitration in the EU? Journal of Information, Law and Technology, University of Warwick, 2004-2005, p. 3 et seq., here p. 3.

[30] Cf. Section 25(2) of the ArbAct [CZE] which reads as follows (cit.:) "(2) *The arbitral award must contain reasoning unless the parties had agreed that reasoning can be dispensed with [...]*".

arbitral award. Whether the review of an arbitral award is possible or not,[31] the ECJ has ruled that the consumer must be guaranteed the right to file a motion with a court, after the arbitration, in respect to certain fundamental issues and in special cases. Depending on the approach of the national arbitration laws, such proceedings may also include proceedings on a motion to set aside an arbitral award (which is the case in most situations). These proceedings are not a regular appellate review, nor do they constitute *appellate proceedings* with respect to the trial before arbitrators,[32] yet the consumer may exercise certain fundamental rights provided to him or her in this position. In practice, it is principally the potential for jurisdictional challenge against the arbitrators which, according to most arbitration laws as well as the standard of the UNCITRAL Model Law, also constitutes grounds for annulment of an arbitral award. The specific quality of consumer protection under EU law inheres in the fact that the consumer is not limited by whether he or she pleaded lack of jurisdiction (due to invalidity of an arbitration agreement which violates consumer protection laws) previously during the arbitral proceedings or not.[33] Consequently, such review basically requires that the arbitral award rendered in a consumer dispute always be substantiated by reasons and that it indicate whether and to what extent the arbitrators debated the respective issue,[34] because the court may deal with the issue only to the extent the court is familiar with the factual and legal circumstances of the case.[35] These circumstances ought to be presented not only in the motion for annulment of the arbitral award and the reply (if any), but primarily in the arbitral award (in the reasons) challenged by the consumer.

116.   Consequently, if the subject of the arbitration is a consumer dispute, the arbitrators (at least specifically in consumer disputes) are obliged to fully apply the applicable law,[36] including its conflict-of-law rules. Generally

---

[31] The general rule is that arbitration is mostly and principally a single instance procedure (no appeal) and where the arbitral award can be subject to review, the parties avail themselves of this option only exceptionally. This arrangement rests on the postulate that *review proceedings*, or any review of a decision in the merits, minimizes the advantage of expeditious arbitral proceedings over litigation.

[32] Cf. *Růžička, K.* Odvolání v rozhodčím řízení? [Title in translation: Appeal in Arbitration?] Právní praxe v podnikání, 2000, No. 4, p. 11 et seq., Bělohlávek, A. Druhá instance v rozhodčím řízení. [Title in translation: Appellate Proceedings in Arbitration]. Právní zpravodaj, 2003, No. 6, pp. 5–7 et al.

[33] See the ECJ judgment in *Mostaza-Claro*.

[34] Although not directly in connection with arbitration, but with conclusions that are largely applicable generally, see *Balík, S.* Písemné odůvodnění rozhodnutí jako součást práva na spravedlivý proces. [Title in translation: Written Explication of the Reasons Underlying the Decision as a Component of the Right to a Fair Trial]. In: *Vostrá, L.* (ed.) Pocta Antonínu Kandovi k 75. narozeninám [In Honor of Antonín Kanda's 75th Birthday], Plzeň: Aleš Čeněk, 2005, pp. 213–218.

[35] See the ECJ judgment in *Pannon GSM*.

[36] Cf. *Sokol, T.* Vázanost rozhodce právem ČR ve vnitrostátním sporu. [Title in translation: The Extent to Which Arbitrators Are Bound by Czech Law in Domestic Disputes]. Právní fórum, 2008, Vol. 5, No. 4, pp. 134–139, *Kennedy, D.* Form and Substance in Private Law Adjudication. Harvard

we could, in isolated cases, consider the possibility of decision-making according to the principles of equity (*ex aequo et bono*), by an arbitrator acting as *amiable compositeur*[37] (where the *lex arbitri* allows such procedure), but strictly within the framework delimited by the applicable substantive rules, primarily consumer protection rules. The standard of protection afforded to the consumer by applicable substantive law cannot be restricted in any manner. Consequently, we would principally have to proceed as follows: first, determine the applicable law, the scope and the limits of consumer protection guaranteed by the applicable law, and then the arbitrators would be allowed to make decisions following the principles of equity, strictly within the limits defined thereby.[38]

III.4. EC Recommendation No. 98/257/EC of 30 March 1998, regarding the resolution of consumer disputes

117. The somewhat negative approach of the EC to consumer arbitration does not extend to post-dispute arbitration agreements[39] (arbitration agreements post-ante). The EC supports all ADR mechanisms, including arbitration, as the preferred method of consumer dispute resolution. The developments of consumer dispute resolution in the global EU context aimed at the replacement of the individual partial national

---

Law Review, 1976, Vol. 89, p. 1685 et seq., *Mann, F. A.* Lex facit arbitrum. In: International Arbitration. In: Liber amicorum Martin Domke, 1967, pp. 157–183 et al.

[37] Cf. *Herboczková, J.* Amiable compositeur v mezinárodním rozhodčím řízení. [Title in translation: Amiable Compositeur in International Arbitration]. Právní rozhledy, 2008, Vol. 16, No. 17, pp. 632–637 et al.

[38] It is generally unclear what exactly this principle means and what procedure it enables. The proponents of one theory maintain that arbitrators are not bound by any generally-binding laws and regulations and the only governing principle is their understanding of the general principles of equity in legal relationships. The proponents of the other theory believe that arbitrators are always obliged to identify the limits of the fundamental principles of the legal system and the substantive rules on the basis of the substantive law determined and established by them, and to make their decisions within the limits of the space defined thereby, even though they are not obliged to respect the wording of the specific provisions regulating the issues they are supposed to rule on. Some models combine both approaches. In any case, even if these methods were hypothetically applicable in the resolution of consumer disputes, the first alternative is clearly out of the question. On the contrary, the arbitrators would have to clearly determine the applicable law and principally always proceed in compliance with the substantive law; they could depart from the substantive law, following the *principles of equity*, only if the applicable non-binding rules allowed such deviations (which is, in connection with consumer contracts, clearly a very limited possibility). Cf. also *Loquin, E.* L'amiable composition en droit comparé et international: Contribution à l'étude du non-droit dans l'arbitrage commercial international, Paris: Travaux du CREDIMI, 1980; *Gill, J.* The arbitrator's role in bringing about a settlement – An English view. In: *Wirth, M.* (ed.) Best Practices in International Arbitration, ASA Special Series No. 26, Collection of Papers from the Conference Organized by ASA Swiss Arbitration Association (27 January 2006 / Zurich), Basel: ASA, 2006 (July), pp. 155–165.

[39] Cf. Section 2(3)(a) of the ArbAct [CZE].

systems by a uniform regime, is perceived as a potential stimulus for the development of trading in the entire single market.[40]

118.   The **EC** *Recommendation* of 30 March 1998 respects the significance of an out-of-court settlement of disputes and **recommends that the following principles be observed**:

▶ **Independence of the decision-making body.** When the decision is taken by an individual,[41] the **EC** emphasizes the sufficient duration of his or her office as well as his or her independence of professional associations or enterprises. When the decision is taken by a body other than an ordinary court of law, i.e. especially by an arbitral tribunal, the **EC** emphasizes the significance of an equal representation of consumers and professionals with respect to the composition of such bodies.

▶ **Transparency.** This principle entails, inter alia, the requirement of written (codified and stable) procedural rules, including any rules governing the determination of the amount and the method of settlement of and compensation for the costs of proceedings, clear rules defining the nature of the decision-making body, and the consequences of the decisions rendered in such proceedings in terms of their binding force (finality and enforceability). At the same time, the *Recommendation* stipulates the obligation to publish annual reports regarding the activities of the permanent institutions handling and / or organizing the resolution of consumer disputes. However, the very principles underlying arbitration, i.e. especially as concerns the confidentiality of arbitration and the status of arbitral panels within the framework of the jurisdiction vested in *permanent arbitral institutions*, limit the possibility of enforcing these requirements to an absolute minimum. This aspect of the requirement of *transparency* can therefore be largely accepted without reservations in connection with state-established dispute resolution organizations, whether they are authorities directly vested

---

[40] See *Drahozal, C. et Friel, R. A.* A Comparative View of Consumer Arbitration. Arbitration, 2005, Vol. 2, p. 133. This, however, is only a vision currently lacking any specific shape. With regard to the developments in the discussions over the potential broadening of the scope of the *Brussels I Regulation* in the past three years or so, the differences in opinion among the individual Member States and between the Member States and the EU are obvious.

[41] "*Authority*" must be interpreted in a broader sense, i.e. not only as a "public authority" but as any entity which is under the applicable laws endowed with the authority to conduct proceedings and render binding and enforceable decisions. We could mention, for instance, an analogy with EU legislation in some other areas. A comparison can be made with the term "court" as defined in Article 2 of Regulation 1346/2000 on the one hand, i.e. court as a public authority, and "court" under Article 15 of the same Regulation (Regulation 1346/2000), on the other hand, which has a much broader scope, i.e. an authority in the wider sense.

The *Recommendation* is also referred to in ECJ Judgment, Joined Cases C-317/08 through C-320/08 of 18 March 2010 (*Rosalba Alassini* /C-317/08/ *et Filomena Califano* v. *Wind SpA* /C-318/08/ *et Lucia Anna Giorgia Iacono* v. *Telecom Italia SpA* /C-319/08/ *et Multiservice Srl* v. *Telecom Italia SpA* /C-320/08/), published in: *OJ* C 134, 22 May 2010.

with public authority, *quasi* public authorities or not. In connection with arbitration, however, these requirements can only be accepted to a very limited extent – which is actually not even principally disputed by interpretation at the *Community* level.

▶ **Adversarial principle.** This principle demands that all arguments presented by the parties be taken into consideration and that the decision-making body properly determine [all] circumstances of fact and [all] legal aspects of the case based on the evidence and considering all the evidence put forward by the parties to the case.

▶ **Effectiveness.** The principle of effectiveness means the expeditious resolution of disputes (or quickly provided protection) which ought to be cost-effective, require no mandatory legal representation, and perform an active role in the body competent to solve the dispute or to examine the consumer protection issues in ascertaining the factual and legal circumstances decisive for the respective case.

▶ **Principle of legality.** This principle means that the consumer may not be deprived of the protection afforded by the mandatory provisions of *lex fori*; in the case of cross-border disputes (disputes with an international dimension), however, the consumer may not be deprived of the protection afforded by the mandatory provisions applicable under the law of the state in which he or she is habitually resident. **This principle is of elementary significance from the perspective of the conflict-of-law rules incorporated into the body of private international law.**

▶ **Principle of liberty.** This principle is based on the presumption that the decision may be binding on the parties only if they were informed of its binding nature in advance. Some experts maintain that this means that an agreement on the resolution of disputes from consumer contracts other than through regular courts is only permissible in the form of a post-dispute arbitration agreement, i.e. an agreement made only in connection with a particular dispute. But this opinion must be seen as ill-founded. The practice of many countries both as concerns arbitration in consumer matters and as concerns analogous mechanisms for the resolution of other, very similar disputes (labor disputes, etc.), indicates that it is more than easily imaginable that the consumer is advised of the nature of such mechanisms and the nature of the resultant decisions in advance. Only the manner of giving advice or instructions must be examined individually in each particular case and with due regard being taken of all relevant circumstances, especially the facts of the case attending the conclusion of the contract. Basically, the same approach must be adopted vis-à-vis the choice-of-law agreements.

▶ **Principle of representation.** The consumer is always allowed to have a representative if that is his or her voluntary decision; however, representation must not be a mandatory condition for the enforcement of consumer protection.

119.   The *Recommendation* is especially **addressed** to the bodies responsible for the out-of-court settlement of consumer disputes, to any natural or legal person responsible for the creation or operation of such bodies, as well as to the Member States, to the extent that they are involved in the establishment or operation of such systems (or the individual institutions for the resolution of the disputes).[42] The reference to Member States would also include state courts with jurisdiction to conduct consumer arbitrations in the above-mentioned cases. The list of all institutions for an out-of-court resolution of disputes which meet the conditions stipulated in the *Recommendation* can be found at the website of the Directorate General (EU) for Health and Consumers.[43]

120.   It must be emphasized that the EC *Recommendation* must be regarded as a collection of **independent recommendations** addressed to both private entities and the Member States.[44] The purpose of the *Recommendation* according to the EC is to allow the institutions to make their views known and to suggest a line of action without imposing any legal obligation on those to whom it is addressed.[45] However, recommendations as instruments of a specific expression of the EC's opinion can be, and have already been in certain cases, a kind of *overture* to the future legislative incorporation of the respective principles, where the EC concludes that its recommendation has not been followed and that it is necessary (and possible) to regulate the respective issues in the form of a *Community* legal instrument.

III.5.   Other sources of EU law

III.5.1.   Directive 98/27/EC of the European Parliament and of the Council of 19 May 1998

121.   Other **EC** laws relevant to the resolution of consumer disputes, especially outside the jurisdiction of courts, include Directive 98/27/EC[46] of the EP and of the Council of 19 May 1998 on injunctions for the protection of consumers' interests.[47,48] This Directive regulates the

---

[42] Commission Recommendation No. 98/257/EC, last paragraph (unnumbered).
[43] See http://ec.europa.eu/consumers/redress_cons/schemes_en.htm [last access 9 January 2012]. For information about the application of the schemes in individual EU countries, including information about additional schemes in respect to which the *Commission* was not informed, see the 2009 study of the Directorate General (EU) for Health and Consumers 2009 available at: http://ec.europa.eu/consumers/redress_cons/adr_study.pdf [last access 9 January 2012].
[44] EC Treaty, Article 249.
[45] See http://eur-lex.europa.eu/en/droit_communautaire/droit_communautaire.htm.
[46] CELEX No. 31998L0027.
[47] In the Czech Republic [CZE], this was implemented by Act No. 634/1992 Coll., on Consumer Protection, as subsequently amended, and by Act No. 99/1963, Code of Civil Procedure, as subsequently amended.
[48] Published in: *OJ* L 166, 11 June 1998, p. 51 et seq.

mechanisms employed by consumer protection organizations as concerns the applicable measures aimed at preventing activities detrimental to the collective interests of consumers. The *Directive* also includes a provision on cross-border actions.

III.5.2. Liability for defective products

122. Consumer protection has a special role in safeguarding the standards of goods and services. This primarily involves liability for defective products. This department may be understood as one governed predominantly by public law, as opposed to the general consumer protection concerning terms in consumer contracts. Safety of the market is one of the duties of the public sector. We can therefore consider not only the application of *public interest*, but also the application of *public policy (ordre public)*.[49]

123. The reservation regarding *public policy* usually adjusts the result of the application of foreign law to comply with domestic (national) ideas of legal standards. At the general level, we can (at least in theory) envisage that in liability for defective products, the application of national standards and conflict-of-laws criteria of private international law may even result in the application of foreign law regulating such liability,[50] even in those cases in which the attained liability standard will not be comparable to the national (domestic) standard. In this connection, we refer to the degree, or the reasonable degree, of such liability which need not always be completely identical to domestic standards but should provide a comparable range of remedies against the producer. Consequently, the particular result of the application of foreign law must always be located within a certain range of acceptability, and exceeding the corresponding benchmarks is an individual affair.

124. The standards of liability for defective products sometimes perform the role of protective measures. Many countries view the principles enshrined in these rules as a component of (at least domestic) *public policy (ordre public)*. Clearly, at least in the context of EU law, within their territorial scope and with the application of the principles of the

---

[49] Protection against unfair terms in consumer contracts is, conversely, the domain of civil (contract) law. Compared with substantive conflict-of-law rules (the rules of private international law), it is more reasonable to assume that consumer protection rules have the nature of overriding mandatory rules (see, for instance, Article 9 of the *Rome I Regulation*) rather than the reservation regarding *public policy* (see, for instance, Article 21 of the *Rome I Regulation*). Conversely, liability for defective products is classified as public law, and the rules can therefore be assumed as falling under the *public policy (ordre public)* category.

[50] Cf. *Freitag, R.* Der Einfluss des Europäischen Gemeinschaftsrechts auf das internationale Produkthaftungsrecht. Max Planck-Institut für ausländisches und internationales Privatrecht. Studien zum ausländischen und internationalen Privatrecht – No 83. Tübingen: Mohr Siebeck, 2000, p. 409.

single market (especially the free movement of persons, goods,[51] services,[52] capital, and the freedom of residence and establishment), we can hardly advocate the view that liability for defective products would still represent a part of *public policy*. In the course of time (with the development of interpretation practice applicable to *Community* law, or EU law), the principle of equal treatment[53] has been surpassed at the *Community* level and the preferred rules are now the standards prescribed by the countries from where the goods come,[54] providing the goods meet these standards.

125. The principle cited in the preceding paragraph was voiced, for instance, in the ECJ's ruling in *Cassis*,[55] as well as in the ECJ's decision in *Dassonville*.[56] Such developments correspond to the application of the principle the objective of which is to eliminate any legal differences and create a single market, which is also one of the fundamental objectives of the *Community*, or of the single market.[57] These developments alone deny that the protection of the country's own consumers and the protection of the market manifested in the laws regulating the liability for defective products would in fact be the subject of *public policy*.

---

[51] Cf. *Millarg, I.* Schranken des freien Warenverkehrs in EG, Baden-Baden: Nomos, 2001; *Szcekalla, P.* Grundfreiheiten Schutzpflichten – eine "neue" Funktion der Grundfreiheiten des Gemeinschaftsrechts, DVBl, 1998, p. 219 et seq.; *Keßler, J.* Das System der Warenverkehrsfreiheit im Gemeinschaftsrecht, Berliner Juristische Universitätsschriften Zivilrecht, Vol. 16, 1997; *Kieninger, E. M.* Verbot des Multi-Level-Marketing – Verstoß gegen die Warenverkehrsfreiheit ? EWS, 1998, p. 277 et seq.; *Solbach, T.* Staatliche Regelungen von Verkaufsmodalitäten als Maßnahmen gleicher Wirkung wie mengemässige Beschränkungen im Sinne des Art. 30 EGV. München: Herbert Utz Verlag, 1996; *Cremer,W.* Das Verhältnis der Beihilferegeln gemäß Art 92 f. EFV zur Warenverkehrsfreiheit. EuR, 1996, p. 225 et seq. et al.

[52] Cf. *Hradil, J.* Princip země původu – změny v oblasti volného poskytování služeb. [Title in translation: The Principle of the Country of Origin – Changes in the Free Movement of Services]. Právní rozhledy, 2006, No. 1, p. 10 et seq.; *Streinz, R. et Leible, S.* Die unmittelbare Drittwirkung der Grundfreiheiten. EuZW, 2000, p. 459 et seq.; *Völker, S.* Passive Dienstleistungsfreiheit im Europäischen Gemeinschaftsrecht, Berlin: Duncker & Humblot, 2000; *Ganten, T. O.* Die Drittwirkung der Grundfreiheiten, Berlin: Duncker & Humblot, 2000; *Jarass, H. D.* Elemente einer Dogmatik der Grundfreiheiten II. EuR, 2000, p. 705 et seq.; *Schöne, F. J.* Dienstleistungsfreiheit in der EG und deutsche Wirtschaftsaufsicht, Köln: Heymann, 1989.

[53] Cf. *Pauknerová, M.* Evropské mezinárodní právo soukromé. [Title in translation: European Private International Law]. Prague: C. H. Beck, 2008, pp. 100–101.

[54] Cf. *Mankowski, P.* Das Herkunftslandprinzip als Internationales Privatrecht. ZvglRWiss, 2001, p. 100 et seq.; *Thünken, A.* Das kollissionsrechtliche Herkunftslandprinzip. Studien zum vergleichenden und internationalen Recht. Bd. 93, Frankfurt am M.: Peter Lang, 2003.

[55] ECJ Ruling Case No. 120/78 (*Rewe v. Bundesmonopolverwaltung für Branntwein*, the *Cassis* case), published in: ECR 1979, p. 649 et seq.

[56] ECJ Judgment, Case 8/74 (*Dassonville*), published in: ECR 1974, p. 837 et seq.

[57] Cf. *Basedow, J.* Zielkonflikte und Zielhierarchien im Vertrag über die Europäische Gemeinschaft. In: Liber Amicorum, Baden-Baden: Nomos, 1995, p. 49 et seq.; *Schubert, T.* Der Gemeinsame Markt als Rechtsbegriff. München: C. H. Beck, 1999; *von der Groeben, H.* Probleme einer europäischen Wirtschaftsordnung. In: Liber Amicorum Börner, 1992, p. 99 et seq., *Müller-Graff, R.* Verfassungsziele der EG/EU. In: *Dauses, M.* (ed.) EU-Wirtschaftsrecht, 1999, Part A.I.; *Jarass, H. D.* Europäisches Energierecht, Berlin: Duncker & Humblot, 1996 et al.

However, liability for defective products can be a component of *national public policy*. But if the application of the country of origin principle negates the postulate that such protection of the market represents a component of the *national public policy*, it cannot be a component of *EU public policy*, let alone *international public policy*. The reason is that *EU public policy* or *international public policy* may not include any principle which is not capable of being a component of *national public policy*. Thus, this issue is not very important, neither from the perspective of the resolution of disputes between a consumer and a professional, nor from the perspective of arbitration (for instance, in the application of the reservation regarding *public policy* as a reason for annulment of the arbitral award). The reason is that the grounds for a refusal to recognize and enforce a foreign arbitral award pursuant to Article V(2)(b) are aimed at the protection of procedural *public policy* whereas liability for defective products is regulated under substantive law.

III.5.3. EU laws with no impact on consumer arbitration

126. Even though Regulation 44/2001 (*Brussels I Regulation*) on jurisdiction and the recognition and enforcement of judgments in civil and commercial matters (originally the *Brussels Convention*) may at first sight appear significant, arbitration is explicitly excluded from its scope. In *Marc Rich* v. *Impianti*[58] the ECJ construed the exclusion in very broad terms. The ECJ ruled that it *"extends to litigation pending before a national court concerning the appointment of an arbitrator, even if the existence or validity of an arbitration agreement is a preliminary issue in that litigation."*[59]

127. The *Rome Convention* and the *Rome I Regulation* also exclude arbitration agreements (determination of the law applicable to arbitration agreements) from their scope. They do, however, contain [substantive] conflict-of-law rules applicable to consumer contracts.

---

[58] ECJ Judgment, Case C-190/89 of 21 July 1991 (*Marc Rich* v. *Impianti*), published in: ECR 1991, p. I–3855. The ECJ's conclusions can be briefly summarized as follows: (1) Litigation pending before a national court concerning the appointment of an arbitrator is excluded from the scope of the *Brussels Convention* (today the *Brussels I Regulation*). (2) Preliminary issues concerning the validity of an arbitration clause do not allow application of the *Brussels Convention* (similarly the *Brussels I Regulation*). (3) Whether the case falls within the scope of the *Brussels Convention* (similarly the *Rome I Regulation*) or, conversely, within the negative definition of the scope excluding arbitration, must be decided according to the subject of the proceedings. (4) The validity of an arbitration agreement must be examined both pursuant to international agreements and pursuant to national laws. (5) It is possible that litigation and arbitration will both be conducted simultaneously in different Member States if the arbitration agreement is accepted by the arbitral tribunal in one Member State and another Member State concludes, conversely, that it is invalid (this point was criticized for instance in: *van Houtte, H.* Why Not Include Arbitration in the Brussels Jurisdiction Regulation? Arb. Int.), 2005, Vol. 21, No. 4, p. 509 et seq., see especially p. 512).

[59] ECJ Judgment, Case C-190/89 of 25 July 1995, published in ECR 1989, p. I–03855.

III.6. Concept of single European Contract Law (contractual framework)

III.6.1. Genesis and development[60]

128. In its 2001 Communication on European Contract Law,[61] the European Commission (*Commission*) opened public consultations regarding problems resulting from divergences in contract law between the Member States. Following the Communication, in 2003, the *Commission* drew up an action plan[62] and proposed to create a common frame of reference containing common principles, terminology, and model rules. A year later, the *Commission* adopted another document[63] which proposed to review the Union's *acquis* in consumer contract law, with the aim of removing inconsistencies and filling regulatory gaps. The result of the review was a proposal for a directive on consumer rights[64] which the *Commission* submitted in October 2008.

129. The Draft Common Frame of Reference of 2008[65] covers principles, definitions and model rules of civil law, including contract law, and tort law. The DCFR also deals with commercial and consumer contracts. The DCFR was based on the previously drafted *Principles of European Contract Law* (PECL). The *Commission* highlighted, for instance, the success of the Vienna Convention on Contracts for the International Sales of Goods (as an UNCITRAL project), the UNIDROIT Principles of International Commercial Contracts as the model rules on sales of goods and provision of services, etc. But the *Commission* emphasized that these instruments cannot restrict the application of national mandatory rules and the unification of the national rules is the desired objective of the *Commission*'s initiative. An instrument of European Contract Law

---

[60] For more details, see also the Green Paper analyzed in the following Chapter.

[61] Communication from the *Commission* on European Contract Law of 11 July 2001. CELEX: 52001DC0398. Available online through prelex.eu at: http://ec.europa.eu/prelex/detail_dossier_real.cfm?CL=cs&DosId=166261 [last access 22 August 2011].

[62] Communication from the *Commission* of 12 February 2003 "A More Coherent European Contract Law – An Action Plan." CELEX: 52003DC0068. Available online at: http://ec.europa.eu/prelex/detail_dossier_real.cfm?CL=cs&DosId=180632 [last access 22 August 2011].

[63] Communication from the *Commission* of 11 October 2004 "European Contract Law and the Revision of the Acquis: The Way Forward." CELEX: 52004DC0651. Available online at: http://ec.europa.eu/prelex/detail_dossier_real.cfm?CL=cs&DosId=191807 [last access 22 August 2011].

[64] Proposal for a Directive on Consumer Rights CELEX 52008PC0614. Available online at: http://ec.europa.eu/prelex/detail_dossier_real.cfm?CL=cs&DosId=197477 [last access 22 August 2011]. This directive (now in the form of a proposal) is to be adopted by the co-decision procedure. As concerns the present situation, the proposal was subject to the first reading in the EP and is currently awaiting the Council's statement regarding the amendments incorporated by the EP in the original proposal. If the directive were adopted, it would replace Directives 85/577/EEC, 93/13/EEC and 1999/44/EC as concerns consumer protection.

[65] *Von Bar, C., Clive, E. et Schulte-Nölke, H.* (eds.) Principles, Definitions and Model Rules of European Private Law. Draft Common Frame of Reference. München: Sellier, 2009. Available online at: http://webh01.ua.ac.be/storme/DCFRInterim.pdf [last access 22 August 2011].

should, according to the *Commission*, help the EU to meet its economic goals and recover from the economic crisis. The Stockholm Programme (EU) for 2010–2014 states that the European judicial area should serve to support economic activity in the internal market. The actions are proposed as an *optional* contract law *instrument*, in particular as regards the common practice of the electronic (*online*) conclusion of contracts.

III.6.2. The *Green Paper*

130.   The *Green Paper*[66] analyzed the possibilities of facilitating cross-border transactions, i.e. transactions with an international dimension.[67] The *Green Paper* proposes seven options for the choice of the most suitable instrument of European Contract Law, without any further burdens or complications for consumers and/or businesses. In addition, it should ensure a high level of consumer protection. **The proposed options of resolving the issues of European Contract Law are as follows** (arranged according to their binding or non-binding nature and normative force):[68]

▶ **Publication of the results of the Expert Group:** This solution would only contribute to a better awareness of the differences between the individual legal systems, without shaping the contract law by new norms.

▶ **An official "toolbox" for the legislator, either** in the form of a *Commission* act, or in the form of an inter-institutional agreement. This would not represent any norm either.

▶ *Commission* **Recommendation on European Contract Law** as an *encouragement* to incorporate the attached instrument into the national laws of the EU Member States. The following **alternatives** are envisaged: **(i)** replacement of national laws with the recommended European instrument[69] or **(ii)** the European Contract Law instrument would be incorporated as an alternative to national law (law of national origin).

▶ **Regulation setting up an optional instrument of European Contract Law;**[70] an alternative which would in each Member State provide the parties with an option between this optional instrument

---

[66] *Green Paper* of 1 July 2010 on policy options for progress towards a European Contract Law for consumers and businesses. CELEX: 52010DC0348. The alternatives proposed by the *Green Paper* served as the basis for the EP's Resolution of 8 June 2011.

[67] In connection with consumer protection, see *Bělohlávek, A.* Spotřebitelská smlouva z pohledu mezinárodního práva soukromého. [Title in translation: Consumer Contracts from the Perspective of Private International Law]. Právní rádce, 2005, No. 8, pp. 4–7.

[68] Cf. *Břicháček, T.* Zelená kniha o smluvní právu. [Title in translation: Green Paper on Contract Law]. Právní fórum, 2011, Vol. 8, No. 10, pp. 476–-484.

[69] The *Green Paper* is compared to the American Commercial Code (*Uniform Commercial Code* [USA]).

[70] This possibility was chosen by the EP from the individual potential alternatives and has therefore been analyzed in greater detail in this book.

and the domestic law (law of national origin).[71] The instrument could be applicable both to contracts with an international dimension (cross-border contracts) and to purely domestic contracts. According to the *Commission*, the instrument should guarantee that the **consumers'** rights would not be compromised; as a necessary precondition, the relation to the *Rome I Regulation* and to other instruments **with a guarantee of high consumer protection** would be clarified as well.[72] In other words, it would be a parallel regime to the laws of national origin. **This particular alternative has been preferred and articulated in the EP Resolution.**[73] Public debates are to be opened now with the aim of understanding the directions and soliciting the opinions of the parties on the possible policies in European Contract Law.[74] The consultations are open to all interested parties.

▶ **Directive on European Contract Law** for the purpose of harmonizing the European Contract Law on the basis of minimum standards *(the minimum harmonization regime).*

▶ **Regulation establishing a European Contract Law** which ought to replace the national laws and introduce a uniform set of substantive rules which should, inter alia, guarantee a high level of protection for the weaker party. This regulation would replace national substantive rules in transactions with an international dimension (cross-border transactions) (directly applicable substantive rules).

▶ **Regulation establishing a European Civil Code**, i.e. introduction of a single European Contract Law.

III.6.3. EP *Resolution* of 8 June 2011 (the *"Resolution"*)

(a) Contents of the EP *Resolution*

131. The crucial objective of the **EP *Resolution*** of 8 June 2011[75] is to support cross-border transactions, especially for small and medium-sized enterprises. It also mentions craft manufacturing which, in the EP's opinion, has a significant economic importance (refers to the *Small*

---

[71] This collection of contract law rules would be incorporated in the national laws of each Member State also for the purposes of private international law.

[72] See Article 12 TFEU concerning the obligation to have regard to the consumer protection requirements in defining and implementing EU policies and other activities.

[73] European Parliament *Resolution* of 8 June 2011 on policy options for progress towards a European Contract Law for consumers and businesses (2011/2013 [INI]), available at the European Parliament website at: http://www.europarl.europa.eu/sides/getDoc.do?pubRef=-//EP//TEXT+TA+P7-TA-2011-0262+0+DOC+XML+V0//CS&language=CS [last access 19 August 2011].

[74] *Green Paper*, pp. 13 and 14.

[75] See also *Bělohlávek, A. et Šrotová, E.* Jednotné evropské smluvní právo – usnesení Evropského parlamentu z 8. června 2011 nastartovalo novou etapu. [Title in translation: Uniform European Contract Law – The European Parliament Resolution of 8 June 2011 Triggered a New Phase]. Právní rádce, 2011, Vol. 19, No. 11, pp. 24–30 et al.

Business Act;[76] SBA). The EP invokes the recently published feasibility study (the *"Feasibility Study"*)[77] on the basis of which the EP supported the creation of an **optional instrument in the form of a regulation, complemented by a "toolbox" and contractual terms**. It calls for the creation of European standard contract models linked to an alternative dispute resolution (ADR) system carried out online. These standard contract models would guarantee very high consumer protection and would exist **in two forms** – **(i)** as *business-to-business* contracts (*"B2B"*) and **(ii)** as *business-to-consumer* contracts (*"B2C"*). In the EP's view, all interested parties would have the option to choose either the optional instrument or, conversely, their own national law *(opt-in)*.

(b) Legal nature of the instrument of European Contract Law

132. The European Parliament (EP) asked the *Commission* to continue discussions as to how the *Feasibility Study* could be used. The EP acknowledged the need for further progress in contract law and favored, amongst other options, "Option 4," i.e. setting up an optional instrument by means of a regulation (after an impact assessment and a clarification of the legal basis), possibly complemented by a *toolbox* that could be endorsed by means of an inter-institutional agreement. The EP thereby called for the **creation of standard European contract models, translated into all EU languages, linked to an alternative dispute resolution system carried out** *online*, which would have the advantage of being a cost-effective and simpler solution for both contractual parties and the *Commission*.[78]

---

[76] The *Small Business Act* was adopted in June 2008 and reflects the *Commission's* approach to small and medium-sized enterprises (*"SMEs"*) which, according to the *Commission*, play a central role in the European economy. The objective is to improve the general approach to business, incorporate the *"Think Small First"* principle in the process of creating policies and supporting the growth of small and medium-sized enterprises, together with support in overcoming obstacles preventing their growth. SBA applies to all independent businesses with no more than 250 employees – these represent 99 % of all companies.

[77] The *Feasibility Study* was drafted by a team of lawyers, ex-judges, and academics from the entire EU; the group was summoned by the *Commission* in April 2010. The group focused on analyzing the possibilities of improving contract law in the EU. The group met each month and consulted the representatives of enterprises (including small and medium-sized businesses), consumer organizations, and legal experts. The meetings were also attended by observers from the *EP* and the *Council*. The study addresses the important practical problems of contractual relationships, such as claims relating to defective products and rules governing the determination of unfair contract terms. The results were published on 3 May 2011. Adopted from: EU in the Czech Republic (2011): Cross-border Transactions. The European Commission published a feasibility study concerning European Contract Law; available online at: http://ec.europa.eu/ceskarepublika/press/press_releases/11_523_cs.htm [last access 19 August 2011].

[78] Some countries have adopted a rather cautious approach to that intent, including the Czech Republic [CZE] (see the information published in: Obchodněprávní revue, 2011, No. 8, p. 246.). The Czech Minister of Justice stated at an informal meeting of the Justice and Home Affairs Council in July 2011 that the Czech Republic [CZE] does not support the adoption of this instrument; one of the reasons was that the solution would give rise to complex issues with respect to the relationship with

133. The EP selected the legal form of regulation, because it believes that only this legal form can guarantee the necessary clarity and legal certainty. The form of regulation would also improve the functioning of the internal market because of the direct effect, with benefits for businesses (reduced costs as a result of obviating the need for conflict-of-law rules), consumers (legal certainty, confidence, high level of consumer protection) and Member States' judicial systems (it would no longer be necessary to examine foreign laws). In that connection, however, it is important to point out the negative effect which is usually absent from documents drafted at the EU level, namely the necessity of strengthening the role of the judge at the national level. The judge is the person who safeguards the protection of the parties in the individual adjudicated disputes and any limitation of the role of national judges (courts) would be very harmful. The instruments mentioned above (unless accompanied by analogous measures supporting the national decision-making process, ideally at the lowest level) often tend to suppress the importance of the role of the judge. According to the EP, the chosen option should support the subsidiarity principle, without prejudice to the legislative powers of the Member States in contract and civil law. The instruments (*toolbox*) could possibly be put into practice step-by-step, starting as a *Commission* tool, and being converted, once agreed between the institutions, into a tool for the Union legislator. The *toolbox* should, in the EP's opinion, provide the necessary legal backdrop and underpinning against which an optional instrument and standard terms and conditions could operate. The *toolbox* should be **based on an assessment of the national mandatory rules of consumer protection** not only within but also outside the existing *acquis*.

134. The EP believes that all parties, be it in B2B or B2C transactions, should be free to choose or not to choose the optional instrument as an alternative to national or international law (*opt-in*). The European Parliament (EP) therefore called on the *Commission* to clarify the intended relationship of the optional instrument with the *Rome I Regulation* and international conventions including the United Nations Convention on Contracts for the International Sale of Goods (*Vienna Convention*, CISG). The European Parliament (EP) also mentioned the need to ensure that the optional instrument offers protection to consumers and small businesses given their position as the weaker contracting partner and that any confusion is avoided when making a choice of law. The EP therefore called on the *Commission* to complement the optional instrument with additional information which would explain in clear, precise and comprehensible language what the consumer's rights are and that they will not be compromised, in order to

---

national law and could ultimately be misused to evade national law. This view could be agreed with. Although criticism is by no means rare, it depends on whether it will prevail and to what extent.

increase their confidence in the optional instrument and to put them in a position to make an informed choice as to whether they wish to conclude a contract on this alternative basis. It appears, however, that this could have negative effects in the form of enhancing consumer protection by special legal instruments (contract law instruments); such practice should be considered to be generally harmful. Intensification of the interpretation, elaboration, and development of current legal institutions within the existing legal framework and supporting their application, instead of introducing special institutions would be preferable. This is apparently the development at which the European Contract Law is targeted (as current instruments adopted at the *Community* / EU level prove) and which, due to its mandate and inability to take account of the position of the other contracting party (the professional), often result in their abuse. The final effect is frequently directly opposite to the officially proclaimed outcome, i.e. a more onerous administrative and formal burden on the economy, depressed competition, and lessened economic flexibility.

135.   The European Parliament (EP) mentioned certain advantages, such as the ECJ's consistent case law and the elimination of linguistic barriers, because the instruments would exist in all EU languages. In that connection, the EP emphasized enhanced awareness, including the introduction of online translation tools. The *Commission* was also invited to draw up mechanisms for regular monitoring and review to ensure that the optional instrument keeps up with the existing *acquis* in contract law, particularly (though not exclusively) the *Rome I Regulation.*

(c) Scope of application of the instrument

136.   The EP believes that both business-to-business (*B2B*) and business-to-consumer (*B2C*) contracts should be covered by the proposal. According to the EP, the optional instrument should offer a very high level of consumer protection, in order to compensate consumers for the protection that they would normally enjoy under their national law; the level of consumer protection should therefore be higher than the minimum protection provided by the consumer *acquis*.[79] Unfortunately, the level of such protection has never been defined, and no instrument stipulates the limits (if any) of such protection in terms of obstacles barring any abuse thereof. In addition, the protection provided by the optional instrument should also cover national mandatory rules. The EP notes that this high level of consumer protection is also in the interests

---

[79] Cf. *Tomášek, M.* Pokračování evropské diskuse o pojmu "spotřebitel." [Title in translation: Continuing European Discussion over the Concept of "Consumer"]. Evropské právo, 2003, No. 10, pp. 8–11.

of businesses as they will only be able to reap the benefits of the optional instrument if the consumers of all the Member States are confident that choosing the optional instrument will not deprive them of the protection they would otherwise enjoy. Arguably this conclusion is mere speculation and, without a thorough analysis which has yet to be implemented, it is doubtful, or at least evasive.

137. The essential components of consumer law applied to contracts are already spread across various sets of European rules, and important parts of the consumer *acquis* are likely to be consolidated in the Consumer Rights Directive (CRD); this directive would provide a uniform body of law which consumers and businesses could readily identify; therefore, it is important to await the outcome of the CRD negotiations before any final decision is made.

138. As concerns the nature of the optional instrument in cross-border situations, the EP believes that the optional instrument should first be available as an opt-in. It would also be necessary to create the required guarantees that the Member States will be able to prevent any misuse of the optional instrument in non-genuine cross-border scenarios. The effects of a domestic opt-in on national bodies of contract law merit specific analysis. The EP points out in its *Resolution* that there could be merit in introducing certain limits when applying the optional instrument in the first instance, and until sufficient experience of its application has been accumulated.

139. The EP emphasizes the particular importance of facilitating e-commerce in the EU, given that this sector is underdeveloped. The European Parliament (EP) intends to make the scope of the *toolbox* quite broad, any optional instrument should be limited to core contractual law issues, whereas the *toolbox* should include among its "tools" concepts from a diverse range of legal traditions within the EU, including rules derived from, inter alia, the academic Draft Common Frame of Reference (DCFR), the *Principes contractuels communs,* and *Terminologie contractuelle commune;*[80] the recommendations should be based on a genuinely high level of consumer protection. The EP therefore called on the *Commission* and the Expert Group to clarify what the core contractual law issues are considered to be.

140. The EP sees the main benefits in an optional instrument containing specific provisions for the most frequent types of contract, in particular for the sale of goods and the provision of services; insurance contracts (particularly small-scale insurance contracts) would also

---

[80] *Fauvarque-Cosson, B. et Mazeaud, D.* (eds.) Droit privé comparé et européen, Vol. 6 and Vol. 7, 2008.

benefit.[81] The EP urges caution with regard to the inclusion of financial services at this stage.[82]

141. According to the EP, however, some specific issues in connection with which an optional instrument might be beneficial have been raised, such as digital rights and *beneficial ownership*. However, this particular area could encounter major problems. "Trust" is a typical example of the inconsistency among concepts adopted by the legal systems of the individual Member States.[83] The EP considers that, on the other hand, there might be a need to exclude certain types of *complex public law contracts*. The EP calls for the Expert Group to explore the option of including contracts on authors' rights (copyright agreements) with the aim of improving the position of authors who are often the *weaker party* in the contractual relation.

(d) Application of the instrument in practice

142. Although the optional instrument is supposed to be a single body of [substantive] law, there will still be a need to seek the provision of standard terms and conditions of trade which can be produced in a simple and comprehensible form, to strengthen consumer confidence. These optional contract terms and conditions based upon an optional instrument should offer greater legal certainty than EU-wide standard terms based upon national laws which would increase the danger of differing national interpretations.

143. Cross-border **alternative dispute resolution (ADR)**, which is speedy and cost-effective in particular for SMEs, remains a priority. The EP emphasizes that, if the parties use one body of law provided by an optional instrument, the application of the ADR mechanisms will be further facilitated. The EP noted that the UNCITRAL Working Group on *Online* Dispute Resolution has also shown interest in an optional instrument as a means to facilitate ADR. The EP has therefore recommended that the *Commission* follows developments within other international bodies.

---

[81] Moreover, preliminary works concerning insurance contracts have been completed – see the Principles of European Insurance Contract Law (PEICL). The objective of the PEICL is to create an optional legal regime for insurance contracts in the EU. To view in greater detail, see the website of the University of Innsbruck, manager of the project; available online at: http://www.restatement.info/ [last access 22 August 2011].

[82] The specifics of the financial services are to be elaborated by an expert group which the *Commission* was requested to appoint.

[83] Cf. *Bělohlávek, A.* Trust jako institut (ne)známý z pohledu mezinárodního práva soukromého (Věcný rozsah nařízení č. 593/2008, o právu rozhodném pro smluvní závazkové vztahy – Nařízení Řím I). [Title in translation: "Trust" as an Instrument (Un)known to Private International Law (Scope of Regulation No. 593/2008 on the Law Applicable to Contractual Obligations – Rome I Regulation)]. Obchodněprávní revue, 2009, Vol. 1, No. 8, pp. 181–188 et al.

144. The EP suggested that improvements to the functioning and effectiveness of cross-border dispute resolution systems (including redress systems) could be facilitated by a direct linkage between the optional instrument and the European Order for Payment Procedure and the European Small Claims Procedure. The EP believes that an *electronic letter before action*[84] should be created to assist companies in protecting their rights, in particular in intellectual property and the European Small Claims procedure.

145. The EP noted concerns that consumers seldom feel they have a choice with regard to contract terms and are confronted with a "*take it or leave it*" situation. Complementing an optional instrument with a toolbox and a set of standard terms and conditions, translated into all languages, should encourage new entrants into markets, thereby strengthening competition, and broadening the overall choice available to consumers. One could argue that, if unsupported by an analysis, this conclusion is very speculative and rather populistic.

(e) Importance of the *Resolution*

146. The *Resolution* proposes the creation of uniform standard contract models known as the optional instrument, complemented with a *toolbox*. This should result in the development of a parallel legal system, alongside national laws. A comparison is made with the CISG, i.e. the parties could always opt for this regime, identical for the entire EU, or for the national law. Regrettably, however, this analogy does not fit. The CISG represents a broad global consensus and only complements national legal regimes. The EP may be seen as attempting to compare something incomparable. This is because if the alternative regime proposed by the EP should play a role similar to that played by the CISG, further application of the national law would be inevitable and the system would only get more complicated. Conversely, if the alternative legal framework should cover all issues, it would develop into an alternative complete contract law system which would, however, lack any connection with other laws incorporated intothe national legal systems. Civil law does not exist separately from the legal framework into which it is incorporated in the national environment. The concern is that the current situation may get more complicated. Indeed, the EP itself mentions that domestic law (law of national origin) could afford an advantage to the party whose law was

---

[84] See *Mišúr, P.* Evropský parlament přijal usnesení k výhledu evropského smluvního práva. [Title in translation: The European Parliament Adopted a Resolution Regarding the Prospects of European Contract Law]. Obchodněprávní revue, 2011, Vol. 3, No. 8, pp. 245–246. However, this informative article erroneously refers to "electronic signature." These are naturally two completely different things.

chosen;[85] the EP therefore believes that the instrument could be successful. One of the central ideas associated with the optional instrument is supposed to be a high level of consumer protection, which could somewhat diminish its attractiveness to certain professionals in concluding contracts with consumers. The marketing potential in the presentation of businesses, as emphasized by the EP, may be considered rather doubtful, although it could, of course, play its role.

147.   The text of the *Resolution* does not clarify how the applicable legal regime would be chosen; the EP urges the *Commission* to focus on this issue. This particular issue could have a major impact on consumer protection. It would therefore be desirable to make sure that situations when the consumer is de facto deprived of his or her choice do not occur with respect to the choice of the applicable legal regime. The EP's idea that the applicable legal regime would be chosen by the consumer appears somewhat naive. Knowledge possessed by the consumer (*average consumer*) can never reach the level (despite the utmost efforts to enhance the consumer's awareness) which would guarantee that the consumer would be able to make a real assessment of the advantages and disadvantages of the individual options. It appears somewhat objectionable that the professional should face a situation in which the professional will depend on a decision that could be influenced by the customer's random choice or aspects other than real legal reasons. Consequently, the view taken by EP that with regard to the optional nature of the regime for the parties, we need not worry about disrupting the principle of freedom of contract or autonomy of will seems untenable. Such consequences are precisely what should be anticipated; indeed, such consequences always occur in strongly protectionist environments. After all, the countries of Central and Eastern Europe have had recent and very negative experience with restrictions on the freedom of contract.

148.   The optional instrument is to be adopted in the **form of a regulation**, subjecting it to the ECJ's interpretation. Regulations apply and have direct effect in the Member States.

149.   It is necessary to emphasize, however, that consumers must be properly informed of this option so they understand that this alternative is advantageous for them and that they need not be afraid to avail themselves of this possibility; Dissemination of this information could be arranged, for instance, by an EU-wide advertising campaign. Potential problems could arise at the stage of formulating these standard contract models (as an optional instrument). The contract law in the individual

---

[85] The EP says that the advantage benefits the party whose law was chosen. This premise probably applies in normal situations; it does not possess general validity, though. It is possible to imagine opposite scenarios, and they are by no means rare in practice.

Member States is not unified and, moreover, some countries are based on different legal traditions; this fact could have a negative impact on the wording of this optional instrument. On the other hand, several regulations have already been adopted which prescribe contract law rules applicable in the EU, or rather rules regulating contractual and non-contractual obligations (*Rome I Regulation* and *Rome II Regulation*), albeit "only" in conflict-of-law rules. However, the terminology of the *Rome I Regulation* and the *Rome II Regulation* could be taken as the basis, because the case law derived from these two instruments has already been evolving; so too can also guidance be drawn from the *Rome Convention* and its application in practice.

150. What precisely the EP means by an electronic letter before action remains completely unclear. The concept has been entirely neglected in the text of the *Resolution* as well as in the materials from the preceding debates.

III.6.4. Influence of the EP's *Resolution* on arbitration

151. The optional instrument should probably be connected to an alternative dispute resolution (ADR) system carried out *online*. The *Resolution* provides no further details.

152. The *online* system of dispute resolution should, if properly carried out, secure benefits both for the consumer and for the professional. *Online* resolution of disputes is cheaper, especially in cross-border transactions. Considering the text of the *Resolution*, cooperation with the UNCITRAL Working Group, which has been interested in the development of this dispute resolution method, is to be expected.

153. As concerns the persons who would resolve disputes arising from the application of the optional instrument, one can imagine a procedure with certain pre-set restrictions for the consumer in securing consumer protection. Considering that the optional instrument ought to safeguard a high level of consumer protection, the consumer's position could be quite strong.

154. The concept does not explicitly refer to arbitration, which has been considered as a permissible alternative dispute resolution method by European law.[86] It is unclear whether any space, and how much, will be allocated to arbitration. With respect to current developments, one should rather presume that the preferred methods of amicable resolution will be mediation or conciliation, as opposed to arbitration which is an adversarial model resembling more the traditional finding of the law by courts. Mediation certainly is not an unsuitable method. But its forcible

---

[86] See ECJ Judgment, Case C-168/05 in *Mostaza Claro*.

introduction in certain countries and in certain legal environments is often more of a disadvantage and complicates the interest in the expeditious resolution of disputes. In the countries of Central and Eastern Europe, there are many reasons why mediation still does not meet its potential, which would allow it to fulfill its purpose in the form of a universal and efficient mechanism. Failure to understand the specifics of certain countries is the weakness plaguing any search for efficient mechanisms at the international level (for instance, at the EU level).[87]

III.7. Proposals of the European Commission regarding the alternative resolution of consumer disputes and regarding online consumer disputes of 29 November 2011

155.   In late November 2011 (29 November 2011) the European Commission (the *"Commission"*) issued several documents relating to alternative dispute resolution and online resolution of disputes for cross-border consumer contracts. Namely: **(i)** the Communication from the Commission on alternative dispute resolution for consumer disputes in the Single Market;[88] **(ii)** the Proposal for a Directive on alternative dispute resolution for consumer disputes[89] (the *"ADR Directive"*); **(iii)** Proposal for a Regulation on online dispute resolution for consumer disputes[90] (the *"ODR Regulation"*). An analysis of these documents will be attempted both from the perspective of their contents and from the perspective of their implications for the existence and functioning of the arbitration system in the EU.

III.7.1. Legal context of the *Commission's* legislative proposals

156.   According to the *Commission's* press release[91] accompanying the issue of documents, in 2010 one in five European consumers encountered

---

[87] For a very fitting description of these problems, see *Nowaczyk, P.* Comment: The Condition of Polish Commercial Mediation. World Arbitration & Mediation Review, 2010, Vol. 4, No. 1, pp. 87–94.

[88] *Commission*: Communication from the Commission to the EP, the Council and the European Economic and Social Committee. Alternative dispute resolution for consumer disputes in the Single Market, 29 November 2011. Available online at: http://ec.europa.eu/consumers/redress_cons/docs/communication_adr_cs.pdf [last access 5 December 2011].

[89] *Commission*: Proposal for a Directive of the European Parliament and of the Council on alternative dispute resolution for consumer disputes and amending Regulation (EC) No 2006/2004 and Directive 2009/22/EC; date of the proposal: 29 November 2011. Available online at: http://ec.europa.eu/consumers/redress_cons/docs/directive_adr_cs.pdf [last access 5 December 2011].

[90] Proposal for a Regulation of the European Parliament and of the Council on online dispute resolution for consumer disputes, 29 November 2011. Available online at: http://ec.europa.eu/consumers/redress_cons/docs/odr_regulation_cs.pdf [last access 5 December 2011].

[91] European Commission (2011): Consumers: Commission puts forward proposals for faster, easier and cheaper solutions to disputes with traders. Available online at: http://europa.eu/rapid/pressReleasesAction.do?reference=IP/11/1461&format=HTML&aged=0&language=EN&guiLanguage=en [last access 5 December 2011].

problems when buying goods and services in the single market. The *Commission* mentioned, by way of example, the refusal to repair a *laptop* which broke down when under guarantee and the denial of a refund for a ruined holiday. The *Commission* noted that these problems could be sorted out without going to court. But out-of-court dispute resolution in the EU is possible only for some business sectors or in some EU territories. The documents published by the *Commission* are supposed to ensure that in the future, all European consumers will have the opportunity to solve their problems without going to court, regardless of the kind of product or service and regardless of where the goods (services)[92] were bought, that is, in the consumer's home country or in another EU country. Further, the *Commission* declared its interest in ensuring that consumers who bought their goods online could resolve their disputes out-of-court and online, within 30 days of purchase.

157.   The Commission reasons that alternative dispute resolution (ADR) for consumers is faster, cheaper, and easier to pursue than court litigation. It is estimated that access to ADR will save consumers of up to 22.5 billion EUR/year. It will also help businesses facilitate the resolution of disputes with consumers and boost their corporate image. The *Commission* wants to facilitate consumer access to the single market by granting better access to wider choice and better prices; this should ultimately contribute to the growth of the EU economy.

158.   It is worth noting, however, that **alternative dispute resolution (ADR)** as understood by the *Commission* in connection with these legislative proposals means any out-of-court resolution of disputes based on a decision or any qualified activity of an impartial third party, such as an **arbitrator,** mediator, or ombudsman. In other words, it is a rather major change, because the previous concepts of alternative dispute resolution did not count on **arbitration,** and arbitration was interpreted as a dispute resolution method closer to judicial decision-making.[93]

159.   According to the *Commission's* findings, there are 750 ADR *entities* in the EU today. However, in some Member States ADR is available only in some sectors (e.g. financial services or telecommunications, etc.). This obstacle, together with low consumer and business awareness regarding ADR, prevents an effective use of all the possibilities offered by alternative dispute resolution. As concerns online dispute resolution, there is no cross-border system which would allow the resolution of

---

[92] Unless specified otherwise below, "goods" shall include services.
[93] Cf. *Bělohlávek, A.* Alternativní způsoby řešení civilních a obchodních sporů (tzv. „ADR") v evropském kontextu. [Title in translation: Alternative Methods of the Resolution of Civil and Commercial Disputes ("ADR") in the European Context]. Evropské právo – Annex Právní rozhledy, 2003, No. 6, pp. 8–11 et al.

disputes arising from the purchase of goods via the Internet. The *Commission* estimates that the cost of unresolved consumer disputes is currently at 0.4 % of the EU's GDP. This includes the money lost by consumers due to problems when shopping in the EU; these *losses* are estimated to be between 500 million and 1 billion EUR. Unfortunately, the proclamations justifying these legislative proposals do not avoid economic-ideological methods typical for Union structures, using data from statistics without any further explanation. Hence, the figures quoted in the statement, unsupported by any closer reasoning or by any figures with respect to the proposals' negative effects, are rather nonsensical and can be taken as a typical example of how often the Brussels administration presents a great number of proposals only to justify its own existence.

III.7.2. Proposed legislative procedure

160. The European Parliament and the Council undertook to adopt the package of legislative proposals by the end of 2012 in connection with the strengthening of the single market.[94] After adoption, the EU Member States will have 18 months to implement the *ADR Directive*. Consequently, EU citizens should have guaranteed access to ADR by the second half of 2014. The single EU-wide platform for online dispute resolution should become fully operational six months after ADR becomes available to all European consumers, i.e. in the first half of 2015.

III.7.3. *Commission* Communication on alternative dispute resolution for consumer disputes in the Single Market

161. The *Commission* argues that a deeper and extended internal market is vital and could result in growth and job creation. One of the means of strengthening the internal market is through consumers. Consumers lack confidence, because their problems related to the purchase of goods in the single market are not backed by an efficient dispute resolution system. The *Commission* has therefore decided to support the alternative and online resolution of disputes which, in the *Commission's* opinion, guarantees swift, cheap, and effective dispute resolution. This will

---

[94] This commitment is based on the *Single Market Act*, a document adopted by the *Commission* on 13 April 2011. The Act considers it necessary to boost the internal market, which is the *heart* of the EU and which remains the strongest weapon against economic recession and an instrument which can secure new, more environmentally-friendly, and internally-intensive growth. The Act claims that it is necessary to support the single market by twelve instruments, such as access to finance for small and medium-sized enterprises; strengthening the mobility of the workforce in the single market; enhancing the protection of intellectual property rights; augmenting the role of consumers in the single market; reducing the administrative burden on enterprises, etc. For more details, see Twelve Projects for the 2012 Single Market: Together for New Growth. Available online at: http://europa.eu/rapid/pressReleasesAction.do?reference=IP/11/469&format=HTML&aged=1&language=CS&guiLanguage=en [last access 5 December 2011].

enhance consumers' confidence in the single market, and consumers will have a better opportunity of reaping the benefits of the market, i.e. wider choice of products, more effective price and quality competition, etc.

162. Cross-border transactions, which should constitute a significant part of the single market, remain a challenge both for consumers and for businesses, because the EU has not yet achieved a high level of protection of consumer rights. Empirical data show that before bringing a case to court, consumers estimate how much time, money, and effort will be required to obtain redress and then weigh these considerations against the value of the claim. Faced with the complexity of the laws governing their disputes, in particular disputes relating to cross-border transactions, consumers are frequently not convinced that going to court would offer them a viable solution, and hence in most cases, they will discard this option if an initial contact with the trader has proved to be unsuccessful. Similarly, businesses, in particular small businesses, are concerned by the risk that they may have to deal with legal and judicial systems with which they are unfamiliar (outside their home country). Therefore, traders often abstain from venturing into new markets which would give them access to new customers. This lack of confidence has an impact on the competitiveness of businesses. The premise is certainly correct, but somewhat unilaterally presented, because the *Commission* fails to mention what costs will have to be spent by the Union, and especially its Member States, to introduce and especially to operate and maintain the dispute resolution system. The reason is that it is only one of many measures which ultimately burden public budgets and result in the tragic budget crises we have currently been witnessing in the EU Member States. This is a typical example of the exquisite concepts cooked up in the Brussels kitchen – unfortunately, the great chef forgets, when drawing up his lavish gourmet menu that the stock-keeper is rapidly running out of basic necessities for simple potato soup, let alone expensive items like chateaubriand. Indeed, Union legislation has been eternally, brilliantly, and successfully avoiding discussion of any of the ramifications which the implementation of these magnificent ideas will have on the increasingly strained budgets of the individual Member States.

163. One of the methods of enhancing the enforcement of rights in the internal market is, according to the *Commission*, improving the availability and further use of out-of-court dispute resolution entities. Alternative dispute resolution is a low-cost and fast alternative for consumers and businesses seeking to resolve disputes. The vast majority of alternative dispute resolution procedures are either free of charge for consumers or of moderate cost (below 50 EUR). Most disputes submitted to alternative dispute resolution entities are decided within 90 days. Undoubtedly the premises underlying these conclusions are

correct. As mentioned above, the flaw in the EU concept inheres in the absence of any solution as to the sources of financing the costs spent on this dispute resolution. The idea that 50 EUR would suffice to cover the actual costs associated with this mechanism is somewhat naive. In addition, the idea that a single mechanism could serve the entire EU market remains unrealistic due to the varying procedural regimes and customs which –although the Brussels legislation sometimes claims differently – diverge on fundamental issues.

164. The *Commission* also claims that most consumers who have used alternative dispute resolution recall it as a straightforward and transparent process where support and advice were provided. Hence, the reasoning is that consumers are more willing to resolve disputes through alternative dispute resolution than through court proceedings. Businesses also prefer resolving disputes through alternative dispute resolution, and so it is believed those businesses which have already used ADR would use it again in the future. Again, these claims presented by the *Commission* cannot be accepted without reservations. For instance, whereas in certain West European countries, and especially in the United States, dispute resolution methods other than the authoritative methods are fairly successful, in the countries of Central and Eastern Europe, as well as in many West European countries and many countries outside Europe, such alternative dispute resolution methods are principally refused.[95] If the *Commission's* new legislative proposals do indeed interpret ADR as including arbitration (as opposed to the previous concepts), then only arbitration is probably enjoying wider recognition as an alternative to court litigation. The principally different experience with *alternative methods* in the individual countries clearly indicates that any attempt at the introduction of a uniform system or a uniform concept is somewhat detached from reality.

165. However, the diversity and uneven geographical and sectoral availability of ADR entities prevent consumers and businesses from fully exploiting their potential. In some Member States ADR entities have not yet been introduced. In other Member States existing ADR entities cover only part of the territory or are only competent in specific sectors in the retail market. This has generated complexity, which has an adverse impact on their efficiency and dissuades consumers and businesses from using them. Furthermore, consumers and businesses are often unaware of the option of referring their disputes to an existing ADR entity, or they do

---

[95] It is necessary to emphasize that whereas the American doctrine traditionally includes arbitration within "Alternative Dispute Resolution" (ADR), most European countries, especially (but not exclusively) *civil law* countries, de facto classify arbitration, as an alternative equal to litigation, among authoritative methods of dispute resolution, analogous to litigation in court, not among alternative methods attempting to find by various means a consensus between the differing opinions of the parties.

not know whether their dispute would fall within the scope of application of a given ADR entity. The *Commission*'s proposals aim at making it easier for consumers to secure redress in the Single Market whether they are buying *online* or *offline*, and, therefore, they effectively contribute to growth and economic stability through enhanced consumer demand.

166.   The proposed legislation covers **contractual disputes between consumers and traders arising from the sale of goods or the provision of services.** This includes complaints filed by consumers against traders but also complaints filed by traders against consumers. However, the proposals do not cover disputes between businesses (business-to-business disputes). In the *Commission*'s opinion, the B2C relationship is different from the B2B relationship because of the asymmetries in the relationship between traders and consumers caused by specific rules on consumer protection, including rules on mandatory consumer information. During the public consultations conducted by the *Commission* all stakeholders (businesses, consumers, and national authorities) expressed the view that these specificities should also be reflected in EU legislation on ADR which should provide for specific measures on ADR for consumer disputes. It is quite common, though, that the *Commission* usually fails to mention those who would voice their criticism regarding the very basis of EU concepts, and commonly tries to present the results of all discussions as a harmonious conclusion.

167.   The *Commission* is proposing two interlinked initiatives – **(i)** a directive on ADR (*ADR Directive*) and **(ii)** a regulation on ODR. The two proposals complement each other. The implementation of the *ADR Directive* will make quality ADR entities available across the EU for all consumer complaints related to contractual disputes arising from the sale of goods or the provision of services. This is a key requirement for the functioning of the *ODR* platform, which will be set up by the regulation.

168.   In order to ensure the smooth implementation of the *ADR Directive*, the proper functioning of ADR entities providing quality services for consumers and traders will be closely monitored in each Member State. National competent authorities will, inter alia, assess whether a given ADR entity respects the quality requirements laid down by the *ADR Directive*. In addition, they will publish regular reports on the development and functioning of ADR entities. Every three years, the *Commission* will draw up a report on the application of the *ADR Directive* and communicate it to the European Parliament and the Council.

169.   The *Commission's* Communication continues with an analysis of the methods of enhancing the awareness of ADR and ODR and their

promotion among consumers and businesses. Once these proposals are adopted and implemented, the *Commission* expects that consumers will have access to quality ADR entities for contractual disputes resulting from transactions, whether *online* or *offline*, cross-border or domestic. They will be able to easily identify the ADR entity which is competent to deal with their dispute. The confidence of consumers to engage in cross-border transactions and to extend their sphere of interest beyond the borders of their Member States will be strengthened.

170. The implementation of the legislative package will also have, in the *Commission*'s opinion, significant advantages for traders. They will be able to avoid time-consuming and expensive court procedures while maintaining and enhancing their business reputation. According to the *Commission*, traders can be expected to have better opportunities to offer a greater variety of products and services via the Internet when knowing that an effective *online* system for redress is in place. Consequently, businesses, and in particular SMEs, will also have more incentives to improve their internal complaint handling systems. This will also secure better competition in the Single Market.

III.7.4. Proposal for a Directive on alternative dispute resolution for consumer disputes (*"ADR Directive"*)

171. As described above, the *Commission* is trying to enhance the position of consumers in the Single Market. Despite a generally high level of consumer protection guaranteed by EU legislation, the *Commission* is of the opinion that consumers encounter problems when using the Single Market, which are often left unresolved, because court proceedings would be too costly or lengthy. The *Commission* has adopted two recommendations on consumer ADR and established two networks dealing with ADR (ECC-NET[96] and FIN-NET[97]). Much EU sector-specific legislation contains a clause on ADR, and the *Mediation Directive* promotes the amicable settlement of disputes, including consumer disputes. However, the *Commission*'s analysis of the current situation identified the following main shortcomings which hinder the effectiveness of ADR: **(i)** gaps in coverage, **(ii)** insufficient consumer and business awareness, and **(iii)** uneven quality of ADR procedures.

III.7.5. Legal elements of the Proposal

172. Under the Proposal for the *ADR Directive*, each Member State is supposed to ensure that **all disputes between a consumer and a trader**

---

[96] The European Consumer Centres Network (ECC-Net) ought to facilitate the consumers' access to a suitable ADR-provider in another Member State in cross-border disputes.
[97] The FIN-Net consists of alternative dispute resolution systems which resolve cross-border disputes between consumers and providers of financial services.

arising from the sale of goods or the provision of services can be submitted to an ADR entity, including through *online* means. The method of implementation of this intent is at the discretion of the Member States; they may use existing ADR entities and adjust their scope of application, or they may create new ADR entities.

173.   The present proposal covers consumer disputes, i.e. disputes between consumers and traders, irrespective of who opens the proceedings. It also applies to ADR entities and mainly covers various mediation procedures. It also covers non-judicial procedures involving the nature of arbitration, such as procedures before consumer complaint boards, traditional arbitration, and conciliation procedures. The Proposal for the *ADR Directive* does not, however, apply to consumer complaint handling systems operated by the trader nor to dispute resolution entities where the natural persons in charge of dispute resolution are employed exclusively by the trader. It also excludes direct negotiations between the parties. When disputes arise, the *ADR Directive* should ensure that consumers are able to quickly identify which ADR entities are competent to deal with their dispute. To this end, the Proposal ensures that **consumers will be able to find information on the competent ADR entity in the main commercial documents provided by the trader and, where a trader has a website, on that website.** In addition, traders will be bound to inform consumers on whether or not they commit to use alternative dispute resolution in relation to complaints lodged against them by a consumer. This obligation will act as an incentive for traders to use ADR more frequently. What must be subject to criticism, though, is that the *ADR Directive* again broadens the obligation of traders to provide information to consumers, which means further costs to be paid by the traders. What the presenters of the Proposal unfortunately fail to understand is that too much information provided to a consumer is often counterproductive. It has become common knowledge that consumers already do not now read the information currently presented to them because of its excessive volume.

174.   Under the present Proposal, Member States shall ensure that consumers can obtain assistance when they are involved in a cross-border dispute. Member States may delegate responsibility for this task to their centers of the European Consumer Centre Network (ECC-net) which currently performs the function of guiding consumers to the ADR entities competent to deal with their cross-border disputes. But the truth is that this network is basically left unused, and its function is moreso academic than practical.

175.   Under the Proposal, ADR entities should be encouraged to become members of networks of ADR entities in sector-specific areas when they deal with disputes in that area. In addition, the present Proposal should

encourage cooperation between ADR entities and the national authorities entrusted with the enforcement of consumer protection legislation. The Proposal for the *ADR Directive* also aims at ensuring that **ADR entities respect the quality principles of impartiality, transparency, effectiveness, and fairness.** Such principles have been laid down in two *Commission* recommendations. Now they are to be given binding effect.

176. The transparency of ADR entities should guarantee that the parties receive all the information they need to make an informed decision before engaging in the (ADR) procedure. ADR procedures should be effective and address certain shortcomings associated with court procedures, such as costs, length,[98] and complexity. Based on the results of existing studies, the Proposal for the *ADR Directive* requires that **disputes should be resolved within 90 days.** At the same time, that ADR procedures remain accessible to all consumers should be ensured; and the cost to consumers should be moderate or free of charge.

177. In order to ensure that ADR entities properly function and provide quality services for consumers and traders, they should be closely monitored. In each Member State, the competent authority will be in charge of monitoring the functioning of ADR entities established in its territory. The competent authorities will, inter alia, assess whether a given ADR entity respects the quality requirements laid down by the *ADR Directive* (or the relevant national laws). In addition, the competent authorities will publish regular reports on the development and functioning of ADR entities. Every three years, the *Commission* will report to the European Parliament and the Council on the application of the *ADR Directive*.

III.8. Proposal for a Regulation on online dispute resolution for consumer disputes ("*ODR Regulation*")

III.8.1. Premises of the proposed Regulation

178. This Proposal, together with the Proposal for a Directive on alternative dispute resolution for consumer disputes, is to be seen, according to the explanatory memorandum, in the context of the efforts to improve the functioning of the retail Internal Market, in particular by enhancing consumer redress linked to cross-border e-commerce transactions. At present, the offer of ADR schemes to resolve consumer disputes related

---

[98] Cf. *I. A.* Council of Europe, Venice Commission. Can Excessive Length of Proceedings Be Remedied? (Science and Technique of Democracy) 164. (2007). This publication issued by the Council of Europe contains a detailed analysis with national reports filed by the Member States of the ECHR. It is easy to see that a situation regarding the length of proceedings, procedural obstacles, and other problems with the exercise (enforcement) of rights in courts exists in most countries.

to e-commerce transactions is scattered and incomplete. In addition, while half the existing ADR schemes offer consumers the possibility of submitting their complaint by means of distant communication (*online*), very few offer consumers the possibility of conducting the entire procedure *online*. Handling the entire process *online* would produce time savings and ease communication between the parties.

179.   The lack of effective redress for complaints resulting from cross-border *online* transactions has adverse consequences both for consumers and businesses. Consumers lose out by not being able to shop online across borders; they thus miss the opportunity of comparing the costs of products in the wider EU market and of buying them where they are less expensive. Businesses, in particular small and medium-sized enterprises, are deterred from acquiring the administrative capacity needed to deal with disputes with consumers residing in another Member State. This hinders the development of the digital Internal Market. In view of the problems identified, the proposed *ODR Regulation* aims at establishing an EU-wide system of resolving disputes *online* that will facilitate the resolution of disputes related to the cross-border *online* sale of goods or provision of services between trader and consumer.

III.8.2. Legal elements of the Proposal

180.   The Proposal for the *ODR Regulation* aims at **establishing a European** *online* **dispute resolution platform**. This ODR platform takes the **form of an interactive website** which offers a single point of entry to consumers and traders who seek to resolve out-of-court a dispute which has arisen from a cross-border e-commerce transaction. **The platform should be accessible in all official languages of the EU, and its use will be free of charge.** Alternative dispute resolution schemes established in the Member States about which the *Commission* has been notified in accordance with the *ADR Directive* will be electronically registered with the ODR platform.

181.   Consumers and traders will be able to **submit their complaints through an electronic complaint form** which will be available on the platform's website in all official languages of the EU. The platform will check if a complaint can be processed and will seek the agreement of the parties to transmit it to the ADR scheme which is competent to deal with the dispute. The competent ADR scheme will seek the resolution of the dispute in accordance with its own rules of procedure within 30 days from the date of receipt of the complaint. The ADR scheme must notify the platform of some data in relation to the development of the dispute (date when the parties were notified of the complaint, date when the dispute was resolved, the outcome of the dispute, etc.).

182.   Under the Proposal, a **network** of *online* dispute resolution **facilitators** should be established, which will consist of one contact point for online dispute resolution in each Member State. The ODR facilitators' network will provide support for the resolution of disputes submitted via the ODR platform.

183.   The Proposal requires traders established within the EU that engage in cross-border ecommerce to **inform consumers** about the ODR platform. This information shall be made easily, directly, prominently, and permanently accessible on the traders' websites. An annual activity report will be drawn up on the operation of the platform. The compliance by ADR schemes with the obligations set out in this *ODR Regulation* will be monitored by the competent authorities to be established in the Member States in accordance with the *ADR Directive*. Every three years, the *Commission* will report to the European Parliament and the Council on the application of the *ODR Regulation*.

III.8.3. Implications of the proposed EU legislation for arbitration

184.   The changes to be introduced by the proposed EU legislation, despite a number of negative aspects mentioned in this study elsewhere, might still have a positive influence, at least on arbitration, which the *Commission* newly classifies under ADR. In particular, arbitration could be used more frequently in consumer disputes. This confirms that the EU itself does not consider arbitration as a mechanism conflicting with consumer protection. Consumer disputes are in some EU countries currently considered as non-arbitrable, which the adoption of the *ADR Directive* might not change, because the *ADR Directive* only refers to ADR as a whole. The objective of the *ADR Directive* will therefore be fulfilled if it becomes possible to resolve consumer disputes by other mechanisms (for instance, mediation). Nonetheless, we must caution against placing too much hope in mediation and other similar dispute resolution methods. This is only a fashionable trend which cannot be forced upon the parties to the dispute. Besides, the result of mediation is not enforceable, unless accepted in full by the parties. Contrary to these dispute resolution methods, arbitration has the advantage of being binding – an arbitral award is binding on the parties and constitutes an enforceable decision. At the international level, it is enforceable under the *New York Convention*.

185.   However, the Proposal for the *ADR Directive* does not clearly indicate whether the Member States must secure access to more types of ADR, or whether a single procedure will suffice, providing it is universally applicable to all consumer disputes. This question is apparently left at the discretion of the individual Member States. The Proposal for the

ADR Directive does, though, contain certain **minimum standards which all ADR procedures must meet.** Namely, these are: **(i)** expertise, **(ii)** impartiality, **(iii)** transparency, **(iv)** effectiveness, and **(v)** fairness. These are rather abstract requirements which, however, must be interpreted as **autonomous concepts** of EU law, i.e. independent of the national legal systems of the Member States.

186. Unfortunately, the proposed legislation also stipulates other requirements be imposed on professionals (traders) regarding the information to be provided to consumers about the available ADR procedures. How to resolve a situation in which the consumer prefers to use an ADR entity other than the entity which the professional (trader) has proposed to the consumer, or about which the professional (trader) has informed the consumer, however, is not clear. Jurisdictional issues are, consequently, entirely dismissed by the proposed EU legislation, and its implementation in the national laws promises to be very complicated. This appears to be an almost irresolvable problem when the mechanisms are to be applied at the international level within the EU, due to the absence of a uniform platform for the resolution of potential jurisdictional disputes. As the *Commission* itself reports, there are currently approximately 750 ADR entities. The consumer, just like the professional (trader), should himself or herself have the option of choosing the entity authorized to *"administer the resolution of his/her dispute,"* naturally if, and only if, the entity meets the requirements laid down by the *ADR Directive*. The proposed legislation, however, hardly envisages such a system in practice, especially at the international level. This is because the *ADR Directive* does not answer the question of whether it is possible to choose an ADR entity from a Member State which has no relation to the contractual relationship between the consumer and the professional. It is likely the solution to the problem will significantly depend on the definition of the jurisdiction vested in the individual entities, which the *ADR Directive* leaves at the discretion of the individual Member States, without any means of securing the necessary harmonization at the international level.

187. The language of the proceedings could be another problem in cross-border transactions. Ordering goods from an e-shop, which could be done without any knowledge of the language, is not the same as commencing ADR. Translations are by no means cheap, especially legal translations where the main emphasis is laid on precise and accurate formulations and the ability to express the intended contents of the relevant facts of the case and legal arguments. There is no simple solution to the problem, because it is not possible to "prescribe" one EU language as the communication language for cross-border transactions.

188. As concerns the application of the ADR system, it will probably be contingent on a better awareness of this option and its benefits, including primarily efficiency (resolving disputes within 90 days) and low costs.

189. The Proposal for establishing a European *online* dispute resolution platform offers a very simple solution for the resolution of disputes. The success of the ODR platform will depend, however, on whether the interactive website will also be simple and comprehensible. Otherwise it may well deter, rather than attract users. Again, it is important to point out certain problems such as the language of communication.

III.8.4. Assessment of the proposals presented by the EU Commission

190. Thus the conclusion here is that a number of the premises underlying the new legislative proposals presented by the *Commission* cannot be denied their real value. But it must be argued that the proposals are in many respects significantly detached from reality. First of all, the *Commission* has entirely dismissed the issues of who will pay for setting up the mechanisms and from what funds. The disputes are principally private-law disputes, and it is hardly imaginable that the mechanisms could generate enough money to finance themselves. Furthermore, no account is taken of the national procedural rules and the need to establish connections with national procedural regimes of dispute resolution. Such connections are vital. This applies all the more if the mechanisms are supposed to include arbitration. The concept is also somewhat schizophrenic with respect to other EU concepts, primarily in connection to arbitration. Regarding arbitration, the ECJ's current case law concerning the application of the *Directive* requires strict adherence to the law, i.e. valid and applicable law, in the resolution of consumer disputes, and specifically the exclusion of methods such as decision-making according to the principles of equity. Although the concept of November 2011 does not explicitly mention this, it basically clearly tends towards something like this. It appears proverbially *as if the left hand doesn't know what the right hand is doing*, or as if the EU, having discovered that it will not succeed in taking control over arbitration through an amendment to the *Brussels I Regulation* due to the opposition voiced by most Member States, has surreptitiously tried to invade the same legal territory through a number of "backdoors" and attempted to erode the fairly comprehensive internationalized structure of arbitration in the international environment by means of many other mechanisms. In any case, it is a rather piecemeal concept, very fragile and one suffering from many systemic errors, to which the Union administration is apparently blind. The obstacle preventing the strengthening of the Single Market is not lack of a consumer protection

mechanism but, conversely, an unprecedented degree of protectionism which "puts" the real "spoke in the wheels." Rather than planning additional consumer protection mechanisms, the development of the EU market would benefit more from effective rules of enforcement of protection against unfair competition, and especially the effective and expeditious enforcement of claims between professionals. These two improvements might perhaps represent a bigger stimulus for the development of the Single Market than further increasing consumer protection.

III.9. Case law of the ECJ concerning arbitration and interpretation of the *Directive* and other consumer protection instruments

III.9.1. Case law of the ECJ in mutual comparison

191.   Since the first decision rendered in which the ECJ (formerly the Court of Justice of the European Communities, the "ECJ") ruled on the unfairness (validity/invalidity) of arbitration clauses in consumer contracts, several landmark decisions have been delivered by the said *forum*; these rulings analyze the issue of arbitrability of consumer disputes, including the autonomy of the parties in the case of consumer contracts, with respect to the possibility of submitting disputes to arbitration. These rulings naturally concern unfair terms in consumer contracts. Although the first explicit reference by the ECJ to consumer contracts dates back to 2006 (the *Mostaza Claro* case) the ECJ's legal opinions are based on older case law. The arbitrability of consumer disputes and the arbitration clauses in consumer contracts must be perceived not only in the context of legal opinions on unfair terms in consumer contracts, but also in conjunction with, for instance, opinions on the choice-of-court clauses in consumer contracts which share many identical features with arbitration clauses; both types of clauses are primarily connected by their similar purpose and nature. Historically, the first decision on which the analysis of arbitration (as well as choice-of-court) clauses in consumer contracts can be based, is the **Océano Grupo** case.[99] That case did not concern arbitration clauses but the fairness (or lack thereof) of choice-of-court clauses. Nonetheless, the conclusions regarding choice-of-court clauses are, in the context of the issues analyzed in this publication, basically fully applicable to arbitration clauses. In said case, the ECJ ruled that **a national court is entitled to determine of its own motion (*sua sponte*) whether a choice-of-court clause before it is unfair when making its preliminary assessment, especially when examining its**

---

[99] ECJ Judgment, Case C-240/98 through C-244/98 of 27 June 2000 (*Océano Grupo Editorial SA et al.*), CELEX 61998CJ0240.

jurisdiction to hear and resolve the case.[100] The ECJ supported its conclusion by the fact that **the consumer's position is weak, both due to his or her weaker bargaining power and his or her lack of knowledge; the court's intervention is necessary to eliminate this imbalance.**

192. In another decision, *Cofidis*,[101] the ECJ primarily concentrated on the issue of whether the **defense of unfairness of a particular term can be limited by an extinctive prescription period.** The Court concluded that such limitation **was not possible,** because it would deprive the consumer of the protection conferred by the *Directive*; the professional (the business) would simply wait and sue the consumer after the expiration of the limitation period.[102] However, the ECJ ruled in the *Cofidis* case that **based on the principle of procedural autonomy, an EU Member State was allowed, observing the principle of equivalence, to maintain and adopt its own procedural rules.** The ECJ maintained that limiting the option of raising the defense by subjecting it to an extinctive prescription period would, if the **principle of equivalence** were duly observed, comply with *Community* law (now EU law); the ECJ highlighted, though, that each case had to be examined individually and with due consideration of the factual and legal specifics of the particular case. The ECJ expressed its opinion only with respect to the extinctive prescription period, which erodes the system of protection under the *Directive*; it did not clarify, though, the decisive moment when the unfair term ceases to bind the consumer, i.e. whether a successful plea (defense) is a conditio sine qua non for the invalidity of the term. The ECJ analyzed this issue in the *Pannon GSM* decision.

193. The *Mostaza Claro*[103] case was a landmark decision; the ECJ approved the use of arbitration clauses in consumer contracts (subject to the

---

[100] It is necessary to emphasize that otherwise the ECJ also honors the principle that, as a rule, it is for the parties to take the initiative in the proceedings and that the court is able to act of its own motion only in *exceptional cases* where the *public interest* requires such intervention. See :
➤ ECJ Judgment, Case C-430/93 of 14 December 1995 (*Jeroen van Schijndel et Johannes Nicolaas Cornelis van Veen* v. *Stichting Pensioenfonds voor Fysiotherapeuten*), published in: ECR, p. I–4705, marg. (21), CELEX: 61993J0430;
➤ ECJ Judgment, Joined Cases C-222/05 through C-225/05 of 7 June 2007 (*J. van der Weerd et al.* /C-222/05/, *H. de Rooy Sr. et H. de Rooy Jr.* /C-223/05/, *Maatschap H. et J. van 't Oever et al.* /C-224/05/ *et B. J. van Middendorp* /C-225/05/ v. *Minister van Landbouw, Natuur en Voedselkwaliteit*), published in: ECR p. I–4233, para. (35), CELEX: 62005CJ0222.
[101] ECJ Judgment, Case C-473/00 of 21 November 2002 (*Cofidis SA* v. *Jean-Louis Fredout*), CELEX 62000CJ0473, published in ECR 2002, p. I–10875.
[102] As concerns arbitration, however, we need to point out that stipulating an extinctive prescription period for petitions for the setting aside of arbitral awards complies with consumer protection under EU law, as the Court held, for instance, in *Asturcom.*
[103] ECJ Judgment, Case C-168/05 of 26 October 2006 in *Elisa María Mostaza Claro* v. *Centro Móvil Milenium SL*), CELEX: 62005CJ0168, published in: ECR 2006, p. I–1421. For a detailed annotation of the decision, see below.

conditions listed in the directive), if allowed under national law. As concerns the arbitrability of consumer disputes, the EU Member States were therefore free to exercise their autonomy. In the *Mostaza Claro* case, the ECJ also held that even if the laws of national origin did not provide the court with the option of assessing the fairness of the arbitration clause, the court could perform such an assessment at least in the proceedings for annulment of the arbitral award. As early as in the *Eco Swiss*[104] case, the ECJ ruled that if a national court was obliged to set aside, at the request of a party, an arbitral award conflicting with the national mandatory rules (laws of national origin), such an obligation also applied to Article 81 TEC (Article 101 TFEU[105]).[106] In the *Mostaza*

---

[104] ECJ Judgment, Case C 126/97, 1981, *Eco Swiss China Time* v. *Benetton International N.V.*, CELEX: 61997J0126, published in: ECR 1999, p. I–03055. This case, however, did not concern a consumer contract; the ECJ was called upon to rule on issues regarding the protection of competition. According to the consistent standpoint of the ECJ, the protection of competition constitutes European [*Community*] *public policy*. This category, however, is very controversial.

[105] Article 101 TFEU (ex Article 81 TEC) (cit.): "1. *The following shall be prohibited as incompatible with the internal market: all agreements between undertakings, decisions by associations of undertakings and concerted practices which may affect trade between Member States and which have as their object or effect the prevention, restriction or distortion of competition within the internal market, and in particular those which:* (a) *directly or indirectly fix purchase or selling prices or any other trading conditions;* (b) *limit or control production, markets, technical development, or investment;* (c) *share markets or sources of supply;* (d) *apply dissimilar conditions to equivalent transactions with other trading parties, thereby placing them at a competitive disadvantage;* (e) *make the conclusion of contracts subject to acceptance by the other parties of supplementary obligations which, by their nature or according to commercial usage, have no connection with the subject of such contracts. 2. Any agreements or decisions prohibited pursuant to this Article shall be automatically void. 3. The provisions of paragraph 1 may, however, be declared inapplicable in the case of:* (-) *any agreement or category of agreements between undertakings,* (-) *any decision or category of decisions by associations of undertakings,* (-) *any concerted practice or category of concerted practices, which contributes to improving the production or distribution of goods or to promoting technical or economic progress, while allowing consumers a fair share of the resulting benefit, and which does not:* (a) *impose on the undertakings concerned restrictions which are not indispensable to the attainment of these objectives;* (b) *afford such undertakings the possibility of eliminating competition in respect of a substantial part of the products in question.*"

[106] *Eco Swiss* concerned a claim for damages made by the licensee (*EcoSwiss China*) against the licensor. The subject matter of the licensing agreement was the right to label the claimant's watches and clocks as *Benetton by Bulova*. The licensing agreement was prematurely terminated by the licensor (three years before the expiration of the agreed period) and the licensee (the claimant, *EcoSwiss China*) instituted arbitral proceedings in the Netherlands [NDL], in compliance with an arbitration agreement incorporated in the licensing agreement. The claimant (the licensee) was successful in the proceedings; the claimant also prevailed in the proceedings on the declaration of enforceability of the arbitral award (both interim and final) before the competent Dutch court. Subsequently, the Dutch Supreme Court (*Hoge Raad* [NDL]) made a reference to the ECJ for a preliminary ruling based on the respondent's objection; the respondent argued that the licensing agreement was contrary to *Community public policy* (*ordre public*) for violating the rules of European competition law. Paradoxically, this ECJ ruling was not so important, even as concerns the issue of *public policy* (*ordre public*) which has been the subject matter of a number of other cases, especially in connection with competition law. The ECJ held that the obligations in terms of Article 81 TEC [Article 101 TFEU] are a component of *European public policy*; but the Court failed to provide any clear guidance as concerns the issue of whether and to what extent this *public policy* must be taken into consideration in arbitration; nonetheless, the ECJ itself principally found the

Claro case, the ECJ broadened the scope of the obligation to cover *Community* legislation (EU laws), the nature of which is similar to *public policy* (providing the national court has jurisdiction to set aside an arbitral award which is contrary to *public policy*). Here again, however, it appears that the ECJ did not mean *public policy* but [*only*] a specific *public interest* expressed through absolute mandatory rules (internationally binding rules, i.e. overriding mandatory rules from the perspective of private international law), which is not a component of *public policy*. This is an obvious demonstration of the fact that even the ECJ itself (unfortunately often due to terminological reasons and due to the legal and cultural diversity of the composition of the ECJ) does not consistently distinguish between *public policy* and a *[mere]* specific *public interest* which is expressed through (overriding) mandatory rules but is not a component of *public policy*.

194.   Neither does the **Pannon GSM**[107] case concern arbitration directly; the ECJ was called upon to assess an agreement on the jurisdiction of a court different from the court that would otherwise have jurisdiction if the decisive criterion were the place of residence of the consumer (the respondent in this case). As opposed to the Spanish law applied in *Mostaza Claro* and *Asturcom*, the Hungarian law required that the unfairness of the contractual term be challenged by the contracting party in its briefs (defense). The Hungarian Code of Civil Procedure [HUN] stipulated that the court shall examine its territorial jurisdiction of its own motion; but, unless the case concerns exclusive jurisdiction, the defense of improper venue cannot be raised after the respondent lodges his or her first submission on the merits. The Hungarian court therefore referred a question to the ECJ for a preliminary ruling asking whether the court was obliged, even in this particular case, to examine its territorial jurisdiction of its own motion. The ECJ ruled that an unfair term in a consumer contract was invalid per se, i.e. the invalidity is not contingent on the respondent successfully raising the relevant defense in court. The ECJ noted, though, that the *Directive* does not prescribe an obligation on the national court to exclude the application of the relevant unfair term if the consumer, having been properly advised by the court, does not intend to challenge it. Consequently, the ECJ leaves it at the consumer's discretion if he or she will be bound by the unfair

---

resulting situation controversial, especially considering that the procedural rules of the *Community* do not apply to arbitration at all or only to a limited extent, at least in cases concerning regular adversarial proceedings. Above all, the ECJ ruled that the arbitrators themselves were not in a position to request the ECJ give a preliminary ruling under Article 234 TEC [Article 267 TFEU]. However, the ECJ allowed the option of adopting such procedure through the medium of courts within the scope of their jurisdiction in the particular arbitral proceedings, in terms of the courts' supportive and control duties vis-à-vis arbitrators.

[107] ECJ Judgment, Case C-243/08 of 4 June 2009 (*Pannon GSM Zrt v. Sustikné Györfi Erzsébet* [*Pannon GSM*]), CELEX: 62008CA0243, the judgment was published in: ECR 2009, p. I–04713.

term. Article 6 of the *Directive*, however, stipulates that the states are obliged to ensure that consumers are not bound by unfair terms. Paradoxically, it is not certain to what extent the ECJ ruling is compatible with the *Directive* – if the consumer decides to insist on the validity of a term which, in the court's opinion, is unfair. In actual fact, the *Directive* would be breached, because the consumer would still be bound by the unfair term. A contractual term in a consumer contract, although unfair per se, is only voidable (its invalidity is *conditional*). The ECJ's interpretation, and consequently also the autonomous interpretation required in the application and/or consideration of EU legal standards, principally does not prescribe the consequence which some legal systems designate as absolute invalidity (ineffectiveness, nullity, etc.).[108] **This means invalidity examined by the court of its own motion.** However, even these situations **require that the consumer perform an act aimed at raising the defense of such invalidity, after the consumer was properly advised of the court's legal opinion (informed / specially advised consumer). The consumer's conduct (actions or omissions) can *ex post* validate the invalidity caused by the unfairness.** This particular conclusion, however, often conflicts with a national concept adopted in the countries which prescribe the consequence of *absolute invalidity* (or a similar effect) which prevents the subsequent validation of this kind of invalidity. The ruling in the *Pannon GSM* case specifically requires (while also applying the autonomous interpretation), in those cases in which the national concept prescribes the "absolute consequence", to proceed by evaluating the cause of the *invalidity* with respect to: the circumstances attending the conclusion of the contract, the approach of the parties to their performance under the contract, and the behavior of the parties in the proceedings (any proceedings) regarding their claims arising from the contract, especially with respect to the **conduct of the specially informed consumer**. This does not erode the concept of *absolute invalidity* (or any other similar concept incorporated in the relevant legal system); it broadens the scope of circumstances which must be taken into account when assessing the *fairness* of the term and the genuine will of the parties. From this perspective, even the *Pannon GSM* decision can be considered a landmark decision, although it prima facie appears to merely follow the ECJ's previous case law. Besides, the Madrid Appeals Court [ESP] arrived at the same conclusion in *Juan*

---

[108] This is especially so with terminological differences and, partially, with differences in the concept itself. See:

[AUT] – Austrian law – *ineffectiveness for the consumer* [*Unwirksamkeit für den Verbraucher*],

[CZE] – Czech law – *absolute invalidity*,

[DEU] – German law – *invalidity* (literally *nullity* [*Nichtigkeit*]),

[SVK] – Slovak law – *absolute invalidity*, etc.

Pedro v. Metrovacesa S.A.[109] The unfairness of the term incorporated in a consumer contract, i.e. the consequences with respect to the validity of the term, cannot be assessed merely in relation to the moment of conclusion of the contract; the subsequent conduct of and the approach adopted by the parties (especially the consumer) must be taken into consideration, too. Their approach ought to significantly influence the determination of whether the parties' expression of will at the conclusion of the arbitration agreement was free and serious or not.

195.   In the *Asturcom*[110] case, the situation was unique in that Ms. *Rodríguez Nogueira* was completely passive both in the course of the arbitration and during the court proceedings – the case got before the Spanish court only because the claimant requested enforcement of the arbitral award. In said case, the ECJ ruled that it was not possible to extend the protection afforded by the *Directive* to those cases in which the consumer is completely passive and fails to challenge the arbitral award; nonetheless, the Court found a way which would allow the courts to set aside the arbitral award – the same procedure as in *Mostaza Claro*.

196.   The Court arrived at that conclusion by applying the principle of equivalence and effectiveness to national laws – if the *Directive* lacks any procedural rules, the Member States are free to adopt their own procedural rules (the principle of procedural autonomy). In other words, if the national court has the option of reviewing the compliance of the arbitral award to *public policy*, the court must also have the option of reviewing the compliance of the arbitral award to *Community* laws, the nature of which is similar to *public policy*. The ECJ failed to add, though, whether the arbitral award issued on the basis of an unfair term ought to be set aside; the Court only held that it is up to the national court to adopt measures which are prescribed for those cases by its national law. Contrary to *Pannon*, the ECJ did not clarify whether the consumer's will to (not) be bound by an unfair term (if any) could be taken into consideration or not.

---

[109] Decision of the Madrid Appeals Court [ESP], Case No. 28079370102010100498 of 12 November 2010 (*Juan Pedro v. Metrovacesa S.A.*); for a detailed annotation of this Spanish decision, see the excursion into Spanish law elsewhere in this book. In the Spanish decision, the Madrid Appeals Court went even further and held, inter alia, that the principle of good faith protects both the consumer and the professional; the Court refused to protect the consumer if he had previously had the opportunity of raising the corresponding objections during the arbitral proceedings. The Court principally refused to deal with the application of consumer protection laws and to consider the alleged invalidity of the arbitration agreement which did not comply with these laws, if the arbitration had in fact been initiated by the consumer himself or herself.

[110] ECJ Judgment, Case C-40/08 of 6 October 2009 (*Telecomunicaciones SL v. Cristina Rodríguez Nogueira* [*Asturcom*]), CELEX 62008CA0040; the judgment was published in: ECR 2009, p. I–09579.

197.   In the **Caja de Ahorros**[111] case, the ECJ confirmed that the standards of consumer protection prescribed by the *Directive* were only the minimum standard, which did not prevent the individual states from adopting their own national laws for securing a higher level of protection for consumers.

198.   The **Pannon GSM** case was followed by the ECJ ruling in **VB Pénzügyi Lízing**[112] in which the ECJ broadens, in the case of choice-of-court clauses, the obligations of the court which discovers a potentially unfair term in a contract. The national court called upon to hear and resolve the case, is – according to the ECJ – obliged to conduct an investigation allowing the court to determine whether the term falls within the scope of the *Directive*, and if so, whether it is unfair. The ECJ also confirms its jurisdiction to interpret an *"unfair term,"* but at the same time the Court **restricts** this power **to a general interpretation only**; the assessment of (un)fairness of contractual terms in individual cases is always the task of the national court. Nonetheless, just like the *GSM Pannon* case, the ruling in the *VB Pénzügyi Lízing* case confirms that the court is obliged to **examine** whether the particular term is actually unfair or not. In other words, the court is obliged to examine any and all circumstances of the contract and primarily the circumstances attending the conclusion of the contract. Both these decisions, however, **warn** against a very common trait in the practice of lower courts (usually not found in the practice of supreme judicial authorities), i.e. an **unduly undiscriminating interpretation**; both decisions emphasize the **necessity of (i) investigation / examination and (ii) an individual assessment of the factual and legal findings.**

199.   As concerns the **Pohotovosť**[113] case, the reference to the ECJ for a preliminary ruling was apparently unnecessary, because the answer to the question could have been inferred from the current case law; this is the reason why the ECJ resolved the case by a reasoned order, not a judgment. The facts of the case are basically identical to the *Asturcom* case. Both cases concerned arbitration terminated by an arbitral award against the consumer, after which the claimant filed a petition for the enforcement of the arbitral award; the response of the competent national court was a reference for a preliminary ruling. The consumers in both cases were passive. The ECJ again confirmed that national courts were entitled to assess the (un)fairness of a contractual term of their

---

[111] ECJ Judgment, Case C-484/08 of 3 June 2010 (*Caja de Ahorros y Monte de Piedad de Madrid* v. *Asociación de Usuarios de Servicios Bancarios [Ausbanc]*). This decision is only briefly annotated in connection with an analysis of the *Directive*.
[112] ECJ Judgment, Case C-137/08 of 9 November 2010 (*VB Pénzügyi Lízing Zrt.* v. *Ferenc Schneider*), CELEX: 62008CA0137, the ECJ judgment was published in: *OJ* C 13, p. 2.
[113] ECJ Order, Case C-76/10 of 16 November 2010 in *Pohotovosť s.r.o.* v. *Iveta Korčkovská [Pohotovosť]*), CELEX: 62010CB0076, *OJ* C 30, p. 12.

own motion, providing that they had the necessary factual and legal findings at their disposal and that such possibility was allowed under the national procedural rules. The ECJ also ruled that the ECJ could not assess the (un)fairness of any particular contractual term, because the Court did not have jurisdiction over that issue; a specific assessment is always the task of the relevant national court. The national court, if it concludes that the contractual term is (un)fair, must adopt the measures prescribed for such cases by national law; the desired result is to make sure that the consumer is not bound by unfair terms. In this particular case, therefore, the ECJ does not at all address the possibility that the consumer would voice his or her opinion regarding the unfair term and whether he or she wishes to be bound by it.

200. In the *Pohotovost'* case, the ECJ also expressed its opinion on the connection between Directive 87/102/EEC and the *Directive*; satisfaction of the requirement posed by Directive 87/102/EEC to mention the APR(C) (annual percentage rate of charge in consumer credit agreements) may be a decisive factor in the assessment of whether the terms of a consumer credit agreement are understandable under the *Directive*. In addition, the national court has the option of directly applying the rules of the national law which implements Directive 87/102/EEC; in such a case, the court would not have to assess the (un)fairness under the *Directive* at all.

III.9.2. ECJ Judgment, Case C-168/05 of 26 October 2006 (*Elisa María Mostaza Claro* v. *Centro Móvil Milenium SL*) [114]

(a) Conclusions of the ECJ

201. Ms. *Mostaza Claro* was the respondent in arbitration in which she failed to plead unfairness of the arbitration clause, although, according to the Spanish court, there are no doubts that the clause was indeed unfair. After the arbitration was over, Ms. *Mostaza Claro* contested the arbitral award before a civil court. She pleaded unfairness of the arbitral award in the proceedings on annulment of the award. The ECJ concluded that the special consumer protection regime under the *Directive* would be breached if the national court did not have the option of setting aside the arbitral award only because the consumer, whose position is weaker compared to the seller or the supplier of services, failed to plead the unfairness of the arbitration clause with his or her first act in the arbitral proceedings. In response to an argument that such an approach would interfere with the efficiency of arbitration, the ECJ noted that where a

---

[114] The judgment is published in: ECR 2006, p. I–1421. CELEX 62005CJ0168. Language of the case: Spanish.

national court has the option of annulling an arbitral award for failure to observe the *public policy* rules, the court must also have such an option in the case of *Community* (EU) rules of this type. In this particular case, the condition was met. According to the ECJ, a court seized with an action for annulment of an arbitral award must determine whether the arbitration clause is (un)fair, even though the consumer has not pleaded unfairness with his or her first act in the arbitral proceedings but only during the course of litigation.

(b) Facts of the case

202. On 2 May 2002, a mobile telephone contract for prepaid services was concluded between *Centro Móvil Milenium SL* ("*Centro Móvil*") and Ms. *Mostaza Claro*.[115] The contract contained an arbitration clause under which any disputes arising from the contract were to be referred for arbitration to the *Asociación Europea de Arbitraje de Derecho y Equidad* (approximate translation of the name of the institution: *European Association of Arbitration in Law and in Equity*; AEADE). As Ms. *Mostaza Claro* did not comply with the minimum subscription period, *Móvil* initiated arbitration before the AEADE.

203. By a letter of 25 July 2003, *AEADE* granted Ms. *Mostaza Claro* a period of 10 days in which to refuse arbitration proceedings (file a jurisdictional challenge). *AEADE* stated that in the event of refusal she could bring legal proceedings. Ms. *Mostaza Claro* did not avail herself of this option but, conversely, presented arguments on the merits of the dispute. She did not challenge the validity of the arbitration agreement. The arbitrator found against her in the merits of the dispute.

204. After the arbitration was over, Ms. *Mostaza Claro* filed a request for annulment of the arbitral award. Ms. *Mostaza Claro* confirmed the invalidity of the arbitration agreement due to its unfairness under Spanish law.

205. The court *(Audiencia Provincial de Madrid* [ESP]*)* stated that there was no doubt that the arbitration agreement was an unfair contractual term and was therefore null and void. However, Ms. *Mostaza Claro* did not plead that the agreement was invalid in the context of the arbitral proceedings. The *Audiencia Provincial de Madrid* therefore stayed the proceedings and referred the following **question** to the ECJ **for a preliminary ruling**: "*May the protection of consumers under Council Directive 93/13/EEC [...] require the court hearing an action for*

---

[115] The Czech version of the judgment refers to "*účastnická smlouva k lince mobilní telefonie*" and the English version to "*mobile telephone contract*". The Spanish version (original wording) is "*un contrato de abono a una línea de telefonía móvil*", while the Polish version is "*umowę o abonament w sieci telefonii komórkowej.*"

annulment of an arbitration award to determine whether the arbitration agreement is void and to annul the award if it finds that that arbitration agreement contains an unfair term to the consumer's detriment, when that issue is raised in the action for annulment but was not raised by the consumer in the arbitration proceedings?"

(c) The ECJ's reasoning and conclusions

206. The ECJ based its decision on the conclusions reached by *Audiencia Provincial de Madrid* on the unfairness[116] of the agreed arbitration clause under the *Directive*. The ECJ did not itself analyze the issue. The ECJ also noted that the ECJ may not rule on the application of general criteria used by the *Community* legislature in order to define the concept of "unfair term" in a particular situation, which must be considered in light of the particular circumstances of the case in question.

207. According to settled case law, in the absence of relevant *Community* rules, the detailed procedural rules designed to ensure the protection of the rights which individuals acquire under *Community* law are an internal affair of each Member State (the principle of *procedural autonomy*), provided that such rules are not less favorable than those governing similar domestic situations (*principle of equivalence*) and that they do not render impossible or excessively difficult the exercise of rights conferred by *Community* law (*principle of effectiveness*).

208. The system of protection introduced by the *Directive* is based on the idea that the consumer is in an unequal position vis-à-vis the seller or supplier. This applies both to his or her bargaining power and level of knowledge. This unequal position leads to the consumer agreeing to terms drawn up in advance by the seller or supplier without being able to influence the content of those terms.[117] Such an imbalance may only be corrected by positive action unconnected with the actual parties to the contract.[118]

209. It is on the basis of those principles that the ECJ ruled that the national court's power to determine of its own motion whether a term is unfair constitutes a means both of achieving the result sought by Article 6 of the *Directive* (preventing an individual consumer from being bound by

---

[116] In this respect, not all language versions employ accurate terms. The Czech version of the judgment uses the term *"abusive"* (*"zneužívající"*). The correct word ought to be *"unfair"* (*"nepřiměřenost"*). See the English *"unfair,"* Spanish *"abusive,"* Polish *"nieuczciwy,"* etc. It is probable that all or most language versions (except the Czech one) employ the same term as the *Directive*.

[117] The ECJ invokes its decision in the *Océano Grupo* case, namely para. (25). The decision will be analyzed below.

[118] ECJ Judgment in *Océano Grupo*, para. (27). See a separate annotation and analysis below.

an unfair term), and of contributing to achieving the aim of Article 7 of the *Directive*. Consequently, the examination undertaken by the national courts may act as a *deterrent* and contribute to *preventing* unfair terms in consumer contracts.[119] That power of the national court is necessary for ensuring that the consumer enjoys effective protection. The reason is the real risk that he or she is unaware of his/her rights or encounters difficulties in enforcing them.[120]

210.   Article 6 of the *Directive* stipulates that the states are obliged to ensure that consumers are not bound by unfair terms. This result could not be achieved if the court seized with an action for annulment of an arbitral award was unable to determine whether that award was void solely because the consumer did not plead invalidity of the arbitration clause during the course of the arbitration proceedings. Such an omission by the consumer could not be compensated for by an action on the part of persons not a party to the contract. The regime of special consumer protection established by the *Directive* would be ultimately undermined. In the present case, the ECJ therefore subordinated the effectiveness of arbitration to the requirements of consumer protection; the former principally requires that the scope for challenging and/or assessing the validity of the arbitration clause be limited and based on a defense raised by the respondent at a particular stage of the arbitral proceedings.[121]

211.   *Centro Móvil* and the German government (surprisingly) submitted that, if the national courts were allowed to determine whether an arbitration clause is void where the consumer did not raise such an objection during the arbitral proceedings, this would seriously undermine the effectiveness of arbitration. It follows from that argument that it is in the interest of efficient arbitral proceedings that the review of arbitral awards should be limited in scope and that annulment of or refusal to recognize an award should be possible only in exceptional circumstances.

212.   The ECJ had previously ruled that, where the domestic rules of procedure require a national court to grant an application for annulment of an arbitral award where such an application is founded on the failure to observe mandatory rules, it must also grant such an application where

---

[119] ECJ Judgment in *Océano Grupo*, para. (25). See a separate annotation and analysis below.
ECJ Judgment in *Cofidis*, para. (32). See a separate annotation and analysis below.
[120] ECJ Judgment in *Océano Grupo*, para. (26). See a separate annotation and analysis below.
ECJ Judgment in *Cofidis*, para. (33). See a separate annotation and analysis below.
[121] Cf. *Lurger, B. et Augenhofer, S.* Österreichisches und Europäisches Konsumentenschutzrecht. 2nd ed., Wien / New York: Springer, 2008, p. 116. But Lurger and Augenhofer venture even further in their conclusions when they claim, literally, as follows (approximate translation, cit.:) "*In this particular decision the ECJ gave precedence to the requirements of consumer protection over the effectiveness of arbitration; the effectiveness of arbitration principally requires that arbitral awards cannot be challenged and set aside, save to a very limited extent.*" It appears Lurger and Augenhofer somewhat confused the purpose with the means of achieving the purpose of arbitration.

it is founded on a failure to comply with *Community* rules of this type (i.e. EU law).[122] The importance of consumer protection has in particular led the *Community* legislature to lay down the rule in Article 6(1) of the *Directive* as a mandatory provision taking into account the weaker position of one of the parties. The aim of the provision is to replace the formal balance between the rights and obligations of the parties with an effective balance which re-establishes equality between them.

213.   The aim of the *Directive* is to strengthen consumer protection. It is therefore a measure essential to the accomplishment of the tasks entrusted to the *Community* and, in particular, to raising the standard of living and quality of life within the *Community*.[123] The nature and importance of the *public interest* underlying the protection which the *Directive* confers on consumers justify the national court being required to assess of its own motion whether a contractual term is unfair, compensating in this way for the imbalance which exists between the consumer and the seller or supplier of services.

214.   Having regard to the foregoing, the answer to the question referred to must be that the *Directive* must be interpreted as meaning that a national court seized of an action for annulment of an arbitration award must determine whether the arbitration agreement is void and annul that award where that agreement contains an unfair term, even though the consumer has not pleaded that invalidity during the course of the arbitration proceedings, but only during the action for annulment.

(d)   Notes on the judgment

215.   The ruling of the ECJ, however important and undoubtedly fundamental, still fails to answer many as yet open questions. One question involves the situation where the consumer's arguments during arbitration are limited to the merits of the case and the consumer counts on raising the defense of invalidity only if he or she fails in the merits. Indisputably such an approach and the shielding of the consumer in such cases not only exceeds the purpose of the *Directive*, it is in fact an abuse of law. Indeed such an approach should not enjoy any protection. The solution to the problem, though by no means the only solution and far from the universal solution, could be drawing the distinction between those consumers who are represented by legal counsel in the arbitral proceedings and those who are not. Although the opinions on such distinctions differ, when assessed from the perspective of the equality of the parties and other legal principles, this solution is familiar

---

[122] ECJ Judgment, Case C-126/97 of 1 June 1999 (*Eco Swiss China Time Ltd* v. *Benetton International NV*), para. (37). ECR 1999, p. I–03055. CELEX 61997CJ0126.

[123] ECJ Judgment, Case C-126/97 of 1 June 1999 (*Eco Swiss China Time Ltd* v. *Benetton International NV*), para. (36). ECR 1999, p. I–03055. CELEX 61997CJ0126.

to many legal systems. Consumer protection is undoubtedly important and its incorporation in EU law is a hardly contestable fact. However, consumer protection in practice often borders on the unbearable, and it would be naive to believe that no consumer is trying to find ways to abuse the standard. After all, practical experience provides enough proof of such abuse. The purpose of the *Directive* can be also used as an argument in those cases where the national legal systems introduce procedural measures aimed against the abuse of these mechanisms.

III.9.3. ECJ Judgment, Cases C-240/98 through C-244/98 of 27 June 2000 (*Océano Grupo Editorial SA*)[124]

(a) Conclusions of the ECJ

216. According to the ECJ, **an agreement on jurisdiction can be considered an unfair term if (i)** it has not been individually negotiated, **(ii)** it was concluded between a consumer on the one hand and a seller or supplier of services (professional) on the other hand, and **(iii)** it confers jurisdiction (venue) on a court or tribunal closer to the principal place of business of the party which is not the same as the consumer's jurisdiction. As concerns the court's option of determining of its own motion whether an agreement on jurisdiction is unfair when making its preliminary assessment, this possibility is necessary for the creation of the system of protection envisaged under Articles 6 and 7 of the *Directive*; the consumer is the weaker party in that regime, which causes an imbalance in the parties' rights and obligations. This imbalance may only be corrected by positive action unconnected with the actual parties to the contract. The national court is therefore vested with the authority to determine of its own motion whether a contractual term is already (un)fair during the preliminary proceedings.

(b) Facts of the case

217. Between 4 May 1995 and 16 October 1996, each of the respondents, all of whom are resident in Spain [ESP], entered into a contract for the purchase of encyclopedias. It was a purchase for personal use, i.e. a typical consumer contract. The encyclopedias were to be supplied in installments. The claimants were the sellers of the encyclopedias. The

---

[124] ECJ judgments in the following cases:
- Case C-240/98, *Océano Grupo Editorial SA* v. *Roció Murciano Quintero*;
- Case C-241/98, *Salvat Editores SA* v. *José M. Sánchez Alcón Prades*;
- Case C-242/98, *José Luis Copano Badillo*;
- Case C-243/98, *Mohammed Berroane*;
- Case C-244/98, *Emilio Viñas Feliú*.

The judgment in the joined cases of 27 June 2000 was published in: ECR 2000, p. I–04941. CELEX 61998CJ0240. Collectively referred to as "*Océano Grupo.*" Language of the case: Spanish.

contracts contained a term conferring jurisdiction on the courts in *Barcelona* [ESP]. The group of consumers who entered into the above-mentioned contract was sued with reference to the jurisdiction clause conferring jurisdiction on the courts in *Barcelona* [ESP]. However, none of the respondents was domiciled in *Barcelona* [ESP]; conversely, the claimant (professional) had its principal place of business there.

218. The purchasers did not pay the purchase price on the agreed due date. Consequently, between 25 July 1997 and 19 December 1997, the seller brought an action in the trial court in *Barcelona* (*Juzgado de Primera Instancia No 35 de Barcelona* [ESP]) to obtain an order that the respondents should pay the sums due. Notice of the claims was not served to the respondents, since the court had doubts as to whether it had jurisdiction over the actions in question. On several occasions the Spanish Supreme Court (*Tribunal Supremo* [ESP]) had held jurisdiction clauses of the kind at issue in these proceedings to be unfair. However, according to the court, the decisions of the courts were inconsistent on the question of whether the court may, in proceedings concerning consumer protection, determine of its own motion whether an unfair term is void.

219. The court in *Barcelona* [ESP] therefore stayed the proceedings and referred to the **ECJ for a preliminary ruling on the following question:** "*Is the scope of the consumer protection provided by Council Directive 93/13/EEC of 5 April 1993 on unfair terms in consumer contracts such that the national court may determine of its own motion whether a term of a contract is unfair when making its preliminary assessment as to whether a claim should be allowed to proceed before the ordinary courts?*"

(c) The ECJ's reasoning and conclusions

220. The ECJ ruled that where the contested contractual term was not individually negotiated and was included in a contract concluded between a consumer and a seller or supplier of services within the meaning of the *Directive*, it satisfies all the criteria enabling it to be classed as unfair. However, the ECJ did not hold any particular provision in the respective case to be unfair.

221. A term of this kind, the purpose of which is to confer jurisdiction on the court closer to the principal place of business of the seller, obliges the consumer to submit to the exclusive jurisdiction of a court which may be geographically distant from his domicile. This may make it difficult for him or her to make an appearance. In the case of disputes concerning limited amounts of money (*petty disputes*), the transportation costs could be a deterrent and cause him to forgo any

legal remedy or defense. Such a term thus falls within the category of terms which have the effect of excluding or hindering the consumer's right to take legal action (see subparagraph (q) of paragraph 1 of the Annex to the *Directive*).

222. As to the question of whether a court seized of a dispute concerning a consumer contract may determine of its own motion whether a term of the contract is unfair, it should be noted that the system of protection introduced by the *Directive* is based on the idea that the consumer is in a weak position vis-à-vis the professional, as regards both his bargaining power and his level of knowledge. This leads to the consumer agreeing to terms (a contract) drawn up in advance by the professional without being able to influence the content of the terms.[125]

223. Article 6 of the *Directive* requires Member States to lay down that unfair terms are not binding on the consumer. This aim cannot be achieved if the consumer were himself obliged to raise the unfair nature of such terms. In disputes where the amounts involved are often limited, the lawyers' fees may be higher than the amount at stake. This may deter the consumer from contesting the application of an unfair contractual term. While it is the case that in a number of Member States procedural rules enable individuals to defend themselves in such proceedings without legal counsel,[126] there is a real risk that the consumer, particularly due to ignorance of the law, will not challenge the term pleaded against him on the grounds that it is unfair. It follows that effective protection of the consumer may be attained only if the national court acknowledges that it has the power to evaluate terms of this kind of its own motion (*ex officio*). Moreover, the system of protection laid down by the *Directive* is

---

[125] However, as the case law from various EU Member States indicates, this obviously does not mean that the text would actually have to be formulated as late as during the negotiation between the consumer and the professional. Such an interpretation would be illogical, although the parties do sometimes argue along these lines in court disputes. After all, such interpretation would prevent any flexibility in the negotiation of any contracts.
Cf. :
➤ Judgment of the Federal Court of Justice (BGH [DEU], Case No. III. ZR 164/06 of 1 March 2007 (There is a detailed annotation elsewhere in this book, especially in the excursus into German law [DEU]),
➤ Judgment of the Federal Court of Justice (Supreme Court [DEU]), Case No. III ZR 265/93 of 13 January 2005 (There is a detailed annotation elsewhere in this book, especially in the excursus into German law [DEU]; in this decision, the BGH [DEU] also quotes extensively from related case law),
➤ To a great extent, this also concerns the Judgment of the Supreme Court CR [CZE], Case No. 23 Cdo 1201/2009 of 29 June 2010 (See the detailed annotation in the excursus into Czech law [CZE]), et al.
The only requirement is that the consumer must be informed in advance, i.e. before the conclusion (execution of the contract / intersection of the consensus of the expressions of will), about the arbitration agreement and the importance thereof. See also the *Recommendation*.
[126] For instance, this is so in the Czech Republic [CZE].

based on the notion that the imbalance between the consumer and the professional may only be corrected by positive action unconnected to the actual parties to the contract. That is why Article 7 of the *Directive* requires Member States to implement means to prevent the use of unfair terms, including the right of authorized consumer associations to take action in order to obtain a decision as to whether contractual terms drawn up for general use (general contract terms) are unfair. The court's power to determine of its own motion whether a term is unfair must be regarded as constituting a proper means both of achieving the result sought by Article 6 of the *Directive* (preventing an individual consumer from being bound by an unfair term), and of contributing to achieving the aim of Article 7 of the *Directive* (deterring the use of unfair terms in consumer contracts). It follows from the above that the protection provided for consumers by the *Directive* entails the national court being able to determine of its own motion whether a term of a contract before it is unfair when making its preliminary assessment as to whether a claim should be allowed to proceed before the national courts.[127]

224. As regards the situation where the *Directive* has not been transposed, the ECJ's case law clearly suggests that, when applying national law, the national court called upon to interpret that law must do so, as far as possible, in light of the wording and purpose of the *Directive* so as to achieve the result pursued by the *Directive*. The requirement for an interpretation of the national law in conformity with the *Directive* requires the court to favor the interpretation that would allow it to refuse jurisdiction [conferred on a different authority] stipulated in an unfair term.

---

[127] According to the author, and as confirmed by the case law of certain Member States (see, for instance, the case law of the BGH [DEU], extensively annotated and quoted elsewhere in this book), it is not possible to accept any breach of the *"Kompetenz-Kompetenz"* principle in connection with arbitration. Where the court delivers its ruling before the arbitrators have had the opportunity to consider the validity of the arbitration agreement in making a decision on their jurisdiction and unless the validity of the arbitration agreement can be assessed without taking evidence and without considering the facts of the case (especially the circumstances attending the conclusion of the agreement), the *"Kompetenz-Kompetenz"* principle must also be allowed to apply in arbitration. See the Judgment of the BGH [DEU], Case No. III ZR 265/03 of 13 January 2005 et al. Many national decisions which can be applied to the problem, such as the above-mentioned decision of the BGH [DEU], have addressed this issue long after the ECJ's ruling in *Océano Grupo Editorial SA,* and it is reasonable to presume that the national courts were well-acquainted with the ECJ's ruling.
The circumstances attending the conclusion of the contract have also been explicitly classified as issues of fact by the SC CR [CZE] in its Judgment Case No. 23 Cdo 1201/2009 of 29 June 2010 (see the excursus into Czech law), et al. This is directly related to the opinion that the *"Kompetenz-Kompetenz"* principle should apply. Cf. see also *Fouchard, Ph.* Clause abusives en matière d'arbitrage. Rev. arb., 1995, p. 149, who bases his interpretation primarily on French law and French practice.
For the same conclusion (outside EU law), see the decision of the Supreme Court of the Canadian Province of Quebec [CAN] in *Rogers Wireless, Inc.* v. *Muroff,* 2007 SCC 35.

III.9.4. ECJ Judgment, Case C-473/00 of 21 November 2002 (*Cofidis SA* v. *Jean-Louis Fredout* [*Cofidis*])[128]

(a) Conclusions of the ECJ

225.   Mr. *Fredout* ([FRA]) was sued in a French court for outstanding installments due on a consumer credit account. The court held that some of the contractual terms were unfair. However, the defense of unfairness was subject to a two-year limitation (extinctive prescription) period under French law, and the court thus could not hold the respective term invalid. Consequently, the French court referred to the ECJ for a preliminary ruling on the question of whether the limitation (extinctive prescription) period can be taken account of. The ECJ held that the court's power to determine of its own motion whether a term is (un)fair constitutes a means necessary for ensuring that the consumer enjoys effective protection under the *Directive*. This applies all the more so if the consumer encounters difficulties in enforcing his or her rights or if the enforcement is made unduly complicated. The protection would be undermined if the consumer were bound by a period [of limitation] limiting the defense of unfairness. According to the ECJ, the professional is usually the claimant in the proceedings. The professional would therefore, in theory, merely have to wait until the expiry of the time-limit before filing an action. The consumer would thereby be deprived of the protection under the *Directive*. The *Directive* must therefore be interpreted as prohibiting the Member States from stipulating limitation periods applicable to the plea of unfairness which would restrict the court's potential to subject such (unfair) terms to assessment.

(b) Facts of the case

226.   By a contract of 26 January 1998, the French company *Cofidis SA* ("*Cofidis*") granted Mr. *Fredout* the opening of a credit account. When installments remained unpaid, *Cofidis* brought an action against him on 24 August 2000 in the *Tribunal d'instance de Vienne* [FRA] for payment of the sums due.

227.   According to the national court's judgment, the offer of credit took the form of a leaflet printed on both sides, with the words "*Free application for money reserve*" in large letters on the front, while the references to the contractual interest rate and a penalty clause were in fine print on the reverse.   The trial court therefore concluded that the financial clauses lack legibility and that that lack of legibility is to be contrasted with the word "free" in a particularly obvious form. Its conclusion was

---

[128] ECJ Judgment, Case C-473/00 of 21 November 2002 (*Cofidis SA* v. *Jean-Louis Fredout*), CELEX 62000CJ0473, published in ECR 2002, p. I–10875. Language of the case: French, also available in English; not available in the languages of the Member States that acceded in 2004 or later.

that the leaflet was therefore likely to mislead the consumer and that the financial clauses could be regarded as unfair. However, as the dispute was one concerning a consumer contract, the *Tribunal d'instance de Vienne* [FRA] considered that the limitation (extinctive prescription) period of two years under Article L. 311-37 of the Consumer Code [FRA] *(Code de la consommation)*[129] applied and prevented it from annulling the terms it had found to be unfair.

228. In those circumstances, the court decided to stay the proceedings and refer the following question to the ECJ for a preliminary ruling:

229. Since the protection conferred by the *Directive* implies that a national court, applying the provisions of national law previous or subsequent to that *Directive*, is to interpret them so far as possible in light of the wording and purpose of the *Directive*: *"Does that requirement of an interpretation in conformity with the system of consumer protection under the Directive require a national court, when hearing an action for payment brought by a seller or supplier [professional] against a consumer with whom he has contracted, to set aside a procedural rule on pleas in defence, such as that in Article L. 311-37 of the Consumer Code [FRA] (Code de la consommation[130]), in so far as it prohibits the national court, either on the application of the consumer or of its own motion, from annulling any unfair term which vitiates the contract where the latter was made more than two years before the commencement of proceedings, and in so far as it thereby permits the seller or supplier [professional] to rely on those terms before a court and base its action on them?"*

(c) The ECJ's reasoning and conclusions

230. *Cofidis* expressed doubts as to the relevance of the question for the outcome of the main proceedings and hence the admissibility of the reference for a preliminary ruling. *Cofidis* submitted that the terms held to be unfair by the national court were not within the scope of the *Directive*. As financial terms in a credit contract, they relate to the definition of its main subject matter. They are therefore excluded from the scope of the *Directive* under Article 4(2) [of the *Directive*]. The terms in question cannot be accused of lack of clarity, since they merely reproduce a model contract drawn up by the national legislature, which under Article 1(2) of the *Directive* is not subject to its provisions.

231. *Cofidis* further submitted that the national court was wrong to hold that the two-year limitation (extinctive prescription) period applied to unfair

---

[129] The excursus into French law elsewhere in this book includes a summary of currently applicable French rules.
[130] The excursus into French law elsewhere in this book includes a summary of currently applicable French rules.

terms. The French government observed that that question was indeed in doubt and that the French Supreme Court (Cass. [FRA]) had not yet had occasion to rule on the point. It is settled case law that it is solely for the national court to determine whether there is any need for a preliminary ruling by the ECJ. A request from a national court may be dismissed only where it is obvious that the national court's request has no bearing on the case in question.

232.   In the present case, there is no prima facie evidence that the disputed contract terms did not fall within the scope of the *Directive*. To fall within the scope of the *Directive*, those terms must satisfy the conditions set out in Article 3(1) of the *Directive*, that is, they must not have been individually negotiated and must, contrary to the requirement of good faith, cause a significant imbalance in the parties' rights and obligations arising under the contract, to the detriment of the consumer. Although the national court had not provided any information on the nature of the contested contract terms, it cannot be excluded that those conditions were satisfied. As to the question of whether or not the two-year limitation (extinctive prescription) period applied to unfair terms that was a question of national law which as such was not within the jurisdiction of the ECJ. The ECJ held that it is not obvious that the question referred has no bearing on the decision in the merits, as argued by *Cofidis*. The ECJ therefore proceeded with the case.

(d)   Assessment of the merits

233.   *Cofidis* and the French government argued that the present case was to be distinguished from *Océano Grupo*.[131] In the *Océano Grupo* case, the ECJ, by allowing a national court to determine of its own motion whether a jurisdiction clause is unfair, merely allowed the court to decline jurisdiction. In the *Cofidis* case, however, the question is whether or not the national court must apply a limitation (extinctive prescription) period laid down by the national legislature.

234.   *Cofidis* and the French government also submitted that in the absence within the *Directive* of any provision concerning a limitation period or a prescription period the question of the application of such a period is covered by the principle of the procedural autonomy of the Member States. Member States regulate these issues themselves providing the rights of the individual guaranteed by *Community* law are respected and providing the principles of equivalence and effectiveness are observed. The ECJ has on several occasions ruled that limitation (extinctive prescription) periods shorter than the two-year period under the Consumer Code (*Code de la consommation* [FRA]) are compatible with those principles.

---

[131] The judgment is annotated elsewhere in this book.

235. Conversely, Mr. *Fredout* submitted that the judgment in *Océano Grupo* should be interpreted broadly. Mr. *Fredout* argued that in the *Océano Grupo* case, the ECJ regarded the national court's power to determine of its own motion the (un)fairness of contract terms as a means of achieving the result laid down in Article 6 of the *Directive* of ensuring that unfair terms do not bind the consumer. That result cannot be achieved if that power is subject to a time-limit. In the case of consumer credit contracts, the majority of actions are brought by the lender, and he would merely have to wait for the expiry of that time-limit to bring an action for payment, thus depriving the consumer of the protection conferred by the *Directive*.

236. The Austrian government [AUT] also submitted its arguments in the case. While accepting that the *Directive* leaves the Member States a wide margin of interpretation, the Austrian government [AUT] argued that it is doubtful that the nature of the limitation (extinctive prescription) period, combined with the shortness of the period, would allow the result prescribed by Article 6 and 7 of the *Directive* to be attained.

237. The *Commission* which, together with Mr. *Fredout*, supported a broad interpretation of *Océano Grupo*, submitted that fixing a time-limit was contrary to the objectives of the *Directive*. To allow the Member States to introduce such time-limits, which might differ from each other, would also be contrary to the principle of the uniform application of *Community* law.

238. The ECJ ruled in *Océano Grupo* that the national court's power to determine of its own motion whether a term is unfair constitutes a means both of achieving the result sought by Article 6 of the *Directive*[132] (i.e. preventing an individual consumer from being bound by an unfair term), and of contributing to achieving the aim of Article 7 of the *Directive*. The decision-making of the national courts may contribute to preventing unfair terms in consumer contracts. That power of the national courts has been regarded as necessary for ensuring that the consumer enjoys effective protection, particularly in view of the real risk that he is unaware of his rights or encounters difficulties in enforcing them.

239. The protection which the *Directive* confers on consumers thus extends to cases in which a consumer has concluded a contract with a professional containing an unfair term, but who fails to raise the unfair nature of the term before the court, either because he is unaware of his rights or because he is deterred from enforcing them on account of the costs which judicial proceedings would involve. It is therefore apparent that in court proceedings aimed at the enforcement of unfair terms

---

[132] ECJ judgment in *Océano Grupo*, para. (28).

brought by professionals against consumers, the fixing of a time limit on the court's power to examine the (un)fairness of the contract terms, is liable to affect the effectiveness of the protection intended by Articles 6 and 7 of the *Directive*. To deprive consumers of the benefit of that protection, professionals would have to merely wait until the expiry of the time-limit. A procedural rule which prohibits the national court, upon expiry of a limitation period, from finding of its own motion or following a plea raised by a consumer that a contract term is (un)fair is therefore liable to render application of the protection intended to be conferred on consumers by the *Directive* excessively difficult. That interpretation of the *Directive* is not contradicted by the fact that the ECJ has on several occasions ruled that limitation periods / prescription periods shorter than two years are not incompatible with the protection of rights conferred on individuals by *Community* law. In each case that raises the question as to whether a national provision renders the application of law impossible or excessively difficult, reference must be made in the analysis to the role played by that provision in the court procedure, its progress, and special features. This postulate is very important. It has become somewhat *fashionable* to rely on one's individual arguments on the ECJ's rationes decidendi, however removed from their context. The same applies to the particular interpretation of the national law and its individual provisions. Consequently, arbitration also requires examination of the entire context and the importance of the individual rules. The status of arbitration in individual countries differs as to its actual significance for the resolution of disputes, including consumer disputes. Whereas in certain countries the importance of arbitration for consumer disputes (or civil disputes in general) is negligible, in other countries any major restrictions on arbitration would basically paralyze the actual situation in the resolution of such disputes. For instance, the estimate for the Czech Republic [CZE] is[133] that the number of disputes heard and resolved in arbitration each year ranges between 100,000 and 150,000 and some estimates of arbitral awards are even higher.

240.   The ECJ therefore ruled as follows: "*In those circumstances, the answer to the national court's question must be that the protection conferred on consumers by the Directive precludes a national provision which, in*

---

[133] After the arbitral awards are served on the parties, they automatically become enforceable decisions (eligible for enforcement/execution) – Section 28 of the ArbAct [CZE]. No *exequatur* is necessary (with respect to domestic arbitral awards). More accurate statistics are therefore available only with respect to execution which requires court approval (enforcement executed by court executors) or a resolution opening the execution (enforcement executed by courts). By far, not all arbitral awards are submitted for execution. It is reasonable to assume that a more significant interference with arbitration by subjecting it to restrictions could affect the enforcement of the law, as such. For instance, a simple thing, like mandatory *exequatur* with respect to all arbitral awards to be performed by courts, could result in a collapse of the judiciary.

proceedings brought by a seller or supplier against a consumer on the basis of a contract concluded between them, prohibits the national court, on expiry of a limitation period, from finding, of its own motion or following a plea raised by the consumer, that a term of the contract is unfair." Indeed, the ECJ's conclusions voiced in *Mostaza Claro* v. *Centro Móvil* apparently follow this reasoning as concerns the restriction imposed on the consumer and prohibiting him or her to plead the unfairness of an arbitration clause after a particular stage of the proceedings has lapsed, especially limiting the plea only to the arbitral proceedings. It is necessary to underscore that the conclusion made by the ECJ (in the *Cofidis* case which did not concern arbitration but which is obviously an important decision in connection with arbitration in consumer matters) only applies to actions brought by professionals against consumers. This conclusion obviously does not apply to actions brought by consumers against professionals.

III.9.5. ECJ Judgment, Case C-40/08 of 6 October 2009 (*Telecomunicaciones SL* v. *Cristina Rodríguez Nogueira [Asturcom]*)[134]

(a) Conclusions of the ECJ

241. Ms. *Rodríguez Nogueira* was the respondent before *Asociación Europea de Arbitraje de Derecho y Equidad* (approximate translation of the name of the institution: *European Association of Arbitration in Law and in Equity*; AEADE),[135] under an arbitration clause incorporated in a consumer contract. After the arbitral award was rendered, Ms. *Rodríguez Nogueira* did not initiate proceedings for annulment of the arbitration award, and it therefore became final and binding. The claimant (*Asturcom*) brought an action before the court for **enforcement** (execution) of the arbitration award. The enforcement court addressed the ECJ with the question of whether the court should, of its own motion, assess the (un)fairness of contract terms in enforcement proceedings if the court determines that the arbitration clause is an (un)fair term. The ECJ ruled that **limitation of the consumer by a limitation (extinctive prescription) period prescribed for the application of annulment of an arbitral award is not incompatible with *Community* law.**

242. Courts may compensate for an omission on the part of a consumer as concerns a plea of unfairness of an arbitration clause in arbitration, but they cannot make up for total inertia on the part of the consumer who has neither participated in the arbitration proceedings at all, nor brought

---

[134] CELEX 62008CA0040, the judgment was published in: ECR 2009, p. I–09579. Language of the case: Spanish.
[135] It was therefore the same *permanent arbitral institution* as in *Mostaza-Claro* v. *Centro Móvil*.

an action for annulment of the arbitration award. Based on the principle of equivalence, however, the ECJ concluded that if the court had the option of setting aside, of its own motion, a final arbitral award which is contrary to *public policy*, the same option must exist with respect to *Community* laws of the same kind, such as in this case. Consequently, if the court concludes that an arbitration clause, on the basis of which the arbitral award was rendered, is unfair, then the court must establish all the consequences thereby arising under the national law, in order to ensure that the consumer is not bound by an unfair clause.

(b) Facts of the case

243. On 24 May 2004, a subscription contract for a mobile telephone was concluded between *Asturcom Telecomunicaciones SL* (*Asturcom*) and Ms. C. *Rodríguez Nogueira*. The contract contained an arbitration clause under which any dispute concerning the performance of the contract was to be referred for arbitration to the AEADE. The seat of that arbitration tribunal, which was not specified in the contact, was located in *Bilbao* [ESP].

244. Since Ms. *Rodríguez Nogueira* had failed to pay a number of bills and terminated the contract before the agreed minimum subscription period had expired, *Asturcom* initiated arbitration proceedings (filed a request for arbitration) against her before the AEADE. The arbitration award, made on 14 April 2005, ordered Ms. *Rodríguez Nogueira* to pay the sum of 669.60 EUR. Since the respondent did not initiate proceedings for annulment of the arbitration award, it became final. On 29 October 2007, the claimant (*Asturcom*) brought an action before the court (*Juzgado de Primera Instancia No 4 de Bilbao* [ESP]) for enforcement of the arbitration award.

245. In its order for reference to the ECJ, the Spanish court stated that the arbitration clause in the contract was unfair, particularly in view of the fact that, first, the costs incurred by the consumer in travelling to the seat of the arbitration tribunal were greater than the amount at issue in the dispute in the main proceedings. Next, according to that court, that seat was located at a considerable distance from the consumer's place of residence, and its location was not indicated in the contract. Last, that body (AEADE) itself drew up the contracts which were subsequently used by telecommunications firms.

246. The referring court also pointed out, first, that arbitrators are not permitted under valid and applicable Spanish Arbitration Law[136] to examine of their own motion whether unfair arbitration clauses are void,

---

[136] The Spanish Arbitration Act, Ley 60/2003 de Arbitraje [ESP], of 23 December 2003; the Act was published in: BOE No. 309 of 26 December 2003, pp. 46097–46109.

and, second, the Spanish Law 1/2000 [ESP] does not contain any provision dealing with the assessment to be carried by the court or tribunal having jurisdiction as to whether arbitration clauses are unfair when adjudicating on an action for enforcement of an arbitration award that has become final. In those circumstances, since it entertained doubts as to whether the national legislation, in particular its domestic procedural rules, is compatible with *Community* law, the Spanish court (*Juzgado de Primera Instancia No 4 de Bilbao* [ESP]) decided to stay the proceedings and to refer to the ECJ the following question for a preliminary ruling:

247. *"In order that the protection given to consumers by Directive 93/13* [Directive] *should be guaranteed, is it necessary for the court hearing an action for enforcement of a final arbitration award, made in the absence of the consumer, to determine of its own motion whether the arbitration agreement is void and, accordingly, to annul the award if it finds that the arbitration agreement contains an unfair arbitration clause that is to the detriment of the consumer?"*

(c)   The ECJ's reasoning and conclusions

248. The ECJ noted that the system of protection introduced by the *Directive* is based on the idea that the consumer is in a weak position vis-à-vis the seller or supplier, as regards both his bargaining power and his level of knowledge. This leads the consumer to agree to terms drawn up in advance by the seller or supplier without being able to influence the content of those terms.[137]

249. Article 6(1) of the *Directive* provides that unfair terms are not binding on the consumer. As is apparent from case law, that is a mandatory provision which aims to replace the formal balance, which the contract establishes between the rights and obligations of the parties, with an effective balance, which re-establishes equality between them.[138]

250. In order to guarantee the protection intended by the *Directive*, the ECJ had also stated on a number of occasions that the imbalance which exists between the consumer and the professional may only be corrected by positive action unconnected with the actual parties to the contract.[139] Consequently, due to this positive effect, these are overriding mandatory rules even from the perspective of the conflict-of-law rules – as opposed

---

[137] The ECJ referred to its judgments in the following cases: (i) *Océano Grupo*, para. (25) and (ii) *Mostaza Claro*, para. (25). Both decisions are annotated in great detail elsewhere in this publication.
[138] The ECJ referred to its judgments in the following cases: *(i) Mostaza Claro*, para. (36) and (ii) *Pannon GSM*, para. (25). The judgment in *Pannon GSM* is annotated below.
[139] The ECJ referred to its judgments in the following cases: *(i) Océano Grupo*, para. (27) and (ii) *Mostaza Claro*, para. (26).

to *public policy* which has negative effects.[140] In light of those principles, the ECJ held that the national court was required to assess of its own motion whether a contractual term was unfair.[141]

251. However, the present case can be distinguished from that which gave rise to the judgment in *Mostaza Claro* in that Ms C. *Rodríguez Nogueira* **did not in any way become involved in the various proceedings relating to the merits of the dispute and, in particular, did not bring an action for annulment of the arbitration award.** Consequently, the

---

[140] From the perspective of this approach, it was also incorporated in Article 9 of the *Rome I Regulation*, it is the *traditional view* of the nature, function, and contents of the overriding mandatory rule according to *Savigny* who defined the relationship of these rules vis-à-vis *ordinary mandatory rules* as the *ius cogens* of the overriding mandatory nature, or as the *ius cogens of the positive*, or even the *strictly positive overriding mandatory nature*. *Savigny* also employs terms such as *exceptional laws, absolute laws,* etc. Cf. *Bělohlávek, A.* Římská úmluva / Nařízení Řím I [Title in translation: Rome Convention / Rome I Regulation], Prague: C. H. Beck, 2009, marg. 09.59, 09.60, 09.94, 09.123; *Bogdan, M.* Foreign Public Law and Article 7(1) of the Rome Convention: Some Reflections from Sweden, w: Vers de nouveaux équilibres entres orders juridiques. Liber amicorum Hélène Gaudemet-Tallon, Dalloz 2008, p. 681; *Pauknerová, M.* Přímá aplikace administrativněprávních norem v mezinárodním právu soukromém. [Title in translation: The Direct Application of Administrative Provisions in Private International Law]. Studie z mezinárodního práva [Studies in International Law], Prague, 1984; *Pauknerová, M.* Přímá aplikace administrativněprávních norem v mezinárodním právu soukromém. [Title in translation: The Direct Application of Administrative Provisions in Private International Law]. Studie z mezinárodního práva [Studies in International Law], Vol. 18, Prague: Univerzita Karlova [Charles University], 1984, p. 145 et seq.; *Pauknerová, M.* Přímo použitelné administrativněprávní normy a mezinárodní právo soukromé. [Title in translation: The Directly Applicable Administrative Provisions and Private International Law]. Právník, 1983, pp. 477–489; *Pauknerová, M.* Státní příslušnost právnických osob v českém právu. [Title in translation: The Nationality of Legal Entities in Czech Law]. Právník, 1997, No. 6, p. 465 et seq.; *Pauknerová, M.* Svoboda usazování obchodních společností a mezinárodní právo soukromé ve světle novějších rozhodnutí Evropského soudního dvora. [Title in translation: The Freedom of Establishment for Companies and Private International Law in Light of More Recent Decisions of the European Court of Justice]. Právník, 2004, No. 12, pp. 1161–1184; *Pauknerová, M.* Tzv. nutně použitelné normy před Rozhodčím soudem při HK ČR a AK ČR. [Title in translation: The Overriding Mandatory Rules Before the Arbitration Court Attached to the Economic Chamber of the Czech Republic and Agricultural Chamber of the Czech Republic]. Právní praxe v podnikání, 1996, Nos. 7–8, p. 16 et seq.; *Pauličková, A.* Slovenská koruna a prijatie euroópskej meny. [Title in translation: The Slovak Crown and the Adoption of the European Currency]. In: The First Virtual Conference: "Inovační procesy ve světě a jejich vliv na evropskou integraci (historie, realita, vize)" [Title in translation: Innovative Processes in the World and Their Influence on European Integration (History, Reality, Vision)]. Collection of papers. Kunovice: Evropský polytechnický institut [European Institute of Polytechnics], 2005, pp. 151–156; *Pazdan, M.* Przyrzeczenie publiczne w polskim prawie prywatnym międzynarodowym. Państ. Prawo, 1989, No. 1, pp. 68–77; *Růžička, K.* Nové právní předpisy v oblasti zahraničního obchodu – Povinnosti dovozců při uvádění výrobků na tuzemský trh. [Title in translation: New Laws in Foreign Trade – Obligations of Importers in Introducing Products to the Domestic Market]. Právo a podnikání, 1997, Nos. 7–8, p. 5 et seq.; *Schnyder, A. K.* „Zwingendes Recht" im internationalen Wirtschaftsrecht nach der neueren Rechtsprechung de EuGH. In: *Baur, J. F. et Mansel, P.* (eds.) Systemwechsle im eurpäischen Kollisionsrecht, München: C. H. Beck, 2002, p. 89 et seq.; *Schnyder, A. K.* "Zwingendes Recht" im internationalen Wirtsrecht nach der neueren Rechtsprechung de EuGH. In: *Baur, J. F. et Mansel, P.* (eds.) Systemwechsel im europäischen Kollisionsrecht, München: C. H. Beck, 2002, p. 89 et seq.

[141] The ECJ referred to its judgment in *Mostaza Claro*, para. (38).

arbitral award now has the force of res judicata. Accordingly, it was necessary to determine whether the need to replace the formal balance between the rights and obligations of the parties with an effective balance which could re-establish equality between them required the court or tribunal responsible for enforcement to ensure that the consumer is afforded absolute protection, even where the consumer has not brought any legal proceedings to assert his rights. This issue also concerned the **relationship with national laws on res judicata.**

252. According to the established case law of the ECJ, it is compatible with *Community* (EU) law to lay down reasonable time limits for bringing proceedings in the interests of legal certainty. Such time limits are not liable to make it virtually impossible or excessively difficult to exercise rights conferred by EU laws. It was therefore necessary to ascertain whether it was reasonable to impose a two-month time limit, such as that laid down in Article 41(4) of the Spanish Arbitration Law (Act [ESP] 60/2003),[142] for filing an application for annulment of an arbitral award. The limitation period of 60 days for filing an action for annulment is not objectionable per se. The ECJ was of the opinion that the period was reasonable and enabled both an assessment as to whether there were grounds for challenging an arbitration award and whether the action for annulment of the award was to be prepared.[143] It should also be pointed out that in the present case it had not been alleged that the national procedural rules governing the bringing of an action for annulment of an arbitration award, in particular the ruling imposing a two-month time limit for that purpose, were unreasonable. Moreover, it is also worth noting that Article 41(4) of the Spanish Law 60/2003 [ESP][144] provides that the time limit starts to run from the date of notification of the arbitration award. Therefore, in the action in the main proceedings, it was not possible for the consumer to have found herself in a situation in which the limitation period had started to run, or had expired, without even being aware of the effects of the unfair arbitration clause upon her. In such circumstances, such a time limit for filing an action is consistent with the principle of effectiveness, since it is not in itself likely to make it virtually impossible or excessively difficult to exercise the consumer's rights.

---

[142] Arbitration Act [ESP] (approximate translation, cit.): Article 41 – "[...] 4. *An application for the declaration of invalidity of an award must be filed within two months after the award was pronounced or, if a correction, interpretation or supplementation of the award was requested, after the decision on the request was pronounced or after the time limit for the issue of any such decision expired."*

[143] It is a three-month time limit in most countries but exceptions exist. Cf. the three-month limit under the ArbAct [CZE].

[144] Cited above in a footnote in this part of the book.

253. In any event, the need to comply with the **principle of effectiveness** cannot be stretched so far as to mean that, in circumstances such as those in the original proceedings (in the *Asturcom* case), a national court is required not only to compensate for a procedural omission on the part of a consumer who is unaware of his/her rights,[145] but also to fully make up for total inertia on the part of the consumer concerned.

254. In light of the foregoing considerations, it must be held that the procedural rules laid down by the Spanish system for the protection of consumers against unfair terms in contracts does not make it impossible or excessively difficult to exercise the rights conferred on consumers by the *Directive*.

255. Next, in accordance with the **principle of equivalence**, the conditions imposed by domestic law under which the courts and tribunals may apply a rule of EU law of their own motion must not be less favorable than those governing the application by those bodies of their own motion of rules of domestic law of the same ranking. Article 6(1) of the *Directive* is a mandatory provision. The ECJ also specifically noted that, according to the ECJ's case law, the *Directive* as a whole constitutes a measure which is essential to the accomplishment of the tasks entrusted to the *European Community* (nowadays the EU) and, in particular, to raising the standard of living and the quality of life throughout the Single Market.[146] Accordingly, in view of the nature and importance of the *public interest* underlying the protection which the *Directive* confers on consumers, Article 6 of the *Directive* must be regarded as a provision of equal standing to national rules which rank, within the domestic legal system, as mandatory rules which the court must or may apply of its own motion. It follows from this that, **inasmuch as the national court or tribunal seized of an action for enforcement (of a final arbitration award) is required, in accordance with domestic rules of procedure, to assess of its own motion whether an arbitration clause is in conflict with *public policy*, it is also obliged to assess of its own motion whether that clause is unfair in light of Article 6 of the *Directive*, where it has available to it the legal and factual elements necessary for that task.**[147] In other words, this procedure does not follow from EU law, it depends on a standard incorporated in national law; consequently, it does not fall within the minimum standard defined by the *Directive*. Therefore, it does not mean that the court would be obliged to examine the factual and legal circumstances ex officio.

---

[145] This was the same as in *Mostaza Claro*.
[146] The ECJ invoked its judgment in *Mostaza Claro*, para. (37).
[147] The ECJ invoked its judgment in *Pannon GSM*, para. (32).

256.   The national court or tribunal is also under such an obligation where, under the domestic legal system, it has the discretion whether to consider of its own motion if such a clause is in conflict with *public policy*. As regards the case in the main proceedings, according to the Spanish government, the court or tribunal responsible for enforcement has the jurisdiction to assess of its own motion whether an arbitration clause in a contract concluded between a consumer and a professional is null and void on the ground that such a clause is contrary to *public policy*. Moreover, a number of recent judgments of the *Audiencia Provincial de Madrid* and the *Audiencia Nacional* have acknowledged that jurisdiction.[148] Consequently, the referring court in the *Asturcom* case is entitled to give due effect, in accordance with national law, to any finding in relation to the arbitration award that an arbitration clause is unfair, so long as the clause is not capable of binding the consumer (i.e. it is null and void).

257.   In light of the foregoing considerations, the answer to the question referred is that the *Directive* must be interpreted as meaning that a national court or tribunal, hearing an action for the enforcement of an arbitration award which has become final and was made in the absence of the consumer, is required to assess of its own motion – where it has available to it the legal and factual elements necessary for that task – whether an arbitration clause in a contract concluded between a seller or supplier and a consumer is unfair, in so far as, under national rules of procedure, it can carry out such an assessment in similar actions of a domestic nature. If that is the case, it is for that court or tribunal to establish all the consequences thereby arising under national law, in order to ensure that the consumer is not bound by that clause.

III.9.6. ECJ Judgment, Case C-243/08 of 4 June 2009 (*Pannon GSM Zrt* v. *Sustikné Győrfi Erzsébet* [*Pannon GSM*])[149]

(a)   Conclusions of the ECJ

258.   Ms. *Sustikné Győrfi* was sued by *Pannon GSM* in a court other than the court which would have jurisdiction according to the place of her residence, based on a choice-of-court agreement. The court referred the following three questions to the ECJ for a preliminary ruling: **(1)** As concerns the answer to the **first question**, the ECJ held that **an unfair contract term was not binding on the consumer**, and it was not necessary, in that regard, for that consumer to have successfully contested the validity of such a term beforehand. **(2)** As concerns the

---

[148] Such decisions are mentioned, without any further details, in the statement of the Spanish government.
[149] CELEX: 62008CA0243, the judgment was published in: ECR 2009, p. I-04713. Language of the case: Hungarian.

second question, the ECJ concluded that the **national court was required to examine, of its own motion, the unfairness of a contractual term where it had available to it the legal and factual elements necessary for that task.** Where it considers such a term to be unfair, it must not apply it, except if the consumer opposes that non-application. That duty is also incumbent on the national court when it is ascertaining its own territorial jurisdiction. **(3)** The ECJ's answer to the **third question** was that **it was for the national court to determine whether a contractual term satisfies the criteria to be categorized as unfair** within the meaning of Article 3(1) of the *Directive*.

(b) Facts of the case

259. On 12 December 2004, Ms. *Sustikné Győrfi* entered into a subscription contract with *Pannon GSM Zrt.* (*Pannon GSM*) for the provision of mobile telephone services. The contract was concluded on the basis of a form[150] supplied by *Pannon*. The form stipulated that, by signing the contract, Ms. *Győrfi* acknowledged the general contractual conditions forming an integral part of the contract and accepted their content. Under those terms and conditions, the parties accepted that the court for the place where *Pannon GSM* has its principal place of business has jurisdiction for any dispute arising from the contract or in relation to it. That term conferring jurisdiction was not individually negotiated by the two parties. Taking the view that Ms. *Győrfi* defaulted on her payment obligations, *Pannon GSM* applied to the *Budaörsi Városi Bíróság* (court) for an order for payment, it being the court in the territorial jurisdiction of which *Pannon* has its principal place of business (the registered office of the claimant). That court made the order sought by the claimant. Ms. *Győrfi* filed, within the prescribed time limit, a statement of opposition to that order. At that moment, the court focused on its jurisdiction and found out that Ms. *Győrfi's* place of residence was not within its jurisdiction. Ms. *Győrfi*, who receives invalidity benefits, had her place of residence 275 km from the seat of the court, and there was no direct train or bus service. According to general procedural rules on

---

[150] Regarding standard form contracts see:
- ➤ Judgment of the BGH [DEU], Case No. III ZR 265/03 of 13 January 2005 which is annotated in detail in the excursus into German law [DEU]; the court unequivocally held that the form does not eo ipso constitute unfairness and impropriety;
- ➤ Judgment of the BGH [DEU], Case No. III ZR 164/06 of 1 March 2007, also annotated in detail in the excursus into German law [DEU].
- ➤ A standard form contract was also concluded in a case handled by the SC CR [CZE] – see the annotation of the Judgment of the SC CR [CZE], Case No. 23 Cdo 1201/2009 of 29 June 2010, which is annotated in detail in the excursus into Czech law [CZE].
- ➤ In connection with American practice [USA], see *Korobkin, R.* Bounded Rationality, Standard Form Contracts and Unconscionability. University of Chicago Law Review, 2003, Vol. 70, p. 1203 et seq. et al.

jurisdiction, the court with territorial jurisdiction would be the court for the place where Ms. *Győrfi* resided.[151]

260. Hungarian procedural laws provide that under the given circumstances, the court must raise, of its own motion, the issue of territorial jurisdiction. However, as jurisdiction is not exclusive, it is no longer possible to raise (challenge) that issue after the first filing by the respondent of her defense to the substance of the dispute. Applicable rules stipulate that the court which is seized may examine the accuracy of the facts relied on, to establish that it has jurisdiction, only where they are inconsistent with self-evident facts or facts of which the court has knowledge *ex officio*, or if such facts are improbable or the other party disputes them.

261. In those circumstances, the court, entertaining doubts as to the possible unfairness of the term conferring jurisdiction, decided to stay proceedings and refer **the following questions to the ECJ** for a preliminary ruling:
   ▶ [1] Can Article 6(1) of the *Directive* – pursuant to which Member States are to provide that unfair terms used in a contract concluded with a consumer by a seller or supplier shall, as provided for under their national law, not be binding on the consumer – be construed as meaning that the non-binding nature vis-à-vis the consumer of an unfair term introduced by the seller or supplier does not have effect *ipso jure* but only where the consumer successfully contests the unfair term by lodging the relevant application?
   ▶ [2] Does the consumer protection provided by the *Directive* require the national court of its own motion – irrespective of the type of proceedings in question and of whether or not they are contentious – to determine that the contract before it contains unfair terms, even where no application has been lodged, thereby carrying out, of its own motion, a review of the terms introduced by the seller or supplier in the context of exercising control over its own jurisdiction?
   ▶ [3] In the event that the second question is answered in the affirmative, what are the factors which the national court must take into account and evaluate in the context of exercising this control?

(c) Arguments of the ECJ

(aa) The first question: Examination of unfairness ex officio (of the court's own motion)

262. The system of protection introduced by the *Directive* is based on the idea that the consumer is in an unequal position vis-à-vis the professional. This applies both to the consumer's bargaining power and his or her level of knowledge which leads to the consumer agreeing to

---

[151] Court: Battonyai Városi Bíróság [HUN] (Municipal Court in Battonyai [HUN]).

terms drawn up in advance by the seller or supplier without being able to influence the content of those terms.[152] The ECJ has already held before[153] that the aim of Article 6 of the *Directive* would not be achieved if the consumer were himself obliged to raise the unfairness of contractual terms, and that effective protection of the consumer may be attained only if the national court acknowledges that it has the power to evaluate terms of this kind of its own motion.

263. If that power is to be granted to the national court, Article 6(1) of the *Directive* cannot be interpreted as meaning that it is only in the event that the consumer has brought a specific application in relation to it, that an unfair contract term is not binding on that consumer. Such an interpretation would rule out the possibility of the national court assessing, of its own motion, in the context of examining the admissibility of the action which is before it, and without a specific application from the consumer to that effect, the unfairness of a contractual term.

264. As regards the legal effects of an unfair term, the ECJ stated before[154] that the importance of consumer protection has led the *Community* legislature to lay down, in Article 6(1) of the *Directive*, that unfair terms used in a contract concluded with a consumer by a seller or supplier shall not be binding on the consumer. The ECJ emphasized that it is a mandatory provision which, taking into account the weaker position of one of the parties to the contract, aims to replace the formal balance, which the latter establishes between the rights and obligations of the parties, with an effective balance, which re-establishes equality between them.

265. Therefore, the reply to the first question is that Article 6(1) of the *Directive* must be interpreted as meaning that an unfair contract term is not binding on the consumer, and it is not necessary, in that regard, for that consumer to have successfully contested the validity of such a term beforehand.

(bb) The second question: Examination of unfairness where the court has sufficient factual and legal information

266. The Court has already held[155] that the protection which the *Directive* confers on consumers extends to cases in which a consumer fails to raise the unfairness of the term, whether because he is unaware of his rights or because he is deterred from enforcing them on account of the costs

---

[152] See the ECJ judgment in *Océano Grupo*.
[153] See the ECJ judgment in *Océano Grupo*, para. (26).
[154] See the ECJ judgment in *Mostaza Claro*, para. (36).
[155] See the ECJ judgment in *Cofidis*, para. (34).

which judicial proceedings would involve. The nature and importance of the *public interest* underlying the protection which the *Directive* confers on consumers justify the national court being required to assess of its own motion whether a contractual term is unfair, compensating in this way for the imbalance which exists between the consumer and the professional.[156] The court seized of the action is therefore required to ensure the effectiveness of the protection intended to be given by the provisions of the *Directive*. Consequently, the role thus attributed to the national court is not limited to a mere power to rule on the possible unfairness of a contractual term, but **also consists of the obligation to examine that issue of its own motion, where it has available to it the legal and factual elements necessary for that task,** including when it is assessing whether it has territorial jurisdiction. In carrying out that obligation, the national court is not, however, required under the *Directive* to exclude the possibility that the term in question may be applicable, **if the consumer, after having been informed of it by that court, does not intend to assert its unfair or non-binding status.** This conclusion is very important for the determination of the limits of *consumer protection*. Consumer protection is the subject of *public interest*; it is not, however, the subject of *public policy*. *Public policy* basically prohibits waiver of the requirements of *public policy*. *Public policy* is integrated in the *pillars* on which a particular legal system rests; it has absolute effects, irrespective of the will of the parties. Due to the strength of the *public interest* involved in consumer protection, the laws regulating such protection have the nature of mandatory rules; from the perspective of private international law, overriding mandatory rules. But if it is not a component of *public policy*, the breach of these rules does not constitute grounds, at the national level, for the refusal of a foreign arbitral award.

267. The reply, therefore, to the second question is that the national court is required to examine, of its own motion, the unfairness of a contractual term where it has available to it the legal and factual elements necessary for that task. Where it considers such a term to be unfair, it must not apply it, except if the consumer opposes that non-application. That duty is also incumbent on the national court when it is ascertaining its own territorial jurisdiction.

(cc) The third question: Circumstances decisive for the assessment of (un)fairness and (im)balance

268. In referring to concepts of *"fairness"* and the *"significant imbalance between the rights and obligations of the parties,"* Article 3 of the *Directive* merely defines in a general way the factors that render unfair a

---

[156] See the ECJ judgment in *Mostaza Claro*, para. (38).

contractual term **that has not been individually negotiated.**[157] The Annex to which Article 3(3) of the *Directive* refers contains only an indicative and non-exhaustive list of terms which may be regarded as unfair.[158] Article 4 of the *Directive* provides that the unfairness of a contractual term is to be assessed taking into account the nature of the goods or services for which the contract was concluded and by referring, at the time of conclusion of the contract, to all the circumstances attending the conclusion of it.[159]

269.   However, as regards the term which is the subject matter of the dispute in the original proceedings, it should be borne in mind that the ECJ has held[160] that a term which was not subject to individual negotiation and was concluded between a consumer and a professional within the meaning of the *Directive*, satisfies all the criteria necessary for it to be judged unfair. As the ECJ also stated before,[161] a choice-of-court agreement obliges the consumer to submit to the exclusive jurisdiction of a court which may be geographically distant from his domicile, which may make it difficult for him to enter an appearance. In the case of disputes concerning limited amounts of money, the costs relating to the consumer's entering an appearance could be a deterrent and cause him to forgo any legal remedy or defense.[162] Such a term falls within the category of terms which have the object or effect of excluding the consumer's right to take legal action, a category referred to in subparagraph (q) of paragraph 1 of the Annex to the *Directive*.

270.   In those circumstances, the reply to the third question is that it is for the national court to determine whether a contractual term, such as that which is the subject matter of the dispute in the main proceedings, satisfies the criteria to be categorized as unfair within the meaning of Article 3(1) of the *Directive*. In so doing, the national court must take account of the fact that a term, contained in a contract concluded

---

[157] ECJ Judgment, Case C-237/02 of 1 April 2004 (*Freiburger Kommunalbauten GmbH Baugesellschaft & Co. KG* v. *Ludger Hofstetter* et *Ulrike Hofstetter*, published in: ECR 2004, p. I–03403. CELEX: 62002CJ0237. See para. (19) of the judgment.

[158] ECJ Judgment, Case C-237/02 of 1 April 2004 (*Freiburger Kommunalbauten GmbH Baugesellschaft & Co. KG* v. *Ludger Hofstetter et Ulrike Hofstetter*), para. (20).

[159] The same principle was applied in the case law of national courts, namely the following decisions (inter alia):
Judgment of the Court of Appeal, Queen's Bench Division – Technology and Construction Court [GBR-ENG], No. HT-07-106 of 18 December 2007 in *Heifer International Inc* v. (1) *Helge Christiansen* (2) *Christiansen Arkitekter KS MAA PAR* (3) *Haslev-Hansson VVS* (4) *Stevns El-Service A/S* et (5) *Listed El-Teknik APS*; [2007] EWHC 3015 (TCC), annotated and analyzed in connection with the law applicable to arbitration agreements with an international dimension. See also, the Judgment of the Supreme Court CR [CZE], Case No. 23 Cdo 1201/2009 of 29 June 2010 (There is a detailed annotation in the excursus into Czech law in this book.).

[160] See the ECJ judgment in *Océano Grupo*, paras. (21) through (24).

[161] See the ECJ judgment in *Océano Grupo*, para. (22).

[162] See the ECJ judgment in *Océano Grupo*, para. (22).

between a consumer and a seller or supplier, which has been included without being individually negotiated and which confers exclusive jurisdiction on the court in the territorial jurisdiction of which the seller or supplier has his principal place of business may be considered to be unfair.

(d) Obligation of arbitrators to instruct the parties about the unfairness of a contractual term

271. The *Pannon GSM* ruling is important, because it allows the consumer to validate an unfair term (whether by his or her act of omission or commission) if the consumer himself/herself fails to plead the unfairness after being instructed about the [potential] unfairness. This conclusion is logical if we simultaneously consider that the court also assesses the unfairness only on the basis of the factual and legal elements of the case available to the court. The court therefore often instructs the consumer based on the court's preliminary assessment, and it is up to the consumer, having been properly instructed, to plead the invalidity and, as the case may be, adduce circumstances supporting the conclusion of unfairness and refusing the application of the contractual term for its invalidity.

272. The question that needs to be asked, however, is whether the obligation to provide instructions to the parties applies to the arbitrators as well. Although it is a generally recognized principle that unpredictable decisions ought to be prevented both in litigation and in arbitration, arbitrators in the international arena are not principally bound by any such obligation to provide instructions; the same applies in a number of countries. The Czech Republic [CZE] is probably an exception in this regard; with respect to the voluminous case law,[163] the obligation to provide instructions to the parties is considered to be one of the principles of civil procedure applicable both in litigation and in arbitration. The unfairness of a contractual term and the consequences thereof are not based on procedural laws but on consumer protection laws, i.e. substantive law. Consequently, if an arbitral tribunal under Czech law is bound by an obligation to provide instructions in preventing surprise decisions in the merits, then the obligation should also apply to the assessment of the potential unfairness of a contractual term. EU law stipulates that arbitration in consumer disputes is principally acceptable (unless the arbitrability of consumer disputes is excluded by national law, i.e. the law of national origin), providing the arbitrators are also bound by the obligation to apply valid law. Failure to perform the obligation to provide instructions should not, however, have

---

[163] See the Judgment of the ConCourt CR, Case No. I ÚS 3227/07 of 8 March 2011, annotated in detail in the excursus into Czech law, as well as in the voluminous case law of Czech courts [CZE].

any practical consequences if the consumer, even in the absence of such instructions, always has the option of challenging the arbitral award in court, and it is only at that stage that the court must assess the unfairness of its own motion and inform the consumer about the court's preliminary conclusion on unfairness. Consequently, failure to perform the obligation to provide instructions regarding the [potential] unfairness of a contractual term during arbitral proceedings cannot be interpreted as grounds for annulment of the arbitral award for failure to allow the party to plead his or her case, as construed by Czech case law in connection with preventing *unpredictable decisions* in the merits. Decisions in the merits are not, as a rule, subject to review. Although the invalidity of an arbitration clause caused by its unfairness in a consumer contract relies on substantive law, its consequence is the lack of jurisdiction of arbitrators. However, jurisdiction is an exclusively procedural category, at least in continental *civil law*. The possibility cannot be ruled out, however, that a different view could be accepted under *common law* which treats jurisdiction as a category of substantive law. Consequently, applying a strict interpretation of the ECJ's case law (for instance, in the *Pannon GSM* case), *common law* is paradoxically less favorable to arbitration, because the arbitrators should perform the obligation of providing instructions regarding a potential defense of unfairness of contract.

III.9.7. ECJ Order, Case C-76/10 of 16 November 2010 (*Pohotovosť s.r.o.* v. *Iveta Korčkovská* [*Pohotovosť*])[164]

(a) Summary

273. Ms. *Korčkovská* accepted a consumer credit line from *Pohotovosť, s.r.o.* ("*Pohotovosť*"). Neither the credit agreement nor the general terms and conditions mentioned the annual percentage rate of charge (APR) of 95.6%. The agreement also contained a provision on the daily default interest of 0.25% of the due and outstanding amount (91.25% per annum); the maximum default interest rate according to Slovak law is 9% per year. Ms. *Korčkovská* defaulted on the credit, and *Pohotovosť* initiated arbitration; subsequently, the company filed for enforcement of the arbitral award. The Slovak court referred several questions to the ECJ for a preliminary ruling.

274. The ECJ resolved the case by a reasoned order, not a judgment, because the answer to the questions could have been inferred from preceding case law. The ECJ has repeatedly held that a national court may assess of its own motion whether a contractual term is (un)fair under Articles 3 and 4 of the *Directive*, where it has available to it the legal and factual

---

[164] *OJ* C 30, p. 12. CELEX: 62010CB0076. Language of the case: Slovak.

elements necessary for that task and where the national rules of procedure allow such an assessment. The ECJ also held that absence of the APR may be the decisive factor for the national court when assessing the clarity of the contractual term under Article 4 of the *Directive*. Where this is not the case, the court may of its own motion assess the (un)fairness pursuant to Articles 3 and 4 of the *Directive* or apply the national law implementing Directive 87/102/EEC, according to which the absence of APR in the consumer credit agreement renders the credit interest-free and free of charge.

(b) Factual and legal findings

275. On 26 February 2008 Ms. *Korčkovská* and *Pohotovosť* s.r.o. entered into a credit agreement for 20,000 SKK (= 663.88 EUR). The charges relating to the credit amounted to 19,120 SKK (634.67 EUR). Ms. *Korčkovská* was obliged to pay back the principal amount and the charges within one year, in monthly installments of 3,260 SKK (= 108.21 EUR). According to the national court, the APR on the credit therefore amounted to 95.6%. The amount of the APR was not, however, specified in the agreement or in the general terms and conditions.

276. Pursuant to Article 4 of the general terms and conditions in the case, the entire debt becomes immediately due and payable if the debtor defaults on two consecutive installments, or part thereof. Article 6 of the general terms and conditions also stipulated that the daily default interest was 0.25% of the amount due and outstanding and that the debtor was obliged to pay it from the first day of delay until full payment of the debt due and outstanding. This interest rate corresponds to an annual rate of 91.25%. The national court held that Slovak law prohibits any default interest in civil-law contracts which *exceeds* the prime interest rate of the European Central Bank (currently 1%) plus 8%, i.e. 9% in total.

277. Article 17 of the general terms and conditions also contained an arbitration clause. According to the arbitration clause, any disputes arising from the agreement shall be decided either by Stály rozhodcovský súd (the Permanent Arbitral Institution) in Bratislava, or a court of competent jurisdiction **chosen by the claimant.** The relations between the creditor and the debtor shall be governed by the Commercial Code [SVK]. The national court added that the agreement also contained a power of attorney authorizing a lawyer to represent Ms. *Korčkovská*.

278. Ms. *Korčkovská* defaulted on two consecutive installments, and *Pohotovosť* submitted a request for arbitration with Stály rozhodcovský súd (the Permanent Arbitral Institution); on 3 November 2008, the arbitral tribunal rendered an arbitral award which ordered Ms. *Korčkovská* to pay to *Pohotovosť* 48,820 SKK (= 1,620.53 EUR) with a

default interest of 39,120 SKK (= 1,298.55 EUR) and compensation for the costs of proceedings amounting to 9,928 SKK (= 329.55 EUR). The award became final on 15 December 2008 and enforceable on 18 December 2008.

279. The award was used by the enforcement officer as the basis for an application of 9 March 2009 filed with Okresný súd Stará Ľubovňa (Stará Ľubovňa District Court) [SVK], requesting that the enforcement officer be entrusted with the enforcement proceedings for 3,467 EUR. On 31 July 2009 the court issued an order staying the enforcement proceedings arguing that the compensation for the claimant's legal costs claimed in the enforcement proceedings (more than 94.61 EUR) was contra bonos mores. Apart from that, the court also held the default interest contra bonos mores, because the agreed daily default interest rate was 0.25% per day on the amount of 1,298,52 EUR from 21 July 2008 until the expiration of the debt.

280. On 26 August 2009 *Pohotovosť* appealed the order with the Krajský súd v Prešove (Regional Court in Prešov) [SVK]. The Regional Court accepted that the *Asociácia spotrebiteľských subjektov Slovenska* (Slovak Association of Consumers) [SVK] may submit a statement supporting Ms. *Korčkovská's* case, in which the Association informed the court, inter alia, about a significant number of enforcement proceedings initiated by *Pohotovosť* in Slovakia [SVK]. The Association therefore believed that the general terms and conditions applicable to credits extended by the company contain unfair terms and constitute unfair business practices; the Association therefore proposed that the court refer to the ECJ for a preliminary ruling.

281. The Regional Court decided to stay the proceedings and **referred the following questions to the ECJ for a preliminary ruling:**
    (1) (a) Is the information regarding the total costs payable by the consumer (in percentage terms) (APR) so important that its absence in the agreement renders the price of the consumer credit non-transparent and insufficiently clear and unintelligible? **(b)** Does the scope of the consumer protection guaranteed under the *Directive* allow for the designation, due to lack of transparency and clarity, as an unfair term in a consumer credit agreement the price itself if the agreement lacks information on the APR and the price is expressed only as an amount consisting of several charges specified both in the agreement and in the general terms and conditions?
    (2) (a) Must the *Directive* be interpreted as meaning that a national court or tribunal hearing an action for the enforcement of an arbitration award, which has become final and was made in the absence of the consumer, is required, where it has available to it the legal and factual elements necessary for that task, to assess of its

own motion whether a penalty in an agreement concluded between a credit provider and a consumer is unfair, in so far as, under the national rules of procedure, it can carry out such an assessment in similar actions of a domestic nature? **(b)** As concerns the unfair penalty for the violation of the consumer's obligations, is the court called upon to establish all the consequences thereby arising under national law, in order to ensure that the consumer is not bound by the unfair penalty? **(c)** Can the penalty of 0.25% per day from the amount due and outstanding of the credit, i.e. 91.25% per year, be assessed as an unfair term?

(3) If an agreement evaded the consumer protection laws in the provision of consumer credits and in a situation where the enforcement of an arbitral award based on the agreement has already been initiated, does the framework of consumer protection allow the court, when applying EU laws (the *Directive* and Directive 2008/48/EC) to consumer credit agreements, to terminate the enforcement or permit the enforcement at the creditor's expense only up to the amount of the due and outstanding balance of the credit where the domestic rules allow such an assessment of the arbitral award and the court has the necessary legal and factual elements available to it?

(c)   Form of the ECJ's ruling

282.   Article 104(3) of the Rules of Procedure of the ECJ stipulates that if the answer to the question may be clearly deduced from existing case law and the ECJ has heard the Advocate General, the ECJ may give its decision by reasoned order. According to the ECJ, this was the situation in the present case.

(d)   Permissibility of the preliminary reference procedure

283.   *Pohotovost'* argued that the answers to some of the questions referred for a preliminary ruling could be provided in the form of an order adopted pursuant to Article 104(3) of the Rules of Procedure of the ECJ. It also maintained, however, that the first and the third question do not concern the interpretation of EU law and that the national court failed to abide by its obligation to deal with issues of domestic (national) law before making a reference to the ECJ for a preliminary ruling. The ECJ noted that even if it might be suitable under certain circumstances to resolve the issues relating exclusively to national law at the moment the court makes the reference for a preliminary ruling, the national courts are not limited in the option of referring to the ECJ if they believe that the case poses questions concerning the interpretation or assessment of the validity of EU law which requires their ruling. As concerns the questions referred, the ECJ held that these questions do concern EU law.

(e) Arguments of the ECJ

(aa) The first question: Information in the agreement about total annual costs of the credit

284. As concerns the necessity of specifying the APR in the agreement, the ECJ pointed out that considering the day of conclusion of the agreement, the situation must be assessed according to Directive 87/102/EEC,[165] not according to Directive 2008/48/EC.[166]

285. The ECJ believed that APR, as information about the total costs of the credit in the form of a rate calculated according to a uniform mathematical formula, was crucial. This information, which – according to Directive 87/102/EEC – must be previously announced in the advertising for the credit, which contributes to the transparency of the market, because it allows the consumer to compare individual credit offers. Furthermore, the APR allows the consumer to consider the scope of his or her commitment.[167] Consequently, the absence of the APR in the credit agreement may be a decisive factor in the assessment by a national court of whether a term of a consumer credit agreement concerning the cost of that credit – in which no mention of the APR is made – is written in plain, intelligible language within the meaning of Article 4 of the *Directive*.

286. If this is not the case, the national court is entitled to assess the unfair nature of the term within the meaning of Article 3 of the *Directive*. Although the term could be considered as excluded from the scope of the *Directive*, the ECJ pointed out that the terms listed in Article 4(2) of Directive 87/102/EEC, falling within the scope of the *Directive*, are excluded from the assessment of their unfair nature only to the extent the competent national court believes, based on the examination of the individual cases, that they were articulated by the seller or supplier in a plain and intelligible language.[168] In this case the unfair nature of the term included in the credit agreement which lacked information on the APR could be assessed from the perspective of the *Directive*; consequently, the national court has the option of determining the

---

[165] Council Directive of 22 December 1986 on the approximation of laws, regulations and administrative provisions of the Member States concerning consumer credit, published in: OJ L 42, 12. 2. 1987, pp. 48–53. CELEX: 31987L0102.

[166] Directive 2008/48/EC of the European Parliament and of the Council of 23 April 2008 on credit agreements for consumers and repealing Council Directive 87/102/EEC. OJ L 133, 22. 5. 2008, pp. 66–92. CELEX 32008L0048.

[167] ECJ Judgment, Case C-264/02 of 4 March 2004, *Cofinoga Mérignac SA* v. *Sylvain Sachithanathan*, published in: ECR 2004, p. I–02157. CELEX 62002CJ0264. Language of the case: French.

[168] ECJ Judgment, Case C-484/08 of 3 June 2010, *Caja de Ahorros y Monte de Piedad de Madrid* v. *Asociación de Usuarios de Servicios Bancarios* (Ausbanc), para. (32). The judgment was published in: ECR 2010, p. 00000. Language of the case: Spanish.

(un)fairness of the term of its own motion. As mentioned above, the Court of Justice could not examine the unfairness of a particular contractual term; it was therefore the task of the national court to determine, with respect to all legal and factual elements, whether the omission to specify the APR could have the result of rendering the contractual term on the costs of the consumer credit unfair within the meaning of Articles 3 and 4 of the *Directive*.

287. The information provided by the national court indicated however that in Slovak law according to Section 4 of Act [SVK] No. 258/2001,[169] which implemented Directive 87/102/EEC, a consumer credit agreement must contain the APR. Absence of the APR in the consumer credit agreement renders the credit interest-free and free of charge.

288. Article 14 of Directive 87/102/EEC imposes on the Member States the obligation to ensure that credit agreements do not derogate, to the detriment of the consumer, from the provisions of national law implementing or corresponding to Directive 87/102/EEC. Consequently, in the circumstances such as in the present case and without the need to examine from the perspective of the *Directive* the unfair nature of the term lacking the APR, Directive 87/102/EEC was to be interpreted as meaning that the national court may of its own motion apply the provision implementing in the national law Article 4 of Directive 87/102/EEC, which stipulates that in the absence of the APR the credit shall be deemed to be interest-free and free of charge.

289. Consequently, the answer to the first question was that in circumstances such as those in the present case, the failure to mention the APR in a consumer credit agreement, the mention of the APR being essential information in the context of Directive 87/102/EEC, may be a decisive factor in the assessment by a national court of whether a term of a consumer credit agreement concerning the cost of that credit in which no such mention is made is (not) written in plain, intelligible language within the meaning of Article 4 of the *Directive*. If that is not the case, that court has the power to assess, of its own motion, whether, in light of all the circumstances attending the conclusion of that contract, the failure to mention the APR in the terms of that contract concerning the cost of that credit is likely to confer on that term an unfair nature within the meaning of Articles 3 and 4 of the *Directive*. However, notwithstanding the power which is given to assess that contract in light

---

[169] Act [SVK] No. 258/2001 Coll., on Consumer Credits and Amending and Supplementing Act of the Slovak National Council No. 71/1986 Coll., on Slovak Trade Inspection, as subsequently amended. Author's note: This Act [SVK] was repealed as of 11 June 2010 by Act [SVK] No. 129/2010 Coll., on Consumer Credits and Other Credits and Loans for Consumers and Amending and Supplementing Selected Legislation.

of the *Directive*, Directive 87/102/EEC is to be interpreted as allowing national courts to apply of their own motion the provisions transposing Article 4 of Directive 87/102/EEC into national law and as providing that the failure to mention the APR in a consumer credit agreement means that the credit granted is deemed to be interest-free and free of charge.

(bb) The second question: Sub-par. (a)

290. The ECJ held that the system of consumer protection introduced by the *Directive* is based on the idea that the consumer is in a weak position as regards both his bargaining power and his level of knowledge; this leads to the consumer agreeing to terms drawn up in advance by the professional without being able to influence the content of these terms.[170]

291. Considering this weaker position of the consumer, Article 6 of the *Directive* provides that unfair terms are not binding on the consumer. It is a mandatory provision which aims to replace the formal balance between the parties with an effective balance.[171] The imbalance between the consumer and the professional may only be corrected by positive action unconnected with the actual parties to the contract.[172] The national court may therefore decide of its own motion on the (un)fairness of a contractual term.[173]

292. Consequently, if a national court, hearing an application for the enforcement of a final arbitral award, must according to domestic rules of procedure, of its own motion, assess any potential conflict of the arbitration clause with *public policy*, the court must of its own motion examine the nature of the arbitration clause with respect to Article 6 of the *Directive* immediately after the court has available to it the necessary legal and factual elements of the case.[174]

293. The ECJ held that according to the information provided by the national court, the national laws on arbitration (ArbAct [SVK]) seem to impose on the court the obligation to terminate the enforcement of the arbitral award ordering payment if the performance is prohibited by law or if it is contra bonos mores. Furthermore, the national court opined that any unfair term in a consumer contract is contra bonos mores under Slovak law, because it causes an imbalance in the rights and obligations of the parties to the detriment of the consumer, in breach of the principle of good faith.

---

[170] See the ECJ judgments in *Océano Grupo*, para. (25), and *Mostaza Claro*, para. (25).
[171] See the ECJ judgments in *Mostaza Claro*, para. (36), and *Pannon GSM*, para. (25).
[172] See the ECJ judgments in *Océano Grupo*, para. (27), *Mostaza Claro*, para. (26), and *Asturcom*, para. (32).
[173] See the ECJ judgment in *Asturcom*, para. (32).
[174] See the ECJ judgments in *Asturcom*, para. (53), and *Pannon GSM*, para. (32).

294. Consequently, similarly to the *Asturcom* case, the ECJ ruled that a court, hearing an application for the enforcement of an arbitral award, may of its own motion terminate the enforcement if the award orders performance which is objectively impossible, prohibited by law, or contra bonos mores. If this is the case and the court has available to it information on the factual and legal elements, the court may of its own motion assess in the enforcement proceedings the unfair nature of the penalty contained in the consumer credit agreement.

295. Consequently, the answer to the second question, sub-par. (a), was that the *Directive* must be interpreted as meaning that a national court or tribunal hearing an action for the enforcement of an arbitration award, which has become final and was made in the absence of the consumer, is required, where it has available to it the legal and factual elements necessary for that task, to assess of its own motion whether a penalty contained in a contract which is the subject matter of the proceedings is unfair, in so far as, under national rules of procedure, it can carry out such an assessment in similar actions of a domestic nature [i.e. if the national laws permit such an assessment during enforcement proceedings].[175]

(cc)   The second question: Sub-pars. (b) and (c)

296. In response to the second question, the ECJ held that with respect to the concept of good faith and a significant imbalance in the rights and obligations of the parties, **Article 3 of the *Directive* only generally defines the elements of an unfair contractual term** which was not individually negotiated. The ECJ may, however, within the limits of its power to interpret EU law under Article 267 TFEU, interpret the general conditions employed by EU legislation only for the purposes of defining the concept of an unfair term. It may not comment on the application of these terms to a particular contractual term; this is possible only depending on the circumstances of each individual case. Consequently, if the national court concludes that the respective term is unfair within the meaning of the *Directive*, Article 6(1) of the *Directive* prescribes that the term cannot be binding on the consumer subject to the conditions stipulated by national law. Article 6 of the *Directive* also demands that the national court, when confronted with an unfair contractual term, must assess whether the contract can exist without that term. The national court must subsequently establish on the basis of the unfair contractual term all the consequences thereby arising under national law and ensure that the consumer is not bound by the unfair term.[176]

---

[175] See the ECJ judgment in *Asturcom*.
[176] See the ECJ judgment in *Asturcom*, para. (59).

297.   Consequently, the ECJ's answer to the second question, sub-pars. (b) and (c) was that it is for the national court concerned to determine whether a term in a credit agreement stipulating, according to the findings of that court, the consumer pay a disproportionately high penalty must, in light of all the circumstances attending the conclusion of the contract, be regarded as unfair within the meaning of Articles 3 and 4 of the *Directive*. If that is the case, it is for that court to establish all the consequences thereby arising under national law, in order to ensure that the consumer is not bound by that term.

(dd)   The third question: Assessment of the unfairness of the contract in proceedings on enforcement of a foreign arbitral award

298.   As concerns the third question, the ECJ noted that the ECJ is not allowed to apply EU law to a particular case; it may only comment on the interpretation of the TEC and the acts adopted by EU institutions. The national court tried to get an answer from the ECJ on the question of whether in circumstances such as those in the present case and considering the ECJ's answers to the first and the second questions, the court may under EU law and national law limit enforcement of the final arbitral award, contested in the merits, to the remaining due and outstanding balance of the credit extended under the credit agreement.

299.   Considering that the answer to the question would result in the ECJ commenting on a particular application of the provisions interpreted under the first two questions to the facts of the case, and considering that in any case the answers to those questions provided to the national court the interpretation tools necessary for the resolution of the dispute at hand, the ECJ did not find any reason to answer that question.

III.9.8. ECJ Judgment, Case C-137/08 of 9 November 2010 (*VB Pénzügyi Lízing Zrt.* v. *Ferenc Schneider*): Unfairness of a choice-of-court clause

(a)   Conclusions of the ECJ

300.   The ECJ reached, inter alia, the **following conclusions:**[177]
   ▶ The obligation of the national court to inform the Minister of Justice when a decision to refer a question [to the ECJ] is sent does not breach EU law.
   ▶ The jurisdiction of the ECJ extends to the interpretation of the concept of an "*unfair term*" within the meaning of the *Directive*.

---

[177] CELEX: 62008CA0137, the ECJ judgment was published in: *OJ* C 13, pp. 2-2. Language of the case: Hungarian.

However, it is always for the national court to determine whether a particular contractual term is actually unfair in the circumstances of the case.

▶ The *Directive* applies to any term conferring the exclusive territorial jurisdiction of a court appearing in a contract concluded between a professional and a consumer which was not individually negotiated. In order to safeguard the effectiveness of the consumer protection intended by the EU legislature, **the national court must thus, in all cases and whatever the rules of its domestic law, determine whether or not the contested term was individually negotiated.**

▶ When assessing the (un)fairness of a choice-of-court clause, **the national court must investigate of its own motion whether the choice-of-court term (clause)**[178] **which is the subject of a dispute before it, falls within the scope of the *Directive*.** If it does, the court must assess of its own motion (*ex officio*) whether such a term is unfair.

(b) Factual and legal findings

301.   On 14 April 2006, Mr. *Schneider* and *VB Pénzügyi Lízing Zrt.* concluded a loan contract to finance the purchase of a car. Mr. *Schneider* ceased to fulfill his contractual obligations (ceased to pay the lease installments). Consequently, the lease company terminated that loan contract and brought an action before the referring court (identified in the choice-of-court clause) – a Budapest court (*Budapesti II. és III. kerületi bíróság*) for the repayment of a debt of 317,404 HUF with interest and costs. The choice-of-court clause stipulated the jurisdiction of a court different from the court corresponding to the place where the respondent (consumer) lived. The court issued a payment order in uncontested proceedings. At that stage (uncontested proceedings for a payment order), Hungarian law does not require the court to hold a hearing or hear the other party; the court therefore did not examine its territorial jurisdiction. Mr. *Schneider* appealed against the order for payment without, however, stating any grounds for that appeal. The consequence under Hungarian law was that the proceedings became contentious (*inter partes*) and were then governed by the provisions of the general law on civil procedure.

(c) Preliminary reference procedure

302.   The Budapest court found that Mr. *Schneider* did not live within its territorial jurisdiction, although the rules of civil procedure provide that the court which has the jurisdiction to hear a dispute such as that before

---

[178] In this connection, the author emphasizes that the purpose of arbitration clauses and choice-of-court clauses is of the same nature.

it is the court within whose jurisdiction the respondent lives. The court therefore stayed the proceedings and referred the following questions to the ECJ for a preliminary ruling:

▶ **The first question:** Does the consumer protection guaranteed by the *Directive*[...] require that – irrespective of the type of proceedings and whether they are *inter partes* or not – in the context of the review of their own competences, the national courts are to assess, of their own motion, the unfair nature of a contractual term before them even if not specifically requested to do so?

▶ **The second question:** If Question 1 is to be answered in the affirmative, what criteria may the national courts take into account in the context of that review, in particular in case the contractual term (clause) does not grant jurisdiction to the judicial body corresponding to the registered office of the service provider (professional), but to a different judicial body which is located close to that registered office [of the professional]?

▶ **The third question:** Pursuant to the first paragraph of Article 23 [of the Protocol on the Statute of the ECJ], is the possibility precluded for the national courts to inform the Ministry of Justice of their own Member State that a reference for a preliminary ruling has been made at the same time as making that reference?

303.   On 13 February 2009, the proceedings before the ECJ were stayed pending delivery of the judgment in the *Pannon GSM* case.[179] Following the delivery of the judgment in the *Pannon GSM* case, the referring Budapest court informed the ECJ that it no longer considered it necessary for the Court of Justice to reply to the first and second questions; the referring court stated, however, that it still wished to obtain an answer to the third question. In the view of the Budapest court, the indications given by the ECJ in its judgment in *Pannon GSM* did not make it possible to decide the question of whether the national court may examine the unfairness of a contractual term of its own motion only where it has available to it the legal and factual elements necessary for that task, or, **rather, whether examining the unfairness of a term of its own motion implied that in the course of that examination the national court was also required to establish of its own motion the facts and the law** necessary for that examination. Having regard to those considerations, the Budapest court decided to refer the following **additional questions** to the ECJ:

▶ Do the powers of the ECJ under Article [267 TFEU] include that of interpreting the concept of an "unfair term" referred to in Article 3(1) of the *Directive*[...] and the terms listed in the Annex to that *Directive*?

---

[179] The ECJ judgment in *Pannon GSM* is annotated in detail elsewhere in this book – see above.

▶ If the answer to the first question is in the affirmative, can a reference for a preliminary ruling seeking such an interpretation – in the interest of the uniform application in all Member States of the level of protection of consumer rights guaranteed by the *Directive* – ask what aspects the national court may or must take into account should the general criteria laid down in the *Directive* apply to a particular individual term?

▶ If the national court itself observes, where the parties to the dispute have made no application to that effect, that a contractual term is potentially unfair, may it undertake, of its own motion, an examination with a view to establishing the factual and legal elements necessary to that examination where the national procedural rules permit that only if the parties so request?

(d) The ECJ's reasoning and conclusions

(aa) Conclusions regarding the third question originally referred: Informing the Minister of Justice

304. The ECJ first dealt with the answer to the third question originally referred. The ECJ held that the fact that the referring court simultaneously informed the Minister of Justice is not capable of influencing the mechanism of the dialogue between the courts in the form of the preliminary reference procedure, nor does it deter the national courts from referring preliminary questions.

(bb) The first and the second additional questions: The jurisdiction of the ECJ to interpret the concept of "unfair term" and the obligation of the national court to apply the interpretation to the facts of a particular case

305. The ECJ pointed out that it had jurisdiction to give a preliminary ruling on the interpretation of the treaties and the acts of the bodies, institutions, and other entities of the European Union without exception. Accordingly, the ECJ may be called upon by a national court to interpret concepts appearing in an instrument of secondary law, such as the concept of an "unfair term". Articles 3(1) and 4(1) of the *Directive*, taken as a whole, define the general criteria permitting an assessment as to whether the contractual terms subject to the provisions of the *Directive* are unfair.[180]

---

[180] The ECJ invoked its Judgment Case No. C-484/08 of 3 June 2010 (*Caja de Ahorros y Monte de Piedad de Madrid* v. *Asociación de Usuarios de Servicios Bancarios* [Ausbanc]), para. (33). The judgment in the *Ausbanc* case is briefly annotated in a footnote in the chapter on EU law / the *Directive*.

306.   Article 3 of the *Directive* merely defines in a general way the factors that render unfair a contractual term that has not been individually negotiated. **The Annex to which Article 3(3) of the *Directive* refers contains only an indicative and non-exhaustive list of terms which may be regarded as unfair.** Article 4 of the *Directive* provides that the **unfairness of a contractual term is to be assessed while taking into account the nature of the goods or services** for which the contract was concluded and by referring, at the time of conclusion of the contract, to all the circumstances attending the conclusion of it.[181] Against that background, it is for the national court to determine whether a contractual term satisfies the criteria of being categorized as "unfair".

307.   The ECJ therefore held that Article 267 TFEU must be interpreted as meaning that the jurisdiction of the ECJ extends both to the interpretation of the concept of *"unfair term"* used in Article 3(1) of the *Directive* and in the Annex thereto and to the criteria which the national court may or must apply when examining a contractual term in light of the provisions of the *Directive*. This examination must be conducted while bearing in mind that it is for that court to determine, in light of those criteria, whether a particular contractual term is actually unfair in the circumstances of the case.

(cc)   The third additional question: The obligation of the court to undertake an *ex officio* review

308.   Referring to its previous case law (the ECJ's decisions in *Océano Grupo, Mostaza Claro,* and *Asturcom*), the ECJ held that the national court must ascertain whether a contractual term which is the subject of the dispute before it falls within the scope of that *Directive*. If it does, that court must assess that term, if necessary, of its own motion, in light of the requirements of consumer protection laid down by that *Directive*.

309.   As regards the **first stage of examination** to be carried out by the national court, it appears from Article 1 in conjunction with Article 3 of the *Directive* that the *Directive* applies to any term conferring exclusive territorial jurisdiction appearing in a contract concluded between a professional and a consumer which was not individually negotiated. In order to safeguard the effectiveness of the consumer protection intended by the EU legislature, the national court must thus, in all cases and whatever the rules of its domestic law, determine whether or not the contested term was individually negotiated. The author believes that the same rule will clearly apply to arbitration clauses as well.

---

[181] The ECJ invoked its Judgment Case No. C-243/08 of 4 June 2009 (*Pannon GSM Zrt v. Sustikné Győrfi Erzsébet [Pannon GSM]*), paras. (37) through (39).

310.	As regards the **second stage of that examination**, it must be found that the contractual term which is the subject of the dispute in the main proceedings provides, as the referring court states, for the exclusive territorial jurisdiction of a court, which is neither the court in whose jurisdiction the respondent lives nor the court with jurisdiction for the place where the applicant has its registered office but the court, which is situated close to the registered office of the applicant **both geographically and in terms of transport links.** As regards a term, which is included without being individually negotiated in a consumer contract within the meaning of the *Directive*, where it confers **exclusive jurisdiction on a court** in the territorial jurisdiction of which the professional has his principal place of business, the ECJ held that it follows that such a term must be regarded as unfair within the meaning of Article 3 of the *Directive* in so far as it causes, **contrary to the requirement of good faith, a significant imbalance in the parties' rights and obligations arising under the contract, to the detriment of the consumer.**[182] The national court must investigate of its own motion whether a term conferring exclusive territorial jurisdiction falls within the scope of the *Directive*. If it does, the court shall assess of its own motion whether such a term is unfair.

III.10   Requirements imposed on EU Member States

311.	The Treaty on the EC (TEC) requires that the Member States implement directives in their national law. Whereas material incorporation is mandatory, the form and method of the implementation of directives depend on the approach adopted by the Member State concerned.[183] Although the *Directive* did, to some extent, lay down the fundamental principles regarding arbitration in consumer disputes, the national laws on arbitration adopted in the individual states (i.e. the EU Member States) exhibit major differences. As analyzed below, these differences also have a significant impact on court proceedings conducted in connection with arbitration and on the resolution of consumer disputes.

An excursus into individual national laws, including the laws of many EU countries, follows in the next chapter of this book.

---

[182] The ECJ invoked its previous case law, namely the Judgment of the ECJ, Joined Cases C-240/98 through C-244/98 *Océano Grupo Editorial SA et Rocío Murciano Quintero and between Salvat Editores SA et José M. Sánchez Alcón Prades et al*, para. (24). The judgment was published in: ECR [2000] I-4941. This decision is annotated above.
[183] Article 288 TFEU, ex Article 249 TEC.

IV. Consumer Arbitration in Selected Countries

IV.1. [AUT] [AUSTRIA]

IV.1.1. Principles and sources of consumer protection (substantive-law basis)

312.   The Austrian General Civil Code (ABGB [AUT]) has traditionally laid down rules for protection against **immoral contractual terms**. In 1979, the Code was supplemented with special provisions which stipulated that the other party to the contract must be **explicitly informed about any irregular and [potentially] detrimental terms**. Section 879(3) of the ABGB [AUT] stipulates that a contractual term is invalid if the obligation is significantly detrimental to one of the parties. The Consumer Protection Act (KSchG [AUT]), in effect since 1979, contains special provisions regulating **public supervision over the contents of contractual terms** exercised by consumer protection organizations and associations.

313.   General provisions (*general clause*) are primarily incorporated in Section 2(2) of the KSchG [AUT] which stipulates that a term is without effect if it departs, to the detriment of the consumer, from the rules incorporated in that chapter of the Consumer Protection Act. However, Austrian law, namely consumer protection laws (especially the Consumer Protection Act – KSchG [AUT]), is based on several levels of consumer protection mechanisms. Section 6(1) of the KSchG [AUT] generally declares as non-binding on the consumer *[für den Verbraucher... nicht verbindlich]* any terms which impair the position of the consumer vis-à-vis the professional (unacceptable provisions *[unzulässige Vertragsbestandteile]).* In conjunction with Section 879 of the AGBG [AUT], this constitutes invalidity *[Nichtigkeit,* i.e. literally *nullity]* which some legal systems classify as "absolute invalidity" (an absolute type of invalidity) assessed by the court of its own motion *(ex officio).* Other terms (other than those listed in Section 6(1) of the KSchG [AUT]) give rise to a burden of proof which requires the professional to prove that the contested contractual term was individually negotiated with the consumer. Another level of consumer protection mechanisms is incorporated in Section 6(3) of the KSchG [AUT] which declares ineffective *[unwirksam]* any unclear or unintelligible term in [general] contract terms and conditions or in standard form contracts; it is therefore a category analogous to *voidability* as enshrined in other legal systems (for instance, Czech law [CZE], etc.). However, if we return to the requirement of transparency *[Transparenzgebot],* the absence of *transparency* renders the relevant terms unfair, i.e. again absolutely invalid *(Nichtigkeit).* In certain cases, though, Austrian law de facto applies the concept of voidability which is based on the principles of autonomy, especially in those cases where the parties perform under their contract and express their interest in

abiding by the rules they have agreed on.[1] Choice-of-court agreements with consumers are without legal effects under Austrian law.[2]

IV.1.2. Consumer arbitration

314. Austria, whose legal rules are principally based on the UNCITRAL Model Law, amended its laws on arbitration (ZPO [AUT]) in 2005, with effect since 1 July 2006.[3] The arbitration laws in Austria [AUT] apply universally to both domestic and international disputes.[4] Rules on arbitrability are generally set forth in Part II of the ZPO [AUT].[5] The rules are obviously similar to German rules (the scope of which is even wider). In general, Austrian rules on arbitrability are more lenient as concerns the condition consisting in the possibility of a settlement regarding the subject matter of the dispute – in general, this possibility is de facto optional; it is mandatory only with respect to other than property claims. Conversely, Austrian law (when compared to German law or Czech law, for instance) is significantly more restrictive as concerns the arbitrability of consumer disputes. The current Austrian *lex arbitri* (ZPO [AUT]) contains special rules restricting consumer arbitration. Section 617 of the ZPO [AUT] reads as follows (approximate translation, cit.):[6] *(1) Arbitration agreements between an entrepreneur and a consumer may validly be concluded only for disputes that already exist. (2) Arbitration agreements to which a consumer is a party must be contained in a document which has been personally signed by the consumer. This document must not contain any other agreements other*

---

[1] Cf. Section 5e(4) of the KSchG [AUT] which reads as follows (approximate translation, cit.): *"Invalidity of the contract can be invoked only by the consumer. The professional cannot claim payment of the price or any partial consideration [orig. Wertminderung, i.e., literally, depreciation, meaning here partial compensation for the advantage supplied] for any performance provided by the professional despite the invalidity [ineffectiveness] of such contracts. The consumer may demand that the professional return any and all money and other performance accepted by the professional contrary to this provision."*

[2] Section 14 of the KSchG [AUT]. See also below, regarding special Austrian provisions concerning arbitration agreements with consumers.

[3] The Austrian Arbitration Act, 2006 (Sections 577–618 of the Austrian Code of Civil Procedure), in English published by J. Power, Austrian Arbitration Act 2006, Vienna (2006).

[4] This is just like in the Czech Republic [CZE], Germany [DEU], and in many other countries.

[5] ZPO-[AUT] (approximate translation, cit.) – Section 582 – *"(1) Any pecuniary claim that lies within the jurisdiction of the courts of law can be the subject of an arbitration agreement. An arbitration agreement on non-pecuniary claims shall be legally effective insofar as the parties are capable of concluding a settlement concerning the matter in dispute. (2) Claims in matters of family law as well as all claims based on contracts that are even only partly subject to the Austrian Landlord and Tenant Act (Mietrechtsgesetz) or to the Austrian Non-profit Housing Act (Wohnungsgemeinnützigkeitsgesetz), including all disputes regarding the conclusion, existence, termination and legal characterization of such contracts and all claims resulting from or in connection with the ownership of apartments may not be made subject to arbitral proceedings. Statutory provisions which are not included in this Chapter and according to which disputes may not or may only under certain circumstances be made subject to arbitral proceedings shall not be affected."*

[6] See the website of VIAC [AUT]. The translation to Czech of the text at the website was provided by the author of this book.

than such that refer to the arbitration proceedings. **(3)** *In arbitration agreements between an entrepreneur and a consumer, the consumer must, prior to the conclusion of the arbitration agreement, receive written legal advice on the significant differences between arbitration proceedings and proceedings before a court of law.* **(4)** *In arbitration agreements between entrepreneurs and consumers, the place of arbitration must be stipulated. The arbitral tribunal may only meet at a different place for an oral hearing or for the taking of evidence, if the consumer has approved or if considerable difficulties stand against the taking of evidence at the place of arbitration.* **(5)** *Where an arbitration agreement was concluded between an entrepreneur and a consumer and where the consumer at the time of concluding the arbitration agreement or at the time when the claim becomes pending, does not have his domicile, usual place of residence or place of employment in that state where the arbitral tribunal has its place of arbitration, the arbitration agreement shall only be of relevance if the consumer relies on the arbitration agreement.* **(6)** *An arbitral award shall also be set aside if in arbitration proceedings to which a consumer is party:* **1.** *Mandatory provisions of the law have been violated the application of which may not be waived by the choice of law of the parties, even in cases with international relevance; or* **2.** *The requirements of Article 530, paragraph (1), Numbers 6 and 7 [ZPO/AUT]* [7] *are fulfilled, according to which a judgment of a court of law could be appealed by means of an application for revision; in this case the time period for the filing of the action for setting aside shall be judged under the respective provisions regarding the application for revision.* **(7)** *Where the arbitration proceedings took place between an entrepreneur*

---

[7] ZPO [AUT] (approximate translation, cit.:) Section 520 – "(1) *Any proceedings terminated by a final decision on the merits may be reopened upon motion by any party, 1. if the underlying document was forged or altered; 2. if a witness, expert witness or the counterparty committed perjury* (Section 288 of the StGB [AUT; Austrian Criminal Code]) *and the decision is based on their testimony; 3. if the decision was affected by misleading information* (Section 108 of the StGB [AUT]), *embezzlement* (Section 134 of the StGB [AUT]), *fraud* (Section 146 of the StGB [AUT]), *forgery* (Section 223 of the StGB [AUT]), *forgery of specifically protected documents* (Section 224 of the StGB [AUT]) *or of public verification clauses* (Section 225 of the StGB [AUT]), *indirectly erroneous notarization or certification* (Section 228 of the StGB [AUT]), *suppression of a document* (Section 229 of the StGB [AUT]) *or relocation of border marks* (Section 230 of the StGB [AUT]) *committed by a counsel for a party, counterparty or his or her counsel; 4. if the judge committed a criminal offence of official misconduct when delivering a decision or a prior decision which served as the basis for the decision relating to the subject of the dispute, to the detriment of any party; 5. if a decision in a criminal case on which the decision relies was quashed by another final judgment; 6. if a party discovers a preceding final decision on the same cause of action or the same legal relationship or if it becomes possible to use a decision which establishes justice between the parties to the trial de novo; 7. if a party discovers new circumstances or evidence or if it becomes possible to use new evidence the invocation and application of which in the previous proceedings could result in a decision more favorable to the party. (2) Trial de novo on the grounds stipulated in paras. 6 and 7 is permissible only if the party, due to no fault of its own, did not have the opportunity to invoke the legal force and effect of the decision or the new circumstances or evidence before the closing of the hearing in which the trial court's decision was rendered.*" Adopted from: *http://www.viac.eu/images/stories/documents/en/New_Code_of_Civil_Procedure.pdf* [last access: 19 March 2012].

*and a consumer, the arbitral award is also to be set aside if the consumer
did not receive written legal advice as stipulated in paragraph (3).*

315. The principle laid down in the first sentence of the provision on
consumer arbitration incorporates a prohibition of arbitration clauses
(Section 617(1) of the ZPO [AUT]).[8] This principle is followed by
requirements regarding the formal requisites of an arbitration
agreement, which must be included in a separate document. The
arbitration agreement cannot be signed if the consumer did not receive
information (also in writing) about the differences between arbitration
and litigation. The arbitration agreement must also contain information
about the seat of the arbitral tribunal which should administer the
arbitration. As concerns consumer contracts concluded via the Internet,
it appears that this procedure of formation of a contract excludes the
possibility that the requirements for the form of the consensus of the
parties regarding the arbitration agreement could be fulfilled by mere
access to a website.[9] The generally recognized principle is that the
requirement of a written form is also fulfilled if the contract is concluded
by means of electronic communication.[10] This makes sense, considering
their current widespread use. After all, a number of new arbitration laws
refer to various types of electronic communications. The explicit
requirement of a document (separate document, etc.) clearly requires
the conclusion of the contract with the use of traditional instruments.

316. Consumers must be **supplied with the following information**: **(i)** a
concluded arbitration agreement which excludes the jurisdiction of
national courts in the merits of the dispute; and indicates **(ii)** that the
arbitrator shall be appointed by the contracting parties; **(iii)** that the
parties have only limited legal remedies to challenge the arbitral award
(above all, the impossibility of challenging the decision on the merits);
and includes **(iv)** a warning that the costs may differ from proceedings
before national courts and are not, usually, covered by legal liability
insurance, i.e. legal expenses insurance.[11]

---

[8] Quoted above in this book.

[9] As opposed to, for instance, the Canadian practice where consent with the arbitration agreement
given by electronic means was approved by the Supreme Court of Canada in its Decision Case No.
31067 of 13 July 2007 (*Dell* v. *Union des Consommateurs et Olivier Dumoulin*). An intervenor in the case
(a third party to the proceedings): Canadian Internet Policy and Public Interest Clinic, Public Interest
Advocacy Centre, ADR Chambers Inc., ADR Institute of Canada, Inc., and London Court of
International Arbitration. Cited under the Ref.: [2007] 2 S.C.R. 801 or 2007 SCC 34. Language of the
case: French. English translation available at: http://scc.lexum.org/en/2007/2007scc34/2007scc34.html.

[10] For instance, an amendment to the ICC Rules drawn up and approved in 2010 omits references to
an exchange of fax messages, which appear to be consigned to history, and explicitly introduces rules
regulating briefs submitted via Internet.

[11] *Riegler, T. et al.* Arbitration Law of Austria: Practice and Procedure. Huntington (New York):
JurisPublishing, 2007, p. 595.

317. Section 617 of the ZPO [AUT] also incorporates provisions on international consumer arbitration; if the consumer does not have his or her residence in the state where the respective arbitral tribunal resides (seat of arbitration), only the consumer may demand application of the arbitration agreement. The consumer's permanent residence is examined both at the time of conclusion of the arbitration agreement and pending the proceedings.[12]

318. These special rules are complemented by general consumer protection rules which generally provide for voidability (to be invoked by the consumer) of unfair terms in consumer contracts (Section 6 of the KSchG [AUT]).[13] However, a special regime applies with respect to agreements on jurisdiction; any such agreement is invalid and is assessed as invalid ex officio if the court chosen under the agreement is not the court which would have had jurisdiction according to the place of the consumer's residence (Section 14 of the KSchG [AUT]). Paragraph (7) of Section 6(2) of the KSchG [AUT] stipulates that arbitration clauses between the parties must be negotiated individually. Fulfillment of this requirement must be proven by the professional.[14]

319. The amendment to Austrian [AUT] civil procedure, i.e. the extensive amendment to the ZPO [AUT] implemented in 2002, principally supports arbitration. This concept was also supported by another amendment to the ZPO [AUT] of 2005 which reformed arbitration laws (*lex arbitri*) incorporated in the ZPO [AUT]. Domestic support for arbitration has been reflected in the institutionalization of arbitral tribunals associated with economic chambers. The special rule under para. (7) of Section 6(2) of the KSchG [AUT] is intended to guarantee that the consumer does not *overlook* the change in court jurisdiction, or rather the method of dispute resolution. The OGH [AUT] has held that the seat of arbitration must not be contrary to Section 14 of the KSchG [AUT] (residence of the consumer).[15]

320. The case law of Austrian courts has been fairly clear on whether consumer protection could be regarded as a component of *international public policy* and on whether it is possible to refuse recognition and

---

[12] *Riegler, T. et al.* Arbitration Law of Austria: Practice and Procedure. Huntington (New York): JurisPublishing, 2007, p. 595.

[13] Invalidity ex tunc pursuant to Section 6 of the KSchG [AUT] in conjunction with Section 879 of the AGBG [AUT]. However, this Austrian concept which originally tried to restore a balanced relationship between a "*reasonable professional*" and an "*average consumer*" is subject to interpretation mainly in connection with the ECJ's case law which stipulates the obligation of review ex officio.

[14] *Lurger, B. et Augenhofer, S.* Österreichisches und Europäisches Konsumentenschutzrecht. 2nd ed., Wien / New York: Springer, 2008, p. 116.

[15] *Lurger, B. et Augenhofer, S.* Österreichisches und Europäisches Konsumentenschutzrecht. 2nd ed., Wien / New York: Springer, 2008, pp. 130–131 (This is with reference to the consistent case law of the OGH [AUT], but without any further specification thereof.).

enforcement of a foreign arbitral award if such principles were breached in the place of the proceedings (in the place where the arbitral award was rendered) – the answer is negative. The landmark decision, and the most elaborate decision at the international level, is probably the decision of the Austrian Supreme Court (OGH [AUT]) Case No. 3 Ob 144/09m of 22 July 2009.[16] The Austrian Supreme Court (OGH [AUT]) has concluded that consumer protection is not a component of *international public policy*; it is not even a component of *EU public policy*. The court thus confirmed the conclusions reached by the ECJ in *Asturcom*, i.e. that consumer protection under EU standards does not interfere with the cross-border area in the enforcement and recognition of foreign arbitral awards. For a detailed annotation and analysis of this Austrian decision in this book, see the chapter on the enforcement of arbitral awards in connection with consumer protection.

IV.2. [BEL] [BELGIUM]

IV.2.1. Principles and sources

321.   Belgium [BEL] **allows** both arbitration and mediation in consumer disputes. Special authorities for the resolution of consumer disputes were set up in certain areas, such as the Arbitration Board for Travel, the Reconciliation Board for Construction, the Mediation Board for Banks-Credits-Investments and an Ombudsman for Telecommunications.[17]

IV.2.2. Arbitration

322.   Arbitration in Belgium is regulated by the Judicial Code [BEL] *(Code Judiciare)*, Articles 1676 through 1723.[18] This part of the Judicial Code [BEL] **contains no special provisions which would concern arbitration in consumer disputes**. The Belgian Judicial Code [BEL] stipulates that all disputes are arbitrable which can be subject to settlement, whether existing or potential future disputes. An arbitration clause (arbitration agreement) must be concluded in writing or in the form of another document binding on the party, which is an expression of their intent to submit their dispute to arbitration. Article 1678(1) of the Judicial Code [BEL] stipulates that an arbitration clause is invalid if it

---

[16] Decision of the OGH [AUT], Case No. 3 Ob 144/09m of 22 July 2009. Published in: (i) SZ 010/21 (Öhlberger) and in: (ii) the Bulletin of the Austrian Arbitration Association (ArbAut) at: http://www.cm.arbitration-austria.at/newsletter_detail.php?archiv_id=44 [last access 3 July 2010].

[17] European Consumer Centre Belgium Guide to solving your consumer issue. Online text, available at the website of the European Consumer Centre Belgium, 2006. Available online at: http://www.eccbelgium.be/images/downloads/Justice_en_1106%281%29.pdf [last access 21 December 2011].

[18] Available in the official languages and in English at the website of the Belgian Centre for Mediation and Arbitration, CEPANI (http://www.cepina.be/EN/Default.aspx?PId=859) [last access 21 December 2011].

grants advantages to one of the parties in the appointment of arbitrators. The number of arbitrators must be odd; it is possible to appoint a sole arbitrator. If the number of arbitrators in the arbitration clause is even, another arbitrator must be appointed so that the number is odd. In the absence of the parties' agreement on the number of arbitrators, the dispute shall be resolved by three arbitrators. The parties may either appoint the arbitrator(s) directly, or they may agree on a third party who/which will appoint the arbitrator(s) *(appointing authority)*.

IV.2.3. Mediation

323. Mediation is provided for in Articles 1724 through 1737 of the Mediation Act.[19] Like arbitration, any dispute which can be settled (the subject matter of which can be subject to settlement) can be subject to mediation. The relevant provisions of the Judicial Code [BEL] contain no special rules on mediation in consumer disputes. The Judicial Code [BEL] distinguishes (i) voluntary mediation from (ii) court-instigated mediation. Voluntary mediation can be initiated at the request of any party irrespective of any pending arbitration or litigation; the parties must agree on the mediator, or they can authorize a third party to select a mediator for them.

324. The court may order mediation if the parties explicitly request it, or if they at least agree with such procedure. The latter is possible only until the hearing in the case is over. The parties must agree on the mediator; the mediator must, however, also be approved by the Federal Mediation Commission [BEL]. The commission accredits mediators and thereby guarantees their expertise and professionalism. The parties may also propose a person who is not an accredited mediator; in such case, however, they must ask the court for approval and provide reasons for their request. The court agrees if it comes to the conclusion that the proposed person meets the conditions for an accredited mediator and if the parties have proven that no accredited mediator is available.

IV.3. [BGR] [BULGARIA]

IV.3.1. Arbitration

325. Arbitration has a longstanding tradition in Bulgaria. The legal framework for arbitration is very detailed, and has been further developed in voluminous case law (important examples of which are cited below in this chapter) and literature.[20] Bulgarian arbitration

---

[19] Available in English at the website of the Belgian Centre for Mediation and Arbitration, CEPANI (http://www.cepina.be/EN/Default.aspx?PId=950) [last access 21 December 2011].
[20] *Dragiev, A.* Meždunarodno pravoradavanije [Title in translation: Resolution of International Disputes], Sofia: Sibi 2006; *Zidarova, J.* Avtonomija na voljata – starodaven i svremenen princip na meždunarodnoto častno pravo. In: Avtonomija na voljata v meždunarodnoto častno pravo [Title in

practice is based on the contractual theory of arbitration. It does not consider arbitral tribunals as public authorities or special jurisdiction authorities.[21] It does not allow for a judicial review of arbitral awards on the merits, based on the assumption that the two systems are entirely separate and subject to different procedural rules,[22] even though the very basis of the possibility of excluding the jurisdiction of courts and replacing it with the jurisdiction of arbitrators rests upon provisions concerning civil litigation.[23]

326. Bulgarian law does not contain any rules explicitly regulating arbitration in consumer disputes. We must, however, take as the basis the principle broadly applied by Bulgarian courts according to which the nature of an arbitration agreement (arbitration clause) is similar to a choice-of-court agreement.[24] As concerns cross-border consumer disputes, deciding the

---

translation: Autonomy of Will – A Traditional and Contemporary Principle of Private International Law, In: Autonomy of Will in Private International Law]. Sofia: Sibi, 2008; *Petrov, R.* Sd´ili arbitraž pri meždunarodnite trgovski sporove [Title in translation: Litigation or Arbitration in International Commercial Disputes]. Sofia: Sibi, 2006; *Tomov, L.* Bulgaria – National Report. In: Arbitration 2010, Getting the Deal Through, London: Global Arbitration Review, Law Business Research 2010, pp. 68–73; Bulgaria – National Report and Note of the General Editor. In: *Paulsson, J.* (ed.) International Handbook on Commercial Arbitration, Last updated in March 2010, Supplement No. 58, KLI, 1984, (update) 2010, pp. i–ii and in many other publications.

[21] Judgment of the Bulgarian Supreme Court [Върховен съд)] No. 327, Civil Case No. 257/92 of 14 January 1993. Source: APIS 7 PRAVO [АПИС 7 ПРАВО legal information system]; Case Law, Bulletin of the Bulgarian Supreme Court, 1993, Vol. 2, No. 14, p. 12.

[22] For example:

> Judgment of the Bulgarian Supreme Court [Върховен съд)] No. 327, Civil Case No. 257/92 of 14 January 1993. Source: APIS 7 PRAVO [АПИС 7 ПРАВО legal information system]; Case Law, 2 Bulletin of the Bulgarian Supreme Court, 1993, Vol. 12, No. 14. For a detailed annotation, see also *Bělohlávek, A. et Rozehnalová, N.* CYArb – Czech (& Central European) Yearbook of Arbitration. Huntington (New York): JurisNet, 2011, Vol. I, pp. 329–330.

> Judgment of the Bulgarian Supreme Court [Върховен съд)] No. 440, Civil Case No. 286/94 of 29 June 1994. Source: APIS 7 PRAVO [АПИС 7 ПРАВО legal information system]; *Case law*, Bulletin of the Bulgarian Supreme Court, 1994, Vol. 3, No. 6. For a detailed annotation, see also *Bělohlávek, A. et Rozehnalová, N.* CYArb – Czech (& Central European) Yearbook of Arbitration. Huntington (New York): JurisNet, 2011, Vol. I, pp. 331–332.

> The fundamental requirement of a choice-of-court agreement under the general rules of Bulgarian civil procedure laws, similar to an agreement on the jurisdiction of arbitrators, is the absence of the exclusive jurisdiction of Bulgarian courts and a written agreement of the parties valid under the laws of the state of the forum. In other words, Bulgarian law is based on the principal importance of the seat of litigation, similar to the seat of arbitration.

> Cf. also Judgment of the Supreme Court of Cassation No. 9, Commercial Case No. 704/2008 of 16 February 2009; Source: APIS 7 PRAVO [АПИС 7 ПРАВО legal information system]. For a detailed annotation, see also *Bělohlávek, A. et Rozehnalová, N.* CYArb – Czech (& Central European) Yearbook of Arbitration. Huntington (New York): JurisNet, 2011, Vol. I, pp. 329–330.

[23] See Section 9 of the Bulgarian Code of Civil Procedure [BGR].

[24] See Section 9(3) of the Code of Civil Procedure [BGR]; approximate translation (cit.): "[...] (3) *(new, promulgated in the Coll., No. 55 of 1992) Subject to the conditions stipulated in paras. 1 and 2, the parties may apply to a foreign court to resolve a case which is not reserved for the exclusive jurisdiction of a Bulgarian court providing the parties give their consent in writing and the consent is effective under the law of the state in the territory of which the court resides. Subject to the same conditions, a*

choice-of-court is permissible only after the dispute arises.[25] In other words, arbitration and consumer disputes are subject to analogous restrictions.

IV.3.2. Mediation

327. Mediation in Bulgaria is a fairly new and rarely used method of alternative dispute resolution. The Bulgarian Act on Mediation[26] was adopted in 2004. Mediation is a voluntary and confidential procedure for the out-of-court resolution of disputes. As a rule, mediation can be used in parallel to both litigation and arbitration. The disputes submitted to mediation may include civil, commercial, employment, or family disputes, or even **consumer protection disputes**,[27] as well as other disputes between

---

Bulgarian court can be authorized to resolve a dispute falling within the jurisdiction of a foreign court." In other words, the parties are given the option of agreeing on the jurisdiction of court (*a choice-of-court agreement*).

[25] See Section 16 of the Act on Private International Law [BGR]; approximate translation (cit.:) Section 16. *"(1) Bulgarian courts also have jurisdiction to hear and resolve claims filed by consumers, save for the cases pursuant to Section 4, if the consumer's habitual residence is in the territory of the Republic of Bulgaria and the requirements under Section 95(2) are met. (2) An agreement on the choice of the competent court is allowed only if concluded after the dispute arose."* The same applies by analogy to employment disputes (Section 17 of the Act on Private International Law [BGR]). The law applicable to consumer contracts with an international dimension is provided for in Section 95 of the Act on Private International Law [BGR]. The relevant provision reads as follows: [approximate translation (cit.):] Section 95 – *"(1) Within the meaning of this Act, a 'consumer contract' means a contract under which one of the parties is a person who acquires goods, uses services, or receives a loan or credit to satisfy his or her own [personal] needs or the needs of his or her family, rather than for sale, production or practice of a trade. (2) A consumer contract shall be governed by the law chosen by the parties. The choice of the applicable law must not deprive the consumer of the protection afforded to him or her by the mandatory rules of the State in which the consumer is habitually resident, providing: 1. The conclusion of the contract in that State was preceded by a specific invitation addressed to the consumer or by advertising, and the consumer had taken in that State all the steps required for the conclusion of the contract, or 2. The other party or an agent of the party received the consumer's order in that State, or 3. The contract is for the sale of goods and, for the purpose of inducing the consumer to buy goods, the seller arranged the consumer's journey to another State where the consumer placed his or her order. (3) In the absence of choice of the applicable law by the parties, the contracts entered into in the circumstances described in para. (2) shall be governed by the law of the State in which the consumer is habitually resident. (4) The provisions of paras. (2) and (3) shall not apply to contracts of carriage nor to contracts for the supply of services where the services are to be supplied to the consumer exclusively in a State other than that in which the consumer is habitually resident. Any such contracts shall be governed by Sections 93 and 94. (5) The contracts which, for an inclusive price, provide for a combination of travel and accommodation, shall be governed by the law determined as the applicable law pursuant to paras. (2) and (3)."*
The original title of the Bulgarian Act on Private International Law [BGR]: Кодекс на международното частно право. Published in State Gazette [DV / ДВ - Държавен вестник], Edition No. 42 of 17 May 2005, as amended by the law published in: DV No. 59 of 20 July 2007, and the amendment published in: DV No. 47 of 23 June 2009.
[26] Published in the State Gazette No. 110/17.12.2004 of 17 December 2004. The text of the Act is also available in English at: http://medierea.ro/wp/?p=68 [last access 30 November 2010].
[27] Srbinova, D. Princip za zaščita na ikonomičeski po-slabata strana kato ograničitel na avtonomija na voljata pri potrebitelskite dogovori. In: Avtonomija na voljata v meždunarodnoto častno pravo [Title in translation: The Principle of Protecting the Weaker Economic Party as a Factor Limiting the

natural persons (individuals) and legal entities. Mediation cannot be used if another dispute resolution method is obligatory by law.

IV.4. [CAN] [CANADA]

IV.4.1. The approach adopted by certain provinces

328. The consumer arbitration regime in Canada [CAN] has two different levels – the level of the individual provinces and the federal level. Arbitration in consumer disputes in the individual provinces is governed by very detailed rules. In the *Stefan Kanitz* v. *Rogers Cable Inc.*[28] case of 2002, the **Ontario** Superior Court of Justice ruled that class actions were permissible. Subsequently, the province of Ontario [CAN] adopted a Consumer Protection Act whereby all prearbitration clauses in contracts concluded after 30 July 2005 were invalidated. Consumers may still, however, negotiate post-dispute arbitration agreements.

329. Arbitration clauses are similarly prohibited under the Consumer Protection Act adopted in the province of **Québec** [CAN]. The law explicitly prohibits any agreement which could limit the consumer's right to a class action in court.[29] The only province whose legal system is based on civil law principles is Québec [CAN]. In addition, Section 1437 of the Civil Code of Québec generally abolishes any clause in a consumer contract which unlawfully discriminates against the consumer; this provision also applies to arbitration clauses. Pursuant to Section 1453 of the same Code, the consumer must be informed about external terms which become part of consumer contracts, including arbitration clauses.[30] In the Dell case (*Union des consommateurs* v. *Dell Computer Corp.*),[31] the courts of Québec ruled that the external arbitration clause could not be enforced against the consumer.

330. The province of **Alberta** [CAN] has adopted a more lenient approach. It prescribes the obligation of a **fair approach to consumers**. Adherence to this principle can always be subject to examination. According to the applicable laws of Alberta [CAN], only arbitration clauses explicitly approved by laws can be incorporated in consumer contracts.

Autonomy of Will in Consumer Contracts, In: Autonomy of Will in Private International Law], Sofia: Sibi, 2008.

[28] [2002] O.J. No. 665. In academic literature, cited as the *"Kanitz"* case.
See *Svantesson, D.* Kanitz v. Rogers Cable Inc. – Time to rethink Article 4 of the proposed Hague Convention? 2002; available online at: http://www.cyberlawcentre.org/Articles/Research_Associates/Svantession_Kanitz_020627CLSR.htm [last access 10 September 2011].
[29] See *IA*. Options Consommateurs. L'arbitrage collectif : une solution pour les consommateurs? Etude présentée au Bureau de la consommation d'Industrie Canada, June 2007, p. vi.
[30] See *IA*. Options Consommateurs. L'arbitrage collectif : une solution pour les consommateurs? Etude présentée au Bureau de la consommation d'Industrie Canada, June 2007, p. 26.
[31] 2007 SCC 34.

IV.4.2. The federal approach

331. The federal level of the Canadian [CAN] system is similar to that of the United States. Nonetheless, the trend of subjecting arbitration in consumer disputes to certain restrictions is undeniable, and even though the decision in the *Dell* case was made in Québec [CAN], the only civil law province of Canada, it has been respected in other provinces, too. Moreover, in the *Seidel* v. *Telus Communications*[32] proceedings before the Federal Supreme Court of Canada, in May 2010, a requirement was voiced to recognize the decision in the *Dell* case as a source of law at the federal level.[33]

IV.4.3. Case law – Decision of the Supreme Court of Canada, Case No. 31067 of 13 July 2007 (*Dumoulin et Union des consommateurs* v. *Dell Computer Corp.*)

(a) Basic conclusions

332. The Canadian court[34] **made the following rulings** in the case:[35]
 ▶ The foreign element (dimension) must be a point of contact that is legally relevant to a foreign country, which means that the contact must be sufficient to play a role in determining whether a court has jurisdiction.[36]
 ▶ An arbitration clause is not in itself a foreign element (dimension) warranting the application of the rules of [Québec] private international law.
 ▶ Arbitration that contains no foreign element (dimension) in the true sense of the word is domestic arbitration.
 ▶ The neutrality of arbitration as a [procedural] institution is one of the fundamental characteristics of this alternative dispute resolution mechanism.

---

[32] 2009 BCCA 104. The case was heard in the Canadian Supreme Court in May 2010.
[33] *Schafler, M.* Arbitration trends in Canada: Deferring to arbitration with arbitrators in the driver's seat. IBA Arbitration News, March 2011, pp. 139–141, here especially p. 141. Available online at: http://www.bazilmcnulty.com/IBA_March_2011.pdf [last access 10 September 2011].
[34] Supreme Court of Canada.
[35] *Dell Computer Corp.* v. *Union des consommateurs.*
[36] Concerning the definition of the foreign element (international dimension), the Court quoted: *Talpis, J. A. et Castel, J. G.* Interpreting the rules of private international law. In: Reform of the Civil Code, Vol. 5B: Private International Law. Translation – *Altschul, S.* Material prepared for: Barreau du Québec and the Chambre des notaires du Québec. Montréal: Barreau du Québec, 1993, p. 38; *Walker, J.* Castel & Walker: Canadian Conflict of Laws. Vol. 1. Markham, Ont.: LexisNexis / Butterworths, 2005 (card catalog, here after an update in 2007, Edition No. 7), Vol. 1, pp. 1-1; see also *Wyler, É. et Papaux, P.* Extranéité de valeurs et de systèmes en droit international privé et en droit international public. In: *Wyler, É. et Papaux, A.* (eds.) L'extranéité ou le dépassement de l'ordre juridique étatique. Paris: Éditions A. Pédone, 1999, p. 239 et seq., here p. 256 (approximate translation, cit.): "*The foreign element must be a point of contact which is legally relevant to a foreign country, which means that the contact must be sufficient to play a role in determining whether a court has jurisdiction.*"

171

► Arbitration is an institution without a forum and without a geographical basis.

► The choice of procedure does not alter the institution of arbitration. The rules become those of the parties, regardless of where they are taken from.

► The facts that the applicable rules of the American [USA] arbitration organization provide that arbitrations will be governed by a U.S. statute and that English will be the language used in the proceedings are not relevant foreign elements (dimensions) for the purposes of the application of [Québec] private international law.

► In a case involving an arbitration agreement, any challenge to the arbitrator's jurisdiction must first be resolved by the arbitrator. A court should depart from the rule of systematic referral to arbitration only if the challenge to the arbitrator's jurisdiction is based solely on a question of law.[37]

► Where questions of mixed law and fact are concerned, the court must refer the case to arbitration unless the questions of fact require only superficial consideration of the documentary evidence in the record.

► The arbitration clause at issue, which could be accessed by means of a hyperlink in a contract entered into via the Internet, is not an external one (a separate term) within the meaning of Art. 1435 of the Civil Code of Québec and is valid.

► Access to the clause in electronic format must be no more difficult than access to its equivalent on paper. Otherwise, it would be an external clause.

► A contracting party cannot argue that a contract clause is binding unless the other party had a reasonable opportunity to read it.

► The traditional test of physical separation, which is applied to determine whether contractual stipulations in paper documents are external, cannot be transposed without qualification to the context of an arbitration clause negotiated via a website and an Internet hyperlink and its nature of a separate document. To determine whether clauses on the Internet are external clauses, therefore, it is necessary to consider another rule, i.e. the precondition of accessibility.

► The mere fact that a party (such as Mr. *Dumoulin)* decides to bring the matter before the courts by means of a class action rather than as an individual action does not affect the admissibility of his action.

---

[37] For the general rule, see Article 943 of the Québec Code of Civil Procedure [CAN] (approximate translation, cit.): "*The arbitrators may decide the matter of their own competence.*" For an exception to the general rule, see Article 940.1 of the Québec Code of Civil Procedure [CAN] (approximate translation, cit.): "*Where an action is brought regarding a dispute in a matter on which the parties have an arbitration agreement, the court shall refer them to arbitration on the application of either of them unless the case has been inscribed on the roll or it finds the agreement null.*"

Access to the clause in electronic format must be no more difficult than access to its equivalent on paper.

▶ The choice of procedural rules in the arbitration agreement (arbitration clause) is not an essential requirement. An invalid agreement on procedural rules applicable to arbitration does not entail the invalidity of the entire arbitration agreement. If such individual term is invalid (for instance, under consumer protection laws), the agreement on jurisdiction of the arbitral tribunal continues to apply and the arbitration shall be governed by general rules.

▶ The decision on whether private international law applies to the given case, whether there is any eligible foreign element, and whether consumer protection laws should apply, as well as the assessment of other issues important for the interpretation of consumer protection laws, requires an examination of the facts of the case. For this purpose, the arbitrators are endowed with the same qualifications and the same instruments as courts and, if in doubt about the validity of the arbitration clause, the court should in such cases leave the decision of these issues primarily to the arbitral tribunal in compliance with the *"Kompetenz-Kompetenz"* principle.

(b) Factual and legal findings

333. Due to erroneous data at the website of the *Dell* company some products were offered for prices which were several times lower than the company intended to sell them for (namely, computers for $89 instead of $379, or for $118 instead of $549). One day after the offer was published, the company blocked access to the erroneous order pages through the usual address. Mr. *Dumoulin*, however, had at his disposal the *"deep link"* (i.e. the full original URL address leading to the final website with the original offer). The original address enabled him to access the original order pages with the erroneous data. He therefore ordered a computer at the lower price. The company then posted an announcement that it would not process orders for computers at the erroneous prices. When *Dell* refused to honor the order, the *Consumers' Union (Union des consommateurs)* and Mr. *Dumoulin* filed a motion for authorization to institute a class action against *Dell. Dell* applied for referral of the claim to arbitration pursuant to an arbitration clause and for dismissal of the motion for authorization to institute a class action. The Superior Court and the Court of Appeal held, for different reasons, that the arbitration clause could not be set up against Mr. *Dumoulin*. The Supreme Court overruled the decisions and allowed *Dell*'s appeal; the Supreme Court also held that the claim should be referred to arbitration and the motion for authorization to institute a class action should be dismissed.

(c) Arguments of the parties and the Court's legal conclusions

334. The trial court as well as the appellate court refused to recognize the arbitration clause and ruled, although for different reasons, that the arbitration clause could not be set up against the consumer. The Superior (trial) Court based its decision on the fact that the arbitration under the clause was to be governed by the rules of an institution[38] located in the United States. This led the court to conclude that there was a foreign element for purposes of the rules of Québec private international law and that the prohibition under Art. 3149 of the Civil Code of Québec [CAN][39] should apply, according to which the arbitration clause is invalid. The Supreme Court did not, however, agree with the basic premise, i.e. that the dispute involved a foreign element (dimension). The Supreme Court held that the seat of the arbitral institution, to the rules of which the arbitration clause referred, is not legally relevant for the determination of the foreign element (dimension). The seat of the arbitral institution has no impact on the disputes in which its rules are used. Another potential foreign element (dimension) was found in the fact that the applicable rules provide that, unless the parties agree otherwise, arbitrations and arbitration procedures are governed by the U.S. Federal Arbitration Act [FAA [USA]]). However, by interpreting Article 3111 of the Civil Code of Québec [CAN],[40] the Supreme Court concluded that the determination of applicable law by the parties does not in itself constitute a foreign element (dimension). And the choice of English as the language of proceedings in Canada could not, in the Court's opinion, be characterized as a foreign element (dimension), although the Court agreed that the use of a language with which the consumer is not familiar may cause difficulties.

335. Contrary to the trial court, the Court of Appeal disagreed with the application of the rules of private international law. This court accepted the statement presented by the *Consumers' Union* which classified the arbitration clause as an *external* clause, rendering the clause invalid, which enabled the Court of Appeal to apply Art. 1435 of the Civil Code of *Québec* [CAN],[41] which declares such a clause invalid. According to

---

[38] National Arbitration Forum (NAF).

[39] Civil Code of the Province of Québec [CAN], Article 3149 (approximate translation, cit.): "*A Québec authority also has jurisdiction to hear an action involving a consumer contract or a contract of employment if the consumer or worker has his domicile or residence in Québec; the waiver of such jurisdiction by the consumer or worker may not be set up against him.*"

[40] Civil Code of the Province of Québec [CAN], Article 3111 (approximate translation, cit.): "*A juridical act, whether or not it contains any foreign element, is governed by the law expressly designated in the act or the designation of which may be inferred with certainty from the terms of the act.* [...]"

[41] Civil Code of the Province of Québec [CAN], Article 1435 (approximate translation, cit.): "*An external clause referred to in a contract is binding on the parties. In a consumer contract or a contract*

the Court of Appeal, *Dell* had not proven that the arbitration clause had been explicitly brought to the consumer's attention. The Supreme Court first highlighted that the case at bar was the first in which the Québec Court of Appeal had had to consider whether a contract clause that can be accessed by means of a hyperlink in a contract entered into via the Internet can be considered to be an external clause. Previous disputes concerning the external nature of contractual stipulations had concerned paper (printed) documents. This is the reason why the traditional test of physical separation could not be applied to the determination of the external nature of an arbitration clause.[42] The Supreme Court therefore, conversely, applied the precondition of accessibility which it considered a suitable instrument for electronic documents. Thus, a clause that requires operations of such complexity that its text is not *reasonably accessible* cannot be regarded as an integral part of the contract. The Supreme Court argued that access to the arbitration clause in electronic format must be no more difficult to access than its equivalent on paper. In the present case, the evidence showed that the consumer could access the website containing the arbitration clause directly by clicking on the highlighted hyperlink entitled *"Terms and Conditions of Sale,"* and this link reappeared on every page the consumer accessed. The Court therefore found the arbitration clause sufficiently accessible. Consequently, the Court held that the clause was not an *external arbitration clause* within the meaning of Art. 1435 of the Civil Code of Québec [CAN][43] but a valid clause. The *Consumers' Union* also submitted, however, that the above-mentioned procedural rules were also a type of an external clause. According to the *Consumers' Union*, the hyperlink merely led to the home page of the American Arbitration Association [AAA US], whereas the procedural rules themselves had to be searched for by the consumer himself/herself. Although the Supreme Court was not sure whether such a document could be designated as an external clause, the Court held that even if the procedural rules were in fact an external clause (i.e. a clause null and void pursuant to Art. 1435 of the Civil Code of Québec [CAN]), that would not affect the validity of the arbitration clause as such. The arbitration procedure would then simply be governed by the Code of Civil Procedure. Consequently, the Supreme Court concluded that the choice of certain procedural rules is not an essential requirement of an arbitration agreement and that it is a separable term even as concerns the consequences of invalidity of such an individual term.

---

of adhesion, however, an external clause is null if, at the time of formation of the contract, it was not expressly brought to the attention of the consumer or adhering party, unless the other party proves that the consumer or adhering party otherwise knew of it."

[42] When dealing with the test of physical separation, the Supreme Court of Québec cited: *Lluelles, D. et Benoît, M. Droit des obligations.* Montréal: Thémis, 2006, p. 748 (approximate translation, cit.): *"A clause is external if it is physically separate from the contract."*

[43] The provision is quoted above.

336. The Supreme Court was primarily concerned with the nature of the arbitration clause, as well as of the arbitration as such. Specifically, the Court was called upon to determine whether the arbitration clause contained a foreign element (dimension), or how to distinguish domestic arbitration from international arbitration. In the reasons for its decision, the Court referred to, inter alia, the structure of the Civil Code of Québec [CAN]. The Court held that in order to ensure the internal consistency of the Civil Code, it is necessary to adopt a contextual interpretation that limits the scope of the provisions of the title on the "International jurisdiction of Québec authorities," under the "Private International Law" book, to situations with a relevant (legally significant) foreign element (dimension). The prohibition in Art. 3149 of the Civil Code of Québec [CAN] against waiving the jurisdiction of Québec authorities to the detriment of the consumer is found in that title and accordingly only applies to situations with a relevant foreign element (dimension). The Court also supported the limitation by reference to an opinion voiced in the preceding case law[44] according to which the incorporation of the provision in the law manifests the legislature's intent to protect the more vulnerable persons, namely consumers or workers. Because the Court held that an arbitration clause itself does not constitute a foreign element (dimension) which would be significant for the determination of jurisdiction, the provision cannot apply. The choice of the rules of procedure or the language of arbitration has no bearing on the fact that arbitration is a neutral institution without a forum and without a geographical basis.[45] Saying that arbitration itself establishes a connection to a given territory would be in outright contradiction to the very essence of the institution of arbitration: its neutrality. This means that the Court interprets the rules for arbitration agreed on by the parties when they concluded the arbitration clause as the rules chosen by these particular parties,[46] not as the rules of a particular institution even if the parties had adopted the rules from the institution. The choice of the English language as the language of the proceedings and the choice of the AAA Rules [USA] as the rules for arbitration is not in itself a foreign element (dimension) for the purposes of applying Québec

---

[44] See the decision delivered by the judge of the Québec Court of Appeal in the Dominion Bridge case (approximate translation, cit.): *"In my view, it is clear that the legislature intended to ensure that employees could not be required to go abroad to assert rights under a contract of employment."*

[45] See *Guillemard, S.* Le droit international privé face au contrat de vente cyberspatial. Cowansville, Qué.: Yvon Blais, 2006, p. 77; *Thuilleaux, S.* L'arbitrage commercial au Québec: Droit interne — Droit international privé. Cowansville, Qué.: Yvon Blais, 1991, p. 145.

[46] Concerning the nature of arbitration as an expression of the principle of autonomy of the parties, the court quoted another Canadian decision in *Laurentienne-vie, compagnie d'assurance inc.* v. *Empire, compagnie d'assurance-vie*, [2000] R.J.Q. 1708 (C.A.), specifically paras. (13) and (16) (approximate translation, cit.): *"Arbitration is a creature that owes its existence to the will of the parties alone."*

private international law, nor can such proceedings be considered as international arbitration.[47]

337. In the dissenting opinion of some of the judges, however, a different view was expressed, namely that one should not attach any significance to the structure of the Civil Code of Québec or the Code of Civil Procedure when interpreting the substantive provisions under review here. According to the dissenting opinion, the Civil Code of Québec [CAN] constitutes an ensemble which is not meant to be parceled out into chapters and sections that are not interrelated. The opinion of the dissenting judges also departed from the majority opinion as concerns the nature of the arbitration clause itself. According to the dissenting opinion, the arbitration clause itself does not constitute a foreign element (dimension) necessary for the application of private international law. No arbitrator selected by a contract can be a Québec authority within the meaning of Art. 3149 of the Civil Code of Québec [CAN] and, similarly, no arbitrator bound by U.S. law can be such an authority either. The fact that the arbitration is to be conducted in English only supports this conclusion. According to the dissenting opinion, we should therefore apply Art. 3149 of the Civil Code of Québec [CAN]. These *dissenting opinions*, however, did not prevail over the majority opinion of the judges.

338. The general rule of the Code of Civil Procedure, which the respondent company unsuccessfully invoked in the Court of Appeal, stipulates that *"the arbitrators may decide the matter of their own competence."*[48] Pursuant to another provision[49] of the same Code, the court must refer the parties to arbitration on the application of either of them, unless it finds the arbitration clause null.[50] According to the Court, this exception

[47] The court noted, however, that the determination of the foreign element (dimension) with respect to international arbitration is different from the determination of whether the case concerns international commerce or not. An ordinary contract may have foreign elements (dimensions) without involving any matters of extraprovincial or international commerce. And although the resulting arbitration will not be considered an international arbitration, it will nonetheless be subject to the rules of private international law.
[48] Code of Civil Procedure of the province of Québec [CAN], Article 943 – The provision is quoted in a footnote above.
[49] Code of Civil Procedure of the province of Québec [CAN], Article 940.1 – The provision is quoted in a footnote above.
[50] In that connection, the court also referred to the practice of the courts in Québec [CAN] which often recognize or refuse the validity of arbitration clauses but not with the required degree of attention. See the following decisions:
> *C.C.I.C. Consultech International* v. *Silverman*, [1991] R.D.J. 500 (C.A.);
> *Banque Nationale du Canada* v. *Premdev inc.*, [1997] Q.J. No. 689 (QL) (C.A.);
> *Acier Leroux inc.* v. *Tremblay*, [2004] R.J.Q. 839 (C.A.);
> *Robertson Building Systems Ltd.* v. *Constructions de la Source inc.*, [2006] Q.J. No. 3118 (QL), 2006 QCCA 461;
> *Compagnie nationale algérienne de navigation* v. *Pegasus Lines Ltd. S.A.*, [1994] Q.J. No. 329 (QL) (C.A.).

is justified by the courts' expertise in resolving such questions and by the rule that an arbitrator's decision regarding his or her jurisdiction can be reviewed by a court. In this particular dispute, the court applied the exception to the general rule in a situation where the arbitrator's jurisdiction was challenged, and it held that the exception must be interpreted as saying that the court should depart from the rule of systematic referral to arbitration only if the challenge to the arbitrator's jurisdiction is based solely on a question of law. If, however, the jurisdictional challenge requires the production and review of factual evidence, the court should normally refer the case to arbitration, as arbitrators have, for this purpose, the same resources and expertise as courts. In the case at bar, the parties raised questions of law relating to the application of the provisions on private international law, determining the existence of a foreign element (dimension) or the assessment of the external nature of the arbitration clause. The Court was of the opinion, though, that this requires not only the interpretation of the legal rule, but also an analysis of the facts and a review of documents and hearing of witnesses. Consequently, the Supreme Court concluded that the case should have been referred to arbitration. According to the dissenting opinion of certain courts, however, the courts below were correct to fully consider, at the request of the claimant, Mr. *Dumoulin*, the validity of the arbitration agreement and to rule on the agreement based on the application of Art. 3149 Civil Code of Québec [CAN]. According to the dissenting legal opinion, which did not prevail in the resulting opinion, the court should rule on the validity of the arbitration agreement only if it is possible to do so on the basis of documents and pleadings filed by the parties without having to hear evidence or make findings about its relevance and reliability. The dissenting opinion argued that the present case was primarily concerned with the interpretation of the law, whether it would have been a more suitable solution if the courts had decided the issue themselves. At the same time, the *dissenting judges* pointed out that in some circumstances, particularly in international commercial arbitration, it may be more efficient to submit all questions regarding jurisdiction for the arbitrator to hear at first instance.

339. Finally, the authors of the dissenting opinion considered the nature of the *adhesion contract*; specifically, they criticized the arguments presented by the respondents in the proceedings before the Supreme Court (Mr. *Dumoulin* and the *Consumers' Union*) according to which the principle of the autonomy of the parties was not applied, because the arbitration clause formed part of a contract of adhesion. In other words, they claimed that Mr. *Dumoulin* should not be bound by the arbitration clause, because he did not truly consent to be bound by the contract in which the clause is incorporated. The dissenting judges pointed out that, although the adhesion contract means that one of the parties cannot

negotiate its terms, this party still has the option of deciding to enter into the contract or not. They therefore supported the view according to which the will of the parties to an adhesion contract is only reduced to a minimum, but it is not a unilateral juridical act, it is a valid contract.[51]

IV.5. [CZE] [CZECH REPUBLIC]

IV.5.1. Arbitration laws

(a) Legal basis and importance of arbitration in the Czech Republic

340.   Arbitration has a long tradition in the Czech Republic and enjoys strong legislative support; it is regulated under a separate law – the Arbitration Act (Act [CZE] No. 216/1994 Coll., on Arbitration and Enforcement of Arbitral Awards, as amended – "ArbAct [CZE]"). Following a lengthy and somewhat quarrelsome debate, an extensive Amendment to the Arbitration Act was adopted and came into effect on 1 April 2012 ("Amendment to the ArbAct [CZE]"). The purpose of the amendment was to define conditions for arbitral proceedings relating to consumer disputes (disputes arising under contracts entered into by consumers), which, for all intents and purposes, could and still can in the Czech Republic be settled through arbitration (such disputes are arbitrable). The text of the Arbitration Act (ArbAct [CZE]) effective until 31 March 2012, however, did not contain any provision to this effect, causing numerous doubts as to the arbitrability of consumer contracts, and as to whether or not Czech law requires arbitration clauses in consumer contracts to be generally considered as unfair and consequently invalid in the sense of the *Directive* and the substantive rules of Czech consumer protection legislation.[52] Until recently, interpretation according to the *lex arbitri* [CZE] was based on the "*Kompetenz-Kompetenz*" principle.[53] The quite extensive case law of [general] Czech courts and of the Constitutional Court, annotated in detail in the final section of this excursion into Czech law, contains relatively frequent references to this issue. Despite the fact that it is somewhat ambiguous and not always consistent, the case law contains numerous references that indicate that arbitration clauses in consumer contracts are

---

[51] See *Jobin, P.-G.* (ed.) Baudouin et Jobin: Les obligations, 6th ed. Cowansville, Qué.: Yvon Blais, 2005, p. 79.

[52] For an excursus into the substantive provisions regulating consumer protection in the Czech Republic [CZE], especially with respect to the interpretation of arbitration clauses and other similar provisions – see below.

[53] See *Rozehnalová, N.* Zásada autonomie a zásada rozhodování rozhodců o své pravomoci – dvě stránky jednoho problému. [Title in translation: The Principle of Autonomy and the Principle of Jurisdiction Decisions Adopted by Arbitrators – Two Sides to a Single Problem]. Časopis pro právní vědu a praxi. 2008, No. 2, pp. 112–121.

essentially acceptable and that consumer disputes are generally arbitrable, i.e. may be submitted to arbitration.[54] The ambiguity concerns the approach to the assessment of unfairness of such clauses with respect to specific contracts and specific disputes. In light of the number of disputes settled through arbitration in the Czech Republic, another aspect that needs to be considered is that the issue is sensitive from a political viewpoint. Due to the absence of the exequatur procedure in relation to domestic arbitral awards,[55] which serve as the basis for enforcement after their delivery to the parties (after they become final) only if approved by a court, there are no exact statistics as to the number of disputes resolved in the Czech Republic. According to the estimates of the Czech Ministry of Justice, however, some 150,000 disputes are heard and settled through arbitration every year, where most of them are resolved in *ad hoc* proceedings, and most concern consumer contracts (contracts entered into by consumers). Such a unique popularity of arbitration shows how important this issue is, and explains why the discussion preceding the Amendment to the ArbAct [CZE] was so extensive.

341.   According to Section 2(1) of the ArbAct [CZE], **all property disputes may be submitted to arbitration if such disputes can be subject to settlement, with the exception of disputes related to the enforcement of decisions and incidental disputes**.[56] In determining whether a private dispute may be settled in arbitration, Czech law does not take into account the status and nature of the contracting parties (parties to the dispute);[57] thus, there are no specific criteria for contracts under which one of the parties acts as a consumer. Until the adoption of the Amendment to the ArbAct [CZE], Czech law contained no explicit exception in relation to consumer disputes and their settlement in arbitration. The only interpretation regarding the validity of arbitration clauses in consumer contracts was therefore possible based on the substantive rules of consumer protection laws that protect consumers

---

[54] Lower courts often considered arbitration clauses as invalid ex lege, irrespective of the circumstances of the individual cases, and their decisions were being overruled only in the appeal proceedings or in the cassation appeal proceedings in the Supreme Court of the Czech Republic [SC CR [CZE]). Conversely, the SC CR [CZE] usually did not (at least at the general level) find arbitration clauses contrary to consumer protection laws (see Resolution of the SC CR [CZE], Case No. 32 Cdo 1590/2008 of 30 March 2009). This issue was also frequently referred to by the Constitutional Court of the Czech Republic [CZE] ("ConCourt CR [CZE]").

[55] The concept is similar to Austrian law. However, Austrian law is – as concerns the arbitrability of consumer disputes – rather restrictive and principally excludes arbitration clauses in consumer disputes (see the separate excursus into Austrian law).

[56] This concerns disputes over the scope of the bankrupt's assets in insolvency proceedings.

[57] This applies except for disputes from agreements entered into by public, non-profit health care facilities established under a special law. Such disputes are not arbitrable under Section 1(2) of the ArbAct [CZE]. This is the only exception recognized by Czech arbitration laws as an exception to arbitrability contingent on the status (nature) of a contracting party.

against unfair contractual terms. Nonetheless, the arbitrability of such disputes has never been principally excluded.

(b) Amendment to the Arbitration Act (Czech arbitration law in effect since 1 April 2012)

(aa) Concept of the Amendment to the ArbAct [CZE]

342. The new law preserves the existing scope of the ArbAct [CZE] which continues to apply to consumer disputes. The ArbAct [CZE], however, now contains explicit provisions intended to protect consumers. A comparable conceptual approach can be found, for example, in German law, which is very similar to the principles of current Czech legislation. At the same time, the Amendment to the ArbAct [CZE] takes into account the elements proposed in the *Recommendation* (EC).

343. Effective as of 1 April 2012, the new arbitration law in the Czech Republic (Amendment to the ArbAct [CZE]) explicitly introduced especially the following **new elements of consumer protection** (with regard to arbitration agreements entered into by consumers):

▶ An arbitration agreement must be contained in a **document separate** from the terms that define the other rights and obligations of the contracting parties, i.e. an arbitration agreement must be in a document separate from the "*main contract*" (a failure to comply with this requirement may render such an agreement invalid).[58]

▶ The amendment defines the **minimum mandatory content of an arbitration agreement**.

▶ The new legislation introduces **stricter requirements for arbitrators** in relation to consumer disputes.

▶ The law now expressly states that disputes under **contracts entered into by consumers may only be resolved according to valid laws**, and that all arbitral awards **must contain reasons**.[59]

▶ An arbitral award relating to a **consumer dispute must include an explicit instruction** that a **motion may be filed** demanding a court annul (set aside) the award.[60]

▶ The amendment introduces a **publicly available list of arbitrators** who have the (sole) authorization to settle **consumer disputes** (this

---

[58] As emphasized elsewhere in this book, we cannot dismiss the necessity of an extensive examination of the behavior of a specifically informed consumer, not only at the conclusion of the contract (although this particular moment is usually crucial) but also at the stage of performing the contract and making claims under the contract. For more details regarding this issue, see Chapter III.9 of this book in connection with the ECJ's ruling in *Pannon GSM*.

[59] If the dispute arises from a contract other than a consumer contract, the present rules apply, i.e. the parties may agree that the dispute will be resolved according to the principles of equity (*ex aequo et bono*) and may also request that the arbitral award be issued without reasons.

[60] The second sentence of Section 25(2) of the ArbAct [CZE] as amended by the Amendment to the ArbAct [CZE].

list is intended to provide information on whether individual arbitrators are eligible for resolving disputes of this kind, and at the same time, whether they are subject to the supervision of the Czech Ministry of Justice).

▶ During proceedings pertaining to the **annulment of an arbitral award**, a court **may examine** whether an arbitrator or a *permanent arbitral institution* resolved a consumer dispute contrary to consumer protection laws, clearly in violation of good morals, or contrary to *public policy*. There has been an extensive debate about the proposed legislation regarding the option of reviewing the merits of the case, i.e. whether the award has been delivered in accordance with substantive law. Such a procedure would involve a special review conducted by a court; arbitrators would in such case essentially deliver rulings corresponding to judgments delivered by courts in trial. **However, the option of reviewing arbitral awards relating to the merits of consumer disputes**, which was strongly advocated by certain political groups and was to be, understandably, restricted to consumer disputes, **was not accepted during the discussion on the proposed requirements for arbitral awards.**

344. These measures expand the possibilities of protecting the consumer, and increase his or her awareness of the nature and procedure of arbitration. Like other types of cases, however, consumer disputes **observe the basic principles of arbitral proceedings,** influenced by the autonomy of will of the parties. First, the stronger party must, previously during the stage preceding a potential dispute, fulfill mandatory conditions that consist of providing information to the prescribed extent, and second, the law introduces **stricter requirements for arbitrators** and their impartiality. At the same time, however, the consumer must be aware of the potential consequences of negotiating an arbitration agreement, i.e. the waiver of his or her right to have a dispute heard and settled by a court. Hence, the law does not protect persons (consumers) who, despite all the information they receive, act in a careless and negligent manner.[61]

345. Beyond mechanisms targeting consumer protection, the Amendment to the ArbAct [CZE] also deals with some other problems that have emerged during the application of the *lex arbitri* in the past. Probably the most important issue that has been causing much *turmoil* in Czech arbitration practice for the past several years is the functioning of

---

[61] Refusal to protect a consumer who behaves in such manner is also approved by the case law of the Supreme Court of the Czech Republic, see:
➢ Judgment of the SC CR [CZE], Case No. 23 Cdo 1201/2009 of 29 June 2010;
➢ Resolution of the SC CR [CZE], Case No. 23 Cdo 4895/2009 of 28 April 2010.
According to the SC CR [CZE] (cit.): *"Consumer protection has its limits; it can in no case be interpreted as a defense of the consumer's recklessness and irresponsibility."*

arbitration centers.[62] These are entities that do not meet the conditions set out in the ArbAct [CZE] for *permanent arbitral institutions,* but these *arbitration centers* nonetheless organize the settlement of disputes (they formally provide resources to arbitrators in *"ad hoc"* proceedings). Czech arbitration laws have been based on the notion that *permanent arbitral institutions* may only be established based on the law,[63] where a strict distinction exists between proceedings before such *permanent arbitral institutions* and proceedings before *ad hoc* arbitrators. This principle has not only been preserved, but also strengthened by the following explicit stipulation that aims to prevent interpretation problems (cit.): *"Permanent arbitral institutions may only be established under another law or only if another law expressly allows their establishment."*[64] At the same time, the law explicitly prohibits the use of designations in the names of legal entities based on which such entities could be mistaken for *permanent arbitral institutions.*[65] In addition, the Amendment to the ArbAct [CZE] expands the objective arbitrability of disputes. This is because, up till now, only disputes falling within the jurisdiction of courts could be resolved through arbitration. Even though this issue had been controversial for some time, disputes falling within the jurisdiction of other authorities had been excluded from objective arbitrability. The Arbitration Act now allows the hearing of such disputes, but only on the condition that special laws contain provisions to this effect. Together with the Amendment to the ArbAct [CZE], the legislators also approved an amendment to the Electronic Communication Act,[66] which allows negotiating arbitration agreements regarding financial disputes arising under said Act (disputes with operators, in particular). Expanding the application of the Act (objective arbitrability) is therefore subject to a direct modification of special laws, which will allow negotiating arbitration clauses in disputes that are not in the general jurisdiction of courts.

346.   Other changes introduced by the Amendment to the ArbAct [CZE] concern:

> ▶ Release from the obligation of confidentiality, the procedure defines the course of action to be taken in the event the whereabouts of an arbitrator are unknown;

---

[62] These issues are very controversial, as the number of disputes to which they gave rise confirms. Some of the important rulings of the [lower] courts as well as the Constitutional Court of the Czech Republic [CZE] are annotated in the final part of this chapter on Czech law (*"Case Law"*).

[63] Section 13(1) of the ArbAct [CZE], the version applicable until 31 March 2012.

[64] Section 13(1) of the ArbAct [CZE], the version applicable since 1 April 2012 (Amendment to the ArbAct [CZE]).

[65] Section 13(4) of the ArbAct [CZE], the version applicable since 1 April 2012 (Amendment to the ArbAct [CZE]).

[66] Act [CZE] No. 127/2005 Coll., on Electronic Communications and Amending Certain Related Legislation, as subsequently amended.

▶ Termination of the arbitral proceedings; and

▶ New grounds for deferring the effect of an arbitral award if it is apparent that a motion to annul the arbitral award is justified and will be allowed,[67] etc.

(bb) Arbitration agreement concluded by a consumer (arbitration agreement for consumer disputes)

347.   The Amendment to the ArbAct [CZE] is based on the idea that, in an arbitration agreement, the contracting parties waive their right to have a consumer dispute heard before a court and delegate this jurisdiction to a private entity. Consumer disputes will be subject to a separately negotiated arbitration agreement (separate document) which will not be included among the terms of the main contract (a failure to comply with this requirement may invalidate the contract). Such an approach will prohibit a situation in which an arbitration clause is included, for instance, in the business terms and conditions.

348.   An arbitration agreement for consumer disputes must specify the following obligatory data (the data must be accurate and complete):

▶ Information on the arbitrator or the fact that the arbitral award will be delivered by a *permanent arbitral institution*,

▶ Information on the manner in which arbitration proceedings are to be initiated and conducted,

▶ Information on remuneration paid to the arbitrator, the anticipated types of costs the consumer may incur in the arbitral proceedings, and the rules for successfully claiming compensation for such costs,

▶ Information on the seat of arbitration,

▶ Information on the method of service of the arbitral award to the consumer, and

▶ Information stating that a final arbitral award is enforceable.

349.   If the parties agree to the jurisdiction of a *permanent arbitral institution*, it is considered sufficient if the arbitration agreement contains a reference to the statutes and rules of such *permanent arbitral institutions*.[68]

350.   The Amendment to the ArbAct [CZE] has defined in a more exact manner and, in relation to **consumer disputes, has also introduced stricter requirements for the discharge of the arbitrator's duties of office**.[69] As before, arbitrators must conform to the general age

---

[67] The objective of this particular point in the Amendment to the ArbAct [CZE] is to prevent manifest excesses, such as the possibility of an enforceable arbitral award issued without any underlying arbitration agreement.

[68] These must be published in the *Business Journal* (just like under the previous provisions).

[69] Section 4 of the ArbAct [CZE].

requirements and be fully qualified for legal (juridical) acts.[70] In addition, arbitrators must have a **clean criminal record**.[71] Beginning 1 April 2012, the law will also require arbitrators handling consumer disputes to possess a **master's degree in law** obtained at a university in the Czech Republic or abroad, provided that such education is recognized by the Czech Republic [CZE] as equivalent to the applicable qualification in the Czech Republic based on an international treaty. Alternatively, such foreign education can be recognized under a special law which requires that the content and extent of such education correspond to the general education that is obtained in a master's law program at a university in the Czech Republic. These special conditions will be assessed by the Ministry of Justice of the Czech Republic during the registration of a person in the registry of arbitrators authorized to settle consumer disputes.[72] Such registration is a prerequisite for the discharge of the duties of office of an arbitrator handling disputes arising from contracts entered into by consumers. Another condition for entry into this registry is that the person to be registered must not have been stricken out from the list of arbitrators during the past five years based on a decision of the Ministry of Justice.[73]

(cc) Independence and impartiality of arbitrators

351. The new law that took effect on 1 April 2012 also introduces more precise and, in relation to consumer disputes, stricter conditions regarding the independence and impartiality of arbitrators. Compared to current legislation, the amendment preserves the obligation of an arbitrator to disclose to the parties information on any circumstances liable to raise doubts about the arbitrator's impartiality.[74] As to **consumer disputes**, arbitrators must inform the parties prior to hearing a case whether they have rendered a decision in any dispute involving one of the parties in the past three years (Section 8(3) of the ArbAct [CZE]).[75] In the event qualified information is provided to the parties

---

[70] The requirement of legal capacity for foreigners (i.e. persons other than citizens of the Czech Republic) is governed by their *lex patriae*. It shall suffice, however, if he or she has legal capacity under the laws of the Czech Republic. (Section 4(2) of the ArbAct [CZE] as amended by the Amendment to the ArbAct [CZE].)

[71] The requirement of no criminal record requires that the person must have no previous final and conclusive conviction for a criminal offence unless the person's criminal record is expunged and the person is deemed never to have been convicted. (Section 4(3) of the ArbAct [CZE] as amended by the Amendment to the ArbAct.)

[72] Section 35(1) of the ArbAct [CZE] as amended by the Amendment to the ArbAct.

[73] Section 35(1)(d) of the ArbAct [CZE] as amended by the Amendment to the ArbAct.

[74] Section 8(2) of the ArbAct [CZE].

[75] ArbAct [CZE] (cit.): Section 8 – "[...] (3) *When deciding consumer disputes, the arbitrator is obliged to inform the parties before the hearing whether he or she has made or participated in the making of an arbitral award in the past 3 years or whether he has been an arbitrator in a pending arbitration over a dispute to which any of the parties is or was a party. The time limit under the preceding sentence shall be calculated from the day when the arbitration covered by the reporting obligation*

(information on circumstances suggesting that an arbitrator should be excluded as biased), the parties may agree on another arbitrator. If no agreement is reached, however, a motion can be filed with a court in accordance with Section 12(2) of the ArbAct [CZE] to dismiss the arbitrator.[76]

IV.5.2. Protection of consumers under substantive law

(a) Sources and principles of consumer protection in contemporary legislation (CC [CZE])

352. Consumer contracts in the Czech Republic [CZE] are regulated under the Consumer Protection Act and under Act [CZE] No. 40/1964 Coll., Civil Code, as subsequently amended (Sections 52–57 of the CC [CZE]). Part One, Chapter Five of the CC [CZE] implements into Czech law most of the provisions of the European directives regulating consumer protection.[77] The directives are also partially implemented in other laws and regulations.[78]

353. From the perspective of the system incorporated in the CC [CZE], this solution is not very suitable. Neither EU law, nor the laws of other than EU Member States perceive consumer contracts as a special type of contract. Hence, if consumer contracts are incorporated in a separate chapter of the CC [CZE], the same arrangement should have been adopted with respect to the general provisions on contracts (Sections 43

---

terminated to the day of commencement of the arbitration in which the arbitrator is bound by the reporting obligation."

[76] Section 12 of the ArbAct [CZE]. The rules regulating the replacement of a disqualified arbitrator have not been changed by the Amendment to the ArbAct [CZE] at all.

[77] In particular, see the following directives:

➢ Council Directive 85/577/EEC of 20 December 1985 to protect the consumer in respect of contracts negotiated away from business premises;

➢ Council Directive 93/13/EEC of 5 April 1993 on unfair terms in consumer contracts (the "*Directive*");

➢ Directive 97/7/EC of the European Parliament and of the Council of 20 May 1997 on the protection of consumers in respect of distance contracts;

➢ Directive 94/47/EC of the European Parliament and the Council of 26 October 1994 on the protection of purchasers in respect of certain aspects of contracts relating to the purchase of the right to use immovable properties on a timeshare basis (*time-sharing*);

➢ Directive 2000/31/EC of the European Parliament and of the Council of 8 June 2000 on certain legal aspects of information society services, in particular electronic commerce, in the Internal Market;

➢ Directive 2002/65/EC of the European Parliament and of the Council of 23 September 2002 concerning the distance marketing of consumer financial services and amending Council Directive 90/619/EEC and Directives 97/7/EC and 98/24/EC.

[78] See:

➢ Act [CZE] No. 124/2002 Coll. on Payment Transactions, as subsequently amended;

➢ Act [CZE] No. 480/2004 Coll., on Certain Information Society Services, as subsequently amended;

➢ Act [CZE] No. 37/2004 Coll., on Insurance Contract, and others.

through 51 of the CC [CZE]), or alternatively Chapter Five should have been entitled "contracts" and further divided so as to include special provisions on consumer contracts (contracts concluded with consumers). These requirements have been clearly reflected in the NCC [CZE] as the new Civil Code (see the brief excursus below, in connection with consumer protection). The provisions on consumer contracts in the CC [CZE] are arranged as follows: Sections 53 and 54 of the CC [CZE][79] regulate distance contracts, Section 57 of the CC [CZE][80] regulates contracts concluded away from the professional's business premises, and Sections 55 and 56 of the CC [CZE][81] contain general provisions common to all contracts concluded between a professional and a consumer.[82] The current law therefore does not follow any clear conception[83] and is not sufficiently transparent, neither from the perspective of the concept of consumer protection at the *Community* level, nor from the perspective of legal theory.[84]

354.   The benchmark for the assessment of (un)fairness of terms incorporated in consumer contracts as well as choice-of-court agreements and arbitration clauses is, similar to the other EU Member States, the *Directive*, namely Articles 3, 6 and 7 of the *Directive*. The *Directive* was transposed into Czech law by the amendment to the Civil Code (CC [CZE]) No. 367/2000 Coll.; the transposition was rather inaccurate and probably incomplete.[85] The *Directive* was primarily implemented through Sections 55 and 56 of the CC [CZE]. The former stipulates that contractual terms in consumer contracts may not depart from the law (statute) to the detriment of the consumer. The legislator therefore

---

[79] Implementing especially Directive 97/7/EC on the protection of consumers in respect of distance contracts.

[80] Implementing especially Directive 97/7/EC on the protection of consumers in respect of distance contracts.

[81] Implementing especially Directive 93/13/EEC on unfair terms in consumer contracts (referred to as the "*Directive*" in this book).

[82] Cf. *Wright, I.* Spotřebitelské smlouvy. [Title in translation: Consumer Contracts]. Juristic.cz. Available online at: http://obcanskepravo.juristic.cz/69897/ [last access 2 May 2009] et al.

[83] Cf. *Wright, I.* Spotřebitelské smlouvy. [Title in translation: Consumer Contracts]. Juristic.cz. Available online at: http://obcanskepravo.juristic.cz/69897/ [last access 2 May 2009] et al.

[84] Unfortunately, the amendment to the CC [CZE] implemented by Act [CZE] No. 367/2000 Coll. did not literally adopt the government proposal which distinctly divided consumer contracts into three categories entitled adhesion contracts, contracts concluded away from business premises, and distance contracts. The fact that adhesion contracts were omitted is particularly astonishing, because this topic definitely should have been included in the CC [CZE] (cf. for instance the government proposal to the subsequently promulgated Act No. 367/2000 Coll.) (cit.): "[...] *adhesion contracts made out completely or to a substantial extent in writing must be expressed in a simple language and in a generally comprehensible manner. If in doubt about the meaning of the terms of adhesion contracts, the interpretation more favorable to the consumer shall apply.*[...]"

[85] *Raban, P.* Drobní dlužníci a zakázaná smluvní ujednání. [Title in translation: Small Debtors and Prohibited Contractual Terms]. Online text. Available online at: http://www.premyslraban.cz/drobni-dluznici.html [last access 10 August 2011].

presumed that the provisions of the statute (whether mandatory or optional) guarantee that the mutual rights and obligations of the parties will be balanced. Consumer contracts are submitted to the general clause in Section 56 of the CC [CZE] which stipulates that consumer contracts may not contain terms which, contrary to the requirement of good faith, cause a significant imbalance in the parties' rights and obligations to the detriment of the consumer. This provision is supplemented in Section 56(3) of the CC [CZE] by a list of contractual terms which are *"especially"* (i.e. *"usually"* and *"inter alia"*) considered unfair. In this regard, the provisions are based on the Annex to the *Directive* containing an indicative list of such terms. The Czech provisions contain 11 such examples, whereas the Annex to the *Directive* contains 17 examples. The Czech legislator has apparently eliminated some examples, especially subparagraphs (e) and (q) of para. (1) of the Annex to the *Directive*.[86]

(b) Consequences of unfair terms in consumer contracts

355. The concept of the consequences of unfair terms in consumer contracts was significantly influenced by the 2010 amendment to the Civil Code (CC [CZE]) and the Consumer Protection Act [CZE] (effective date 1 August 2010).[87] The prohibition of such terms in a consumer contract which depart from the law (statute) to the detriment of the consumer was preserved (Section 55(1) of the CC [CZE]).[88] What has changed, however, is the concept of the consequences affecting the *terms detrimental to the consumer* under Section 55(2) of the CC [CZE]. Before 1 August 2010,[89] the terms were considered voidable[90] (invalid if

---

[86] Annex to the *Directive* (cit.): Paragraph 1 "[...] (e) *requiring any consumer who fails to fulfil his obligation to pay a disproportionately high sum in compensation* [...] (q) *excluding the consumer's right to take legal action or exercise any other legal remedy, particularly by requiring the consumer to take disputes exclusively to arbitration* [...]."

[87] Act [CZE] No. 155/2010 Coll., Amending Certain Laws in Order to Improve Their Application and Alleviate the Administrative Burden Imposed on Entrepreneurs.

[88] CC [CZE] (cit.): Section 55 – "(1) *Contractual terms in consumer contracts may not depart from the law to the detriment of the consumer. In particular, the consumer may not waive the rights guaranteed to him or her by the law or impair his or her contractual position in any other manner.* [...]"

[89] CC [CZE], version applicable until 31 July 2010 (cit.): "[...] (2) *Clauses in consumer contracts falling within the definition in Section 56 are voidable by the consumer (Section 40a). However, if the clause directly affects other terms of the contract, the consumer may invoke the invalidity of the entire contract.* [...]"

[90] This Section was directly connected with Section 40a of the CC [CZE]; the latter, as applicable until 31 July 2010, read as follows (cit.): Section 40a – "*If a legal (juridical) act is invalid under the provisions of Section 49a, Section 55, Section 140, Section 145(2), Section 479, Section 589, Section 701(1), Section 775, and Section 852b(2) and (3) of the CC [CZE]], the act shall be deemed valid unless the person affected by the act invokes the invalidity thereof. Invalidity cannot be invoked by the person who caused the invalidity. The same applies if a legal (juridical) act is not performed in the form required by the agreement of the parties (Section 40 of the CC [CZE]). If a legal (juridical) act violates the generally applicable law governing prices, it shall be invalid only to the extent to which it violates such law if the person affected by the act invokes the invalidity thereof.*" Section 55(1) of the CC

their validity was challenged by the consumer); after 1 August 2010,[91] the law is based on absolute invalidity. As a result of this change, the court examines the unfairness of the terms in consumer contracts *ex officio*, because the contracts are considered absolutely invalid. After the 2010 amendment, the court must therefore examine of its own motion whether the consumer contract departs from the *"common standard of rights and obligations offered by the optional provisions of the law"* to the detriment of the consumer and, if in the affirmative, hold the relevant terms invalid.[92] The courts should, however, take as their basis the concept of the common (*average*) consumer and keep in mind that an excessively restrictive interpretation of contracts, meaning maximum favors for the consumer, could have the result of rendering the entire system of the law of obligations nonfunctional. **Hence, as concerns arbitration agreements,** [any] **arbitration agreement concluded with a consumer cannot automatically be presumed to be** [*a priori*] **invalid** when, for instance, the Amendment to the ArbAct [CZE] which took effect on 1 April 2012 is, conversely, based on the permissibility of arbitration agreements in relations between a consumer and a professional. In this regard, **the concept and the standard incorporated in the amendment to the Arbitration Act** [Amendment to the ArbAct CZE] **have become an important benchmark** since 2012. Special consumer protection, as prescribed for instance under Section 55 of the CC [CZE], certainly interferes with the parties' freedom of contract, and it is important to make sure that unfair terms in consumer

---

[CZE], followed by Section 55(2) of the CC [CZE], could have been interpreted in a number of ways until the 2010 amendment [see Selucká, M. Ochrana spotřebitele? Nenápadná změna se zásadními dopady. [Title in translation: Consumer Protection? An Inconspicuous Amendment with Major Implications]. Právní rozhledy, 2010, Vol. 18, No. 14, p. 513 et seq., Adopted from the cited source]: (i) The fact that Section 55(1) of the CC [CZE] causes absolute invalidity (the reference to the entire Section 55 of the CC [CZE]) in Section 40a of the CC [CZE] and the entire Section 55 of the CC [CZE] is an error and, considering the wording of Section 55(2) of the CC [CZE], has been interpreted as applicable to deviations from the binding rules as well as deviations from the nonbinding rules). The relationship of Section 39 of the CC [CZE] and Section 55(1) of the CC [CZE] is a lex specialis relationship, i.e. it covers both deviations from the binding rules and deviations from the nonbinding rules; (ii) Section 55(1) of the CC [CZE] causes voidability – with respect to the explicit list in Section 40a of the CC [CZE]; the renvoi incorporated only in Section 55(2) of the CC [CZE] is disregarded. The relationship of Section 39 of the CC [CZE] and Section 55(1) of the CC [CZE] is interpreted as follows: Section 39 of the CC [CZE] regulates deviations from binding rules whereas Section 55(1) of the CC [CZE] regulates only deviations from nonbinding rules. After the 2010 amendment of the CC [CZE], we have been facing a problem which does not concern deviations from binding rules but deviations from nonbinding, optional rules which could benefit the professional rather than the consumer (see also *Selucká, M.* Ochrana spotřebitele? Nenápadná změna se zásadními dopady. [Title in translation: Consumer Protection? An Inconspicuous Amendment with Major Implications]. Právní rozhledy, 2010, Vol. 18, No. 14, p. 513 et seq.).

[91] CC [CZE], the version applicable since 1 August 2010 (cit.:) "[...] (2) *Clauses in consumer contracts specified in Section 56 are invalid.* [...]"

[92] *Selucká, M.* Ochrana spotřebitele? Nenápadná změna se zásadními dopady. [Title in translation: Consumer Protection? An Inconspicuous Amendment with Major Implications]. Právní rozhledy, 2010, Vol. 18, No. 14, p. 513 et seq.

contracts will be interpreted *reasonably* and adequately by the courts in individual cases. Besides, the very fundament of the relevant provisions of Czech law, namely Section 55(1) of the CC [CZE], has no explicit basis in any provision of secondary EU law; consequently, it is more likely a legislative initiative of the national (domestic) legislator of the EU Member State. The principle of proportionality is best served (in the sense of *de lege ferenda*) by a balance between absolute invalidity prescribed solely for contractual terms breaching mandatory rules[93] and voidability (subject to an objection raised by a party) for all other cases, i.e. where the contractual term does not violate any mandatory provision. Consequently, the developments in consumer protection laws in the Czech Republic in the form of the 2010 amendment to Section 55(2) of the CC [CZE] are best described as a politically motivated *transition from one extreme to the other*, unfounded on any considerations compatible with a constitution which would be motivated by an interest in stability and the proportional protection of all rights.

356.   Indeed, the ConCourt CR [CZE] itself has analyzed the issue in great detail in its decision of 9 February 2011,[94] in connection with the request for repealing certain parts of Section 40a of the CC [CZE] and Section 55(2) of the CC [CZE], as applicable before the 2010 Amendment to the CC [CZE]. Notwithstanding the fact that the Constitutional Court [CZE] dismissed the application, because it was made at the time the legislator was passing the above-mentioned conceptual amendment to the CC [CZE], the Court commented on unfair terms in consumer contracts in the reasons for its decision [in dismissing the application]. The Constitutional Court [CZE] held [that] *"it fully shares in the opinion of the applicant who perceives the concept of voidability of consumer contracts as inconsistent with Czech constitutional laws, namely with the principles of equality, fairness and legal certainty, i.e. as a concept violating the commitments of the Czech Republic arising from international treaties,[95] which is incompatible with the essence and the purpose of legal provisions that ought to manifest the principle of protection of the de facto weaker contracting party (the consumer), correcting the application of the principle of autonomy of will in private law. In order to fulfill these constitutional prerequisites, it is necessary to connect the breach of statutory rules, incorporated in* Section 55 of the CC [CZE] *and* Section 56 of the CC [CZE] *as a means of balancing the de facto inequality, with absolute invalidity laid down by law (a statute) which the court applies ex officio, without the consumer having to plead*

---

[93] Within the meaning of Section 2(2) of the CC [CZE] and Section 39 of the CC [CZE].
[94] Decision of the ConCourt CR [CZE], Case No. Pl. ÚS 1/10 of 9 February 2011, available at the website of the ConCourt CR [CZE] and published in: Výběr rozhodnutí ÚS ČR [Selected Case Law of the ConCourt CR], 2011, Ref. No. 520.
[95] The ConCourt CR [CZE] invoked Article 1(1) and (2) of the Constitution [CZE] and Article 1 and Article 3(1) of the Charter [CZE].

the invalidity." The Constitutional Court of the Czech Republic [CZE] is of the opinion that the concept of voidability (applicable until 31 July 2010 according to the previous wording of Section 55(2) [CZE]) formerly had unacceptable legal consequences and caused manifest injustice, allowing professionals to breach the rights of consumers and subsequently generate substantial profit as a result of this unlawful behavior.[96] Hence, the Constitutional Court of the Czech Republic [CZE] concluded that if Section 55 of the CC [CZE] had not been amended (until 31 July 2010, Section 55 of the CC [CZE] was based on the concept of voidability), the ConCourt CR [CZE] would have had no choice but to declare the relevant provision incompatible with the Constitution of the Czech Republic and with the Charter [CZE].[97] The Constitutional Court of the Czech Republic [CZE] thereby expressed its opinion regarding the requirement for a higher level of consumer protection in terms of the *absolute invalidity* of unfair terms.[98] This

[96] The ConCourt CR [CZE] held that the typical cases concerning loan agreements (credit contracts) mentioned by the claimant in the proceedings had become a phenomenon which had long been troubling the entire society. If, for instance, consumer contracts commonly contain or used to contain terms which deprive the consumer of his or her right to determine which debt ought to be settled from the consumer's performance before all other debts (because payment of the principal amount halts further accrual of interest and contractual penalties), this commonly results in a spiral of other debts, and the consumers are totally unable to pay their debts because the resultant increase of their debt exceeds their capabilities. Moreover, if consumer contracts provide for combined or accumulated penalties – applicable only to consumers – or contain provisions allowing the supplier to unilaterally change the terms of the commitment, or choice-of-court clauses which provide for the jurisdiction of the court in the place where the supplier has its registered office (as a result of which the consumers are deprived of the possibility of defending their claims in a court situated in the place of their residence), such contemptible, indeed usurious, contracts must be considered unlawful and the statutory provisions sanctioning such contracts as unconstitutional.
[97] With reference to Article 1(1) and (2) of the Constitution [CZE] and Article 1 and Article 3(1) of the Charter [CZE].
[98] Indeed, this view has already been adopted by the lower Czech courts [CZE] in numerous decisions, although their approach has not always been uniform. Cf.:
➢ Judgment of the SC CR [CZE], Case No. 33 Cdo 2330/2009 of 29 November 2010, in which the Court held that a term in a consumer contract for work is invalid for violating Section 55(1) of the CC [CZE] if the term stipulates that the client (consumer) who cancels the contract is obliged to pay to the contractor (apart from the price of the works which have already been carried out and a compensation for reasonable costs in terms of Section 642(1) of the Civil Code) a financial penalty constituting a disadvantage for which no compensation is provided under the contract. The parties cannot agree in their contract that one (or both) of them will have the right to cancel the contract by providing a cancellation payment after the party has already performed or accepted performance, or part thereof, under the contract (Section 497 of the CC [CZE]). In said case, the court classified the binding rule in Section 55 of the CC [CZE] as a unilaterally mandatory feature of otherwise nonbinding rules.
➢ Judgment of the SC CR [CZE], Case No. 33 Cdo 4601/2008 of 16 September 2010: In that decision, the Court expressed a somewhat less rigorous and more balanced (in the author's opinion) view when the Court held that a contractual penalty in a consumer contract which causes an imbalance between the contracting parties within the meaning of Section 56(1) of the CC [CZE], is not in itself invalid but must be assessed in the context of other contract terms which, in their entirety, may ultimately support the conclusion that the contractual penalty is invalid.

rather radical opinion was nonetheless corrected by the Constitutional Court of the Czech Republic [CZE] itself in its later case law (especially case law from 2011) in which the Court analyzed issues of proportionality and the relation between freedom of contract and consumer protection (protection of the weaker contracting party) and exhibited a highly balanced approach in doing so.[99] This case law is partly analyzed in the chapter dealing with the case law of Czech courts and of the Constitutional Court of the Czech Republic [CZE] – see below (in this excursus into Czech law).

357.   Although EU law leaves to the discretion of the individual Member States which concept of the consequences of unfair terms in consumer contracts they opt for, it is necessary to emphasize that the ECJ's case law is usually not so strict and does not prescribe the requirement of absolute invalidity. It only stipulates the obligation of the court to examine the nature of the contractual term of its own motion and, especially, to lay emphasis on the awareness of and the information provided to the consumer. In the *Pannon GSM*[100] case, the ECJ underlined that the respective contractual terms could not always be held invalid, even if the objective circumstances of the contract (the relevant term) could support such conclusion, and that it was also necessary to take account of the subjective factors of the case. It is primarily important to take into consideration the interest of both parties (mainly the consumer) in the performance of the contract, including the interest in the fulfillment of terms which might appear invalid (as a result of *unfairness*). This is primarily about the assessment of the conduct of an average and informed consumer in the performance of the contract, which also applies to the stage of enforcing the party's contractual claims in court, or before *another authority*. Neither EU law, nor the ECJ's case law interferes with the individual concept of consumer protection applied by the Member State; but as the *Pannon GSM* case shows, it is important to adopt a highly individual approach and take into account any and all factors relating to the conclusion of the contract, as well as the events following its conclusion, including all stages (fora and instances) of the resolution of disputes arising from the contract.

We must emphasize, though, that the [quoted] decisions focused on the examination of facts (contracts) relating to the period preceding the 2010 amendment of the CC [CZE].

[99] See the Judgment of the ConCourt CR [CZE], Case No. II. ÚS 2164/10 of 1 November 2011, which is annotated in detail below in this excursus into Czech law ("*Case Law*").

[100] ECJ Judgment, Case C-243/08 of 4 June 2009 (*Pannon GSM Zrt v. Sustikné Győrfi Erzsébet* [*Pannon GSM*]), CELEX: 62008CA0243, the judgment was published in: ECR 2009, p. I–04713. The ECJ's ruling is annotated in detail in Chapter III.9 of this book and also referred to elsewhere. Unfortunately, the decision is often interpreted inconsistently, especially as concerns the necessity to have regard for the approach of the parties to the performance of their obligations and the exercise of their rights under the contract.

(c)   Proposal for a new Civil Code (NCC [CZE])

358.   From the substantive-law perspective, consumer protection in the Czech
Republic is currently regulated primarily by the Civil Code (CC [CZE]).
In 2011, however, an expert team finished work on a brand new code –
the New Civil Code ("NCC [CZE]"). The proposal was passed by the
Chamber of Deputies of the Parliament of the Czech Republic on 9
November 2011, and subsequently by the Senate of the Parliament of the
Czech Republic on 25 January 2012. It is to be expected that the Code
will take effect on **1 January 2014**.[101] The NCC [CZE] has adopted many
of the consumer protection rules incorporated in the present Civil Code
("CC [CZE]") and the Commercial Code ("ComC [CZE]"), in which the
necessary *Community* directives were transposed, and completed the
transposition. The NCC [CZE] also implements the new Directive
2008/122/EC of the EP and of the Council of 14 January 2009 on the
protection of consumers in respect of certain aspects of timeshare, long-
term holiday product, resale and exchange contracts. But the NCC
[CZE] has not introduced many changes in the position of consumers.
Most Czech consumer protection rules have been taken over from
Community (EU) legislation. The NCC [CZE] is therefore not much
different from the present CC [CZE]. Some of these rules include: the
same time limits for the cancellation of contracts, the right to keep
goods which were not ordered, the application of consumer-friendly
interpretation, etc. In certain cases, the NCC [CZE] introduces more
precise rules compared to the current provisions of the CC [CZE].

359.   The concept of "consumer" goes hand in hand with the concept of
"professional." The currently applicable Civil Code (CC [CZE]) contains
two definitions of "consumer": **(i)** Section 52(3) of the CC [CZE] defines
a consumer as a person who enters into and provides performance
under contracts for purposes which are outside his or her commercial or
other professional capacity, and **(ii)** Section 54a(4)(c) of the CC [CZE]
defines a consumer as a natural person who acts outside his or her
commercial or other professional capacity when entering into and
providing performance under financial services distance contracts. The
main drawback is that these differing definitions disadvantage business
in the industries which are subject to the general provisions of Sections
53 and 54 of the valid and applicable Civil Code (CC [CZE]). Such
industries are disadvantaged not only compared to the sector of financial
services contracted by means of distance communication but also
compared to sectors regulated under special laws, such as Act [CZE] No.
145/2010 Coll., on Consumer Credit [Section 3(a)], and Act [CZE] No.

---

[101] Transitional provisions are based on the principle that statutes are not retroactive and that the
new statute only applies to the rights and obligations which come into existence after the statute
takes effect. Contractual obligations which arise until the effective date of the NCC [CZE] are
therefore subject to the current legislation (CC [CZE] or ComC [CZE]).

127/2005 Coll., on Electronic Communications [Section 2(1)(d)], which define a consumer as a natural person. The NCC [CZE] defines "consumer" as the opposite of "professional" and vice versa.[102] The **definition of consumer** in the NCC [CZE] reads as follows (cit.): *"a man or a woman who enters into a contract or deals with a professional outside his or her trade or profession."*[103] Consistent with the current CC [CZE], the NCC [CZE] **does not include legal persons in the category of consumers**. The new law defines a consumer in the same way as EU law, especially as concerns **(i)** the *Directive*, **(ii)** Directive 85/577/EEC to protect the consumer in respect of contracts negotiated away from business premises, **(iii)** Directive 97/7/EC on the protection of consumers in respect of distance contracts, etc. A broad interpretation of consumer which includes legal persons is inconsistent with the ECJ's case law. The ECJ has ruled that only a natural person can be a consumer; in certain other cases, the ECJ has ruled that more rigorous consumer protection must be considered an erroneous implementation of directives which disrupts the internal market of the European *Community*.[104] Nonetheless, the above-quoted provisions also limit the definition of professional by connecting the professional's personal status with the conclusion and performance of a contract. This is not quite accurate. In compliance with the applicable directives as well as the trends at the supranational level (proposal for a European Civil Code; *Draft Common Frame of Reference*), the NCC is based on the general concept that a consumer is a natural person who enters into a contract or deals with a professional; "dealing with" means both factual and legal actions. But the consumer is only a man or a woman who deals with the professional outside his or her own trade.[105] The rules incorporated in the NCC [CZE] are connected to other consumer protection rules. The new Civil Code of the Czech Republic (NCC [CZE]), however, neither excludes the protection of legal persons, or professionals who could be in the position of the weaker party, although their protection is guaranteed under the general provisions and not under the special consumer protection rules. The interpretation of "professional" for the purposes of consumer protection under the NCC [CZE] is to become broader in order to be consistent with European law. Consumers must be protected even if they negotiate transactions with a person for whom the criterion of profit is not important; this applies, for instance, to the provision of public services or general welfare services supplied by persons who do not have the status of professional with respect to the services, because – for instance – they belong to the

---

[102] See Section 412 of the NCC [CZE]. Similarly, Sections 13 and 14 of the BGB [DEU].

[103] See Section 412 of the NCC [CZE].

[104] Judgment of the ECJ, Joined Cases C-541/99 (*Cape Snc* v. *Idealservice*) and C-542/99 (*Idealservice MN RE Sas* v. *OMAI sRL*) of 22 November 2001; CELEX: 61999J0541.

[105] Similarly, see: (i) Section 13 of the BGB [DEU], (ii) Article 7:5 BW [NDL] et al.

public sector.[106] The NCC [CZE] is based on the expression "every person" which is supposed to indicate that the person's status under private or public law is not important in that connection; the important thing is that he or she negotiates contracts with a particular content.

360. The NCC [CZE] also contains provisions which apply to **arbitration clauses in consumer contracts,** namely Section 1803(j) of the NCC [CZE][107] which is basically a **transcript** of the *Directive*.[108] This provision of the NCC [CZE] **principally prohibits two types of arbitration clauses: (i)** arbitration clauses which deprive the consumer of the right to take legal action or exercise any other legal remedy and **(ii)** arbitration clauses which require the consumer to exercise his or her rights exclusively with an arbitrator who is not bound by consumer protection laws. **The Amendment to the ArbAct [CZE] which has taken effect in the meantime has, however, rendered this provision of the NCC [CZE] unnecessary.** Hence, the relation of the NCC [CZE] to the ArbAct [CZE] can be considered as the relation of general rules to special rules, because the NCC [CZE] only stipulates a general principle which is then developed in detail in the ArbAct. Since the special law (ArbAct [CZE]) expressly permits arbitration in consumer disputes (subject to explicitly stipulated conditions), the incorporation of the indicative rules of the *Directive* in the Civil Code is rather confusing and will certainly give rise to doubts. It shows how uncoordinated the legislative process in the Czech Republic was when the new Civil Code and the extensive Amendment to the ArbAct [CZE], adopted in late 2011, were being drafted. In any case, the special provisions incorporated in the ArbAct [CZE] which explicitly permit arbitration in consumer disputes require that the discrepancy between the NCC [CZE] and the ArbAct [CZE] be interpreted in compliance with the ArbAct [CZE]. Section 1803(j) of the NCC [CZE] will have to be interpreted in compliance with European practice and consistent with Section 1802 of the NCC [CZE], i.e. an arbitration clause in a consumer contract will be considered invalid if, contrary to the requirement of fairness, it causes a significant imbalance in the rights or obligations of the parties to the detriment of the consumer. Consequently, an arbitration clause in a consumer contract is, as a rule, not invalid if it meets the requirements of Article 2(3) of the ArbAct [CZE] (as amended by the Amendment to the ArbAct [CZE]).

---

[106] For instance, the *Directive* employs the term *"publicly owned"* entity in this connection.
[107] NCC [CZE] (cit.): Section 1803 – *"Specifically prohibited clauses include [...] (j) excluding or hindering the consumer's right to take legal action or exercise any other legal remedy, or requiring the consumer to submit disputes exclusively to arbitration or arbitrator that are not bound by consumer protection laws."*
[108] Council Directive 93/13/EEC of 5 April 1993 on unfair terms in consumer contracts.

361.   **Adhesion contracts** are not a special type of contract, and the designation of the contracts as *"adhesion"* contracts is not accurate either. The word *"adhesion"* relates to the method of concluding the contract, not to the contract itself. Consequently, the relevant provisions refer to *"contracts concluded by adhesion."* The principle is that the contract is not formed by mutual negotiations between the parties but by one of the parties presenting the complete text of the contract to the other party who has the option to take the offer or decline it (i.e. "take it or leave it"). The NCC [CZE] does not refuse this perspective but, conversely, accepts the reality, i.e. that many contracts are concluded in such manner; it also takes account of the perspective of economic usefulness. The NCC [CZE] introduces more detailed provisions which would not only be based on the general principles for the resolution of complicated situations where the stronger party *forces* the terms on the *weaker* party. It has been inspired by some foreign civil codes, as well as international projects such as the proposal for the European Contract Code (*Code europeen des Contrats. Avant-projet*) and the *Draft Common Frame of Reference* for a European Civil Code.

362.   The NCC [CZE] requires that **all notices** from the professional to the consumer be clear and intelligible and made out in the **language in which the contract is concluded.**[109] It is necessary to bear in mind that this legal requirement is different from the legal requirement of clarity and intelligibility of an expression of will, and it has different legal consequences. Article 5 of the *Directive* requires that the consumer must be properly informed. Unless the consumer is supplied with clear and intelligible information in the proposed manner, the contract is not ipso facto invalid, but the breach of the duty to provide information to the consumer might give rise to his or her right to cancel the contract under more favorable conditions, pursuant to the following provisions. Ambiguous formulations allowing for varying interpretations also result in an interpretation of the contract more favorable to the consumer.[110] Applied to arbitration clauses, we could conclude that an arbitration clause would be invalid if it stipulated that the arbitral proceedings will be conducted in a language different from the language in which the contract was concluded (or, naturally, different from the mother tongue of the consumer or the official language of the place of the consumer's habitual residence). Naturally, however, the NCC [CZE] has no explicit provision dealing with the language of the proceedings concerning

---

[109] Refers to:
➤ Article 5 of the *Directive* and
➤ Articles 4 and 5 of Directive 97/7/EC on the protection of consumers in respect of distance contracts.
[110] These are special benefits reserved for consumers; they cannot be claimed by persons who have a legitimate interest in consumer protection under domestic laws (for an exception, see Article 5 in conjunction with Article 7 of the *Directive*).

consumer disputes and, as a substantive-law code, it does not regulate any procedural issues. The NCC [CZE] is based on the mandatory nature of consumer protection provisions. If the parties depart from the provisions by agreement, the agreement is disregarded. This means that such deviation from the rule is legally irrelevant, without prejudice to the validity of the other provisions of the contract. This also applies if there is no specific agreement, but the consumer unilaterally waives his or her subjective right accorded to the consumer under the provisions of the applicable part of the NCC [CZE].

363.   The principle of *proportionality*, currently incorporated in Section 56(1) of the CC [CZE], is also included in the NCC [CZE] and the rules are analogous.[111] The requirement of proportionality applies to all contractual terms and all rights and obligations of the parties; the court will have to examine whether the imbalance (if any) is to the detriment of the consumer and whether this particular imbalance is fair or not. Terms which exclude or limit the professional's liability for actions that cause an injury or death to the consumer are impermissible; the same applies to terms which limit or exclude the consumer's rights to make claims from defects, including a claim for damages. Terms which stipulate that the contract binds the consumer ipso facto whereas the professional's obligations under the contract are subject to a condition precedent to the fulfillment of which depends solely on the professional's will are also impermissible. Similarly impermissible are those terms which allow the professional to keep what the consumer had provided to him or her in case the consumer does not enter into the contract with the professional or rescinds (cancels) the contract. Terms which only allow the professional to cancel the contract without having any grounds for doing so or to terminate by notice an obligation agreed for an indefinite period of time without a reasonable notice period are also impermissible. Terms which the consumer did not have an opportunity to get acquainted with before the conclusion of the contract and which allow the professional to modify the contract or the term unilaterally and without having any grounds for doing so are also impermissible. Terms which stipulate that the final price shall only be determined at the moment of performance, without the consumer's option of cancelling the contract if the agreed price for the goods or services is significantly higher, are also impermissible. Terms which breach these mandatory provisions shall be disregarded. Exceptions apply to terms negotiated individually, i.e. not as adhesion terms.

---

[111] See Section 1802 of the NCC [CZE], in compliance with Article 3(1) of the *Directive*. It is to be expected that this requirement will include the general principle of the parties acting in good faith and exercising their rights in good faith, including good morals.

364. The NCC [CZE] stipulates that **an expression of will of a party has legal effects vis-à-vis the other party only after the expression of will reaches the other party, i.e. reaches the sphere of the other party.** But the NCC [CZE] provides for an exception in case the **consumer cancels the contract.** In these cases, it is sufficient if the consumer **at least dispatches** the notice of cancellation to the professional by the stipulated deadline.

365. Current civil law provisions [CZE][112] require that certain information **be provided** to the consumer **in writing.** This requirement is sometimes construed by lawyers as requiring that the notification be provided in a written form, i.e. that it must be an expression of will which meets all the requirements stipulated for a written form, including the signature of the party. But neither the *Directive*, nor any other EU laws require that these notifications to consumers have the form of a written expression of will. It is **only necessary to make sure that the consumer is informed by available means and with the use of such means of communication which allow the consumer to display and preserve the information.** This is a major difference, and the requirements have been inaccurately transposed into the laws of a number of EU Member States. Consequently, the NCC [CZE] clearly distinguishes these two levels. The notification to the consumer must therefore be on paper or another durable medium, so that it can be preserved and displayed again at any time.

366. Special protection must be afforded to the consumer if the contract with him or her is entered into **using the means of distance communication.** Sections 1808 through 1816 of the NCC [CZE] implement Directive 97/7/EC of the European Parliament and of the Council on the protection of consumers in respect of distance contracts. They also take account of the requirements laid down by Directive 2002/65/EC concerning the distance marketing of consumer financial services. Both directives are also reflected in the currently applicable Civil Code (CC [CZE]).[113] The consumer has the right to cancel the contract within 14 days of accepting performance. The NCC [CZE] also stipulates other time limits for cancellation. The new law explicitly highlights the consumer's right to cancel the contract without giving any reasons and without any penalties. If the professional fails to provide the required information to the consumer, the time limit for cancellation of the contract by the consumer is extended to three months. If the professional provides the required information in the course of this three-month period, the time limit is interrupted and a new 14-day time limit starts to run. The consumer's right to cancel the contract is based on the presumption that the consumer does not have the opportunity of

---

[112] For instance, Section 53(6), Section 54b(8), Section 60(1) and (2) of the CC [CZE].
[113] Sections 53 through 54d of the CC [CZE].

seeing and trying out the goods or of checking the nature or the quality of the service before entering into the contract.

367.   The consumer protection provisions relating to **financial services** are now incorporated in Sections 54a through 54d of the CC [CZE].[114] Just like the present law, the NCC [CZE][115] also especially implements Directive 2002/65/EC concerning the distance marketing of consumer financial services. It is therefore focused on banking and credit services, payment transactions services, as well as investment and insurance services. The purpose of the proposed legislation is to guarantee protection to the consumer – to make sure that he or she has the necessary information, to provide him/her with a defense against unsolicited services and with the right to cancel the contract within a defined time limit, etc. The consumer has the right to ask the professional anytime after the conclusion of the contract for a printed account of the stipulated information, as well as the right to change the means of distance communication used, unless this is incompatible with the nature of the financial service provided.

368.   Special rules concern **contracts negotiated away from business premises**. The new law principally implements Directive 85/577/EEC to protect the consumer in respect of contracts negotiated away from business premises.[116] The NCC [CZE] basically adopts the present provisions.[117,118] The new rules concern door-to-door selling and other situations in which either the professional negotiates the contract with the consumer away from the professional's business premises or in which the professional does not have any permanent business premises at all. This usually includes situations in which the consumer does not expect an offer to enter into a contract and is unprepared for the negotiation, does not have sufficient opportunity to check the quality of the offered performance, compare the price and other terms of the offer with other offers in the market. The consumer therefore has the right to cancel the contract within 14 days or, if no performance was provided

---

[114] See Sections 54a through 54d of the CC [CZE].
[115] See Sections 1817 through 1827 of the NCC [CZE].
[116] See ECJ Judgment, Case C-412/06 of 10 April 2008 (*Annelore Hamilton* v. *Volksbank Filder eG.*), CELEX: 62006CJ0412, published in: ECR, p.I-2383, para. (32), which reads as follows (cit.): " [...] *the objective of the Directive – as expressed specifically in the fourth and the fifth recital in the Preamble – is to protect consumers against the risks arising from the conclusion of contracts away from business premises, because the special feature of these contracts is that as a rule it is the trader who initiates the contract negotiations, and the consumer is totally unprepared for a door-to-door sales call, especially because the consumer did not compare the quality and price of the offer with other available offers.*" With respect to arbitration clauses, though, there is no special difference between contracts concluded away from the business premises of the trader, contracts concluded by means of distant communication, and other contracts concluded by the consumer as *adhesion contracts*.
[117] See Section 57 of the CC [CZE].
[118] See Sections 1828 through 1830 of the NCC [CZE].

under the contract, within one month, without stating any grounds and without any penalty. The professional must notify the consumer of his or her right of cancellation, on paper or on another durable medium, at the time of conclusion of the contract (the provision also lists the mandatory content of the notification). This does not apply if the consumer explicitly requested the professional's visit.

369.   Sections 1831 through 1846 of the NCC [CZE] concerning **timeshare contracts and other holiday services** implement Directive 2008/122/EC on the protection of consumers in respect of certain aspects of timeshare, long-term holiday product, resale and exchange contracts. These contracts do not represent a unified type of contract. They may be formed by the conclusion of contracts establishing rights in rem or obligations or nominate or innominate contracts. Hence, the NCC [CZE] does not treat these contracts as a special type of contract but incorporates special provisions which protect the consumer **irrespective of what type of contract** has given rise to the right to the timeshare or other services benefiting the consumer. These special provisions apply to contracts concluded for a **duration of more than one year.** The rules in the NCC [CZE] also extend to other services relating to timeshare contracts and contracts for other holiday services. Consumer protection also extends to contracts in which the professional only undertakes to assist the consumer in the conclusion of a timeshare contract or a contract for other holiday services, or to contracts under which the consumer, for consideration, joins an exchange system connected with the right to a timeshare or other services. These rules also apply to agreements on future contracts. Directive 2008/122/EC is based on the principle of maximum harmonization, i.e. it does not allow the Member States to depart from its provisions.

370.   The consumer is also protected by the fact that the professional must provide to the consumer, before the conclusion of the contract, certain information, an exhaustive list of which is incorporated in the new law, which the professional cannot unilaterally change at any later occasion. In compliance with Article 3(2) and (3) of Directive 2008/122/EC, the new law stipulates the obligation to indicate in the invitation to any promotional event the nature and the purpose of the event, as well as the professional's obligation to make the information available to the consumer before the conclusion of the contract. The information must be provided to the consumer on a special form, a template of which is incorporated in a cabinet regulation. The professional shall also explicitly notify the consumer of his or her right of cancellation, the deadline for the cancellation, and of the prohibition to pay or secure any advance or other payments during the deadline for cancellation. Such information must also be included in the contract, and each of these provisions must be signed by the consumer separately. The consumer

has the right to receive the information in a language of the country where the consumer has his or her residence or whose national the consumer is, depending on the consumer's choice. The requirement of a written form of the contract is based on the need to ensure that its terms are clear and unambiguous. In compliance with Directive 2008/122/EC, the new law also articulates special terms which the contract must contain. The contract must include a form for the potential cancellation of the contract. The template of the form is again prescribed by a cabinet regulation. The terms of the contract must comply with and must not depart from the pre-contractual information which the professional provided to the consumer on paper or on another durable medium (i.e. in a form which allows the terms to be repeatedly displayed). This does not apply if the inconsistency is caused by *force majeure* or if the parties explicitly agree. If it is clear before the conclusion of the contract that the terms of the contract will differ from the information, the professional must notify the terms to the consumer in the same manner as the pre-contractual information; the professional must also highlight the changes in the contract. Mandatory rules regarding holiday product contracts with the consideration payable in installments should also contribute to consumer protection. The installments may only be divided into equal annual payments. The professional is always obliged to request the consumer to pay at least 14 days in advance. The request for payment is a condition for the installment to become due and payable. If the professional's request is delayed, the payment shall become due and payable within 14 days after the consumer received the request. Beginning with the third installment payment, the consumer also has the right to cancel the contract within the period in which the professional requested the consumer to pay the installment; the cancellation period shall expire together with payment of the installment.

IV.5.3. Case law

(a) **Judgment of the Constitutional Court of the Czech Republic [CZE], Case No. IV. ÚS 2157/08 of 24 September 2008**[119]

(aa) **Legal opinion of the Constitutional Court**

371. ▶ **Arbitration clauses shall be interpreted** with the use of the standard methods of interpretation [of contracts].[120] These methods

---

[119] Available online from the website of the ConCourt CR [CZE] at: http://nalus.usoud.cz/Search/ResultDetail.aspx?id=59950&pos=1&cnt=1&typ=result [last access 20 August 2011].
[120] See also Resolution of the SC CR [CZE], Case No. 32 Odo 977/2005 of 14 June 2006, which reads as follows (cit.): "(1) *Lack of jurisdiction of the court is one of the procedural prerequisites the absence of which has the result of termination of the proceedings pursuant to Section 104(1) of the CCP [CZE]. The court lacks jurisdiction to hear the case if a particular case is excluded by law from the jurisdiction of courts until the proceedings before a different authority are terminated, as well as if the*

shall also apply to the interpretation of the unambiguity of the arbitration agreement.

▶ If the arbitration clause is valid,[121] the arbitration does not violate the Constitution in terms of depriving the party of his or her **lawful judge**.

▶ The possibility of the parties to a private-law relationship [contracting parties] to resolve their disputes in arbitration is envisaged by the law[122] and is certainly allowed under constitutional laws. The arbitration agreement comes into existence if based on an expression of free will which manifests the consent of the contracting parties to have their dispute resolved outside the judiciary. The fact that [only] after the dispute arises, one of the parties starts to deny the validity of the arbitration clause and disagrees with the content of the arbitral award, cannot change anything in that regard.

▶ An arbitration clause which **allows the claimant to choose between a request for arbitration and a lawsuit in court in no case violates the principle of equality of the parties**, as incorporated in Article 37(3) of the Charter of Rights and Freedoms [CZE]. An arbitration clause is an expression of the free will of the contracting parties and allows them to consider whether (and where) they will file their claims.

(bb) Factual and legal findings

372. In his complaint filed with the ConCourt CR [CZE], the complainant argued that the lower courts had erred[123] in refusing to annul the arbitral award rendered by the Arbitration Court Attached to the Economic Chamber of the Czech Republic and the Agricultural Chamber of the Czech Republic, Case No. Rsp 107/04 of 23 June 2004. The complainant maintained that no valid arbitration clause had been agreed upon; the contract negotiated between the complainant and the joint party contained a term according to which the parties merely declared their

---

case is to be submitted to arbitration according to the agreement of the parties, subject to the conditions stipulated in Section 106(1) of the CCP [CZE]. Section 106(1) of the CCP [CZE] principally differs from the general provisions on lack of jurisdiction in Section 104 of the CCP [CZE] only in that the court does not examine the absence of the procedural requirement of its own motion, but only following a timely objection raised by the respondent. (2) An arbitration clause (arbitration agreement) belongs to bilateral (or multilateral) legal (juridical) acts (cf. Section 34 of the CC [CZE]); its validity in terms of Section 106(1) of the CCP [CZE] must be assessed both from the perspective of the general requirements for legal (juridical) acts (cf. Section 37 et seq. of the CC [CZE]) and from the perspective of other requirements stipulated in the ArbAct [CZE] which regulates arbitration agreements in Sections 2 and 3."

[121] In this particular case, the courts held the arbitration clause valid.

[122] Regulated by Act No. 216/1994 Coll., on Arbitration and Enforcement of Arbitral Awards (ArbAct [CZE]).

[123] The following decisions were rendered in the proceedings before the [lower] courts:

➢ Judgment of the District Court for Prague 1, Case No. 11 C 106/2005-54 of 27 June 2006;

➢ Judgment of the Municipal Court in Prague, Case No. 20 Co 385/2006-80 of 7 December 2006 and

➢ Resolution of the SC CR [CZE], Case No. 32 Cdo 2697/2007-99 of 21 February 2008.

awareness that potential disputes arising in connection with the contract could be solved, inter alia, in arbitration. Such a vague alternative arbitration clause is invalid. The complainant also argued that the courts had violated the principle of equal standing of the parties in the proceedings, because the Municipal Court in Prague concluded that the claimant had the right to choose whether to file his claim with an arbitral tribunal or with a court; in the complainant's opinion, such interpretation confers unacceptable advantages on one of the parties to the dispute.

(cc) Commentary on the judgment of the Constitutional Court

373. The judgment of the ConCourt CR [CZE] has extensive implications.[124] Most of its conclusions can also be applied to the specific department of consumer dispute resolution.

(b) Judgment of the ConCourt CR, Case No. I ÚS 3227/07 of 8 March 2011

(aa) Conclusions and importance of the decision

374. The Constitutional Court of the Czech Republic (ÚS ČR [CZE]) has repeatedly analyzed issues connected with arbitration[125] and the basis for arbitration.[126] The landmark decision is the Judgment of the ConCourt

---

[124] Also cited in: *Hulmák, M. et Tomančáková, B.* Rozhodčí řízení jako vhodný prostředek řešení sporů mezi dodavatelem a spotřebitelem (1. část). [Title in translation: Arbitration as a Suitable Mechanism for the Resolution of Disputes between a Supplier and a Consumer (Part 1)]. Obchodněprávní revue, 2010, Vol. 2, No. 6, pp. 168–173 (see also footnote 9 in the article), etc.

[125] For example:
➢ Resolution of the ConCourt CR [CZE], Case No. III. ÚS 460/01 of 1 November 2001, published in: Sbírka nálezů a usnesení Ústavního soudu České republiky [CZE] [Reports of Judgments and Resolutions of the Constitutional Court of the Czech Republic], Vol. 24, Resolution Ref. No. 41, p. 563 et seq.
➢ Resolution of the ConCourt CR [CZE], Case No. IV: ÚS 174/02 of 15 July 2002, published in: Sbírka nálezů a usnesení Ústavního soudu České republiky [CZE] [Reports of Judgments and Resolutions of the Constitutional Court of the Czech Republic], Vol. 27, Resolution Ref. No. 20, p. 257 et seq.; this particular resolution is invoked by the majority of the subsequent decisions of the ConCourt CR [CZE] until the Judgment of the ConCourt CR, Case No. I ÚS 3227/07 of 8 March 2011, annotated in this book.
➢ Resolution of the ConCourt CR [CZE], Case No. III. ÚS 145/03 of 12 September 2003;
➢ Resolution of the ConCourt CR [CZE], Case No. IV. ÚS 435/02 of 22 October 2002;
➢ Resolution of the ConCourt CR [CZE], Case No. IV. ÚS 511/03 of 4 December 2003;
➢ Resolution of the ConCourt CR [CZE], Case No. I. ÚS 339/02 of 26 January 2004;
➢ Resolution of the ConCourt CR [CZE], Case No. III. ÚS 166/05 of 29 April 2005;
➢ Resolution of the ConCourt CR [CZE], Case No. II. ÚS 2169/07 of 3 September 2007;
➢ Resolution of the ConCourt CR [CZE], Case No. II. ÚS 3059/08 of 15 January 2009 et al.
[126] For more details, see: *Bělohlávek, A. et Profeldová, T.* Arbitration in the Case Law of the Constitutional Court of the Czech Republic with Regard to the Nature and Purpose of Arbitration. In: *Bělohlávek, A. et Rozehnalová, N.* CYArb – Czech (& Central European) Yearbook of Arbitration:

CR, Case No. I ÚS 3227/07 of 8 March 2011,[127] which has brought about a significant material change in the opinions held by the ConCourt CR [CZE]. The preceding constitutional opinion (which appears long outdated, even from the perspective of international practice) was based on the presumption that arbitration was mainly the process of determining the contents of the consensus between the parties to the dispute;[128] in other words, it was based on contractual theory. The opinion expressed in the Judgment of the ConCourt CR [CZE] pushes this theory **a great way towards the jurisdiction theory of arbitration, perceived as a process of finding the law by a private-law entity,** analogous and equivalent to litigation and in compliance with applicable law. It is therefore safe to say that this 2011 decision of the Constitutional Court of the Czech Republic [CZE] overruled the contractual theory[129] and confirmed the jurisdictional basis for arbitration (albeit based on the contractual autonomy of the parties), and thereby confirmed the actual state of affairs that has already been in

---

The Relationship between Constitutional Values, Human Rights and Arbitration, Huntington (New York): JurisNet, 2011, Vol. 1, pp. 343–361; *Rozehnalová, N. et Havlíček, J.* Rozhodčí smlouva a rozhodci ve světle některých rozhodnutí... aneb quo vadis...? [Title in translation – Arbitration Agreement and Arbitrators in Light of Several Judgments ... Or Quo Vadis ...?] Právní fórum, 2010, No. 3, p. 114 et seq.; *Varvařovský, P.* Rozhodčí řízení v judikatuře Ústavního soudu. [Title in translation: Arbitration in the Case Law of the Constitutional Court]. Právní fórum, 2010, No. 3, p. 143 et seq. et al.

[127] The judgment is available online at the website of the ConCourt CR at: http://nalus.usoud.cz/Search/ResultDetail.aspx?id=69584&pos=1&cnt=1&typ=result [last access 110826]. The proceedings before the Constitutional Court were preceded by the following decisions of the [lower] courts: (i) Judgment of the Municipal Court in Prague, Case No. 8 Cm 164/2004-28 of 29 October 2004, (ii) Judgment of the High Court in Prague, Case No. 8 Cmo 80/2005-42 of 7 October 2005 and Resolution of the SC CR [CZE], Case No. 32 Odo 366/2006-64. The arbitral award was rendered in arbitration before the Arbitration Court Attached to the Economic Chamber of the Czech Republic and the Agricultural Chamber of the Czech Republic, Case No. Rsp 352/03 of 30 April 2004.

[128] The previous case law of the ConCourt CR [CZE] was more inclined towards the ratio expressed in the Resolution of the ConCourt CR [CZE], Case No. IV ÚS 174/02 of 15 July 2002, published in: Sbírka nálezů a usnesení Ústavního soudu České republiky [CZE] [Reports of Judgments and Resolutions of the Constitutional Court of the Czech Republic], Vol. 27, Resolution Ref. No. 20, p. 257 et seq. Annotated in great detail in: *Bělohlávek, A. et Profeldová, T.* Arbitration in the Case Law of the Constitutional Court of the Czech Republic with Regard to the Nature and Purpose of Arbitration. In: *Bělohlávek, A. et Rozehnalová, N.* CYArb – Czech (& Central European) Yearbook of Arbitration: The Relationship between Constitutional Values, Human Rights and Arbitration, Huntington (New York): JurisNet, 2011, Vol. 1, pp. 343–361, here pp. 350–354.

[129] After all, legal theory was only rarely inclined towards this approach in modern Czech arbitration; see *Bělohlávek, A. et Pezl, T.* Postavení rozhodčího řízení v systému ochrany práv a ústavního pořádku České republiky a dalších zemí. [Title in translation: Status of Arbitration in the System of the Protection of Rights and the Constitutional Laws of the Czech Republic and Other Countries]. Právní rozhledy, 2004, No. 7, pp. 256–261; *Raban, P.* K odpovědnosti rozhodce a rozhodčího soudu. [Title in translation: Concerning the Liability of Arbitrators and Arbitral Tribunals]. Bulletin advokacie, 2003, No. 1, pp. 25–34. Critical opinions or outright refusals of the theory were more common; see: *Pecha, R.* K právní povaze rozhodčích nálezů. [Title in translation: Concerning the Legal Nature of Arbitral Awards]. Bulletin advokacie, 2003, No. 5, pp. 41–45; *Růžička, K.* K otázce právní povahy rozhodčího řízení. [Title in translation: Concerning the Legal Nature of Arbitral Proceedings]. Bulletin advokacie, 2003, No. 5, pp. 32–40 et al.

place for some time in both arbitration proceedings, as such, and in the judicial practice of the courts. The arbitral tribunal was also classified as a **"different authority"** which is important, especially, because arbitrators are directly bound by applicable law and obliged to apply applicable law. At the same time, however, the Constitutional Court has honored the fact that the arbitrators' jurisdiction can only be established by the agreement of the parties based on their autonomy and within the limits of the applicable statutory rules. This decision is comparable to the modern approach to arbitration and reflects the actual present situation.

375. The Constitutional Court of the Czech Republic [CZE] **expressed its opinion on, inter alia, the following issues**, many of which are essential for the definition of the arbitration agreement, arbitration as such, arbitral proceedings and their relationship to litigation:

▶ Arbitration is a **type of civil procedure.** The fundamental difference from civil procedure in court (i.e. litigation) lies in the definition of the management and decision-making authority. Whereas in court proceedings (litigation) it is the court, in arbitration it is the arbitrator or a *permanent arbitral institution* (hereinafter the "arbitrator").[130]

▶ The fact that arbitration is a type of civil procedure, however, **does not in and of itself mean that courts are allowed to intervene freely in arbitration.**

▶ The arbitrator's power to hear and resolve the dispute is based on the **joint will of the parties to the dispute** expressed in their arbitration agreement. By means of this procedural agreement, the parties exclude the jurisdiction of the courts (with respect to Section 106(1) of the CCP [CZE][131] only conditionally) and establish the jurisdiction of the arbitrator(s).

---

[130] This abbreviation has been employed in the Judgment of the ConCourt CR [CZE] in the present case.

[131] CCP [CZE[(approximate translation, cit.): Examining the procedural requirements – [...] Section 106 – "(1) *As soon as the court discovers, on the respondent's objection lodged together with or before the first act of the respondent in the merits, that the agreement of the parties requires that the case be submitted to arbitration, the court must desist from further examination of the case and terminate the proceedings; the court, however, hears the case if the parties declare that they waive the agreement. The court also hears the case if the court determines that the matter is not arbitrable under the laws of the Czech Republic, or that the arbitration agreement is invalid or non-existent, or that examining the agreement in arbitration proceedings exceeds the scope of jurisdiction vested in the arbitrators by the agreement, or that the arbitral tribunal refused to hear the case. (2) If the court proceedings under Subsection (1) were terminated and the same case was submitted to arbitration, the original petition for commencement of the proceedings retains its legal effects providing the motion for the commencement of the arbitration proceedings is lodged no later than 30 days of service of the court's resolution terminating the proceedings. (3) If the arbitration proceedings were opened before the court proceedings, the court stays the proceedings on the non-existence, nullity or expiration/termination of the agreement until the arbitrator(s) decide on their jurisdiction over the case or in the merits."*

▶ **Based on the voluntary acts of the parties, the arbitrator therefore performs the duties instead of a court,** which would otherwise have to hear and decide the case. However, the rights of the parties to make dispositions with their disputes are even more far-reaching; the parties to the dispute are, for instance, allowed to determine the identity of the arbitrators, the applicable procedural rules, the venue of arbitration, the type of proceedings (oral or written), or even the criteria that should be applied to the merits.[132]

▶ No claim can be subject to both **arbitration and litigation** at the same time, i.e. the two proceedings **cannot be conducted in parallel**; arbitral awards are also endowed with the same effect as final and binding court decisions,[133] which means that arbitral awards constitute *res judicata*, barring the parties from litigating the same claim again in courts.

▶ **In compliance with the principle of autonomy of the parties, the law honors the freely expressed will of the parties who wish to have their dispute heard and decided by an arbitrator**; courts are therefore not allowed to intervene in the arbitral proceedings, except in strictly defined situations specified in the ArbAct [CZE]. On the other hand, this does not mean that the purpose of arbitration is to eliminate or reduce the degree of protection that would otherwise be afforded to the parties in civil litigation; arbitration, just like litigation, aims at the peaceful resolution of the dispute between the parties. The parties only have a special reason (for instance, expeditiousness[134] or confidentiality of the information discussed in

---

[132] The ConCourt CR invoked Section 25(3) of the ArbAct [CZE].
ArbAct [CZE] (cit.): Section 25 – "(1) *The arbitral award must be adopted by a majority of the arbitrators, must be made in writing and signed by at least the majority of the arbitrators. The operative part of the arbitral award must be clear and unambiguous.* (2) *The arbitral award shall be reasoned unless the parties agree to dispense with reasons; this also applies to any arbitral award rendered pursuant to Section 24(2) of the ArbAct* [CZE]. (3) *When making the award, the arbitrators apply the substantive law applicable to the dispute; they may, however, resolve the dispute according to the rules of equity but only if the parties explicitly authorized them to.*"
[133] The ConCourt CR invokes Section 28(2) of the ArbAct [CZE].
ArbAct [CZE] (cit.): Section 28 – "(1) *The written copy of the arbitral award must be served to the parties and after the service stamped with the legal force clause.* (2) *If an arbitral award cannot be subject to review under Section 27 of the ArbAct* [CZE] *or if the time period for filing the petition for review under Section 27 of the ArbAct* [CZE] *expired without the petition having been filed, the award has the effects of a final and binding court judgment and is enforceable by courts upon delivery.*"
ArbAct [CZE] (cit.): Section 27 – "*The parties may agree in their arbitration agreement that the arbitral award can be reviewed by other arbitrators at the request of any or both of the parties. Unless the arbitration agreement stipulates otherwise, the petition for review must be sent to the other party no later than 30 days from the date of delivery of the arbitral award to the party requesting the review. Review of the arbitral award constitutes part of the arbitral proceedings, and it is subject to the provisions of this Act.*"
[134] The ConCourt CR [CZE] has held (cit.): "*Academic writings mention, for instance, the following advantages: more expeditious proceedings due to the usual exclusion of appeal, less formal proceedings, and simpler procedural rules, as well as the fact that the arbitrator can be an expert in the respective field which is the subject matter of the dispute.*"

the proceedings) to believe that arbitration is a more suitable solution for them. From this perspective, the submission of a dispute to arbitration means the transfer [of jurisdiction, legal protection] to **a different decision-making and law-finding authority**, rather than a waiver of legal protection;[135] indeed, any other conclusion would render it conceptually unacceptable to consider arbitration a dispute resolution method alternative to litigation.

▶ The law allows the parties to exclude the jurisdiction of the court by their arbitration agreement and to vest jurisdiction over their dispute in an arbitrator, who will find the law in their respective case and incorporate the result in an authoritative decision – the arbitral award. The conclusion of the agreement is the result of a decision freely made by the parties, who contemplate the advantages and disadvantages of submitting their case to arbitration.

▶ The **autonomy of will** is one of the principles observed by a state honoring the rule of law. This autonomy also applies to the process of negotiating arbitration agreements. The law therefore accepts that the parties do not desire to have their dispute resolved by a court and prefer arbitration.

▶ Hearing the case in arbitral proceedings **does not constitute a denial of legal protection; it only represents the transfer of the latter from the courts to arbitrators.** However, the state cannot entirely waive the possibility of intervening; it must retain certain **supervisory duties** exercised by the courts.[136] The extent of this supervision must be carefully balanced – the rule stipulating that arbitration must also guarantee legal protection must not be eliminated, but on the other hand, the advantages of arbitration and its practical applicability must not be entirely wiped out.

▶ The parties have a broad scope to **agree on procedural rules**[137] governing the arbitral proceedings; on the other hand, though, this scope is not without limits. The Arbitration Act (ArbAct) contains in Section 18 of the ArbAct [CZE][138] a **mandatory provision**

Cf. *Klein, B.* Pozapomenuté výhody rozhodčího řízení. [Title in translation: The Forgotten Advantages of Arbitration]. Právní fórum, 2008, No. 4, p. 128 et seq.

[135] Cf. a similar case in Germany, Judgment of the Federal Court of Justice (Supreme Court; BGH [DEU], Case No. III ZR 265/03 of 13 January 2005. Said decision of the German court is available at: http://juris.bundesgerichtshof.de/cgi-bin/rechtsprechung/document.py?Gericht=bgh&Art=en&nr=31677&pos=0&anz=1 [last access 9 August 2011]. Cited in: *Hulmák, M. et Tomančáková, B.* Rozhodčí řízení jako vhodný prostředek řešení sporů mezi dodavatelem a spotřebitelem (1. část). [Title in translation: Arbitration as a Suitable Mechanism for the Resolution of Disputes between a Supplier and a Consumer (Part 1)]. Obchodněprávní revue, 2010, Vol. 2, No. 6, pp. 168–174 (see Footnote 33 in the article).

[136] Cf. *Klíma, K.* Ústavní právo. [Title in translation: Constitutional Law]. 1st ed. Dobrá Voda u Pelhřimova: Aleš Čeněk, 2002, p. 79.

[137] The ConCourt CR invoked Section 19(1) of the ArbAct [CZE]; this provision is quoted below.

[138] ArbAct [CZE] (cit.): Section 18 – "*The parties have an equal standing in the arbitral proceedings and must be provided with a full opportunity to assert their rights.*"

incorporating the principle of equal standing of the parties; the parties must also be provided with a full opportunity to assert their rights. Any agreement of the parties conflicting with this rule would be null and void. The equality of the parties and the full opportunity to assert their rights are principles that apply even in those cases in which the arbitrator's case management of the proceedings is governed by arbitration rules adopted by a *permanent arbitral institution*, or in which the arbitrators themselves determine the progress of the proceedings. This is clearly articulated in the second sentence of Section 19(2) of the ArbAct [CZE].[139] A breach of mandatory Section 18 of the ArbAct [CZE][140] constitutes grounds for setting aside the arbitral award listed in Section 31(1)(e) of the ArbAct [CZE].[141] If the *equality of the parties* was not honored or if any of the parties was denied a full opportunity to assert his or her rights, the party was undoubtedly denied the opportunity to plead his or her case before the arbitrators within the meaning of this provision.

▶ **Unpredictable acts of the arbitrator** could also constitute such denial of a full opportunity to assert the party's rights. The result of this is that the party, for instance, would not be able to plead their case with respect to all relevant circumstances. Or, the party may not be able to supplement their statements regarding any facts that the party did not consider relevant from the perspective of their own legal opinion, but which are relevant from the perspective of the arbitrator's legal opinion, and to propose the relevant evidence. **Eliminating any unpredictability** in the arbitrators' decision is all the more exigent, because arbitration, as a rule, does not allow appeals.[142] This constraint prevents the parties from responding to

---

[139] ArbAct [CZE] (cit.): Section 19 – "*(1) The parties have a right to agree on how the arbitrators shall case manage the proceedings. Matters regarding the case management of the proceedings may be resolved by the chairman of the tribunal providing he or she was authorized to do so by the parties or by all arbitrators. (2) Unless the parties negotiated an agreement pursuant to Subsection (1), the arbitrators shall case manage the proceedings in any manner they shall see fit. They case manage the arbitral proceedings in such manner that the facts of the case necessary for the resolution of the dispute are sufficiently ascertained, without any unnecessary formalities and while giving all parties equal opportunity to plead their case.*"

[140] Cited above.

[141] ArbAct [CZE] (cit.): Section 31 – "*At the request of any party the court sets aside an arbitral award if (a) the award was rendered in a case which is not arbitrable (cannot be the subject of a valid arbitration agreement), (b) the arbitration agreement is null and void for other reasons, was cancelled or does not apply to the dispute, (c) one or more arbitrators involved in the resolution of the dispute was/were not authorized to make decisions in the case under the arbitration agreement or otherwise, or lacked the capacity to act as arbitrator(s), (d) the arbitral award was not passed by the majority of arbitrators, (e) one or more parties did not have the opportunity to plead their case before the arbitrators, (f) the arbitral award orders a party to provide performance which was not requested by the creditor or which is not possible or allowed under domestic law, (g) it transpires that there are grounds which would otherwise justify a motion for reopening the proceedings (trial de novo) in civil litigation.*"

[142] See Section 27 of the ArbAct [CZE] (cit.): Section 27 – "*The parties may agree in their arbitration agreement that the arbitral award can be reviewed by other arbitrators at the request of any or both of*

---

any surprising legal opinion, at least *ex post facto*. **The arbitrator cannot play the role of a merely passive element; he or she must case manage the proceedings in such manner that his/her decision is not a surprise to the parties.** To that end, civil court proceedings prescribe that courts must give instructions to the parties; there is no reason to absolve the arbitrator of that obligation in arbitral proceedings, considering the fact that in such proceedings the arbitrator acts as the decision-making authority instead of the court. **The duty of the arbitrator to give instructions to the parties** does not conflict with the nature of arbitration; in other words, the specific features of arbitration cannot justify the conclusion that arbitrators do not need to ensure that their decisions are predictable.

▶ The Arbitration Act [CZE] (ArbAct [CZE]) does not lay down the arbitrator's obligation to give instructions; it is therefore legitimate **to reasonably apply the Code of Civil Procedure** (CCP [CZE]).[143]

---

the parties. Unless the arbitration agreement stipulates otherwise, the petition for review must be sent to the other party no later than 30 days from the date of delivery of the arbitral award to the party requesting the review. Review of the arbitral award constitutes part of the arbitral proceedings, and it is subject to the provisions of this Act."

[143] The ConCourt CR invokes Section 30 of the ArbAct [CZE] and subsequently Section 118 of the CCP [CZE]. The Court simultaneously confirms the opinion expressed in the Judgment of the SC CR [CZE], Case No. 32 Odo 1528/2005 of 25 April 2007 and in the Judgment of the SC CR [CZE], Case No. 23 Cdo 3749/2008 of 26 May 2010.

CCP [CZE] (cit.): Section 118 – *"(1) After opening the hearing the chairman of the panel requests the claimant (petitioner) to present his or her claim (petition for opening the proceedings) or summarize the contents thereof, and requests the respondent (or all other parties to the proceedings) to present his or her defense or written pleadings or summarize the contents thereof; submissions lodged by absent parties shall be read or the contents thereof summarized by the chairman of the panel. The respondent (other party to the proceedings) who has not lodged his or her written pleadings shall be invited by the chairman of the panel to make a statement in the case. If necessary, the chairman of the panel also invites the party or parties to supplement their statements and to propose evidence supporting their case. (2) Having performed the acts under Subsection (1), the chairman of the panel reports the results of the preparatory stage of the proceedings and informs the parties accordingly which legally significant statements of fact presented by the parties can be considered uncontested, which legally relevant statements of fact remained contested and what evidence proposed so far shall be heard or read and what evidence shall be heard or read despite the fact that the parties did not propose to hear or read the evidence. (3) Unless the law stipulates otherwise, the chairman of the panel shall case manage the proceedings depending on the circumstances of the case."*

CCP [CZE] (cit.): Section 118a – *"(1) If it transpires during the hearing that a party has not yet presented all relevant statements of fact or has presented them only insufficiently, the chairman of the panel invites the party to supplement its statements and gives him or her instructions as to which statements are to be supplemented and what the consequences of noncompliance are. (2) If the chairman of the panel opines that the court's legal opinion of the case could differ from the party's legal opinion, the chairman invites the party to supplement the relevant statements of fact to the necessary extent; the chairman shall proceed similarly to Subsection (1). (3) If the chairman of the panel discovers during the hearing that a party has not yet proposed evidence necessary to prove all of his or her contested statements, the chairman invites the party to identify such evidence without undue delay and gives him or her instructions regarding the consequences of noncompliance. (4) During the hearings, the chairman of the panel also gives to the parties instructions regarding other procedural rights and duties of the parties; this does not apply if the party is represented by an attorney or a notary public to the extent of the notary's authorization under special laws."*

▶ If the courts in the proceedings on setting aside an arbitral award failed to address the objection that the arbitrator(s) did not discharge their duty to give instructions to the parties in the course of the arbitral proceedings, the ConCourt CR [CZE] cannot (materially) address this objection either, because the Constitutional Court would thereby violate its duty to act as a protector of constitutionally guaranteed fundamental rights and freedoms, and would interfere with and unduly substitute for the conduct of the courts. In such cases, however, the court may grant the constitutional complaint and annul the decisions of the lower courts for violating the party's right to a fair trial.[144]

▶ Although it might be constitutionally relevant in certain cases that the legislator failed to lay down rules regulating a particular issue, this does not apply if the list of grounds for annulment of an arbitral award[145] does not include a conflict with substantive law or *public policy*. Permitting the review of arbitral awards by the court[146] due to a breach of substantive law is doubtful both from the perspective of interpreting the grounds for annulment of arbitral awards and from the theoretical perspective.

▶ Proceedings on setting aside an arbitral award by the court can never be structured similarly to remedial civil court proceedings, let alone regular appellate proceedings. If the court were allowed to review an arbitral award from the perspective of its compliance with substantive law, it would deny the existence of arbitration. **The supervisory role of the courts** can therefore only concentrate on **examining the crucial procedural issues**, for instance, whether arbitration could actually have been conducted, whether any important procedural rights were denied to the parties, or whether the arbitral award itself is free of any procedural flaws (for instance, it was not passed by the majority of the arbitrators).

(bb) Factual and legal circumstances of the case and court decisions regarding setting aside an arbitral award

376. Proceedings at the ConCourt CR [CZE] were held following the proceedings on setting aside the arbitral award, which was rendered in the Czech Republic in April 2004. The Arbitration Court Attached to the Economic Chamber of the Czech Republic and the Agricultural Chamber of the Czech Republic dismissed the claimant's claim for the payment of [CZK *xxx.xxx.xxx*], and stated that the arbitral award was

---

[144] Consequently, the case was remanded to the trial court which will have to examine whether the duty to give instructions was breached in the arbitral proceedings and whether there are grounds for setting aside the arbitral award or not. We have had no new information about the new trial in the lower courts and the results thereof until the day of drafting this annotation.

[145] The grounds are listed in Section 31 of the ArbAct [CZE]; the provision is quoted above.

[146] Cf. *Pohl, T.* K problematice přezkoumání rozhodčích nálezů soudem. [Title in translation: Regarding the Review of Arbitral Awards by Courts]. Právní fórum, 2008, No. 4, p. 158 et seq. et al.

final and binding, having the effect of a final judgment as soon as it was served on both parties, and was enforceable by the court. The Arbitration Court reasoned that the claimant was not entitled to claim the respective amount of money from the respondent; consequently, the claimant's motion was dismissed.

377. The complainant[147] argued that the principle of predictability of decisions was breached in the arbitral proceedings due to the violation of the duty to give instructions, which the arbitrators refused to apply. According to the complainant, the arbitral tribunal breached the duty to give instructions by adopting a different legal opinion on two issues without having informed the claimant thereof, and by failing to invite the claimant to propose evidence proving the complainant's allegations regarding the interpretation of a contract according to the intention of the parties, which was – considering the award finally rendered by the arbitrators – fundamental. The complainant argued that the true will of the parties should have been ascertained by interrogating witnesses.[148] The complainant actually proposed the examination of witnesses, without being requested to do so by the arbitrators; the arbitrators, however, rejected this evidence without providing any grounds justifying such rejection. The complainant in the complainant's constitutional complaint alleged that the courts groundlessly refused (in the proceedings on setting aside the arbitral award) to apply the principle of predictability incorporated in Section 118a of the CCP [CZE],[149] and thereby violated Article 36(1) of the Charter [CZE][150] and Article 37(3) of the Charter [CZE].[151]

---

[147] The complainant was a bank, namely *Česká spořitelna a.s.*
Regarding some aspects of the connection between contracts negotiated in the financial area and arbitration according to Czech laws see also *Krč, R. et Marek, K. Smlouva o otevření akreditivu.* [Title in translation: Letter of Credit Agreement]. Právní rozhledy, 1998, No. 7, p. 361 et seq.
[148] As concerns the significance of such evidence, the complainant invokes the Judgment of the ConCourt CR [CZE], Case No. I. ÚS 220/98 of 6 June 2000, published in: Sbírka nálezů a usnesení Ústavního soudu České republiky [CZE] [Reports of Judgments and Resolutions of the Constitutional Court of the Czech Republic], Vol. 18, reg. no. N 85, p. 219 et seq.
[149] The provision is quoted above in the annotation of this judgment.
[150] Charter [CZE] (approximate translation, cit.): Chapter Five – The Right to Judicial and Other Legal Protection – Article 36 – "(1) *Everyone may assert, through the legally prescribed procedure, his or her rights before an independent and impartial court or, in specified cases, before a different authority.* (2) *Unless the law provides otherwise, a person who claims that his or her rights were curtailed by a decision of a public administrative authority may turn to a court for review of the legality of that decision. However, judicial review of decisions affecting the fundamental rights and basic freedoms listed in this Charter may not be removed from the jurisdiction of courts.* (3) *Everyone is entitled to compensation for damage sustained by him or her as a result of an unlawful decision of a court, another state authority, or a public administrative authority, or as a result of an improper official procedure.* (4) *Conditions and detailed provisions are laid down by statute.*"
[151] Charter [CZE] (approximate translation, cit.): Chapter Five – The Right to Judicial and Other Legal Protection – [...] Article 37 – "[......] (3) *All parties to the proceedings are equal.* [......]"

378. The complainant also argued that the arbitral award grossly violated substantive law, as a result of which the decision was unpredictable. The complainant's main argument was the acceptance of the contractual theory by the Constitutional Court of the Czech Republic [CZE] (according to a number of decisions rendered in the past).[152] The complainant claimed that if the duty of the arbitrator was [only] to establish (settle) an obligation (relationship) between the parties, rather than to find the law (as opposed to the duties of courts, as the contractual theory of arbitration would demand), the law-finding activity of courts should not be prejudiced by arbitration, and courts should be allowed to review the arbitral award from the perspective of its compliance with substantive law. This conclusion is also supported, in the complainant's view, by the fact that arbitrators are not "**different authorities**" in terms of Article 36(1) of the Charter [CZE].[153] Both the arbitral proceedings and the arbitral award are of a private law nature; arbitral awards should therefore be reviewable from the perspective of their compliance with substantive law. They are not, however, and the complainant considers this state of affairs unconstitutional. Section 31 of the ArbAct [CZE], as opposed to other laws, does not even allow the courts to annul the arbitral award for fundamental procedural irregularities,[154] or for breach of *public policy* or the fundamental principles of Czech law [CZE]. The complainant argued that this violates the complainant's right to a fair trial, and this situation can only be remedied by including in Section 31 of the ArbAct [CZE] the possibility to set aside an arbitral award for failure to comply with substantive law. The complainant therefore suggested amending the ArbAct [CZE], so that the list of grounds for setting aside an arbitral award is no longer an exhaustive list but becomes merely illustrative.

379. As concerns the facts of the case, the complainant pointed out that the award did not comply with substantive law, because the Restructuring Agreement negotiated between the parties did not stipulate the due date

---

[152] The ConCourt CR [CZE] also invoked the contractual theory, and the complainant refers specifically to:

➤ Resolution of the ConCourt CR [CZE], Case No. III. ÚS 460/01 of 1 November 2001, published in: Sbírka nálezů a usnesení Ústavního soudu České republiky [CZE] [Reports of Judgments and Resolutions of the Constitutional Court of the Czech Republic], Vol. 24, Resolution Ref. No. 41, p. 563 et seq.

➤ Resolution of the ConCourt CR [CZE], Case No. IV: ÚS 174/02 of 15 July 2002, published in: Sbírka nálezů a usnesení Ústavního soudu České republiky [CZE] [Reports of Judgments and Resolutions of the Constitutional Court of the Czech Republic], Vol. 27, Resolution Ref. No. 20, p. 257 et seq. and

➤ Resolution of the ConCourt CR [CZE], Case No. IV. ÚS 435/02 of 22 October 2002.

[153] Cited above in the annotation of this judgment.

[154] The grounds for setting aside an arbitral award are (inter alia) identical to the grounds for a trial de novo in court proceedings (see Section 31(g) of the ArbAct [CZE]), but not to the grounds constituting an *irregularity of proceedings*.

on which the motivation fees were to be paid. From this perspective, the award conflicted with the Restructuring Agreement and breached the principle of *pacta sunt servanda*, as well as the statutory rules regulating the interpretation of the parties' expression of will. The courts failed to protect the complainant against an award rendered in violation of substantive law, by which the courts breached Article 36(1) of the Charter [CZE].

380.   However, the complainant argued, in particular, that the arbitral proceedings also suffered from other procedural irregularities. The arbitral tribunal failed to hear the evidence proposed by the complainant and based its decision merely on the allegations of the joint party (i.e. respondent in the original arbitral proceedings, hereinafter the "respondent"). Even though the complainant proposed interrogating witnesses, whereby the true will of the parties was to be determined, the arbitral tribunal dismissed the proposal and thereby de facto deprived the complainant of the possibility of pleading the complainant's case; the tribunal based its decision merely on the unsubstantiated allegations of the respondent. The lower courts concluded that the failure to hear or read evidence did not constitute grounds sufficient for setting aside an arbitral award pursuant to Section 31(e) of the ArbAct [CZE]; this conclusion conflicts with Article 36(1) of the Charter [CZE][155] and Article 37(3) of the Charter [CZE].[156]

381.   The trial court[157] dismissed the complainant's motion for the annulment of the arbitral award. The court maintained that the arbitral tribunal's refusal to hear the evidence did not constitute grounds for setting aside the arbitral award pursuant to Section 31(e) of the ArbAct [CZE] (failure to provide an opportunity to plead one's case in the arbitral proceedings). The court of appeals upheld the decision of the trial court.[158] The court of appeals maintained that the arbitral tribunal had discussed the case with the parties in an oral hearing, and the parties had had full opportunity to present their statements and propose evidence. Setting aside an arbitral award for the tribunal's failure to hear or read evidence proposed by a party would only be possible if the arbitrators, without any justification, refused to hear or read the evidence or examined it only insufficiently. The court, however, cannot evaluate such evidence with regard to its potential impact on the result of the proceedings; such an evaluation is reserved for the arbitrators.[159] The

---

[155] Cited above in the annotation of this judgment.
[156] Cited above in the annotation of this judgment.
[157] Judgment of the Municipal Court in Prague [CZE], Case No. 8 Cm 165/2004 of 11 January 2005 (unpublished).
[158] Judgment of the High Court in Prague [CZE], Case No. 8 Cmo 80/2005-42 of 7 October 2005.
[159] The court of appeals also discovered that the arbitrators had in fact analyzed the grounds for rejecting the respective evidence (interrogation) and had issued resolutions regarding that issue.

cassation appeal to the Supreme Court challenging the decisions mentioned above was dismissed.[160] The Supreme Court upheld the preceding decisions of the lower courts, especially as concerns the opportunity of the party to plead his or her case in the arbitral proceedings. The Supreme Court mainly emphasized that the parties have no right to have all the evidence (which they proposed) heard or read, not even under civil procedure rules regulating litigation.

(cc) Decision of the Constitutional Court on merits

382. According to the ConCourt CR [CZE], both arbitrators and *permanent arbitral institutions* are *different authorities* (from the courts), which resolve disputes between the parties, and in so doing apply applicable law. They do not, however, become public authorities as a result thereof. Arbitrators are still private persons whom the parties to the dispute endow with the power to hear and decide their dispute according to their procedural agreement. If the arbitrator or the *permanent arbitral institution* is not a public authority, then their decision or any other intervention cannot be directly challenged by a constitutional complaint. The ConCourt CR [CZE] therefore dismissed the part of the complainant's constitutional complaint in which the complainant directly challenged the arbitral award (the Constitutional Court refused to set aside the arbitral award). Indeed, the complainant actually admitted that the part of the constitutional complaint challenging the arbitral award was only included because the complainant wished to proceed cautiously. The Constitutional Court therefore concentrated exclusively on the arguments challenging the court decisions rendered in the proceedings on setting aside the arbitral award.

383. The constitutional complaint was joined with the motion to repeal the part of Section 31 of the ArbAct [CZE] that stipulates that the list of grounds for the annulment of an arbitral award is exhaustive. The complainant pointed out that a conflict with substantive law was missing as a ground for annulment, as well as other situations such as a breach of *public policy*. The complainant did not suggest, though, that the absence of these grounds curtailed the complainant's constitutional rights. It was the absence of any arguments regarding any potential violation of the

---

[160] Resolution of the Supreme Court of the Czech Republic [CZE], Case No. 32 Odo 366/2006-64 of 11 September 2007. Published at the SC CR [CZE] website at: http://www.nsoud.cz/ JudikaturaNS_new/judikatura_prevedena2.nsf/WebSearch/71F12800CB05F81AC12575FF007A036C ?openDocument [last access 26 August 2011]. The Supreme Court (SC CR [CZE]) points out, inter alia, that the Code of Civil Procedure (CCP [CZE]) does not grant the parties the right to have the evidence heard or read which they had proposed; it is the court that decides what evidence (proposed by the parties) shall be admitted in the proceedings. The party is not deprived of the opportunity to plead his or her case before the court by the mere fact that the court refuses to hear or read the evidence proposed by that party, providing the court justifies its refusal to take the evidence. This interpretation can be extrapolated to Section 31(e) of the ArbAct [CZE].

complainant's specific constitutional rights that resulted in dismissing the motion as prima facie groundless. The refusal to review the merits of arbitral awards has also been analyzed by the ConCourt CR [CZE], thoroughly and from the comparative (international) perspective.[161] The Constitutional Court concluded, however, that the courts had failed to sufficiently address the issue of whether or not the duty to give instructions had been duly discharged, and in the latter case, if the arbitrators had thereby violated the party's right to a fair trial or, as the case may be, deprived the party of the opportunity to plead its case in the arbitral proceedings. Despite avoiding any decision on the merits, i.e. the annulment of the decisions of the lower courts and remanding of the case for a new trial in order to find out whether the duty to give instructions was duly discharged, the ConCourt CR [CZE] provided an unusually thorough and comprehensive analysis of the majority of the fundamental issues relating to the nature of the arbitration agreement, the substance of arbitration, the fundamental principles of arbitration, and its relation to the process of finding the law and to the acts of courts. Without exaggeration, it is a landmark decision, which offers a new and clear definition of these fundamental issues from the perspective of constitutional law and constitutional principles. However, it is by no means a *surprising decision*. Legal professionals and a large number of academics have clearly confirmed that the definition of the substance of arbitration as previously articulated by the Constitutional Court, especially in the 2002 resolution, and as subsequently adhered to, is no longer sustainable; the Constitutional Court de facto treated arbitration as an equal alternative to litigation from the perspective of many fundamental procedural principles and from the perspective of finding the applicable law in arbitration.[162] It is therefore probably the *proverbial end* of the 15-year search for a constitutional opinion on arbitration after the ArbAct [CZE] was adopted in 1994 (effective date 1 January 1995), and arbitration was thereby opened for the majority of civil disputes and disputes without international dimensions, which were the only arbitrable disputes prior to 1995.[163]

(dd) Correlation between decision and consumer protection

384. The respective dispute was not a consumer dispute. However, the Constitutional Court (ConCourt CR [CZE]) modified its case law and explicitly stated that arbitrators were an "institution" that finds and must

---

[161] The Court made a comparison with Article 34 of the UNCITRAL Model Law, Section 1059 of the ZPO [DEU] and Section 40 of the ArbAct [SVK].

[162] Cf. Rozehnalová, N. Rozhodčí řízení – alternativa k řízení soudnímu. [Title in translation: Arbitration – An Alternative to Litigation]. Právní fórum, 2008, No. 4, p. 121 et seq.

[163] Pursuant to Act No. 98/1963 Coll., on Arbitration in International Commerce and on the Enforcement of Arbitral Awards.

find the applicable law. It is a significant shift in the case law of the ConCourt CR [CZE] from 2002. Indeed, the ConCourt CR [CZE] thereby also provided a clear answer to the question of what the arbitrators' duty in the arbitral proceedings actually is. Arbitrators are persons (albeit with private-law status) who apply applicable law, and there is consequently no reason to suspect that the requirements of consumer protection under European (Union) law should not be fulfilled in this regard. Indeed, the same conclusion regarding this issue in connection with consumer protection was also articulated, for instance, by the German Federal Court of Justice (Supreme Court, BGH [DEU]). On the other hand, it is necessary to point out that the ConCourt CR [CZE] did not attempt to disguise its rather cautious approach to arbitration clauses in consumer contracts. The Court stated that the law indeed allowed the parties to exclude, in their arbitration agreement, the jurisdiction of the court and to vest jurisdiction over their dispute in an arbitrator who would find the law in their respective case and incorporate the result in an authoritative decision – the arbitral award. The conclusion of the agreement is the result of a decision freely made by the parties, who contemplate the advantages and disadvantages of submitting their case to arbitration. The Constitutional Court, however, explicitly emphasized that the complainant was not a consumer, and therefore the Court had not analyzed arbitration clauses incorporated in arbitration agreements that (cit.): "*are often abused and frequently have the nature of unreasonable (unfair) terms,*" Apparently, the Court reserved the right to draw specific conclusions, should it be called upon to review a case concerning a consumer dispute in the future. Moreover, the decision was adopted at a time when the Cabinet was finalizing an extensive Amendment to the ArbAct [CZE], the purpose of which was, inter alia, to lay down rules applicable in consumer arbitration. It is therefore laudable that the ConCourt CR [CZE] at that time refrained from voicing any explicit opinion on arbitration clauses in consumer disputes, and left the entire field of law to the legislator. The Court's reservation (as concerns consumer disputes) is thus constitutionally conformant and strategic. On the other hand, the *critical remark* went rather too far (this is a general negative trait of the Czech decision-making practice). It is clear that in its future decisions, the ConCourt CR [CZE] might apply very strict criteria (to say the least) in connection with arbitration clauses in consumer contracts and with respect to consumer protection. Indeed, the Court's possible future approach to consumer arbitration can be deduced from numerous paragraphs of the present judgment, especially the Court's conclusion regarding full autonomy, which, however, means the expression of a **joint** (i.e. *genuine, true* – author's note) **will of the parties**. The arbitration agreement entered into between the parties must therefore clearly indicate that it represents an expression of will of both (all) parties to the agreement. The Constitutional Court of the Czech Republic [CZE] also repeatedly emphasized the equality of the parties and pointed out that any agreement of the parties to the contrary would be null and void. This necessarily means that any agreement that would award more procedural rights to one of the parties, to the detriment of others, would be null and void.

385. The emphasis placed on the **duty to give instructions** as protection against surprising decisions is probably a feature specific to Czech law (Czech *lex arbitri*). The requirement to furnish both parties with the necessary instructions had previously and repeatedly been voiced, especially (though not exclusively) in the case law of the Supreme Court of the Czech Republic [CZE]. Although there are certain trends even in the international arena that have the objective of eliminating *unpredictable decisions*, prevailing international practice has adopted a rather distrustful approach to any duty to give instructions in arbitration and has stressed the principle of maximum liability of the parties for the protection of their rights, arguing that a duty to give instructions tends to conflict with the principle of independence and impartiality of arbitrators. Consequently, it is certainly a specific feature of the Czech *lex arbitri* and Czech civil procedure in which this [*duty to give instructions*] imposed on the courts [or arbitrators, as the case may be] is considered a *principle*, thanks to the case law of the lower courts, as well as the Constitutional Court. This principle becomes all the more important in connection with consumer disputes, although it applies to arbitration generally.

(c) Resolution of the Constitutional Court of the Czech Republic, Case No. II. ÚS 3057/10 of 5 October 2011

(aa) Conclusions of the Constitutional Court

386. The Constitutional Court of the Czech Republic arrived at the **following conclusions, inter alia:**[164]

▶ The Constitutional Court [CZE] has repeatedly **accentuated the principle of freedom of contract, also in relation to arbitration clauses. The mere incorporation of arbitration clauses in the laws and regulations is not considered a restriction of access to court**, i.e. no violation of Article 36(1) of the Charter.[165] However, it is

---

[164] The decision is available at the website of the ConCourt CR [CZE]. The litigation involved the following decisions:
➤ Resolution of the District Court for Prague 2 [CZE], Case No. 18 C 218/2009-59 of 29 October 2010,
➤ Resolution of the Municipal Court in Prague [CZE], Case No. 58 Co 332/2010 of 16 July 2010.
[165] Charter [CZE] (cit.): Chapter Five – The Right to Judicial and Other Legal Protection – Article 36 – "(1) *Everyone may assert, through the legally prescribed procedure, his or her rights before an independent and impartial court or, in specified cases, before a different authority. (2) Unless the law provides otherwise, a person who claims that his or her rights were curtailed by a decision of a public*

desirable that the **waiver of the right to have the dispute reviewed by a court be permissible, unambiguous, and made through one's own free will.** [166] This requirement entails the obligation of the court to examine the arbitration clause, in each particular case, from the perspective of the reasonability of the clause (see the *Directive*), taking into account the unequal position of the consumer as a party to the arbitration agreement.

▶ Autonomy of will and freedom of individual conduct are primarily based on Section 2(1) of the ArbAct [CZE].

▶ The method of entering into, and the wording of, arbitration agreements (or arbitration clauses, as the case may be) in consumer contracts regulated under Section 52 et seq. of the CC [CZE] must be subject to a special approach. These provisions are based on the *Directive* which was adopted with the aim of enhancing the protection of consumers against unfair contractual terms. Article 3(1) and Article 6(1) of the *Directive* indicate that a national court is authorized to examine an arbitration clause incorporated in a contract concluded between a consumer and a trader (professional) in light of the *Directive*, even if the consumer himself or herself did not plead unfairness of the clause.

▶ Article 3(1) of the *Directive* in conjunction with paragraph 1(q) of the Annex to the *Directive* stipulate that **arbitration clauses can also be considered unfair terms in consumer contracts.**

▶ Section 56 of the CC [CZE] stipulates that consumer contracts must not contain terms causing a **significant imbalance in the parties' rights and obligations.** Terms which (i) were not individually negotiated or which (ii) simultaneously cause a significant imbalance in the parties' rights and obligations are invalid.

▶ The court examines all circumstances of the case. Despite the fact that arbitration clauses are not explicitly listed in the indicative list of

---

administrative authority may turn to a court for review of the legality of that decision. However, judicial review of decisions affecting the fundamental rights and basic freedoms listed in this Charter (Charter [CZE]) may not be removed from the jurisdiction of courts. (3) Everyone is entitled to compensation for damage sustained by him or her as a result of an unlawful decision of a court, another state authority, or a public administrative authority, or as a result of an improper official procedure. (4) Conditions and detailed provisions are laid down by statute."

[166]The ConCourt [CZE] invokes the judgment of the ECHR in the case of Complaint No. 1643/06 of 28 October 2010 (*Suda* v. *The Czech Republic*) in which the right to a fair trial under Article 6(1) of the ECHR was subject to examination. *Suda* v. *The Czech Republic* concerned a Czech citizen living in the Czech Republic (the complainant). He was a minority shareholder in a joint stock company. His shares were redeemed by the majority shareholder in compliance with the provisions of the Commercial Code [CZE], which anticipated the possibility that the compensation for the shares would in such cases be reviewed by an arbitral tribunal instead of a court. The complainant argued that his fundamental right to a fair trial had been violated in these cases, because he was bound by an arbitration clause which he himself had not negotiated. Cf. *Roodt, Chr.* Conflicts of Procedure Between Courts and Arbitral Tribunals with Particular Reference to the Right of Access to Court. African Journal of International and Comparative Law, 2011, Vol. 19, pp. 236–282.

potential unfair terms in consumer contracts as specified in the CC [CZE],[167] the court may conclude that a particular arbitration clause must be classified as unfair.

▶ If the arbitration clause is incorporated in a consumer contract, the wording of the clause must be subject to a more rigorous assessment; the same applies to the criteria regarding the arbitrators who might be called upon to resolve potential future disputes between the contracting parties – the method of their appointment must be subject to a particularly rigorous test. **Considering the nature of consumer contracts, it is necessary to lay special emphasis on the rule that both parties must have equal rights in selecting their arbitrators.**

▶ In the case of an arbitration clause [in a consumer contract] which is, contrary to the law, clearly aimed at causing detriment to the "weaker" contracting party, the principle of party autonomy must not be (mis)used to negate the protection of that party. A democratic country honoring the principle of the rule of law must not give up the protection of the rights and legitimate interests which could be jeopardized in alternative proceedings conducted in lieu of litigation.[168]

▶ Assessment of the validity of an arbitration clause must **take into account the importance of arbitration** as a dispute resolution method, including the appointment of the arbitrator, i.e. the person who **the parties choose** because they have confidence in him or her. **The principle of selecting one's arbitrator is not fulfilled by a mere reference to a list of arbitrators.**

▶ Section 2(1) of the ArbAct [CZE] provides that an arbitration agreement (or [an arbitration] clause incorporated in the main contract, as the case may be) **must include the parties' agreement on either an "ad hoc" arbitrator(s) or a *permanent arbitral institution* established under the law.**[169] The *ad hoc arbitrator,*

---

[167] Section 56(2) of the CC [CZE] as amended. We ought to mention that the New Civil Code (NCC [CZE]) expressly broadens this non-exhaustive list to include arbitration clauses.

[168] In this case, the Constitutional Court of the Czech Republic agreed with the opinion expressed in the Decision of the Grand Panel of the Civil Law Division and the Commercial Law Division of the Supreme Court of the Czech Republic, Case No. 31 Cdo 1945/2010 of 11 May 2011.

[169] See the ArbAct [CZE] (as applicable on the day this arbitration clause was concluded, cit.): Section 13 – Permanent Arbitral Institutions – "(1) *Permanent arbitral institutions can be established only under the law.* (2) *Permanent arbitral institutions can issue their own statutes and rules which must be published in the Business Journal; these statutes and rules may determine the method of appointment and the number of arbitrators and may stipulate that the arbitrators shall be selected from a list administered by the permanent arbitral institution. The statutes and rules may also determine how the arbitrators shall case manage the proceedings and render their decisions and resolve other issues connected with the activities of the permanent arbitral institution and the arbitrators, including rules regulating the costs of proceedings and remuneration for the arbitrators.* (3) *If the parties agreed on the jurisdiction of a particular permanent arbitral institution and failed to agree otherwise in the arbitration agreement, they shall be deemed to have submitted to the*

always a natural person (Section 4 of the ArbAct [CZE]),[170] can be identified (*by his, her, or their name(s), should there be more than one arbitrator, directly in the arbitration agreement*), or the arbitration agreement (clause) can define the method of appointment and the number of arbitrators – Section 7(1) of the ArbAct [CZE].

▶ Section 19 of the ArbAct [CZE][171] provides that the parties may agree on how the arbitrators shall case manage the proceedings, and, in the absence of such agreement, the arbitrators shall case manage the proceedings in any manner they shall see fit (the proceedings are oral unless the parties agree otherwise). **As opposed to arbitrators appointed** *ad hoc, permanent arbitral institutions* **may issue their own rules (statutes and rules) which may set forth the process of appointment and determine the number of arbitrators (the arbitrators can be selected from a list), as well as stipulate the manner whereby the arbitrators shall case manage the proceedings and the costs of arbitration payable by the parties.** Such rules must be published in the *Business Journal [Obchodní věstník]*.[172] Decisions[173] are rendered pursuant to the above-

---

regulations specified in Subsection (2), as applicable on the day the request for arbitration is filed with the permanent arbitral institution." With effect from 1 April 2012, an Amendment to the ArbAct [CZE] modifies Section 13 of the ArbAct [CZE] by amending Subsection (1) and inserting a new Subsection (4) in Section 13 [a new subsection] of the ArbAct [CZE] (cit.): Section 13 – Permanent Arbitral Institutions – "(1) *Permanent arbitral institutions can be established only by another law or if their formation is explicitly allowed by another law.* [...] (4) *No entity may carry out its activities using a name which evokes a misleading impression that the entity is a permanent arbitral institution under this law unless a different law or regulation or an international agreement integrated in the legal system authorizes the entity to use the name.*" Subsections (2) and (3) of Section 13 of the ArbAct [CZE] continue to apply unamended.

[170] ArbAct [CZE] (as applicable on the day this arbitration clause was concluded, cit.): Part Two – Arbitrators – Section 4 – "(1) *Any citizen of the Czech Republic who is of legal age and has legal capacity can serve as an arbitrator unless a special law stipulates otherwise. (2) A foreigner can serve as an arbitrator if he or she has legal capacity under the laws of his or her country; it shall suffice, however, if he or she has legal capacity under the laws of the Czech Republic.*"
With effect from 1 April 2012, an Amendment to the ArbAct [CZE] modifies Section 4 of the ArbAct [CZE] with respect to arbitration in consumer disputes; the entire Section 4 of the ArbAct [CZE] is amended as follows (cit.): Section 4 – "(1) *Any citizen of the Czech Republic who is of legal age, has no criminal record and has legal capacity can serve as an arbitrator unless a special law stipulates otherwise. (2) A foreigner may serve as an arbitrator if he or she meets the condition of majority, no criminal record and legal capacity; the requirement of legal capacity shall be governed by the person's lex patriae. It shall suffice, however, if he or she has legal capacity under the laws of the Czech Republic. (3) In order to meet the requirement of no criminal record under Subsections (1) and (2), the person must have no previous final and conclusive conviction for a criminal offence unless the person's criminal record is expunged and the person is deemed never to have been convicted. (4) An arbitrator designated by an arbitration clause to resolve disputes arising from consumer contracts must be registered in the list of arbitrators administered by the Ministry of Justice (the 'Ministry').*"
[171] Quoted below in a footnote to the annotation of this decision.
[172] See Section 13(2) of the ArbAct [CZE]. Regarding the conditions for the formation of "*permanent arbitral institutions,*" see Section 13(1) of the ArbAct [CZE]. The provision is cited elsewhere in a

mentioned rules issued by the *permanent arbitral institution*, as applicable on the day the request for arbitration is filed with the arbitral institution.

▶ If an entity other than a *permanent arbitral institution* under the ArbAct [CZE] carries out activities which, according to the ArbAct [CZE], are reserved for *permanent arbitral institutions*, **logic dictates** that this entity **clearly and intentionally violates the law.** It is a manifest attempt to impose conditions which raise **reasonable and justified doubts regarding the perspective of an independent and impartial dispute resolution.**

▶ If the arbitration agreement lacks any direct identification of an *ad hoc* arbitrator, or a **specific description of the method of his or her appointment,** but **only refers to a selection made by a "tribunal" or "court,"** i.e. a legal entity (corporation) other than a *permanent arbitral institution* established under the law, **the arbitration agreement is invalid.**

▶ **The arbitration clause is also likely to be classified as invalid if the clause refers to a legal entity whose company name contains the words** *"arbitral," "court," "institution," or "tribunal"* **when it is not in fact a *permanent arbitral institution*** pursuant to Section 13 of the ArbAct [CZE], because such a reference can be considered a fraudulent **term misleading the consumer** as a deceitful company name.

▶ The parties may also agree to depart from the rules issued and published by the *permanent arbitral institution*; in the absence of such agreement, however, the *permanent arbitral institution* follows the rules.

(bb) From the facts of the case; decisions of the lower courts

387. The case concerned an arbitration clause which read as follows (cit.): *"[a]ny and all disputes arising from or in connection with this contract shall be submitted to and resolved in arbitration before [... company name of the legal entity.... with its registered office in Prague...], by a single arbitrator selected by the Court from the list of arbitrators administered by the Arbitration Court of the Czech Republic. The arbitral proceedings shall follow the Rules of Procedure, the Tariff and other rules adopted by the Arbitration Court of the Czech Republic*

---

footnote to the annotation of this decision, together with information regarding the changes to be implemented with effect from 1 April 2012.

[173] Although the Constitutional Court of the Czech Republic in its resolution speaks of the *"decision-making subject to the respective rules,"* the Constitutional Court means especially the *entire procedure* which only the final decision brings to an end. It is a somewhat inaccurate statement incorporated in the reasons for the resolution adopted by the ConCourt CR [CZE]; it does not appear though that it will cause any problems with the interpretation of the ruling.

(rozhodcisoud.net). The parties have explicitly agreed that these rules, as applicable on the day the arbitration was initiated, shall be followed in the arbitral proceedings, within the meaning of Section 19(1) [of the ArbAct (CZE)];[174] *the parties authorize the arbitrator selected by the Court to resolve the dispute following the principles of equity.*[175] *The parties have explicitly agreed that no oral hearings before the arbitrator are necessary.*"[176] This arbitration clause was incorporated in the main contract (the reservation contract). The legal entity referred to in the arbitration clause as the administrator of the dispute was not a *permanent arbitral institution* within the meaning of the definition of the latter under Section 13 of the ArbAct [CZE].[177] The consumer, as one of the contracting parties, filed a lawsuit with a court (i.e. started litigation) based on the contract.

---

[174] ArbAct [CZE] (as applicable on the day this arbitration clause was concluded, cit.): Section 19 – *"(1) The parties have a right to agree on how the arbitrators shall case manage the proceedings. Matters regarding the case management of the proceedings may be resolved by the chairman of the tribunal providing he or she was authorized to do so by the parties or by all arbitrators. (2) Unless the parties negotiated an agreement pursuant to Subsection (1), the arbitrators shall case manage the proceedings in any manner they shall see fit. They shall case manage the arbitral proceedings in such manner that the facts of the case necessary for the resolution of the dispute are sufficiently ascertained, without any unnecessary formalities and while giving all parties equal opportunity to plead their case."* With effect from 1 April 2012, an Amendment to the ArbAct [CZE] modifies Section 19 of the ArbAct [CZE] by amending Subsection (2) of Section 19 of the ArbAct [CZE] and inserting a new Subsection (4) in Section 19 of the ArbAct [CZE] (cit.): Section 19 – "[...] (2) *Unless the parties negotiated an agreement pursuant to Subsection (1) or unless the procedure is determined pursuant to Subsection (4), the arbitrators shall case manage the proceedings in any manner they shall see fit. They shall case manage the arbitral proceedings in such manner that the facts of the case necessary for the resolution of the dispute are sufficiently ascertained, without any unnecessary formalities and while giving all parties equal opportunity to plead their case.* [...] (4) *The parties may also determine the procedure to be followed in the rules regulating the arbitral proceedings, providing the rules are enclosed with the arbitration agreement, without prejudice to the application of rules adopted by a permanent arbitral institution."* Subsections (1) and (3) of Section 19 of the ArbAct [CZE] continue to apply unamended.

[175] ArbAct [CZE] (as applicable on the day this arbitration clause was concluded, cit.): Section 25 – *"[...] (3) When making the award, the arbitrators apply the substantive law applicable to the dispute; they may, however, resolve the dispute according to the rules of equity but only if the parties explicitly authorized them to."* With effect from 1 April 2012, an Amendment to the ArbAct [CZE] modifies Section 25 of the ArbAct [CZE] with respect to consumer arbitration by amending Subsections (2) and (3) of Section 25 of the ArbAct [CZE] as follows: Section 25 – "[...] (2) *The arbitral award shall be reasoned unless the parties agree to dispense with reasons; this also applies to any arbitral award rendered pursuant to Section 24(2). An arbitral award rendered in a dispute arising from a consumer contract must always contain reasons and instructions regarding the right to file a petition with the court for annulment of the award.* [...] (3) *When making the award, the arbitrators apply the substantive law applicable to the dispute; they may, however, resolve the dispute according to the rules of equity but only if the parties explicitly authorized them to. In disputes arising from consumer contracts, the arbitrators shall always abide by consumer protection laws and regulations."* Subsection (1) of Section 25 of the ArbAct [CZE] continues to apply unamended. There is no change in cases which do not concern consumer contracts (contracts concluded by a consumer / a consumer-type contract).

[176] This arbitration agreement (in the form of an arbitration clause) was concluded on 12 May 2007.

[177] Section 13 of the ArbAct [CZE] is cited above in a footnote to the annotation of this decision, including information about the change to be implemented with effect from 1 April 2012.

388.   **The trial court** held that the *Directive* itself and its horizontal effect did not suffice to render the arbitration agreement invalid. The trial court also held that the arbitral proceedings must abide by the law even if the parties agree on how the arbitrator shall case manage the proceedings. Consequently, an arbitration clause incorporated in a consumer contract cannot *per se* impair the consumer's position. The trial court therefore terminated the proceedings based on the respondent's defense (objection) of lack of jurisdiction (the respondent invoked the arbitration clause). However, the court of appeals reversed the decision of the trial court and terminated the proceedings.

389.   In the appeal challenging the decision of the trial court, the claimant argued that an arbitration clause in a consumer contract is automatically invalid pursuant to the application of Section 55(1) of the CC [CZE].[178] **The court of appeals** concluded[179] that it was an unfair term contrary to consumer protection laws and, consequently, an invalid provision. The court of appeals maintained that the respective arbitration clause caused an imbalance between the contracting parties to the detriment of the claimant as the consumer pursuant to Section 56 of the CC

---

[178] CC [CZE] (cit.): – Section 55 – "(1) *Contractual terms in consumer contracts may not depart from the law to the detriment of the consumer. In particular, the consumer may not waive the rights guaranteed to him or her by the law or impair his or her contractual position in any other manner. (2) Clauses in consumer contracts specified in Section 56 are invalid. (3) When in doubt as to the meaning of consumer contracts, the interpretation that is more favorable to the consumer shall apply."* Section 56 – "(1) *Consumer contracts may not contain terms which, contrary to the requirement of good faith, cause a significant imbalance in the parties' rights and obligations to the detriment of the consumer. (2) Subsection (1) shall not apply to contractual terms which define the subject of the performance under the contract or the price of the performance. (3) Inadmissible contractual terms are, in particular, contractual terms (a) excluding or limiting the legal liability of a supplier in the event of the death of a consumer or personal injury to the latter resulting from an act or omission of that supplier, (b) excluding or limiting the consumer's rights to make claims under liability for defects or liability for damage, (c) stipulating that an agreement is binding on the consumer whereas the supplier's performance is subject to a condition whose realization depends on the supplier's own will alone, (d) permitting the supplier to retain the performance provided by the consumer even if the latter does not conclude a contract with the supplier or cancels the contract, (e) authorizing the supplier to cancel the contract without any contractual or statutory reason where the same facility is not granted to the consumer, (f) enabling the supplier to terminate a contract of indeterminate duration without reasonable notice except where there are serious grounds for doing so, (g) obliging the consumer to fulfill conditions which he or she had no opportunity to get acquainted with prior to the conclusion of the contract, (h) enabling the supplier to alter the terms of the contract unilaterally without a valid reason which is specified in the contract, (i) providing for the price of goods or services to be determined at the time of delivery or allowing a supplier of the goods or services to increase their price without in both cases giving the consumer the corresponding right to cancel the contract if the final price is too high in relation to the price agreed when the contract was concluded, (j) obliging the consumer to fulfill all his or her obligations where the supplier does not perform his or hers, (k) giving the supplier the possibility of transferring his or her rights and obligations under the contract, where such transfer jeopardizes the enforceability of the consumer's claim or the guarantees for the consumer, without the latter's agreement."*

[179] The decision of the court of appeals is not available, and the conclusions were taken over from the summary incorporated in the reasons given by the ConCourt CR [CZE].

[CZE].[180] The clause effectively restricts the fundamental constitutional right of the claimant as a citizen and a consumer to assert his or her rights before an independent tribunal (Article 36(1) of the Charter [CZE][181]); the claimant's fundamental right is restricted in a manner which the claimant could not control due to the fact that the contract was an adhesion contract (Article 3(2) of the *Directive*). The Municipal Court in Prague, as the court of appeals, also held that the invalidity in the present case was irreparable, i.e. absolute invalidity,[182] and rejected the possibility of voidability, with reference to the provisions of Article 6(1) of the *Directive* and the interpretation thereof in the ECJ's case law. In the ensuing proceedings before the ConCourt CR [CZE], the complainant objected, inter alia, that the court of appeals had failed to address the issue of whether the case law of the ECJ was binding on the citizens of the Czech Republic and that the court of appeals had failed to quote, or at least refer to, the ECJ's relevant rulings.

(cc) Constitutional complaint and conclusions adopted by the Constitutional Court in its ruling, including the reasons[183]

390. The claimant filed a constitutional complaint and demanded setting aside the decision of the court of appeals. The claimant argued, inter alia, that consumer disputes clearly belonged to the category of disputes which could be submitted to arbitration (they are arbitrable). These disputes meet all the conditions prescribed by the ArbAct [CZE]; in particular, they are property disputes capable of settlement. The claimant highlighted that its clients had not been forced to accept the arbitration clause and that the provision excluding the jurisdiction of courts was being regularly struck out at the clients' request. The claimant's contracting practice was therefore open to proposals for changes intended to modify the *basic contract offer* presented by

---

[180] The provision is cited above in a footnote to the annotation of this decision.

[181] Charter [CZE] (cit.): Chapter Five – The Right to Judicial and Other Legal Protection – Article 36 – "(1) *Everyone may assert, through the legally prescribed procedure, his or her rights before an independent and impartial court or, in specified cases, before a different authority. (2) Unless the law provides otherwise, a person who claims that his or her rights were curtailed by a decision of a public administrative authority may turn to a court for review of the legality of that decision. However, judicial review of decisions affecting the fundamental rights and basic freedoms listed in this Charter (Charter [CZE]) may not be removed from the jurisdiction of courts. (3) Everyone is entitled to compensation for damage sustained by him or her as a result of an unlawful decision of a court, another state authority, or a public administrative authority, or as a result of an improper official procedure. (4) Conditions and detailed provisions are laid down by statute.*"

[182] However, the decision of the Municipal Court predates the effective day of the 2010 amendment to the CC [CZE] which laid down the absolute invalidity of *unfair terms* in consumer contracts from 1 August 2010 (Section 55(2) of the CC [CZE]) – see the analysis of the substantive rules regulating consumer protection in Czech law.

[183] Further conclusions of the ConCourt CR [CZE] are summarized in the opening part of this annotation.

potential clients. The conclusion of arbitration agreements must therefore be considered an expression of free will, because the consumer (just like other potentially concerned consumers) did not request any changes in this regard.

391.   The Constitutional Court principally dismissed the constitutional complaint, especially because any other decision would constitute undue interference with the decision-making of the [lower] courts; the Constitutional Court also highlighted its exceptional status according to which the ConCourt [CZE] is not part of the general court structure. The Constitutional Court is called upon to protect constitutionality, not to control "common" legality, and it therefore does not examine whether the [lower] courts interpreted and applied "simple (sub-constitutional) law" correctly. Nonetheless, the ConCourt CR [CZE] did provide comments on several important issues.

392.   Above all, the Constitutional Court CR [CZE] principally agreed with the conclusion adopted by the [lower] court in the present case (i.e. the court of appeals). **The Constitutional Court, however (following its previously voiced opinions), did not classify arbitration clauses in consumer contracts as automatically invalid.** The Court only confirmed that **courts are entitled to review the validity of such arbitration clauses in particular cases,** even if the parties themselves do not plead the invalidity. If the courts conclude that, in the given case, the clause is unfair, they shall hold the clause invalid.

393.   The ConCourt CR [CZE] emphasized the rule which is often neglected (and such neglect stems from an unduly undiscriminating approach). The problem is that arbitration clauses in consumer contracts are not automatically invalid; even the fact that the arbitration agreement (as a part of the main contract) was concluded as an adhesion contract does not automatically render the agreement invalid. Invalidity is a penalty for an arbitration clause which, **in the particular case**, causes a significant imbalance between the parties, to the detriment of the consumer (providing all of these conditions are met). The Constitutional Court CR [CZE] referred to its previous rulings, according to which an arbitration clause negating the jurisdiction of the courts does not violate the right to judicial protection if the content thereof corresponds to the **expression of will of both contracting parties.**[184] This opinion complies with the case law protecting the autonomy of will and the freedom of individual action. The expression of will must be entirely free, permissible, and unambiguous. The courts are therefore obliged to assess each arbitration clause individually.

---

[184] Resolution of the ConCourt CR [CZE], Case No. II. ÚS 2682/08 of 6 November 2008, whereby a complaint against the resolution of the SC CR [CZE], Case No. 32 Cdo 2282/2008 of 31 July 2008, was dismissed.

394.   In connection with the rules applicable to arbitration, the Constitutional Court held that only *permanent arbitral institutions* are allowed to issue their own rules as standard procedural guidelines. At the same time, however, the Court expressed an opinion which probably does not feature very prominently in the respective decision. The fact is that even the parties to the proceedings conducted before a *permanent arbitral institution* which issued its procedural rules *(Rules)* and published those Rules in the *Business Journal* may agree to depart from the Rules. This legal opinion has been widely recognized in the Czech Republic, but it has never been clearly confirmed. The reason is that none of the three *permanent arbitral institutions* in the Czech Republic incorporates provisions in its Rules which are common in a number of international arbitral institutions in other countries, i.e. provisions which often enable these institutions to reject a request for arbitration if, for instance, the agreement of the parties is irreconcilable with certain procedural standards which the *permanent arbitral institution* considers essential.

395.   Just like in many other cases handled by the ConCourt CR [CZE], in the practice of the lower courts, and in the rich case law of the SC CR [CZE], the focal point was the position of the *arbitration centers*, i.e. entities *organizing* arbitration, whose status does not meet the conditions stipulated for *permanent arbitral institutions* under Section 13 of the ArbAct [CZE]. In the present case, the arbitration clause stipulated that the arbitrators shall be chosen by the *arbitration center* from its own list of arbitrators, without this center being a *permanent arbitral institution*.[185] In its constitutional complaint, the complainant disagreed with the legal opinion which classifies such an arrangement as an evasion (circumvention) of the law (namely the provision regulating *permanent arbitral institutions*); the complainant argued that the ArbAct [CZE] is a private law regulation, not subject to the principle of implied prohibition (whatever is not explicitly permitted by the law, is prohibited). Conversely, the complainant argued that the private law

---

[185] In that connection, it is necessary to say a few words about the basically global discussion regarding the issue of whether *permanent arbitral institutions* should administer any *lists* of arbitrators at all. Many important *permanent arbitral institutions* have abandoned this practice over the years past, and a number of them have not been, as a rule, administering any *lists* at all. In that connection, we need to mention an extensive discussion in Austria [AUT] concerning the issue of whether the list of arbitrators ought to be renewed at all after the *validity* of the previous document expired in 2009. It is true that a new (updated) list was published again in 2010 but only as an *indicative list* of experts in international arbitration. Besides, even those arbitral institutions which have maintained the practice of lists, have to some extent abandoned at least the requirement of the partially binding nature of these lists. We must emphasize, though, that in the countries of Central and Eastern Europe it is still a fairly common practice, with its disadvantages, but with certain advantages, too. Nonetheless, in the present case handled by the ConCourt CR [CZE] the key issue was not a *list* administered by an entity which would meet the statutory requirements of a *permanent arbitral institution* under Section 13 of the ArbAct [CZE] (this provision is quoted above in a footnote to this annotation).

nature of the Arbitration Act clearly requires that the application of this law must be subject to the principle of implied permission pursuant to Article 2(4) of the Constitution CR [CZE] (and Article 2(3) of the Charter [CZE]),[186] i.e. whatever is not explicitly prohibited by the law is therefore permitted. The complainant in the present case expressed an opinion that neither the ArbAct [CZE], nor any other law prohibits *ad hoc* arbitrators [appointed for the given proceedings] to organize in the arbitration centers; the complainant even claimed this to be the arbitrators' constitutional right.[187] The complainant also disagreed with the opinion of the Grand Panel of the SC CR [CZE], Case No. 31 Cdo 1945/2010 of 12 May 2011, whereby the Supreme Court supported the opinion articulated in the Decision of the High Court in Prague, Case No. 12 Cmo 496/2008 of 28 May 2009. The latter maintains that the activities of the *arbitration centers* which do not meet the stipulated requirements in order to qualify as *permanent arbitral institutions*, as well as their practice of issuing *Rules* and lists of arbitrators, constitute unlawful evasion (circumvention) of the law.[188] In the present case, the ConCourt CR [CZE] identified with the conclusion of unfairness of the given [particular] arbitration clause. In particular, the consumer may not waive the rights guaranteed to him or her by the law, or otherwise impair his or her contractual position. The Constitutional Court of the Czech Republic [CZE] upheld the conclusions of the court of appeals and agreed that, considering the terms of the main contract in this particular case (the reservation contract) which can be **subsumed under the general category of consumer contracts**, the wording of the arbitration clause incorporated therein must be measured according to a more rigorous standard; the same applies to the criteria relating to the arbitrators who will decide any eventual future dispute between the contracting parties, especially the method of their appointment. Considering the nature of consumer contracts, it is necessary to lay special **emphasis on the rule that both parties must have equal rights in selecting their arbitrators. Consequently, the principle of selecting one's arbitrator is not, in this particular case, fulfilled by a mere reference to the list of arbitrators.**

396.   In this case, the parties had agreed that the disputes would be resolved in arbitration before [*a legal person other than a permanent arbitral institution under Section 13 of the ArbAct /CZE/*] "[...] *a single arbitrator selected by said Court.* [...]" However, this "Court" is not a *permanent arbitral institution* within the meaning of the Arbitration Act. Section

---

[186] Charter [CZE] – Article 2 – [...] "(3) *Everyone may do that which is not prohibited by law; and no one may be compelled to do that which is not imposed upon him or her by law.*"

[187] With reference to Article 20(1) of the Charter [CZE] (cit.): "*The right of association is guaranteed. Everyone has the right to associate together with others in clubs, societies, and other associations.*"

[188] Here an intentional partial summary.

7(1) of the ArbAct [CZE] stipulates that the arbitration agreement should, as a rule, determine the number of arbitrators and identify them by their names, or stipulate the method whereby the number and the identity of the arbitrators shall be determined. The final number of arbitrators must always be odd. Subsection (2) of the respective provision stipulates that if the arbitration agreement does not set forth the requirements specified in Subsection (1), each party shall appoint one arbitrator, and these arbitrators shall elect the chairman of the arbitral panel. Section 13(1) of the ArbAct [CZE] stipulates that *permanent arbitral institutions* can only be established by law. Section 13(2) of the ArbAct [CZE] stipulates that *permanent arbitral institutions* can issue their own *statutes* and *rules* which must be published in the *Business Journal*; these statutes and rules may determine the method of appointment and the number of arbitrators and may stipulate that the arbitrators shall be selected from a list administered by the *permanent arbitral institution*. The statutes and rules may also determine how the arbitrators shall case manage the proceedings and render their decisions, as well as resolve other issues connected with the activities of the *permanent arbitral institution* and the arbitrators, including rules regulating the costs of proceedings and remuneration for the arbitrators. With respect to the terms of the particular arbitration clause and taking into account whether the parties agreed in said clause that any of their eventual future disputes (considering the fact that the legal person referred to in the clause is not a *permanent arbitral institution* which can only be established under the law) would be solved by an *ad hoc* arbitrator, the fact that the **selection of the respective arbitrator was entrusted directly to this "Court"** (i.e. the legal person in question) cannot be dismissed. However, this legal person (a corporation) is not a *permanent arbitral institution*[189] in terms of applicable law, and it is not entitled to issue *statutes* and *rules* which would, inter alia, provide for rules regulating the case management of the arbitral proceedings or, as the case may be, determine the method of appointment of arbitrators, etc. If the entity carries out activities which, according to the ArbAct [CZE], are reserved for *permanent arbitral institutions,* **logic dictates** that this entity **clearly and intentionally violates the law**. It is a manifest attempt to impose conditions which raise reasonable and justified doubts regarding the perspective of independent and impartial dispute resolution. That the parties had perhaps agreed on having their eventual dispute resolved by an *ad hoc* arbitrator cannot even be postulated, because no such arbitrator was identified in the arbitration agreement, or rather the arbitration agreement contained no clear terms, in compliance with the law, which would provide for the method of selecting the respective arbitrator. The previously mentioned

---

[189] The line of business registered in the Companies Register for the given legal person was *brokering trade and services.*

reference to the appointment of an arbitrator by the "Court" cannot be accepted as an alternative (substitute) method of appointing the *ad hoc* arbitrator due to the reasons specified above, as well as with respect to the principle of equality of the parties.

397.   The Constitutional Court of the Czech Republic [CZE] also held that the conclusion regarding the misleading, even fraudulent, nature of the clause could also be derived from the fact that the arbitration clause referred to (whether to the *Rules* or in connection with the appointment of the arbitrator) a legal person whose name (*company name*) included the words "*arbitration court,*" despite the fact that it was not a *permanent arbitral institution* under Section 13 of the ArbAct [CZE]. In that connection, it is important to add that an extensive Amendment to the ArbAct has been passed in the meantime, taking effect on 1 April 2012. The Amendment, inter alia, incorporates into the ArbAct [CZE] a new Section 13(4) which explicitly prohibits the use of such a *misleading* name by entities other than those having the status of a *permanent arbitral institution*.[190] This basically constitutes an enactment of the principle which had already been articulated by Czech courts in their previous rulings.[191]

(d)   Judgment of the Constitutional Court of the Czech Republic, Case No. II. ÚS 2164/10 of 1 November 2011: Correlation between the protection of autonomy in negotiating arbitration agreements and the protection of the weaker contracting party (consumer protection)

(aa)   Conclusions of the Constitutional Court

398.   The Constitutional Court of the Czech Republic **arrived at the following conclusions, inter alia**:[192]

---

[190] Section 13(4) of the ArbAct [CZE], the version which takes effect on 1 April 2012 (cit.): "*(4) No entity may carry out its activities using a name which evokes a misleading impression that the entity is a permanent arbitral institution under this law unless a different law or regulation or an international agreement integrated in the legal system authorizes the entity to use the name.*"

[191] See the Resolution of the High Court in Prague, Case No. 7 Cmo 136/2010 of 22 July 2010, according to which corporations are not allowed to choose a *company name* which would include the words "*arbitral*" or "*arbitration*", unless they are indeed a *permanent arbitral institution* established under a special law. This was a decision rendered by the court of appeals on appeal from a resolution adopted by the trial court administering the Companies Register; the trial court dismissed the petition for the registration of a changed company name of the corporation, because the new name was supposed to include the words "*arbitral office.*" The decision was annotated in and the cited ratio decidendi is adopted from: Soudní rozhledy, 2011, Vol. 17, No. 3, Decision Ref. No. 31, pp. 100–101. As concerns the general principles governing company names for corporations, the High Court referred to the opinion expressed in the Resolution of the SC CR [CZE], Case No. 29 Cdo 201/2007 of 15 April 2008.

[192] The decision is available at the website of the ConCourt CR [CZE]. The litigation involved the following decisions:

▶ Courts are primarily obliged to interpret procedural rules and principles from the perspective of the purpose and the sense of protecting constitutionally guaranteed fundamental rights and freedoms.

▶ An *ad hoc* arbitrator must always be a natural person.

▶ An arbitration agreement in consumer disputes is valid if the rule regulating the appointment of the arbitrator is transparent and unambiguous.

▶ Respect for and protection of the autonomy of will are the elementary prerequisites for the functioning of the material rule of law; it is a *"matrix"* of the relationship between an individual and the state authority, in the sense of a *"constant which encompasses the individual fundamental rights articulated by positive law in response to their massive violation by authoritarian or totalitarian regimes."* Consequently, the principle of autonomy allows the parties to an arbitration agreement to waive, freely and intentionally, their right to submit their dispute to an independent and unbiased court.[193]

▶ The consumer protection laws aim primarily at the protection of the weaker contracting party (the consumer); this is a distinct trend in our modern private law.

▶ However, the protection of **autonomy** of will cannot be absolute **in a situation involving another fundamental right of the individual or a constitutional principle or another constitutionally approved** *public interest* which are capable of **proportionately restricting** the autonomy of will.[194]

▶ If the particular case concerns a relationship between a professional and a consumer, **the arbitration clause must primarily be viewed from the perspective of the consumer's right to protection.**

▶ Arbitration clauses must also be subject to examination as potentially unfair and unacceptable terms. It is irrelevant if the law (CC [CZE]) includes arbitration clauses in the indicative list of unfair (abusive) terms or not.[195]

▶ An unfair term is a term which causes an increased disproportional imbalance between the parties (their rights and obligations) and is

---

> Resolution of the District Court for Prague 10 [CZE], Case No. 16 C 295/2009-9 of 19 October 2009,
> Resolution of the Municipal Court in Prague [CZE], Case No. 22 Co 565/2009-20 of 15 June 2010. The decision was also analyzed in literature; see Gojová, J. Rozhodčí doložka ve spotřebitelské smlouvě a její ústavněprávní limity. [Title in translation: Arbitration Clause in a Consumer Contract and its Limits under Constitutional Law]. Právní fórum, 2012, Vol. 9, No. 1, pp. 46–48.

[193] The ConCourt CR [CZE] invoked its prior rulings such as:
> Resolution of the ConCourt CR [CZE], Case No. I. ÚS 2619/08 of 18 November 2008.
> Resolution of the ConCourt CR [CZE], Case No. II. ÚS 805/06 of 8 January 2007.

[194] The Constitutional Court of the Czech Republic [CZE] invoked its prior ruling, namely the Judgment of the ConCourt CR [CZE], Case No. II. ÚS 3/06 of 6 November 2007.

[195] See Section 56(3) of the CC [CZE], as subsequently amended, which does not include arbitration clauses in the indicative list of [*potentially*] abusive, i.e. unfair, terms.

ultimately capable of resulting in a significant procedural disadvantage for one of the parties. Such imbalance can also be the result of decision-making following the *principles of equity* which deprive the consumer of legal protection.

▶ **The right to a lawful judge** (Article 38(1) of the Charter) is also reflected in arbitration, albeit in a simplified form. This principle is reflected in arbitration through the medium of **transparent and unambiguous rules regulating the appointment of arbitrator.**

(bb) Factual and legal findings

399. The parties entered into a loan agreement and an agreement on the security transfer of right. The contract contained an arbitration clause according to which the dispute between the parties could have been heard by any of the two arbitrators named therein with whom the request for arbitration would be filed. In particular, the arbitration clause stipulated that *"[a]ny and all disputes will be finally resolved by an arbitrator appointed by the claimant from a list of members of the Arbitrators Association, or appointed by the Chairman of the Arbitrators Association if the claimant does not exercise his or her right to appoint the arbitrator, in arbitration pursuant to the Arbitration Rules of the Arbitrators Association; the parties agree that the arbitral proceedings will be conducted only on the basis of written materials, without a hearing, and that the dispute will be resolved according to the rules of equity."*[196] The request for arbitration was initially filed with the first of the agreed arbitrators, but the arbitrator refused to resolve the dispute between the parties. The other arbitrator agreed to by the parties, the *Arbitrators Association* with its registered office in Prague [CZE], has not [yet] refused to hear the case and resolve the dispute. However, in the meantime, a lawsuit has been filed with a court.

400. **The trial court** terminated the proceedings on the determination of invalidity of the contract based on a timely jurisdictional challenge, i.e. due to the existence of the arbitration agreement.[197]

401. **The court of appeals**, on appeal against the trial court's decision, upheld the resolution of the trial court, because the court found no reason prohibiting the hearing and the resolution of the case in arbitration. The court held that the parties had failed to exploit all possibilities to have the dispute resolved in arbitration (the court had no information available to it suggesting that the other arbitrator agreed by the parties refused to hear the case).

---

[196] The interpretation of arbitration clauses was adopted from the reasons for the Judgment of the ConCourt CR [CZE].
[197] See Section 106(1) of the CCP [CZE].

(cc) Constitutional complaint and conclusions adopted by the Constitutional Court in its ruling, including reasons[198]

1. Result of the proceedings

402. In his constitutional complaint, the complainant primarily pleaded violation of his right to judicial protection and right to fair trial pursuant to Article 36(1) of the Charter [CZE], arguing that the courts should have heard the case pursuant to the second sentence of Section 106(1) of the CCP [CZE]. The complainant claimed that the arbitration clause did not stipulate that if one of the arbitrators refused to hear the case, the party was obliged to file the request for arbitration with the other arbitrator, as the courts held. The complainant emphasized that an arbitration clause could not name as an arbitrator a *legal person*, i.e. an *unidentified arbitrator*, and was therefore invalid. The courts should have taken the invalidity into account.

2. Contractual autonomy and consumer protection

403. In his reply to the other party's statement and the statement filed by the joint party, the complainant opposed the argument that the arbitration clause represented a free expression of will of both parties by claiming that he had de facto no possibility of influencing the terms of the contract. The contractual autonomy in this case was limited to the possibility of either signing the contract or not, i.e. the parties were only *formally* equal. The complainant also complained about the low standard of the arbitrators and their financial dependence on the outcome of the proceedings which, in the complainant's opinion, predetermines the outcome of the arbitration.

404. First of all, the Constitutional Court concluded that the case could concern a consumer relationship, i.e. a consumer contract negotiated between a professional and a consumer. At the same time, however, the Court reiterated the theory long-established in its case law, namely the maximum scope for autonomy. In the present case, the Court was obliged to rule on the correlation between the protection of autonomy and the protection of other fundamental rights. The Court has concluded that contractual autonomy is not unlimited (absolute) if there is another fundamental right, constitutional principle, or approved *public interest*. In the present case, it is the principle of protection of the weaker contracting party, enshrined in the consumer protection laws. The Constitutional Court also noted that the principle of consumer protection prevails over the protection of autonomy of will.

---

[198] Further conclusions of the ConCourt CR [CZE] are summarized in the opening part of this annotation.

3. EU-compliant interpretation of consumer protection law

405.   Consumer protection was (also) transposed into Czech law on the basis of the *Directive*. Although the *Directive* has no horizontal direct effect (i.e. between the parties themselves) in Czech law, it can be employed for the purpose of an **EU-compliant interpretation of Czech law** in order to support our conclusions. Section 51a of the CC [CZE] constitutes the basis for the application of an EU-compliant interpretation in consumer contracts.[199] This provision is important from the perspective of interpretation. When applying the EU-compliant interpretation, or the interpretation following the *"Von Colson"* principle, the objective of the European rule (typically a directive) ought to serve as the principal guideline for the courts in the interpretation of national law (rules of domestic origin).[200]

406.   According to the Constitutional Court, the aim of the *Directive* was to enhance the protection of consumers against unfair contractual terms. The assessment of an arbitration clause as an unfair term (within the meaning of depriving the consumer of his or her right to litigate) is based on the previous rulings of the ConCourt CR [CZE] in which the Court held that arbitration was not the process of finding the law, but the completion of the contractual relationship between the parties. In other words, arbitration clarifies and settles the parties' mutual rights; the arbitrator is authorized to do so by the parties, based on their contract whereby the parties delegated their will to the arbitrator.[201] The

---

[199] CC [CZE] (cit.): Section 51a – *"This Chapter integrates the relevant applicable law of the European Community and regulates consumer protection in consumer contracts and certain duties associated with the conclusion of consumer contracts."*

[200] The ConCourt CR [CZE] invokes the following rulings of the ECJ:
➢ ECJ Judgment, Case 14/83 of 10 April 1984 (*Sabine von Colson et Elisabeth Kamann* v. *Land Nordrhein-Westfalen*), CELEX: 61983CJ0014 and
➢ ECJ Judgment, Case 79/83 of 10 April 1983 (*Dorit Harz* v. *Deutsche Tradax GmbH*), CELEX: 61983J0079&lg.

[201] The Constitutional Court of the Czech Republic [CZE] invoked its prior rulings, namely:
➢ Resolution of the ConCourt CR [CZE], Case No. I. ÚS 339/02 of 26 January 2004,
➢ Resolution of the ConCourt CR [CZE], Case No. IV. ÚS 511/0 of 5 December 2003,
➢ Resolution of the ConCourt CR [CZE], Case No. III. ÚS 166/05 of 29 April 2005,
➢ Resolution of the ConCourt CR [CZE], Case No. Pl. ÚS 37/08 of 28 January 2009.
But we can also mention the following decisions:
➢ Resolution of the ConCourt CR, Case No. III. ÚS 460/01 of 1 November 2001, published in: Sbírka nálezů a usnesení ÚS ČR [Reports of Judgments and Resolutions of the ConCourt CR], Vol. 24, Resolution Ref. No. 41, p. 563 et seq.
➢ Resolution of the ConCourt CR, Case No. IV: ÚS 174/02 of 15 July 2002, published in: Sbírka nálezů a usnesení ÚS ČR [Reports of Judgments and Resolutions of the ConCourt CR], Vol. 27, Resolution Ref. No. 20, p. 257 et seq.; this particular resolution is invoked by the majority of the subsequent decisions of the ConCourt CR until the Judgment of the ConCourt CR, Case No. I ÚS 3227/07 of 8 March 2011, annotated in this section.
➢ Resolution of the ConCourt CR, Case No. III. ÚS 145/03 of 12 September 2003;

ConCourt CR [CZE] maintains that based on this approach, the inevitable conclusion is that arbitration does not constitute proceedings of a judicial nature. Consequently, it is also reflected in the generally more rigorous requirements imposed on arbitration clauses and their essential terms, the objective of which is to ensure that they do not constitute unfair terms in consumer contracts (e.g., do not deprive the consumer of his or her right to litigate).

4. Internal inconsistencies in the reasons for the judgment regarding the nature of arbitration and manifest conflict with other rulings of the Constitutional Court

407. The conclusion expressed in the preceding paragraph is **most surprising,** especially with respect to the **Judgment of the ConCourt CR [CZE], Case No. I ÚS 3227/07 of 8 March 2011**[202] which has brought about an apparent change of opinion. The opinion expressed in the Judgment of the ConCourt CR [CZE] of 8 March 2011 **pushes the theory considerably towards the jurisdictional theory of arbitration, perceived as a process of finding the law by a private-law entity**, analogous and equivalent to litigation and in compliance with applicable law. The Judgment of the ConCourt [CZE], Case No. I. ÚS 3227/07 of 8 March 2011 thus basically abandoned the contractual theory – as corroborated, after all, by the view adopted by lawyers as well as, more or less, the case law of lower courts.[203] The decision confirmed the

---

➢ Resolution of the ConCourt CR, Case No. IV. ÚS 435/02 of 22 October 2002;
➢ Resolution of the ConCourt CR, Case No. II. ÚS 2169/07 of 3 September 2007;
➢ Resolution of the ConCourt CR, Case No. II. ÚS 3059/08 of 15 January 2009 et al.
For more details, see *Bělohlávek, A. et Profeldová, T.* Arbitration in the Case Law of the Constitutional Court of the Czech Republic with Regard to the Nature and Purpose of Arbitration. In: *Bělohlávek, A. et Rozehnalová, N.* CYArb – Czech (& Central European) Yearbook of Arbitration: The Relationship between Constitutional Values, Human Rights and Arbitration, Huntington (New York): JurisNet, 2011, Vol. 1, pp. 343–361; *Rozehnalová, N. et Havlíček, J.* Rozhodčí smlouva a rozhodci ve světle některých rozhodnutí... aneb quo vadis...? [Title in translation – Arbitration Agreement and Arbitrators in Light of Several Judgments ... Or Quo Vadis ...?] Právní fórum, 2010, No. 3, p. 114 et seq.; *Varvařovský, P.* Rozhodčí řízení v judikatuře Ústavního soudu. [Title in translation: Arbitration in the Case Law of the Constitutional Court]. Právní fórum, 2010, No. 3, p. 143 et seq. et al.
[202] The Judgment is available online from the website of the ConCourt CR at: http://nalus. usoud.cz/Search/ResultDetail.aspx?id=69584&pos=1&cnt=1&typ=result [last access 26 August 2011]. The proceedings before the ConCourt CR [CZE] were preceded by the following decisions of the [lower] courts [CZE]: (i) Judgment of the Municipal Court in Prague, Case No. 8 Cm 164/2004-28 of 29 October 2004, (ii) Judgment of the High Court in Prague [CZE], Case No. 8 Cmo 80/2005-42 of 7 October 2005 and (iii) Resolution of the SC CR [CZE], Case No. 32 Odo 366/2006-64. The arbitral award was rendered in arbitration before the Arbitration Court Attached to the Economic Chamber of the Czech Republic and the Agricultural Chamber of the Czech Republic, Case No. Rsp 352/03 of 30 April 2004.
[203] After all, legal theory was only rarely inclined towards this approach in modern Czech arbitration; see *Bělohlávek, A. et Pezl, T.* Postavení rozhodčího řízení v systému ochrany práv a ústavního

jurisdictional basis of arbitration (albeit based on the contractual autonomy of the parties). Moreover, the decision of the ConCourt CR [CZE] basically confirmed and approved the actual state of affairs existing in both arbitration itself and in the decision-making practice of the courts. The crucial reason is that in its decision of 8 March 2011, – both a correct and a landmark decision, the Constitutional Court of the Czech Republic defined the arbitrator (arbitral tribunal) as **"another authority."** This definition influences not only the status of arbitrator, but also the fact that the arbitrator is directly bound by valid and applicable law and has an obligation to apply it.[204] It almost appears as if Panel II of the ConCourt CR [CZE] (which rendered the decision annotated in this chapter) was not aware of the judgment of 8 March 2011 rendered by Panel I of the ConCourt CR [CZE]. **Both decisions are fundamentally different as concerns the definition of the nature of arbitration.** The judgment of 8 March 2011 may be seen as reflecting the actual situation in the Czech Republic, in a most accurate and sensitive manner, and has managed to strike the perfect balance between the role played by arbitration in reality,[205] the right to judicial protection, and the specific type of an alternative law-finding process which arbitration undoubtedly is, although performing the same function as litigation.[206] Hence, it is legitimate to ask whether perhaps the essence of arbitration in the Czech Republic should not be made subject to another plenary opinion of the ConCourt CR [CZE]. In this connection, the judgment of the ConCourt CR [CZE] of 1 November 2011 (the decision annotated in this chapter) is even more surprising, because the Constitutional Court notes, in the final part of the reasons, that

---

pořádku České republiky a dalších zemí. [Title in translation: Status of Arbitration in the System of Protection of the Rights and the Constitutional Laws of the Czech Republic and Other Countries]. Právní rozhledy, 2004, No. 7, p. 256–261; *Raban, P.* K odpovědnosti rozhodce a rozhodčího soudu. [Title in translation: Concerning the Liability of Arbitrators and Arbitral Tribunals]. Bulletin advokacie, 2003, No. 1, pp. 25–34. Critical opinions or outright refusals of the theory were more common; see *Pecha, R.* K právní povaze rozhodčích nálezů. [Title in translation: Concerning the Legal Nature of Arbitral Awards]. Bulletin advokacie, 2003, No. 5, pp. 41–45; *Růžička, K.* K otázce právní povahy rozhodčího řízení. [Title in translation: Concerning the Legal Nature of Arbitration]. Bulletin advokacie, 2003, No. 5, pp. 32–40 et al.

[204] For a detailed annotation of the judgment of the ConCourt CR [CZE] (also in connection with consumer protection), see *Bělohlávek, A.* Ústavní soud České republiky opustil striktní smluvní výklad koncepce rozhodčího řízení [Title in translation: The Constitutional Court of the Czech Republic Has Abandoned Its Strict Contractual Interpretation of the Concept of Arbitration]. Bulletin advokacie, 2011, Vol. 22, No. 12, pp. 40–43.

[205] Judgment of the ConCourt CR [CZE], Case No. I. ÚS 3227/07 of 8 March 2011: *"Arbitration is a type of civil procedure. The fundamental difference from civil procedure in court (i.e. litigation) lies in the definition of the managing and decision-making authority. Whereas in court proceedings (litigation) it is the court, in arbitration it is the arbitrator or a permanent arbitral institution."*

[206] Judgment of the ConCourt CR [CZE], Case No. I. ÚS 3227/07 of 8 March 2011: *"Based on the voluntary acts of the parties, the arbitrator therefore performs the duties instead of a court which would otherwise have to hear and decide the case."* Elsewhere, for instance: *"Hearing the case in arbitral proceedings does not constitute denial of legal protection; it only represents the transfer of the latter from courts to arbitrators."*

arbitration entails **delegation of the jurisdictional power of the state** (court) to private law entities – arbitrators.[207] In the same paragraph, however, the Constitutional Court states that the arbitrators' decision complements the legal relationship between the parties to the contract. This negates the conclusion of the phrase "delegated jurisdictional power." The expression "completion of a legal relationship" eo ipso excludes "jurisdictional activity" as decision-making on the "fair application of the law," i.e. making decisions on what is and what is not lawful.

408. However, the most serious excess in the judgment may be found in the fact that the ConCourt CR [CZE] basically defines the arbitrator as a *representative of a party*. Although the Constitutional Court employed rather *metaphorical* words in order to emphasize the *contractual basis* of arbitration, the fact that arbitrator(s) must be principally independent, which fundamentally conflicts with the position of a person who is supposed to *represent* (= *defend*) the interests of a party cannot be dismissed. **The independence of the arbitrator, excluding the interpretation of his or her position as a representative of a party**, is in many respects explicitly emphasized in the ArbAct [CZE] itself;[208] it is also confirmed by extensive international practice which even perceives the absolute independence of arbitrators as a widely internationally recognized principle of arbitration.

---

[207] Para. (26) of the reasons for the judgment of the ConCourt CR [CZE].

[208] See primarily Section 8 of the ArbAct [CZE], but also Section 1(1), Section 11, Section 12 and Section 31(c) of the ArbAct [CZE] (except Section 8 of the ArbAct [CZE], the other provisions mentioned above continue to apply unamended even after the Amendment to the ArbAct [CZE] which takes effect on 1 April 2012).
ArbAct [CZE] (as applicable on the day this arbitration clause was concluded and as applicable on the day of the annotated judgment of the ConCourt CR [CZE] cit.): Section 8 – "*The candidate to be selected as or appointed arbitrator or who was selected as or appointed arbitrator must notify the parties or the tribunal without delay of any and all circumstances which could give rise to legitimate doubts regarding the candidate's impartiality which would disqualify the candidate as arbitrator.*"
The first of April 2012 is the effective date of the Amendment to the ArbAct [CZE] which enhances the independence of arbitrators and amends Section 8 of the ArbAct [CZE] by replacing the provision with the following provision which reads as follows (cit.): Section 8 – "(1) *The arbitrator is disqualified from hearing and resolving the case if his or her connection to the case, the parties or their representatives gives rise to doubts about his or her impartiality. (2) The candidate to be selected as or appointed arbitrator or who was selected as or appointed arbitrator must notify the parties or the tribunal without delay of any and all circumstances which could give rise to legitimate doubts regarding the candidate's impartiality which would disqualify the candidate as arbitrator. (3) When resolving disputes from consumer contracts, the arbitrator is obliged to inform the parties before the hearing whether he or she has made or participated in the making of an arbitral award in the past three years or whether he has been an arbitrator in a pending arbitration over a dispute to which any of the parties is or was a party. The time limit under the preceding sentence shall be calculated from the day when the arbitration covered by the reporting obligation terminated to the day of commencement of the arbitration in which the arbitrator is bound by the reporting obligations.*"

5. Proportionality of fundamental rights in consumer contracts and the requirement of transparency

409.   The Constitutional Court concluded that, in this particular case, the arbitration clauses meet the defining criteria of unfair terms, because they cause an **increased disproportionate imbalance between the parties (in the sense of their rights and obligations)**, which is ultimately capable of resulting in a significant procedural disadvantage for one of the parties. This procedural imbalance may also be caused by the fact that the consumer is deprived of the benefits afforded to him or her by the consumer protection rules incorporated in the applicable laws, for instance by **decision-making following the principles of equity.**

410.   In this connection, one should note that the Amendment to the ArbAct [CZE], effective date 1 April 2012, excludes the possibility of decision-making following the principles of equity in consumer disputes, although otherwise the Amendment (Section 25 of the ArbAct [CZE]) does not exclude the possibility of resolving consumer disputes in arbitration, subject to certain statutory requirements.[209]

411.   The Constitutional Court held that this case did not meet the requirement of a transparent agreement for the arbitrator or the method of his or her appointment, which is the basic prerequisite for the option of negotiating an arbitration agreement in a consumer dispute. The Constitutional Court specifically highlighted that the arbitration clauses allowed only one of the parties to choose the arbitrator and that all disputes were to be finally resolved by an arbitrator appointed by the claimant from a list of members of the *Arbitrators Association*, or appointed by the Chairman of the *Arbitrators Association* if the claimant

---

[209] ArbAct [CZE] (as applicable on the day this arbitration clause was concluded and as applicable on the day of the annotated judgment of the ConCourt CR [CZE] cit.): Section 25 – "[...] (2) *The arbitral award shall be reasoned unless the parties agree to dispense with reasons; this also applies to any arbitral award rendered pursuant to Section 24(2). (3) When making the award, the arbitrators apply the substantive law applicable to the dispute; they may, however, resolve the dispute according to the rules of equity but only if the parties explicitly authorized them to.*"
With effect from 1 April 2012, an Amendment to the ArbAct [CZE] modifies Section 25 of the ArbAct [CZE] with respect to consumer arbitration by amending Subsections (2) and (3) of Section 25 of the ArbAct [CZE] as follows (cit.): Section 25 – "[...] (2) *The arbitral award shall be reasoned unless the parties agree to dispense with reasons; this also applies to any arbitral award rendered pursuant to Section 24(2). An arbitral award rendered in a dispute arising from a consumer contract must always contain reasons and instructions regarding the right to file a petition with the court for annulment of the award.* [......] (3) *When making the award, the arbitrators apply the substantive law applicable to the dispute; they may, however, resolve the dispute according to the rules of equity but only if the parties explicitly authorized them to. In disputes arising from consumer contracts, the arbitrators shall always abide by consumer protection laws and regulations.*" Subsection (1) of Section 25 of the ArbAct [CZE] continues to apply unamended. There was no change in cases which do not concern consumer contracts (contracts concluded by a consumer / a consumer-type contract).

did not exercise his or her right to appoint the arbitrator, in arbitration pursuant to the Arbitration Rules of the *Arbitrators Association*; the parties agreed that the arbitral proceedings would be conducted only on the basis of written materials, without a hearing, and that the dispute would be resolved according to the rules of equity. Consumer arbitration must generally guarantee procedural rights comparable with the rights guaranteed in litigation which would be conducted if the consumer did not enter into the arbitration agreement (oral and direct hearing, appeal, no obstacles preventing the exercise of the consumer's right); the arbitration conducted subject to the conditions stipulated in the present case definitely does not provide such a guarantee.

6.   Requirement of appeal

412.   The requirement of *appeal*, as articulated by the Constitutional Court as a requirement for procedural rights which must be guaranteed in case the consumer exercises his or her rights, may be considered potentially controversial. Although Section 27 of the ArbAct [CZE][210] allows the parties to agree on a review of the arbitral award in arbitration, such a procedure is rather unusual in practice. From the international perspective, one may even argue that such a procedure is only exceptionally incorporated in national arbitration laws. Elaboration on the suitability of such a procedure is not intended here; but some authors maintain that it dissolves the generally recognized advantage of arbitration, namely its expeditiousness. The opinion of the Constitutional Court, as *interpreted* in the preceding paragraph, would thus necessarily suffer from an internal conflict. If, on the one hand, the Constitutional Court generally allows arbitration in consumer disputes, it cannot, on the other hand, require that the arbitral award be principally subject to review. An arbitral award should not be, as a rule, subject to appeal, and an agreement of the parties on a review of the decision in the merits ought to only be an exception to the general rule. After all, this approach is also recognized by the Czech arbitration rules (*lex arbitri*). The fact that the Amendment to the ArbAct [CZE], effective date 1 April 2012, still allows arbitration in consumer disputes also means that the legislator not only accepts, in principle, this method of resolution of consumer disputes, but also approves the fundamental principles of this type of proceedings vis-à-vis consumer disputes. One must therefore disagree with the view that the possibility of appeal is a procedural principle which would have to be insisted on as the

---

[210] ArbAct [CZE] (cit.): Section 27 – *"The parties may agree in their arbitration agreement that the arbitral award can be reviewed by other arbitrators at the request of any or both of the parties. Unless the arbitration agreement stipulates otherwise, the petition for review must be sent to the other party no later than 30 days from the date of the delivery of the arbitral award to the party requesting the review. Review of the arbitral award constitutes part of the arbitral proceedings, and it is subject to the provisions of this Act."*

procedural *ordre public.* To some extent, however, decision-making following the principles of equity could limit the possibility of review with respect to the issue of whether the arbitration managed to guarantee those rights of the consumer which are considered an essential component of consumer protection. It is worth mentioning, though, that elsewhere in the judgment[211] the Constitutional Court held (cit.:) *"arbitration represents a 'departure' from traditional litigation, the results of which can only be subject to court review under very limited circumstances."*[212] Surprisingly, the reasons for the judgment of the ConCourt CR [CZE] are full of internal contradictions, inconsistencies, and conflicts with other recent decisions of the Constitutional Court; the other decisions are, conversely, mostly consistent and in line with long-established [practices].

413. The Constitutional Court has generally concluded that the respective arbitration clauses do not guarantee a transparent approach and, consequently, must be classified as unacceptable (in a consumer contract). If the arbitration clauses have the result of the parties waiving the right to judicial protection guaranteed by the state, it does not mean that they allow for arbitrariness. An arbitral award is an enforceable decision; consequently, state authority applies to arbitration as well – it can only be exercised in situations within the limits and in the manner stipulated by law while honoring fundamental rights and freedoms. From the perspective of constitutional law, negotiations about the arbitration clause in a consumer contract can be permitted only if the terms of appointment of the arbitrator and the agreed procedural rules guarantee equal treatment to the parties. According to the Constitutional Court, this means (vis-à-vis the consumer) increased protection of the weaker party (consumer) as well as the fact that the agreed procedural rules will guarantee a fair trial, including the possibility of reviewing the arbitral award by other arbitrators, as allowed under the applicable arbitration act. As already mentioned above, this requirement could be successfully contested. This is confirmed by the Amendment to the ArbAct [CZE] which was drafted after protracted discussions and extensive legislative work, with the assistance of experts, including representatives of the judiciary, authorities supervising the protection of consumer rights, etc. After all, the main objective of the Amendment to the ArbAct [CZE] (after 1 April 2012) was the incorporation of mechanisms which would guarantee the specific protection of consumers in arbitration.

---

[211] Para. (28) of the reasons for the judgment of the ConCourt CR [CZE].

[212] With reference to Section 31 of the ArbAct [CZE] which contains an exhaustive list of grounds justifying an application for annulment of an arbitral award, or setting aside of an arbitral award by a court.

7. Right to a lawful judge and rules concerning the appointment of arbitrator

414. As an *obiter dictum*, the Constitutional Court added that arbitration clauses in consumer contracts must be subject to more rigorous requirements than arbitration agreements in other contracts. The main emphasis is laid on a transparent choice of arbitrator who should resolve the dispute. No rules may be waived in consumer arbitration. The Constitutional Court also noted, as an *obiter dictum*, that just as litigation is subject to the **right to a lawful judge** (Article 38(1) of the Charter [CZE]) as one of its fundamental principles, a **similar requirement can be extended to arbitration.** Although arbitration entails simplified proceedings, it should also pursue the objective of a just and fair decision in the case, which primarily requires transparent and unambiguous rules concerning the appointment of an arbitrator.

Paragraph (27) of the reasons for the judgment of the ConCourt CR [CZE] annotated in this chapter is somewhat unclear. The relevant part of the decision of the Constitutional Court of the Czech Republic [CZE] reads as follows (cit.:) *"[i]f the decision in the case is to be rendered by an entity (legal person) other than a permanent arbitral institution established under the law* (Section 13 of the ArbAct [CZE]), *the arbitrator ought to be clearly identified, either by his or her name, or by a clear specification of the method of his or her appointment."* This sentence seems to suggest that the *"dispute could be resolved by a legal entity."* Although *lex arbitri* does not explicitly require that only a "natural person" (or a group of natural persons – arbitral panel) can act as an arbitrator, i.e. *the person making the factual and legal findings and delivering a decision in the merits,* such a requirement can clearly be inferred from Section 4 of the ArbAct [CZE]. Indeed, other decisions of the ConCourt CR [CZE] articulate the requirement regarding the determination of the arbitral forum by stipulating that the parties may either agree on a *permanent arbitral institution* or a particular natural person, or they can agree on a [transparent] procedure of appointment of this individual (natural person) as arbitrator in *ad hoc* proceedings.[213] The Constitutional Court adds that the wording of the law[214] clearly *prefers* the requirement of individualization (specification) of the arbitrator (cf. *"[...] disputes are decided by independent and impartial arbitrators,"*[215] *"[...] ought to be resolved by one or more arbitrators [...]"*[216] or *"the arbitration agreement usually ought to determine the*

---

[213] This somewhat unclear conclusion of the ConCourt CR [CZE] is even more surprising in light of the fact that the Constitutional Court ruled on the issue approximately three weeks before, in its Resolution (ConCourt CR [CZE]), Case No. II. ÚS 3057 of 5 October 2011.
[214] Refers to Section 1, Section 2(1), Section 7(1) of the ArbAct [CZE].
[215] Section 1 of the ArbAct [CZE].
[216] Section 2(1) of the ArbAct [CZE].

number of arbitrators and their identity").[217] At the end of the relevant paragraph of the reasons, however, the Constitutional Court concludes that the arbitrator must be a natural person. Hence, it is not quite clear what, in fact, was the purpose of this excursus in para. (27) of the reasons. Due to the fact that, as opposed to litigation, the possibility of reviewing an arbitral award is limited to the exhaustive list of grounds for annulment of arbitral awards,[218] the dispute must be resolved by an arbitrator chosen according to transparent rules. In the present case, however, the choice of arbitrator was at the discretion of one party only – the claimant was to select the arbitrator from a list administered by an entity other than a *permanent arbitral institution*. The list of arbitrators applicable at the moment of filing the request for arbitration can be entirely different from the list applicable at the moment the arbitration clause was concluded. Consequently, the choice of arbitrator need not at all depend on the will of the party addressing the entity, it could be much more influenced by the entity administering the list (for instance, by including specific individuals in the list or, conversely, striking out others). In the Constitutional Court's opinion, this prevents a transparent choice of arbitrator. The Constitutional Court [CZE] noted that the autonomy of the parties in negotiating arbitration agreements is not entirely unlimited. The Court also highlights that the right to choose the arbitrator must not be abused to the advantage of only one of the parties. In such case, the autonomy of will is limited by Article 2(3) of the Charter [CZE] which stipulates that everyone may do that which is not prohibited by law, and no one may be compelled to do that which is not imposed upon him or her by law. In other words, the parties have the right to freely choose the method of review of a particular legal relationship, but this right is limited by fundamental procedural rules and principles. The Constitutional Court concluded that a choice of arbitrator approved by both parties could be considered as permissible, because the choice **would not be at the exclusive discretion of only one party**; otherwise, the arbitration clause could create an imbalance in the parties' rights and obligations. This conclusion, albeit only as an *obiter dictum*, is not entirely persuasive either. It could be persuasive only if the Constitutional Court clearly distinguished between a *permanent arbitral institution* and *ad hoc* proceedings, albeit organized (*administered*) by a legal entity other than a *permanent arbitral institution*. Specifically, the Constitutional Court failed to address the importance of Section 7 of the ArbAct [CZE], which allows the parties to agree on the method of appointment of arbitrator. The parties may agree on the entity which will *choose* the arbitrator for them (the *appointing authority*) – such an agreement is principally allowed and

---

[217] Section 7(1) of the ArbAct [CZE].
[218] From this perspective, it is not entirely clear what the Constitutional Court meant by stipulating the requirement of observing the progress of the case through the individual court instances, as described above in the annotation to this judgment of the ConCourt CR [CZE].

widely accepted in the international arena. The conclusions of the Constitutional Court can be generally accepted; but the circumstances of the issues in question must be perceived from a more comprehensive perspective. The crucial issue is what criteria of independence should be met by the *third party* who/which appoints the *independent arbitrator* vested with the authority to hear and resolve the dispute. The criteria, especially the guarantee of independence of this *appointing authority*, ought to be the key factor. Unfortunately, this has been entirely neglected by the Constitutional Court. The Court's conclusion that the appointment of arbitrator from the *list of arbitrators* conflicts with constitutional principles, namely the requirement of transparency, is highly questionable as well. Limitations applicable to the selection of arbitrators are, as a rule, nothing unusual. Although a number of *permanent arbitral institutions* abroad have recently abandoned the practice of administering a *list of arbitrators*, it is still a fairly common practice in arbitral proceedings conducted in the countries of Central and Eastern Europe. It is hardly acceptable that the possibility of changes in these *lists of arbitrators* after the conclusion of the arbitration agreement and before the opening of the proceedings (appointment of arbitrator) should play any major role. Such changes are natural, and they do not limit the statutory prerequisite that the arbitrator (albeit selected from the *list of arbitrators*) must meet the requirement of independence. The important thing is that the *appointing authority* also meets the requirements of independence, i.e. in the choice of an independent and impartial arbitrator. Naturally, one may also agree that the fundamental principles applicable to arbitration prohibit that the right to appoint or even influence the choice of arbitrator belongs only to one party. Whether this is the situation in a particular case or whether, conversely, the requirements of equality of the parties are met, must be assessed according to the particular circumstances of each individual case. However, those situations where the respondent is passive, and, consequently, the arbitrator can be appointed only by one party must not be forgotten. This happens when, for instance, the arbitration clause provides for a *sufficient and reasonable period* in which the respondent is supposed to comment on the claimant's proposal and, in the absence of any comments, i.e. the respondent neither confirms nor refuses the proposal, his/her consent is presumed. Nonetheless, such a situation must be explicitly agreed, and the agreement must guarantee that the counterparty had a sufficient and reasonable possibility to evaluate the proposal. It therefore constitutes acceptance of the opposite version of the civil law principle according to which, conversely, *silence does not mean consent*. This procedure complies with the requirement of proportionality, because we must also accept the interest in preventing the respondent from obstructing the hearing and resolution of the dispute. We can also fully agree that the fulfillment of the proportionality principle in consumer disputes must be subjected to an especially rigorous test. Surprisingly, the Constitutional Court failed to ask these very questions, or failed to answer them; conversely, the Court articulated opinions which could be labeled superficial and especially internally inconsistent and conflicting with the current case law of the ConCourt CR [CZE]. We can undoubtedly agree with the final conclusion of the Constitutional Court in the present case. But as mentioned above, this decision is – and the author is much surprised at the fact – excessive in many respects, because otherwise the case law of the ConCourt CR [CZE] is fairly constant and balanced.

(e) Judgment of the Supreme Court CR [CZE],[219] Case No. 23 Cdo 1201/2009 of 29 June 2010[220]

(aa) Conclusions of the Supreme Court

415.   The Supreme Court [CZE] was called upon to decide on a cassation appeal.[221] The case concerned court proceedings on the annulment of an arbitral award in a dispute with a consumer. The following conclusions can be derived from the proceedings (the relevant part):

▶ If, in proceedings on the annulment of an arbitral award, a court finds that the relation between the parties constitutes a consumer contract, the court must base its findings regarding the purported conflict with consumer protection laws (and the inevitable invalidity of the arbitration clause) on the application of consumer protection laws (i.e., in the present case, on Section 55(1) of the CC [CZE][222] and Section 56(1) of the CC [CZE]), not just only on the general requirements concerning arbitration agreements pursuant to Section 3(2) of the ArbAct [CZE],[223] on Arbitration and the Enforcement of Arbitral Awards, as subsequently amended.

---

[219] In the cassation appeal proceedings (as an exceptional remedial measure) against the resolution of the Municipal Court in Prague, Case No. 21 Co 245/2008-86 of 11 November 2008 (as the court of appeals). The proceedings concerned the annulment of an arbitral award.

[220] Available at the website of the SC CR [Supreme Court of the Czech Republic]. Also annotated in: *Bělohlávek, A. et Rozehnalová, N.* CYArb – Czech (& Central European) Yearbook of Arbitration. Huntington (New York): JurisNet, 2011, Vol. I, pp. 271–276. The original text of the decision is available online at: http://www.nsoud.cz/JudikaturaNS_new/judikatura_prevedena2.nsf/WebSearch/71A7DDD7C6E4054CC1257761003CDF9F?openDocument [last access 18 August 2011].

[221] The preceding stages of the litigation involved the following decisions:

  ➤ Trial court: Judgment of the District Court for Prague 4, Case No. 43 C 48/2006 of 19 February 2008 and

  ➤ Court of appeals: Judgment of the Municipal Court in Prague, Case No. 21 Co 245/2008-86 of 11 November 2008.

[222] CC [CZE] (cit.): – Section 55 – "(1) *Contractual terms in consumer contracts may not depart from the law to the detriment of the consumer. In particular, the consumer may not waive the rights guaranteed to him or her by the law or impair his or her contractual position in any other manner.* (2) *The clauses in consumer contracts specified in Section 56 are invalid.* (3) *When in doubt as to the meaning of consumer contracts, the interpretation that is more favorable to the consumer shall apply.*"

[223] ArbAct [CZE] (cit.:) Section 3 – "(1) *The arbitration agreement must be executed in writing; otherwise it is null and void. The arbitration agreement is also considered executed in writing if it is*

▶ The Czech Act on Arbitration and the Enforcement of Arbitral Awards (Section 3(2) of the ArbAct [CZE])²²⁴ does not condition the valid conclusion of an arbitration agreement on the requirement that the contract containing the arbitration clause must indicate in any specified manner that the arbitration clause was also agreed on.²²⁵ It suffices that the arbitration clause is *[simply]* incorporated in the principal (main) contract.

▶ Section 3 of the ArbAct [CZE] merely stipulates the formal requirements for arbitration agreements. It does not regulate other issues relating to the formation (conclusion) of an arbitration agreement.

▶ In other words, Section 3 of the ArbAct [CZE] does not set forth any general requirements concerning the terms of the arbitration agreement or the method of its formation²²⁶ but, in the form of an

---

negotiated by telegraph, fax, or any electronic means enabling the recording of its content and identification of the individuals or entities who concluded the arbitration agreement. (2) However, if the arbitration clause is incorporated in the terms and conditions governing the main contract to which the arbitration clause applies, the arbitration clause is also considered validly negotiated if a written offer of the main contract with the arbitration clause was accepted by the other party in any manner clearly indicating the latter party's consent with the contents of the arbitration agreement."
²²⁴ ArbAct [CZE] (cit.:) Section 3 – "[...] (2) *However, if the arbitration agreement is incorporated in the terms and conditions governing the main contract to which the arbitration clause applies, the arbitration clause is also considered validly negotiated if a written offer of the main contract with the arbitration clause was accepted by the other party in any manner clearly indicating the latter party's consent with the contents of the arbitration agreement."*
The first of April 2012 is the effective date of the Amendment to the ArbAct [CZE] the main purpose of which is to incorporate special rules on consumer protection in arbitration; the Amendment keeps the current Subsections (1) and (2) of Section 3 unamended and introduces special rules on arbitration agreements concluded with consumers in Subsections (3) through (6) of Section 3, which read as follows (cit.): Section 3 – "[...] (3) *An arbitration agreement for the resolution of disputes arising from consumer contracts must be negotiated separately, not integrated in the terms and conditions governing the principal contract; otherwise the arbitration agreement is invalid. (4) The professional shall provide the consumer with a proper explanation reasonably preceding the conclusion of the arbitration clause so that the consumer can assess the potential consequences of the conclusion of the arbitration clause for the consumer. Proper explanation shall be interpreted as meaning the explication of all consequences of the arbitration clause. (5) The arbitration clause concluded pursuant to Subsection (3) must contain truthful, accurate, and complete information about* (a) *the arbitrator or about the fact that the dispute will be resolved by a permanent arbitral institution,* (b) *the method of commencement and the form of case management of the arbitral proceedings,* (c) *the arbitrator's fees and anticipated types of costs which the consumer might incur in the arbitration, and about the rules governing the award of the costs,* (d) *the seat of arbitration,* (e) *the method whereby the arbitral award will be served on the consumer and* (f) *the fact that a final arbitral award is enforceable.* (6) *If the arbitration clause vests the jurisdiction to resolve the dispute to a permanent arbitral institution, the requirements under Subsection (5) are also fulfilled by a reference to the statutes and rules of permanent arbitral institutions issued under Section 13."*
²²⁵ This conclusion must be corrected with respect to the special rules contained in the Amendment to the ArbAct [CZE] taking effect on 1 April 2012.
²²⁶ The SC [CZE] is of the opinion that this is where the court of appeals (the Municipal Court as the court of appeals) erred. We must emphasize, though, that this conclusion corresponded to the law before the Amendment to the ArbAct [CZE]. The Amendment to the ArbAct also stipulates requirements as concerns the terms of an arbitration agreement concluded with a consumer (see

exemption from the rule, sets out the conditions under which a written offer to conclude the principal (main) contract containing the arbitration clause may be accepted by the other party other than in writing (i.e. the offer must be accepted in a form which makes the other party's consent with the terms of the arbitration agreement clear and obvious). If the arbitration agreement (or, as the case may be, the principal contract which also contains the arbitration clause) was made in writing, the requirement of written form pursuant to Section 3(1) of the same Act [ArbAct (CZE)] has been fulfilled. Consequently, there is no reason to examine whether the prerequisites for the exemption from the rule set out in Section 3(2) of the ArbAct [CZE] were met, let alone to conclude, based on said provision, that the arbitration clause is invalid.

▶ As concerns the issue of whether the contract in question is an individually agreed agreement or a standard form (adhesion) contract, we need to examine, for instance, the scope, structure, and choice of font of the contract. Adhesion contracts are typically formed in long and unclear texts in miniature, hard-to-decipher fonts, or a mere reference to general terms of business of the same design.[227]

▶ In circumstances where the arbitration clause is contained in the text as a separate (and, in fact, the penultimate) provision, the first words of which (*"Potential disputes"*[...]) are highlighted, and the immediately following point occupies a single line, followed by the space reserved for the applicant's signature, there can be no doubt that the recipient of the contract offer (the accepting party) consented both to the principal (main) contract and to the arbitration clause contained therein. The parties have therefore signed the agreement beyond any doubt.[228] In this situation, the claimant (*applicant*) must have known that he was also entering into an arbitration agreement (clause); this conclusion is also inevitable when applied to the *average consumer*.[229] Consumer protection has

---

Section 3(5) of the ArbAct as amended by the Amendment to the ArbAct). We need to ask, though, whether this is a conceptual solution and whether perhaps the special requirements concerning the terms of an arbitration agreement concluded with a consumer should not be incorporated in Section 2 of the ArbAct – which the author would support. Nonetheless, Section 3 of the ArbAct as amended by the Amendment to the ArbAct does not prescribe any requirements regarding the individual terms of arbitration agreements other than those negotiated between a professional and a consumer; the only mandatory prerequisites concern the form of the arbitration agreement or the method of conclusion of the agreement.

[227] In other words, the Supreme Court of the CR [CZE] neither upheld the conclusion of the court of appeals in that the contract was a standard form contract, nor an adhesion contract, which is sometimes negotiated between a professional and a[n] [end] consumer.

[228] In this regard, the Supreme Court [SC CR] [CZE] invoked its conclusions reached in Resolution Case No. 23 Cdo 4895/2009 of 28 April 2010.

[229] The Supreme Court [SC CR] [CZE] held that the conclusion applied all the more if the respective contracting party (addressee of the contract offer / applicant) was a holder of a university degree.

its limits; it can in no case be interpreted as a defense of the consumer's recklessness and irresponsibility.[230] Consequently, the consumer cannot successfully plead that the arbitration clause was placed among the general terms in the contract without being specifically entitled or highlighted, and that he or she was not made aware of the term, not even verbally.

► The conclusion of whether the party intended to perform a specific legal (juridical) act (i.e. whether the party wanted to express its will aimed at the formation, amendment, or extinguishment of rights and obligations associated with such an expression by law)[231] is a finding of fact.[232] If the document recording the expression of will did not itself suffice to allow the conclusion that the text contained therein indeed expressed the party's will, the court would have to examine: the circumstances attending the conclusion of the contract,[233] the

---

This conclusion must be approved, i.e. we must always individually assess the relevant contracting party, as well as all other circumstances of the case.

[230] In connection with this conclusion, the SC CR [CZE] invokes another authority, namely the published commentary on the Civil Code – Švestka, J., Spáčil, J., Škárová, M., Hulmák, M. et al. Občanský zákoník [Title in translation: Civil Code], Vol. I, Prague: C. H. Beck, 2008, p. 408.

[231] The provision is quoted above in the footnotes to the annotation of this court decision.

[232] For an identical opinion, see *Fouchard, Ph.* Clause abusives en matière d'arbitrage. Rev. arb., 1995, p. 149, *Fouchard* (especially with regard to French laws and French practice) emphasizes that the courts should not automatically hold an arbitration agreement invalid where the case requires the examination of the circumstances attending the conclusion of the contract. The courts should treat the issue as a question of fact. Questions of fact should be heard and proved or disproved in arbitration, and the courts should therefore follow the "*Kompetenz-Kompetenz*" principle and leave the primary resolution of these questions to the arbitrators.

Indeed, the same conclusion was reached, outside the EU, by a Québec court [CAN] in *Rogers Wireless, Inc.* v. *Muroff;* 2007 SCC 35. See *Caplow, S. P.* Arbitration Class Action Waivers in the United States and Canada. Arbitration, 2008, Vol. 74, No. 1, pp. 57–64, here p. 63–64. The Canadian decision is fully annotated elsewhere in this book.

[233] Concerning the moment relevant for the assessment of unfairness, see *Maisonneuve, M.* Le droit américain de l'arbitrage et la théorie de l'unconscionability. Rev. arb., 2005, p. 101. He also concludes that it is a question of fact which should be examined at the stage of admitting evidence and assessing the merits. According to *M. Maisonneuve*, the assessment should relate to the moment of conclusion of the contract; he therefore challenges the practice in the United States. Conversely, one could maintain that as concerns this particular issue, the practice of the American courts [USA] is not principally different from the practice pursued by most European countries, i.e. most European courts (for instance [FRA], but also [CZE] and [DEU]).

The ECJ has also addressed these issues in its case law. Indeed, the ECJ's case law indicates that the (un)fairness of a contractual term must be assessed with respect to the nature of the performance and the circumstances attending the conclusion of the contract, relating specifically to the act of formation of the contract. See:

➢ ECJ Judgment, Case C-237/02 of 1 April 2004 (*Freiburger Kommunalbauten GmbH Baugesellschaft & Co. KG* v. *Ludger Hofstetter et Ulrike Hofstetter*), para. (20), as well as;

➢ ECJ Judgment, Case C-243/08 of 4 June 2009 (*Pannon GSM*), which is annotated in detail elsewhere in this book and which refers to ECJ Judgment, Case C-237/02 of 1 April 2004.

An identical approach, including all consequences and with a meticulous examination of the purpose and the circumstances attending the conclusion of the contract, was also adopted by an English court – see the Judgment of the Court of Appeal, Queen's Bench Division – Technology and Construction Court, No. HT-07-106 of 18 December 2007 in *Heifer International Inc* v. (1) *Helge Christiansen* (2)

subsequent behavior of the parties,[234] or other such facts which
would permit this (or another) conclusion regarding the party's will.
Alternatively, the court would have to (upon hearing or reading the
proposed relevant evidence) make a reasoned conclusion that the
party failed to meet the burden of proof. Attaching one's signature to
a document containing an arbitration agreement constitutes consent
with the arbitration agreement (unless specifically proven otherwise).
Consequently, it is not possible to conclude that the arbitration
clause is invalid, because it was not executed in a special, defined
manner. The law's only requirement is that of the written form.[235]

(bb) Factual and legal findings

416. The case concerned a motion for annulment of an arbitral award. The
claimant was a consumer, the respondent was a professional. The
parties' dispute was previously resolved by an arbitral award. The
claimant demanded annulment of the arbitral award rendered by the
arbitrator [XY] on 31 January 2006 under Case No. R-610/2005, whereby
she was ordered to pay to the respondent [xxx,xxx.xx CZK] with
interest. The claimant pleaded invalidity of the arbitration clause
contained in an agency agreement of 26 November 2004. Under the
agency agreement, the respondent undertook to mediate for the
claimant the sale of her family house. The claimant argued that the
arbitration agreement was ambiguous (it did not clearly indicate the
precise number of arbitrators) and contra bonos mores. The claimant
considered it *immoral* that the arbitrator was to be appointed by an
association in which one of the parties to the dispute was a member. The
claimant was not presented with the list of arbitrators, and it is not clear
whether it actually existed in the relevant period. The claimant also
argued that it was not acceptable to conduct the proceedings pursuant
to the unclear internal rules of this "association," without the parties
having the opportunity to get acquainted with the rules at or before the
conclusion of the arbitration clause. The respondent, as a member of the
Association of Real Estate Agencies [CZE] (in this annotation
hereinafter referred to as the "Association"), therefore enjoyed an
advantage in the arbitration. The claimant referred to Section 56(1) of

---

Christiansen Arkitekter KS MAA PAR (3) *Haslev-Hansson VVS* (4) *Stevns El-Service A/S et* (5) *Listed El-Teknik APS*; [2007] EWHC 3015 (TCC), [2008] Bus LR D49; [2007] APP.L.R. 12/18, [2008] All ER (D) 120 (Jan) available online from the website at: (i) http://www.bailii.org/ew/cases/EWHC/TCC/2007/3015.html [last access 27 August 2011] or (ii) http://www.nadr.co.uk/articles/published/ArbitLRe/Heifer%20v%20Helge%202007.pdf [last access 27 August 2011]. This decision is also annotated in detail and repeatedly analyzed elsewhere in this book.
[234] See also ECJ Judgment, Case C-243/08 of 4 June 2009 (*Pannon GSM Zrt v. Sustikné Győrfi Erzsébet [Pannon GSM]*), CELEX: 62008CA0243, The judgment was published in: ECR 2009, p. I–04713. This decision of the ECJ is annotated in detail in Chapter III.9.
[235] The Supreme Court [SC CR] [CZE] again departed from the conclusion of the court of appeals (Municipal Court in Prague [CZE] as the trial court).

the Civil Code (CC [CZE]), the *Directive* and the *Recommendation*. The claimant insisted that Czech law and EC law classify as invalid, in consumer disputes, any contractual terms the objective or consequence of which is a substantial impairment of the consumer's position. This is what happened in the present case, according to the claimant, because she was deprived of appellate proceedings. The arbitration clause was articulated in such a manner that, as an *average consumer*, she could not evaluate the consequences of accepting it, and the arbitration clause transferred the jurisdiction over the case from the court competent to hear the case according to her place of residence to an arbitrator in Prague. She emphasized that arbitration should not circumvent court proceedings; it should be conducted only by specialized institutions, and the consumer should not enter into an arbitration clause before the dispute arises. The claimant also asserted that the arbitrator in the present case was biased, because he is a permanent advisor to a professional organization in which the respondent is also a member.

(cc)   Decisions of the trial court and the court of appeals

417.   The trial court dismissed the claim. The court concluded that – with reference to the binding legal opinion of the court of appeals – the arbitrator challenge does not constitute grounds for annulment of the arbitral award. The court held the arbitration clause valid. The trial court ruled that the contract, in which the clause was incorporated, was not a standard form contract[236] which would, for instance, contain a number of terms written in small print and be difficult to read even for a person with perfect vision. The fact that the arbitration clause was included among the miscellaneous provisions of the agency agreement does not in itself render the clause invalid. The relevant page of the contract (in which the arbitration clause is printed) contains other essential terms, such as the subject matter of the contract and the fees, and the words *"potential disputes"* are actually highlighted. Consequently, the claimant should have gotten acquainted with the text of the contract; indeed, the claimant herself did not claim that she had not read the contract. The trial court did not find the arbitration clause immoral or contrary to the consumer protection laws. The trial court did remark that, in the court's opinion, arbitration as a method of

---

[236] Regarding standard form contracts, see:
➤ Judgment of the BGH [DEU], Case No. III ZR 265/03 of 13 January 2005 which is annotated in detail in the excursus into German law [DEU]; the court unequivocally held that the (this) form does not eo ipso constitute unfairness and impropriety;
➤ Judgment of the BGH [DEU], Case No. III ZR 164/06 of 1 March 2007, also annotated in detail in the excursus into German law [DEU];
➤ A standard form contract was also the subject matter of a case before the ECJ – see ECJ Judgment, Case C-243/08 of 4 June 2009, [*Pannon GSM*], CELEX: 62008CA0243 which is annotated in detail in Chapter III.9 and elsewhere in this book.

resolution of consumer disputes generally brings only disadvantages to the consumer; in the present case, however, the conditions were the same for both parties, i.e. neither of them enjoyed any advantages. According to the findings made by the trial court, the "Association" did administer a list of arbitrators, and the arbitrator was included in the list at the relevant time. The court did not find the arbitration clause vague, because it stipulated the method of determining the number and the identity of the arbitrators.

418.　Conversely, the court of appeals overturned the judgment of the trial court and, simultaneously, set aside the arbitral award, i.e. granted the claim. The court of appeals referred to its preceding cassation decision in which the court highlighted the necessity of examining the validity of the arbitration clause with respect to Section 3(2) of the ArbAct [CZE]. The court of appeals held that the agency agreement entered into by and between the parties pursuant to Section 774 of the CC [CZE] is a type of a consumer contract, and, consequently, its regime should not conflict with: the consumer protection provisions of the CC [CZE], the consumer directives of the EP and of the Council (EC), especially the *Directive*, or Directive 98/27/EC. Section 3(2) of the ArbAct [CZE] anticipates a certain method of accepting the arbitration agreement which will indicate the other party's consent with the terms of the arbitration agreement; it can only be interpreted as meaning that the other party must have known that the arbitration clause was being concluded and gave its consent with the arbitration clause.[237] The court highlighted that the respective contract was a **standard form contract in which most of the terms are determined in advance and**[238] **the other party, usually a consumer, has basically no possibility of introducing any changes to the text**. The first page is to be filled out with the specific identification data of the party interested in concluding the contract, and the second page contains "general terms of the agency agreement." This second part contains the arbitration clause as its penultimate provision. The court of appeals concluded that the claimant's signature on that page could not be interpreted as meaning that her signature also signified her consent with the arbitration clause.

---

[237] With reference to the Judgment of the ConCourt CR [CZE], Case No. II. ÚS 3/2006 of 6 November 2007.

[238] The fulfillment of both prerequisites is important. Naturally, the fact that the contract was prepared in advance as a contract offer does not ipso facto entail violation of the principles of consumer protection. Cf.
➤ Judgment of the Federal Court of Justice (BGH [DEU]), Case No. III. ZR 164/06 of 1 March 2007 (annotated in detail elsewhere in this book, especially in the excursus into German law [DEU]);
➤ Judgment of the Federal Court of Justice (Supreme Court [DEU]), Case No. III ZR 265/93 of 13 January 2005 (a detailed annotation elsewhere in this book, especially in the excursus into German law [DEU]; in this decision the BGH [DEU] provides extensive quotations from related case law) and in other rulings.

If the respondent acted in compliance with the principles of honest business transactions, the respondent would have highlighted the arbitration clause, albeit incorporated in the general terms of the agency agreement in order to make it obvious that it is a different term. The signature under such a provision would clearly indicate the claimant's consent with the provision. However, the respondent did not proceed honestly, because the arbitration clause was included among the general terms of the agency agreement. It is true that the beginning of the relevant article is highlighted, but the graphic elements used are the same for all initial words in all the remaining provisions of the general terms. Consequently, the arbitration clause is visually no different from the other general terms of the contract and does not draw the reader's attention. **The court of appeals assessed the visual differentiation of the text as insufficient to sustain the validity of the clause and concluded that the claimant's signature on the document cannot ipso facto constitute her consent with the terms of the arbitration agreement; the arbitration clause is therefore invalid**, which constitutes grounds for annulment of the arbitral award pursuant to Section 31(b) of the ArbAct [CZE].

(dd) Conclusions of the court of appeals and the subsequent decision of the Supreme Court, including reasons

419.   Based on its findings that the agency agreement entered into between the parties was a consumer contract, the court of appeals (i.e. the Municipal Court in Prague) therefore focused on the general interpretation of Section 3(2) of the ArbAct [CZE]; the court interpreted the provision as stipulating that the method of accepting an arbitration clause must clearly indicate that the other party knew that an arbitration agreement was being entered into and granted its consent therewith. Based on the assessment of the case pursuant to this provision, the court of appeals concluded that the requirements for the conclusion of an arbitration agreement were not fulfilled, because the claimant's signature of the agency agreement could not, ipso facto, constitute her consent with the terms of the arbitration agreement. In other words, the court of appeals held that the signature itself could not be interpreted as meaning that the claimant knew (must have known) that she was entering into the arbitration clause and gave her consent with the arbitration clause.

420.   Consequently, the SC CR [CZE], in the proceedings on the cassation appeal, focused solely on the question of whether the assessment summarized in the preceding paragraph was correct or not; the Supreme Court did not concentrate on the issues on which the court of appeals did not base its decision. The Supreme Court [SC CR] [CZE] concluded that the lower court's interpretation of Section 3(2) of the ArbAct [CZE]

was not correct and held that the court of appeals erroneously applied the law, i.e. its decision must be vacated. The Supreme Court neither excluded the possibility, though, that consumer protection laws could impose other requirements on the conclusion of arbitration agreements, i.e. on the validity of an arbitration clause contained in the principal (main) contract. However, such a conclusion would have to be made, if necessary, on the basis of the interpretation and application of consumer protection laws (especially the Civil Code), not only on the basis of the general arbitration laws of the Czech Republic [CZE] which do not prescribe any such requirement for special consent with an arbitration clause incorporated in the principal contract.

421.   In interpreting Section 3 of the ArbAct [CZE],[239] the Supreme Court concluded that the purpose of the provision was concentrated solely on the definition of formal requirements for arbitration agreements. The arbitration agreement must be executed in writing; otherwise it is invalid. The arbitration agreement is also considered executed in writing if it is negotiated by telegraph, fax, or any electronic means enabling both the recording of its content and the identification of the individuals or entities who concluded the arbitration agreement.[240] However, if the arbitration agreement is incorporated in the terms and conditions governing the principal (main) contract with which the arbitration clause is connected, the arbitration clause is also considered validly negotiated if a written offer of the principal contract with the arbitration clause was accepted by the other party in any manner which clearly indicates the latter party's consent with the contents of the arbitration agreement.[241] Section 3(1) of the ArbAct [CZE] prescribes that the arbitration agreement must be, on penalty of invalidity, made in writing, and sets forth the technical means of communication which may be used to meet the requirement of the written form. The second subsection then stipulates the prerequisites for an exemption from the requirement of the written form where the arbitration agreement has been incorporated in the principal (main) agreement (i.e. where the arbitration agreement takes the form of an arbitration clause).[242]

---

[239] This provision of the Act on Arbitration and the Enforcement of Arbitral Awards also applied, without modifications, at the time when the examined arbitration clause was concluded or when the agency agreement containing the relevant arbitration clause was concluded.

[240] The SC CR [CZE] quotes Section 3(1) of the ArbAct [CZE].

[241] The SC CR [CZE] invokes Section 3(2) of the ArbAct [CZE].

[242] Here the reasoning of the SC CR [CZE] refers to the following publications:
Rozehnalová, N. Rozhodčí řízení v mezinárodním a vnitrostátním obchodním styku. [Title in translation: Arbitration in International and National Commerce]. Prague: ASPI Publishing, 2002, p. 85 and Bělohlávek, A. Zákon o rozhodčím řízení a o výkonu rozhodčích nálezů. Komentář. [Title in translation: Act on Arbitration and the Enforcement of Arbitral Awards. Commentary]. Prague: C. H. Beck, 2004, p. 48.

422. For this reason, the Supreme Court of the Czech Republic [CZE] overturned the decision of the court of appeals (i.e. quashed the decision on annulment of the arbitral award) and remanded the case for a new trial.

(f) **Resolution of the SC CR [CZE], Case No. 31 Cdo 1945/2010 of 11 May 2011: Arbitration clause which impairs the position of the "weaker" contracting party; permanent arbitral institutions versus "ad hoc" arbitrators**

(aa) Conclusions of the Supreme Court

423. The Supreme Court reached the following conclusions in the present case:[243]

▶ The principle of **party autonomy must not be (mis)used** to negate the consequences consisting in the invalidity of arbitration clauses which violate the law and which **clearly indicate an intention to harm the "weaker" contracting party (a party to the contractual relationship).**[244] A democratic country honoring the principle of the rule of law must not surrender the protection of the rights and legitimate interests which could be jeopardized in alternative proceedings conducted instead of litigation.

▶ If the arbitration agreement lacks any direct identification of an *ad hoc* arbitrator, or a specific description of the method of his or her appointment, and refers to *"Rules on Arbitration"* issued by a legal entity (corporation) other than a *permanent arbitral institution* established under the law, the arbitration agreement is invalid pursuant to Section 39 of the CC [CZE].[245]

▶ Section 2(1) of the ArbAct [CZE][246] indicates that an arbitration agreement (or a clause incorporated in the principal contract, as the

---

[243] Available from the website of the SC CR [CZE] at: http://www.nsoud.cz/JudikaturaNS_new/ judikatura_prevedena2.nsf/WebSearch/35D7A1839F99F5BAC1257899002EA885?openDocument [last access 12 January 2011]. Also published in Sbírka soudních rozhodnutí [Court Reports], 2011, Ref. No. 121. Cited in: *Tomsa, M.* K problematice právní úpravy rozhodčího řízení. [Title in translation: Regarding Laws on Arbitration]. Obchodněprávní revue, 2011, Vol. 3, No. 9, pp. 267–270, here p. 269. This decision is also referred to in certain later rulings, for instance in the Resolution of the SC CR [CZE], Case No. 30 Cdo 4415/2010 of 27 July 2011, etc.

[244] The SC CR [CZE] held that this was the case here.

[245] This ratio decidendi was adopted from the database of the SC CR [CZE] (in the section regarding the decision published at the court's website).
CC [CZE] (cit.): Section 39 – *"A legal (juridical) act is invalid if the content or the purpose thereof violates or evades the law or is inconsistent with good morals."*

[246] ArbAct [CZE] (as applicable on the day this arbitration clause was concluded, cit.): Section 2 – "(1) *The parties may agree that their disputes over property, except disputes arising from the enforcement of decisions and except incidental disputes, which would otherwise fall within the jurisdiction of the courts, shall be decided by one or more arbitrators or by a permanent arbitral institution (arbitration agreement)."*

case may be) must include the parties' agreement on either (an) "*ad hoc*" arbitrator(s) or a *permanent arbitral institution* established under the law.

▶ The *ad hoc* arbitrator must always be a natural person (Section 4 of the ArbAct [CZE]).[247]

▶ The *ad hoc* arbitrator(s) must be identified [by his, her, or their name(s)], or the arbitration agreement (arbitration clause) may define, in compliance with Section 7(1) of the ArbAct [CZE], the method of appointment and the number of arbitrators.

▶ As opposed to *ad hoc* appointed arbitrators, [only] *permanent arbitral institutions* may issue their own rules (statutes and rules) which may set forth the process of appointment and determine the number of arbitrators (the arbitrators can be selected from a list), as well as stipulate the manner whereby the arbitrators shall case manage the proceedings and the costs of arbitration payable by the parties. Such rules must be published in the *Business Journal* [*Obchodní věstník*].

▶ If an entity other than a *permanent arbitral institution* established under a special law (Section 13 of the ArbAct [CZE]) carries out activities which, according to the ArbAct [CZE], are reserved for *permanent arbitral institutions*, logic dictates that this entity clearly and intentionally violates the law.

▶ **Proceedings before a *permanent arbitral institution* also allow that the parties may agree to depart from the rules adopted by the *permanent arbitral institution*.** Unless the parties agree otherwise,

---

With effect from 1 April 2012, an Amendment to the ArbAct [CZE] also partially modifies (supplements) Section 2(1) of the ArbAct [CZE]; the respective provision, as amended by the Amendment to the ArbAct [CZE], reads as follows (cit.): Section 2 – "[...] (1) *The parties may agree that their disputes over property, except disputes arising from the enforcement of decisions and except incidental disputes, which would otherwise fall within the jurisdiction of the courts or which are subject to arbitration under special laws, shall be decided by one or more arbitrators or by a permanent arbitral institution (arbitration agreement). [...]*"

[247] ArbAct [CZE] (as applicable on the day this arbitration clause was concluded, cit.): Part Two – Arbitrators – Section 4 – "(1) *Any citizen of the Czech Republic who is of legal age and has legal capacity can serve as an arbitrator unless a special law stipulates otherwise. (2) A foreigner can serve as an arbitrator if he or she has legal capacity under the laws of his or her country; it shall suffice, however, if he or she has legal capacity under the laws of the Czech Republic.*"
With effect from 1 April 2012, an Amendment to the ArbAct [CZE] modifies Section 4 of the ArbAct [CZE] with respect to arbitration in consumer disputes; Section 4 in its entirety of the ArbAct [CZE] is amended as follows (cit.): Section 4 – "(1) *Any citizen of the Czech Republic who is of legal age, has no criminal record and has legal capacity can serve as an arbitrator unless a special law stipulates otherwise. (2) A foreigner may serve as an arbitrator if he or she meets the condition of majority, no criminal record and legal capacity; the requirement of legal capacity shall be governed by the person's lex patriae. It shall suffice, however, if he or she has legal capacity under the laws of the Czech Republic. (3) In order to meet the requirement of no criminal record under Subsections (1) and (2), the person must have no previous final and conclusive conviction for a criminal offence unless the person's criminal record is expunged and the person is deemed never to have been convicted. (4) An arbitrator designated by an arbitration clause to resolve disputes arising from consumer contracts must be registered in the list of arbitrators administered by the Ministry of Justice (the 'Ministry').*"

the arbitrator(s) shall follow the rules adopted by the *permanent arbitral institution,* as applicable on the day the request for arbitration is filed with the *permanent arbitral institution.*

(bb) Factual and legal findings and decisions of the trial court and the court of appeals

424. The parties entered into a real estate purchase contract (real estate transfer contract); the contract contained an arbitration clause. The arbitration clause stipulated that "[a]*ny and all disputes which arise or could arise between the parties or any other claims **shall be resolved in arbitration before a single arbitrator, in compliance with Act No. 216/1994 Coll., pursuant to the Rules on Arbitration and the Tariff adopted by [XY, s.r.o.];*[248] *the valid version of these documents is available at the website of the above-mentioned association of arbitrators.*"[249] The relevant issue is that [XY, s.r.o.] is not an entity which could be classified as a *permanent arbitral institution* pursuant to Section 13 of the ArbAct [CZE].[250]

425. The subject matter of the dispute was the determination of the (ownership) title to real property; the claimant argued that the purchase contract was invalid. The District Court in Frýdek-Místek, as the trial court, terminated the proceedings initiated by the petition for

---

[248] Name withheld by the author. The decision mentions a specific entity.

[249] The arbitration agreement is not available. This is adopted from the interpretation articulated in the reasons for the resolution of the SC CR [CZE], in the part summarizing the contents of the claimant's cassation appeal; the text is *reconstructed* from the information regarding various parts of this arbitration clause.

[250] ArbAct [CZE] (as applicable on the day this arbitration clause was concluded, cit.): Section 13 – "(1) *Permanent arbitral institutions can be established only under the law. (2) Permanent arbitral institutions can issue their own statutes and rules which must be published in the Business Journal; these statutes and rules may determine the method of appointment and the number of arbitrators and may stipulate that the arbitrators shall be selected from a list administered by the permanent arbitral institution. The statutes and rules may also determine how the arbitrators shall case manage the proceedings and render their decisions, as well as resolve other issues connected with the activities of the permanent arbitral institution and the arbitrators, including rules regulating the costs of proceedings and remuneration for the arbitrators. (3) If the parties agreed on the jurisdiction of a particular permanent arbitral institution and failed to agree otherwise in the arbitration agreement, they shall be deemed to have submitted to the regulations specified in Subsection (2), as applicable on the day the request for arbitration is filed with the permanent arbitral institution.*"
With effect from 1 April 2012, an Amendment to the ArbAct [CZE] modifies Section 13 of the ArbAct [CZE] by amending Subsection (1) and inserting a new Subsection (4) in Section 13 of the ArbAct [CZE] as follows (cit.): Section 13 – Permanent Arbitral Institutions – "(1) *Permanent arbitral institutions can be established only by another law or if their formation is explicitly allowed by another law.* [......] (4) *No entity may carry out its activities using a name which evokes a misleading impression that the entity is a permanent arbitral institution under this law unless a different law or regulation or an international agreement integrated in the legal system authorizes the entity to use the name.*" Subsections (2) and (3) of Section 13 of the ArbAct [CZE] continue to apply (even after the Amendment to the ArbAct [CZE]) unamended.

the determination of the (ownership) title to the particular real estate[251] filed with said court; the reason for the termination was a timely jurisdictional challenge. The Regional Court in Ostrava [CZE], as the court of appeals, upheld the trial court's decision.[252] An arbitration clause covers not only the rights arising from legal relationships established directly by the contract, but also the issue of the legal validity of these relationships as well as the rights associated therewith. If the arbitration agreement is included in a real estate purchase contract (real estate transfer contract), the arbitration clause also covers disputes over the determination of the (ownership) title to the real estate.

(cc)   Cassation appeal

426.   In her appeal, the claimant argued, inter alia, that the courts had erroneously interpreted the first sentence of Section 7(1) of the ArbAct [CZE]. The claimant emphasized that the parties had only agreed on the number of arbitrators (a single arbitrator), without identifying any particular arbitrator. If we applied the second part of the sentence in Section 7(1) of the ArbAct [CZE] to the present case, then considering the relevant arbitration clause we could conclude that the method of determining the number of arbitrators and identifying the individual arbitrators stipulated therein was not agreed in the present case either. The signing of the purchase contract containing the arbitration clause does not imply that the claimant got acquainted with the *"Rules on Arbitration and the Tariff of [XY, s.r.o.]"* to which the arbitration clause refers. The claimant therefore argued that the arbitration clause violated Section 2(1) of the ArbAct [CZE] and Section 7(1) of the ArbAct [CZE] and was an invalid legal (juridical) act. The claimant also argued that if her petition in the merits pleaded invalidity of the purchase contract, it entailed a plea of invalidity of the arbitration clause contained therein.

427.   The claimant also argued that in criminal proceedings conducted before the same court[253] a connection had transpired between the legal counsel for the respondent and [X.Y., s.r.o.] in other similar cases, which unacceptably violates the principle of impartiality of any eventual arbitral proceedings. The claimant argued that her conclusion regarding the invalidity of the purchase contract itself is supported by the acts of a

---

[251] Resolution of the District Court in Frýdek-Místek [CZE], Case No. 15 C 238/2008-18 of 2 February 2009.
[252] Resolution of the Regional Court in Ostrava [CZE], Case No. 57 Co 150/2009-51 of 15 February 2010.
[253] District Court in Frýdek-Místek, Case No. 1 T 97/2008; the current status of the proceedings was not specified.

particular natural person [*M.T.*] for which the person was convicted;[254] the person is still being prosecuted for another part of the committed act relating to the subject matter of the purchase contract. The claimant also emphasized that she could not abide by the *Rules on Arbitration and the Tariff* issued by an entity which was not authorized to do so, because it was not a *permanent arbitral institution*. The respondent therefore challenged the legal conclusions of the court of appeals as concerns the validity of the arbitration agreement.

(dd) Decision of the cassation court and the cassation court's arguments

428.   The three-member panel No. 30 of the SC CR [CZE], which was called upon to hear and decide the cassation appeal according to the court's schedule, arrived at a legal opinion which departs from the preceding decisions.[255] The Supreme Court of the CR [CZE] concluded that the decision of the court of appeals was not correct.

429.   The Supreme Court of the CR [CZE] analyzed the issue of whether the arbitration clause in the present case required that the resolution of the eventual dispute between the parties be entrusted to (an) *ad hoc* arbitrator(s); the Supreme Court highlighted that both the trial court and the court of appeals in the present case had actually answered the question in the affirmative (despite no detailed analysis of said issue).

---

[254] Judgment of the District Court in Frýdek-Místek [CZE], Case No. 80 T 127/2009 of 3 February 2010. There is no information on whether the judgment is final.

[255] Judgment of the SC CR [CZE], Case No. 32 Cdo 2312/2007 of 21 January 2009. In said decision, the cassation court adopted, inter alia, a legal opinion according to which "[*i*]*f the court of appeals in the given case held that the terms of the arbitration agreement had been validly negotiated by reference to the rules specified therein (Rules of Arbitration Procedure adopted by Společnost pro rozhodčí řízení a.s.), such a provision appears, to say the least, as a vague and ambiguous provision, in that the rules were made for ad hoc arbitral proceedings and were not incorporated in the arbitration agreement and, as opposed to statutes issued by permanent arbitral institutions (Section 13(2) of the ArbAct), these rules were not published in the Business Journal.*" The opinion voiced in said decision corresponds to the Resolution of the High Court in Prague, Case No. 12 Cmo 496/2008 of 28 May 2009, annotated elsewhere in this book.

However, this decision was preceded by another decision, namely Resolution of the SC CR [CZE], 32 Cdo 2282/2008 of 31 July 2008, which reads as follows (cit.): "*The parties to the agreement may validly agree that the disputes arising from their agreement will be decided by an arbitrator selected by the complainant from a list of arbitrators administered by a private entity other than a permanent arbitral institution established within the meaning of Section 13 (of the ArbAct [CZE]) and that the arbitral proceedings will follow the rules adopted by such a private entity.*"

See also: *IA*. An overview of decisions rendered by the Supreme Court of the Czech Republic in 2010 which were not selected for publication. In: Sbírka soudních rozhodnutí a stanovisek [Court Reports]. Soudní rozhledy, 2011, Vol. 17, No. 2, pp. 41–47, here p. 44; *Kocina, J.* Rozhodčí doložky sjednané ve prospěch „soukromých rozhodčích soudů". [Title in translation: Arbitration Clauses Vesting Jurisdiction in "Private Arbitration Courts"]. Bulletin advokacie, 2011, Nos. 7-8, pp. 48–49; *Sokol, T.* K aktuálním problémům rozhodčího řízení. [Title in translation: Regarding Contemporary Problems in Arbitration]. Právní rádce, 2011, Vol. 19, No. 9, pp. 4–14, here p. 9 et al.

430. At the same time, the Supreme Court emphasized that what could not be dismissed was the fact that the selection of the respective arbitrator was subjected to the regime of [X.Y., s.r.o.] which, however, had never been authorized to issue statutes and rules that would, inter alia, regulate the way in which the arbitrator(s) case manage(s) the arbitral proceedings or determine(s) the method of appointment of the arbitrator(s), etc. [X.Y., s.r.o.] is a corporation; the line of business of that corporation in the decisive period was specified as follows: consultancy services for arbitrators in arbitration, services provided by organizational and economic consultants relating to the services for arbitrators and arbitration, and, lastly, agency services for arbitrators and arbitration.

431. The Supreme Court described such a situation, i.e. when entities other than *permanent arbitral institutions* issue their own rules which also provide for the method of appointment of arbitrators, as a manifest imposition of conditions which raise reasonable doubts as to the perspective of independent and impartial dispute resolution.

432. The court also held that the parties' possible agreement on having their eventual dispute resolved by an *ad hoc* arbitrator could not be postulated, because no such arbitrator was identified in the arbitration agreement, or rather the arbitration agreement contained no clear terms, compliant with the law, which would provide for the method of selecting the respective arbitrator; the previously mentioned reference (and a very general reference at that) to the rules adopted by [X.Y., s.r.o.] cannot be accepted as an alternative (substitute) method of appointing the *ad hoc* arbitrator due to the reasons specified above. The SC CR [CZE] held that the respective arbitration clause had been a clear attempt to impair the position of the weaker contracting party. This is the first case in which such an opinion was explicitly voiced, at the general level, with respect to arbitration agreements, i.e. not only in connection with contracts concluded by consumers. Although any details regarding the terms of the main contract concluded in the present case may be unknown, it might prove difficult to infer that the contract was a typical consumer contract. Consequently, the Supreme Court based its conclusions not on the special protection afforded to consumers but on general legal principles [civil law principles], which constitute a principle superior to the special protection of consumers (though not endowed with higher *force*).

433. Both the trial court's and the appellate court's decisions were overturned, and the case was remanded to the trial court for a new hearing.

(g) Resolution of the Supreme Court of the Czech Republic [CZE],[256] Case No. 30 Cdo 4415/2010 of 27 July 2011

(aa) Conclusions of the Supreme Court

434. ▶ It is permissible to file a cassation appeal against the decision of the court of appeals which upheld the trial court's termination of the proceedings due to the existence of an arbitration agreement (pursuant to Section 106(1) of the CCP [CZE][257]).[258]

▶ If the arbitration agreement lacks any direct identification of an *ad hoc* arbitrator (i.e. by his or her name),[259] or a specific description of the method of his or her appointment, and merely stipulates that the **arbitrator will be appointed by one of the contracting parties from a list of arbitrators administered by a legal entity other than a *permanent arbitral institution*[260]** and that the arbitration will be conducted pursuant to the rules issued by the legal entity, **the arbitration agreement is invalid for evading (circumventing) the law.**

(bb) Factual and legal findings

435. The trial court terminated the proceedings initiated by an action for determination of (ownership) title to real property. The claimants pleaded absolute invalidity of the contract for the security transfer of (ownership) title. The court proceedings were terminated based on the respondent's defense. The respondent challenged the jurisdiction of the court and supported his argument by reference to an arbitration agreement.[261] It is necessary to point out that the arbitration clause

---

[256] Decisions in the preceding stages of the proceedings were delivered by the following courts:
➢ District Court for Prague 5 as the trial court – Resolution Case No. 34 C 542/2009-53 of 13 November 2009,
➢ The Municipal Court in Prague as the court of appeals – Resolution Case No. 17 Co 103/2010-73 of 9 August 2010.
The SC CR [CZE] overturned both decisions of the lower courts and remanded the case to the trial court for a new hearing.

[257] OSŘ [CZE]: Section 106 – "(1) *As soon as the court discovers, on the respondent's objection lodged together with or before the first act of the respondent in the merits, that the agreement of the parties requires that the case be submitted to arbitration, the court must desist from further examination of the case and terminate the proceedings; the court, however, hears the case if the parties declare that they waive the agreement. The court also hears the case if the court determines that the matter is not arbitrable under the laws of the Czech Republic, or that the arbitration agreement is invalid or non-existent, or that examining the agreement in arbitration proceedings exceeds the scope of jurisdiction vested in the arbitrators by the agreement, or that the arbitral tribunal refused to hear the case. [...]"*

[258] The SC CR [CZE] invoked the Resolution of the SC CR [CZE], Case No. 29 Cdo 1051/2004 of 28 April 2005.

[259] That is, outside the jurisdiction of a *permanent arbitral institution* under Section 13 of the ArbAct [CZE].

[260] Pursuant to Section 13 of the ArbAct [CZE].

[261] The arbitration clause read as follows: "*The parties undertake to submit any and all property disputes which arise from this contract in the future to arbitration before a single arbitrator, in*

referred to the rules of arbitration issued by an entity other than a *permanent arbitral institution* pursuant to Section 13 of the ArbAct [CZE]. The court of appeals upheld the decision. The court of appeals held that establishing the jurisdiction of a single arbitrator by reference to the rules issued by an entity identified in the arbitration clause fully suffices and that the arbitration clause was articulated in plain and intelligible language. The court of appeals rejected the arguments of the claimants challenging the validity of the arbitration clause due to the absence of any rules regulating the appointment of the arbitrator, together with their reference to the decision of the High Court in Prague [CZE], Case No. 12 Cmo 496/2008.[262] The court of appeals also argued that if the arbitration agreement does not set forth the method of appointment of the arbitrator(s), it is governed by Section 7 of the ArbAct [CZE] as a subsidiary provision, and referred to the Resolution of the SC CR [CZE], Case No. 32 Cdo 95/2006.[263] The court of appeals held that the claimants' plea of invalidity of the (main) contract of

---

compliance with Act No. 216/1994 Coll. [ArbAct (CZE)], pursuant to the Rules on Arbitration and the Tariff."

[262] In this case, the High Court in Prague [CZE] in its Decision Case No. 12 Cmo 496/2008 of 28 May 2009 concluded that if the arbitration agreement lacked any direct identification of an *ad hoc* arbitrator (i.e. outside the jurisdiction of an entity which has the status of a *permanent arbitral institution* under Section 13 of the ArbAct [CZE]), or a specific description of the method of his or her appointment, and merely referred, as concerns the selection of the arbitrator and determination of the rules of arbitration, to a legal entity other than a *permanent arbitral institution* established under the law, and referred to statutes and rules adopted by that corporation which provide for the appointment and selection of arbitrators, as well as the case management of arbitration and the rules governing the costs of proceedings, the arbitration agreement was invalid pursuant to Section 39 of the Civil Code for evading (circumventing) the law. Consequently, the High Court in Prague [CZE] held the arbitration clause in the case invalid.

[263] Decision of the SC CR [CZE], Case No. 32 Odo 95/2006 of 28 March 2007: Section 7(1) of the ArbAct [CZE] stipulates that the arbitration agreement should, as a rule, determine the number of arbitrators and identify them by their names, or stipulate the method whereby the number and the identity of the arbitrators shall be determined. The final number of arbitrators must always be odd. If the arbitration agreement lacks a provision corresponding to Subsection (1), each party shall appoint one arbitrator, and these arbitrators shall elect the chairman of the arbitral panel (Section 7(2) of the ArbAct [CZE]). In the present case, the arbitration clause stipulated a precise number of arbitrators (three). The seat of arbitration was Prague. Hence, the arbitration clause met the requirements of Section 3 of the ArbAct [CZE] which prescribes a written form, and Section 17 of the ArbAct [CZE], i.e. the agreed place where the arbitration is to be held, i.e. Prague in this particular case; the arbitration clause also determined a specific number of arbitrators and the method of appointing the arbitrators in terms of Section 7 of the ArbAct [CZE]. The appellant's defense that Article 9 of the contract was ambiguous, i.e. that no Arbitration Court Attached to the Economic Chamber in Vienna existed, the rules of which should have been observed by the arbitrators, could not influence the validity of the arbitration clause. In the absence of any specification in the arbitration agreement of the method of appointing the arbitrators, Section 7 of the ArbAct [CZE] applies, i.e. each party shall appoint one arbitrator and the two arbitrators elect the chairman of the arbitral panel. The court of appeals correctly deduced that in the present case, the parties had agreed that their disputes should be resolved by arbitrators (i.e. an *ad hoc* arbitral tribunal), not by a *permanent arbitral institution* within the meaning of Section 13 of the ArbAct [CZE]. An agreement on the rules which the arbitrators ought to abide by, within the meaning of Section 19 of the ArbAct [CZE], is not an essential term of an arbitration clause.

[*dd.mm.2007*], in which the arbitration clause was incorporated, was irrelevant. The court of appeals maintained that even if this was the case, then considering the alleged grounds of invalidity, the part of the contract which contains the entirely separate arbitration agreement (in the form of an arbitration clause) still continues to apply.[264] **The court** of appeals **also examined the arbitration agreement pursuant to the** *Directive* **and did not find any conflict with the** *Directive.* The claimants filed a cassation appeal with the SC CR [CZE]. They argued that the arbitration clause did not contain any direct identification of the arbitrator or a specific description of his or her appointment, but merely referred, as concerns the selection of the arbitrator and determination of the rules of arbitration, to a legal entity other than a *permanent arbitral institution* established under the law (Section 13 of the ArbAct [CZE]).

(cc)   Subject matter of the proceedings before the SC CR [CZE]

436.   The review proceedings in the SC CR [CZE] focused on the legal issues specified in the cassation appeal, i.e. the validity of the arbitration clause which did not identify any individual arbitrator but (only) stipulated the method of his/her appointment by reference to internal documents drafted by an entity other than a *permanent arbitral institution*. In connection with the arbitration agreement, the SC CR [CZE] was also dealing with the question of whether arbitration ought to be governed by the internal rules of a legal entity other than a *permanent arbitral institution*.[265]

(dd)   Reasons for the decision

437.   The Supreme Court (SC CR [CZE]) primarily invoked the Decision of the High Court in Prague, Case No. 12 Cmo 496/2008 of 28 May 2009,[266] and the Judgment of the SC [CZE], Case No. 31 Cdo 1945/2010 of 11 May 2011.[267] An arbitration clause which refers to rules issued by an entity (legal entity) other than a *permanent arbitral institution* (Section 13 of the ArbAct [CZE]), and the method of appointing arbitrators chosen from a list administered by the legal entity were held invalid. **The reason for the invalidity was an evasion (circumvention) of the law.**

---

[264] The court of appeals adhered to the principle of separability of the principal (main) contract from the incidental agreement.

[265] Interpretation of Sections 2, 7 and 13 of the ArbAct [CZE].

[266] This decision of the High Court in Prague [CZE] was also selected for publication in the Sbírka soudních rozhodnutí a stanovisek [Court Reports] [CZE] under No. 45/2010, for the purpose of unifying case law.

[267] The decision was issued by the Grand Panel of the Civil and Commercial Section of the SC CR [CZE].

438. The SC CR [CZE] did not explicitly challenge the conclusions of the court of appeals regarding its assessment of compliance with the *Directive*. But the Court critically addressed the situation which allows only one of the parties (albeit only de facto) to appoint the arbitrator. Such a situation must be assessed as directly conflicting with the *Directive*. Consequently, it was de facto also taken into account by the SC [CZE] in its decision, although the resolution of the Court does not explicitly say so.

IV.6. [DEU] [GERMANY]: Friendly approach to consumer arbitration

IV.6.1. Legal control of contractual terms

439. The concept of protection against unfair terms in consumer contracts has been promoted in Germany [DEU] since 1977. The Act on the Regulation of the Law on General Business Terms (AGBG [DEU])[268] incorporated comprehensive provisions regulating these issues in German law. Not only the consumer, but any natural or legal person who enters into a contract and thereby accepts the standard contract terms of the other party, benefited from the protection under the Act (AGBG [DEU]) and still continues to enjoy the same protection under the new law replacing the AGBG [DEU]. These provisions thus have a much wider scope, which automatically covers consumer protection as well. Hence, the law also included relationships governed exclusively by commercial law. Part of the Act ceased to have effect as a result of an extensive amendment to the law of obligations, effective date 1 January 2002, and was replaced by Sections 305–310 of the BGB [DEU] and Section 1 et seq. of the UKlaG [DEU].

440. The primary objective of the implementation of the *Directive* in Germany [DEU] was to secure sufficient control over [general] contractual terms presented by one of the parties. The law (AGBG [DEU]), however, did not cover terms other than general business terms and conditions. The rules were subsequently complemented with the so-called gray list of standard contractual terms; the unfairness of these terms is considered likely, but their actual nature depends on the assessment of particular circumstances. Another list, the so-called black list, contains types of provisions which are automatically considered unfair. Contractual terms which were not included in any of these two lists were assessed according to the general clause. The wording of the clause was, however, somewhat different from the definition contained in the *Directive*. The clause stipulates that those terms which constitute

---

[268] *Gesetz zur Regelung des Rechts der Allgemeinen Geschäftsbedingungen* [In translation: Act on the Regulation of General Business Terms and Conditions].

unjustified disadvantage contrary to the requirement of good faith are invalid. This is a broader definition than the corresponding provision of the *Directive*. The Act was subsequently amended and other terms, which were not included in the [general] contractual terms and conditions, were also subjected to statutory control. Following the reform of the law of obligations in Germany [DEU], effective date 1 February 2002, the German law was supplemented with the rule stipulating that **insufficiently transparent contracts are also invalid.**

441. The contemporary substantive-law concept of consumer protection in Germany is based on the BGB [DEU]. It rests, traditionally, on the power to cancel (rescind) the contract. Failure to meet the standards imposed on the terms of a consumer contract means that the respective (defective) term does not become part of the contract.[269] Hence, the Civil Code (BGB [DEU]) does not principally require that the term be held invalid, but it cannot be invoked and taken into consideration.[270] De facto, however, we can infer (to put it simply) invalidity ab initio. The Act then stipulates that the entire contract ceases to have effect *[Unwirksamkeit]* only in those cases where insistence on the observance of the terms of the contract would constitute an unbearable, unacceptable hardship on the part of the consumer.[271] Consequently, there are two categories of consequences which may befall unfair contractual terms (especially, without limitation, terms incorporated in [general] contract terms and conditions): namely, (i) consequences relating separately to such terms (provisions) irrespective of the validity of the remaining terms of the contract[272] and (ii) consequences in the form of invalidity[273] of the entire contractual term.

---

[269] See Section 305 et seq. of the BGB [DEU].

[270] Indeed, the term *"ineffectiveness"* [*Unwirksamkeit*] in German law can be defined as the same institution which is by certain *civil law* legal systems classified as *(absolute) invalidity*, or where many other legal systems prescribe other types of *invalidity* assessed *ex officio*.

[271] See Section 306 of the BGB [DEU].

[272] See Section 306 of the BGB [DEU] in conjunction with Section 139 of the BGB [DEU] which entails invalidity (*Nichtigkeit*, i.e. literally *nullity*) of a term; the interpretation applied in connection with this concept is combined with Section 134 of the BGB [DEU], and it means invalidity caused by a breach of the law.

[273] Orig. *Unwirksamkeit*, i.e. literally *invalidity*.
The ineffectiveness of unfair terms is referred to in Section 307 of the BGB [CZE]; as concerns unfair terms in consumer contracts, the provision is considered to be the general rule. Procedurally, however, the consequence connected with the effects of an ineffective term (i.e. when the law considers the term *unwirksam*) is in this connection judicially interpreted as raising a claim, or a defense, which must be proven by evidence; in other words, the party who makes the claim, or the defense, as applicable, must present the relevant statements and support them with evidence.

IV.6.2. Tolerant application of the *Directive* and national arbitration laws

442. German courts interpret the *Directive*, in connection with arbitration, less strictly than other Member States of the EC. In a dispute dating back to 2005,[274] German courts concluded that an arbitration clause between a consumer and a professional was valid, in compliance with the national arbitration laws (ZPO [DEU]), as well as with the AGBG [DEU], whereby the *Directive* was implemented.[275] The court held that the arbitration clause did not exhibit any features of a prohibited contractual term. According to the German courts, **arbitration agreements are not "*surprising*"[276] for the consumer**; they are not contrary to the good faith of the parties and are not eo ipso and a priori disadvantageous for the contracting party that accepted the [general] contract terms. The court also held that the **Directive** does **not principally rule out arbitration clauses in consumer contracts and that arbitration (arbitration agreements) complies with the requirements of the Directive.**[277]

443. Arbitration in Germany [DEU] is regulated under the provisions of Book X of the Code of Civil Procedure (ZPO [DEU]). However, the application of the ZPO [DEU] to arbitration in parts other than Book X is strictly limited to the issues explicitly referred to by the Act. Since the extensive amendment to the law implemented with effect from early 1998, arbitration in Germany has enjoyed widespread support. General disputes of a property nature are principally arbitrable, and the definition of *dispute of a property nature* is interpreted very extensively. However, even disputes which lack the property nature are arbitrable, providing the parties are allowed to make a settlement regarding the subject matter of the dispute.[278] Consequently, an

---

[274] BGH [DEU], decision of 13 January 2005, annotated in: (i) NJW, 2005, p. 1125 and (ii) Schieds VZ2005, p. 95 et seq.

[275] In the meantime, this Act was repealed and replaced with rules incorporated in the BGB [DEU].

[276] See:

➤ Decision of the BGH [DEU], Case No. III ZR 265/03 of 13 January 2005, published in: BGHZ, Vol. 162, p. 9 et seq. (for a detailed annotation of the decision, see below);

➤ Decision of the BGH [DEU], Case No. III ZR 164/06 of 1 March 2007, annotated in: NJW-RER, 2007, p. 1456 et seq.;

➤ Decision of the OLG Frankfurt a. M., Case No. Sch 3/06 of 20 July 2007, annotated in: OLG Report Frankfurt a. M., 2008, p. 647 et seq. et al.

[277] See Judgment of the BGH [DEU], Case No. III ZR 256/03 of 13 January 2005 annotated in detail in this book (in this excursus into consumer arbitration in Germany [DEU], see below).

[278] Cf. Article 1030 [ZPO-DEU] which reads as follows (approximate translation, cit.) Section 1030 – Arbitrability – "(1) *Any property claim can be the subject matter of an arbitration agreement. An arbitration agreement providing for other than property claims has effects only if the parties have the right to enter into a settlement regarding the subject matter of the dispute.* (2) *An arbitration agreement regulating legal relationships which are the subject matter of a lease relationship concerning an apartment located in Germany is without legal effect. This shall not apply to*

arbitration agreement governed by German law may not concern issues falling within the scope of criminal law, family law, and issues relating to certain lease relationships. (However, disputes regarding the lease of non-residential premises are arbitrable.) Patent law disputes are also considered arbitrable, together with disputes involving antitrust law (rules providing for the protection against the restriction of competition), which appear more and more frequently at the level of national *lex arbitri*.[279]

444. German law does not principally reject arbitration clauses in consumer contracts, i.e. it is even friendlier than Austrian law which traditionally strongly promotes this method of dispute resolution. Special rules relating to consumer contracts are incorporated only in Section 1032(5) of the ZPO [DEU]. The provision stipulates that arbitration agreements to which a consumer is a party must be contained in a document which has been personally signed by the parties. A written document can be replaced with an electronic one. At the same time, the document containing the arbitration clause must not include other terms, i.e. terms unrelated to arbitration. Exceptions include contracts to which a consumer is a party and which are executed in the form of a notary record.[280] Some legal opinions maintain that these rules apply not only to disputes between a professional and a consumer, but also to disputes (relationships) between two consumers.[281]

---

apartments pursuant to paras. (1) through (3) of Section 549(2) of the BGB. (3) This shall be without prejudice to any rules other than those incorporated in this Book which stipulate that a dispute may not be submitted to arbitration at all, or only under specific conditions."
Similarly, Austrian law, just like German law, requires the option of making a settlement (the right to make dispositions with the subject matter of the dispute) only with respect to other than property disputes. No such condition is required with respect to property disputes.

[279] *Bělohlávek, A.* K úpravě hospodářské soutěže – Zásadní změny v komunitární úpravě hospodářské soutěže od 1. května 2004 – Nařízení rady (ES) č. 1/2003 o provádění pravidel hospodářské soutěže stanovených v článcích 81 a 82 a smlouvy ES a jejich aplikaci v činnosti komise, národních úřadů pro ochranu hospodářské soutěže, soudů a rozhodců. [Title in translation: Concerning Competition Rules – Fundamental Changes in the Community Law Regulating Competition After 1 May 2004 – Council Regulation (EC) No. 1/2003 on the Implementation of the Rules on Competition Laid Down in Articles 81 and 82 of the EC Treaty and Their Application by the Commission, National Competition Authorities, Courts and Arbitrators]. Obchodní právo, 2004, No. 13, pp. 10–17.

[280] Cf. *Tröder, J.* Die Einbeziehung von Schiedsabreden in notarielle Urkunden. Mitteilungen der Rheinischen Notarkammer, 2000, pp. 379–383.

[281] Cf. *Schmitz, P.* Schiedsvereinbarungen in der notariellen Praxis. Theinische Notar-Zeitschrift, 2003, No. 12, pp. 591–612, here p. 601 (in Footnote No. 106 *Schmitz* refers to commentaries to the ZPO [DEU]). *Schmitz* says that the classification of a party to a particular legal relationship as a consumer depends on the nature (on the qualitative assessment) of the potential dispute which is to be submitted to arbitration.

IV.6.3. Case law

(a) Judgment of the Federal Court of Justice (Supreme Court [DEU]), Case No. III ZR 265/03 of 13 January 2005[282]

(aa) Conclusions of the court

445. ▶ The parties to an arbitration agreement cannot establish the jurisdiction[283] of an arbitral tribunal which would allow the arbitral tribunal to assess its own jurisdiction (under the *"Kompetenz-Kompetenz"* principle) where such an assessment would be binding on the courts as well.

▶ Due to the *"Kompetenz-Kompetenz"* principle, the court is not obliged to wait until the issue of jurisdiction is resolved by the arbitral tribunal.[284]

▶ An arbitration agreement **to which a consumer is a party may be executed in the form of a standard form contract** providing the requirements of form stipulated in Section 1031(5) of the ZPO [DEU] are met.[285] **It is not necessary that the consumer have any special reason for submitting the given dispute to arbitration.**[286]

▶ The legislator wished to protect the consumer against terms that could surprise the consumer and establish the jurisdiction of an arbitral tribunal. For example, such a surprising term could be hidden in the "small print" of the contract.[287] If this were the case, it would be necessary – just like in this case – to execute the arbitration agreement in the form of a separate document signed by the

---

[282] The decision is available at: http://juris.bundesgerichtshof.de/cgi-bin/rechtsprechung/document.py?Gericht=bgh&Art=en&nr=31677&pos=0&anz=1 [last access 9 August 2011]. Also mentioned in: *Hulmák, M. et Tomančáková, B.* Rozhodčí řízení jako vhodný prostředek řešení sporů mezi dodavatelem a spotřebitelem (1. část). [Title in translation: Arbitration as a Suitable Mechanism for the Resolution of Disputes between Suppliers and Consumers (Part 1)]. Obchodněprávní revue, 2010, Vol. 2, No. 6, pp. 168–174 (see footnote 33). Also annotated in:
  ➢ NJW, 2005, pp. 1125–1127,
  ➢ DNotZ, 2005, p. 666 et seq.,
  ➢ SchiedsVZ, 2005, p. 95 et seq.,
  ➢ VuR, 2005, p. 236 et seq. et al.
Decisions in the preceding stages were rendered by: (i) the trial court: Landgericht Düsseldorf [DEU]; (ii) the court of appeals: OLG Düsseldorf [DEU] – judgment of 23 July 2003.
[283] Pursuant to arbitration laws under the ZPO [DEU] valid since 1998.
[284] With reference to the first sentence of Section 1040(1) of the ZPO [DEU].
[285] A standard form contract was also concluded in a case handled by the SC CR [CZE] – see the annotation of the Judgment of the SC CR [CZE], Case No. 23 Cdo 1201/2009 of 29 June 2010, which is annotated in detail in the excursus into Czech law [CZE].
A contract in the same form was also concluded, for instance, in cases decided by the ECJ – see ECJ Judgment, Case C-243/08 of 4 June 2009, *Pannon GSM.*
[286] No special motive or reason for the conclusion of an arbitration agreement is required.
[287] Concerning this issue, see also the Judgment of the SC CR [CZE], Case No. 23 Cdo 1201/2009 of 29 June 2010; this judgment is annotated in detail elsewhere in this book – see the excursus into Czech law.

parties.[288] Such a separate document must provide for, and only for, the issues relating to arbitration.[289] Arbitration agreements incorporated in a separate document cannot usually be considered surprising terms (clauses) [for the consumer]. The fact that the arbitration agreement (concluded in a separate document) was prepared in advance by one of the contracting parties (the professional) does not give rise to any doubts either.[290]

▶ An arbitration agreement incorporated in general business terms and conditions does not in itself constitute any unfair disadvantage for the contracting partner.[291] It is not necessary that the parties have any special reason for submitting their disputes to arbitration.[292] Arbitration represents a finding of the law in the broader sense; in other words, it means the resolution of disputes by a neutral third party.[293] The Act recognizes arbitration as a form of resolution of disputes by a **private authority**[294] and also allows arbitration, in principle, in disputes with consumers. The only requirement applicable where the consumer is involved is the special form of an arbitration agreement;[295] the purpose of the requirement is to "warn the consumer" and protect him or her against economic or social preponderance.

▶ The *Directive* is based on the premise that arbitration clauses incorporated in general contract (business) terms and conditions are allowed in consumer contracts. The Annex to Article 3(3) of the *Directive* contains a list of terms which may be held unfair, i.e. invalid. This list also provides warnings and examples.[296] However, the list only concerns arbitration clauses which leave the consumer

---

[288] Paragraph (1) of Section 1029(2) of the ZPO [DEU].

[289] The first part of the third sentence of Section 1031(5) of the ZPO [DEU].

[290] In the reasons for the decision, the BGH [DEU] extensively quotes the available published doctrine. The court also mentions opinions departing from the apparently prevailing opinions. Concerning these issues, see also the Judgment of the Federal Court of Justice (BGH [DEU], Case No. III. ZR 164/06 of 1 March 2007 (a detailed annotation elsewhere in this book, also in this excursus into German law [DEU] and with references in other chapters).

[291] The BGH [DEU] invokes its previous rulings, namely the Resolution of the BGH [DEU], Case No. III ZR 200/85 of 26 June 1986, as well as an unspecified judgment of the BGH [DEU], published in: BGHZ 115, p. 324 et seq. and extensively quotes from academic writings.

[292] For example, as concerns special professional claims, the necessity of which the resolution of potential disputes can be expected.

[293] The BGH [DEU] invokes the Resolution of the BGH [DEU], Case No. III ZB 53/03 of 27 May 2004, published in: NJW, 2004, p. 2226 et seq., here especially p. 2227.

[294] Section 1025 et seq. of the ZPO [DEU].
For a similar definition of the purpose of arbitration, see also the Judgment of the ConCourt CR [CZE], Case No. I ÚS 3227/07 of 8 March 2011; some of the conclusions articulated in the decision of the Czech Constitutional Court are annotated in the excursus into the laws of the Czech Republic.

[295] Section 1031(5) of the ZPO [DEU].

[296] Cf. ECJ Judgment, Case C-478-99 of 7 May 2002 (*Commission of the EC v. Sweden* [SWE]). In connection with this judgment, the ECJ also quotes the BGH [DEU] in the reasons. also EuZW, 2002, p. 465, para. 22 and a published note by *Pfeiffer*.

with no other choice than arbitration and which are not covered by legal provisions.[297] This does not apply to arbitration clauses which are incorporated in general contract terms and conditions and which concern arbitration approved by the law. This does not apply to the present case, especially since the arbitration agreement itself invokes the statutory provisions.[298]

► If the arbitration agreement must comply with the requirement of special form (here analogically in professional-consumer relationships),[299] it is not necessary to meet the requirement of the same special form with respect to an assignment of claims which the arbitration agreement covers. The legal successor (assignee) is bound by the arbitration agreement despite the fact that the assignment (i.e. the assignee's accession to the obligations arising from the arbitration agreement) did not meet the requirements of the special form prescribed for arbitration agreements in the relationships of the given type (i.e. arbitration agreements negotiated between professionals and consumers).[300]

(bb) Factual and legal findings

446. The claimant instituted proceedings against the respondent (a joint stock company and a particular member of its Board of Directors) for compensation of losses sustained as a result of a breach of contract and for compensation for unlawful conduct. On 18 May 1998, the claimant[301] entered into an *"account opening agreement"* (*"Managed Account"*) which was prepared (drafted) in advance by the respondent. The agreement authorized the respondent to execute/close futures or forwards for the account and risk of the claimant (her legal predecessor). The *"account opening agreement"* contained an arbitration clause. On 15 May 1998, the parties entered into a separate arbitration agreement, also in the form of a standard form contract, intended to implement the arbitration clause.[302]

---

[297] Article 1(q) of the Annex to Article 3(3) of the *Directive.*

[298] An explicit reference to Book X of the ZPO [DEU].

[299] It is necessary to point out that German law generally protects the weaker contracting party irrespective of the type of the relationship.

[300] The courts in this case invoked the following decisions:
➢ Judgment of the BGH [DEU], Case No. III ZR 2/96 of 2 October 1997, annotated in: NJW, 1998, p. 371 and in: BGHZ, Vol. 71, p. 162 et seq., here p. 165, and
➢ Resolution of the BGH [DEU], Case No. III ZB 66/01 of 1 August 2002, annotated in: NJW-RR, 2002, p. 1462 et seq., here especially p. 1463.

[301] The claimant was the wife of the original contracting party who assigned his claims to the claimant.

[302] The arbitration agreement read as follows (partly an approximate translation): "1. *Jurisdiction of the arbitral tribunal – any and all disputes arising from the brokering agreement between the company [...] AG [i.e. the respondent], members of the company's Supervisory Body, members of the company's Board of Directors, the company's employees and persons authorized to provide performance and the clients (customers) shall be resolved by an arbitral tribunal to the exclusion of*

447. The claimant deposited in his client account with the respondent the total amount of 281,400 DEM. Later, he received back 20,552.50 USD (= 36,849.24 DEM). He therefore suffered losses amounting to 244,550.76 DEM (= 125,036.82 EUR). The claimant requested the respondent to pay – as a debtor bound by joint and several liability together with the other respondent, a member of the first respondent's Board of Directors who was, in the meantime, found guilty by a final and conclusive verdict – in compensation for the losses consisting in the above-mentioned amount (plus interest). The respondent challenged the jurisdiction of the court due to the existing arbitration agreement. The claimant, conversely, argued that the arbitration agreement was invalid. The trial court and the court of appeals dismissed the claim as inadmissible. The Federal Court of Justice, when deciding on an appeal, upheld the decisions of the lower courts, albeit departing from some of the opinions voiced by the court of appeals.

(cc) Reasons for the decision

448. The Court found the arbitration agreement valid.[303] The arbitration agreement explicitly provided for the authorization of the arbitral tribunal to assess its own jurisdiction (*"Kompetenz-Kompetenz"*). The Court is entitled to review only the validity of this particular term. The agreement on the authorization for the arbitral tribunal to assess its own jurisdiction (the *"Kompetenz-Kompetenz"* clause) does not breach the act on general contract terms and conditions (AGBG [DEU]),[304] because it did not represent an unfair disadvantage for any of the contracting parties (Section 9 of the AGBG [DEU]). The arbitration agreement also complies with Section 28 of the BörsG [DEU] (the Stock Exchange Act, previously applicable); besides, this provision is not applicable in the given case, because the agreed arbitral tribunal is not a "stock exchange arbitral tribunal" within the meaning of said law.

---

regular legal proceedings. The arbitral tribunal shall hear and resolve any and all disputes which might arise from or in direct connection with the brokering agreement, for any legal reason whatsoever (for instance, as a result of non-performance, impossibility of performance, positive breach of obligations, and breach of obligations in the negotiation of the agreement, as a result of disallowed actions, as a result of the anticipated conclusion of a consultancy agreement, and other obligations connected with the brokering agreement, etc.), to the exclusion of regular legal proceedings. [...] Finally, the arbitral tribunal shall also resolve disputes over the effectiveness and the interpretation of this arbitration agreement [...]." Note: *"Positive breach of obligations"* means any breach of a contractual obligation which does not constitute a delay or impossibility of performance. The quotation was adopted from the published reasons for the judgment.

[303] The court also explicitly stated the validity and enforceability against the claimant as the legal successor to the original contracting party. The court of appeals concluded that the special form prescribed for this particular arbitration agreement by Section 1031 of the ZPO [DEU] need not be honored if another party is acceding to the agreement or if the claims from the main contract are being assigned to another party, as the case may be.

[304] In the meantime, the relevant rules were transferred to the new provisions incorporated in the BGB [DEU].

449.   The court of appeals accepted the respondent's defense.[305] The court also concluded that the arbitration agreement and the assignment of claims from the main contract were valid and that the arbitration clause was binding on the assignee. In this connection, it is irrelevant that the assignment (and the accession of the assignee to the arbitration agreement) did not meet the requirements of form prescribed for the conclusion of this particular arbitration agreement itself.[306] Contrary to the court of appeals, the BGH [DEU] concluded that the review of an arbitration agreement was not limited to the validity of the term stipulating that the arbitrators shall themselves assess their jurisdiction, i.e. the validity of the *"Kompetenz-Kompetenz"* clause.[307]

450.   However, by the amendment to the arbitration laws of 22 December 1997,[308] the legislator – intentionally departing from German case law (the current case law of the BGH [DEU]) – ultimately reserved decisions on the arbitral tribunals' jurisdiction for the courts.[309] Consequently, the amendment limited the arbitrators' right to a [potentially] exclusive assessment of their own jurisdiction.

451.   The decision on the jurisdiction of the arbitral tribunal in arbitration is primarily made by the arbitral tribunal itself. It is usually an interim decision (where the jurisdiction of the arbitrators is challenged); exceptionally, the issue can also be resolved by a final arbitral award. If the arbitral tribunal concludes that it lacks jurisdiction to hear the case, the tribunal renders a procedural resolution whereby the claim in the merits is dismissed as inadmissible. The final word, however, is left to the court in the annulment proceedings – both as concerns the interim decision[310] and as concerns the final arbitral award and the procedural decision on the lack of jurisdiction on the part of the arbitrators.[311,312]

452.   Hence, the parties to an arbitration agreement cannot establish the jurisdiction of an arbitral tribunal which would allow the arbitral tribunal to assess its own jurisdiction (under the *"Kompetenz-Kompetenz"* principle) where such an assessment would be binding on

---

[305] Section 1032(1) of the ZPO [DEU].
[306] Section 1031 of the ZPO [DEU].
[307] Concerning this particular right, the arbitration agreement explicitly stipulated, in the fourth sentence of Article 1, as follows (approximate translation, cit.): *"The arbitral tribunal shall also resolve disputes over the effectiveness and the interpretation of this arbitration agreement as well as any potential amendments* [to the arbitration agreement]."
[308] Book X of the ZPO [DEU] – amendment of 22 December 1997, published in: BGBl. [DEU] I p. 3224. The "new" provisions apply since 1998.
[309] The BGH [DEU] refers to the explanatory memorandum drafted by the Federal Government – Federal Gazette 13/5274 p. 26 and p. 44.
[310] The second sentence of Section 1040(3) of the ZPO [DEU].
[311] Section 1059 of the ZPO [DEU].
[312] The BGH [DEU] refers to the explanatory memorandum drafted by the Federal Government – Federal Gazette 13/5274 p. 81.

the courts as well. The BGH [DEU] concluded that the arbitration clause articulated in the respective contract was probably more in line with previous legislation (valid before 1998). But the clause could not, under currently applicable rules, restrict the jurisdiction of the court with respect to the court's authorization to make a final evaluation on the jurisdiction of arbitrators. The term was not an essential term of the arbitration agreement.[313] Consequently, its invalidity does not affect the agreement on jurisdiction over the merits of the dispute. The only restriction is that the arbitrators may not decide on their jurisdiction "with final force and effect."

453. As concerns the binding effect of the arbitration agreement on the legal successor to the original party to the agreement (assignor, consumer), the BGH [DEU] arrived at the conclusion that the arbitration agreement itself meets the formal requirements[314] imposed on arbitration agreements negotiated with a consumer. The arbitration agreement was executed in the form of a separate agreement (a separate document signed by the parties).[315] The document contains only terms relating to arbitration.[316] The fact that it was an "arbitration agreement" prepared (drafted) in advance by the respondent (a professional) does not render the arbitration agreement defective. The law does not prescribe any other requirements as concerns the content or the form.[317]

454. In the present case, the arbitration agreement of 18 May 1998, prepared (drafted) in advance, did not become part of the contract,[318] because it would constitute a *surprising* clause. The arbitration agreement concluded in a separate document met the formal requirements. The arbitration agreement used by the respondent (professional) in the general contract terms and conditions would, in itself, be invalid[319] if it unfairly disadvantaged one of the contracting partners contrary to the principles of honest business transactions. But in this particular case, the

---

[313] The practical application of the rules valid in Germany [DEU] until 1998 was based on the presumption that these are two separate agreements, an agreement on the arbitrators' right to assess their own jurisdiction, and an agreement on the arbitrators' jurisdiction over the resolution of the dispute in the merits. It is all the more necessary, under the new rules, to conclude that an invalid "Kompetenz-Kompetenz" term, which is not an essential term of an arbitration agreement, does not render the arbitration agreement invalid. In this connection, the BGH [DEU] also refers to the explanatory memorandum drafted by the Federal Government – Federal Gazette 13/5274 p. 26 and p. 44, as well as another decision of the BGH [DEU] of 6 June 1991 (no further specifications).

[314] Section 1031(5) of the ZPO [DEU].

[315] Paragraph (1) of Section 1029(2) of the ZPO [DEU] and the first part of the third sentence of Section 1031(5) of the ZPO [DEU].

[316] The first part of the third sentence of Section 1031(5) of the ZPO [DEU].

[317] Section 1031(5) of the ZPO [DEU].

[318] This is according to the previous rules incorporated in Section 3 of the AGBG [DEU]. Analogous rules are now incorporated in Section 305c(1) of the BGB [DEU].

[319] According to the previous rules incorporated in Section 9(1) of the AGBG [DEU]. Analogous rules are now incorporated in Section 307(1) of the BGB [DEU].

parties had negotiated another arbitration agreement, in a separate document. Consequently (*and to the contrary*), if the validity of a standard form arbitration agreement was contingent on – without any statutory provision that would stipulate so – the existence of a special legal interest in the use of such form, the parties would be subjected to major legal uncertainty. Instead of a direct hearing of the merits of the dispute in arbitration, the case would first require court proceedings clarifying whether the use of the general contract terms and conditions has any interest justifying the application of the arbitration clause.

455.   The law does not prescribe any restrictions as concerns the scope of the arbitration agreement. Consequently, if the arbitration clause explicitly refers to "contractual and non-contractual claims," it does not violate the law. Hence, the Court did not find any circumstances which would constitute an unfair disadvantage for the consumer arising from the standard form arbitration agreement. Access to the arbitral tribunal, the right to appoint an arbitrator, as well as the conditions for arbitration were all formulated in a just and fair manner [for both parties]. Both parties had the right to submit their dispute to arbitration. Both parties could participate in the appointment of the arbitral tribunal (arbitral panel), which safeguards the impartiality of the arbitral tribunal. It is not possible to plead procedural errors even if one of the parties fails to appoint an arbitrator by the stipulated deadline or if the arbitrators fail to agree on the chairman of the arbitral panel. In such cases, the right to make an appointment is vested in a neutral authority.[320] The terms of the arbitration agreement regarding the arbitration itself were free of any defects; they basically provided for the application of Book X of the ZPO [DEU]. No unfair disadvantage could be inferred on the basis of fears that the arbitral tribunal would not observe the mandatory provisions of German law to the detriment of the consumer.[321]

---

[320] In this case to the Chairman of the OGH Düsseldorf [DEU] (Article 2(4) of the arbitration agreement).
[321] The BGH [DEU] refers to: (i) Section 52 and Section 53 of the BörsG [DEU] as applicable until 30 June 2002, (ii) Section 764 and Section 762(1) of the BGB [DEU] as applicable before the amendment, (iii) as well as (regarding liability) Section 31, Section 826, Section 823(2) of the BGB [DEU] in conjunction with Sections 263 and 266 of the StGB [DEU].
The BGH [DEU] also invokes the following preceding case law:
➢ Judgment of the BGH [DEU], Case No. III ZR 68/90 of 6 June 1991, annotated in: NJW, 1991, p. 2215 et seq.;
➢ Judgment of the BGH [DEU], Case No. II ZR 41/87 of 21 September 1987, annotated in: WM, 1987, p. 1353 et seq., especially p. 1354;
➢ Judgment of the BGH [DEU], Case No. II ZR 124/86 of 15 June 1987, annotated in: WM, 1987, p. 1353 et seq., especially p. 1154;
➢ Judgment of the BGH [DEU], Case No. II ZR 10/83 of 12 March 1984, annotated in: NJW, 1984, p. 2037 et seq. (regarding the agreement on the jurisdiction of courts);
➢ Resolution of the BGH [DEU], Case No. XI ZR 52/92 of 21 September 1993, annotated in: WM, 1993, p. 2121 et seq.

456. In this particular case, the arbitral tribunal was subject to the laws on domestic (national) arbitration and was obliged to apply German law,[322] because the parties agreed that the arbitration was to take place in Düsseldorf [DEU][323] and, moreover, explicitly agreed on the application of German law. The respective arbitration agreement stipulated that the chairman of the arbitral panel must have the capacity to act as arbitrator under German law. Such an arbitral tribunal cannot be presumed not to abide by the mandatory rules of German law.[324] Considering all the circumstances of the case, the Court concluded that the appeal and the plea of invalidity of the arbitration agreement were unsubstantiated.

(b) Judgment of the Federal Court of Justice (Supreme Court [DEU]), Case No. III. ZR 164/06 of 1 March 2007: Limitation of the right to appoint an arbitrator does not render the arbitration agreement invalid

(aa) Conclusions of the court

457. In said case,[325] the German Federal Court of Justice (BGH [DEU]) held[326] that:

▶ An unfair limitation of the right of one of the parties to appoint an arbitrator conditioned by a standard form contract[327] does not render the arbitration clause invalid.[328]

---

[322] Regarding the arbitrators' obligation to apply valid and applicable law, see also the Judgment of the ConCourt CR [CZE], Case No. I ÚS 3227/07 of 8 March 2011; some of the conclusions articulated in the decision of the Czech Constitutional Court are annotated in the excursus into the laws of the Czech Republic. Although this opinion of the ConCourt CR [CZE] did not concern a *consumer contract* (a consumer dispute), most of it is also applicable to proceedings in which the consumer is a party.

[323] Section 1025(1), Section 1043(1) of the ZPO [DEU].

[324] See Judgment of the BGH [DEU], Case No. III ZR 68/90 of 6 June 1991, annotated in: NJW, 1991, p. 2215 et seq.

[325] The decision is available at: http://juris.bundesgerichtshof.de/cgi-bin/rechtsprechung/document.py?Gericht=bgh&Art=en&nr=39276&pos=0&anz=1 [last access 9 August 2011].

[326] The claimants' appeal to the Federal Court of Justice was dismissed. The following rulings were rendered in the preceding stages of the proceedings:
➢ Decision of the Amtsgericht Unna (as the trial court), Case No. 16 C 170/05 of 31 October 2005 and
➢ Decision of the Landgericht Dortmund (as the court of appeals), Case No. 6 S 16/05 of 28 April 2006.

[327] Regarding standard form contracts, see:
➢ Judgment of the BGH [DEU], Case No. III ZR 265/03 of 13 January 2005, also annotated in detail in the excursus into German law [DEU].
➢ A standard form contract was also concluded in a case handled by the SC CR [CZE] – see the annotation of the Judgment of the SC CR [CZE], Case No. 23 Cdo 1201/2009 of 29 June 2010, which is annotated in detail in the excursus into Czech law [CZE].
➢ This type of contract was also discussed in cases handled by the ECJ – see ECJ Judgment, Case C-243/08 of 4 June 2009, *Pannon GSM*.
➢ Regarding contracts executed in small and indistinct print, see Judgment of the SC CR [CZE], Case No. 23 Cdo 1201/2009 of 29 June 2010; see also the chapter on the assessment of validity of arbitration agreements in *consumer contracts*.

[328] Comparison with the approach adopted by other countries:

▶ The disadvantaged contracting party may petition the court to balance the composition of the arbitral tribunal by its decision.[329]

▶ Unless the parties concluded a different agreement on procedure and unless the provisions of the ZPO [DEU] on arbitration contain specific rules regulating a particular procedural issue, the applicable procedural rules shall be at the arbitrators' discretion. Consequently, the law allows the parties extensive autonomy and, in the absence of the parties' agreement, allows certain autonomy to the arbitrators, too.

▶ Hence, an unclear term in the arbitration agreement regarding applicable procedural rules does not render the arbitration agreement invalid.

(bb)   Factual and legal findings

458.   Based on a contract of 29 February 2000, executed in the form of a notary record, the respondent sold a plot of land to the claimants and built a(n) (extended family) house thereon. The contract contained an arbitration agreement.[330] The claimants demanded that the respondent

---

➤ For example, the doctrine adhered to by Czech courts is in similar situations (probably unnecessarily) much more rigorous, and the courts hold arbitration agreements invalid in these cases.

➤ However, some U.S. courts have adopted the same approach as Czech courts. For instance, the Illinois Supreme Court held in Case No. N.E. 2d of 3 February 2011 (*Carr v. Gateway*; published in 2011 WL 329115, III. Feb. 3, 2011) that the dissolution of a *permanent arbitral institution* (in this case the NAF – National Arbitration Forum) entailed expiration of the arbitration agreement, because the agreement on the NAF as the appointing authority was an integral part of the parties' agreement and dissolution of the venue therefore rendered the entire arbitration agreement impossible to implement. The court thereby refused to apply Section 5 of the FAA [USA] as a subsidiary provision. This stipulates that if it is not possible to appoint the arbitrator, then the arbitrator shall be appointed by the court (providing no other venue is agreed as the appointing authority). Regarding the decision of the Illinois Supreme Court [USA], see *Tager, E. M., Parasharami, Archis A. et Ranlett, K. S.* United States: Illinois Supreme Court Rules that Arbitration Agreement is Unenforceable Because it Selects the National Arbitration Forum, Which No Longer Handles Consumer Arbitrations. Mondaq, 10 February 2011, available online at: http://www.mondaq.com/unitedstates/article.asp?articleid=122638 [last access 27 December 2011].

➤ Hence, the German approach is apparently friendlier to the enforcement of arbitration agreements.

[329] The first sentence of Section 1034(2) of the ZPO [DEU].

[330] The text of the arbitration agreement (adopted from the reasons for the judgment; approximate translation, cit.): Article 1 – *"Any and all disputes between the parties arising from the contract for work and the purchase contract* (Bauträgervertrag*) pursuant to Section I. shall be resolved, if permitted by the law, by an arbitral tribunal, to the exclusion of regular legal proceedings; the arbitral tribunal's decision shall be final and binding."* Article 2 – *"The arbitral tribunal shall consist of a single arbitrator. The arbitrator shall be Mr. [...] R., presiding judge of the District Court [...]. If this arbitrator is not willing or able to discharge the office of arbitrator for factual or legal reasons, a different arbitrator shall be appointed by the Chairman of the High District Court* (Oberlandesgericht) *Hamm [DEU] upon the motion of any of the parties. The arbitrator must in any case be capable of discharging the office of arbitrator. After the commencement of the arbitral*

pay an advance on the expected costs of remedying the defects of the construction,[331] with interest. The respondent pleaded invalidity of the arbitration clause. Both the trial court and the court of appeals dismissed the claim as inadmissible after they had held the arbitration clause valid.[332]

(cc) Reasons for the decision

459. The arbitration clause incorporated in the general business terms and conditions did not, as such, constitute any unfair disadvantage for any of the contracting parties. However, identifying a particular person as the arbitrator in a standard form arbitration agreement could unfairly disadvantage one of the parties, because the party would thereby de facto lose any influence on the composition of the arbitral panel of a different opinion.[333] Such an impermissible limitation of the right of one of the parties to appoint an arbitrator does not, however, render the arbitration clause invalid.[334] If the arbitration agreement grants an advantage to one of the parties in constituting the arbitral tribunal, the disadvantaged party may ask the court for the appointment of a different arbitrator.[335] The arbitration clause is subject to special rules governing the supervision of its contents by the court, also with respect to the composition of the arbitral panel (the individual arbitrators). The court is obliged to make sure that the appointed arbitrators are independent and impartial,[336] and that the composition of the arbitral tribunal is balanced. Hence, the Federal Court of Justice held that the arbitration agreement used by the respondent in the form of a standard form does not, according to the claimants' pleadings, withstand the control of its terms pursuant to the first sentence of Section 2(2) of the AGBG [DEU].[337] Consequently, the arbitration agreement constitutes an unfair disadvantage for the claimant. The reason is that the respondent, who

---

proceedings, a party challenging the arbitrator is obliged to notify its objections to the other party and to the arbitrator within 14 days after the party learns of the commencement of the arbitral proceedings. Otherwise, any objections against the arbitrator after the arbitral proceedings are commenced are inadmissible." Article 3 – "The arbitral tribunal determines, at the tribunal's sole discretion, the rules governing the proceedings according to the applicable provisions of the Code of Civil Procedure [ZPO (DEU)] [...]."

[331] The requested payment was 2,262 EUR.
[332] In terms of the conditions set forth in Section 1031(5) of the ZPO [DEU].
[333] A contrary legal opinion was previously voiced by the OLG Celle [DEU]; annotated in: OLGReport 2000, p. 57 et seq. The previous decision was referred to in the decision annotated here.
[334] Section 1034(2) of the ZPO [DEU].
We cannot entirely rule out that the decision would, in this respect, be more cautious in the case of the recognition and enforcement of a foreign arbitral award.
[335] The first sentence of Section 1034(2) of the ZPO [DEU].
[336] The first sentence of Section 1034(2) of the ZPO [DEU]; the first sentence of Section 1035(5) of the ZPO [DEU].
[337] In the meantime, the Act on General Business Terms and Conditions (AGBG [DEU]) was repealed, but the concept was adopted and incorporated directly in the BGB [DEU].

drafted the arbitration agreement in advance, unilaterally stipulates the presiding judge of the District Court [in] "R." as the sole arbitrator. Moreover, the arbitration agreement did not specify which procedural law ought to apply in relation to the arbitrator. Despite these doubts, however, the Federal Court of Justice (BGH [DEU]) concluded that the **arbitration agreement still continued to apply in these cases**.

460. In other words, the Court (BGH [DEU]) did express certain doubts regarding unclear procedural standards for the resolution of the dispute according to the arbitration agreement, including its doubts regarding the appointment of an arbitrator, but these doubts did not render the agreement invalid.

461. An arbitral award is enforceable if the parties enjoy equal treatment in the course of the arbitral proceedings. The parties must be guaranteed the right to be heard, and it is not possible to exclude the right to professional legal counsel.[338] Unless the parties concluded a different agreement on procedure and unless the provisions of the ZPO [DEU] on arbitration contain specific rules regulating a particular procedural issue, the applicable procedural rules shall be at the arbitrators' discretion.[339] Consequently, the law allows the parties extensive autonomy and, in the absence of the parties' agreement, allows certain autonomy to the arbitrators, too. Hence, an unclear term in the arbitration agreement regarding the applicable procedural rules does not render the arbitration agreement invalid. The autonomy of the arbitrators is not without limits, and it is subject to restrictions stipulated by the law.[340] This in no way exceeds the statutory framework of disposition.

(c) Judgment of the Federal Court of Justice (Supreme Court [DEU]), Case No. XI 349/08 of 8 June 2010 (*M v. N*): Law applicable to arbitration agreement and form of arbitration agreement

(aa) Conclusion of the court

462. The Federal Court of Justice (BGH [DEU]) reached the **following conclusions** in the present case:[341]

▶ Arbitration agreements between a foreign broker and a consumer with his or her habitual residence in Germany [DEU] are governed by German law and thus must comply with the formal requirements set out by Section 1031(5) of the ZPO [DEU].[342]

---

[338] Section 1042(2) of the ZPO [DEU].
[339] The first sentence of Section 1042(4) of the ZPO [DEU].
[340] Section 1042 of the ZPO [DEU].
[341] Annotated in: ITA, 2011, Vol. 11, No. 2, edition of 17 February 2011.
[342] ZPO [DEU] (approximate translation, cit.) Section 1031 "[...] (5) *Arbitration agreements to which a consumer is a party must be contained in a document which has been signed by the parties' own*

▶ This conclusion is contingent on the finding that the party acted as a consumer, i.e. – inter alia – for a purpose different from his or her business or not in connection with his/her business. This conclusion is a finding of fact.

(bb) Factual and legal findings

463. In the proceedings on compensation for losses arising from a contract with a securities broker, conducted before a German court with jurisdiction over the claimants' residence, the respondent pleaded lack of international jurisdiction of the German courts. He maintained that the contract contained an arbitration clause. The BGH [DEU] confirmed (apart from other conclusions) the international jurisdiction of the German court with reference to Section 32 of the ZPO [DEU].[343] The case concerned a claim arising from non-contractual liability. These claims fall within the jurisdiction of German courts if the actions giving rise to the non-contractual liability mainly occurred in Germany. According to the facts of the case established by the court, the actions occurred in Germany.

(cc) Arguments of the court

464. The court of appeals (OLG Düsseldorf [DEU]) concluded that the arbitration agreement could not be invoked, because it was invalid. The arbitration clause was incorporated in the contractual terms and conditions attached to the agreement on opening an account. These terms also stipulated the law of the State of New York [USA] as the governing law. Consequently, the arbitration clause represented an anticipated choice of law for non-contractual obligations, which would be invalid under German law analogically pursuant to Article 42 of the EGBGB [DEU].[344]

(d) Decision of Krefeld District Court, Case No. 6 O 186/95 of 29 April 1996 (*Richard Zellner* v. *Phillip Alexandre Securities and Futures Ltd.*)

465. A conclusion similar to the case before the BGH [DEU] was made by a German court in Case No. XI 349/08 of 8 June 2010,[345] *Richard Zellner*

---

hands. *The written form prescribed under the first sentence may be replaced by electronic means pursuant to Section 126a of the BGB [DEU]. The written or electronic document must not contain any operative terms other than those relating to arbitration; this shall not apply to a notary record."*

[343] ZPO [DEU] (approximate translation, cit.): Section 32 *"Claims arising from unlawful conduct shall be filed with a court with jurisdiction over the district where the unlawful conduct occurred."*

[344] EGBGB [DEU] (approximate translation, cit.): Section 42 *"After the circumstances occur which gave rise to the non-contractual obligation, the parties may choose the law which shall govern their relationship, without prejudice to the rights of third parties."*

[345] For an annotation, see above in this book.

v. *Phillip Alexandre Securities and Futures Ltd.* The arbitration clause in a contract between a German citizen and an English securities broker anticipated the jurisdiction of the LCIA; the contract also stipulated the choice of English law. The German court held the arbitration clause invalid due to the absence of information provided to the consumer in the given case; just like the English courts in a different case, the German court also took into account that the consumer did not have any professional counsel. The conclusion on invalidity of the arbitration clause was also based on the *Directive*, which the court applied in this case. As a matter of fact, the validity of the arbitration clause contained in the contract was also assessed by an English court[346] in subsequent proceedings on the recognition and enforcement of the German decision; the English court arrived at the same conclusions as the German court, i.e. it held the clause invalid, despite the fact that the court applied English law.

466. This decision, compared to subsequent case law and practice in Germany, indicates that Germany has undergone similar developments as in the case law of English courts[347] and, at a more sedate speed, the case law of French courts.[348] Presently, the courts analyze the factual circumstances attending the contract and its conclusion in much greater detail and **refuse any undiscriminating opinions** which *a priori* exclude or accept arbitration agreements in certain types of contracts or relationships. Nonetheless, scrutinizing developments in the case law and other opinions from legal practice over the past 20 years, during which consumer protection has become more and more accentuated, it appears that German law, just like Austrian law and other legal systems in the traditional continental *civil law* systems, are, surprisingly, friendlier to arbitration and the enforcement of arbitral clauses than *common law* legal systems which, somewhat unjustly *praise* themselves for being favorable to and supporting arbitration. The approach adopted by individual legal systems is, to say the least, very balanced, and from the global perspective, arbitration can be said to enjoy general support. From this perspective, Germany is an example of a country that has

---

[346] Decision of the Queen's Bench Division (*Richard Zellner* v. *Phillip Alexandre Securities and Futures Ltd.*), [1997 ILPr 730 (QB); see especially paras. (736) through (738). See also *Hörnle, J.* Legal Controls on the Use of Arbitration Clauses in B2C E-Commerce Contracts. Masaryk University Journal of Law and Technology, pp. 31–32; available online at: http://www.mondaq.com/unitedstates/article.asp?articleid=83370 [last access 27 December 2011].

[347] See developments in English practice [GBR-ENG] which can be deduced from the decisions annotated in detail in connection with the excursus into English law, in the following cases:
➤ *Zealander & Zealander* v. *Laing Homes Limited* of 1999, CILL 1510;
➤ *Picardi* v. *Cuniberti* of 2002, [2002] EWHC 2923 (QB);
➤ *Westminster Building Company Limited* v. *Beckingham* of 2004, [2004] BLR 163 (TCC);
➤ *Allen Wilson Shopfitters and Builders* v. *Buckingham* of 2005, [2005] EWHC 1165 (TCC).

[348] See the decision Cass. (civ. 1er) [FRA] of 30 March 2004 (*Rado* v. *Painewebber*), annotated in: Rev. arb. 2005, p. 115 et seq. See also a separate excursus into French law, below in this book.

undergone substantial developments with respect to arbitration since the major 1998 amendment to the ZPO [DEU]; before the amendment, arbitration was considered an *unnecessarily expensive comedy*, whereas today it has earned the status of an indispensable component of finding the law and resolving disputes. The approach adopted by *civil law* countries has also been supported by much more consistent case law[349] which is fully open to the enforcement of arbitration agreements, even in consumer contracts.

(e) Judgment of the BGH [DEU], Case No. XI ZR 349/08 of 8 June 2010: Arbitration clauses in contracts between a consumer and a foreign securities broker

(aa) Conclusions of the court

467. The German Supreme Court reached, inter alia, the following conclusions:[350]

▶ **The application of special laws aimed at the protection of the weaker contracting party** (the consumer), for instance as concerns the special form and content of the arbitration agreement, **is contingent on the fulfillment of two requirements: (i)** one of the parties is a consumer, and **(ii)** the performance of the (main) contract must take place in the territory of the state whose law prescribes such special requirements. The former (the status of the party as a consumer) is a question of fact, the latter (place of performance) is a question of law.[351]

▶ The obligation of the party keeping the account (as the securities broker) to transfer, after termination, the balance in the account to

---

[349] Very consistent case law is to be found in Austria which, in the author's opinion, is one of the countries that exhibits long-standing support for arbitration, at least as concerns published or adjudicated legal opinions. However, arbitration in consumer disputes is subject to certain statutory limits, as analyzed in a separate excursus into Austrian law in this book.

[350] The annotation here was adopted from the ITA Reporter, KLI, 2011, No. 2 of 17 February 2011, as well as from the summary of the trial court's decision available online at: http://www.justiz.nrw.de/nrwe/lgs/duesseldorf/lg_duesseldorf/j2008/15_O_289_07urteil20080125.ht ml [last access 8 January 2012]. Also cited or annotated in: (i) ZIP, 2010, p. 2505, (ii) WM, 2010, p. 2025, (iii) BB, 2010, p. 2983, (iv) SchiedsVZ, 2011, p. 46, (v) NJW-RR, 2011.
This decision of the BGH [DEU] was also invoked by subsequent decisions of the German Federal Court of Justice (BGH [DEU]), especially:
(i) Decision of the BGH [DEU]), Case No. XI ZR 350/08 of 25 January 2011,
(ii) Decision of the BGH [DEU], Case No. XI ZR 351/08 of 25 January 2011, as well as
(iii) Decision of the BGH [DEU], Case No. XI ZR 352/08 of 17 May 2011.
Similar issues have also been debated in the following decisions:
(iv) Decision of the BGH [DEU], Case No. XI ZR 157/09 of 22 March 2011,
(v) Decision of the BGH [DEU], Case No. XI ZR 22/10 of 22 March 2011,
(vi) Decision of the BGH [DEU], Case No. XI ZR 197/08 of 22 March 2011 and others.

[351] We would maintain that this is not exclusively a question of law, but a question of law and fact mixed.

the client who has his or her residence in Germany [DEU] constitutes a sufficiently **qualified connection** to Germany as the **state of the consumer's residence** so that German laws on consumer protection apply, including special rules on consumer disputes incorporated in the lex arbitri (here Section 1031(5) of the ZPO [DEU]), if the client is a consumer.

▶ **Article II(1) of the New York Convention applies only to the objective arbitrability of disputes.** National laws stipulating that the arbitration clause can, in certain cases, be negotiated only by certain persons (persons with a specific status[352]), is only a limitation of subjective arbitrability to which the *New York Convention* does not apply.

▶ When examining consumer protection in relationships with an international dimension, **the courts must assess the validity of the arbitration clause pursuant to Article VII of the *New York Convention*,** which stipulates that the arbitration clause is valid according to the law applicable to the arbitration agreement.

(bb) Factual and legal findings and decisions of the trial court and the court of appeals

468. In said case, a German client[353] sued an American securities broker in a German court. The claimant demanded compensation for losses sustained as a result of futures and forwards trades on a U.S. stock exchange. In this particular case, the broker acted as both a custodian and a clearing house in the execution of transactions with securities for domestic and foreign agents. The transactions were executed via the respondent's online system. The respondent challenged the jurisdiction of the German courts due to the existence of an arbitration agreement. Conversely, the claimant pleaded invalidity of the arbitration agreement for non-compliance with the special laws on arbitration agreements in consumer relations; the claimant thereby invoked the German consumer protection law requiring the fulfillment of special form requirements applicable to these types of arbitration agreements. The trial court and the court of appeals accepted jurisdiction with reference to German consumer protection laws.

---

[352] In this case, the application of the WpHG [DEU] according to which arbitration agreements concerning future potential disputes arising from capital and financial markets can only be negotiated by professionals or legal persons subject to public law. The relevant rules are quoted below in the annotation of this decision of the BGH [DEU].

[353] In this case, a group of claimants. For the sake of simplicity in this annotation, "claimant" is referred to in the singular.

(cc) Decision and arguments of the Federal Court of Justice (BGH [DEU])

469. The German Federal Court of Justice (BGH [DEU]) vacated the decisions of the trial court and the court of appeals[354] for insufficient consideration of the case. According to the decision of the Federal Court of Justice, the lower courts insufficiently considered the existence of a valid arbitration agreement between the parties, i.e. a valid defense against the jurisdiction of the national court in compliance with German law. The courts should have primarily focused on the questions of fact and law, namely the eligibility of the claimant as a consumer and the connection to Germany in relation to applicability of German laws for the protection of the weaker contracting party (here the consumer).

470. The BGH concluded that the decision of the court of appeals rested on an erroneous assessment of the applicable arbitration clause. The appellant (the securities broker) did not in fact invoke the arbitration clause incorporated in the contractual terms and conditions attached to the statements of account, but invoked an arbitration clause contained in an Option Agreement and in the Approval Form. This particular Agreement did not contain any agreement on the choice of law. The BGH [DEU] held that, as a result thereof, the court of appeals should have examined the validity of the arbitration clause for different reasons. The BGH identified two more reasons of potential invalidity of the arbitration clause. But, as the Court held, even those reasons would not have rendered the clause invalid, because the court of appeals failed to ascertain the facts of the case to a sufficient extent. However, the BGH as the appellate instance could not itself examine the facts of the case; it was only allowed to assess questions of law.

471. According to the BGH [DEU], however, the trial court and the court of appeals should have primarily focused on the issue of whether the arbitration clause was binding pursuant to Section 37h of the Securities Trading Act [*Wertpapierhandelsgesetz*] (WpHG).[355] According to this Act, an arbitration clause (covering potential future disputes) is valid only if it is negotiated between merchants (professionals)[356] or between

---

[354] Decisions: (i) LG Düsseldorf, Case No. 15 O 289/07 of 25 January 2008, (ii) LG Düsseldorf, Case No. 15 O 289/07 of 28 March 2008 and (iii) decision of the OLG Düsseldorf, Case No. 9 U 87/08 of 17 November 2008.

[355] WpHG – Wertpapierhandelsgesetz [*Gesetz über den Wertpapierhandel*] [DEU] (approximate translation, cit.): Section 37 h – Arbitration agreements – "*Arbitration agreements concerning future disputes arising from services regarding securities, ancillary services regarding securities or futures and forwards are binding only if both parties are merchants or legal persons subject to public law.*"

[356] The definition of professional (merchant) is incorporated in the German Commercial Code (HGB [DEU]) – see Sections 1 through 7 of the HGB [DEU]). According to Section 1 of the HGB [DEU]

legal persons governed by public law. The application of the special rules incorporated in the German Securities Act (§ 37h WpHG) is neither excluded by Article II(1) of the *New York Convention*.

472. According to the BGH [DEU], the arbitration clause in the given case did not comply with the formal requirements stipulated in Article II of the *New York Convention*, because it was not signed by both parties, nor was it contained in an exchange of letters. Consequently, the OLG should have ascertained whether the arbitration clause was valid pursuant to Article VII of the *New York Convention*, which stipulates that the arbitration clause is valid according to the law applicable to the arbitration agreement. The conclusions of fact made by the OLG Düsseldorf were not, however, sufficient for the proper assessment of this issue.

473. The BGH [DEU] held that the arbitration clause would be invalid if Section 1031(5) of the ZPO [DEU] were applicable. In order for Section 1031(5) of the ZPO [DEU] to apply, two requirements had to be fulfilled. First, the parties must have signed the agreement in their capacity as consumers. Second, the performance of the contract must have taken place in Germany. While the first question, whether the party to the arbitration agreement is a consumer, is a question of fact that the appellate court is not competent to make a decision on, the second question is purely a question of law.

474. As a consequence of the foregoing, the outcome of the case depended on a factual question, i.e. whether the party had acted in its capacity as a consumer. This would be the case if the dealings in question had been made for private purposes and had not been connected to the party's business activities. Consequently, the Federal Court of Justice remanded the case for a reassessment of the relevant questions.

(approximate translation, cit.): Section 1 – "(1) *Merchant in this Code means any person carrying on a mercantile trade. (2) Mercantile trade means any operation of a mercantile enterprise unless the type or the scope of the trade did not require the operation of the enterprise in a mercantile manner.*" It is worth noting that German terminology employs the term "merchant," not professional; the translation to Czech uses the word "professional" ("podnikatel") which materially corresponds to the scope of the term "merchant" ("obchodník") under German law. The word "merchant" ("obchodník") used in certain Czech laws (certain Czech consumer protection laws, etc.) is an incorrect translation of the term used, especially in the German version as well as in other language versions of EU law.

(f) Judgment of the BGH [DEU], Case No. III ZR 16/11 of 19 May 2011 (*C. v. D.*): Non-performance of formal requirements and impossibility of subsequent validation of the arbitration agreement

(aa) Conclusion of the court

475. The Federal Court of Justice (BGH [DEU]) reached the **following conclusions** in the present case:[357]

▶ Consumers may not invoke arbitration agreements which are invalid for being contrary to the formal requirements of contracts pursuant to Section 1031(5) of the ZPO [DEU].[358] This also applies if the party invoking the invalidity is the professional who drafted the contract offer.

(bb) Factual and legal findings

476. The case concerned a contract with the manager of a dance school (dance classes). The contract contained an arbitration clause. The professional (manager of the dance school) sued his client for remuneration due under the contract. However, the claimant filed his claim with a court, not an arbitral tribunal. The trial court[359] granted the claim despite the fact that the client of the dance school (as a consumer) himself pleaded lack of jurisdiction and invoked the jurisdiction of the arbitral tribunal according to the arbitration clause. The court of appeals[360] granted the respondent's defense motion. Conversely, the Federal Court of Justice vacated the decision of the court of appeals and upheld the conclusions reached by the trial court.

(cc) Arguments of the court

477. Section 1031(5) of the ZPO [DEU] reads as follows (cit.:) *"Arbitration agreements to which a consumer is a party must be contained in a document which has been signed by the parties' own hands. The written form prescribed under the first sentence may be replaced by electronic means pursuant to Section 126a of the BGB [DEU]. The written or electronic document must not contain any operative terms other than those relating to arbitration; this shall not apply to a notary record."* The Federal Court of Justice (BGH [DEU]) held, however, that non-

---

[357] This information was adopted from the annotation published in: *Kreindler, R. H.* In C. v. D., The German Federal Court of Justice held that a consumer may not rely on an arbitration agreement that is invalid for failing to fulfill the form requirements of §1031(5) German Code of Civil Procedure (*Zivilprozessordnung* or *ZPO*) even if the party contesting the invalidity of the agreement was a non-consumer who had drafted the agreement (19 May 2011). ITA Arbitration Reporter, KLI, 2011, Vol. 9, No. 8.

[358] Full citation below.

[359] Amtsgericht Anklam.

[360] Landgericht Stralsund.

compliance with the formal requirements of the arbitration agreement in consumer relations automatically renders the agreement invalid.[361] In these cases, it is not possible to apply the special rules incorporated in Section 1031(6) of the ZPO [DEU] according to which (cit.): *"Lack of form is subsequently validated if the parties start discussing the case before arbitrators."*

IV.7. [DNK] [DENMARK]

478.   In 2005 Denmark passed the Law on Arbitration based on the UNCITRAL Model Law, namely Act [DNK] No. 553 of 24 June 2005.[362] However, the UNCITRAL Model Law was implemented with several modifications. For instance, Danish law introduces the definitions of domestic and international arbitration[363] and applies to all arbitrations with the seat of arbitration in Denmark.

479.   The Law on Arbitration [DNK] contains special provisions concerning consumer disputes: **(i) An arbitration agreement** concerning consumer disputes **must not be negotiated before the dispute arises** on pain of nullity.[364] **(ii)** A jurisdictional challenge must be raised on or before the submission of the statement of defense. In consumer disputes, however, the consumer may also plead invalidity of his or her arbitration agreement in the ensuing proceedings, unless the consumer continued with the arbitration even after he or she was informed that the arbitration agreement was not binding.[365] In this connection, it is appropriate to point out an interesting decision of the Austrian Supreme Court (OGH [AUT]),[366] which ruled on the recognition and enforcement of an arbitral award rendered in a consumer dispute in Denmark [DNK]. This decision was based on an arbitration clause which was apparently contrary to the above-mentioned Danish law on arbitration (*lex arbitri*) and consumer protection laws and indeed, would have been contrary even to Austrian law as well, had the arbitration agreement been governed by Austrian law or had Austria [AUT] been the seat of arbitration.

---

[361] This would constitute "absolute invalidity" under certain legal systems (e.g., under Czech law, etc.) which cannot be subsequently validated by the parties' conduct. The contra proferentem principle shall not apply.

[362] Available in English from the website of the Danish Institute of Arbitration (*Voldgiftsinstituttet*) at: http://www.voldgiftsinstituttet.dk/en/Materiale/Files/Danish+Arbitration+Act+2005. [last access 21 December 2011].

[363] *Schiersing, N.* Denmark. In: *Wegen, G. et Wilske, S.* Arbitration 2011. Published as a part of the edition: Getting the Deal Through, London, 2011, p. 122 et seq.

[364] See Section 7 of the Arbitration Act [DNK].

[365] See Section 16 of the Arbitration Act [DNK].

[366] Decision of the OGH [AUT], Case No. 3 Ob 144/09m of 22 July 2009 which is annotated in detail in Chapter V.4.4. of this book, referred to in other chapters as well.

IV.8. [ESP][SPAIN]

IV.8.1. Spanish approach to consumer arbitration

480. Spanish law contains a positive definition of objective arbitrability which covers any and all relations (disputes) subject to the freedom of contract. In other words, it is a somewhat broader category than the criterion defined as the right to negotiate a settlement regarding the subject of the dispute. This means that employment disputes are arbitrable, too. Also, Spanish law **does not principally exclude arbitration in consumer disputes.** Consequently, consumer disputes in arbitration are subject to the general rules on consumer protection and especially the rules on unfair arbitration clauses. However, special laws limit such arbitration in consumer disputes which should (only) follow the principles of equity.[367]

481. Arbitration in Spain is regulated under the Arbitration Act [ESP] of 2003,[368] which is based on the UNCITRAL Model Law and which applies to all arbitrations held in Spain, and under the Code of Civil Procedure. Consumer disputes are governed by Act [ESP] No. 44/2006 of 29 December 2006, on Improved Consumer Protection,[369] which amended the Consumers and Users General Act [ESP] No. 26/1984 (CUGA).[370]

482. Special rules are incorporated in Book III, Part III of the Spanish Arbitration Act which introduced Article 545 of the Spanish Code of Civil Procedure on court jurisdiction and the form of decisions in the case of mandatory enforcement. The first instance enforcement courts with jurisdiction over arbitral awards are the *Juzgado de Primera Instancia* in the place where the arbitral award was rendered. However, special laws apply where the enforcement is targeted against a

---

[367] Act No. 26/1984 [ESP] of 19 July 1984, on the Protection of Consumers and Users, published in: BOE, No. 175 and No. 176, edition of 24 July 1984. The original version is available online at: http://civil.udg.edu/normacivil/estatal/contract/lgdcu.html [last access 2 November 2009]; see especially the implementing provisions of the Act.
See also Judgment of the Spanish Constitutional Court [ESP] No. 15/1989 of 26 January 1989, published in: Annex to the BOE [ESP], No. 43, edition of 20 February 1989.
[368] Available in English from the Kluwer Arbitration website at: http://www.kluwerarbitration.com/document.aspx?id=ipn25805 [last access 22 December 2011].
[369] Available in Spanish with an English foreword from the Kluwer Arbitration website at: http://www.kluwerarbitration.com/document.aspx?id=ipn80855 [last access 22 December 2011].
[370] Available in English from the website of the Spanish Ministry of Justice at: http://www.google.cz/url?sa=t&rct=j&q=consumers%20and%20users%20general%20act&source=web&cd=3&ved=0CDcQFjAC&url=http%3A%2F%2Fwww.mjusticia.gob.es%2Fcs%2FSatellite%2F1292347027031%3Fblobheader%3Dapplication%252Fpdf%26blobheadername1%3DContent-Disposition%26blobheadervalue1%3Dattachment%253B%2Bfilename%253DRevised_Tex_of_the_General_Law_for_the_Protection_of_Consumers_and_Users_%28Ley_General_para_la_Defensa_de_Consumidores_y_Usuarios%29.PDF&ei=Y2_zTpmeBJHpObvzqa4B&usg=AFQjCNEX67l5Zsm-r0KHpaZK7_vD5KaG-w&sig2=KFNfTTbC03yasKrbO0DK9g&cad=rja [last access 22 December 2011].

consumer. The court competent to hear class actions aimed at the protection of group rights and other important interests of consumers is the court with jurisdiction over the place where the respondent has his/her business premises or, in the absence thereof, the place of the respondent's registered office/residence; if the respondent has no registered office/residence in the territory of Spain, the competent court is the court with jurisdiction over the claimant's place of residence.[371] Disputes concerning insurance, the sale of movable items for personal consumption with the purchase price payable in installments and pursuant to financing contracts, as well as disputes concerning contracts for the provision of services or contracts concerning movable items the conclusion of which was preceded by a public offer, shall be decided in a court with jurisdiction over the place of residence of the insured, the buyer, the debtor, or the recipient of the offer, in this order.

483. Whereas the Arbitration Act [ESP] stipulates that all disputes concerning disposable rights are arbitrable, the Increased Consumer Protection Act [ESP] stipulates more specific criteria governing the arbitrability of consumer disputes. This Act prescribes post-dispute arbitration clauses if jurisdiction over consumer disputes should be vested in institutions other than those established for the protection of consumers[372]. The objective of this provision is to protect the consumer who is in a weaker position vis-à-vis the professional (protection of the weaker party) and could easily succumb to *pressure*. This Act was passed in response to the ECJ judgment which reprimanded Spain for insufficient consumer protection in the *Asunto* case,[373] in which the *Commission* filed a complaint against Spain alleging improper implementation of Article 5 and Article 6(2) of the *Directive*.

484. Chapter II of the Consumers and Users General Act [ESP] sets forth the system of consumer dispute resolution in arbitration. This system ought to be usable for decision-making following the principles of equity unless the parties explicitly agree that they insist on decision-making according to the law (following applicable laws and regulations). Arbitral panels ought to be composed of the representatives of the relevant economic sector, representatives of consumer protection associations and consumers, as well as representatives of public administration. The parties' agreement that the dispute shall be resolved in arbitration

---

[371] These provisions were complemented with Act (Ley) 39/2002 [ESP] of 28 October 2002 which implements into the Spanish legal system various directives of the *Community* concerning the protection of the interests of consumers and users (BOE No. 259, edition of 29 October 2002, pp. 37922–37933).
[372] Institutions set up by law specifically for the resolution of consumer disputes, such as the Consumer Court of Arbitration.
[373] ECJ Judgment, Case C-70/2003 of 9 September 2004 (*Commission* v. *Kingdom of Spain*; the *Asunto* case); CELEX: 62003CJ0070.

following a special system for the resolution of consumer disputes must be voluntary and explicit as well as executed in writing, by electronic means, or by any other permissible means which allow recording the terms thereof. An arbitration agreement cannot be negotiated with and a public offer to arbitrate cannot be accepted if made by insolvent subjects.

485.	Consumer protection in Spain also relies on Article 51 of the Spanish Constitution of 27 December 1978.[374] The Constitution [ESP] mandates that **public authorities guarantee the protection of consumers and users** by implementing efficient procedures protecting the safety, health, and legitimate economic interests of these persons. They also promote their awareness and education, support their organizations, and consult issues with them which could affect them in any manner. In order to fulfill the constitutional mandate, the Consumer Protection Act is primarily based on the objective of providing consumers and users with a legal instrument of protection and defense which does not exclude or substitute for other procedures.

486.	Consumer arbitration under Spanish law was also examined by the ECJ's case law in *Mostaza Claro* and *Asturcom*, which are analyzed in detail elsewhere in this book.

487.	In December 2010, a proposal for an amendment to the Spanish Act on Arbitration and Rules Governing Institutionalized Arbitration was published.[375] The aim of the new law is not only to confirm that the resolution of disputes following the principles of equity (*ex aequo et bono*) is prohibited in consumer disputes, but that, at the same time, this possibility ought to be limited exclusively to international non-consumer disputes. The reasons for the amendment are that the resolution of domestic disputes following the principles of equity should be reserved only for mediation.[376]

---

[374] The original version of the legal provisions is available online at: http://www.constitucion.es/ [last access 3 November 2009]. Constitution of the Kingdom of Spain of 29 December 1978, as subsequently amended (approximate translation, cit.): Article 51 – "(1) *The public authorities shall guarantee the protection of consumers and users and shall, by means of effective measures, safeguard their safety, health, and legitimate economic interests.* (2) *The public authorities shall promote the awareness and education of consumers and users, foster their organizations, and hear them on those matters affecting their members, under the terms established by law.* (3) *Within the framework of the provisions of the foregoing paragraphs, the law shall regulate domestic trade and the system of licensing commercial products.*"

[375] For more information regarding the proposal, see *Angell, J.* Proposed amendments to the Spanish Arbitration Act. IBA Arbitration News, March 2011, pp. 97–101. Also available online at: http://www.bazilmcnulty.com/IBA_March_2011.pdf [last access 10 September 2011].

[376] For more information regarding the proposal, see *Angell, J.* Proposed amendments to the Spanish Arbitration Act. IBA Arbitration News, March 2011, pp. 97–101. Also available online at: http://www.bazilmcnulty.com/IBA_March_2011.pdf [last access 10 September 2011]. See the information on p. 100 where *Angell* criticizes that the proposal is based on an incorrect differentiation

IV.8.2. Case law – Decision of the Madrid Court of Appeals [ESP], Case No. 28079370102010100498, 12 November 2010 (*Juan Pedro* v. *Metrovacesa S.A.*): The principle of good faith protects both the consumer and the professional[377]

(a) Legal opinion of the Court

488. ▶ The principle of good faith prevents the **consumer, who initiated the arbitral proceedings** referring to the arbitration clause incorporated in a consumer contract, to plead invalidity of the arbitration clause in subsequent proceedings on annulment of the arbitral award.

▶ The consumer's defense of invalidity of the arbitration agreement should be rejected, since he had only objected to the validity of the arbitration agreement during the proceedings on annulment of the arbitral award, despite the fact that the consumer had had the opportunity to raise the defense earlier during the arbitral proceedings.

▶ A party which knows of a violation of any non-mandatory provision of the *lex arbitri* and fails to object within the established time limit, or, in the absence of a set time limit, as soon as practicable, will be deemed to have waived its right to object.[378] This also applies to the recourse of pleading invalidity of the arbitration agreement.

(b) Factual and legal findings and other conclusions of the Court

489. The claimant (consumer) in arbitration was also the claimant in the proceedings on annulment of the arbitral award in which he pleaded, inter alia, **invalidity of the arbitration agreement.**[379] **As an ancillary argument, he also referred to the Consumer Protection Act [ESP].**[380]

---

between arbitration and mediation as two different procedures. *Angell* also hopes that the deficiencies in this regard will be eliminated in the course of the legislative process in Parliament [ESP].

[377] Annotation: *Mandilla-Serrano,F.* In: ITA, 2011, Vol. 11, No. 4, edition of 20 April 2011. The rationes decidendi and the basic information regarding the decision were freely adopted from the cited annotation.

[378] The Madrid Court of Appeals [ESP] invoked Article 6 of the Arbitration Act [ESP] (approximate translation, cit:) Article 6. "*Tacit waiver of the right to plea invalidity. Where a party, aware of the non-compliance with any non-binding provision of this Act or any requirement of the arbitration agreement, does not state his objection within the period provided or, in the absence of such a period, as soon as possible, shall be deemed to have waived the right to raise the corresponding defense under this Act.*"

[379] In doing so, the Court invoked Article 41(1)(a) of the Arbitration Act [ESP]. The provision stipulates as follows (approximate translation, cit.): Article 41. Grounds [for annulment of an arbitral award] "1. *An arbitral award may be set aside only if the party making the application alleges and proves:* (a) *that the arbitration agreement does not exist or is not valid,* [...]"

[380] Consumer Protection Act [ESP] No. 1/2007.

490.   Apart from the issues annotated in the above rationes decidendi, the Court also examined the *ultra petita* defense. The Court dismissed this argument on the ground that the claimant was only attempting to have the arbitrators' award reviewed in the merits, which is prohibited. Other arguments presented by the claimant consisted in an improper constitution of the arbitral panel and defective procedure. The Madrid Court of Appeals dismissed these arguments, too. It invoked Article 6 of the Arbitration Act [ESP],[381] i.e. because the claimant failed to plead the defects earlier during the course of the arbitral proceedings themselves despite having had ample opportunity to do so.

(c) Notes on the judgment

491.   This *prima facie* inconspicuous decision is in many respects very important. It confirms that consumer protection is by no means absolute and that the consumer is also obliged to assume responsibility for the exercise of his or her rights. Indeed, the ECJ's decision in the *Pannon GSM* case[382] also indicates that the potential invalidity of an arbitration clause resulting from a breach of consumer protection laws is not absolute.[383] The annotated decision of the Madrid Court of Appeals only confirms this premise. It also emphasizes that the consumer cannot be afforded such protection which would allow him or her to abuse the consumer protection and reserve the plea of invalidity in case the consumer loses in the arbitral proceedings. Moreover, the Spanish decision denied (and correctly so) protection to a consumer who was the claimant in the arbitral proceedings and whose defense of invalidity was solely motivated by his failure in arbitration. This particular case constitutes an abuse of right (the Spanish court employed the argument of *good faith* protecting both parties to the consumer contract). The decision is all the more important, because it was rendered only after a series of the ECJ's decisions which addressed either arbitration clauses or, at least, choice-of-court clauses from the perspective of consumer protection.[384]

---

[381] This provision of the Arbitration Act [ESP] is cited above in the footnote regarding the rationes decidendi of the decision of the Madrid Court of Appeals.

[382] Annotated in detail elsewhere in this book (see the analysis of the ECJ's case law). In the *Pannon GSM* case, which did not primarily concern the arbitration clause but a choice-of-court clause, the ECJ emphasized that the court could not hold the clause invalid if the consumer failed to plea its invalidity despite having the opportunity to do so.

[383] Hence, it is not an institution designated in certain legal systems as *absolute invalidity* ([CZE], [AUT], etc.), elsewhere as *ineffectiveness (Unwirksamkeit)* [DEU], or merely as *nullity (null and void)* [GBR-ENG], etc.

[384] The ECJ's rulings are annotated and analyzed in a separate part of this book, see above the excursus into EU law.

IV.9. [EST] [ESTONIA]

492. On 1 January 2006 a new Code of Civil Procedure [EST] took effect in Estonia; Chapter XIV of the new law regulates arbitration. The majority of the Estonian provisions on arbitration are based on the UNCITRAL Model Law and do not contain any special rules regulating consumer disputes. The Code of Civil Procedure [EST] applies to arbitration in Estonia. Section 718 of the Code of Civil Procedure [EST] stipulates that all property disputes are arbitrable; non-property disputes may be submitted to arbitration only if the parties have the right to negotiate a settlement with respect to such disputes. Section 719 of the Code stipulates that if a consumer is a party to the arbitration agreement, the agreement must contain the consumer's digital or handwritten signature. There are two institutions in Estonia handling the out-of-court settlement of consumer disputes[385]: (i) the Consumer Complaint Committee generally for all disputes between professionals and consumers and (ii) the Insurance Court of Arbitration.

IV.10. [FRA] [FRANCE]

IV.10.1. Legal control of contractual terms

493. Supervision over unfair terms has evolved from precedents. The provisions of the CoCiv [FRA] contained only certain general rules. This situation changed in 1978 with the adoption of Act [FRA] 78-22 the purpose of which was to introduce a system of public law supervision over contractual terms incorporated in contracts concluded with consumers. The Commission des clauses abusives[386] was set up to this end as the competent authority with the power to issue recommendations.[387] However, the attempt did not prove very successful. Consequently, French consumer protection laws were recodified in the early 1990s when the new French Consumer Protection Act was promulgated. The court review of unfair terms in consumer contracts was introduced into French law in 1991 in connection with the new Consumer Protection Act. The right to apply for a review originally only benefited individual consumers. The right to sue, benefiting

---

[385] For more information, see the European Consumer Centre of Estonia Alternative Dispute Resolution, available online from the website of the ECC of Estonia at: http://www.consumer.ee/alternative-dispute-resolution-2/ [last access 9 January 2012].

[386] The commission, however, still exists. For more information online, see at: http://www.clauses-abusives.fr/.

[387] Apart from the recommendations available online at: http://www.clauses-abusives.fr/recom/index.htm [last access 24 May 2009], this commission especially focuses on the supply of information, and it administers a very well-organized, technically well-arranged, and voluminous register of rulings of both the ECJ and, especially, the French courts at all levels which have ruled on unfair terms in consumer contracts (available online at: http://www.clauses-abusives.fr/juris/index.htm; page available in French; [last access 24 May 2009]).

consumer organizations and associations, was only introduced into French law in 1998. The *Directive* was implemented on 1 February 1995 through French Act 95-96, which inserted a new Article L. 132-1[388] into

---

[388] Act [FRA] No. 95-96 of 1 February 1995.
Article L. 132-1 implemented by Act No. 95-96 of 1 February 1995 Article 1, published in the Annex to JORF of 2 February 1995 and Regulation No. 2001-741 of 23 August 2001 Article 16, published in JORF of 25 August 2001 (approximate translation, cit.): *"In contracts concluded between a business and a non-business or consumers, clauses [provisions] which aim to create or result in the creation, to the detriment of the non-professional or the consumer, of a significant imbalance between the rights and obligations of the parties to the contract, are unfair. (•) The Council of State decrees issued upon the advice of the committee set up as per Article L. 132-2, may determine the types of clauses that must be regarded as unfair in the sense of the first paragraph. (•) An annex to this code includes an illustrative and non-exhaustive list of clauses that may be regarded as unfair if they satisfy the conditions posed in the first paragraph. In the event of dispute concerning a contract that includes one such clause, the applicant is not exempt from submitting proof of the unfair nature of this clause. (•) These provisions apply whatever the contract form or medium. This is the case, in particular, for purchase orders, invoices, performance bonds, delivery notes or slips, and travel vouchers or tickets, containing stipulations which may, or may not, have been freely negotiated, or references to general terms fixed in advance. (•) Without prejudice to the rules of interpretation provided for in Articles 1156 to 1161, 1163, and 1164 of the civil code [CoCiv] [FRA], the unfair nature of a [contractual] term is assessed by referring, when the contract is concluded, to all the circumstances surrounding its conclusion, as well as to all the other contractual clauses. It is also evaluated in respect of those contained in another contract where the conclusion or performance of these two contracts are legally dependent upon one another. (•) Unfair terms are deemed to be null and void. (•) Evaluation of the unfair nature of terms in the sense of the first paragraph does not involve either the definition of the main purpose of the contract nor the adequacy of the price of, or remuneration for, the goods being sold or the service being offered, provided that the terms are written in a clear and comprehensible manner. (•) The contract shall continue to be applicable in all its provisions other than those deemed to be unfair if it can continue to exist without the said terms. (•) The provisions of this article are public policy."*
(•) Annex: Terms referred to in the third paragraph of Article L. 132-1:
"1. Terms with the [following] aim or the [following] effect:(a) *of excluding or limiting the business's legal liability in the event of the death of a consumer or personal injury caused to the latter, resulting from an act or omission of this business;* (b) *of inappropriately excluding or limiting the consumer's legal rights in respect of the business or another party in the event of total, or partial, failure to perform, or defective performance by the business of any one of the contractual obligations, including recourse to offsetting debt owed to the business with a credit that it may have against said business;* (c) *of providing for a firm undertaking from the consumer, even though the performance of the business services is subject to a condition which is solely dependent on goodwill;* (d) *of enabling the business to withdraw sums paid by the consumer when the latter has withdrawn from the conclusion or performance of the contract, without providing for the right, for the consumer, to receive compensation of an equivalent amount from the business where it is the latter who withdraws;* (e) *from obliging the consumer who has failed to perform his/her obligations to pay compensation in a disproportionately high amount;* (f) *from authorizing the business to cancel the contract in a discretionary manner if the same option is not given to the consumer, as well as enabling the professional to retain the sums paid in respect of service provisions not yet supplied by him, where it is the professional himself who cancels the contract;* (g) *from authorizing the business to terminate a contract of indeterminate duration without giving reasonable advance notice, without just cause;* (h) *from automatically extending a contract of indeterminate duration in the absence of an expression to the contrary from the consumer, although an excessively remote date has been set as the deadline for the expression of this desire not to extend the contract on the part of the consumer;* (i) *from irrefutably establishing the consumer's adherence to clauses that the latter has not actually had the opportunity to become aware of prior to conclusion of the contract;* (j) *from authorizing the business to unilaterally amend the terms of the*

the French Consumers Act (by the Consumer Protection Act [FRA] / Code de la Consommation [FRA]) of 1 February 1995.[389] The crucial general clause of the Consumer Code does not condition the unfairness of the respective terms on a breach of the requirement of good faith. Individually agreed terms also fall within the scope of protection against unfairness. According to French law, both natural and legal persons can have the status of consumer.

IV.10.2. Consumer arbitration

494.   In France [FRA], consumer protection in international arbitration traditionally differs from domestic disputes. French courts do not intervene in international arbitration to any major extent, and

---

contract without a valid reason being specified in the contract; (k) from authorizing businesses to unilaterally amend, without a valid reason, the characteristics of the product to be delivered or the service to be supplied; (l) from specifying that the price of the goods is to be determined at the time of delivery, or from according the seller of the goods or the supplier of the services the right to increase their prices without, in both cases, the consumer having a corresponding right enabling him/her to cancel the contract should the final price be too high in respect to the price agreed when the contract was concluded; (m) from according the business the right to determine whether the item delivered or the service supplied conforms to contractual stipulations or from according the latter the exclusive right to interpret any one of the clauses of the contract; (n) from restricting the business' obligation to respect the obligations undertaken by its authorized agents or from making its undertakings subject to adherence to a particular formality; (o) from obliging the consumer to fulfill his obligations even though the business may not have fulfilled its obligations; (p) from providing for recourse to transfer, on the part of the business, of the contract, where this is likely to engender a reduction in guarantees for the consumer without the latter's agreement; (q) from canceling or impeding the institution of legal proceedings or means of redress by the consumer, in particular, by obliging the consumer to exclusively refer the case to an arbitration panel not covered by legal provisions, by unduly limiting the means of submitting evidence available to the consumer or by making the latter responsible for providing proof which, by virtue of applicable law, should normally lie with another party to the contract.

2. Scope of points g, j and l: (a) Point g does not pose an obstacle to clauses in which suppliers of financial services reserve the right to unilaterally terminate a contract for an indeterminate period without prior notice in the event of just cause, provided that the obligation to immediately inform the other contracting party, or parties, of this fact lies with the business. (b) Point j does not pose an obstacle to clauses in which suppliers of financial services reserve the right to change the rate of interest owed by the consumer or owed to the latter, or the amount of any other charges appertaining to financial services, without prior notice in the event of just cause, provided that the obligation to inform the other contracting party, or parties, of this fact as soon as possible, lies with the business and provided that said party, or parties, are free to terminate the contract immediately. In addition, point j does not pose an obstacle to clauses in which the business reserves the right to unilaterally change the terms of a contract for an indeterminate period provided that the duty to notify the consumer of this fact in sufficient time lies with the consumer and the consumer is free to cancel the contract; (c) Points g, j and l do not apply to: (•) – transactions concerning securities, financial instruments, and other products and services whose price is linked to fluctuations in currency or in a stock market index or in a financial market rate beyond the business' control; (•) – contracts for the sale or purchase of currency, travelers cheques or international money orders denominated in national currencies; (d) Point l does not pose an obstacle to price indexation clauses provided that these are legal and that the mode of price variation is clearly described." Available at: http://195.83.177.9/code/liste. phtml?lang=uk&c=61&r=2140 [last access 13 August 2011].

[389] The Consumer Protection Act [FRA] also contains conflict-of-law rules, specifically in Article L.135-1 of the Consumer Protection Act.

international arbitration is not subject to so much regulation as in other countries (especially as concerns the intervention of the state in arbitration). Conversely, domestic arbitration is subject to fairly rigorous rules; it is only admitted in disputes between professionals *(commerçants)*.

495.   The new 1995 law basically literally adopts the *Directive*. This means that consumer arbitration is principally permitted unless the consumers prove that the arbitration agreement is unfair. Hence, the special provisions established an exception to the general prohibition of arbitration for parties other than professionals, and consumer disputes arising from domestic transactions can now be resolved in arbitration, as opposed to the past.[390] The arbitrability of consumer disputes is also allowed in disputes with an international dimension, albeit with certain restrictions.[391]

496.   The second stage of implementation involved the amendment of Section 2061 of the French Civil Code (CoCiv [FRA]).[392] This provision no longer refers to the commercial nature of arbitration and stipulates that arbitration agreements are valid if concluded for the benefit of a business relationship (in connection with business). This excludes all relations between a professional and a consumer. Some lawyers argued that this provision applied exclusively to arbitration agreements negotiated before the new law took effect, i.e. before 15 May 2001.[393]

---

[390] *Fouchard, Ph.* Clause abusives en matière d'arbitrage. Rev. arb., 1995, p. 149.

[391] See the decisions of the French courts:
➢ Cour de appel de Paris of 24 March 1995 (*Bin Saud Abdel Aziz* v. *CIC Paris*), decision published in: Rev. arb., 1996, p. 259 et seq., here especially p. 263 and
➢ Cour de appel de Paris of 7 December 1994 (*Jaguar* /V2000/), published in: Rev. arb., 1996, p. 245 and subsequently the decision Cass. of 21 May 1997 (the same case, i.e. *Jaguar* /V2000/), published in: Rev. arb., 1997, p. 537.

[392] CoCiv [FRA], Section 2061, as amended by Act [FRA] No. 2001-420 of 15 May 2001 (approximate translation, cit.): Article 2061 – "*Unless stipulated otherwise by mandatory provisions, an arbitration agreement is valid in contracts concluded by reason of a professional activity.*" The original wording (cit.:) "*Sous réserve des dispositions législatives particulières, la clause compromissoire est valable dans les contrats conclus à raison d'une activité professionnelle.*", Act No. 2001-420 of 15 May 2001 was published in: JORF [FRA] of 16 May 2001. This provision of the CoCiv [FRA] is also referred to in: (i) Decree No. 2000-810 [FRA] of 24 August 2000 – Annex V, Part V, (ii) Regulation No. 2004-604 [FRA] of 24 June 2004 – Articles 57 and 58.

[393] Decision of the Cour de commerce de Paris [FRA] of 2004 in *AGRR* v. *ACE Insurance*, published in Rev. arb., 2004, p. 641 et seq. Adopted from: *Poudret, J. F., Besson, S. et Birti, S.* Comparative Law of International Arbitration. 2nd ed., London: Sweet & Maxwell, 2007, p. 43. This decision (*AGRR* v. *ACE Insurance*) was subject to criticism; see Orléans. Les Cahiers de l'Arbitrage No 2004/1/2, Gaz. Pal, 21–22 May 2004, p. 24 or IA. Paris Commercial Court. Rev. arb., 2004, p. 451 et seq. The latter held that Article 2061 of the CoCiv [FRA], despite its incorporation in the CoCiv [FRA], is a procedural provision and, consequently, must be applied to all arbitration agreements negotiated after the effective date of the provision. Developments in the interpretation of Article 2061 of the CoCiv [FRA] are also mentioned in *Poudret, J. F., Besson, S. et Birti, S.* Comparative Law of International Arbitration. 2nd ed., London: Sweet & Maxwell, 2007, p. 43.

However, according to the 2005 case law of the French Supreme Court (Cass. [FRA]),[394] the provision also applies to arbitration agreements negotiated before the [new] law took effect. The provisions do not apply to contracts with an international dimension.[395] This approach has also been criticized in academic sources;[396] it appears, nonetheless, that we should expect that the French courts will continue to follow this course in the future. The question is how this provision will be interpreted in conjunction with the Commercial Code, i.e. whether consumer contracts are invalid as a result of the amended Section 2061 of the CoCiv [FRA] or whether they are subject to a special regime, namely the amended Article L.132-1 of the Commercial Code. French case law has not yet clearly answered this question.

497.   As concerns international arbitration, recent case law indicates that French courts are more and more open to the recognition and enforcement of arbitration clauses in consumer disputes.[397] A typical example involves arbitration clauses concluded between self-employed professionals (especially lawyers-attorneys) and their clients, including disputes over attorney fees.[398]

---

[394] Decision of the Cass. [FRA] in *SCP Ménard-Quimbert* v. *Beauchard*, published in Rev. arb., 2005, p. 1011 et seq. Adopted from: *Poudret, J. F., Besson, S. et Birti, S.* Comparative Law of International Arbitration. 2nd ed., London: Sweet & Maxwell, 2007, p. 43.

[395] Cf. *Loquin, E.* L'arbitrage des litiges du droit de la consommation. In: *Osman, F.* (ed.) Vers un code européen de la consommation, Bruxelles: Bruylant, 1998, p. 359 et seq.; *Kaufmann-Kohler, G.* Online Dispute Resolution and its Significance for International Commercial Arbitration. In: Liber Amicorum in honour of Robert Brinner, Paris: ICC Publishing, 2005, Publication 693, p. 445; *Deggos, L.* Les nouvelles dispositions de la loi française relative à la clause compromissoire. IBLJ/RDAI, 2001, Vol. 12, p. 653 et seq.

See the following decisions:

➢   Cass (civ., 1re) of 21 May 1997 (*Meglio* v. *V2000*), annotated (author: *Hauzé, V.*) in: RCDIP, 1998, p. 87 et seq. and

➢   Cass. (civ., 1re) of 21 May 1997 (*Renault* v. *V2000*), annotated (author: *Jarrosson, C.*) in: Rev. arb., 1997, p. 537 et seq.

Both of these decisions are also mentioned by (adopting the same source) *Kaufmann-Kohler, G.* Online Dispute Resolution and its Significance for International Commercial Arbitration. In: Liber Amicorum in honour of Robert Brinner, Paris: ICC Publishing, 2005, Publication 693, p. 445 (Footnote No. 22).

[396] Cf. *Delebecque, P.* Arbitrage et droit de la consommation. Droit & Patrimoine, May 2002, No. 104, p. 50. The criticism is also mentioned by, without further commentary and, inter alia, with reference to the same source, *Kaufmann-Kohler, G.* Online Dispute Resolution and its Significance for International Commercial Arbitration. In: Liber Amicorum in honour of Robert Brinner, Paris: ICC Publishing, 2005, Publication 693, p. 445 (Footnote No. 22).

[397] See the decision Cass. (civ. 1er) of 30 March 2004 (*Rado* v. *Painewebber*). Annotated in: Rev. arb., 2005, p. 115 et seq.

Similarly, the English and German courts which have probably proceeded much further than the French courts.

[398] See the following rulings of the French Supreme Court (Cass. [FRA]):

➢   Cass., Civ. 1er, Case No. 97-41.860 of 4 May 1999, published in: Bulletin Cass. [FRA], Ref. No. C112945; available online at: http://www.easydroit.fr/jurisprudence/Cour-de-Cassation-Chambre-sociale-du-4-mai-1999-97-41-860-Publie-au-bulletin/C112945/ [last access 25 December 2011].

IV.11. [GBR] [UNITED KINGDOM]

IV.11.1. Sources and principles of consumer protection

498.   English law experienced a major landmark in consumer protection law in 1999 when the Unfair Terms in Consumer Contracts Regulation 1999 was adopted; inter alia, the 1999 Regulation incorporated in the law of the United Kingdom **the principle of good faith** promoting consumer protection,[399] as enshrined in Article 3 of the *Directive*. A similar approach was adopted with respect to the principle of the most favorable interpretation of contractual terms benefiting the consumer pursuant to Article 5 of the *Directive*.

IV.11.2. Consumer arbitration

499.   Some countries have adopted consumer protection rules exceeding the required standard under the *Directive*. This applies, for instance, to the United Kingdom [GBR] which implemented, for *England and Wales*, the part of the *Directive* relating to consumer arbitration through the Arbitration Act 1996 (AA [GBR-ENG]). This Act combines the principles of the *Directive* and the idea that "standard" arbitration is not suitable for the resolution of disputes for small claims, which are indeed often submitted to arbitration. The Arbitration Act (AA [GBR-ENG]) itself, however, does not establish an irrefutable presumption for the conclusion that an arbitration agreement is unfair if relating to disputes the value of which is below a certain benchmark. Arbitration clauses in other cases are assessed in terms of the standards pursuant to the *Directive*.

> Cass., Civ. 1er, Case No. 04-11.384 of 22 November 2005, published in: Bulletin Cass. [FRA], Ref. No. C51400; available online at: http://www.easydroit.fr/jurisprudence/Cour-de-Cassation-Chambre-civile-1-du-22-novembre-2005-04-11-384-Publie-au-bulletin/C51400/ [last access 25 December 2011].

> Cass., Civ. 1er, Case No. 04-12.655 of 22 November 2005, published in: Bulletin Cass. [FRA], Ref. No. C51402; available online at: http://www.easydroit.fr/jurisprudence/Cour-de-Cassation-Chambre-civile-1-du-22-novembre-2005-04-12-655-Publie-au-bulletin/C51402/ [last access 25 December 2011].

> Cass., Civ. 1er, Case No. 04-20.350 of 4 June 2006, published in: Bulletin Cass. [FRA], Ref. No. C51437; available online at: http://www.easydroit.fr/jurisprudence/Cour-de-Cassation-Chambre-civile-1-du-7-juin-2006-04-20-350-Publie-au-bulletin/C51437/ [last access 25 December 2011].

> Cass., Civ. 1er, Case No. 03-16.640 of 20 June 2006, published in: Bulletin Cass. [FRA], Ref. No. C51135; available online at: http://www.easydroit.fr/jurisprudence/Cour-de-Cassation-Chambre-civile-1-du-20-juin-2006-03-16-640-Publie-au-bulletin/C51135/ [last access 25 December 2011].

The overview of the rationes decidendi and other rulings are also available at: http://www.easydroit.fr/codes-et-lois/article-2061-du-Code-civil/A54610/ [13 August 2011].

[399] The same principle was also observed in connection with certain categories of commercial agency contracts. See Commercial Agents (Council Directive) Regulations 1993 as the national British law implementing Directive 86/653/EEC.

500. The UK Office of Fair Trading (OFT [GBR]) published an "Unfair contract terms guidance" (the "Guidance") which includes the following provision: "17.2 *Under Section 91 of the Arbitration Act 1996 [AA /GBR-ENG/], a compulsory arbitration clause is automatically unfair if it relates to claims of £5,000 [GBP] or less.*" This is a unique example of a term that is always unfair under the Regulations regardless of circumstances. A compulsory arbitration clause forbidden by the AA [GBR-ENG] is both legally ineffective and open to regulatory action in all cases.

501. Potential problems include the possibility that the parties to the consumer contract may not know whether the arbitration agreement is valid or not until a claim is filed concerning a particular dispute.

502. As concerns the corresponding consequences, the OFT [GBR] recommends that the professional either excludes the arbitration clause or at least explains that consumers have the right to go to court, just like they have the right to submit the dispute to arbitration.[400] According to the Guidance: "17.3 *If an arbitration clause* [provision] *is to be used, it should be free from the element of compulsion. Such a clause can, for example make clear that consumers (or both parties) have a free choice as to whether to go to arbitration or not. Arbitration in the UK is fully covered by legal provisions, and so noncompulsory arbitration clauses are unlikely to encounter objections provided they are in clear language and not misleading.*" It is necessary to point out, though, that the words "*covered by legal provisions*" are the source of certain doubts.

503. Consumer arbitration is governed by the *Directive*, with the exception of small claims.[401] Despite the strictness of this regime in the United Kingdom [GBR] where the Authorized Chamber of Arbitrators deals with consumer arbitration programs, arbitration in these types of disputes is not very common (as opposed to the U.S.).[402]

---

[400] *Drahozal, C. et Friel, R. A.* A Comparative View of Consumer Arbitration. Arbitration, 2005, Vol. 2, p. 134.
[401] See the following decisions in which the fundamental principles according to the *Directive* were applied:
  ➤ *Zealander & Zealander* v. *Laing Homes Limited*, 1999, CILL 1510. (invalidity of an arbitration agreement – for more information, see below);
  ➤ *Heifer* v. *Christiansen et al.*, Decision of the Queen's Bench, Technology & Construction Court, Case No. HT-07-106 of 18 December 2007. (The conclusion in this decision was, conversely, that consumer protection standards were not breached.)
[402] See *Drahozal, C. et Friel, R. A.* A Comparative View of Consumer Arbitration. Arbitration, 2005, Vol. 2, p. 131.

IV.11.3. Case law

(a) Decision in *Zealander & Zealander v. Laing Homes Limited* of 1999

504. The case concerned the assessment of the nature of contractual terms under the 1994 consumer protection laws.[403] The case concerned a contract under which the claimant purchased real property from the respondent. The contract contained an arbitration clause. The respondent's motion for termination of the court proceedings was dismissed, because the arbitration clause was found contrary to consumer protection laws. After a thorough assessment of the applicable laws, the judge held the arbitration agreement invalid. The reason supporting the conclusion on invalidity of the arbitration agreement was that the claimant (purchaser) was not provided with an opportunity to consider or to negotiate the terms of the arbitration clause. The clause limited or even excluded the claimant's right to legal protection by means of a claim in court and, as such, was found contrary to consumer protection laws.[404]

(b) Decision in *Picardi v. Cuniberti* of 2002, *Westminster Building Company Limited v. Beckingham* of 2004 and *Allen Wilson Shopfitters and Builders v. Buckingham* of 2005: Importance of the information provided to consumer

505. *Westminster Building Company Limited* v. *Beckingham* of 2004[405] and *Allen Wilson Shopfitters and Builders* v. *Buckingham* of 2005[406] indicate that since the 1990s,[407] English legal practice has also undergone certain developments; courts are now trying to assess the facts of the case and, on the basis of examination thereof, draw individual conclusions on the (in)validity of arbitration clauses.[408] Both cases concerned construction contracts negotiated with a consumer. The Court accepted the validity of the arbitration clause, because the Court concluded that the consumers had received enough information regarding the content of the contract and the meaning of the terms

---

[403] Unfair Terms in Consumer Contract Regulations 1994. This law only applies to contracts where at least one of the parties was a consumer.

[404] Cf. *Andrews, N.* Contract Law. CUP, 2011, p. 428; *Selby, J.* United Kingdom: Are Contract Terms Really Binding? Part II. Mondaq, 16 April 2007, available online at: http://www.mondaq.com/article.asp?articleid=47440 [last access 14 August 2011] et al.

[405] [2004] BLR 163 (TCC).

[406] [2005] EWHC 1165 (TCC).

[407] See the decision in *Zealander & Zealander* v. *Laing Homes Limited* of 1999, CILL 1510; this decision was annotated above.

[408] Similarly, also in Germany [DEU], as we demonstrated in detail in the excursus into German law, as well as in France [FRA], as indicated by the decision Cass. (civ. 1er) [FRA] of 30 March 2004 (*Rado v. Painewebber*), annotated in: Rev. arb. 2005, p. 115 et seq.

incorporated therein. It sufficed that the consumers had professional counsel. Indeed, the same conclusion was reached by the Court in *Picardi v. Cuniberti* of 2002;[409] in this case, conversely, the Court did not accept the validity of the arbitration agreement due to the lack of information which had been provided to the consumer[410] and, as opposed to both of the 2004 and 2005 cases mentioned above, the consumer had no counsel.[411] The Court *(Queen's Bench Division)* highlighted the importance of the information which limits or restricts the consumer's right to file his or her claim in court.[412]

IV.12. [HRV] [CROATIA]

506.   After Croatia separated in 1991, the provisions regulating arbitration have been firmly incorporated in the federal laws of this former Yugoslav Federation.[413] The former Yugoslav *lex arbitri* was incorporated both in **(i)** civil court procedure laws and in **(ii)** private international law provisions. Croatia adopted both legislative acts and the relevant provisions applied throughout the 1990s. However, the need for conceptual changes was obvious. Current Croatian arbitration laws are based on the UNCITRAL Model Law; this law combines both domestic and international arbitration. The current Croatian Arbitration Act [HRV] of 28 September 2001 has applied since 19 October 2001.[414] It is loosely based on the UNCITRAL Model Law which has, however, been substantially adapted to the domestic environment.[415]

---

[409] [2002] EWHC 2923 (QB).

[410] [2002] EWHC 2923 (QB), para. (127).

[411] Cf. also the Decision of the [German] District Court in Krefeld [DEU], Case No. 6 O 186/95 of 29 April 1996 (*Richard Zellner* v. *Phillip Alexandre Securities and Futures Ltd.*) and the following decision of the English court – (Queen's Bench Division) – (in the same case, i.e. *Richard Zellner* v. *Phillip Alexandre Securities and Futures Ltd.*), [1997 ILPr 730 (QB). For a brief annotation and a summary, see the excursus into German law above. It appears that German and English practice have, in this regard, followed similar developments as concerns the thorough examination of the circumstances attending the conclusion of the contract, the facts of the case, and the refusal of any unduly undiscriminating assessment. The author believes, however, that the approach adopted by German courts is more consistent, stable, and therefore easily foreseeable; surprisingly, the German approach is, in its consequences, more supportive of arbitration than the approach adopted by many common law countries (for more details, see also the excursus into German law).

[412] See also *Hörnle, J.* Legal Controls on the Use of Arbitration Clauses in B2C E-Commerce Contracts. Masaryk University Journal of Law and Technology; available online at: http://www.mondaq.com/unitedstates/article.asp?articleid=83370 [last access 27 December 2011].

[413] *Uzelac, A.* Croatia, in: *Paulsson, J.* (ed.). International Handbook on Commercial Arbitration, (Kluwer Law International 1984. Last updated: December 2009. Supplement No. 57) pp. 1–56; adopted from the website at: http://www.kluwerarbitration.com/document.aspx?id=KLI-KA-201004001-n [last access 21 December 2010].

[414] Published in the Collection of Laws (Narodne novine): No. 88/2001, edition of 11 October 2001.

[415] Cf. *Uzelac, A.* Croatia. In: *Paulsson, J.* (ed.). International Handbook on Commercial Arbitration, KLI, 1984 Last updated: December 2009, Supplement No. 57, pp. 1–56. Available online at: http://www.kluwerarbitration.com/document.aspx?id=KLI-KA-201004001-n [last access 21 December 2010].

507. Consumer arbitration is not the subject of any special provisions of the Croatian Arbitration Act [HRV]. The only specific feature is the requirement imposed on the conclusion of the arbitration agreement. Article 6(6) of the Arbitration Act [HRV] stipulates as an exception to the general rules that if the dispute arose or could arise from a consumer contract, **the arbitration agreement must be contained in a separate document signed by both parties to the dispute.** Unless the document is executed by a notary public, the document must not contain any provisions other than those relating to arbitration.

IV.13. [HUN] [HUNGARY]

508. The basic source of arbitration in Hungary is Act No. LXXI of 1994 on Arbitration [HUN], adopted on 8 November 1994,[416] which contains comprehensive provisions on arbitration in Hungary. Upon entering into effect, this Act repealed previous legislation contained in Chapter XXIV of the Act on Civil Procedure (Act No. III of 1952 [HUN] on Civil Procedure).[417]

509. In terms of the conditions of arbitrability, Hungary's arbitration legislation adopted the provisions of the UNCITRAL Model Law essentially unchanged. Under Section 7(2) of the Hungarian Civil Code[418] (Act No. IV of 1959 [HUN] on the Civil Code of the Republic of Hungary, as subsequently amended) and under the Arbitration Act [HUN], arbitration is permitted as an alternative to judicial proceedings for the resolution of civil disputes: **(i)** if at least one of the parties is a person engaged in economic activities as a profession (within the scope of his or her line of business) and the dispute is associated with these activities, **(ii)** if the parties can freely dispose of the subject matter of the proceedings, and **(iii)** the parties have entered into an arbitration clause. An arbitration agreement may be concluded even if the condition set out in (i) has not been met, provided that the law so permits.[419] Section 4 of the Arbitration Act [HUN] sets out those cases in which the jurisdiction

---

[416] The Arbitration Act [HUN] took effect on 13 December 1994. The English translation is available online from the website of the Court of Arbitration Attached to the Hungarian Chamber of Commerce and Industry at: http://www.mkik.hu/index.php?id=1409 [last access 21 December 2010].
[417] In the meantime, this Act was subject to several amendments. Major modifications were implemented especially in 1997 and 1999. See *Kengyel, M.* Die Revision im ungarischen Zivilprozeß. Zeitschrift für Zivilprozess, 1994, No. 2, pp. 191–192; *Kőrös, A.* Perújítás. In: *Petrik, F.* (ed.). Polgári eljárásjog. Kommentár a gyakorlat számára. Budapest: HVG-ORAC, 2006, 504/2; *Gáspárdy, L.* Quo Vadis Hungarian Civil Procedure Law? In: Studi di diritto processuale civile in onore di Giuseppe Tarzia, Milano: Giuffrè, 2005, p. 2673 et seq. et al.
[418] Section 7(2) of the Hungarian Civil Code (approximate translation, cit.): "(2) *Parties may resort to arbitration instead of litigation if at least one of them is professionally engaged in an economic activity* [business], *if the legal dispute is in connection with that activity, and if the parties are able to freely dispose of the subject of the proceeding.*"
[419]See Section 3 of the Arbitration Act [HUN].

of an arbitral tribunal is precluded (the absence of *objective arbitrability*, e.g. the subject matter of the dispute cannot be submitted to arbitration). These include matters of personal status, matters subject to administrative law, and proceedings concerning a payment order. In the assessment of whether an arbitration agreement applies to a dispute, the determining factor is the actual merits of the claim (*facticity*) rather than how the statement of claim is worded.[420]

510.   The above conditions **do not preclude the consumer from becoming a party to arbitration.**[421] The Arbitration Act [HUN] does not prescribe any special provisions for consumer protection. Hence, the general rule is that individuals (natural persons) must [only] have full legal capacity under the civil law rules in order to conclude an arbitration agreement.

511.   The relatively broad scope of the Arbitration Act [HUN] does not preclude a consumer from becoming a party to arbitration. However, the Arbitration Act [HUN] contains no specific provisions on consumer protection. Nevertheless, it is necessary to bear in mind that in this area Hungary [HUN], as an EU Member State, is obliged to reflect EU law and the case law of the ECJ. As a matter of principle, EU law leaves the issue of whether to permit the negotiation of arbitration agreements in consumer contracts up to the national law. Hungarian law, by not precluding this possibility, admits the conclusion of arbitration agreements in consumer contracts. However, it must reflect the principles of consumer protection arising from the relatively high standard of consumer protection in the EU (both under EU law and under the ECJ's case law). Therefore, courts ex officio examine (in proceedings on the annulment or on the recognition and enforcement of arbitral awards) whether an arbitration clause constitutes an unfair term in a consumer contract. This right cannot be contractually waived by consumers.

512.   It is also necessary to note that under certain circumstances, Hungarian practice also **views legal entities**, i.e. all professionals, **as consumers** (as do some other countries, although this does not stem from EU law[422]).[423]

---

[420] Decision of the Hungarian Supreme Court [HUN], Case No. 13. Gf. 40.483/2007/7 of 2008. Source: (Complex – A legal information system) No. EBH 2008.1789.

[421] Indeed, the *Directive* does not exclude it either. The same conclusion could be found in German case law which has analyzed these issues in great detail. See Judgment of the BGH [DEU], Case No. III ZR 256/03 of 13 January 2005, annotated in detail in this book (in the part concerning arbitration in consumer disputes in Germany [DEU]).

[422] See ECJ Judgment, Joined Cases C-541/99 and 542/99 of 22 November 2001 in *Cape Snc.* v. *Idealservice Srl.* and *Idealservice MN RE Sas* v. *OMAI Srl*. Cf. also *Tomášek, M.* Pokračování evropské diskuse o pojmu "spotřebitel." [Title in translation: The Continuing European Discussion over the Concept of "Consumer"]. Právní rozhledy – Evropské právo, 2003, No. 10, pp. 8–11 and *Palla, T.* 63811. Právnická osoba jako spotřebitel? Už ne. [Title in translation: Legal Person as a Consumer? Not Any More]. epravo.cz. 16 July 2010. Available online at: http://www.epravo.cz/top/clanky/pravnicka-osoba-jako-spotrebitel-uz-ne-63811.html [last access 26 August 2011].

Entrepreneurs, according to case law, should be regarded as consumers if they can be considered to be the final recipients (*final consumers*) of goods.[424]

513. In connection with consumer protection, it should be observed that Hungary [HUN] has introduced certain penalties for breaches of obligations to consumers committed by professionals. Thus, for example, in extreme cases failure by a travel agency to provide information to a customer in accordance with the *Directive* may, in Hungary [HUN] (as in Greece [GRE]), be penalized by the withdrawal of the agency's license.[425] This is true even though, as regards the method of penalization of an infringement of this kind, EU law essentially gives Member States a free hand in implementing these standards in their domestic law.

IV.14. [CHE] [SWITZERLAND]

514. Swiss law [CHE] ranks among the rather restrictive regimes. Consumer arbitration is regulated under the Federal Court Jurisdiction Act [CHE][426] and the Private International Law Act (IPRG [CHE]).[427] Generally, the arbitrability of Swiss domestic disputes is limited by the right of the parties to make dispositions with the subject of their disputes and the exclusive jurisdiction of courts. Employment disputes are, with certain exceptions, arbitrable as well. **However, consumer disputes may be decided only by the authorities whose jurisdiction is agreed in a particular case; prearbitration clauses in consumer disputes are not allowed.** Swiss laws do not allow arbitration clauses, but they do permit, for instance, the conclusion of arbitration agreements on disputes which have already arisen between a professional and a consumer (subject to statutory restrictions).[428]

---

[423] This approach has been adopted by certain countries on top of the requirements stipulated by EU law. This typically includes situations when the subject matter of the contract does not concern the person's regular business activity, when he or she does not have free opportunity to negotiate the terms, etc.

[424] Decision of the Hungarian Supreme Court [HUN] (dec.), Legf. Bír. Kfv., No. III. 37.675/2003 of 2004. Source: (Complex – A legal information system) No. BH 2004.1093. In the original Hungarian version, the Court concludes (cit.): Végül a Legfelsőbb Bíróság megjegyzi, hogy alaptalanul hivatkozott az alperes felülvizsgálati kérelmében az 191999/44/ES /EK irányelvre, mert az Fgytv. indokolása utal arra, hogy a fogyasztó fogalmának definíciója összhangban van az Európai Unió közösségi szintű joggyakorlatával. See also *Bělohlávek, A.* Rome Convention / Rome I Regulation. Commentary: New EU Conflict-of-Laws Rules for Contractual Obligations. Vol. I. Huntington (New York): JurisPublishing, 2010, marg. 06.142.

[425] *Selucká, M.* Ochrana spotřebitele v soukromém právu. [Title in translation: Consumer Protection in Private Law]. Prague: C. H. Beck, 2008.

[426] Federal Court Jurisdiction Act [CHE] of 24 March 2000, RS 472.

[427] The IPRG [CHE] only applies to relationships (disputes) with an international dimension.

[428] See *Favre-Bulle, X.* Arbitrage et Règlement alternative des litiges (ADR): une autre justice pour les consommateurs? In: *Théovenoz, L. et Reich, N.* (eds.). Droit de la consommation, Liber Amicorum Bernd Stauder, Genève: Schulthess, 2006, p. 97 et seq., here pp. 101–103.

IV.15. [ITA] [ITALY]

515.   Consumer protection in Italy is regulated under the Consumer Code [ITA].[429] Arbitration in Italy is regulated under the Code of Civil Procedure [ITA], namely Book Four, Part VIII.[430] These provisions do not distinguish between international and domestic arbitration. Article 806 of the Italian Code of Civil Procedure[431] contains only a negative definition of arbitrability in connection with disputes concerning intellectual property, competition, antitrust law, transfer of securities, and disputes among corporations and associations. Italian law does not, however, contain any special provision which would concern the arbitrability of consumer disputes. Consumer disputes are principally arbitrable. The Consumer Code stipulates that out-of-court dispute resolution may also be employed in relations between consumers and professionals. Nonetheless, it is only possible to use procedural methods which meet the principles stipulated in the *Recommendation*.[432] An agreement on the resolution of disputes before a different authority may be considered unfair to the consumer.[433] Article 139 of the Consumer Code stipulates that an association of consumers, together with other entities from the list administered by the Ministry of Productive Activities, may act in the interest of consumer protection. Furthermore, pursuant to Article 140 of the same Code, these entities may also file a class action, whereas individual consumers are endowed with no such right. They may also use mediation.[434]

---

[429] Available from the website of the European Consumer Centre Italy at: http://www.ecc-netitalia.it/inglese/Legislation/Legislative%20Decree%206%20September%202005%20no.206%20,%20 Consumer%20Code.pdf [last access 22 December 2011]. The concept of the Code is also substantially similar to the Czech Act [CZE] No. 634/1992 Coll., on Consumer Protection.

[430] In English available from the Kluwer Arbitration website at: http://www.kluwerarbitration.com/ document.aspx?id=ipn28151 [last access 22 December 2011].

[431] Code of Civil Procedure [ITA] (approximate translation, cit.): Article **806** – Arbitrability of Disputes – "*The parties may submit the disputes arising between them to arbitrators providing the disputes do not concern inalienable rights; this shall not apply if the law contains an explicit prohibition. * Disputes regulated under Section 409 [of the Code of Civil Procedure /ITA/] may be resolved by arbitrators only if permitted by the law, a collective agreement or a contract.*"

[432] Their list is available from the website of the Health and Consumers Directorate at: http://ec.europa.eu/consumers/redress_cons/ecc_italy_en.htm [last access 9 January 2012].

[433] It ought to be mentioned that a choice-of-court agreement vesting jurisdiction in a court other than the court which would have jurisdiction according to the consumer's residence (domicile) is invalid (see Article 33(2)(u)) of the Consumer Code.

[434] As concerns mediation in Italy, we must distinguish between "conciliazione" and "mediazione." Before the Mediation Act No. 28 of 4 March 2010, mediation was known as "conciliazione," because mediation (mediazione) had another traditional meaning connected with family law and agency. The 2010 Act introduced the term "mediazione" for mediation which quickly caught on and was also used in the official Italian translation of Directive 2008/52/EC on certain aspects of mediation in civil and commercial matters. Today, the word "mediazione" is employed in civil, commercial, corporate, financial, banking, insurance, family, and criminal disputes. It is also used for disputes relating to the environment and social security. Conversely, "conciliazione" is still used for intra-judicial,

IV.16. [LTU] [LITHUANIA]

516.   The basic source of the law on arbitration is the Code of Civil Procedure [LTU][435] which entered into force on 1 January 2003, and the Arbitration Act [LTU][436] which entered into force on 2 May 1996. These laws apply to all arbitrations conducted in Lithuania. The Lithuanian law on arbitration is based on the UNCITRAL Model Law, albeit with certain differences.[437]

517.   Article 11 of the Arbitration Act [LTU] stipulates that **consumer disputes are not arbitrable**, just like disputes arising from constitutional, employment, family and administrative relations; disputes concerning competition, patents, trademarks, service marks, and disputes relating to insolvency are not arbitrable either.

IV.17. [LVA] [LATVIA]

IV.17.1. Latvian arbitration laws

518.   Arbitration in Latvia is regulated under Part D of the Code of Civil Procedure [LVA][438] which does not contain any special provisions concerning consumer disputes. Paragraph 7 of Section 6(3) of the Consumer Rights Protection Act[439] stipulates that terms which exclude or limit the consumer's[440] rights to avail himself or herself of the protection provided by consumer protection institutions or courts and which stipulate compulsory arbitration for the consumer's dispute are considered unfair. Such terms are without effect. From the legal perspective, this ineffectiveness constitutes an irrefutable presumption. Nevertheless, it is possible to conclude that consumer arbitration is permitted under Latvian law providing the consumer may, apart from

---

employment and consumer disputes. *Bruni, A.* Mediation in Italy. Part. I, 2011, available online at: http://www.mediate.com/articles/BruniA1.cfm [last access 9 January 2012].

[435] In English available from the Kluwer Arbitration website at: http://www.kluwerarbitration.com/ document.aspx?id=KLI-KA-1020005-n [last access 22 December 2011].

[436] In English available from the Kluwer Arbitration website at: (http://www.kluwerarbitration.com/ document.aspx?id=KLI-KA-1020004-n) [last access 22 December 2011].

[437] For more details, see *Audzevicius, R.; Samulevicius, T. et Juozaitis, M.* Lithuania. In: *Wegen, G. et Wilske, S.* Arbitration 2011. Published as a part of the edition: Getting the Deal Through, London, 2011, p. 276 et seq.

[438] In English available from website of Kluwer Arbitration at: http://www.kluwerarbitration.com/ document.aspx?id=KLI-KA-201004007-n [last access 22 December 2011].

[439] In English available from the website of the Consumer Rights Protection Center at: http://www.ptac.gov.lv/page/271[last access 9 January 2012].

[440] The consumer is defined as a natural person who intends to purchase, does purchase, could purchase, or use goods which are by no means connected with his or her business or trade; see the judgment of the Latvian Supreme Court, Case No. SPC-35/2006, cited in: *Zukova, G. et Kacevska, I.* (2010): Latvia. In: *Mistelis, L. et Shore, L* .World Arbitration Reporter. Second Edition, Huntington (New York): JurisNet, 2010, pp. LAT 18-19.

arbitration, also go to court. Neither theory nor practice has yet answered the question of the validity of such arbitration clauses. Consequently, when petitioned to enforce an arbitral award in a consumer case, Latvian courts go so far as subjecting the award to a review in the merits or they refuse enforcement of the award.[441] If the contractual term allows both arbitration and litigation and if it is contained in a standard type contract, the courts are rather cautious when interpreting such terms. The reason is that these terms are *ex iure* considered contractual terms which have not been individually negotiated, i.e. contrary to the Consumer Rights Protection Act. According to a decision of the Latvian Supreme Court,[442] however, an arbitration clause in a consumer contract is valid if the consumer explicitly gives his or her consent with the clause or if he or she proposed the clause himself/herself. The burden of proof in such cases is imposed on the professional.[443] In principle then, Latvian courts have a *unique*[444] jurisdiction to hear and resolve consumer disputes.

IV.17.2. Case law - Judgment of the Latvian Constitutional Court, Case No. 2004-10-01 of 17 January 2005[445]

519. The case concerned a petition for a repeal of the first part of Section 132(3) and of Section 233(6) of the Code of Civil Procedure [LVA]. In terms of Article 9 of the Constitution [LVA], the Latvian Constitutional Court held that the provisions complied with the constitutional laws.

520. The Court assessed the admissibility of and the conditions for the conclusion of an arbitration agreement in consumer contracts. Following the case law of the ECtHR as well as the case law of the ECJ,[446] the Latvian Constitutional Court held that anyone may choose from standard market conditions and either accept or refuse the conclusion of

---

[441] *Zukova, G. et Kacevska, I.*: Latvia. In: Mistelis, L. et Shore, L. World Arbitration Reporter. Second Edition, Huntington (New York): JurisNet, 2010, pp. LAT 18-19.

[442] Decision of the Latvian Supreme Court, Case No. SPC-13/2007.

[443] For more information on the case law of the Supreme Court concerning arbitration clauses, see the compilation in Latvian issued by the Supreme Court and available from the website of the Latvian Supreme Court at: http://www.google.cz/url?sa=t&rct=j&q=spc-13%2F2007&source=web&cd=1&ved=0CB4QFjAA&url=http%3A%2F%2Fwww.at.gov.lv%2Ffiles%2Fdocs%2Fsummaries%2F2008%2Fapkopojums%2520par%2520skirejtiesam.doc&ei=jAgMT7fIMMni4QS73LnsDA&usg=AFQjCNFJYdnuuhpZayg2UtSCWKUHRNdutQ&cad=rja [last access 10 January 2012].

[444] The term "exclusive jurisdiction" has been deliberately avoided; the term used instead is intended to highlight the actual state of affairs rather than the exclusive jurisdiction prescribed by law.

[445] Judgment of the Latvian Constitutional Court, Case No. 2004-10-01 of 17 January 2005; available online at: http://www.satv.tiesa.gov.lv/upload/2004-10-01E.rtf [last access 11 July 2008].

[446] At that time in compliance with the ECJ ruling, Cases C-240/98 through 244/98 in *Océano Grupo Editorial SA v. Rocío Murciano Quintero*, published in: ECR [2000] I-4491. According to this decision of the ECJ, arbitration agreements contained in consumer contracts are principally allowed, and it is only necessary to assess the conditions attending the conclusion of the arbitration agreement (especially the part containing the arbitration clause) in terms of Article 3 of the *Directive*.

a contract and specific contractual terms. In other words, no one is forced to enter into a contract. *The invisible hand of the market* (as explicitly referred to by the Constitutional Court [LVA] in the reasons for the decision) influences the terms of the negotiated contracts. The market itself provides an opportunity to the parties (here the consumers) to decide whether to enter into the contract or not. Consequently, they must bear both the positive and the negative consequences of their decisions. If any market participant abuses his or her position with the aim of imposing his or her terms on other market participants which they would not accept if no such abuse occurred, it is necessary to seek protection exclusively in the mechanisms provided on the basis of laws against anti-competitive conduct. The Latvian Constitutional Court, fully in compliance with the case law of the ECtHR (especially in terms of the decision in *Suovaniemi v. Finland* [FIN] and other rulings), also addressed the issue of disqualifying an arbitrator for lack of impartiality.

IV.18. [MEX] [MEXICO]

521. One of the current trends in Mexican [MEX] legislation is that special provisions concerning arbitration are being inserted in a number of laws. Frequently, these laws have a connection with consumer protection, either fully or at least as regards their main objective. To wit these are: the Consumer Protection Act, the Financial Services Act, some civil codes,[447] as well as laws and rules regarding the provision of public and private health care. These laws are now beginning to explicitly support arbitration.[448]

IV.19. [NLD] [NETHERLANDS]

522. Arbitration is regulated under the Code of Civil Procedure [NLD][449] and applies to all arbitrations conducted in the Netherlands [NLD]. The Dutch arbitration law was inspired by the UNCITRAL Model Law, without, however, adopting it literally. The law provides that all disputes are arbitrable which have arisen or could arise in the future between the parties to a certain legal relationship, irrespective of whether the relationship is a contractual one or not. The Dutch Code of Civil Procedure does not contain any special rules regulating consumer disputes. Nonetheless, it is possible to use them as a basis for the

---

[447] Mexico [MEX] is specific for the fact that the civil law rules applicable in the individual territories are different.

[448] For information regarding this proposal, see *Castro Pereznieto, L. et Graham, J.* A recent ruling in Mexico raises serious and troubling questions about amiable composition. IBA Arbitration News, March 2011, pp. 117–118, here especially p. 117. Also available online at: http://www.bazilmcnulty.com/IBA_March_2011.pdf [last access 10 September 2011].

[449] In English available from the Kluwer Arbitration website at: http://www.kluwerarbitration.com/document.aspx?id=ipn26248 [last access 22 December 2011].

interpretation of arbitration clauses in consumer contracts. Part 6.5.3. BW [NLD] entitled "Standard Terms and Conditions" contains the so-called "*black list*" (Article 6:236 BW [NLD]) and the "*gray list*" of contractual terms. Whereas the contractual terms included in the "*black list*" **are always considered** unreasonably burdensome, terms included in the "*gray list*" **may, but need not, be considered** unreasonably burdensome. Unreasonably burdensome terms are voidable; the factors taken into consideration are primarily: the nature and content of the contract, the method whereby the standard terms and conditions were negotiated, the interest of both contracting parties obvious to both of them, and other circumstances of the case. Paragraph (n) in the "*black list*" stipulates that a term is always considered unreasonably burdensome if it provides for the settlement of a dispute other than by a court with jurisdiction pursuant to law or by one or more arbitrators, unless it allows the respondent to choose for a settlement of the dispute by a court with jurisdiction pursuant to law and this choice can be made within a period of at least one month after the professional has invoked the stipulation in writing.[450] Apart from regular ADR methods, disputes in the Netherlands [NLD] are also resolved with the use of the binding advice of a third party, a method frequently employed to resolve consumer disputes. The parties agree that they will consider the recommendation made by the third party binding. This advice then becomes part of the contractual obligation of the parties and failure to perform the obligation may subsequently result in a lawsuit (see Article 7:900 BW [NLD]).Thirty years ago, the Foundation for Dispute Committees for Consumer Cases was set up (*Stichting Geschillencommissie voor Consumentenzaken*, SGC),[451] focused on the expeditious, cheap, and simple resolution of disputes between professionals and consumers.[452]

---

[450] Available in English at: http://www.dutchcivillaw.com, specifically at: http://www.dutchcivillaw.com/civilcodebook066.htm) [last access 12 January 2012]. For information about the implementation of the *Directive* see, http://www.eu-consumer-law.org, especially the study by *Martin Ebers* at http://www.eu-consumer-law.org/consumerstudy_part2c_en.pdf [last access 11 January 2012]. See also *Jongbloed, A. W.* Access to Justice, Costs and Legal Aid. In: Electronic Journal of Comparative Law, Vol. 11.1 (May 2007), p. 18, para. 3.6, available online at: http://www.ejcl.org/111/art111-14.pdf [last access 10 January 2012].

[451] http://www.degeschillencommissie.nl/english. Note: The whole website is in Dutch, only one page is in English.

[452] At present, the Foundation has 33 commissions active in the following sectors: banking, child care, real estate, public welfare enterprises, postal services, travel, telecommunications, cleaners, and hospitals. Each commission is composed of 3 members – the Chairman (a lawyer), a member appointed by consumers (*Consumentenbond*), and a member appointed by an organization advocating the interests of the professional. All commissions are recognized by the government, and they are organized according to impartial principles. The average length of proceedings is, according to the data available, five months.

IV.20.   [NOR] [NORWAY]

IV.20.1.   Arbitration

523.   Norwegian arbitration law (*lex arbitri*) is incorporated in the Arbitration Act (*Voldgiftsloven*)[453] of 1 May 2005. The law stipulates that a pre-dispute arbitration agreement is not binding on the consumer. The consumer may in such case challenge the jurisdiction of the arbitral tribunal and, in doing so, is not bound by the time limits prescribed for such defense by the law.[454] Consequently, arbitration clauses in consumer disputes are possible, but not binding on the consumer.[455] The consumer must be informed in advance about the meaning of arbitration, the arbitral award, and the possibility of review.

524.   Arbitration agreements negotiated with a consumer must be concluded in a separate document and signed by both parties.[456] Norwegian law even explicitly allows the conclusion of the agreement by electronic means, providing the parties use a reliable method to secure the authenticity and safe recording of the terms of the parties' agreement.[457]

IV.20.2.   Mediation

525.   The out-of-court settlement of consumer disputes in Norway [NOR] has been entrusted to the Consumer Disputes Committee.[458] The nine members of the Committee (the Chairman as a neutral member plus four representatives of consumers and four representatives of professionals) are appointed by the Minister of Children and Family Affairs (on behalf of the King). The scope of the Committee's jurisdiction covers disputes over the supply of goods, services provided in connection with the purchase of goods, craftsmen's services, and disputes over the right to cancel a contract in the case of distance selling

---

[453] Act No. 25 of 14 May 2004 – Arbitration Act (*Lov om voldgift*) promulgated in the Collection of Laws in 2004, Book 6, on 14 May 2004. This Act was subsequently amended by Act No. 90 of 17 June 2005 and Act No. 127 of 21 December 2007. The current law has been in effect since 1 January 2008.
[454] Arbitration Act [NOR], Section 11(2).
Arbitration Act [NOR], (approximate translation, cit.): Section 18(3): *"Jurisdictional challenge must be raised on or before the submission of the statement of defense in the merits; this shall not apply to consumer disputes in which the arbitration clause is not binding on the consumer (Section 11(1)). However, the arbitral tribunal may allow that the jurisdictional challenge be heard later if it is principally not the fault of the party that the plea was not made earlier. The respective provision (Section 11(3)) explicitly stipulates that the right to raise the challenge does not expire if the party actively participated in the appointment of the arbitral panel without making the challenge. The extinguishment of the right (in terms of the relevant general provision) is principally connected with the first submission in the merits."*
[455] Arbitration Act [NOR], Section 11(1).
[456] Arbitration Act [NOR], Section 11(2).
[457] Arbitration Act [NOR], Section 11(2).
[458] FTU-Forbrukertvistutvalget, Postboks 45906 Nydalen, N-0404 Oslo, Norway. Further information is available at: http://www.forbrukertvistutvalget.no/ [last access 14 August 2011].

and sales outside ordinary sales outlets. The value of the dispute is irrelevant. Proceedings before the Committee are not arbitration; it is a type of ADR analogous to mediation.[459] The Committee's decision constitutes an enforceable title unless any of the parties files a lawsuit in court within four weeks.

IV.21. [POL] [POLAND]

IV.21.1. Tradition of consumer protection in Poland

526.   As early as 1939, the Polish Code of Obligations[460] already contained rules providing for protection against unfair contractual terms. The concept of the Code was, however, different from the requirements articulated by the *Directive*. The Code stipulated that the Ministerial Commission was authorized to define, in the form of directives, certain types of [contractual] terms – a normative standard focused, as necessary, on consumer protection. But the Ministerial Commission issued only one such directive. Since 1990 a party arguing that a particular contractual term is grossly unfair and constitutes an advantage benefiting the person who has used the term has had the right to go to court and demand that the court hold the [contractual] term invalid *inter partes*. The *Directive* was implemented into Polish law by the Act on the Protection of Competition and Consumers [POL] of 16 February 2007[461] whereby the Polish Civil Code (K.c. [POL]) was amended. However, the definition of *"consumer"* incorporated in the 2000 Act does not fully correspond to the relevant definition in the *Directive*. The reason is that the definition of consumer also includes any person that enters into a contractual obligation which is only indirectly related to a person's business and professional activities. This definition certainly cannot be considered contrary to the *Directive*. We can rather conclude that its material or subjective scope is broader than in the *Directive*. Therefore, the concept of the respective provisions can be considered largely analogous to the German provisions (under the BGB [DEU] as modified by the 2002 amendments) which apply to unfair terms in contracts and contractual terms and conditions, or to contracts in general, irrespective of whether the contracts were concluded with a consumer or not. As a result of the implementation of the *Directive*, Polish procedural law also stipulates that consumer associations have the right to file petitions for review (annulment) of certain contractual terms.

---

[459] More information about the proceedings is available at: http://baseswiki.org/en/Consumer_Disputes_Committee,_Norway [last access 14 August 2011].
[460] Act No. 379 of 30 June 1939. Ustawa [POL], nr. 379 z dnia 30. czerwca 1939 r. Dz. U. [POL], nr. 58, poz. 379, pp. 908-916.
[461] Ustawa z dnia 16 lutego 2007 r., o ochronie konkurencji i konsumentów (Dz.U. [POL], 2007 r. Nr. 50 poz. 331).

527.   Consumer protection in Poland is entrusted to consumer associations and the Polish ombudsman for the protection of consumer rights (*Rzecznik konsumentów*[POL])[462]; these issues also fall within the competence of the Chairman of the Office for the Protection of Competition and Consumers (*Urząd Ochrony Konkurencji i Konsumentów*[POL])[463] and other authorities pursuant to the above-mentioned Polish law.[464] If the consumer court with special jurisdiction in Warsaw prohibits any particular contractual term, the decision is published in the Economic and Legal Bulletin and entered into a special register (*Rejestr klauzul niedozwolonych*)[465] administered by the Chairman of the Office for the Protection of Competition and Consumers.   Once the decision is published and entered into the register, it has effects *erga omnes*. The register is publicly accessible and presently contains approximately 950 contractual terms.[466]

IV.21.2. Conditions for consumer arbitration

528.   Consumer arbitration is widely used in Poland. However, a consumer dispute is arbitrable only if the arbitration agreement (arbitration clause) was individually negotiated with the consumer. Otherwise the agreement, or clause, as the case may be, is invalid. This is how EU law influences Polish law and legal practice. According to the applicable case law of the ECJ, arbitration in consumer disputes is not prohibited (depending on the relevant national concept in the individual Member States). It is necessary to make sure, however, that the party had an opportunity to negotiate the terms of the arbitration agreement; there are also other requirements which must be met (it must not contain an unfair provision in consumer contracts).

---

[462] The local level is represented by regional and municipal ombudsmen (presently approximately 360 ombudsmen). In Warsaw see website at: http://www.konsument.um.warszawa.pl/ [last access 9 August 2011].

[463] The website of the office is available at: http://www.uokik.gov.pl/.

[464] Consumer protection tasks pursuant to the Act on the Protection of Competition and Consumers [POL] Chairman of the Office (Prezes Urzedu; Section 29 et seq. of the Act; authority with jurisdiction pursuant to Article 4(1) of Regulation 2006/2004/EC), Local Self-Government (Samorząd terytorialny; Sections 38 and 39 of the Act), Regional Council of Ombudsmen for the Protection of Consumer Rights (Krajowa Rada Rzeczników Konsumentów; Section 44 of the Act) and Organization for the Protection of Consumer Rights (Organizacje konsumenckie; Section 45 of the Act).

[465] The register is available at: http://www.uokik.gov.pl/rejestr_klauzul_niedozwolonych2.php [last access 9 August 2011].

[466] *Bělohlávek, A. J.* Rome Convention / Rome I Regulation: New EU Conflict-of-Laws Rules for Contractual Obligations. Vol I, marg. 06.75 and marg. 06.76 (JurisPublishing, Huntington, NY 2010); *Stefanicki, R.* Ochrona konsumenta w swietle ustawy o szczególnych warunkach sprzedazy konsumenkiej (Wolters Kluwer Polska, Warsaw, 2006); *Wegrzynovwski, L.* Niedozwolone postanowienia umowne jako srodek ochrony slabszej strony umowy obligacyjne. Warsaw: C. H. Beck, 2006.

529. According to the case law of the Polish Supreme Court (SN [POL]), a breach of the fundamental principles of consumer protection also constitutes grounds for a refusal of the recognition and enforcement of a foreign arbitral award pursuant to the *New York Convention*. This is an important decision (from the perspective of consumer protection) of 22 February 2007[467] which must be annotated in a broader context. The decision demonstrates to what extent Polish law requires the observance of the fundamental imperatives of EU law, fundamental constitutional principles, and to what extent it also applies to the procedure pursuant to the *New York Convention*. The Polish Supreme Court held:

530. If any proceedings governed by Section 1162(2)[468] of the K.p.c. [POL] were initiated after the effective date of the Amendment, Section 2[469] of the K.p.c. [POL] allows such procedure, and the entire basis of the submission regarding the arbitration clause, which is a combination of a substantive and a procedural contract, does not prevent the application of intertemporal provisions contained in the procedural contract. The constitutional order of priority in the application of laws (Article 91(1) of the Polish Constitution[470]) calls for an examination of the formal requirements primarily pursuant to the *New York Convention*, Article II(1) and (2), which articulate the requirement of the written form in very broad terms; hence, the provision also includes an exchange of letters or telegrams.

531. Application of the arbitration clause was at the discretion of the professional – the respondent company – without any reference to the

---

[467] Decision of the SN [POL], Case No. No IV CSK 200/06 of 22 February 2007. The decision is also available online at: (i) http://dokumenty.e-prawnik.pl/orzecznictwo/sad-najwyzszy/izba-celna/1ivcsk06200.html [last access 9 August 2011], (ii) http://static.e-prawnik.pl/pdf/orzeczenia/1_IV_CSK_06_200.pdf [last access 9 August 2011], (iii) http://arbitraz.laszczuk.pl/orzecznictwo/234,postanowienie_sadu_najwyzszego_z_dnia_22_lutego_2007_r_iv_csk_200_06.html [last access 9 August 2011].
[468] K.p.c. [POL] (approximate translation, cit.): Section 1162 – "(1) *The arbitration agreement must be executed in writing.* (2) *The requirement as to the form of the arbitration clause is also satisfied in the case of a clause included in any written communication or representation exchanged between the parties or made through means of remote communication allowing a record to be made of the contents thereof. Any reference in a contract made to the document containing the provision on submitting disputes for resolution by an arbitration court shall satisfy the requirement as to the form of the arbitration clause, provided that the contract is made in writing and the reference is made in such manner that the clause is incorporated into the contract.*"
[469] K.p.c. [POL] (approximate translation, cit.): Section 2 *"Arbitral proceedings and court proceedings regarding the effectiveness and enforceability of an arbitral award or regarding a challenge to the arbitral award initiated prior to effective date [of the Act] proceed in line with the previous provisions."*
[470] Constitution [POL] (approximate translation, cit.): Article 91(1) – *"A ratified international agreement published in the Journal of Laws of the Republic of Poland forms a part of the national legal order and is indirectly applied, unless the application thereof is subject to issuing an act."*

rules regulating the decision-making of the AAA [USA].[471] The contract also anticipated the application of foreign law, which represented substantially different legal conditions for the consumer than those prescribed by the European legal framework. The contract also represented additional problems for the consumer as concerns his participation in the proceedings, specifically with regard to the distance he would have to travel to the place of the proceedings, as well as the costs and the generally recognized problems in obtaining an entry visa to the United States. These are all circumstances which must be considered as constituting an unfair term within the meaning of the *Directive*. An arbitration clause which constitutes an unfair (unjust) contractual term for the respondent and constitutes circumstances violating Article 6(2) of the *Directive* justifies the conclusion that the case must not be subject to compulsory arbitration.

532.   The interpretation of Article II(2) et seq. of the *New York Convention* does not allow the conclusion, without the arbitral award being set aside, that the arbitration agreement does not meet the requirement of a proper written form. There is also no reason to presume that the terms of an agreement displayed on a website are not equivalent to the terms presented in an agreement concluded in a written form. This especially holds true for the application of the *New York Convention*, which only requires the written form and does not contain any specific rules regarding issues such as the moment of conclusion of the contract (for instance, between parties present at the same time), the place, and the manner of acceptance of the *"online"* offer.

533.   Section 1162(2) of the K.p.c. [POL] stipulates that the requirements of the written form of a submission filed in arbitral proceedings (for instance, the statement of claim) are met if the arbitration clause was contained in an exchange of letters and in messages exchanged by means of distance communication which enable their contents to be recorded, or in a written agreement negotiated in the form of a separate document containing an agreement on submitting the dispute to arbitration. Visiting a website with a draft contract addressed to an unspecified group of potential addressees and confirming online one's will to enter into the contract does not constitute an expression which would enable recording a particular expression of will with respect to a specific individualized contractual relationship. In the given case, a computer "confirmation" of a contract – as opposed to a standard electronic signature which at least safeguards a minimum degree of credibility – does not constitute a basis for the identification or reproduction of the contents of such an expression of will. The

---

[471] Cf. also *Drahozal, Chr. R. et Zyontz, S.* An Empirical Study of AAA Consumer Arbitration. Ohio St. J. on Disp. Resol., 2010, Vol. 25, p. 843 et seq.

requirement would be met if a specific expression of will were at least sent by an individual electronic mail (e-mail) which would enable identification of the sender.

IV.22 [PRT] [PORTUGAL]

534. Provisions on arbitration in Portuguese law are primarily incorporated in Act [PRT] No. 31/86, on Arbitration[472]; the Act is not based on the UNCITRAL Model Law. Portuguese law does not prescribe any special rules for consumer disputes. All disputes are arbitrable if they concern rights with which the parties may freely dispose (as opposed to inalienable rights), unless they are subject to the exclusive jurisdiction of courts or compulsory arbitration. Consumer disputes are arbitrable under Portuguese law, and there are six regional arbitral centers in the country.[473] Apart from these centers which can be used for any and all sectors, there are also specialized centers, for instance for disputes concerning contracts for utilities, etc.[474]

IV.23 [RUS] [RUSSIA]

535. Russian arbitration laws distinguish between domestic and international arbitration. International arbitration is regulated under the International Arbitration Act of 1993 [RUS][475] and domestic arbitration under the Federal Act on Arbitral Tribunals in the Russian Federation [RUS] of 2002. As a rule, all civil disputes are arbitrable under Russian law, unless the law stipulates otherwise.[476] The law does not specifically provide for consumer disputes, nor does it contain any prohibition against submitting such disputes to arbitration. However, Russian practice has no experience with the resolution of consumer disputes in arbitration. Moreover, these courts have repeatedly ruled that arbitration clauses in consumer disputes breach the consumer's right to a choice of forum.[477]

---

[472] In English available from the Kluwer Arbitration website at: http://www.kluwerarbitration.com/ document.aspx?id=ipn26684 [last access 22 December 2011].

[473] For example: Centro de Arbitragem de Conflitos de Consumo de Lisboa, Centro de Arbitragem de conflitos de Consumo do distriro de Coimbra ad.

[474] *Commission:* Consumer Redress – Portugal. Available online at: http://ec.europa.eu, and specifically at: http://ec.europa.eu/consumers/redress_cons/docs/MS_fiches_Portugal.pdf [last access 11 January 2012].

[475] In English available at: http://www.kluwerarbitration.com/document.aspx?id=KLI-KA-1128007-n [last access 22 December 2011].

[476] *Marisin, E. et Khodykin, R.* Russian Federation. In: *Mistelis, L. et Shore, L.* World Arbitration Reporter. Huntington (NY): Juris, p. Rus-35 et seq.

[477] *Koroloev, S.* Towards the Non-arbitrability of Consumer Disputes in Ukraine. Available online from the website of the CIS Arbitration Forum, 2010, at: http://cisarbitration.com/2011/ 03/06/towards-non-arbitrability-of-consumer-disputes-in-ukraine/#more-426 [last access 11 January 2012].

IV.24. [SVK] [SLOVAKIA]

IV.24.1. Sources and principles of consumer protection

536. Similar to the Czech Republic [CZE], Slovak law [SVK] did not contain any private law rules on the protection of consumers against unfair terms until the implementation of the *Directive*. The Slovak Civil Code (CC [SVK]) was amended in 2004, and the *Directive* was almost literally adopted into it. The amendment of the CC [SVK] was followed by an amendment to the Consumer Protection Act, which was necessitated by the required harmonization of definitions and the incorporation of the status of consumer protection organizations. The Slovak provisions are special as concerns the **definition of consumer – it also includes legal persons.** Cooperation between governmental authorities and non-governmental consumer protection organizations has attained a very high level of effectiveness.

IV.24.2. Consumer arbitration

537. Arbitration in Slovakia is regulated under Act No. 244/2002 Coll., on Arbitration (ArbAct [SVK]).[478] Consumer disputes in Slovakia are not arbitrable. Consumer protection requires that consumer disputes are subject to the exclusive jurisdiction of courts.

538. In 2010 the Slovak Parliament (*Slovenská národná rada* (Slovak National Council) [SVK]) debated a landmark Amendment to the ArbAct [SVK].[479] However, the amendment has not yet entered into force, because the President of the Slovak Republic has refused to sign the amending bill. From its inception, the new law has been received with distrust; the main objections have focused on its excessively rigorous regulation of arbitral proceedings. Critics have argued that, considering the limitations to be newly introduced by the amendment, it could have the result of depriving this method of alternative dispute resolution of any attractiveness. The amendment required stricter supervision over

---

[478] The ArbAct [SVK] was passed on 3 April 2002 and took effect on 1 July 2002; it has subsequently been amended in 2005 (Act No. 521/2005 Coll. [SVK]) and in 2009 (Act No. 71/2009 Coll. [SVK]). The ArbAct [SVK] is primarily based on the UNCITRAL Model Law, with which it shares and from which it adopts a great number of elementary principles. Nevertheless, it is not an Act which would formally adopt the UNCITRAL Model Law. Similar to arbitration law in the Czech Republic [CZE], Slovak law (ArbAct [SVK]) is substantially compatible with the UNCITRAL Model Law, but it is not an implementation of the UNCITRAL Model Law. In 2010 the Slovak Parliament passed a very important Amendment to the ArbAct [SVK] which was heavily criticized, and the President of Slovakia refused to sign it.
[479] The amendment was passed on 9 March 2010, and it was supposed to take effect on 1 July 2010. See also *Bělohlávek, A. et Profeldová, T.* Amendment to the Slovak Arbitration Act of 9 March 2010 Has Not Been Signed by the President of the Slovak Republic. In: *Bělohlávek, A. et Rozehnalová, N.* (eds.) CYArb – Czech (& Central European) Yearbook of Arbitration, Huntington (New York): JurisNet, 2011, Vol. I, pp. 445-448.

permanent arbitral institutions, especially with respect to arbitral tribunals and arbitral proceedings, the subject matter of which would be disputes involving **consumer contracts and employment disputes.** The control powers of the Ministry of Justice of the Slovak Republic, as the authority supervising *permanent arbitral institutions,* were to be enhanced (including the power to impose sanctions). The fundamental importance of the *[planned]* amendment was to consist in a new method of founding *permanent arbitral institutions,* namely on the basis of law.[480] Presently, Slovakia is one of the countries with a fairly free regime for founding arbitral tribunals as *permanent arbitral institutions* (similar to the Russian Federation [RUS] as well as some other countries in Central and Eastern Europe). The amendment has clearly been inspired by the laws applicable in the *Czech Republic* [CZE], where *permanent arbitral institutions* may only be founded on the basis of law.[481] Some opinions have maintained that this control function of the state, together with the effort to introduce and enforce certain minimum standards to be observed by all arbitrators, would in future enable transferring the resolution of disputes arising from certain types of obligations/legal relationships to arbitration, with an explicitly stipulated jurisdiction of the *permanent arbitral institutions* over these disputes. Under such circumstances, there would probably be no doubt that jurisdiction over particular disputes is delegated by the state to arbitrators, which implies a jurisdictional approach to arbitration.

539.   The amendment intended to introduce the liability of the founder of an arbitral tribunal for the observance of any and all obligations imposed on the arbitral tribunal. The amendment was to explicitly introduce the power to file complaints against steps taken by the arbitral tribunal. The complaint was to be directed: against the violation of the right to have one's case heard without undue delays, against the breach of the principles of dignity of the arbitral proceedings by persons participating in the performance of the arbitral tribunal's duties, or against other shortcomings in the arbitral tribunal's activities relating to cases before the tribunal or to the steps taken by the arbitrators, the Board of the arbitral tribunal, members of the Board of the arbitral tribunal, or other persons participating in the activities of the arbitral tribunal. The handling of the complaints and the requests for a review of the procedure, whereby the complaint directed against the proceedings of the arbitral tribunal was resolved, were to be explicitly subjected to the reasonable application of the provisions of a special law which is

---

[480] See Section 12(1) of the Slovak Arbitration Act which was newly supposed to finish with the sentence (cit.:) *"A permanent arbitral institution can also be founded by statute and attached to a legal person which, for the purposes of this Act, is considered the founder."*
[481] See Section 13 of the ArbAct [CZE].

otherwise applicable to court proceedings.[482] At the request of the *Ministry of Justice of the Slovak Republic,* the founder of the arbitral tribunal would be obliged to present the Ministry with information regarding the founder's activities and the activities of the *permanent arbitral institution* established by the founder and its arbitrators. Arbitral tribunals would also be obliged to submit annual reports regarding the handling of consumer disputes to the *Ministry of Justice of the Slovak Republic.*[483]

540.   **Special provisions were to be introduced with respect to the resolution of *consumer disputes.*** The amendment planned to introduce special powers for *consumer protection associations* which would be newly authorized to petition the competent court for a court order requiring the founder of the arbitral tribunal to ensure that any *permanent arbitral institution* set up by the founder abstains from the resolution of consumer disputes. Such a court order would be issued if the arbitral tribunals repeatedly violated consumer rights and the consumers thereby sustained losses exceeding the total amount claimed in the proceedings. In such cases, the consumer protection association would be entitled to file an application for a preliminary injunction with the same negatory effect as concerns the competence of the arbitral tribunal over consumer disputes. The court would especially consider whether the arbitral tribunal had already been reprimanded for breaching the rights of the parties to a consumer dispute by a court or the supervisory authority and whether the founder of the arbitral tribunal could have known about it. Apart from that, the amendment was supposed to introduce special requirements for the form and contents of the arbitration clauses in consumer contracts (no longer an arbitration clause, but only an agreement incorporated in a separate document). Considering the discussion of the nature of arbitration in *Slovakia* [SVK], it is especially necessary to emphasize that the draft

---

[482] Sections 63 through 70 of Act [SVK] No. 757/2004 Coll., on Courts and Amending and Supplementing Other Acts, as subsequently amended, and Act No. 9/2010 Coll. [SVK], on Complaints. The reference to the Courts Act, or rather its analogous application, clearly indicates that the legislator interprets arbitration in the jurisdictional sense. This is further supported by the power to request that the complaint be reviewed by the Ministry of Justice, if the complaint concerns proceedings regarding a consumer contract and the complainant is not satisfied with the way his or her complaint was handled by the arbitral tribunal / or the founder of the arbitral tribunal.

[483] See Section 15b(2) of the ArbAct [SVK] in terms of the 2010 Amendment which reads as follows (cit.): *"Based on the documents of the arbitral tribunal founded by the Founder, the Founder is obliged to draw up and submit to the Ministry a report on the activities of the permanent arbitral institution with respect to the resolution of consumer disputes in arbitration for the given calendar year; the report shall be submitted on or before 31 March of the following calendar year; the report must also include information about complaints which have been filed complaining about the procedures of the arbitral tribunal, how they were handled and resolved, and if they were justified or not. The Founder is also obliged to submit the dispute by the same deadline to other public authorities if required to do so under special laws."*

amendment planned to reserve the resolution of consumer disputes exclusively for *permanent arbitral institutions* which would obtain, and maintain valid throughout the proceedings over the dispute, a license to resolve consumer disputes from the *Ministry of Justice of the Slovak Republic*. It is also necessary to point out that the granting of the license was to be subject to and contingent on the fulfillment of rather stringent requirements. For instance, the founder would be obliged to maintain a deposit of 200,000 EUR securing the performance of the financial obligations connected with the founder's liability for the activities of the *permanent arbitral institution*. The amendment intended to impose specific requirements concerning the qualification of arbitrators dealing with consumer disputes (eligibility criteria stipulated directly by law, not requirements for arbitrators which would be agreed by the parties to the dispute according to their interests) and significantly limit the freedom of the parties as concerns an agreement on the case management of their dispute – the amendment stipulated, without exceptions, that the rules for arbitration in consumer disputes must never depart from the rules regulating civil procedure (CCP [SVK]), litigation in trial court, to the detriment of the consumer. Similar restrictive intervention of the state was to be introduced with respect to the resolution of employment disputes. The amendment has never entered into force and, after the Slovak president's veto, has never been debated by the Slovak legislator again.

IV.24.3. Case law – Resolution of the Regional Court in Prešov [SVK], Case No. 17CoE/99/2010 of 15 February 2011

(a) Conclusions of the court

541. The Regional Court in Prešov [SVK], upholding the decision of the trial court (District Court in Kežmarok [SVK]) **arrived, inter alia, at the following conclusions:**[484]

▶ An arbitration clause which is not the result of a consumer's active negotiation of the terms of the contract and which does not provide the consumer with any choice as to whether to accept or decline the clause is unacceptable and consequently contra bonos mores.

▶ If the arbitral award was delivered on the basis of **an unacceptable arbitration clause, the court may decline to give its consent to the enforcement (execution) of the award or to terminate currently pending enforcement proceedings (execution).**

---

[484] Adopted from the annotation: *Horváth, E.* Neprijateľná rozhodcovská doložka [Title in translation: Unacceptable Arbitration Clause], najpravo.sk, 24 March 2011. Available online at: http://www.najpravo.sk/judikatura/obcianske-pravo/spotrebitelske-zmluvy/neprijatelna-rozhodcovska-dolozka.html?print=1 [last access 2 January 2012].

► **The absolute commercial transaction** which is obligatorily subject to the provisions of the Commercial Code can also be classified as a consumer contract (a contract concluded by a consumer) which is **subject to special consumer protection.** Such contracts are also subject to the special consumer protection regime in terms of the *Directive.*

► The consumer is no doubt the weaker contracting party, whether due to his or her lack of the necessary information or due to his or her weaker negotiating position.[485]

► The protection of consumers against unacceptable contractual terms entails absolute nullity, and there is no justification for such terms. In this regard, the European Union promoted the status of consumer protection up to the level of *national public policy* rules.[486]

► A situation in which the consumer can either accept the contract or refuse it as a whole offers no choice to the consumer, here in the sense of choosing arbitration over litigation in case of a dispute, or vice versa.

► If the obligor breached his or her obligations the obligee has the right to enforce his or her protection. Such enforcement, however, must be exercised using legitimate means of protection, which do not include procedures based on unacceptable terms in consumer contracts.

► **Acknowledgment of debt** by the obligor entails only substantive law effects and does not validate unacceptable terms in a contract (in the present case, an agreement on the method of enforcing claims under an unacceptable arbitration clause).

---

[485] The Regional Court in Prešov [SVK], as the court of appeals, invoked in this connection the ECJ's judgment in *Mostaza Claro*, para. (25); the ECJ's ruling is annotated in great detail elsewhere in this book. The Court also invoked Article 3 of the *Directive.*

[486] The Court invoked ECJ Resolution, Case C-76/10 of 16 November 2010 (*Pohotovosť*), para. (50) which is annotated in great detail elsewhere in this book. The relevant paragraph (50) reads as follows (cit.): "*Considering the nature and the importance of public interest which is the basis of the protection afforded by Directive 93/13 to consumers, Article 6 of the Directive must be considered a provision equal to national rules with the status of mandatory rules under the respective national legal system (the cited judgment in Asturcom Telecommunicaciones, para. 52).*"
We cannot agree with the conclusion regarding *public policy* – see the commentary to the decision in the final part of this annotation.
The consequence consisting in absolute invalidity is not required under EU law; nor is it clearly prescribed by the ECJ's case law. This is often a somewhat simplified interpretation, sometimes used by the case law of the courts, primarily *lower courts*. The ECJ's interpretation in a number of its decisions (see the detailed analysis above) stipulates only one clear requirement, namely that the courts address the nature of the contract ex officio (of their own motion). This is indeed an obligation connected with potential absolute invalidity, but it in no way anticipates that this type of invalidity must be the outcome of the respective case. On the contrary, the ECJ's case law invites the courts to thoroughly analyze all circumstances of the contract, both the circumstances attending the conclusion of the contract and the subsequent events relating to the conduct of the parties with respect to performance under the contract and the proceedings regarding claims made under the contract. See the judgment of the ECJ in the *Pannon GSM* case, analyzed in detail in Chapter III.9 and referred to elsewhere in this book.

▶ The characteristic of a judgment as final and conclusive is its essential quality, because it is associated with the important principle of legal certainty resulting from a final and conclusive decision in the merits (*res judicata*). However, in certain cases, the law itself explicitly provides that a final and conclusive judgment can be subject to review (for instance, by way of exceptional remedial measures). Such legally approved exceptions to the rule include the court's power to dismiss a petition for enforcement or to terminate currently pending enforcement proceedings pursuant to special laws (pursuant to the Arbitration Act[487]).

(b) Factual and legal findings and reasons for the trial court's decision

542. The present case concerned a claim arising from a consumer credit provided by means of a bank credit card. The District Court in Kežmarok [SVK] (as the trial court) dismissed the executor's application for an authorization to enforce the arbitral award. The reason was that the respective contract contained an unacceptable (unfair) term, an arbitration clause in a standard form contract.[488] The court invoked the basic characteristic features of consumer contracts.[489] The court highlighted that one of the characteristic features of a consumer contract is that the contract is drafted in advance and the consumer has no opportunity to negotiate the terms of the agreement or make any changes to the offer. This was the case here. The court also invoked the ArbAct [SVK][490] which stipulates that the court shall terminate the enforcement proceedings (execution) at the obligor's motion or of its own motion: **(i)** for any of the reasons stipulated by special laws, or **(ii)** if the arbitral award suffers from defects in terms of Section 40(a) and (b)

---

[487] Section 45 of the ArbAct [SVK]. The provision will be quoted below in the footnotes relating to the annotation of this decision.

[488] In the present case, the arbitration clause was incorporated in the bank's business terms and conditions (cit.): "*Any potential dispute between the bank and the client arising from or in connection with the legal relations between the bank and the client, which the parties fail to solve by their mutual agreement, will be submitted for resolution to the Permanent Arbitration Court of the Banking Association established in Bratislava ("Arbitration Court").*" This arbitration clause was concluded on 17 June 2004.

[489] Section 52 et seq. of the CC [SVK].

[490] Section 45 of the ArbAct [SVK] (cit.): "*(1) The court with jurisdiction over enforcement or execution under special laws shall terminate the enforcement or execution proceedings at the request of the respondent against whom the enforcement of the arbitral award or the enforcement of the judgment or the execution were initiated (a) out of the grounds stipulated in a special law, (b) if the arbitral award suffers from a defect specified in Section 40(a) and (b), or (c) if the arbitral award orders a party to the arbitration to provide performance which is objectively impossible, unlawful or contra bonos mores. (2) The court with jurisdiction over enforcement or execution shall terminate the enforcement of the arbitral award or the execution of its own motion (sua sponte) if the court discovers that the arbitration suffered from defects specified in Subsection 1(b) or (c). (3) The court decisions under Subsections 1 and 2 can be appealed.*"

of the ArbAct [SVK],[491] or (**iii**) if the arbitral award orders impossible or unlawful performance or performance contra bonos mores. The court also invoked the indicative list of unacceptable contractual terms in the CC [SVK],[492] which also includes arbitration clauses that order the

---

[491] ArbAct [SVK] (cit.): Part Seven – Annulment of Arbitral Awards – Section 40 – Grounds for Filing a Petition with the Court – *"(1) A party to arbitration may file a petition with the competent court demanding that a domestic arbitral award be set aside only if (a) the arbitral award was delivered in a matter which cannot be submitted to arbitration (a non-arbitrable matter) (Section 1(3)), (b) the arbitral award was delivered in a matter which had already been decided by a final and conclusive court decision delivered in litigation or by a final and conclusive award of an arbitral tribunal delivered in different arbitral proceedings, (c) one of the parties to the arbitral proceedings challenges the validity of the arbitration agreement, (d) the arbitral award deals with a matter which was not covered by the arbitration agreement and the party to the arbitral proceedings raised such an objection in the arbitration, (e) the party to the arbitration who must have a statutory representative did not have such a representative or a party to the arbitration was represented by an unauthorized person and the person's acts were not subsequently approved, (f) the arbitral award was delivered by an arbitrator who was disqualified by a decision rendered under Section 9 for lack of impartiality, or the party to the arbitration could not have the arbitrator disqualified before the arbitral award was issued without the party's fault, (g) the principle of equality of the parties to arbitration was violated (Section 17), (h) there are reasons justifying a petition for a trial de novo under special laws or (i) the arbitral award was affected by a criminal offence committed by the arbitrator(s), party(ies) to the arbitration or expert(s) which the perpetrator was found guilty of by a final and conclusive judgment, (j) the arbitration violated generally binding laws and regulations on the protection of consumer rights. (2) If a party to the arbitration files a petition with the competent court, the contested arbitral award remains final and conclusive. The court called upon to adjudicate on the petition may suspend the enforceability of the arbitral award at the request of a party."*
[492] Section 53(4) of the CC [SVK]. CC [SVK] (cit.): Section 53 – *"(1) Consumer contracts must not contain terms which cause a significant imbalance in the rights and obligations of the contracting parties to the detriment of the consumer ("unfair term"). This shall not apply as concerns contractual terms which relate to the main subject matter of the performance and to the adequacy of the price, in so far as these contractual terms are in plain intelligible language or if these unfair terms were individually negotiated. (2) A term shall not be regarded as individually negotiated even if the consumer had an opportunity to get acquainted with the term before signing the contract, unless the consumer was able to influence the substance of the term. (3) Unless the supplier proves otherwise, contractual terms agreed between the supplier and the consumer shall not be regarded as individually negotiated. (4) The following terms in a consumer contract shall especially be considered as unfair, i.e. terms (a) requiring the consumer to perform with which the consumer did not have the opportunity to get acquainted before the conclusion of the contract, (b) giving the supplier the power to transfer his or her rights and obligations under the contract to a different supplier without the consumer's consent, where the transfer would jeopardize the enforceability or reduce the guarantees for the consumer, (c) excluding or limiting the legal liability of the supplier in the event of the death of the consumer or personal injury to the latter resulting from an act or omission of that supplier, (d) excluding or limiting the consumer's rights when invoking the supplier's liability for defects or liability for damage, (e) permitting the supplier to retain performance provided by the consumer even in case the latter does not conclude or cancels the contract with the supplier, (f) permitting the supplier to cancel the contract without any contractual or statutory reason where the same facility is not granted to the consumer, (g) enabling the supplier to terminate a contract of indeterminate duration without reasonable notice except where there are serious grounds for doing so, (h) obliging the consumer to fulfill all his or her obligations where the supplier does not perform his or hers, (i) enabling the supplier to alter the terms of the contract unilaterally without a valid reason agreed upon in the contract, (j) providing for the price of goods or services to be determined at the time of delivery or allowing the supplier to increase the price of his or her goods or services without in both cases giving the consumer the right to cancel the contract if the final price is too high in relation to the price agreed when the contract was concluded,*

(k) *requiring any consumer who fails to fulfill his or her obligation to pay a disproportionately high sum as a penalty for defaulting on the consumer's obligation, (l) restricting the consumer's access to evidence or imposing on him or her a burden of proof which, according to applicable law, should lie with another party to the contract, (m) inappropriately excluding or limiting the power of the consumer to enforce his or her rights vis-à-vis the supplier in the event of total or partial non-performance by the supplier, including the consumer's right to offset a debt owed to the supplier against any claim which the consumer may have against the supplier, (n) automatically extending the validity of a contract of fixed duration after the expiration of the period for which the contract was concluded while giving the consumer an unreasonably short period to express his or her consent with the prolongation of the contract, (o) giving the supplier the right to determine whether the goods or services supplied are in conformity with the contract, or giving him or her the exclusive right to interpret any term of the contract, (p) limiting the supplier's liability if the contract was concluded by his or her agents or requiring that a contract concluded by the supplier's agent meet a particular formality, (r) requiring the consumer to take disputes exclusively to arbitration, subject to the arbitration clause agreed by the parties. (5) Unfair terms in consumer contracts are invalid. (6) If the subject matter of the consumer contract is the provision of finances, the remuneration must not significantly exceed a remuneration commonly required on the financial market for consumer credits in similar cases. The assessment of similarity between the cases shall primarily include the consideration of the consumer's financial situation, the manner and the extent to which his or her obligation is secured, the volume of the finances provided by the supplier, and the due date. (7) Securing an obligation arising from a consumer contract by a security transfer of rights to real property is not allowed in consumer contracts. (8) If the supplier provided performance to the consumer and the consumer had not ordered the performance, the consumer is not obliged to return or retain the performance; the supplier shall not have any other claims against the consumer either. Unrequested performance also includes any repeated performance provided to the consumer under a contract concluded by means of distant communication if the consumer had not explicitly requested such performance. Unless the supplier proves the opposite, repeated performance shall always be considered unrequested. (9) In the case of performance under a consumer contract which is supposed to be provided in installments, the supplier may exercise his or her right under Section 565 only after three months following the consumer's default on the payment of an installment and providing the supplier warned the consumer of the exercise of said right with no less than a 15-day notice. (10) The unfairness of contractual terms shall be assessed taking into account the nature of the goods or services for which the contract was concluded and all the circumstances attending the conclusion of the contract, at the time of conclusion of the contract, and to all the other terms of the contract or of another contract on which it is dependent. (11) The terms of a consumer contract of indeterminate duration according to which the supplier of financial services under a special law reserves the right to terminate the contract unilaterally without any notice period where there is a serious objective reason shall not be considered an unfair term under Subsection (4)(g) providing there is a serious objective reason which was not caused by the supplier, which the supplier could not foresee or avert and which prevents the supplier from performing under the contract, and on condition the supplier agreed in the contract that the supplier would notify the consumer of the termination of the contract and the reason for the termination without undue delay and in writing. (12) Subsections (4)(g) and (i) on unfair terms shall not apply to a consumer contract the subject matter of which is (a) a transaction in transferable securities, financial instruments, and other products or services where the price is linked to fluctuations in rates and indices on the regulated market or to a market rate that the supplier does not control, (b) a purchase or sale of foreign currency, traveler's cheques, or international money orders denominated in foreign currency. (13) The following terms shall not be considered as unfair under Subsection (4)(i), i.e. terms according to which (a) a supplier of financial services under special laws reserves the right to alter the rate of interest or the amount of other charges for financial services under special laws payable by the consumer or the supplier without notice where there is a serious objective reason, provided that the supplier undertakes to inform the consumer without undue delay and in writing of the alteration and of the consumer's right to terminate the consumer contract and provided that the latter is free to dissolve the contract immediately and free of charge, (b) a supplier of financial services under special laws reserves the right to unilaterally alter the conditions of the consumer*

consumer to solve his or her disputes with the professional exclusively via arbitration.[493]

543. The trial court held that the arbitration clause prevented an arbitral award rendered on the basis thereof from becoming an enforceable decision, because it prevented the consumer from choosing either arbitration or litigation. The arbitration clause was, in the present case, not the result of any active negotiation of the terms of the contract in which the consumer would participate; in other words, the consumer had no choice when accepting the contractual terms. The consumer could only "take it or leave it" as a whole. The trial court therefore terminated the proceedings,[494] because the arbitration clause was found unacceptable and consequently contra bonos mores.

contract for an indeterminate duration provided that the supplier is obliged to inform the consumer without undue delay and in writing of the alteration and of the consumer's right to terminate the contract and provided that the latter is free to dissolve the contract immediately and free of charge. (14) Subsection (4)(j) on unfair terms shall not apply to a consumer contract the subject matter of which is (a) a transaction in transferable securities, financial instruments, and other products or services where the price is linked to fluctuations in rates and indices on the regulated market or to a market rate that the supplier does not control, (b) a purchase or sale of foreign currency, traveler's cheques, or international money orders denominated in foreign currency, (c) a price-indexation clause, where explicitly permitted under special laws and provided that the method by which prices vary is explicitly described in the clause."

[493] It is basically a literal transcript of the list of contractual terms specified in the Annex to the *Directive*. See Section 53(4)(r) of the CC [SVK]; these provisions were incorporated in the Slovak Civil Code by Act [SVK] No. 568/2007 Coll., effective date 1 January 2008 (cf. the analysis of the new substantive rules regulating consumer protection in the Czech Republic [CZE] in connection with the New Civil Code – NCC [CZE]). The trial court also invoked the conclusions of the joint session of the Department for Civil Law and the Department for Commercial Law of the Regional Court in Prešov [SVK] held on 27 September 2010; the judgment analyzed in this annotation quotes the following passage from the opinion adopted by the joint session: "*A contractual term in a standard form contract concluded after 31 December 2007 or in general business terms and conditions incorporated in such a contract which was not individually negotiated by the consumer and which requires the consumer to resolve his or her disputes with the supplier exclusively in arbitration prevents the arbitral award issued on the basis of the term from becoming an enforceable decision which would give the supplier the right to demand authorization for an executor to conduct the execution. The term qualifies as an unfair contractual term even if it gives the consumer the right to choose between arbitration and litigation, providing that the clause also allows that if the arbitration is initiated by the supplier, the consumer will be obliged to submit to arbitration or will be obliged to file a petition with the court in case the consumer wishes to prevent arbitration. There are no reasons preventing the court from adopting an analogous approach if the contract was concluded before 1 January 2008.*" The reasons justifying the opinion further read as follows (also adopted from the annotation of the trial court's decision): "*The high rate of abuse and the manifest preference for efficiency over an objective decision-making process fully justify the increasingly intensive focus on arbitral awards as enforceable decisions. [According to our jurisprudence ([...])] "[f]rom the consumer's perspective it is irrelevant whether the resolution of his or her disputes in arbitration is imposed on him or her by a standard contractual clause or by the supplier's conduct. The consumer ought to be protected from both. The power of the supplier to impose his or her will in the contractual relationship was the reason why the entire mechanism of consumer protection against standard form contracts was created.*"

[494] With reference to Section 39 and Section 53(5) of the CC [SVK] and to Section 45(1)(c) and (2) of the ArbAct [SVK].

(c) Decision and arguments of the court of appeals

544. The Regional Court in Prešov, as the court of appeals, upheld the conclusions reached by the trial court. The obligee's appeal was therefore dismissed. The court of appeals had no doubt that the contract in the present case was a standard adhesion contract, i.e. a standard form contract being repeatedly concluded by the professional. The same applies to the contractual terms as well as to the fact that the credit facility was provided (as a financial service) in connection with the creditor's business. The court of appeals thereby rejected the obligee's arguments – the obligee claimed in its appeal that the contract was not a consumer contract, because the special provisions regulating *"consumer contracts"* do not apply to *absolute business transactions* (in the present case, a credit contract), which are subject to the provisions of the Commercial Code. These arguments were rejected by the court of appeals with reference to the *Directive*. The court also analyzed the consumer protection rules applicable before 1 January 2008 with respect to standard form contracts (pre-formulated standard contracts);[495] these rules prohibited contractual terms *"which establish a manifest disproportion between the rights and obligations of the contracting parties, to the detriment of the consumer."* Consequently, it is not necessary to resort to the indirect effect of the *Directive* in order to conclude that the obligee, as the professional, was at the time of conclusion of the contract explicitly prohibited from contracting such terms in his or her standard form contracts which would establish a significant imbalance between the parties' rights and obligations, to the detriment of the consumer.[496] The court of appeals concluded that an arbitration clause requiring the consumer to submit to arbitration as the only option was unacceptable.[497]

545. The obligee's argument invoking the Act on Banks was not successful either. The Act on Banks stipulates that the bank is obliged to instruct the client (and be able to prove it did so) about the consequences of entering into the proposed arbitration agreement and give him or her the **right of choice**.[498] The court concluded, however, that the bank had offered no such choice to the consumer.

---

[495] The case primarily concerned the application of Section 23a of Act No. 634/1992 Coll., on Consumer Protection, as applicable on the day the contract was concluded (the standard form contract is *a contract which is supposed to be concluded in more cases if it is usual that the consumer has no substantial control over the terms of the contract*).

[496] See Section 53 et seq. of the CC [SVK]. This provision is quoted in a footnote elsewhere in this annotation of the decision of the Slovak court.

[497] The court invoked, similarly to the trial court, the conclusions of the joint session of the Department for Civil Law and the Department for Commercial Law of the Regional Court in Prešov [SVK] held on 27 September 2010, just like the conclusions of the session were referred to by the trial court (quoted in a footnote above).

[498] Section 93b(1) of Act [SVK] No. 483/2001 Coll., on Banks. The court extensively elaborated on the obligations binding on the professional under the Slovak Act on Banks as the court responded to the

546. The court of appeals also rejected the claimant's (the professional's) arguments regarding the importance of acknowledgment of debt by the consumer. The court correctly held that the instrument of acknowledgment of debt is regulated under substantive law which has effects with respect to the expiration of time periods, legal fiction regarding the existence of the debt, etc. Such acknowledgment, however, has no influence on the validity (or subsequent validation, as the case may be) of unacceptable terms in a consumer contract which are consequently, in the court's opinion, null and void.

(d) Notes on the judgment

547. The Slovak court's decision is not surprising. Besides, it is clear that Slovakia [SVK] belongs to those countries which have not only implemented, but have also applied the *Directive* rather strictly. Nonetheless, the judgment is in certain respects controversial. First of all, we need to point out that **the Slovak court classifies consumer protection in the European Union (under EU law) as a component of** *public policy.* However, according to the analysis in chapter II, consumer protection is a **component of a [qualified]** *public interest.* **Both concepts (*public policy* v. *public interest*) must be principally distinguished,** also from the perspective of the protection associated therewith. These **two different categories** are often used interchangeably even in the case law of courts; but the effects, and especially the effects, of both categories are significantly different. Besides, it appears that the Slovak court adopted a rather undiscriminating approach and rejected the arbitration clause without meticulously analyzing the facts of the case, especially the circumstances attending the conclusion of the contract.[499] This does not appear to comply with current European practice either, including the ECJ's case law and important opinions prevalent in most European countries. Slovakia [SVK] has apparently been undergoing certain developments (together with some other countries, especially EU Member States)

---

claimant's (professional's) arguments. In the end, however, the court ruled against the claimant (professional) by stating that the claimant had failed to meet the conditions prescribed under the Act on Banks. The quoted provision of the Slovak Act on Banks stipulates the obligation to submit the offer of the contract (in the present case, the offer of the arbitration agreement) in advance. In a later amendment to the law, this particular provision of the Slovak Act was amended to clearly stipulate that the bank must let its client *choose.* The court ruled that the claimant had *offered no choice* in the present case.

[499] It is important to mention that only the source cited in the opening part of this annotation which summarizes the respective court decision was available. The full text of the decision of the trial court and, especially, of the court of appeals could not be obtained. It needs to be emphasized (see also the footnote above) that the Slovak court apparently did address the circumstances attending the conclusion of the contract to some extent, as evidenced by its conclusions regarding the performance (in the present case, *failure to perform*) of the professional's obligations under the Slovak Act on Banks vis-à-vis the client (consumer).

which most other countries have already put behind them, i.e. moving from a strict rejection of arbitration clauses in consumer contracts in the past to a very cautious and careful examination of the facts of the case and all circumstances attending the conclusion of the contract,[500] which can be the only decisive factor in determining whether a particular contractual term is unacceptable or not and consequently in determining the legal effects of such a factual situation.

548.   Nonetheless, the sources available do not offer any detailed information regarding the course of the arbitral proceedings in the present case, and especially as to whether the opportunity to request annulment of the arbitral award was or wasn't available to the consumer and used. While the decision does mention that the consumer *did not plead* invalidity of the arbitration clause during the arbitration itself, it does not, however, indicate what opportunity the consumer had to raise such an objection and whether, and to what extent, the consumer was or wasn't an active participant in the arbitral proceedings. This significantly affects the applicability of the ECJ's legal opinion voiced in *Asturcom*, as well as in *Océano Grupo*, which the Slovak court invokes, both cases of which are annotated in greater detail elsewhere in this book. The Slovak courts (neither the trial court nor the court of appeals) do not address this issue at all, or do so only to an insignificant extent (based on the available annotation), and do not therefore answer the question of **what opportunity the consumer had to raise his or her objections (if any) in the course of and immediately after the arbitration.** The court based its arguments on the *absolute invalidity* of an unacceptable term in a consumer contract. But as explained elsewhere in this book (see the detailed analysis of the ECJ's case law), EU interpretation practice does not necessarily impose the requirement of absolute invalidity, especially not *a priori* in connection with arbitration agreements. On the contrary, EU law leaves the particular consequences of the concept adopted by the individual Member States at their discretion. At the same time, however, case law highlights the necessity of an individual assessment of all circumstances of the contract, the conclusion thereof, as well as of the conduct of the parties at the conclusion of the contract and in the exercise of their claims under the contract. Case law is also based on the concept of an informed consumer. The Slovak decision, just like many of the decisions adopted, for instance, by Czech courts [CZE], invokes its own (national) substantive law and the concept of the absolute invalidity of unfair terms in consumer contracts. "*In the same breath,*" however, it invokes the *Directive* and the effects of the *Directive*. In that connection, many of the decisions of the national (domestic) courts fail to adhere to the EU interpretation which would also allow an interpretation in favor

---

[500] See especially the excursus into the law of Germany [DEU] which appears to have progressed most of all, in the European context, but also into the law of France [FRA], United Kingdom [GBR], etc.

of *voidability*. This would be depending on the opportunity which the **informed consumer** had in the course of and immediately after the arbitral proceedings to raise his or her objections and the extent to which the consumer actually availed himself or herself of that opportunity (if at all). Thus there may be certain doubts as to whether, and to what extent, the Slovak court actually addressed these issues in the present case.

IV.25.   [SWE] [SWEDEN]

III.25.1. Sources and principles of consumer protection

549.   In 1971 Sweden [SWE] adopted the Act on Contractual Terms in Consumer Relationships which mostly contained commercial law rules. The Act authorized the **consumer ombudsman** to conduct discussions with consumer organizations and to prohibit the use of unjustified terms and conditions. The ombudsman is authorized to adopt measures prohibiting the use of particular contractual terms which were assessed as unjustified. Such cases are handled by the consumer ombudsman, the Swedish Consumer Agency, and the Commercial Court as the only authorities authorized to adopt the final decision. Together with the accession of Sweden to the EU, the 1971 Contractual Terms Act was replaced with Act [SWE] of 15 December 1994 (the Obligations Act) which only regulates relations between professionals and consumers. The new Swedish Obligations Act features two differences from the laws of other countries. **First**, it takes into account the facts of the case at the moment of conclusion, or before the conclusion of the contract; circumstances which occurred after the conclusion are considered only if it is more favorable for the consumer. **Second**, the review of unjustified contractual terms is limited. As concerns unfair terms which were not individually agreed, the consumer has the right to demand that the rest of the contract remain unamended, i.e. that the court refrain from reviewing the other terms.

III.25.2. Consumer arbitration

550.   Arbitration in Sweden is regulated under the Arbitration Act [SWE] of 1999[501] which adopted some of the provisions of the UNCITRAL Model Law. The Act stipulates that a dispute is arbitrable if the parties have the right to negotiate a settlement over the dispute. Section 6 of the Arbitration Act [SWE] further specifies the conditions of the arbitrability of consumer disputes. The provision **prohibits invoking pre-dispute arbitration clauses** if the dispute concerns goods, services, or any other performance provided for personal use. Nonetheless, there

---

[501] In English available from the Kluwer Arbitration website at: (http://www.kluwerarbitration.com/document.aspx?id=ipn22198) [last access 22 December 2011].

are several **exceptions** to the rule: **(i)** this rule shall not apply in the case of a lease relationship where the parties have agreed on the jurisdiction of a special tribunal for such relationships (regional rent tribunal or regional tenancies tribunal) and the Real Estate Act [SWE] does not stipulate otherwise; **(ii)** the case concerns a dispute between the insurer and the policyholder which arose from insurance concluded on the basis of a group contract and was negotiated by the representatives of the group, and **(iii)** this rule shall neither apply if its application would be contrary to the international commitments of Sweden.

IV.26. [USA] [UNITED STATES OF AMERICA]

IV.26.1. Support for consumer arbitration

551.   Arbitration in the United States, at the federal level, is regulated under the Federal Arbitration Act (FAA [USA]).[502] According to the FAA, agreements to arbitrate (whether arbitration clauses or ex ante arbitration agreements) are valid, irrevocable, and enforceable. The English legal system has long been rather cautious in its approach to arbitration (much longer than in the U.S.), which may be attributed to the necessity of securing a uniform legal system around common law. The rather negative approach to arbitration adopted by the courts in England [GBR-ENG] changed only as late as 1996, with the adoption of the *Arbitration Act 1996* ("AA" [GBR-ENG]), which was passed at the time when consumer protection was in the forefront of interest. Conversely, the FAA [USA], which was supposed to reverse the unfriendly approach to arbitration inherited from English law came into existence long before anybody even started to think of special consumer protection rules.[503] Consequently, the FAA [USA] contains no special rules applicable to consumer disputes, as opposed to a number of more recent national arbitration laws. Nonetheless, the U.S. Supreme Court consistently interprets the absence of any special provisions applicable to consumer disputes as a confirmation that the FAA applies to consumer disputes. In the *Allied-Bruce Terminix Cos. v. Dobson*[504] case, the U.S. Supreme Court held[505] that "[*w*]*hen enacting the FAA [USA], the*

---

[502] FAA [USA] – 9 U.S.C. § 1 through 16 (2006); Congress [USA] passed the law in 1925.

[503] See *Drahozal, C. et Friel, R. A.* A Comparative View of Consumer Arbitration. Arbitration, 2005, Vol. 2, p. 137.

[504] Decision of the Supreme Court [USA], Case No. 93-1001 of 18 January 1995 (*Allied Bruce Terminix Companies, Inc. et Terminix International Company, Petitioners* v. *G. Michael Dobson et al.*), in: 513 U.S. 265 (1995). Available online at: http://www.law.cornell.edu/supct/html/93-1001.ZO.html [last access 7 August 2011]. For a detailed annotation, see below in the "U.S. case law" section.

[505] It was an opportunity to change the standard introduced by a decision of the U.S. Supreme Court [USA] in *Southland Corporation* v. *Keating* (465 U.S. 1 (1984). Conversely, however, the Supreme Court of the United States upheld this decision and ruled that the FAA [USA] prevailed over any special provisions adopted by the individual states of the union [USA].

Congress had the needs of consumers, as well as [all] others, in mind."[506] This trend in federal case law was further augmented in the following decision of 2006 in *Buckeye Check Cashing, Inc.* v. *Cardegna,*[507] in which the Court explicitly invoked the separability of the arbitration clause (arbitration agreement) from the main contract in consumer relations.

552.   Arbitration clauses are extensively used in consumer contracts in the U.S. They can be found in contracts which individuals (consumers) enter into on a daily basis, i.e. when providing for their basic needs. For instance, arbitration clauses are commonly used in insurance contracts (especially for disputes between the insured and the insurer, i.e. *first-party insurance claims*) and in contracts between a bank and its clients; arbitration clauses can be found in basically every contract with a pest control company,[508] which is, naturally, a service regularly required by many households, as well as in connection with medical and healthcare services,[509] etc.[510] These developments have introduced numerous arbitration clauses into consumer disputes since the early 1990s, culminating in the late 1990s into the first decade of this century. The AAA [USA], which resolves a great number of consumer disputes, has drawn up guidelines for consumer disputes, the *Consumer Due Process Protocol* (AAA [USA]).[511]

---

[506] See *Drahozal, C. et Friel, R. A.* A Comparative View of Consumer Arbitration. Arbitration, 2005, Vol. 2, p. 134.

[507] 126S.Ct. 1204, 163 L.Ed. 2d 1038 (2006), 546 U.S. 440 (2006). Hence, the validity of the consumer contract and the consequences of its potential invalidity can be assessed by the arbitrators in compliance with the arbitration clause contained in the consumer contract. It confirms that the generally recognized principle of separability of the arbitration agreement from the main contract also applies to consumer relations.
See *MacHarg, J. P. et Bates, A. (Jr.)* Non-Signatories and International Arbitration: Understanding the Paradox. In: *Alibekova, A. et Campbell, D.* (eds.) Comparative Law Yearbook of International Business. KLI, 2007, pp. 3–22, here especially p. 6. *Sheppard, A.* The Moth, the Light, and the United States Severability Doctrine. JIA, 2006, Vol. 23, p. 479 et seq., here especially p. 482; *Samuel,* [...] Separability and the United States Supreme Court Decision in *Buckeye* v. *Cardegna.* JIA, 2006, Vol. 22, p. 477 et seq., *Barnes, R. L.* "Prima Paint" Pushed Compulsory Arbitration under the "Erie" Train. Bepress Legal Repository, The Berkeley Electronic Press, 2006, pp. 3–4, available online at: http://law.bepress.com/cgi/viewcontent.cgi?article=9522&context=expresso&sei-redir=1#search=%22 Buckeye%20Check%20Cashing%2C%20Inc.%20vs%20Cardegna%22 [last access 11 August 2011] et al.

[508] See the following decisions:
> *Allied-Bruce Terminex Co., Inc.* v. *Kaplan* (a 1984 decision), 465 U.S. 1 (1984);
> *Terminex Int'l Co.* v. *Stabbs* (a 1996 decision), 930 S.W.2d 345 (Ark. 1996).

[509] See the following decisions:
> *Sosa* v. *Paulos* (Utah, a 1996 decision), 924 P.2d 357;
> *Engalla* v. *Permanente Medical Group* (California, a 1997 decision), 938 P.2d 903;
> *Buraczynski* v. *Eyring* (Tennessee, a 1996 decision), 919 S.W.2d 314.

[510] Cf. *Huber, S. K. et Trachte-Huber, E. W.* Top ten developments in arbitration in the 1990s. JDI. Available online at: http://findarticles.com/p/articles/mi_qa3923/is_200011/ai_n8955348/pg_2/ ?tag=mantle_skin;content [last access 14 August 2011]. The authors provide the same examples.

[511] Statement of Principles of the National Consumer Disputes Advisory Committee. See *Huber, S. K. et Sheppard, B. H. (Jr.)* (eds.) AAA Yearbook on Arbitration & the Law. 23rd Vol., Huntington (New York): AAA /University of Houston – Law Center/ JurisNet, 2011 (special annex) et al.

553. However, the U.S. courts have already ruled before that arbitration clauses incorporated in contracts of adhesion in the form of a reference to the general contractual terms and conditions **could be invalid in a particular case** if the proceedings (arbitration) entailed **unreasonably high costs** and thereby discouraged the consumer from enforcing his or her rights.[512] The assessment of the validity of the arbitration agreement and its acceptability for the consumer is subject to the application of the *costs test*. This potential defense against an arbitration clause is, however, open to the consumer only with respect to clauses contained in the contracts of adhesion, without any power of modifying the contract.[513] Nonetheless, basically all of the relevant rulings emphasize the necessity of an individual assessment. Let us analyze, for instance, the 1998 decision of the Supreme Court of the State of New York [USA], as the court of appeals, in ***Brower v. Gateway***.[514] The arbitration clause in the consumer contract vested jurisdiction in the ICC Court. The value of the dispute was 4,000 USD (plus the costs of the proceedings). The opening administrative fee alone, payable together with the submission of the statement of claim with the ICC Court and non-refundable fees, amounted to 2,000 USD.[515] The Court found such conditions unreasonable and held, inter alia, that reasonableness must also be assessed in connection with the value of the dispute.[516] The Court in this

---

[512] See the following decisions:
- Supreme Court [USA] in *Green Tree Financial Corp.* v. *Randolph*, 531 U.S. 79 (2000). However, the claimant did not prove in that case that he had incurred any such (unreasonable) costs.
- Court of Appeals of the District of Columbia [USA] in *Cole* v. *Burns International Security Services*, 105 F.3d 1465 (D.C. Cir. 1997). Although, this case concerned an employment dispute. The Court, however, only transferred the costs of the dispute to the employer.
- Court of Appeal of California [USA] in *Gutierrez* v. *Autowest*, 2003 Cal. App. LEXIS 1817 (Ct. App. 2003). The Court admitted the possibility of pleading invalidity of the arbitration clause if the costs of the exercise of the consumer's right (commencement of proceedings) were unreasonable for the consumer.

Similar conclusions (unreasonably high costs as the grounds for pleading invalidity of the arbitration clause) were reached by the courts in the following disputes:
- US Court of Appeal, Ninth Circuit in *Ting* v. *AT&T*, 3190 F.3d 1126, p. 1150 (9th Cir. Cal. 2003);
- *Ingle* v. *Circuit City Stores*, 328 F3d 1165 (especially 1175–1176; 9th Cir. 2003);
- *Szetela* v. *Discover Bank*, 118 cal. Rptr. 2d 862 (see especially 867-68x Ct. App. 2002).

All the above decisions are also mentioned, together with an interesting overview and a comparison with international practice, in *Kaufmann-Kohler, G.* Online Dispute Resolution and Its Significance for International Commercial Arbitration. In: Liber Amicorum in honour of Robert Brinner, Paris: ICC Publishing, 2005, Publication 693, p. 446.

[513] Take-it or leave-it contracts.

[514] Decision of the New York State Supreme Court in *Brower* v. *Gateway* 2000, Inc., 676 N.Y.S. 2d 569, 1998, N.Y. App. Div.

[515] The entry fee currently amounts to 5,000 USD.

[516] Cf. *Mc Laughlin, J. T.* Arbitrability: Current Trend in the United States. Arb. Int., 1996, Vol. 12, p. 123 et seq. or *Alle-Murphy, L.* Are Compulsory Arbitration Clauses in Consumer Contracts Enforceable?: A Contractual Analysis. Temple Law Review, 2002, Vol. 75, p. 125 et seq.; *Zheng, S. Tang* Electronic Consumer Contracts in the Conflict of Laws. Oxford / Portland (Oregon): Hard Publishing, 2009, p. 155 et al.

case also took into account the distance between the consumer's residence and the place of proceedings.[517]

554. A similar approach must also be applied to the assessment of other aspects of such a contract and arbitration clauses contained in contractual terms and conditions. Factors taken into consideration in a particular case include, for instance, the potential significance of public access to court proceedings, as opposed to principally confidential arbitration, etc. In *Trujillo v. Apple Computer*[518] the Court held the arbitration clause inapplicable (ineffective), because the consumer did not have the opportunity to read the agreement incorporated in the cellular phone contract before the conclusion thereof. Probably the most frequent issue in American case law is the extent of the permissible limitation of the consumer in his or her access to *class actions.*[519]

555. Potential *unconscionability* is assessed according to the general principles of contract law, not according to special provisions on consumer protection (with certain exceptions). The courts take into account the bargaining position of the contracting parties.[520] Courts in

---

[517] In the ECJ's preliminary reference decisions, the distance from the place of the proceedings was taken into consideration in the following cases (inter alia):
➢ ECJ Judgment, Case C-40/08 of 6 October 2009 in *Asturcom* (following court proceedings in [ESP]) and
➢ ECJ Judgment, Case C-243/08 of 4 June 2009 in *Pannon GSM* (following court proceedings in [HUN]).
Both of the above-mentioned decisions are annotated in detail in the Chapter on the ECJ's case law.
The distance between the consumer's residence and the place of proceedings in the transcontinental dimension were also considered by the Polish Supreme Court (SN [POL]) – see the Decision of the SN [POL], Case No. No IV CSK 200/06 of 22 February 2007, annotated in the excursus into Polish law.
[518] Judgment of the U. S. District Court for the Northern District of Illinois Eastern Division, Case No. 07 C 4946 of 18 April 2008 (in *Jose Trujillo et al.* v. *Apple Computer, Inc. et AT&T Mobility, LLC*), 578 Supp 2d 979; the judgment is available online at: http://law.justia.com/cases/federal/district-courts/illinois/ilndce/1%3A2007cv04946/212324/93 [last access 27 August 2011]. See also *Zheng, S. Tang* Electronic Consumer Contracts in the Conflict of Laws. Oxford / Portland (Oregon): Hard Publishing, 2009, pp. 155–156.
[519] Cf. *Hörnle, J.* Legal Controls on the Use of Arbitration Clauses in B2C E-Commerce Contracts. Masaryk University Journal of Law and Technology, p. 34.
[520] See the decisions in the following cases:
➢ Judgment of the U.S. Court of Appeals, Second Circuit, Case No. 01-7870, 01-7872 and 01-7860 of 1 October 2002 (in *Christopher Specht, John Gibson, Michael Fagan, Sean Kelly, Mark Gruber, Sherry Weindorf et al.* v. *Netscape Communications Corporation et America Online, Inc.*), 306 F 3d 17 (2d Cir 2002); the judgment is available online at: http://ftp.resource.org/courts.gov/c/F3/306/306.F3d.17.01-7860.01-7872.01-7870.html [last access 27 August 2011]; cf. *Dratler, J. (Jr.)* Licensing of Intellectual Property, Law Journal Press, 1994, § 1.06[1], p. I–50 et al.
➢ Judgment of the U. S. District Court for the Northern District of Illinois Eastern Division, Case No. 07 C 4946 of 18 April 2008 (in *Jose Trujillo et al.* v. *Apple Computer, Inc. et AT&T Mobility, LLC*), 578 Supp 2d 979; the judgment is available online at: http://law.justia.com/cases/federal/district-courts/illinois/ilndce/1%3A2007cv04946/212324/93 [last access 27 August 2011].
➢ *McKee* v. *AT&T*, 164 Wash 2d 372.

certain U.S. states, especially in California,[521] Alabama, and others, have in many cases attempted to apply a restrictive approach and have held arbitration clauses invalid. As the important annotated rulings below shall demonstrate, attempts at the application of a special approach, outside the general principles of the interpretation of contracts, have been repeatedly overruled by the federal United States Supreme Court, which has long favored the priority of the Federal Arbitration Act (FAA [USA]); the Court has therefore always referred to the necessity of applying general evaluation criteria. It has to be emphasized that **only a substantial breach** of the fundamental principles of contract law and an abuse of the position of the stronger party render the agreement *unconscionable*.[522]

556. The courts analyze the **actual process of negotiating the contract** in great detail. Consequently, they usually reject a plea of ineffectiveness of an arbitration clause if the consumer had the opportunity to read the contractual terms and conditions prior to signing[523] but still failed to do so.[524]

➤ Cf. *Zheng, S. Tang* Electronic Consumer Contracts in the Conflict of Laws. Oxford / Portland (Oregon): Hard Publishing, 2009, p. 156.

[521] Cf. the decision of the California Supreme Court in *Ting* v. *AT&T*, 319 F3d 1126 (9th CirCal. 2003) and other decisions which will be cited or annotated below.

[522] See the decision of the Supreme Court of the United States in *Iberia Credit Bureau* v. *Cingular Wireless LLC, Sprint Spectrum Company, Centennial Wireless*; 379 F3d 159, paras. (167) and (168). The Court also held that the principles of contract law were substantially breached by the fact that the stronger party had the opportunity to choose either arbitration or litigation, whereas the other contracting party had no such choice [see paras. (168) and (169) of the same decision]. In this connection, it is necessary to emphasize that the procedure of the "choice of forum" by the claimant is not unusual; it is also a fairly well-known mechanism in the international arena. Even though it is not the best solution, it allows reflection on the specifics of a particular dispute (especially the specifics of the claim); one and the same relationship may include various types of claims, not precisely definable in advance, and it is not possible to determine in advance whether it would be more suitable to resolve the claims in arbitration or in court. However, the choice should generally always be at the discretion of the "claimant", not one of the parties specifically.

[523] Indeed, the practice of the courts in the U.S. is, in this regard, no different from the requirements of EU law. Subparagraph (i) of the *Directive* (see the excursus into EU law) also requires that the consumer *has an objective opportunity to read the contract*, not that the consumer actually reads it. Nonetheless, from the perspective of the fundamental principles of contract law, case law in the U.S. allows a significantly more balanced approach and protection against the abuse of consumer protection by the consumer, because it penalizes, to some extent, a consumer who himself/herself acted *carelessly* and failed to read the contract.

[524] See the decisions in the following cases:
➤ *Grimm* v. *First National Bank of Pennsylvania*, 578 2d 785,
➤ *MA Mortenson* v. *Timberline Software*, 140 Wash 2d 568;
➤ *Mortenson* v. *Timberline Software*, 83 Wash App 819;
➤ *Olle* v. *5401 Western Ave Residential*, 569 F Supp 2d 41;
➤ *US ex rel Wilson* v. *Kellogg Brown*, 525 F3d 370;
➤ *Falbe* v. *Dell*, WL 1588243.
Cf. *Hill, J.* Cross Border Consumer Contracts, Oxford: OUP, 2008, as well as *Zheng, S. Tang* Electronic Consumer Contracts in the Conflict of Laws. Oxford / Portland (Oregon): Hard Publishing, 2009, p. 156 (invoking the above-mentioned book – *Hill, J.*).

557.   Nonetheless, some courts [in the U.S.] have also ruled that generally unfair (unjust) arbitration clauses may constitute an obstacle to the enforcement thereof and the arbitral proceedings as such.[525]

558.   Although individual U.S. states have their own arbitration laws, their legislative powers with respect to consumer protection (in connection with arbitration) are limited. Consequently, the supply of goods and the provision of services between individual U.S. states is primarily subject to federal laws (FAA [USA]), almost without exception. Indeed, the U.S. Supreme Court repealed laws adopted by some individual states which had introduced special provisions on consumer arbitration, namely the acts adopted by Alabama (restricting the power to negotiate arbitration clauses) and Montana (regarding the unfair nature of arbitration clauses in consumer contracts).[526]

559.   Moreover, the Supreme Court of the United States has recently held[527] that if a contract stipulates that all disputes shall be submitted to arbitration in compliance with the AAA [USA] rules,[528] the FAA [USA] shall prevail over national laws (i.e. the laws of the individual states [of the USA]) which would prescribe exclusive court jurisdiction. The Supreme Court of the United States has held that the Act (FAA [USA]) shall apply even if the contract explicitly provided for the application of the law of a particular state of the union [USA]. Similarly, in the *Discover Bank* case, California courts have ruled that in the absence of any explicit provision on dispute resolution in a contract, the FAA replaces the requirement stipulated by the California law *that all contracting parties must have access to law.*[529]

560.   Some authors argue that the varying approach to consumer arbitration in the U.S. on the one hand and in Europe on the other hand is based on two differences.[530] The first is ascribed to the differences in the concept of the legislative protection of consumers and the second to the nature of the American system of dispute resolution.

---

[525] See the decision in *Pine Ridge Homes, Inc.* v. *Stone*, 2004 WL 1730170 (Tex. App. – Dallas 2004).

[526] See *Dauer, E.* Judicial Policing of Consumer Arbitration. Pepperdine Disp. Res. L. J., 2000, Vol. 91, No. 1, p. 6.

[527] See the decision in *Preston* v. *Ferrer*, No. 06-1463 of 20 April 2008, 2008 U.S. Lexis 2011.

[528] The *American Arbitration Association* (AAA [USA]) is, inter alia, specialized in consumer disputes, i.e. disputes over the supply of goods or services between an individual consumer (natural person) and a professional.

[529] See *IA.* Options Consommateurs. L'arbitrage collectif : une solution pour les consommateurs? Etude présentée au Bureau de la consommation d'Industrie Canada, June 2007, p. 23.

[530] See *Drahozal, C. et Friel, R. A.* A Comparative View of Consumer Arbitration. Arbitration, 2005, Vol. 2, p. 131.

561.   The U.S. is said to afford a lesser degree of protection to consumers than European countries under EU law.[531] Legislators (in the U.S.)[532] argue that interference in contractual autonomy is easier in civil law where a certain degree of unfairness is presumed. The second difference is premised on the very organization of the American judicial system. In proceedings before national courts, the parties have the right to plead their case before a jury. The parties very often avail themselves of this right in their court proceedings. It is therefore presumed that the courts often favor the consumer – as a result thereof, litigation as a jury trial loses its appeal for the professional and thereby increases the likelihood of arbitration.

562.   Moreover, the U.S. allows, similar to many other countries, consumers to associate and file class actions which can be lodged on behalf of many disputants without them actually being parties to the proceedings.[533] Professionals welcome arbitration clauses as a means of preventing proceedings based on class actions. The same reason probably explains the prevalence of arbitration clauses in consumer contracts under Canadian law as well. The importance of arbitration clauses in consumer contracts has also been supported by the **Canadian Supreme Court in Dell**[534] in which the Court ruled that arbitration clauses in consumer contracts are valid despite the fact that the consumers thereby lose their right to a class action.

563.   The American judicial and legal system allows punitive damages. This compensation is not based on the actual losses sustained by the consumer, but on the unlawful conduct of one of the parties. Punitive damages can be very high. Arbitration represents a method of limiting the amount of punitive damages, because the general assumption is that arbitrators are less inclined to be in favor of these damages than courts. Consequently, professionals are strongly motivated to conclude arbitration clauses in consumer contracts. Due to the prevalence of contracts of adhesion and the favorable legal environment, arbitration agreements have become a common term in consumer contracts. This especially applies to consumer credits – most of them incorporate an

---

[531] See *Drahozal, C. et Friel, R. A.* A Comparative View of Consumer Arbitration. Arbitration, 2005, Vol. 2, p. 131.

[532] See *Drahozal, C. et Friel, R. A.* A Comparative View of Consumer Arbitration. Arbitration, 2005, Vol. 2, p. 135.

[533] Class actions in consumer disputes resolved in arbitration were allowed by the decision of the U.S. Supreme Court [USA] in *Green Tree Financial Corp.* v. *Bazzle*, 539 U.S. 444 (2003).

[534] See a separate excursus into Canadian law and the approach adopted by certain Canadian provinces.

arbitration clause.[535] According to a group of American consumers, credit card companies adopted in 1999 a joint resolution supporting the widespread use of arbitration clauses in consumer contracts.[536] It is not difficult to enter into such contracts; not only do the companies offer advantages in the form of lower interest rates applicable if the consumer agrees with the arbitration clause,[537] but in *Badie v. Bank of America*[538] a California court[539] ruled in 1998 that consumers were bound by arbitration agreements sent by banks together with regular monthly statements.[540] However, the importance of the California court's conclusion did not reach beyond its borders.

IV.26.2. Limitation of consumer arbitration

564.   Although arbitration in consumer disputes is generally preferred in the U.S., consumers who are not interested in an arbitration agreement in their consumer relations have two arguments available to them which they can use against arbitration. First, there are claims under federal laws. If a party to arbitration is prevented from presenting an effective defense of his or her rights under federal laws,[541] the party has the right to resolve his/her dispute by litigation instead of arbitration. Circumstances preventing the exercise of these rights can include, for instance, the high costs of arbitration or the fact that the arbitration agreement contains a waiver of remedies.[542]

---

[535] See *Hanotiau, B.* L'Arbitrabilité in: Recueil des Cours, 2002, Vol. 296, para. (352) and *Bland, F. P.* Hearing on Mandatory Binding Arbitrations: Are They Fair to Consumers? Testimony Given to the United States House of Representatives Judiciary Committee, 12 June 2007, p. 3.

[536] See Public Citizen, How the Credit Card Companies Ensnare Consumers, September 2007, p. 20; available at http://www.citizen.org/documents/Final_wcover.pdf. This report served as the basis for a lawsuit lodged by San Francisco against the *National Arbitration Forum*, with reference to the decisions of this arbitral tribunal, most of which were in favor of professionals (businessmen) (see the Wall Street Journal Law Blog, 7 April 2008, available at: http://blogs.wsj.com/law/).

[537] See *Rutledge, P.* Testimony Given to the United States House of Representatives Judiciary Committee (Hearing on the Arbitration Fairness Act of 2007), 25 October 2007, p. 15.

[538] Decision of the Court of Appeal of California, First Appellate District, Division Three, Case No. A068753 of 3 November 1998. Neutral citation (published in): (1998) (i) 67 Cal. App. 4th 779; (ii) 79 Cal. Rptr. 2d 273; (iii) 1998 Cal. App. LEXIS 916; (iv) 98 Cal. Daily Op. Service 8189; (v) 98 Daily Journal DAR 11359. Annotated in great detail elsewhere in this book.

[539] California has enacted special rules governing consumer disputes. These rules stipulate, for instance, that California citizens may ask for a release from the obligation to pay the fee for arbitration (exclusive of compensation paid to arbitrators – arbitrator fees) in any consumer disputes handled by the AAA [USA]. See § 1284.3 of the California Code of Civil Procedure which applies to consumers whose monthly income meets the stipulated criteria.

[540] *McLaughlin, J. T.* Arbitrability: Current Trends in the United States. Arb. Int., 1996, Vol. 12, No. 2, p. 213.

[541] *Drahozal, C. et Friel, R. A.* A Comparative View of Consumer Arbitration. Arbitration, 2005, Vol. 2, p. 135, referring to *Green Tree Financial*.

[542] *Drahozal, C. et Friel, R. A.* A Comparative View of Consumer Arbitration. Arbitration, 2005, Vol. 2, p. 135.

565. The second reason for a refusal to arbitrate consumer disputes is the theory of *unconscionability*. This theory requires that the contract be an expression of the [genuine] will of the parties, on pain of unenforceability.[543] Indeed, this theory is not much unlike the European approach (especially under EU law) which does not principally exclude arbitration agreements in consumer disputes[544] (with potential national specifics as concerns the limitation, or even exclusion, of the arbitrability of consumer disputes); however, if the *lex arbitri* enables the conclusion of arbitration agreements (perhaps subject to special requirements, as the case may be), the arbitration agreement must be a genuine expression of will of the parties as a consensus, i.e. the intersection of their expressions of will. The principle of *unconscionability* in the U.S. stipulates that if a contractual term is so unreasonable that the consumer could not have reasonably accepted it, the term is unenforceable.[545]

566. Apart from this, state courts afford a certain level of support to consumers. Whereas at the federal level, the Supreme Court of the United States accepts class actions in cases covered by an arbitration agreement only if the arbitration agreement explicitly provides for this possibility,[546] California courts have ruled that arbitration agreements in consumer relations must not limit the consumer's right to file a class action, and in *Southland Corporation* v. *Keating*[547] the courts ordered the joinder of separate arbitral proceedings.[548] The Court thereby maintained control over arbitration especially as concerns the reasonableness thereof and supervised the hearing of the class action before the arbitrators. The decision in **Southland Corporation v. Keating**[549] has resulted in an unprecedented use of arbitration

---

[543] *IA*. Options Consommateurs. L'arbitrage collectif : une solution pour les consommateurs? Etude présentée au Bureau de la consommation d'Industrie Canada, June 2007, p. 20. Unenforceability under common law can be compared, to some extent and especially from the civil law perspective, to voidability (i.e. invalidity applied at the request of the party).

[544] See Judgment of the BGH [DEU], Case No. III ZR 256/03 of 13 January 2005 annotated in detail in this book (in the part concerning arbitration in consumer disputes in Germany [DEU]). The judgment analyzed the issues in great detail and from the EU perspective (at that time the EC perspective). Opponents of consumer arbitration sometimes avail themselves of a rather simplified argument, i.e. that EU law prohibits arbitration clauses in consumer contracts. Naturally, this is not a valid premise. EU law only prescribes certain conditions which ought to be observed in contracts with consumers in order to comply with the requirement of protection of the "weaker contracting party" (i.e. the consumer).

[545] See *Drahozal, C. et Friel, R. A.* A Comparative View of Consumer Arbitration. Arbitration, 2005, Vol. 2, p. 135.

[546] *IA*. Options Consommateurs. L'arbitrage collectif : une solution pour les consommateurs? Etude présentée au Bureau de la consommation d'Industrie Canada, June 2007, p. 22, referring to Green Tree.

[547] 465 U.S. 1 (1984).

[548] *IA*. Options Consommateurs. L'arbitrage collectif : une solution pour les consommateurs? Etude présentée au Bureau de la consommation d'Industrie Canada, June 2007, p. 21.

[549] 465 U.S. 1 (1984).

agreements in consumer contracts. Hence, arbitration has without a doubt become the most widespread method of resolving consumer disputes. According to a 2004 U.S. survey, 69.2% of respondent businesses confirmed the inclusion of arbitration clauses in their contracts concluded with consumers.[550]

567. The Florida Supreme Court [USA] attempted in the *Buckeye* case to limit the scope of application of the FAA [USA]. The Court held that the FAA [USA] had not replaced the jurisdiction of the court over the validity of the contract.[551] The criticism directed against consumer arbitration has also been addressed by various institutions dealing with arbitration. In response to protests voiced by consumer groups, the AAA [USA], which is otherwise focused primarily on commercial arbitration, published a *Consumer Due Process Protocol*. The Protocol actually allows class actions in arbitration.[552]

568. Finally, under pressure exerted by consumer associations, federal legislators in the U.S. have adopted measures aimed at the limitation of arbitration in consumer disputes. The first step was the proposal for Act No. 107-273 which anticipated the prohibition of arbitration clauses in franchise contracts with sellers of motor vehicles. Although consumers are not parties to franchise agreements, it is possible to identify the stronger party in such relationships; consequently, these agreements represent a certain type of adhesion contract. Apart from these measures, a federal prohibition against arbitration clauses in consumer credit contracts was introduced in 2006 (on pain of criminal prosecution) but only if the credit is provided to members of the U.S. army.[553] It is somewhat unclear what the actual ramifications would be if the prohibition under this Act were breached, because there is no practical experience with application of this law.

IV.26.3. Proposal for a new federal law in the United States (draft Arbitration Fairness Act, AFA [USA])

569. In 2009 the U.S. Congress initiated discussions regarding a special law which would respond to the boom in arbitration agreements in consumer contracts. It was a reaction to the unprecedented expansion of arbitration in consumer disputes; the discussion primarily focused on

[550] *Casey, K. R.* Hot Issues Alerts – Law Firms. Mandatory Consumer Arbitration. The Metropolitan Corporate Counsel, 5 August 2009. Available online at http://www.metrocorpcounsel.com/current.php?artType=view&artMonth=August&artYear=2009&EntryNo=10019 [last access 7 August 2011].
[551] See *IA*. Options Consommateurs. L'arbitrage collectif : une solution pour les consommateurs? Etude présentée au Bureau de la consommation d'Industrie Canada, June 2007, p. 24.
[552] See *IA*. Options Consommateurs. L'arbitrage collectif : une solution pour les consommateurs? Etude présentée au Bureau de la consommation d'Industrie Canada, June 2007, p. V.
[553] 10 U.S.C. 987(e)(3).

consumer rights. The corresponding restrictive provisions were incorporated in the proposal for a new *Arbitration Fairness Act* (AFA [USA]).[554] The discussion over the proposal, centered on the advantages of arbitration as opposed to its potential abuse in consumer disputes, is still ongoing. The Act (AFA [USA]) could introduce limitations in consumer arbitration which might, in certain respects, exceed current trends in the European model; principally, however, they would be similar. This would follow the **Canadian example** – the *Dell*[555] case had the result of limiting arbitration in consumer disputes in several Canadian provinces. In any case, even if the draft AFA [USA] were passed, it would probably only influence certain aspects of consumer arbitration (for instance, the costs of proceedings). However, the discussion also reflects the debate over *class actions* which represent an important phenomenon in American legal and judicial practice.[556] The Act, which is supposed to supplement Part 9 U.S.C., was subject to very extensive discussion. The last version of the proposal was published on 12 May 2011[557] and its scope covers consumer[558] and employment (individual labor) disputes,[559] disputes which are supposed to resolve civil rights, and the limitations of pre-dispute arbitration agreements (clauses).[560]

---

[554] H.R. 1020, 111th Congress (2009).

[555] See a separate excursus into Canadian law and the approach adopted by certain Canadian provinces.

[556] Certain states [in the U.S.] consider any arbitration clauses which prevent consumers from joining class actions as invalid. See the following decisions:

➤ *Oestreicher* v. *Alienware*, 502 FSupp2D 1061 (NDCal 2007),
➤ *Kaltwasser* v. *Cingular Wireless LLC*, 543 FSupp2d 1124 (NDCal 2008),
➤ *Cf. Carideo* v. *Dell*, 520 Supp2d 1241 (WDWash 2007),
➤ *Discover Bank* v. *Superior Court*, 134 Cal App 4th 886 (Cal App 2005).

See *Zheng, S. Tang* Electronic Consumer Contracts in the Conflict of Laws. Oxford / Portland (Oregon): Hard Publishing, 2009, p. 155, Note 29.

[557] Available online at: http://www.gpo.gov/fdsys/pkg/BILLS-112s987is/pdf/BILLS-112s987is.pdf [last access 12 August 2011].

[558] A consumer dispute according to the AFA [USA] is defined as a "*dispute between an individual who seeks or acquires real or personal property, services (including services relating to securities and other investments), money, or credit for personal, family, or household purposes and the seller or provider of such property, services, money, or credit.*"

[559] An employment dispute (a dispute between an employer and employee) is defined by reference to Section 3 of the Fair Labor Standards Act of 1938 (29. U.S.C. 203).

[560] The draft AFA [USA] defines arbitration clauses (predispute arbitration agreements) as "*any agreement to arbitrate a dispute that had not yet arisen at the time of the making of the agreement.*" In other words, a "dispute" is interpreted as a difference of opinion between the parties, a conflict over the interpretation of the contract and the rights and obligations of the parties in general, i.e. as an arbitration agreement regarding potential future disputes in a procedural sense. In the case of a "dispute," as the term is used in the above definition, the question is what European terminology (especially) connects with the term "arbitration clause."

IV.26.4. Enforcement of arbitral awards rendered in the United States in consumer disputes abroad

570. In connection with the enforcement of U.S. arbitral awards rendered in consumer disputes abroad, we can refer to, for instance, the decision of the Polish Supreme Court (SN [POL]) of 22 February 2007.[561] In said case, the Court assessed an arbitration clause in a contract, between a professional from the U.S. and a consumer from Poland which vested jurisdiction in the AAA [USA] with the place of proceedings in the U.S., as an unfair term that significantly discriminated against the Polish consumer. The Polish Supreme Court (SN [POL]) emphasized an important difference from the requirements stipulated by the European legal framework. It needs to be admitted that the arguments presented by the Polish Supreme Court[562] are in many respects very persuasive and could be used as a model solution for similar situations in broader international practice.

IV.26.5. Case law

(a) Decision of the Supreme Court of the United States of America, No. 82-500 of 23 January 1984 (*Southland Corp. et al.* v. *Keating et al.*); 465 U.S. 1 (1984): Special protection afforded to *franchisees*

(aa) Main conclusions of the decision

571. The U.S. Supreme Court [USA], and the lower California courts in the preceding stages of the proceedings,[563] were called upon to assess the special provisions regulating franchise agreements under California law, especially Section 31512[564] of the *California Corporations Code*, namely the part entitled *California Franchise Investment Law*.[565] This provision prohibits and renders void any [contractual] terms whereby the franchisee would waive the application of the law or would be bound to act contrary to the law. The courts focused predominantly on the interpretation of validity of arbitration clauses in franchise agreements regarding claims based on this law (*California Franchise Investment*

---

[561] Decision of the SN [POL], Case No. No IV CSK 200/06 of 22 February 2007. This decision is analyzed in detail in the territorial excursus into consumer arbitration in Poland [POL].

[562] For more details, see the excursus into consumer arbitration rules in Poland [POL].

[563] *Southland Corp.* v. *Keating*; appeal against the judgment of the Supreme Court of California.

[564] California Franchise Investment Law [USA-CAL] (cit.): "31512. *Any condition, stipulation or provision purporting to bind any person acquiring any franchise to waive compliance with any provision of this law or any rule or order hereunder is void.*" (Cal. Corp. Code Ann. 31512 (West 1977).

[565] California Franchise Investment Law is a part of the California Corporations Code, Section 31000 et seq. The California Corporations Code is available at: http://www.leginfo.ca.gov/cgi-bin/calawquery?codesection=corp&codebody=&hits=20 [last access 24 August 2011], franchise laws are available at: http://www.corp.ca.gov/srd/ccfil.asp [last access 24 August 2011].

Law). Section 31512[566] of the Franchise Investment Law is connected with Section 31513[567] of the same law that stipulates certain procedural rights. Concerning arbitration clauses in franchise agreements, the U.S. Supreme Court [USA] ruled on the following issues, inter alia:

▶ Any delay of the review of a state judicial decision on the invalidity of an arbitration agreement until the state court litigation in the merits has run its course would defeat the core purpose of the agreement.

▶ Any interpretation of Section 31512 of the *California Corporations Code* or the relevant part thereof, the *California Franchise Investment Law*[568] suggesting that all claims brought under the statute require judicial consideration and hence cannot be covered by an arbitration clause, directly conflicts with Section 2 of the FAA [USA][569] and thereby violates the *Supremacy Clause* (the principle of precedence in the application of the law).

▶ In enacting Section 2 of the FAA [USA],[570] Congress declared a **national policy favoring arbitration** and withdrew the power of the states to require a judicial forum for the resolution of claims that the contracting parties agreed to resolve by arbitration.

▶ That federal law (FAA [USA]) creates a body of federal substantive law that is applicable in both state and federal courts.[571]

▶ To confine the scope of the Federal Arbitration Act (FAA [USA]) to arbitration clauses sought to be enforced in federal courts would frustrate what Congress intended to be a comprehensive enactment (in the relevant area, i.e. regarding arbitration).

▶ The requirement that the term [vesting jurisdiction in the arbitrators] must "involve commerce"[572] is not to be interpreted as a limitation on the power of the federal courts [to assess the validity of

---

[566] Cited in the footnote above.

[567] California Franchise Investment Law [USA-CAL] (cit.): "31513. *Whenever a person is entitled under this law to a hearing in accordance with the provisions of Chapter 5 (commencing with Section 11500) of Part 1 of Division 3 of Title 2 of the Government Code, a formal hearing before the Department of Corporations may be substituted with the consent of such person and of the commissioner for such hearing before an independent hearing officer; and in that case after such hearing before the Department of Corporations such person shall not be entitled to any further administrative remedy.*" (Cal. Corp. Code Ann. 31513 (West 1977).

[568] For a specification of the Act, see the footnote above.

[569] FAA [USA] (cit.): "§ 2. *Validity, irrevocability, and enforcement of agreements to arbitrate – A written provision in any maritime transaction or a contract evidencing a transaction involving commerce to settle by arbitration a controversy thereafter arising out of such contract or transaction, or the refusal to perform the whole or any part thereof, or an agreement in writing to submit to arbitration an existing controversy arising out of such a contract, transaction, or refusal, shall be valid, irrevocable, and enforceable, save upon such grounds as exist at law or in equity for the revocation of any contract.*" Czech translation published in: Bělohlávek, A. Rozhodčí řízení, ordre public a trestní právo. [Title in translation: Arbitration, Ordre Public and Criminal Law]. Part II, Prague: C. H. Beck, 2008, Annex C, Section XI.1.

[570] Quoted in a footnote above.

[571] See the decision in *Moses H. Cone Memorial Hospital* v. *Mercury Construction Corp.*, 460 U.S. 1.

[572] Quoted in a footnote above.

the arbitration agreement] but as a necessary qualification on a statute intended to apply in state as well as in federal courts.

▶ Since the overwhelming proportion of civil litigation is in state courts [courts of the individual U.S. states /USA/], the legislator could not have intended to limit the FAA [USA] to disputes [proceedings] only subject to federal court jurisdiction.

▶ In creating a substantive rule applicable in state as well as in federal courts, the legislator intended to foreclose state legislative attempts to undercut the enforceability of arbitration agreements.

▶ Not even a special measure (of state legislation) can, at the general level, limit the fundamental principles resulting from arbitration laws, here a federal statute. This case primarily concerned the relationship between federal law [USA] and individual U.S. state legislation. From an even more general perspective, it is an important decision promoting the *"Kompetenz-Kompetenz"* principle in relations in which the law provides special protection to the *weaker* (potentially weaker) party.

(bb) Factual and legal findings

572.   *"7-Eleven"* franchisees filed actions against the franchisor in California Superior Court alleging, among other things, fraud, misrepresentation, and violation of the disclosure requirements of the *California Franchise Investment Law. Keating* also filed a class action on behalf of approximately 800 other franchisees. The respondent pleaded lack of jurisdiction of the court, referring to the existence of an arbitration clause incorporated in all franchise agreements. The Court granted the defense except for those claims which were based on the *Franchise Investment Law.* The respondent appealed from the order as concerns its jurisdictional challenge to the California Court of Appeal. The California Court of Appeal granted the defense, reversed the trial court's decision on jurisdiction and accepted that these special claims were also arbitrable. The *California Franchise Investment Law* [USA-CAL], as a special law governing this special type of contractual relations, affords special protection to *franchisees* as the *weaker contracting party*. Indeed, such protection is also provided under certain EU laws. The Court of Appeal concluded that the special rules governing franchise agreements did not render the arbitration clauses invalid. A contrary interpretation would conflict with Section 2 of the *Federal Arbitration Act* (FAA [USA][573]). The California Supreme Court reversed the ruling of the Court of Appeal and, invoking Section 31512 of the *California Franchise Investment Law*, ruled that all claims asserted under said Act must be heard in court litigation; in other words, the California Supreme Court denied the applicability of the arbitration clause to such claims. The

---

[573] Quoted in a footnote above.

California Supreme Court concluded that the California statute did not contravene the *Federal Arbitration Act* (FAA [USA]). After the last appeal, the U.S. Supreme Court held that such an interpretation of Section 31512 of the California law *(California Franchise Investment Law)* directly conflicts with Section 2 FAA [USA], and thereby violates the *Supremacy Clause* (regarding the legal force of the statutes within their hierarchy). The U.S. Supreme Court held that federal law creates a body of federal substantive law that must be applied by both state and federal courts.[574]

(cc) Arguments of the parties and the Court's legal conclusions

573. When examining the issue of whether the Supreme Court of the United States has jurisdiction to decide whether state legislation conflicts with federal before the state court issues any final decision (which has also been mentioned by opponents), the Court invoked *Cox Broadcasting Corp. v. Cohn*,[575] according to which the Court has jurisdiction if *"a refusal to immediately review the state court decision might seriously erode federal policy."*[576] In the *Southland Corp. et al. v. Keating et al.* case, the effect of the judgment of the California court was to nullify a valid contract made by private parties under which they agreed to submit all contract disputes to arbitration. According to the federal

---

[574] The U.S. Supreme Court invoked its own decision in *Moses H. Cone Memorial Hospital* v. *Mercury Construction Corp.*, 460 U.S. 1 . This decision creates a precedent with respect to the waiver of jurisdiction and the related obligation of the court to abstain from hearing a case. It is the *"abstention doctrine."* The doctrine stipulates that a court of law must in certain cases refuse to hear a case, when hearing the case would intrude upon the powers of another court or authority. This doctrine is usually invoked in connection with lis pendence, where the same issues are brought before a state court and a federal court at the same time. In *Moses H. Cone Memorial Hospital* v. *Mercury Construction Corp.*, the U.S. Supreme Court applied the doctrine to arbitration. This case involved a complicated dispute arising from a construction contract. The court ruled that a hospital in North Carolina must submit its dispute to a company in Alabama, as the contractor (regarding construction work relating to a hospital ward), to arbitration despite litigation currently pending between the same parties (and an architect for the project) in a state court. The subject of the dispute was also covered by special substantive rules (state legislation). The U.S. Supreme Court held that a reference to special legislation cannot serve as a means of circumventing an arbitration clause subjected to federal substantive law (FAA [USA]). Cf. also:
> *Stark, T. L.* Negotiating and drafting contract boilerplate. ALM Publishing, 2003, p. 182;
> *Born, G.* International Civil Litigation in United States Courts: Commentary & Materials. 3rd ed., KLI, 1996, p. 995;
> *Riesel, D.* Environmental enforcement civil and criminal. Law Journal Press, 1997, § 1.04[3], pp. 1–18;
> *Matthias, J. H., Neumeier, M. M. et Burgdoerfer, J. J.* Directors and officers' liability: Prevention, insurance, and indemnification. Law Journal Press (card index), 2000, § 10.03, pp. 10–14 et al.

[575] 420 U.S. 469 (1975). The case concerned the extent of the freedom of the press; a federal court held that a Georgia law prohibiting the release of a rape victim's name was unconstitutional.

[576] See the 1975 Judgment of the Supreme Court [USA] in *Cox Broadcasting Corp. v. Cohn*, 420 U.S. 483 (1975).

court, any delay of the review of such a decision until the state court litigation had run its course would defeat the core purpose of the contract. The Court therefore concluded that it had jurisdiction to make such a decision.

574.   The California court relied on Section 31512 of the *California Franchise Investment Law* which stipulates that any provision requiring the franchisee to act contrary to any provision of the Law is null and void.[577] The California Supreme Court [USA-CAL] interpreted this statute to require judicial consideration and the judicial resolution of claims brought under the [special] state statute, and accordingly the arbitration clause regarding such claims could not be recognized; this should not have been interpreted as meaning that the statute would conflict with the *Federal Arbitration Act* (FAA [USA]). However, the federal court expressed a different opinion – the Court held that in enacting the Federal Act (FAA [USA]), Congress had the power and jurisdiction over state courts on whether or not to insist on the judicial resolution of disputes, irrespective of whether the parties had agreed to an arbitration clause for these cases. The reason is that the Court discerns only two limitations on the validity and enforceability of arbitration provisions (clauses) governed by the Federal Arbitration Act (FAA [USA]). First, they must be part of a *"maritime contract"* or a *"contract evidencing a transaction involving commerce."* Second, an arbitration agreement may be *"revoked*[578] *upon grounds as exist at law or in equity for the revocation of any contract."*[579] The Court did not find anything in the FAA [USA] indicating that the principle could be subject to any additional limitations under state law.[580] Hence, the U.S. Supreme Court held that so interpreted Section 31512 of the *California Franchise Investment Law* directly conflicts with Section 2 of the FAA [USA] and violates the *Supremacy Clause.*[581]

---

[577] Quoted in a footnote above.

[578] To revoke, i.e. to hold invalid.

[579] See Section 2 FAA [USA]; the provision is quoted in a footnote above.

[580] If we abstract from the application of the law to the relationship between federal law [USA] and individual U.S. state law, the conclusion can, to some extent, also apply to the relationship between the Arbitration Act and special rules regulating certain legal relations. But even the special law stipulating special rights which could be invoked by the weaker party under the special rules does not limit the application of the general arbitration laws. This would probably not be the same if the FAA [USA] itself allowed the limitation of the applicability (of the scope) of the Act in certain special cases. However, the FAA [USA] contains no such provision limiting the scope of the Act. And it is not possible to invoke the objective of the special law either. We must remember, however, that the given case primarily concerned the relationship between federal and state law, although the broader impact of the conclusions of the decision on these situations is obvious and fairly apparent.

[581] These are principles primarily relying on Article VI(2) of the Constitution of the United States, the *Supremacy Clause.* See *Drahozal, Ch. R.* The Supremacy Clause: A Reference Guide to the United States Constitution. Praeger, 2004; *Vázquez, C. M.* Treaties as Law of the Land: The Supremacy Clause and the Judicial Enforcement of Treaties. Harvard Law Review, 2008, Vol. 122, pp. 599–695 et al.

575. Referring to other decisions which analyzed, inter alia, the historical[582] or the systematic[583] importance of the respective federal law (FAA [USA]), the Court supported the opinion that this law creates a body of substantive federal law that is applicable in both state and federal courts. The court viewed the "involving commerce"[584] requirement not as a limitation on the power of the federal courts, but as a necessary qualification on a statute intended to apply in both state and federal courts. To confine the Act's scope to proceedings in federal courts would frustrate the legislator's intention, i.e. to **foreclose state legislative attempts to undercut the enforceability of arbitration agreements.**

576. Finally, the Court argues that the interpretation advocated by the California court is also undesirable, because it encourages [undesirable] *forum shopping*, depending on the law which the court applies in a particular case, in order to obtain a more favorable result. According to such an interpretation, the claims based on the California legislation lack arbitrability [only] if they are made in a state court. It is obvious, however, that by filing a claim with a federal district court, the Federal Act (FAA [USA]) would be recognized and the arbitration clause for the claims would be recognized as well. However, the overwhelming majority of civil disputes are resolved in state courts; hence, the federal court does not *believe* that the legislator intended to limit the applicability of the federal Act only to disputes subject exclusively to the jurisdiction of federal courts. The Court noted that such an interpretation would only frustrate the legislator's intent to *"place arbitration agreements upon the same footing as other [contracts]."*[585]

(dd) Notes on the judgment

577. The decision is important for several reasons. Apart from clearly formulating the precedence of federal law, the U.S. Supreme Court also confirms other circumstances: **(i)** the general rules on the interpretation of contracts also apply to special-type contracts, **(ii)** this approach broadly applies even to special provisions focused on the protection of certain contracting parties and **(iii)** confirms the broad conception of arbitrability generally incorporated in the FAA [USA]. After all, special protection is provided under **EU law** as well.[586] The special approach to

---

[582] See the decision in *Prima Paint Corp.* v. *Flood & Conklin Mfg. Co.*; 388 U.S. 395 (1967) (cit.): *"The statute is based upon [...] the incontestable federal foundations of control over interstate commerce and over admiralty."*

[583] See the decision in *Moses H. Cone Memorial Hospital* v. *Mercury Construction Corp.*, 460 U.S., at 1, 25, & n. 32: The Arbitration Act [FAA /USA/] *"creates a body of federal substantive law."*].

[584] See Section 2 FAA [USA]; the provision is quoted above.

[585] H. R. Rep. No. 96, 68th Congress, 1st Sess., 1 (1924).

[586] Cf. *Akyürek-Kievits, H. E. et Mok, M. R.* Verkoopfranchising en art. 85 EEG-verdrag. S.E.W., 1987, pp. 394–399; *Bejček, J.* Existenční ochrana konkurence [Title in translation: Existential Protection of

franchises is enshrined in a number of national laws,[587] and it is an internationally recognized model.[588] As concerns EU law, it is necessary to mention the special conflict-of-law rules incorporated in Article 4(1)(e) of the *Rome I Regulation*.[589] This substantive (conflict-of-law) provision of EU law does not classify *franchises* under consumer relations; it does recognize, though, their commercial nature. Indeed, the term *franchise* was originally employed as a *working* title for a *commercial model*,[590] the essence of which has developed into a more comprehensive legal definition only by a gradual standardization of the legal relations between the parties to the *franchise*. It is necessary to

Competition], Brno: Masaryk University, 1997; *Brzobohatá, M. et Bejček, J.* Franchising. [Title in translation: Franchising]. Právní praxe v podnikání, 1993, Nos. 7-8, p. 11 et seq., *Bělohlávek, A.* Franšíza z pohledu tuzemského, evropského a mezinárodního práva soukromého (franšíza jako zvláštní smluvní koncepce a kolizní úprava Nařízení Řím I - Nařízení EP a Rady /ES/ č. 593/2008). [Title in translation: Franchise from the Perspective of Domestic, European and Private International Law (Franchise as a Specific Contractual Concept and the Conflict-of-Law Rules in the Rome I Regulation – Regulation of the EP and of the Council /EC/ No. 593/2008)]. Obchodní právo, 2009, Vol. 18, No. 3, pp. 2–39; *Bělohlávek, A.* Účinnost licenčních smluv k tzv. průmyslovým právům z daňového hlediska. [Title in translation: Effectiveness of Licence Agreements Regarding Industrial Rights from a Tax Perspective]. Daňová a hospodářská kartotéka (DHK), 1999, No. 2; *Burst, J. J. et Kovar, R.* La mariée est en blanc: Dans l'arrêt Pronuptia la Cour de justice des Communautés européennes " blanchit" le contrat de franchise de distribution. Gazette du Palais, 1986, III Doct., pp. 392–398; *Galán C. E.* Los contratos de "franchising" ante el Derecho comunitario protector de la libre competencia. Revista de Instituciones Europeas, 1986, pp. 687–702; IA EEC Court Leaves Questions on Franchising Unanswered. Business Europe, 1986, No. 8, p. 3 et seq.; *IA.* Jurisprudence communautaire en matière de concurrence. Revue de la concurrence et de la consommation, 1986, No. 34, pp. 42–44 et al.

[587] Cf. *Frignani, A.* Franchising in Italia. Obiter dictum: Electronic Law Journal, 1997, Vol. 3, Ref. No. 3 in the volume; available online at: http://www.jus.unitn.it/cardozo/Review/home.html [last access 20 February 2009]; *Elías-Ostua y Ripoll, de, R.* Franchising con cláusula de exclusividad. Noticias CEE, 1986, No. 14, pp. 121–124; *IA.* Franchising, München: Deutscher Franchise-Verbad e.V., 1992; *Jakubíková, D.* Franchising [Title in translation: Franchising], Plzeň: Vydavatelství Západočeské univerzity [West Bohemia University Press], 1997; *Jamin, Chr.* Le premier arrêt communautaire sur la franchise. La vie judiciaire 1986, No. 2082, p. 1, pp. 5–6; *Jamin, Ch.* Le premier arrêt communautaire sur la franchise. Propriété industrielle (PIBD), 1986, No. 389 II, p. 75 et seq. et al.

[588] Cf. *Houdard, G.* Franchise: L"arrêt "Pronuptia." Propriété industrielle, 1986, No. 389 II, p. 76 et seq.; *IA.* Guide to International Master Franchise Arrangements / UNIDROIT, International Institute for the Unification of Private Law, Rome: International Institute for the Unification of Private Law (Unidroit), 1998; *IA.* UNIDROIT Guide to International Master Franchise Arrangements, 2nd ed., Rome: International Institute for the Unification of Private Law (Unidroit), 2007 et al.

[589] Rome I Regulation (cit.): Article 4 – "1. *To the extent that the law applicable to the contract has not been chosen in accordance with Article 3 and without prejudice to Articles 5 to 8, the law governing the contract shall be determined as follows:* [...]; (e) *a franchise contract shall be governed by the law of the country where the franchisee has his habitual residence;* [...]." Note: *The Rome Convention* did not include any special rule explicitly regulating this type of contract.

[590] *Mendelsohn, M. et Acheson, D.* Franchising – moderní forma prodeje [Title in translation: Franchising – Modern Form of Selling], Prague: Management Press, 1994; *Štensová, A. et Gieratová, Z.* Viete čo je franchising? [Title in translation: Do You Know What Franchising Is?] Bratislava: Vydavateľstvo Elita, 1991; *T: Thieffry, P.* La franchise, la confiance et la raison. Observations sur l'éventuelle influence de la jurisprudence américaine sur l'arrêt Pronuptia de la CJCE. Gazette du Palais, 1986, III Doct., pp. 562–565 et al.

point out, though, that due to the significantly dynamic development of the *model*, as well as due to the fact that it encompasses a number of various synallagmatic and commercially interactive performances,[591] it is not possible to set forth an absolutely clear and all-encompassing definition of a *franchise*. Nonetheless, all of its alternatives are connected by a set of characteristic features which at least allow the definition of the fundamental objectives of a *franchise*, which are subsequently manifested in the legal relationship between the parties in the form of specific obligations.

(b) Decision of the Supreme Court of the United States of America, No. 93-1001 of 18 January 1995 (*Terminix v. Dobson*)

(aa) Main conclusions of the Court

578.   In the present case, the U.S. Supreme Court[592] ruled on certain fundamental issues as follows:

▶ Congress [the legislator] would not have wanted state and federal courts to reach different outcomes about the validity of arbitration agreements in similar cases.[593]

▶ The application of the *Federal Arbitration Act* (FAA [USA]) does not depend on whether the parties contemplated interstate commerce at the conclusion of the contract. It suffices that the transaction (contract) indeed involved interstate commerce.

---

[591] This is not an established or common term in legal terminology. But, the essence of the term is typical for what the business model of a franchise stands for. It is a mutual complex of relatively independent relations which, in their mutual harmony, pursue a particular commercial purpose. At the same time, however, performance within the scope of one relationship influences the performance in another relationship, and one performance significantly shapes the content of other such interconnected relationships. For example, revenue turnover (or another business performance) influences the type, amount, and method of paying rent, the fees for the use of industrial rights, or other rights to intangible assets, etc. It is necessary to realize, though, that it is a mutually interconnected complex which would deserve to be called an "organism." Hence, the term "interactive performance" is by no means so unacceptable for the definition of the subject matter and the content of a franchise as it would appear at first sight. It is an interactive mechanism of a certain kind – as the term (interactive performance) is more common in communication technologies. Cf. *Bělohlávek, A.* Římská úmluva / Nařízení Řím I. Komentář. [Title in translation: Rome Convention / Rome I Regulation. Commentary]. Part I, Prague: C. H. Beck, 2009, marg. 4.461. After all, the term is also used in linguistics, which is, due to the analogy of the term, even more familiar with the concept, considering the mechanism we are trying to label it with in the context of commercial and legal terminology. Cf. *Selting, M.* Beendigung(en) als interaktive Leistung. In: Hausendorf, H. (ed.) Sprache als Prozeß, Tübingen: Narr, 2007, pp. 307–338.

[592] *Allied Bruce Terminix Companies, Inc. et Terminix International Company, Petitioners v. G. Michael Dobson et al.*, review of the decision of the Supreme Court of Alabama (writ of certiorari), In: 513 U.S. 265 (1995). Available online at: http://www.law.cornell.edu/supct/html/93-1001.ZO.html [last access 7 August 2011].

[593] See the decision in *Southland Corp. v. Keating*, paras. (15) and (16); annotated in great detail elsewhere in this book.

▶ The basic purpose of the *Federal Arbitration Act* (FAA [USA]) is to put arbitration provisions on the same footing as a contract's other terms,[594] i.e. to make arbitration clauses universally valid.

▶ The words *"involving commerce"* are broader than *"commercial."* (The court thereby extended the scope of the FAA [USA], so that the courts of the individual U.S. states could not apply any law which would limit, let alone deny, the validity of arbitration clauses; this would conflict with the purpose of the FAA [USA].

▶ State courts may not decide that a contract is fair (*reasonable*) enough to enforce all its basic terms, but not fair enough to enforce its arbitration clause.

▶ Consumers who were under external pressure to enter into a contract with an unwanted arbitration clause may be protected by declaring the arbitration clause invalid using general legal principles upon such *"grounds as exist at law or in equity for the revocation of any contract."* It is unlawful for a state court to decide that the [main] contract is fair enough to enforce all its basic terms, but not fair enough to enforce its arbitration clause. That kind of policy places arbitration clauses on an unequal footing, compared to other contract terms, which is directly contrary to the Act's language and the legislator's intent.

(bb) Factual and legal findings

579.   The respondent, the original owner of a house in Alabama [USA], entered into a pest control agreement specifically aimed at controlling termites with the local office of *Allied Bruce Terminix Companies* (the respondent in the proceedings);[595] the agreement was concluded before the sale of the house. The agreement stipulated that any disputes or claims were to be resolved exclusively by arbitration. Before the sale of the house, the provider inspected the house and issued a clean bill of health (no termites). However, shortly after the sale of the house and the transfer of the termite protection agreement to Mr. and Ms. *Dobson*, the new owners found the house infested with termites. After attempts to treat and repair the house, which the new owners found inadequate, Mr. and Ms. *Dobson* sued the original owner and *Allied Bruce and Terminix* in Alabama [USA] state court. *Terminix*, the respondent, immediately asked the court for a stay, invoking an arbitration clause and Section 2 of the FAA [USA]. The Court denied the defense of lack of jurisdiction and the respondent, *Terminix*, appealed to the Supreme Court of Alabama [USA] which confirmed the previous decision. The Supreme Court of Alabama [USA] considered the FAA [USA] inapplicable to the contract, because the connection between the contract and interstate

---

[594] See the decision in *Scherk* v. *Alberto Culver Co.*, 417 U. S., para. (511).
[595] A franchise of the Terminix International Company with offices in a number of states in the U.S.

commerce was *too slight*. In the view of the Supreme Court of Alabama, the Act applies to a contract only if at the time the parties entered into the [main] contract (including the arbitration clause), they contemplated substantial interstate activity (the present case concerned an interstate service provider and the material used was imported from a state different from Alabama [USA]). However, **the Supreme Court of the United States reversed** the judgment of the Alabama Court and arrived at a different conclusion; in doing so, the U.S. Supreme Court gave precedence to a broader interpretation of the Act (FAA [USA]) and recognized the *de facto* connection between the contract and interstate activity, although the parties probably did not contemplate it at the moment of conclusion. Applying the FAA [USA], the Court recognized the applicability of the arbitration clause to disputes arising from the contract.

(cc) Arguments of the parties and the Court's legal conclusions

580.   When interpreting the FAA [USA], the Court had to decide whether the Act provides a statutory niche to the individual U.S. states in which they remain free to apply their own policy or laws (potentially less favorable to arbitration). The Court employed not only the grammatical, but also the historical and teleological, interpretation methods and concluded that there is no room for the application of the principles and laws of the individual U.S. states. Hence, the Court held that Section 2 of the FAA [USA] stipulates that *"written provision in any maritime transaction or a* **contract evidencing a transaction involving commerce** *to settle by arbitration a controversy thereafter arising out of such contract or transaction, or the refusal to perform the whole or any part thereof, [...] shall be valid, irrevocable, and enforceable, save upon such grounds as exist at law or in equity for the revocation of any contract."*[596] According to the U.S. Supreme Court, the words *"involving commerce"* are broader than *"commercial."* This presumption is only confirmed by the federal Act's legislative history, which obviously indicates the expansive intent of the legislator.[597] By passing the Act in 1925, Congress primarily intended to overcome the unwillingness of the courts of the individual states to recognize arbitration clauses in their attempts to broaden their jurisdiction.[598] This approach originates from the ancient practice of the

---

[596] Put in boldface by the author.
[597] See the explanatory memorandum: H. R. Rep. No. 96, 68th Cong., 1st Sess., 1 (1924) (cit.): *"The Act's control over interstate commerce reaches not only the actual physical interstate shipment of goods but also contracts relating to interstate commerce."*
[598] See the decision in *Bernhardt* v. *Polygraphic Co. of America, Inc.*, 350 U.S. 198, 211, N. 5 (1956), which cites the decision in *United States Asphalt Refining Co.* v. *Trinidad Lake Petroleum Co.*, 222 F. 1006, 1007 (SDNY 1915). This 1915 decision further invokes an even older decision in *Scott* v. *Avery*, 5 H. L. Cas. 811 (1856).

English courts which the U.S. courts subsequently adopted. The Court also pointed out that the broader interpretation is consistent with the **purpose of the federal Act (FAA [USA]), to put arbitration clauses on the same footing as other terms in the contract (the main contract).**[599]

581.   The Court also invoked the decision of the Court in *Southland Corp.* v. *Keating* which also had to resolve a conflict between state and federal law. In that case, the federal Supreme Court held that **state courts may not apply the law of their state which renders arbitration agreements invalid.** The federal Court ruled that Congress would not have wanted state and federal courts to reach different outcomes about the validity of arbitration agreements in similar cases.[600] The opponents in the *Terminix* v. *Dobson* case asked the Court to overrule that decision and thereby permit the Alabama court to apply its state law and deny validity to the arbitration clause. The Court pointed out, however, that in the meantime, no other court had eroded the decision, and Congress, both before and after the decision in the *Southland Corp.* v. *Keating* case, had enacted legislation which, conversely, strengthens arbitrability and also that the parties rely on the consistent application of this approach in a number of contracts. The U.S. Supreme Court denied the opponents' motion and upheld the conclusions made in the previous decision in *Southland Corp.* v. *Keating.*

582.   When interpreting Section 2 of the FAA [USA], the U.S. Supreme Court also interpreted the word *"evidencing,"* i.e. what in particular the contract is supposed to evidence. In this connection, the Court asked whether *"evidencing a transaction"* means only that the transaction (that the contract "evidences") must turn out, *in fact*, to have involved interstate commerce? Or, does the application of the FAA [USA] require anything else? According to Judge Lumbard's decision in a different dispute,[601] it was legally irrelevant whether any commercial exchange actually occurred between individual U.S. states in the course of performance of the terms of the contract; the relevant issue was whether the parties at least contemplated any such interstate commerce at the time they entered into the contract. Cogent evidence indicating the intent of the parties should therefore determine whether the contract falls within Section 2 FAA [USA][602] or not. This interpretation was subjected to vigorous criticism by the U.S. Supreme Court, because it **conflicts with the fundamental purpose of the Act. It begs the**

---

[599] See the decision in *Scherk* v. *Alberto Culver Co.*, 417 U. S., at 511.

[600] See the decision in *Southland Corp.* v. *Keating*, paras. (15) and (16); see also a separate detailed annotation elsewhere in this book.

[601] See the decision in *Metro Industrial Painting Corp.* v. *Terminal Constr. Co.*, 287 F. 2d 382, 387 (1961).

[602] The provision is quoted in a footnote above.

question of what was or was not contemplated by the parties. The process of establishing these facts, however, entails costs and delays in litigation which the Act was supposed to prevent.[603] The Court also suggested that such interpretation would often make the validity of the arbitration clause dependent on a random event, namely whether the parties happened to think to insert a reference to interstate commerce in the contract. The Court noted that in certain cases, this certainly cannot be expected of the parties. Section 2 FAA [USA] stipulates that the parties may, for instance, agree that existing disputes from a previously concluded contract will be submitted to arbitration – however, the criticized interpretation would render the arbitration clause invalid (or impossible to apply the federal Act) only because the parties originally did not anticipate that the relationship arising from the contract would have any interstate dimensions. For these reasons, the U.S. Supreme Court accepted an interpretation which allows a broader application of Section 2 FAA [USA],[604] i.e. an interpretation requiring *"only"* that the contract de facto concern interstate commerce. This applies even if the parties did not contemplate any such thing. According to the Alabama Supreme Court, the parties, when entering into the contract, contemplated and intended to enter into a contract the substance of which involved a local dimension, not an interstate connection. As analyzed above, this is legally irrelevant for the U.S. Supreme Court, and this case still falls within the scope of the FAA [USA]. Therefore, the arbitration clause must be accepted as valid. The federal Court noted, inter alia, that the parties had not contested that the contract in that case involved an interstate element.

583. Finally, the Court emphasized that Section 2 FAA [USA] especially gave the states (i.e. the state courts) a **method for protecting consumers against external pressure to agree to a contract with an unwanted arbitration provision.** The courts may hold the arbitration agreement invalid **using general legal principles upon** *"grounds as exist in law or in equity for the revocation of any contract."* However, the Court subjected to fierce criticism and held unlawful a procedure whereby a state court decides that the [main] contract is fair enough to enforce all its basic terms, but not fair enough to enforce its arbitration clause. That kind of policy places arbitration clauses on an unequal footing, compared to other contractual terms, which is directly contrary to both the Act's language and the legislator's intent.[605]

---

[603] See the decision in *Moses H. Cone Memorial Hospital* v. *Mercury Constr. Corp.*, 460 U.S. 1, 29 (1983).
[604] The provision is quoted in a footnote above.
[605] See the decision in *Volt Information Sciences, Inc.*, 489 U. S., para. (474).

(c) Judgment of the Court of Appeal of California, No. A068753 of 3 November 1998 (*Badie* v. *Bank of America*)

(aa) Conclusions of the Court

584. In the present case, the California court[606] ruled on certain fundamental issues as follows:

▶ Customers' consent to allow the bank to change terms did not constitute consent to the arbitration clause by unilateral notice. The Court reasons that the object, the subject matter or the nature of the original account agreement do not indicate that the claimant intended to assume obligations such as a submission of the dispute to alternative dispute resolution, to the exclusion of court jurisdiction. This applies all the more, because it constitutes a waiver of a right guaranteed under the Constitution.

▶ Ambiguous contract language should be interpreted most strongly against the party who prepared it, particularly in regard to adhesion contracts.[607]

▶ The fact that a contract is one of adhesion does not mean that it is also an "unconscionable" contract.[608]

▶ A modification made "*in accordance with the terms of the contract*" means, at least in part, a modification whose general subject matter was anticipated when the contract was entered into. The Court held that as concerns the procedure of amendment of the contract, it only contained a procedural condition regarding the requirement of "informing" the party about the amendment. Indeed, the existence of the agreement was one of the arguments of the respondent (bank). However, the Court thereby expanded the conditions for the validity of the amendment to the contract by the consensus regarding its terms.

▶ When the claimant fails to raise a point, or asserts it but fails to support it with evidence, we treat the point as waived.

▶ The federal policy favoring arbitration agreements [...] is at bottom a policy guaranteeing the enforcement of private contractual

---

[606] Court of Appeal of California, First Appellate District, Division Three, in *Sandra L. Badie et al.* v. *Bank of America*. Available online at: http://caselaw.findlaw.com/ca-court-of-appeal/1288986.html [last access 25 December 2011].

[607] "*In cases of uncertainty not removed by the preceding rules, the language of a contract should be interpreted most strongly against the party who caused the uncertainty to exist.*" (Civ. Code, § 1654 [USA-CAL]).

[608] The term "*unconscionable*" can in many legal concepts be interpreted as unfair treatment or as an absence of any expression of will. See the 1994 decision of the California Court of Appeal in *California Grocers Assn.* v. *Bank of America*; 22 Cal. App. 4th 205, 215–217; 27 Cal. Rptr. 2d 396.

arrangements.[609] However, it does not substitute for a voluntary consent to arbitration.[610]

▶ Whether there is an agreement to submit disputes to arbitration or reference does not turn on the existence of a *public policy* favoring alternative dispute resolution.

▶ The exercise of discretionary powers conferred onto a party by contract must also be evaluated under the implied covenant to assure that the promises of the contract are effective and in accordance with the parties' legitimate expectations.

▶ If the Bank's performance under the change of terms provision was not consonant with the duty of good faith and fair dealing, then whether the ADR clause, considered in isolation, satisfies the implied covenant makes no difference.

▶ An agreement on alternative dispute resolution is not integral to the relationship between the Bank and the client. Consequently, the change of terms provision cannot apply to such issues. It is necessary to point out, though, that the Court avoids generalization and formulates the sentence so that it clearly indicates that the Court is only referring to this particular arbitration clause. Hence, the general and normative nature of this conclusion is missing.

▶ Waiver of the right to a jury trial is inherent in the decision (expression of will) to resolve disputes in a nonjudicial forum. In this regard, the Court somewhat generalizes the postulate, broadly recognized by American doctrine, and explains the order made by a different court, the wording of which is not so obvious.[611]

▶ Where it is doubtful whether a party has waived his or her constitutionally protected right to a jury trial, the question should be resolved in favor of preserving that right.

(bb) Factual and legal findings

585. The claimants, clients of the Bank, challenged the validity of an arbitration clause which the respondent Bank sought to add to the existing adhesion account agreements between the parties by sending those customers a notification of the amendment. The trial court entered a judgment in favor of the respondent, ruling that the change of terms provision in the original contract permitted the modification of the contract by a unilateral act and, consequently, the addition of the arbitration clause. The trial court held the clause valid. The Court of Appeal reversed that judgment and, applying general rules on the

---

[609] See the decisions in the following cases: (•) *Mitsubishi Motors* v. *Soler Chrysler-Plymouth* (1985) 473 U.S. 614, 625, 105 S. Ct. 3346, 3353, 87 L. Ed. 2d 444; (•)*Volt Info. Sciences* v. *Leland Stanford Jr. U.* (1989) 489 U.S. 468, 478, 109 S. Ct. 1248, 1255, 103 L. Ed. 2d 488.

[610] See the decision of the California court in *Victoria* v. *Superior Court* (1985) 40 Cal. 3d 734, 739, 222 Cal. Rptr. 1, 710 P.2d 833.

[611] This other decision is the decision of the California court in *Madden*; 17 Cal. 3d on p. 714.

B2C Arbitration: Consumer Protection in Arbitration

conclusion and interpretation of contracts, concluded that the consent with the change of terms provision given by the claimants, clients of the Bank, was not intended to enable the respondent to unilaterally add the arbitration clause into their contract. Consequently, the Court of Appeal concluded that the arbitration clause was not integrated into the original contract and could not be enforced against the respondent.

(cc) Arguments of the parties and the Court's legal conclusions

586. According to the Court of Appeal, the claimants' briefs insufficiently addressed the statutory causes of action they brought (for instance, they did not even refer to the statutory provisions on which they based their claims). Consequently, the Court, invoking other decisions, pointed out that *"when a claimant fails to raise a point, or asserts it but fails to support it with reasoned argument and citations to authority, we treat the point as waived."* [612] The Court of Appeal therefore limited its review to the trial court's declaratory determination as to the validity and enforceability of the arbitration clause.

587. The Court of Appeal criticized the trial court for maintaining that the validity of the extension of the contract by the arbitration clause depends on how the alternative dispute resolution and, specifically, arbitration is treated under *California* law. The Court of Appeal held that the validity of the clause does not turn on the existence of a *public policy* favoring alternative dispute resolution. The primary issue to be established is whether the claimants agreed to use some form of alternative dispute resolution to resolve disputes regarding their account agreements with the respondent Bank. In doing so, the Court applied general legal principles that govern the formation and interpretation of contracts. Hence, the Court did not apply any special consumer protection, but carried out interpretation following general legal principles. Indeed, this argument is also fully applicable at the European, or even at the EU level. In Europe, it has also been argued (irrespective of the fundamental legal concept adopted by the individual state) that the special legal protection of consumers is unnecessary, because the same protection could be afforded by a diligent application of general legal principles. This approach merits full support. Of course, the need

---

[612] It is the application of the obligation to state the relevant facts and propose evidence supporting the facts.
The California Court of Appeal especially invoked the following preceding decisions: (•) *People* v. *Stanley*, (1995) 10 Cal. 4th 764, 793 [42 Cal. Rptr. 2d 543, 897 P.2d 481]; (•)*Tiernan* v. *Trustees of Cal. State University & Colleges* (1982) 33 Cal. 3d 211, 216, fn. 4 [188 Cal. Rptr. 115, 655 P.2d 317]; (•) *Muega* v. *Menocal* (1996) 50 Cal. App. 4th 868, 877 [57 Cal. Rptr. 2d 697]; (•) *San Mateo County Coastal Landowners' Assn.* v. *County of San Mateo* (1995) 38 Cal. App. 4th 523, 559 [45 Cal. Rptr. 2d 117]; (•) *Kim* v. *Sumitomo Bank* (1993) 17 Cal. App. 4th 974, 979 [21 Cal. Rptr. 2d 834]).

350

for consumer protection is undeniable; but special rules are unnecessary. The general legal environment is fully capable of securing such protection. Nevertheless, at least in the EU environment, it is necessary to take as the basis the existence, i.e. the mandatory application, of such special rules. However, the decision of the California Court of Appeal is a typical and a very well-articulated demonstration of the American approach to the protection of the contracting parties.

588.   The California Court of Appeal focuses, in this regard, primarily on what the parties intended when they expressed their agreement with the unilateral change of *"terms"* (here of the account agreement) by the Bank. The claimants limited the terms purely to price terms for currently existing services; this interpretation is supported by the fact that all conditions discussed in the original agreements pertain to matters that are integral to the relationship between the claimants (clients) and the respondent Bank, whereas the method of dispute resolution (which the Court considered a matter "collateral," i.e. not inherent in that contractual relationship) is not discussed in the original agreement at all. Conversely, the respondent Bank pointed out that the change of terms provision was articulated very broadly and did not contain any direct limitation of its enforcement. The Court of Appeal agreed with the claimant, arguing that the object, nature, and subject matter of this agreement strongly support the conclusion that the claimants, the Bank's customers, by agreeing to a unilateral change of terms provision, did not intend to give the Bank the power in the future to terminate their right to have disputes resolved in the civil justice system, including their constitutionally based right to a jury trial. In short, the original agreement(s) do(es) not suggest that ADR was one of *"those things concerning which the parties intended to contract."*[613] In this regard, the Court of Appeal also invokes Section 1654 of the California Civil Code.[614] According to said provision, any ambiguities in contract must be interpreted strictly against the drafter. [615] The Court also emphasized the constitutional nature of the right which was limited by the respondent party, and especially the stricter conditions applicable to any waiver of such a right. In this regard, the Court also held that in order to be enforceable, a contractual waiver of the right to a jury trial

---

[613] The California Civil Code, § 1648 (cit.): *"However broad may be the terms of a contract, it extends only to those things [obligations] concerning which it appears that the parties intended to contract."* (Civ. Code, § 1648)].
[614] The California Civil Code, § 1654 (cit.): *"In cases of uncertainty not removed by the preceding rules, the language of a contract should be interpreted most strongly against the party who caused the uncertainty to exist."* (Civ. Code, § 1654)].
[615] Quoted in a footnote above.
See also the following decisions of the California courts [USA]: (•) *Graham* v. *Scissor-Tail, Inc.* (1981) 28 Cal. 3d 807, 819-820, 171 Cal. Rptr. 604, 623 P.2d 165; (•) *Goddard* v. *South Bay Union High School Dist.*, 79 Cal. App. 3d at pp. 105–106.

"[the waiver] must be clearly apparent in the contract and its language must be unambiguous and unequivocal, leaving no room for doubt as to the intention of the parties."[616] The Court of Appeal notes that *"where it is doubtful whether a party has waived his or her constitutionally protected right to a jury trial, the question should be resolved in favor of preserving that right."*[617]

589. The respondent also contended that the contractual term was valid as long as the prescribed procedure for making the modification had been followed. The only procedural requirement set forth in the change of terms provision was that the respondent would notify the other party of the change. This suffices for the modification to be valid; the respondent therefore argued that the modification was valid if it was made *"in accordance with the terms of the contract."* However, the California Court of Appeal concluded otherwise, namely that the term *"in accordance with the terms of the contract"* means, at least in part, a modification whose general subject matter was (or could have been) anticipated when the contract was entered into.[618]

590. When determining whether the respondent, as a party to the contract with a discretionary right to change the rights of the other party, exercised its entitlement in compliance with the duty of good faith and fair dealing, the trial court concluded that the respondent (Bank) duly discharged the obligation when amending the account agreement. The trial court held that the arbitration clause, as a modification of the contract, does not deprive the other party of the anticipated and agreed advantage benefiting the party under the agreement (its contractual status). Conversely, the Court of Appeal criticized this opinion of the trial court. The Court focused on the arbitration clause, in isolation, and concluded that the primary subject of analysis is the exercise of the discretionary right of the respondent to change the contract, not the

---

[616] See the decision of the California Court of Appeal in *Trizec Properties, Inc.* v. *Superior Court* (1991) 229 Cal. App. 3d 1616, 1619, 280 Cal. Rptr. 885 (cit.): "[It] *must be clearly apparent in the contract and its language must be unambiguous and unequivocal, leaving no room for doubt as to the intention of the parties."*

[617] The California Court of Appeal invokes the preceding decision of a California court in *Byram* v. *Superior Court* (1977) 74 Cal. App. 3d 648, 654; 141 Cal. Rptr. 604.

[618] The California Court of Appeal invokes the preceding decisions of California courts in the following cases: (•) *Busch* v. *Globe Industries*, 200 Cal. App. 2d 315, (•) *Clark Equipment Co.* v. *Mastelotto, Inc.* (1978) 87 Cal. App. 3d 88, 150 Cal. Rptr. 79] (•) as well as the decision in *Powell* v. *Central Cal. Fed. Sav. & Loan Assn.* (1976) 59 Cal. App. 3d 540, 130 Cal. Rptr. 635. In said cases, modifications of a contract in its original wording were defined as changes which might be made in the future under certain circumstances (cit.): *"The modifications in question were specifically identified in the original contracts as changes that might be made in the future under certain circumstances."* See also the decision in *Hunt* v. *Mahoney* (1947) 82 Cal. App. 2d 540, 546, 187 P.2d 43, (cit.): *"Extension of time to perform was not a modification requiring a writing [written notification], because the possibility of an extension was provided for in [the] original contract."*

arbitration clause itself. Consequently, it is especially necessary to determine whether the respondent exercised its right in compliance with the duty of good faith and *fair dealing*. The Court of Appeal concluded, however, that if the very exercise of the Bank's right under the change of terms provision did not comply with the duty of good faith and fair dealing, it is irrelevant whether the arbitration clause itself complies with this implicit requirement or not. According to the extensive interpretation advocated by the respondent (Bank), the Bank may exercise its discretionary right (the right to change the contract) with no limitation on the substantive nature of the changes it may make as long as it complies with the de minimis procedural requirement of "notice" [to the other party]. However, such interpretation virtually eliminates the good faith and fair dealing requirement from the Bank's relationship with its customers. Therefore, the Court of Appeal concluded (as opposed to the opinion expressed by the trial court) that the respondent (Bank) had not satisfied the requirement in its exercise of the discretionary right to amend the contract.

(d) Judgment of the United States Court of Appeals, Sixth Circuit, No. 98-028 30 / 99-3854 of 8 September 2000 (*James D. Stout; Shirley A. Brown v. J. D. Byrider*, a/k/a *Docherty Motors, Inc.*; *T & J Acceptance Corporation*, d/b/a *Carnow Acceptance Company*)[619]

(aa) Conclusions of the Court

591. ▶ Consumer protection laws do not prohibit arbitration agreements (arbitration clauses) in consumer credit agreements.

▶ If the parties agree on the jurisdiction of a particular arbitral institution with its own available rules on arbitration, **there is no reason to *a priori* presume that these institutions would fail to provide fair protection to consumers.**

▶ The buyers' (consumers') contention that the sellers would not enter into the purchase contract with them if they did not conclude the arbitration agreement is a speculation; unless there is clear evidence supporting such a conclusion, the assumption must not be accepted and the arbitration agreement must not be rejected.[620]

---

[619] 228 F3d 709 (2000). The judgment is available online at: http://www.leagle.com/xmlResult.aspx?xmldoc=2000937228F3d709_1879.xml&docbase=CSLWAR2-1986-2006 [last access 2 September 2011].
[620] Further conclusions made by the court are mentioned below in connection with the summary of the court's arguments.

(bb) Factual and legal findings

592. The dispute concerned the sale of used cars financed through *CarNow Acceptance Corporation* (CNAC) *franchises*. At the closing of the contracts for the sale of vehicles, a CNAC (seller) representative presented various documents to the buyer, including a separate, written arbitration agreement in bold type. The content of the arbitration agreement was briefly explained at the closing. The seller gave the buyer the opportunity to ask questions and to review the paperwork before signing. The transactions were videotaped.

593. The claims in court were filed by two claimants jointly. Their contracts contained different arbitration agreements, in the first case appointing the AAA [USA], in the second case the *Better Business Bureau*. The claimants alleged violations of the Ohio Consumer Sales Practices Act and fraud. The respondents pleaded lack of jurisdiction and moved to compel arbitration. The claimants argued that Congress did not intend to allow that TILA claims (*Truth in Lending Act* of 1968)[621] could be subject to arbitration and invoked the decision in *Randolph v. Green Tree Financial Corp.*[622]

594. Both claimants filed a class action against *J. D. Byrider* and *CNAC* for the violation of TILA [USA], for violations of the Ohio Consumer Sales Practices Act, and for common law fraud. Both parties moved for summary judgment,[623] and the respondents filed a motion to compel arbitration.

(cc) Arguments of the courts

595. The district court granted the respondent's defense of lack of jurisdiction and compelled arbitration. The court held that the arbitration agreements were valid (*enforceable*) both under Ohio law [USA] and under federal law [USA]. The Court of Appeals, Sixth Circuit, affirmed the orders of the trial court. It found, in reliance on the videotapes, that the claimants had clearly agreed to arbitrate; they reviewed, discussed, read, and signed the arbitration agreements. The Sixth Circuit found that ***Randolph v. Green Tree Financial Corp.*** was

---

[621] The object of the Act is to safeguard the provision of full and accurate information to the recipients of consumer credits. The Act also aims to secure the fair resolution of disputes over installments on consumer credits. The original title of the Act was "*Consumer Credit Protection Act*"; 15 USC Sec. 1473. Available online at: http://www.fdic.gov/regulations/laws/rules/6500-1400.html [last access 2 September 2011] and elsewhere.

[622] In *Randolph* v. *Green Tree Financial Corp.* the Court held the arbitration agreement in a consumer credit agreement invalid for limiting the consumer in the exercise of his/her rights under the TILA [USA].

[623] An institution which means (simply speaking) that the court rules on the entire case or specific (especially) legal issues at the request of the parties without a jury trial.

distinguishable and could not be invoked. In *Randolph* v. *Green Tree Financial Corp.*[624] the parties did not agree on the jurisdiction of an institution which would presume clear rules for the resolution of such disputes. In the present case (*Stout* v. *J. D. Byrider*, a/k/a *Docherty Motors, Inc.*) the situation was different. Consequently, the Court rejected the claimants' arguments. The Court found no evidence that the arbitration agreements were unenforceable adhesion contracts, one-sided or unfair (unconscionable). The claimants presented only speculation that if they refused to sign the arbitration agreements, the respondents would not enter into the vehicle purchase contracts with them. Furthermore, there was no evidence that the arbitration organizations would fail to fairly and equally oversee the claimants' claims.

596.   The claimants argued that the arbitration agreements were unfair and against *Ohio public policy* [USA]. The Court concluded, however, that if the parties had clearly agreed on submitting their contractual and non-contractual claims to arbitration, *"neither this Court nor the Ohio courts have the ability to mandate judicial resolution of these disputes in violation of the parties' agreement."*[625]

(e) **Judgment of the Supreme Court of Arkansas, No. 1981594 of 15 September 2000 (*Alabama Catalog Sales* v. *Harris*): Jurisdiction over the validity of arbitration agreements**

(aa)   **Conclusion of the Court**

597.   The Supreme Court of Alabama held that the trial court, not the arbitrator, must decide the legality and enforceability of contracts containing an arbitration clause and especially arbitration clauses. It was a majority decision, opposed by a minority of the judges in their dissenting opinions; moreover, the conclusion cannot be said to enjoy any major support. On the contrary, the decision is rather exceptional.

---

[624] Judgment of the Supreme Court of the United States, Case No. 98-6055 of 13 March 2001 (in *Larketta Randolph, on behalf of herself and all others similarly situated*, v. *Green Tree Financial Corp. – Alabama et Green Tree Financial Corporation*), 244 F. 3d 814, 819 (11th Cir. 2001). Available online at: http://caselaw.findlaw.com/us-11th-circuit/1453496.html [last access 28 December 2011].

[625] Adopted from: Zuckerman, S., C. Arbitrability of TILA claims. Available online at: http://www.allbusiness.com/legal/mediation/1105777-1.html [2 September 2011] and at: http://findarticles.com/p/ articles/mi_qa3923 /is_200011 / ai_n8957192/pg_2/?tag=mantle_skin;content [last access 14 August 2011]. See also *Maurer, K.* The Truth about Arbitration: Enforcing Consumers' and Employees' Legal Rights, Michigan Bar Journal, May 2003, also available online at: http://www.michbar.org/journal/pdf/pdf4article564.pdf [last access 2 September 2011] et al.

(bb) Factual and legal findings

598. The claimant sued *Alabama Catalog Sales*, a catalog sales company, alleging that it violated the Alabama [USA] Small Loan Act. The claimant argued that the *"payday"* loans were unlawful, the interest was usurious, and the company collected on the loans without a license. The claimant also contended that the arbitration agreements were void for illegality. The respondent company argued that the validity of the arbitration clauses should only be determined by the arbitrators.

(cc) Arguments of the courts

599. The trial court denied the respondent's plea of lack of jurisdiction and denied the motion to compel jurisdiction. A majority of the Alabama High Court affirmed the order.

600. The court ruled that the claimant himself pleaded invalidity of the arbitration clause. Considering the illegality of the agreement, the issue was to be determined by the court. However, several judges argued, in their dissenting opinion, that the contracts were not *facially* void; consequently, they should have been assessed primarily by the arbitrators according to the *"Kompetenz-Kompetenz"* principle.[626]

(f) Judgment of the Supreme Court of Arkansas, No. 99-1398 of 21 September 2000 (*ShowMeTheMoney* v. *Williams*): Requirement of mutuality of arbitration clauses

(aa) Conclusion of the Court

601. ▶ The arbitration clause [here in consumer contracts] must be the **expression of the mutual rights and obligations of the parties.** Genuine mutuality means a requirement of the joint interest of both parties to submit potential disputes to arbitration.

(bb) Factual and legal findings

602. The claimant *ShowMeTheMoney Check Cashers* entered into agreements with customers to pay up to 100 USD cash in return for checks of equal amount.[627] The company promised to collect the amounts specified in the checks on the due date and deposit them with a

---

[626] Adopted from: *Zuckerman, S., C.* Who decides arbitrability. AAA, November 2000 – January 2001. Available online at http://findarticles.com/p/articles/mi_qa3923/is_200011/ai_n8962593/?tag= mantle_skin;content [last access 14 August 2011].

[627] Whereas many countries (especially in Europe) are unfamiliar with paying by check, it is a very common practice in Anglo-Saxon countries, especially in the U.S. Even petty costs and wages are often paid by check. Hence, check collection services are commonly offered.

bank. The company charged a 15 USD fee as a remuneration for the service. The agreements contained an arbitration clause covering potential claims against customers. The claimants obtained cash advances from *ShowMeTheMoney Check Cashers* at closing but did not have their due and payable checks cashed. The claimants alleged that the contracts violated the usury law. The claimants (customers/consumers) filed their claims with a court. The respondents pleaded lack of jurisdiction, referring to the arbitration clauses.

(cc) Arguments of the courts

603. The trial court rejected the jurisdictional challenge. The Arkansas Supreme Court affirmed the order of the trial court, emphasizing the ineffectiveness (invalidity / literally *unenforceability*) for lack of mutuality of the arbitration clause. To satisfy the mutuality requirement, the agreement must fix a real liability on both parties. The Court said that arbitration clauses must not be used as a *shield* against litigation by one party which reserved to itself the sword of court action.[628] The *Arkansas Supreme Court* held that an arbitration clause in a check-cashing agreement that reserved the company's right to sue in court, whereas the company's customers were forced to submit their disputes to arbitration, was unenforceable for lack of mutuality.

(g) Decision of the Supreme Court of the United States, Case No. 09-893 of 11 April 2011 (*Vincent Concepcion & others* v. *AT&T Mobility LLC*): Prevalence of the purpose of arbitration over special consumer protection

(aa) Conclusions of the Court

604. In the present case, the U.S. Supreme Court[629] **reached, inter alia, the following conclusions**:
▶ Special consumer protection[630] consisting, for instance, in the right to join a class action cannot prevail over the main objectives of the

---

[628] Adopted from: *Zuckerman, S. C.* Consumer: Mutuality requirement. Dispute Resolution Journal, Nov 2000 – Jan 2001. Available online at: http://findarticles.com/p/articles/mi_qa3923/is_200011/ai_n8955347/?tag=mantle_skin;content [last access 14 August 2011]. See also *Kennett, A. K.* Case Notes: *Showmethemoney Check Cashers, Inc.* v. *Williams*: Show Me the Mutuality – A New Demand Based on an Old Doctrine Changes the Rules for Enforceability of Arbitration Agreements in Arkansas. Ark. L. Rev., 2001-2002, Vol. 54, p. 621 et seq.

[629] The information was adopted from the annotation published in: *Amirfar, C. M. et Akpa, S. O.* In: *Liza and Vincent Concepcion* v. *AT&T Mobility*, the Supreme Court of the United States held that Section 2 of the *Federal Arbitration Act* preempts California law invalidating class action waivers in certain types of consumer contracts, and that therefore, the waiver in the underlying contract was valid (11 April 2011). ITA Arbitration Reporter, KLI, 2011, Vol. 9, No. 11.

[630] Here as expressed in the decision of the California Supreme Court [USA] in *Discover Bank* v. *Superior Court*, 113 P. 3d 1100 (Cal. 2005).

Federal Arbitration Act (FAA [USA]), i.e. to safeguard the enforceability of arbitration agreements.

▶ Arbitration clauses may be invalidated by generally applicable contract defenses, such as fraud, duress, etc., but not by a defense consisting solely in the disproportionality of the arbitration clause [in consumer contracts].

▶ The law must not be applied so as to disadvantage arbitration.

(bb) Factual and legal findings

605. In February 2002 *Liza and Vincent Concepcion* entered into an agreement with *AT&T Mobility LLC* (AT&T) for the sale and servicing of their cellular (mobile) phones. The contract contained an arbitration clause which excluded classwide arbitration proceedings. Although a final price was declared, AT&T also charged a sales tax.[631] In 2006 the *Concepcions* filed a complaint against AT&T in the federal District Court for the Southern District of California [USA]. The complaint was later consolidated with a putative class action alleging, among other things, that AT&T had engaged in unfair competition, namely false advertising and fraud regarding the price. After the contract was entered into, AT&T incorporated changes in the arbitration clause contained in the contractual terms and conditions. These changes included, inter alia, the minimum compensation for the costs of proceedings sustained by AT&T amounting to 7,500 USD, as well as other changes concerning, for instance, legal fees. In 2008 AT&T initiated arbitration and invoked the amended arbitration clause. The *Concepcions* argued that the arbitration clause was unconscionable and unlawfully exculpatory under California law, because it included a class action waiver.

(cc) Arguments of the courts

606. The trial court denied AT&T's motion, although it held that the arbitration agreement also contained provisions favorable to consumers.[632] The reason was especially the fact that AT&T failed to prove that arbitration as strictly bilateral proceedings would prevail over the deterrent effects of class actions. The federal Court of Appeals[633] affirmed the order and held that the FAA [USA] did not prevail over rules based on the case law of California courts which renders any waiver of class action invalid. The reason is that these rules concern contract law in general, not only arbitration law.

---

[631] An indirect (sales) tax, substitutes for the Value-Added Tax applicable in Europe.
[632] With reference to a preceding decision of the California Supreme Court [USA] in *Discover Bank* v. *Superior Court*, 113 P. 3d 1100 (Cal. 2005).
[633] Federal Court of Appeals, Ninth Circuit.

607.   However, the Supreme Court of the United States reversed the preceding decision and invoked the decision in *Discover Bank* v. *Superior Court.*[634] The Court emphasized that the rule articulated in that case undermines the fundamental objective of the FAA [USA]; consequently, the FAA [USA][635] prevails. The Court also held that arbitration clauses may be invalidated by generally applicable contract defenses, such as fraud, duress, etc., but not by a defense consisting solely in the disproportionality of the arbitration agreement. The U.S. Supreme Court also held that special consumer protection manifested in the *Discover Bank* case and in the right to join a class action cannot prevail over the main objective of the FAA [USA], i.e. to safeguard the enforceability of arbitration agreements. The Court also ruled that law must not be applied so as to disadvantage arbitration. The U.S. Supreme Court emphasized that class actions (albeit in arbitration) significantly differ from individual proceedings and mentioned the disadvantages of class actions[636] such as higher formality, higher costs, slower proceedings, together with higher risks for the consumer.

(dd) Commentary on the decision

608.   The decision is important for the fact that the protection of arbitration clauses and the faith in their enforceability prevailed even at the time of culminating discussions about the future of arbitration agreements in consumer contracts. It is a landmark decision, especially with regard to the time when it was rendered by the U.S. Supreme Court, and it confirms the long-standing trend supporting arbitration. At the same time, the decision indirectly rejects any populist consumer protection and highlights the need to strengthen an awareness of the law and knowledge and observance of the principles of general law; this goes hand-in-hand with the criticism of special protection laws.

---

[634] 30 Cal.Rptr.3d 76. The California Supreme Court found the arbitration clause in the present case unenforceable. The reason was that a class action waiver incorporated in the arbitration clause would exculpate *Discover Bank* from liability for unlawful conduct causing small amounts of damages to the customer. However, the conclusion of the California Supreme Court in this case was overruled and modified in *AT&T* v. *Concepcion*. (AT&T was the appellant before the U.S. Supreme Court; in the trial court, the company was the respondent and the other party was the claimant.)
[635] Section 2 FAA [USA].
[636] The U.S. Supreme Court invoked, for instance, its decision in *Stolt-Nielsen S. A.* v. *Animal Feeds Int. Corp.*, 130 S.Ct. 1758 (2010).

V. Consumer Arbitration as the Subject Matter of Proceedings in Court

609.   If any consumer arbitration issues become the subject of litigation, it is probable that the case will in any connection concern the validity of the arbitration clause. This is the reason why this issue was focused on in the preceding chapters of this book. The following section will concentrate on consumer arbitration problems which the courts commonly handle. The individual subsections are arranged according to the various procedural stages during which the courts may become involved in these matters.

V.1. Validity of arbitration agreements in consumer contracts

V.1.1. Importance of the validity of arbitration agreements

610.   A valid arbitration agreement confers the exclusive jurisdiction to hear and resolve a dispute upon arbitrators. Hence, in most states the arbitration agreement automatically excludes the jurisdiction of courts, if the subject matter of the dispute is covered by the arbitration agreement.[1] According to most national laws, the courts dismiss or reject a claim if the matter is covered by an arbitration agreement unless the arbitration agreement is invalid.

611.   Article II(3) of the *New York Convention* stipulates that the court shall refer the parties to arbitration unless one of the parties claims that the arbitration agreement is *"null and void, inoperative, or incapable of being performed."* Similar rules can be found in most national *leges arbitri*.[2] Besides, Article V(1)(a) of the *New York Convention* stipulates

---

[1] See the CCP [CZE] (cit.): Section 106 – "(1) *As soon as the court discovers, on the respondent's objection lodged together with or before the first act of the respondent in the merits, that the agreement of the parties requires that the case be submitted to arbitration, the court must desist from further examination of the case and terminate the proceedings; the court, however, hears the case if the parties declare that they waive the agreement. The court also hears the case if the court determines that the matter is not arbitrable under the laws of the Czech Republic, or that the arbitration agreement is invalid or non-existent, or that examining the agreement in arbitration proceedings exceeds the scope of jurisdiction vested in the arbitrators by the agreement, or that the arbitral tribunal refused to hear the case. (2) If the court proceedings under Subsection (1) were terminated and the same case was submitted to arbitration, the original petition for commencement of the proceedings retains its legal effects providing the motion for the commencement of the arbitration proceedings is lodged no later than 30 days of service of the court's resolution terminating the proceedings. (3) If the arbitration proceedings were opened before the court proceedings, the court stays the proceedings on the non-existence, nullity, or expiration/termination of the agreement until the arbitrator(s) decide on their jurisdiction over the case or in the merits."* A similar solution can be found in many other legal systems.
[2] See:
 ➢ [FRA]: Section 1458 of the Code of Civil Procedure (before amendment),
 ➢ [GBR-ENG] Section 9(4) of the AA [GBR-ENG],
 ➢ [CHE]: Section 7(b) of the IPRG [CHE].

that recognition and enforcement may be refused if the arbitration agreement is not valid *"under the law to which the parties have subjected it or, failing any indication thereon, under the law of the country where the award was made"* (i.e. under the law of the seat of arbitration). For more details regarding these issues, see below.

V.1.2. Scope of the concept of "validity of an arbitration agreement" in consumer relations

612.   There are two aspects which might influence the validity of arbitration clauses in consumer contracts. First, the material (objective) arbitrability of a consumer dispute, i.e. whether a particular dispute, or the subject matter of the dispute, may be submitted to arbitration or whether it falls within the exclusive jurisdiction of courts. Any issue is arbitrable (may be heard and resolved in arbitration) if applicable law allows the parties to enter into an arbitration agreement covering the respective type of dispute.

613.   The concept of arbitrability *"is connected with the limitations which apply to arbitration as a method of dispute resolution according to public policy. Any country may decide, in compliance with its own economic and social policy, which disputes may be resolved in arbitration and which may not."*[3] Many countries typically exclude from the scope of arbitrability any disputes which concern criminal law issues (especially proceedings in *public law matters*), a number of family law disputes, employment disputes, etc.

614.   The total absence or limitation of the arbitrability of consumer disputes may be defined by applicable law either in negative terms (by denying arbitrability) or in positive terms (by stipulating exclusive jurisdiction for courts or other authorities or prescribing a particular procedure). If the law contains rules exclusively regulating any special procedure applicable to consumer disputes, such disputes may not be resolved in arbitration if at least one of the contracting parties is a consumer. For example, French law stipulates that disputes with an individual/natural person (consumer disputes) are not arbitrable, and an arbitration agreement would in such case be invalid. However, even France has experienced significant developments favoring arbitrability even in disputes with a natural person acting in a capacity other than as a professional.[4] The arbitrability rules in selected countries are discussed above.

---

[3] *Redfern, A. and Hunter, M.* Law and Practice of International Commercial Arbitration, 1991, p. 137.
[4] For more details, see a separate section elsewhere in this book, including references to selected decisions of French courts.

615.   Nonetheless, the validity of arbitration agreements relating to consumer relationships is not limited exclusively to arbitrability issues. Even if the consumer dispute itself is arbitrable, the validity of the arbitration agreement is subject to, and only to, the conditions of its formation.[5] As the ECJ's case law clearly indicates, EU law does not principally rule out the possibility of resolving consumer disputes in arbitration.[6] Even EU law leaves major decisions and conditions at the sole discretion of the Member States. Consequently, EU law does not prescribe the conditions of arbitrability, it merely lays down certain fundamental requirements concerning arbitration agreements negotiated in connection with consumer contracts and the conclusion of such agreements. Hence, EU law cannot be said to prohibit arbitration agreements with respect to consumer contracts. Neither does EU law regulate the form of the arbitration agreement.

616.   Considering the presumed unique nature of arbitration as an exception to the general jurisdiction of courts, national laws (lex arbitri) usually require that the arbitration agreement be concluded following special rules. This arrangement is supposed to guarantee that the expression of will shall also meet specific criteria, as a manifestation of the parties' awareness of the exceptional nature of the procedure. This rule has been significantly simplified especially thanks to the frequent use of distance communication in the conclusion of contracts, as well as in connection with the simplification of repeated legal transactions by using [general] contract terms and conditions. The requirement of written arbitration agreements (printed, or in one and the same document, or as an explicit expression of will, etc.) was therefore alleviated in a number of national laws or based on national case law. An even more significant simplification occurred at the international level. In spite of that, however, the requirement of an expression of will which meets strict formal criteria still exists in a number of legal systems specifically in connection with consumer protection. Such stricter requirements must always be interpreted as special requirements regarding the validity of arbitration agreements in consumer contracts. The validity of arbitration agreements in consumer disputes may be contained both in general arbitration laws [lex arbitri] (and may even depend on general

---

[5] See the decision of the Supreme Court of Canada [CAN], Case No. 31067 of 13 July 2007 in *Dell* v. *Union des Consommateurs et Olivier Dumoulin.* Cited under Ref.: [2007] 2 S.C.R. 801 or 2007 SCC 34. The Supreme Court of Canada has held that the laws of the Province of Québec have never explicitly stipulated that consumer disputes are not arbitrable. The Canadian approach is different. The Consumer Protection Act of Québec [CAN] contains a specific provision regarding the validity, applicability, and effects of arbitration agreements concluded with consumers. See para. (221) of the decision.
[6] See the Judgment of the BGH [DEU], Case No. III ZR 256/03 of 13 January 2005, annotated in detail in this book (in the part concerning consumer arbitration in Germany [DEU]), as well as the ECJ's case law, also annotated in detail in this book.

rules regulating the validity of legal – juridical – acts), and in special rules regulating consumer contracts.

617.   Besides, even under the general standards applicable in the U.S., an arbitration agreement for consumer disputes is *"unconscionable,"* i.e. *"invalid,"* if it requires a financially demanding arbitration or in those cases where the contractual terms are executed in small print.[7, 8]

618.   The *doctrine of unconscionability* excludes the application of the arbitration agreement, or even, in selected states of the U.S., renders the respective arbitration agreement invalid.[9] This doctrine especially applies in those cases where the party which proposed the agreement abused its position and the other party had no other option, under the circumstances, than to sign the agreement. The courts decide whether the arbitration agreement would be entered into if the contractual relationships were entirely free and voluntary. This primarily concerns standard form contracts negotiated in regular legal transactions. This theory does not limit the application of such an approach to selected types of contracts.

V.1.3.   Law applicable to the validity of the arbitration agreement

619.   Arbitration agreements seldom identify the law applicable to them[10] despite the fact that the choice of law by the arbitral panel is important;

---

[7] Concerning said issue, see also Judgment of the SC CR [CZE], Case No. 23 Cdo 1201/2009 of 29 June 2010; this judgment is annotated in detail elsewhere in this book – see the excursus into Czech law.

[8] Some experts argue that, as opposed to EU law (the *Directive*), the unfairness of an agreement in the U.S. is assessed at the moment of conclusion of the agreement, not at the time of the arbitral proceedings. See *Maisonneuve, M.* Le droit américain de l'arbitrage et la théorie de l'unconscionability. Rev. arb., 2005, p. 101. We cannot agree with this conclusion and maintain that the *Directive* also requires that we take account of the situation at the moment of conclusion of the agreement. Indeed, the *Directive* demands that we focus primarily on the circumstances attending the conclusion of the agreement (contract), i.e. the situation at the moment of conclusion thereof. Consequently, we do not identify with this legal opinion as concerns the basic differences between the American approach [USA] and the European approach [EU]. Besides, the Member States themselves are to determine the general imperative as to what legal situation should be taken account of by the court (for instance) in the process of negotiating the contract. The standards of the individual Member States significantly differ in this respect. But if we are supposed to assess the nature of an arbitration clause in a consumer contract and the (un)fairness thereof, the *Directive* requires that we examine the circumstances attending the conclusion thereof.

[9] Cf. *Korobkin, R.* Bounded Rationality, Standard Form Contracts and Unconscionability. University of Chicago Law Review, 2003, Vol. 70, p. 1203 et seq.

[10] For more details concerning this issue, see: *Bělohlávek, A.* Římská úmluva / Nařízení Řím I. Komentář. [Title in translation: Rome Convention / Rome I Regulation. Commentary]. Prague: C. H. Beck, 2009, marg. 01.930 through 01.1289; *Bělohlávek, A.* Rome Convention / Rome I Regulation, Huntington (NY, USA): JurisPublishing, 2010, marg. 01.930 through 01.1289 (as well as other language versions of the same book, for instance in Polish – Warsaw: C. H. Beck, 2010, in Russian – Kiev (Ukraine): Taxon, 2010, the future Romanian version – Bucharest: C. H. Beck, to be issued in

an incorrect choice may ultimately result in annulment of the award by courts in the seat of arbitration. The parties may subject the validity of the arbitration agreement to the following applicable laws: **(i)** law of the place where the agreement was entered into, **(ii)** law of the place where

---

2012, etc.); *Bělohlávek, A.* Právo použitelné na řízení před rozhodci. [Title in translation: The Law Applicable to Arbitration]. Právo a podnikání. 2005, No. 11, pp. 2–9; *Böhm, P.* Zur Rechtsnatur des Schiedsvertrages unter nationalen und internationalen Gesichtspunkten. ZfRV, 1968, p. 262 et seq.; *Cahn, A.* Prozessualle Dispositionsfreiheit und zwingendes materielles Recht. Archiv für die civilistische Praxis, 1998, No. 198, pp. 35–71; *Collins, L.* The law governing agreement and procedure in international arbitration in England. In: *Lew, J. D. M.* (ed.) Contemporary Problems in International Arbitration, Dordrecht/Boston/Lancaster: Martinus Nijhoff Publishers, 1987, p. 127 et seq.; *Derains, Y.* Possible Conflict of Laws Rules and the Rules Applicable to the Substance of the Dispute. In: *Sanders, P.* (ed.) UNCITRAL's Project for a Model Law on International Commercial Arbitration. ICCA Congress Series, 1994, No. 2, p. 169 et seq.; *Ereciński, T. et Weitz, K.* Sąd arbitrażowy, Warsaw: Wydawnictwa Prawnicze LexisNexis, 2008; *Esposito, M.* L'arbitrato tra autonomia privata e giurisdizione (Corte cost. 17 dicembre 1997 n. 410. Giur. cost., 1998, Vol. 43, No. 1, pp. 251–282; *Goldmann, B.* Les conflicts des lois dans l'arbitrage international de droit privé. Recueil des Cours, 1963, p. 352 et seq.; *Gonsorčíková, M.* Právně teoretické aspekty procesní smlouvy jako nástroje upravující rozhodčí řízení. [Title in translation: Legal Theoretical Aspects of Procedural Contracts as Instruments Regulating Arbitration]. iPrávník, available online at: http://www.ipravnik.cz/cz/clanky/civilni-proces/art_3708/pravne-teoreticke-aspekty [last access 21 July 2008]; *Hanefeld, I. et Wittinghofer, M. A.* Schiedsklauseln in Allgemeinen Geschäftsbedingen SchiedsVZ, 2005, Vol. 3, No. 5, pp. 217–229; *Heiskanen, V.* Jurisdiction v. Competence: Revisiting a Frequently Neglected Distinction. Ius Gentium RY – Finnish Yearbook of International Law – Acta Societatis Fennicae Iuris Gentium A-Series, 1994, Vol. 5; *von Hoffmann, B.* Die internationale Schiedsrichtervertrag – eine kollisionsrechtliche Skizze. In: *Platney, A.* (ed.) Festschrift zum Siebzigsten Geburtstag Ottoarndt Glossner, Heidelberg: Verlag Recht u. Wirtschaft, 1994, p. 143; *Macur, J.* Důvody neplatnosti rozhodčí smlouvy. [Title in translation: The Grounds for Nullity of Arbitration Agreements]. Právní rozhledy, 2001, No. 12, pp. 579–583; *Macur, J.* Lze posuzovat procesní jednání stran podle ustanovení hmotného práva o vadách právních úkonů? [Title in translation: May the Procedural Acts of the Parties be Assessed According to Substantive Rules on the Defects of Legal (Juridical) Acts?] Právní rozhledy, 1995, No. 11, pp. 440–443; *Marek, K. et Žváčková, L.* Obchodní podmínky, obchodní zvyklosti a vykládací pravidla. [Title in translation: Business Terms, Business Usages and Interpretation Rules]. Prague: ASPI, 2008; *Myšáková, P.* Autonomie vůle v mezinárodní arbitráži. [Title in translation: Autonomy of Will in International Arbitration]. Právní rádce, 2008, Vol. 16, No. 3, p. 41 et seq.; *Rozehnalová, N.* Určení fóra a jeho význam pro spory s mezinárodním prvkem. [Title in translation: Determination of the Forum and Its Importance for Disputes with an International Dimension]. Bulletin advokacie. 2005, I: No. 4, pp. 16–23 and II: No. 5, pp. 12–16; *Rozumov, K.* The Law Governing the Capacity to Arbitrate. ICCA Congress Series, 1994, No. 7; *Sehnálek, D. et Gonsorčíková, M.* Online Arbitration: Problems with Cyberspace. In: Cyberspace 2003, Normative Framework. Collection of Articles from a Conference, Brno: Masaryk University, 2004; *Seraglini, Ch.* Les parties faibles face à l'arbitrage international: à la recherche de l'équilibre. Gaz. Pal., Cah. de l'arbitrage, 2007, No. 4, p. 5 et seq.; *Wagner, B.* Prozeßverträge, Tübingen: Mohr Siebeck, 1998; *Wagner, G.* Rechtswahlfreiheit im Schiedsverfahren: Ein Probierstein für die juristische Methodenlehre. In: *Roth, H. et Gottwald, P.* Festschrift für Ekkehard Schumann zum 70. Geburtstag, Tübingen: Mohr Siebeck, 2002, p. 535 et seq.; *Walton, A.* Russell on the Law of Arbitration. London: Stevens and Sons, 1979; *Zachariasiewicz, M.* Autonomiczny charakter klauzuli arbitrażowej w międzynarodowym arbitrażu handlowym. In: *Pazdan, M.* (ed.) Problemy Prawa Prywatnego Międzynarodowego, Part I, Katowice: Wydawnictwo Uniwersytetu Śląskiego, 2007, pp. 85–114; *Žilcov, A. H.* Primjenimoje pravo v meždunarodnom kommerčeskom arbitraže (Title in translation: Law Applicable in International Commercial Arbitration), Moscow: 1998. (Title in original: Жильцов, А. Н. Применимое право в международном коммерческом арбитраже, Москва, 1998) et al.

the arbitration took place (seat of arbitration) and **(iii)** law of the place of enforcement of the arbitral award (although a choice of law according to this connecting factor is very rare in practice).

620. It is probable that under the *"Kompetenz-Kompetenz"* principle (i.e. the principle of independence/separability of the arbitration agreement from the main contract, as partially mentioned above and analyzed below) the dispute will first be submitted to an arbitral tribunal supervised by a court of law. Arbitral tribunals may determine that the law applicable to the arbitration agreement is the law chosen by the parties, or the law applicable to the main contract, or the law chosen according to different principles. This will depend on the law applicable to the seat of arbitration.

621. Switzerland [CHE] has adopted a special provision regulating these issues, namely Section 178(2) of the IPRG [CHE]. The provision stipulates that *"the arbitration agreement is valid if it complies with (i) the law chosen by the parties, or (ii) the law applicable to the merits of the dispute, especially the law applicable to the main contract, or (iii) Swiss law."*

622. In France [FRA], international arbitral tribunals (with their seat of arbitration in France [FRA]) may decide on the validity of arbitration agreements not by reference to a particular national law, but simply by reference to the genuine and joint intent of the parties, taking into account *public policy*.[11]

623. Courts will usually determine applicable law according to the conflict-of-law rules of private international law. Most national *lex arbitri* define the subject of arbitrability, i.e. determine the scope of matters [disputes] which may be resolved in arbitration, in compliance with Article II(1) of the *New York Convention*.[12] Consequently, national courts usually tend to conclude that the law applicable to the arbitration agreement is identical to: the law of the main contract in which the arbitration clause is incorporated, the law applicable to the seat of arbitration, or the law applicable to the place where enforcement of the arbitral award is sought.[13] It appears the primary determinant is the seat of arbitration especially if agreed by the parties (which is common in practice). Denying the influence of the place of proceedings in modern society (the so-called manifestations of the denationalization of arbitration) is a

---

[11] See *Gaillard, E. et Savage, J.* (eds.) Fouchard, Gaillard & Goldman, On International Commercial Arbitration, 1999, pp. 228–236 and *Poudret, F. et Besson, S.* Droit comparé de l'arbitrage international, 2002, pp. 134–144.

[12] By way of illustration only: [CHE]: Section 177 of the IPRG [CHE] – all financial claims are arbitrable.

[13] See *Kirry, A.* Arbitrability: Current Trends in Europe. Arbitration International, 1996, p. 377.

chimera. In theory, but also in practice, it is basically impossible to ignore the importance of the fact that state (legislative) power determines the scope of arbitration and the effects (enforceability and the conditions thereof) attributed to arbitral awards. But the arbitration agreement remains a contractual institution and even though one may, to some extent, accept its hybrid nature, the possibility of choosing applicable law is not excluded.

624.   In consumer disputes, however, *public policy* rules must be taken into account. Consumer protection laws are usually (at least) mandatory, or they are a component of *public policy* recognized by the law applicable in the seat of arbitration. In **Austria** [AUT], for instance, consumer protection and the limitation of arbitrability of consumer disputes are regulated by binding provisions. However, Austrian case law excludes these matters from the scope of *public policy*.[14]

625.   Under **EU law**, the *Directive* stipulates that Member States shall take the necessary measures to ensure that the consumer does not lose the protection granted by this *Directive* by virtue of the choice of the rules/regulations of a non-Member country as the rules/regulations applicable to the contract if the latter has a close connection with the territory of the Member States.[15]

626.   In **Slovakia** [SVK], the new prohibition of arbitration clauses (as pre-dispute agreements covering all potential future disputes) in consumer disputes applies retroactively to agreements which have already been entered into.[16] This clearly manifests the strong *public interest* in special provisions governing these issues. It is somewhat questionable, though, whether the nature of *public policy* is such that, from the perspective of private international law, it enables the application of the corresponding reservation.

627.   If the arbitral tribunal does not act in compliance with mandatory consumer protection laws, the arbitral award may be set aside by the courts in the seat of arbitration. The enforcement of the award abroad may be jeopardized.[17] The approach to the enforcement of foreign arbitral awards in such cases is not consistent.

---

[14] Decision of the OGH [AUT], Case No. 3 Ob 144/09m of 22 July 2009. Published in: (i) 010/21 (Öhlberger) and in (ii) the Austrian Arbitration Association (ArbAut) Bulletin at: http://www.cm.arbitration-austria.at/newsletter_detail.php?archiv_id=44 [last access 3 July 2010]. This decision will be annotated in detail in connection with the enforcement of foreign arbitral awards rendered in consumer disputes.

[15] *Directive*, Article 6. The application of Article 6 of the *Rome I Regulation* is excluded by Article 1 of the *Rome I Regulation*.

[16] *Magal, M.* ILO, Newsletter, 10 January 2008, p. 1.

[17] This issue is analyzed below. Cf. the Austrian practice which prohibits refusing the foreign enforcement of an arbitral award only on the grounds that the law limiting arbitrability was violated,

628.	When ruling on the validity of the arbitration agreement for consumer disputes, courts usually apply their own law, i.e. *lex fori*. This especially applies if there is any (specific, not latent) connection to the laws of the forum, such as habitual residence,[18] nationality, or permanent residence of the consumer, as the case may be.

629.	Naturally, it is not possible to rule out a conflict between the law applicable to the seat of arbitration and the law applicable to the arbitration agreement regarding the validity of the arbitration agreement. Each state has its own definition of the essence of *public policy*[19] which may or may not include consumer protection rules.[20] In the former situation, the state's own *public policy* rules may prevail over the *public policy* rules applicable in other countries. Unless the *public policy* rules prohibit or limit the application of a different (foreign) law which the parties may have chosen as the law applicable to their agreement, the arbitral tribunal may, despite the separability of the arbitration agreement from the main contract, consider this chosen law as the law applicable to the arbitration agreement.[21]

---

whether in the place where the arbitration was held or in the country of enforcement. Cf. Decision of the OGH [AUT], Case No. 3 Ob 144/09m of 22 July 2009. Published in: (i) 010/21 (Öhlberger) and in (ii) the Austrian Arbitration Association (ArbAut) Bulletin at: http://www.cm.arbitration-austria.at/newsletter_detail.php?archiv_id=44 [last access 3 July 2010]. This Austrian decision is analyzed below. Conversely, the Polish Supreme Court (SN [POL] refused enforcement of an arbitral award rendered in the U.S. (by the AAA [USA]) on the grounds of a breach of consumer protection laws and invalidity of the arbitration clause. See the Decision of the SN [POL], Case No. No IV CSK 200/06 of 22 February 2007. This decision is also analyzed in great detail elsewhere in this book.

[18] European conflict-of-law rules (EU) primarily use the person's habitual residence as the basic connecting factor.

[19] For a detailed analysis of the delimitation of *public policy* and *public interest*, see above. We have maintained that the protection of the consumer (weaker party) is in most cases the subject of *public interest*, a category different from *public policy* (again personal opinion). It must be admitted, however, that some countries explicitly present such protection as *public policy* (*ordre public*). Of course, one must respect the right of each national legislator to define its *public policy*. Nevertheless, at the general level, and especially in the cross-border context, we are more inclined towards the theory that this issue is not within the purview of *public policy*, especially not *public policy* (*ordre public*) under Article V(2)(b) of the *New York Convention*.

[20] French law, for instance, explicitly classifies consumer protection as part of *public policy*. This postulate is contained in Article L 132-1 implemented by Act No. 95-96 of 1 February 1995, Article 1, published in the Annex to JORF of 2 February 1995 and Regulation No. 2001-741 of 23 August 2001, Article 16, published in JORF of 25 August 2001. Some countries have arrived at this conclusion in their case law or legal doctrine. Conversely, Austria, which allows annulment of an arbitral award for violation of *public policy*, concluded in the decision of the OGH [AUT] that a breach of consumer protection is not a violation of *public policy* which would justify a refusal to recognize and enforce a foreign arbitral award in terms of Article V(2)(b) of the *New York Convention* (see the Decision of the OGH [AUT], Case No. 3 Ob 144/09m of 22 July 2009, which is annotated in great detail elsewhere in this book).

[21] *Favre-Bulle, X.* Arbitrage et Règlement alternative des litiges (ADR): une autre justice pour les consommateurs? In: *Théovenoz, L. et Reich, N.* (eds.) Droit de la consommation, Liber Amicorum Bernd Stauder, Genève: Schulthess, 2006, p. 97 et seq., here p. 104.

630. Nonetheless, even if the arbitration agreement were invalid or the dispute were non-arbitrable under the law applicable to the arbitration agreement, a guarantee that the arbitral tribunal at the seat of arbitration will actually find the agreement invalid is impossible. Take, for instance, the validity of an arbitration clause in a consumer contract governed by Austrian law, with the seat of arbitration in Switzerland.

631. According to **Swiss law**, pre-dispute arbitration agreements (arbitration clauses) in consumer disputes are invalid (null and void). However, the validity of the arbitration agreement is not contingent on Swiss law. Section 178 of the IPRG [CHE] stipulates that arbitration agreements are valid if they comply with any of the following three legal systems, one of which is Swiss law: **(i)** the law chosen by the parties, **(ii)** the law applicable to the subject matter of the dispute, or **(iii)** Swiss law. In order to preserve the validity of the arbitration agreement, it would suffice to subject it to the law of any U.S. state, even if it were invalid under Austrian or Swiss law. But not all legal systems allow similar recourse. For instance, even if the law applicable to the subject matter of the dispute or to the arbitration agreement permits arbitration clauses for consumer disputes, the law of the seat of arbitration may prohibit such agreements and consider them invalid. Consequently, the parties run the risk of annulment of any award rendered in spite of such restrictive rules at the seat of arbitration either on grounds of a breach of *public policy*[22] or due to the absence of material arbitrability. Besides, if in such case the arbitral award were rendered in Switzerland [CHE] and were not challenged in Switzerland [CHE] by a motion for annulment or if the motion for annulment were dismissed by a Swiss court, existing Austrian case law allows[23] the assumption that the Austrian courts would recognize and enforce the award despite the fact that the arbitration agreement would breach Austrian consumer protection laws.

632. Naturally, the law of the place of recognition and enforcement of a foreign arbitral award is also important. Article V(2)(a) of the *New York Convention* stipulates that the recognition and enforcement of a foreign arbitral award may be refused if the subject matter of the difference is not capable of settlement by arbitration (arbitrable) under the law of the country of enforcement of the award (even if it would be arbitrable under the law of the seat of arbitration) or if the award is contrary to *public policy* in the country where recognition and enforcement are sought.[24] Consequently, the arbitral panel may be forced to take into

---

[22] If the laws in the place where the proceedings were held allow such grounds for annulment of an arbitral award.
[23] Decision of the OGH [AUT], Case No. 3 Ob 144/09m of 22 July 2009. This decision is annotated in great detail elsewhere in this book (see the excursus into Austrian law).
[24] Article V(2)(b) of the *New York Convention* must be interpreted as *international public policy*. This must be distinguished from *national public policy*. Although the states ought to exert efforts to unify

consideration the law of the place where enforcement of the award will be sought. It is necessary to point out, though, that the obligation to take into consideration the law of the anticipated or potential place where enforcement of the arbitral award will be sought is by no means generally supported in international theory and practice. Many academics and practitioners argue that the arbitrator may not take account of the [anticipated/potential] place of enforcement of the award. The commonly invoked reason is that the arbitrator simply cannot know where enforcement will be sought and must, conversely, assume that the award will be performed voluntarily.[25] These opinions err in their reasoning; arbitrators should reasonably, and wherever possible, take account of the law of the potential place of enforcement of the award. First, the postulate that the parties will certainly voluntarily perform what they are ordered to is somewhat detached from current reality and indicative of a certain measure of naïveté, and second, the arbitrator should endeavor, as much as possible, to make his or her decision enforceable in the future. In many, if not most, cases, it is even possible to anticipate, with a certain degree of likelihood and knowing the circumstances of the case and the personal status of the parties, in which cases the enforcement of the arbitral award is to be expected.

633. Some rules on arbitration, such as the ICC Rules, require that the arbitrators make sure that their award is enforceable. This issue is analyzed below.

V.1.4. Special arbitration laws and EU courts

634. The *Directive* does not allow the choice of any law other than the law of a Member State as the law applicable to a consumer contract should it prove contrary to the principles enshrined in the *Directive*. As concerns the law applicable to consumer contracts, the *Directive* indicates that the issues were taken into account (albeit in a much more lenient form) in Article 6(2) of the *Rome I Regulation*[26] which, in conjunction with

---

international interpretation, we must naturally count on the fact (and practice confirms this hypothesis) that states might differ in their own interpretation of *international public policy*. A contrary opinion would deny national sovereignty. But it is certainly advisable for the international community and especially the signatories of the individual international treaties to exert every effort and strive for unification in the interpretation.

[25] These opinions are frequently connected with opinions on the delocalization of arbitration. As already mentioned elsewhere in this book, the opinions on delocalization of the place of proceedings cannot be sustained and must be viewed as outdated, considering the importance of state power and especially the legislative power (legislation) and judicial power both in the state of proceedings and in the state of recognition and enforcement.

[26] Rome I Regulation, Article 6(2) (cit.): "*Notwithstanding paragraph 1, the parties may choose the law applicable to a contract which fulfils the requirements of paragraph 1, in accordance with Article 3. Such a choice may not, however, have the result of depriving the consumer of the protection afforded*

Article 6(1) of the *Rome I Regulation*,[27] allows a limited choice of law. It is not explicitly limited to the choice of law of an EU Member State, but the choice (of law) must not deprive the consumer of the fundamental principles of protection.

635. Considering the fact that all Member States are bound by the *Directive*, it might appear that the question of applicable law is rather academic. All courts in the EU Member States would arrive at the same conclusion. But, even though it is true that the implementation of the *Directive* gave rise to a common platform for the assessment of certain issues relating to consumer arbitration (inter alia), the implementation of the *Directive* in the individual EU Member States was not consistent.[28] Hence, an arbitration agreement may be held valid in one EU Member State and invalid in another.

V.1.5. Decision in *Philip Alexander Securities Futures Ltd v. Bamberger* [GBR-ENG]/[DEU]

636. The factual and legal circumstances in ***Philip Alexander Securities Futures Ltd v. Bamberger***[29] were as follows. *Philip Alexander Securities*, a company established in London [GBR-ENG], was doing business with consumers in Germany [DEU]. All contracts contained arbitration clauses with the agreed seat of arbitration in London [GBR]. When a

---

to him by provisions that cannot be derogated from by agreement by virtue of the law which, in the absence of choice, would have been applicable on the basis of paragraph 1."
Similarly, the Rome Convention, Article 5(2) (cit.:) "*Notwithstanding the provisions of Article 3, a choice of law made by the parties shall not have the result of depriving the consumer of the protection afforded to him by the mandatory rules of the law of the country in which he has his habitual residence: (-) if in that country the conclusion of the contract was preceded by a specific invitation addressed to him or by advertising, and he had taken in that country all the steps necessary on his part for the conclusion of the contract, or (-) if the other party or his agent received the consumer's order in that country, or (-) if the contract is for the sale of goods and the consumer travelled from that country to another country and there gave his order, provided that the consumer's journey was arranged by the seller for the purpose of inducing the consumer to buy.*"
[27] Rome I Regulation, Article 6(1) (cit.): "*Without prejudice to Articles 5 and 7, a contract concluded by a natural person for a purpose which can be regarded as being outside his trade or profession (the consumer) with another person acting in the exercise of his trade or profession (the professional) shall be governed by the law of the country where the consumer has his habitual residence, provided that the professional: (a) pursues his commercial or professional activities in the country where the consumer has his habitual residence, or (b) by any means, directs such activities to that country or to several countries including that country, and the contract falls within the scope of such activities.*"
Similarly, the Rome Convention, Article 5(1) (cit.:) "*This Article applies to a contract the object of which is the supply of goods or services to a person ("the consumer") for a purpose which can be regarded as being outside his trade or profession, or a contract for the provision of credit for that object.*"
[28] Nevertheless, Regulation No 2006/2004 of the EP and of the Council of 27 October 2004 attempts to solve the problem by strengthening cooperation between the Member States with respect to the *Directive*.
[29] Court of Appeals, Civil Division, 12 July 1996, Rev. arb. 1997, p. 167.

dispute arose, several consumers commenced proceedings in German courts, whereas the professional challenged the jurisdiction of the German courts and demanded adherence to the arbitration agreements. At that time, the professional filed a motion with English courts and succeeded with his request for an injunction preventing the proceedings. Under the Consumer Arbitration Agreements Act 1988, as applicable at the time, English law accepted arbitration if consumers had their permanent residence outside England [GBR-ENG], and, consequently, the protection afforded under the English Act did not apply to them.[30] The English courts accepted that this might give rise to potentially conflicting decisions rendered by German courts which did not grant the defense of lack of jurisdiction and decided in the merits.[31]

V.1.6. Decision in *Heifer International Inc. v. Helge Christiansen et Christiansen Arkitekter KS MAA PAR et al.* [GBR-ENG]

637. In *Heifer International Inc.*[32] v. *Helge Christiansen*[33] *et Christiansen Arkitekter KS MAA PAR et al.*[34] the English courts were also presented with a claim concerning the provision of services by Danish businessmen to consumers in England [GBR-ENG]; arbitration in the respective cases was initiated in Denmark [DNK].[35] As a result thereof, an award rendered in one Member State would not be challengeable in the place where it was rendered, but would be subject to recognition/enforcement in another country. It is possible that the courts of the EU Member States would be forced to refer the issue of interpretation to the ECJ. The issue of **enforcement of foreign arbitral awards** in consumer disputes has not yet been resolved by the ECJ.

---

[30] The Court of Appeals ultimately decided that protection afforded only to domestic consumers violated the provisions of the EC Treaty on free movement, whereby the conflict was resolved.

[31] Cf. also the Decision of the [German] District Court in Krefeld [DEU], Case No. 6 O 186/95 of 29 April 1996 (*Richard Zellner* v. *Phillip Alexandre Securities and Futures Ltd.*) and the subsequent decision of the English court – Queen's Bench Division) – (in the same case, i.e. *Richard Zellner* v. *Phillip Alexandre Securities and Futures Ltd.*), [1997 ILPr 730 (QB)]. For a brief annotation and a summary, see the excursus into German law and a note in the excursus into English law above.

[32] A company established (registered) in the British Virgin Islands [BVI]. The beneficial owner of the company is a wealthy Russian family living in England [GBR-ENG].

[33] A Danish architect.

[34] Judgment of the Court of Appeal, Queen's Bench Division – Technology and Construction Court, No. HT-07-106 of 18 December 2007 in *Heifer International Inc* v. *(1) Helge Christiansen (2) Christiansen Arkitekter KS MAA PAR (3) Haslev-Hansson VVS (4) Stevns El-Service A/S et (5) Listed El-Teknik APS*; [2007] EWHC 3015 (TCC), [2008] Bus LR D49; [2007] APP.L.R. 12/18, [2008] All ER (D) 120 (Jan) Available online from the following websites at: (i) http://www.bailii.org/ew/cases/EWHC/TCC/2007/3015.html [last access 27 August 2011] or (ii) http://www.nadr.co.uk/articles/published/ArbitLRe/Heifer%20v%20Helge%202007.pdf [last access 27 August 2011]. The decision is annotated in great detail below, in the chapter below on the application of various legal systems to the definition of consumer and to the validity of the arbitration agreement.

[35] High Court of Justice, Queen's Bench Division, Technology and Construction Court, 18 December 2007, Case HT-07-106.

Considering the applicability of the *New York Convention*, the jurisdiction of the ECJ over the issue is questionable.

V.2. Application of various legal systems to the definition of consumer and the validity of an arbitration agreement

V.2.1. Importance of the definition of consumer

638.   The definition of consumer varies in the individual jurisdictions. EU law stipulates that a consumer is a natural person who purchases goods or services for purposes other than trade or business. Such delimitation can be considered the minimum standard of definition. The status of consumer is reserved for the *"final consumer who does not carry on business in connection with the respective contract, nor is the contract supposed to be used for business purposes."*[36] A consumer in Germany is defined as *"any natural person who enters into a transaction for a purpose which could be considered as a transaction outside his or her business."* As a result thereof, German courts have excluded a doctor purchasing a share in his medical practice from the protection applicable to consumer arbitration.[37] It is necessary to emphasize, though, that German law is based on the general protection afforded to the weaker party. A protection analogous to consumer protection under EU standards is therefore provided to a broader category of parties than in most other Member States. According to French law, a businessman entering into a contract outside the scope of his or her business or trade had long been considered a consumer.[38] French courts have excluded such businessmen from the protection provided under the *Directive*.[39]

V.2.2. Decision in *Heifer International Inc. v. Helge Christiansen et Christiansen Arkitekter KS MAA PAR et al.* [GBR-ENG]

639.   The merits of the dispute before the English court in *Heifer International Inc.*[40] v. *Helge Christiansen*[41] et *Christiansen Arkitekter KS MAA PAR et al.*[42] was an order for works relating to the

---

[36] See the following decisions:
➤   ECJ Judgment of 21 June 1978, *Bertrand* v. *Paul Ott*;
➤   Decision Cass., civ. 1ère [FRA] of 18 July 2000, annotated in: Bull. 216.
[37] See the decision of the OLG Düsseldorf [DEU] of 4 May 2004, OLGR Düsseldorf 2004, 345.
[38] See the decision Cass., civ. 1ère [FRA] of 25 May 1992, Bull. 162.
[39] See the decision Cass. Civ. 1ère [FRA] of 24 January 1995, Bull. 54.
[40] A company established (registered) in the British Virgin Islands. The beneficiary owner of the company is a wealthy Russian family living in England [GBR-ENG].
[41] A Danish architect.
[42] Judgment of the Court of Appeal, Queen's Bench Division – Technology and Construction Court, No. HT-07-106 of 18 December 2007 in *Heifer International Inc* v. *(1) Helge Christiansen (2) Christiansen Arkitekter KS MAA PAR (3) Haslev-Hansson VVS (4) Stevns El-Service A/S et (5) Listed*

reconstruction of a house belonging to the owners of the *Heifer* company established in *Surrey* [GBR-ENG]. The contract was entered into by and between *Heifer International and Christiansen Arkitekter KS MAA PAR et al.* The *Heifer* company **gave a power of attorney** to *Helge Christiansen* to enter into contracts with Danish craftsmen and workers as well as to perform other duties in connection with the performance of the contract. Based on the contract, three agreements were negotiated with three workers (by *Helge Christiansen*). Subsequently, the client (*Heifer*) filed a claim for performance in connection with defective work and a return of the money paid under the contract in connection with the defective work. *Helge Christiansen* pleaded that he himself was not a party to the contract concluded with *Heifer* and moved for dismissal of the claim. The workers applied for a stay (termination) of the proceedings due to the existence of an arbitration clause (seat of arbitration agreed in Denmark [DNK]) contained in the contract with *Christiansen Arkitekter KS MAA PAR*. The Court considered the possibility that the owner of the house would not be a consumer if he had purchased the real estate as an investment. *Heifer International Inc.* argued that the arbitration clause was not incorporated into the contract concluded with *Helge Christiansen* and, being cautious, alternatively argued that the arbitration clause was unfair, i.e. not valid (binding) under the Unfair Terms in Consumer Contracts Regulation 1999 No. 2083 [GBR].[43] The judge concluded that *Heifer International* and *Helge Christiansen* had not entered into any contract. **The judge agreed, though, that the claimant was a consumer even though he acted through a company, because the real estate did not have the nature**

El-Teknik APS; [2007] EWHC 3015 (TCC), [2008] Bus LR D49; [2007] APP.L.R. 12/18, [2008] All ER (D) 120 (Jan), available online from the following websites at: (i) http://www.bailii.org/ew/cases/EWHC/TCC/2007/3015.html [last access 27 August 2011] or (ii) http://www.nadr.co.uk/articles/published/ArbitLRe/Heifer%20v%20Helge%202007.pdf [last access 27 August 2011].

[43] Unfair Terms in Consumer Contracts Regulations 1999, SI 1999/2083, Reg 3. The provisions regarding the definition of consumer are based on the object of the contract (the purpose of the transaction). The subjective scope of the provisions is provided to the person whose actions are aimed at the satisfaction of a purpose other than his or her economic, commercial, or professional interests.

The judge followed the trend established by the decision of the Court of Appeal, Civil Division, of 24 January 2007 [GBR-ENG] *Fiona Trust Corp* v. *Privalov*, 2007 EWCA Civ. 20, i.e. that jurisdiction or arbitration clauses in international commercial relationships ought to be assessed with a great degree of discretion. In the present case, the Court concluded that despite the *consumer object (purpose)* of the contracts between *Heifer* and the three Danish entities, the contracts (negotiated by a proxy) had a commercial basis, and it was necessary to apply the AA 1996 [GBR-ENG].

As concerns *Fiona Trust Corp* v. *Privalov*, the case involved the assessment of potential bribery. The English court in the case (*Fiona Trust Corp.* v. *Privalov*) explicitly confirmed that factual circumstances which give rise to the suspicion of corruption can be submitted to arbitration, and thereby confirmed the separability (independence) of the arbitration agreement from the main contract, although the proceedings were conducted according to the preceding lex arbitri, i.e. the English Arbitration Act 1972. See *Bělohlávek, A.* Rozhodčí řízení, ordre public a trestní právo. [Title in translation: Arbitration, Ordre Public, and Criminal Law]. Prague: C. H. Beck, 2008, Part II, marg. 1533; *Grant, T., D.* International arbitration and English courts. ICLL, 2007, Vol. 56, pp. 871–884 et al.

of a mere business investment, as it was intended as a house where the owners (beneficial owners) of *Heifer International Inc.* were to live.[44] The Court concluded, however, that arbitration clauses themselves are not unfair terms, considering all the circumstances regarding their content and the process of negotiation,[45] should it be necessary to assess them according to British consumer protection laws due to the place of performance under the contract. Although the respective terms might have appeared formally unfair, considering the actual facts of the case and the particular circumstances, they were not unfair. The existence and the validity of the clauses must be principally assessed by the Danish arbitral tribunal according to Danish consumer protection laws (the *"Kompetenz-Kompetenz"* principle). The judge also took into consideration that, for instance, *Heifer International Inc.* (or the beneficial owners of the company) followed the advice of its Danish legal counsel[46] when negotiating the contract with *Christiansen Arkitekter KS MAA PAR*. Even though the place where the order was to be realized was England [GBR-ENG], a substantial part of the work was nonetheless performed in connection with the duties of the architect

---

[44] Unfair Terms in Consumer Contracts Regulations 1999, SI 1999/2083, Reg 3; the definition of consumer is based on the object of the contract (purpose of the transaction). The subjective scope of the provisions is provided to the person whose actions are aimed at the satisfaction of a purpose other than his or her economic, commercial, or professional interests. The purpose of the investment in this case was the purchase and reconstruction of a house where the person (*beneficial owner of Heifer*) intended to live with his family, not for the purpose of generating income or preserving the value of capital, notwithstanding the fact that the investment also, but not exclusively, had the nature of capital (preservation of the value of capital). The *commercial basis* of the contracts between *Heifer* and the Danish craftsmen had also been preserved, and it was possible to interpret the contracts fully in compliance with the interpretation rules used in relation to arbitration under the AA 1996 [GBR-ENG].

[45] Indeed, the ECJ's case law also indicates that the (un)fairness of a contractual term must be assessed with respect to the nature of the performance and circumstances attending the conclusion of the contract, relating specifically to the act of formation of the contract. See:
➤ ECJ Judgment, Case C-237/02 of 1 April 2004 (*Freiburger Kommunalbauten GmbH Baugesellschaft & Co. KG* v. *Ludger Hofstetter et Ulrike Hofstetter*, para. (20), as well as
➤ ECJ Judgment, Case C-243/08 of 4 June 2009 in *Pannon GSM*, which is annotated in detail elsewhere in this book and which refers to the ECJ Judgment, Case C-237/02 of 1 April 2004.
Similarly, see also the Judgment of the Supreme Court of the CR [CZE], Case No. 23 Cdo 1201/2009 of 29 June 2010, annotated in the excursus into Czech law.

[46] The importance of professional advice for the assessment of terms incorporated in consumer contracts (especially the arbitration clause) was also highlighted in the following decisions of the English courts (also annotated in a separate excursus into English law, see above):
➤ *Picardi* v. *Cuniberti* of 2002, [2002] EWHC 2923 (QB) (here from the negative perspective, in the absence of such advice or any other professional information provided to the consumer);
➤ *Westminster Building Company Limited* v. *Beckingham* of 2004, [2004] BLR 163 (TCC);
➤ *Allen Wilson Shopfitters and Builders* v. *Buckingham* of 2005, [2005] EWHC 1165 (TCC).
The importance of information and the method of providing information to the consumer were also highlighted in the decision of the [German] District Court for Krefeld [DEU], Case No. 6 O 186/95 of 29 April 1996 (*Richard Zellner* v. *Phillip Alexandre Securities and Futures Ltd.*) and the subsequent decision of the English court – Queen's Bench Division) – (in the same case, i.e. *Richard Zellner* v. *Phillip Alexandre Securities and Futures Ltd.*), [1997] ILPr 730 (QB).

and the preparatory work in Denmark [DNK]. *Heifer* chose only Danish architects and stipulated in the contract that the work be preferably carried out by Danish craftsmen. As concerns the (un)fairness of the arbitration clause for *Heifer International*, classified by the Court as a consumer, the English court also examined whether *Heifer's* access to arbitration in Denmark [DNK] would not be impaired. The arbitration was to be conducted in Danish. The judge did acknowledge that *Heifer* would probably be forced to hire an interpreter, but the financial situation of the company allowed such costs. Neither did the Court find any other reasons which would indicate that *Heifer's* rights might not be afforded fair protection (fair hearing).

V.2.3. International practice

640. Varying definitions of the "consumer" influence the application of consumer protection laws, including the assessment of validity of the arbitration agreement. Before they proceed to the application of consumer protection laws, arbitral tribunals must first define the status of the party as the [potential] consumer.

641. The definition of the "consumer" under national laws (for instance: German citizen or a person with his or her habitual residence in Germany [DEU] is a consumer if he/she meets the definition under German law) would provide consumers with certainty as to their status, but it would result in differing outcomes (for instance: if German and American consumers enter into the same consumer contract with a professional, the two approaches to one and the same contract might differ) and besides, the outcome would be unpredictable from the perspective of the professional. On the other hand, the definition of "consumer" pursuant to the law applicable to the respective consumer contract guarantees that the protection provided to consumer will be assessed on the basis of a contract, not according to the subjective element of the relationship, although the consumers might be denied the protection which they enjoy in their home country. International practice is more inclined to leave the decisions on these issues to the arbitral tribunals. The application of consumer protection laws relating to arbitration by courts usually means the application of mandatory rules which do (or do not) allow a choice of law. In such proceedings, the consumer is defined according to these mandatory rules. The disadvantage is that the definition of consumer may change according to the applicable law, depending on whether it is subject to examination in arbitration or in litigation. This may have the result (by no means exceptional in practice) that the arbitrators determine that the party is not a consumer, whereas the court in proceedings on annulment of the arbitral award concludes that the party is a consumer.

V.2.4. Consequences of the decision on the invalidity of an arbitration agreement

642. If the arbitral panels find the arbitration agreement invalid, they should refuse jurisdiction. If they fail to do so, the courts in the seat of arbitration, when called upon to rule on annulment of the arbitral award, may set aside the award; alternatively, courts in enforcement or exequatur proceedings may refuse recognition or enforcement of the award (pursuant to Article V(2)(a) of the *New York Convention*).

643. If the court holds the arbitration agreement invalid, the consequences of the decision depend on the stage of the proceedings. If the arbitration has not been initiated yet, the court may rule that the arbitral tribunal does not have jurisdiction or that jurisdiction over the dispute is vested in courts. It is possible that the courts of one country conclude that the arbitration agreement is valid, allowing the arbitration to commence or continue, whereas courts in the country of recognition and enforcement reach an opposite conclusion.

644. This may typically happen if the consumer contract includes an arbitration clause with an agreement on the seat of arbitration in the U.S. The consumer, however, files a lawsuit in France, in a court with jurisdiction according to the consumer's habitual residence. The professional challenges the jurisdiction of the French court. The plea is not granted, and, conversely, the court holds the arbitration agreement invalid. The merits of the dispute will be heard and resolved by the French court. However, the professional files a counterclaim with an arbitration tribunal in the U.S. The court and the tribunal will render two decisions which might even completely contradict each other.

645. If arbitration has already been initiated and an arbitral award has actually been rendered, the court may decide on the validity of the arbitration agreement either during the proceedings on annulment of the arbitral award or during the proceedings on recognition and enforcement. If the court holds the arbitration agreement invalid in the annulment proceedings, the arbitral award will be set aside. No future arbitration could be conducted in the country. However, some countries, such as France [FRA], allow the enforcement of an arbitral award despite the fact that it was set aside in the country of its origin. The reason is that the *New York Convention* allows, but does not mandate, the refusal of the recognition and enforcement of the arbitral award if the arbitral award was set aside in the country where it had been rendered. Nevertheless, these cases are rather exceptional, and they usually involve a political element or a major and more significant commercial element. But, if the court decides on the invalidity of the arbitration agreement during exequatur/enforcement proceedings, the

decision always prevents enforcement in the state where such decision was rendered; it does not exclude, however, the enforcement of the arbitral award in a different country (at least according to the *New York Convention*).

V.3. Procedural issues and stages of proceedings

V.3.1. Confirmation or refusal of jurisdiction by the arbitral tribunal / Application of the *"Kompetenz-Kompetenz"* principle

646. Courts are sometimes presented with claims filed by consumers despite the fact that their contract contains an arbitration clause. In such cases, the respondent (professional) usually challenges the jurisdiction of the court. The *"Kompetenz-Kompetenz"* principle stipulates that arbitration tribunals have the right to make decisions regarding their own jurisdiction.

647. Article II(3) of the *New York Convention* stipulates that the court shall refer the parties to arbitration unless the arbitration agreement, invoked by one of the parties, is *"null and void, inoperative or incapable of being performed."* Similar rules can be found in most national arbitration laws (lex arbitri).

648. For instance, **French courts** are under Section 1458 of the NCPC [FRA] are obliged to refuse jurisdiction unless the arbitral tribunal has not been constituted yet and the arbitration clause is apparently invalid. It is clear that the requirement of validity of an arbitration agreement is not fulfilled in many countries, especially in consumer disputes. For example, if the requirements of the *Directive* are to be observed, the determination of validity of the arbitration agreement usually demands the taking of evidence in the merits, so that the circumstances attending the conclusion of the consumer contract containing the arbitration clause are properly clarified. French courts therefore allow the arbitral tribunal to be the first to rule on the issue. The reason is that the circumstances attending the conclusion of the arbitration agreement cannot be assessed without the reading and hearing of evidence. The concept of apparent invalidity (for instance, in connection with arbitration agreements) must be interpreted as invalidity which can be assessed without hearing the parties, without taking evidence, and without assessing the facts of the case.[47] However, the *Directive*, or the

---

[47] The conclusion of a contract is also classified as a factual circumstance in the Judgment of the Supreme Court of the Czech Republic (SC CR [CZE]), Case No. 23 Cdo 1201/2009 of 29 June 2010. For a detailed annotation of this judgment of the SC CR [CZE], see elsewhere in this book (see the excursus into Czech law [CZE]).

applicable EU consumer protection laws, as the case may be, principally allow arbitration agreements in consumer contracts (subject to the observance of the applicable requirements). Consequently, the courts should in such cases conclude that the arbitration clause is not apparently invalid and allow the arbitral tribunal to be the first to assess the validity of the arbitration agreement. This is how French courts would proceed, despite the fairly strong protection of consumers under French law and the restrictive rules on arbitrability in consumer contracts.[48]

649. The same procedure was also adopted by a court in **Québec [CAN] in** *Rogers Wireless, Inc.* v. *Muroff*.[49] A Canadian consumer (residing in the Province of Québec) was obliged to pay four (4) Canadian dollars per minute for a roaming cell phone connection when using his phone in the northeastern part of the U.S. The contract with the telecommunication network operator contained an arbitration clause. The assessment of the arbitration clause depended on a number of questions of fact and law. The court observed the *"Kompetenz-Kompetenz"* principle and left the primary determination of the nature of the arbitration clause and its fairness, i.e. validity, to the arbitrators.[50]

650. However, the procedure whereby the primary decision on the validity of the arbitration agreement is reserved, even in consumer matters, for the arbitrators, i.e. a diligent application of the *"Kompetenz-Kompetenz"* principle, is not generally recognized in consumer disputes. In **Germany**,[51] for instance, which is known for a fairly friendly approach to arbitration (especially after the German *lex arbitri* was amended in 1997, with effect since 1998[52]), including consumer arbitration, a German court (BGH [DEU]) held that despite the *"Kompetenz-Kompetenz"* principle, the courts need not, in disputes arising from consumer contracts, give precedence to the conclusion made by the arbitral tribunal in its primary consideration of the validity of the arbitration agreement.[53]

---

[48] See *Fouchard, P.* Clause abusives en matière d'arbitrage. Rev. arb., 1995, p. 149.

[49] 2007 SCC 35.

[50] See *Caplow, S. P.* Arbitration Class Action Waivers in the United States and Canada. Arbitration, 2008, Vol. 74, No. 1, pp. 57–64, here p. 63--64.

[51] German law [DEU] demands judicial exequatur as a condition for enforceability of arbitral awards even in domestic disputes. The court, however, concentrates only on the observance of the fundamental principles and does not review the merits of the case.

[52] Cf. *Rozehnalová, N.* Nová úprava rozhodčího řízení v SRN. [Title in translation: New Arbitration Law in the Federal Republic of Germany]. EMP, 1999, Vol. 8, No. 5, pp. 15–21; before the amendment, see *Bělohlávek, A. et Jašek, V.* Rozhodčí řízení v SRN. [Title in translation: Arbitration in the Federal Republic of Germany]. Daňová a hospodářská kartotéka, 1996, Vol. 4, No. 4, pp. 37–44 and No. 5, pp. 45–50.

[53] Decision of the BGH [DEU], Case No. III ZR 265/03 of 13 January 2005 (annotated in detail in the excursus into German law).

651. The *"Kompetenz-Kompetenz"* principle is generally, i.e. not only in Germany, widely recognized, but it does not exclude the decision-making autonomy of the courts. Consequently, the relationship between this principle and the autonomy (jurisdiction) of the courts must be interpreted as meaning that the courts examine to what extent the arbitrators addressed the issue and whether the parties' fundamental rights were guaranteed in the application of this principle during the decision-making of the arbitral tribunals.

652. Besides, it is also necessary to mention the special approach under EU law which, specifically in connection with consumer disputes under the ECJ's applicable case law, actually mandates that the courts address the issue of validity of arbitration agreements in consumer disputes. These issues are analyzed in detail especially in the chapter on EU law.

653. The contract, as required by the Court of Justice of the European Union and as described in the previous paragraph, may not (...or would not...) be fully accepted in the United States. U.S. doctrine is strictly based on the contractual nature of arbitration, and the case law of the U.S. courts is based on the premise that the courts' role is to protect any party from a situation where he would *"be required to submit to arbitration any dispute which he has not so agreed to submit."*[54] According to this doctrine, arbitrability is an *"issue for judicial determination"* unless *"the parties clearly and unmistakably provided otherwise."* Consequently, the validity of arbitration agreements in the U.S. is based on general contract law, and the conclusions reached may differ depending on which law applies to the respective contract. Hence, the U.S. courts commonly decide disputes concerning arbitrability[55] while fully respecting the principle of separability of the arbitration agreement from the main contract.[56] Nonetheless, the approach adopted by the U.S. courts is still

---

[54] Decision in *Steelworkers* v. *Warrior & Gulf Nav. Co*, 363 U.S. 574, 582 (1960).

[55] *Caplow, S. P.* Arbitration Class Action Waivers in the United States and Canada. Arbitration, 2008, Vol. 74, No. 1, pp. 57–64, here p. 57, including the cited examples of case law (adjudicated opinions).

[56] Decision of the U.S. Supreme Court (2006) in *Buckeye Check Cashing, Inc.* v. *Cardegna*, 546 U.S. 440 (2006). The Florida Supreme Court granted the claim and acknowledged the invalidity of the main contract, holding that the invalidity also automatically rendered the arbitration agreement invalid (in the given case the contract stipulated unreasonably high fees which violated the principles of contract law; the court held that the invalidity was indeed bordering on a criminal offence). However, the U.S. Supreme Court, which maintains that arbitrability must be assessed according to federal substantive law, found the arbitration agreement valid, because the claimant failed to make a separate plea of invalidity of the arbitration agreement. Hence, the U.S. Supreme Court ruled that the validity of the main contract should be assessed by the arbitrators.
However, U.S. courts have also been called upon to address the opposite situation, i.e. whether a plea of invalidity of the arbitration agreement can in certain cases be considered as encompassing a plea of invalidity of the main contract. See the decision in *Negrampa* v. *Mailcoups, Inc*, 469 F.3d 1257, 1271-77 (9th Cir. 2006).
See also the decisions in the following cases:
➢ *Sanford* v. *Memberworks*, 483 F.3d 956, 962 (9th Cir., 2007)
➢ *Flores* v. *Jewels Marketing and Agribusiness*, 2007 WL 2022042 (E.D.Cal. 9 July 2007) et al.

not much different from the approach adopted by many courts in European countries.

654. In any case, the *"Kompetenz-Kompetenz"* principle and the **New York Convention** give precedence to arbitral tribunals only when deciding on the validity of the arbitration agreement. They do not bestow the power of a monopoly on them. This means that even though courts may refuse to deal with the arguments concerning the validity of an arbitration agreement in consumer disputes, as a matter of fact, the courts always have the last word. They may be called upon to rule on the validity in the subsequent stages of the proceedings, especially at the stage of proceedings on the annulment of the arbitral award.

V.3.2. Consumers' arguments against arbitration agreements

655. If the consumer is faced with a jurisdictional challenge raised by the professional against the court with jurisdiction over the consumer's residence (especially habitual residence), the consumer may argue that a submission of the dispute to arbitration would violate mandatory consumer protection laws and, in certain countries, also *public policy*. This argument would be based on allegations, such as the costs of such proceedings,[57] access to the place where the arbitration ought to take place, complicated procedures to file claims, difficult conditions for the taking of evidence, limited access to affordable legal aid, denial of justice, etc.

V.3.3. Costs of proceedings and availability of legal protection

656. The issue of the costs of proceedings is particularly sensitive. Although arbitration need not necessarily be more expensive than litigation (the costs might be lower due to the usual absence of any regular remedial measure against the decision in the merits, but also due to other factors), arbitration, in its original concept, was not intended as a means of resolving consumer disputes. No free legal aid is available in arbitration, which is otherwise guaranteed by the individual states to natural persons (subject to certain conditions). The party must therefore finance his or her own legal counsel, if necessary, as well as other costs of the arbitral proceedings exclusively from his or her own funds. Besides, a number of rules governing the proceedings in arbitral tribunals, especially in international disputes,[58] are not suitable for the resolution of small (petty) claims. As concerns standard procedures for the resolution of

---

[57] For more details, see the following chapter.

[58] However, many national institutions presume special procedural mechanisms and rules applicable to arbitration or other methods of resolving consumer disputes or disputes over small claims. For instance, see the AAA [USA], Guidelines for Arbitrating Small Claims under the ICC Rules, ArbCourt [CZE].

disputes before international arbitral tribunals, the arbitration rules and institutions such as the ICC, VIAC, LCIA, or the UNCITRAL Rules (applicable to *ad hoc* arbitration in international disputes) usually entail fairly high costs of arbitration.[59] Besides, the costs are due and payable at the commencement of the proceedings, which requires advance payment and might deter the consumer.

657.   According to most international rules of arbitration, the arbitral tribunal is entitled to terminate the arbitral proceedings if the advance on the costs is not paid. Consequently, the consumer might find himself or herself deprived of the possibility to proceed with his/her claim against the professional, because in judicial proceedings he or she would be released from the duty to pay court fees or could receive free legal aid. Courts in European countries are very sensitive to such arguments. For example, a **Norwegian court** [NOR] set aside an arbitration agreement in a consumer relationship, because, inter alia, **the statutory legal costs insurance** (legal liability insurance) **did not cover the costs of arbitration.**[60]

658.   In a different case, a **German court** refused to compel arbitration despite the existence of an arbitration clause and a jurisdictional challenge; the reason was that one of the parties did not have sufficient finances to submit her claims in arbitration. Consequently, legal protection was inaccessible to the consumer in arbitration, although it would be available in litigation.[61] The German Federal Court of Justice (BGH [DEU]) held that the arbitration agreement may in such cases be considered "inoperative" or "unenforceable," and, consequently, the claim could be made in court despite the existence of the arbitration agreement.[62]

659.   In **England** [GBR-ENG], the London Court of Appeal [GBR-ENG] in *Paczy* v. *Haendler & Natterman GmbH* ruled that impecuniosity of one party does not make an arbitration agreement incapable of being performed.[63]

660.   **U.S.** courts have repeatedly ruled that the submission of the consumer's rights to arbitration which would entail unconscionable costs is unacceptable.[64] This applies both to advance payments for the

---

[59] Presently, the minimum non-refundable fee payable together with the statement of claim (request for arbitration) amounts to 5,000 USD in proceedings governed by the ICC Rules.

[60] EFTA Report on the Implementation of the *Directive*, p. 12.

[61] Decision of the BGH [DEU] of 9 April 2000.

[62] Decision of the BGH [DEU], Case No. III ZR 33/00 of 14 September 2000. The BGH [DEU] thereby followed its previous ruling of 12 November 1987 (decision annotated in: NJW, 1987, p. 1215).

[63] *Paczy* v. *Haendler & Natterman GmbH*, [1981] 1 Lloyd's Rep 302.

[64] As concerns these issues, see also the excursus into U.S. law.

arbitrators' costs and to the risk that the consumer will also bear other costs of the proceedings. For instance, in *Blaise Alexander et Gerald Freeman v. Anthony International LLP*[65] the court held that the weaker party bore the risk of being obliged to pay the costs of proceedings, and, consequently, the contract was invalid on grounds of unconscionability. In *Green Tree Financial Corp v. Randolph*, the Supreme Court of the United States held that arbitration is contrary to *public policy* if it is to be conducted in a tribunal where the consumer or the employee is not able to enforce his or her rights.[66] However, the consumer's argument regarding unconscionable costs was rejected only because the consumer failed to meet the burden of proof regarding such unconscionable costs.[67] Conversely, in *James D. Stout; Shirley A. Brown v. J. D. Byrider, a/k/a Docherty Motors, Inc.; T & J Acceptance Corporation, d/b/a Carnow Acceptance Company*,[68] the Court (for the Sixth Circuit) [USA], as the appellate court, refused to apply the conclusions reached in *Green Tree Financial Corp. v. Randolph*. The reason was that in *Stout v. J. D. Byrider* the parties had agreed on the jurisdiction of a specific arbitral institution which published its rules. The Supreme Court rejected a mere hypothesis that such an institution would not justly apply the law and accepted the jurisdiction of the arbitrators.[69]

V.3.4. Consequences of the decision on the invalidity of an arbitration agreement in a consumer contract

661.   If the court finds the arbitration agreement invalid or if it is inapplicable for any other reason, the claimant may file a claim on the merits with a court. Complications may arise at the stage of enforcement of the court decision in countries which consider the arbitration agreement valid.

662.   Consequently, it is not likely that the court decision would be recognized or enforced in a country in which the award was or should have been rendered. This would be favorable to consumers, because they

---

[65] Decision of the U.S. Court of Appeals, Third Circuit, No. 02-3764 of 19 August 2003; 341 F.3d 256 (3. Cir. 2003). However, this case concerned an employment dispute, not a consumer dispute. Available online at: http://caselaw.findlaw.com/us-3rd-circuit/1293059.html [last access 14 August 2011] or at: http://ftp.resource.org/courts.gov/c/F3/341/341.F3d.256.02-3764.html [last access 14 August 2011]. The reference for comparison were the costs of court proceedings.

[66] U.S. Supreme Court [USA], 531 US 79 (2000).

[67] This case concerned the costs which the consumer would have to pay in advance. As concerns the costs of the entire proceedings, see the following decisions [USA]:
➢   *Ingle* v. *Circuit Ciry Stores Inc.*328 F.3d 165, 1179 (9th Cir.); 124 S.Ct. 1169 (2004)
➢   *Al-Satin* v. *Circuit City Stores. Inc.*, 394 F.3d 1254 (9th Cir. 2005).

[68] 228 F.3d 709 (2000). The judgment is available online at: http://www.leagle.com/xmlResult.aspx?xmldoc=2000937228F3d709_1879.xml&docbase=CSLWAR2-1986-2006 [last access 2 September 2011].

[69] This judgment is annotated in detail elsewhere in this book (in the excursus into U.S. law – "Case Law").

are less likely to have assets abroad than professionals. However, such considerations, whether realistic (and to what extent) or not, are somewhat misguided and shortsighted. No party should deliberately disregard the decision and the performance thereof only because it enjoys protection in its domestic environment. Besides, it is probable that the unfavorable decision would be enforced in a country in which the professional carries on his or her regular economic activity, especially if the amount in the dispute were low.

V.3.5. Challenging arbitral awards concerning consumer contracts

(a) Courts in proceedings which are connected with and follow arbitration and the scope of judicial review

663.   An arbitral award may, under certain circumstances, be challenged in a national court at the seat of arbitration. Such applications for annulment of arbitral awards are usually based on exceptional grounds explicitly specified by law. The objective is to make sure that the court sets aside an arbitral award (in total or in part) if any of the fundamental conditions were breached which apply to the commencement and the course of the arbitral proceedings. If this is indeed the case, the arbitral award is usually set aside. According to the *New York Convention* and the UNCITRAL Model Law, the competent court may refuse the recognition and enforcement of an arbitral award which was "set aside" by a court at the seat of arbitration.[70]

664.   Every country which regulates arbitration in its national laws has its own concept of the control (supervision) it intends to exercise over arbitration. The scope of the control differs from country to country. But most states have adopted rules which allow their courts to set aside an arbitral award that is contrary to *public policy*. Such rules are also incorporated in the UNCITRAL Model Law.[71]

665.   The EU Member States are also obliged to make sure that arbitral awards do not conflict with *European public policy*. This was clearly articulated in some of the ECJ's rulings such as *Eco Swiss China* v. *Benetton International N.V.*[72] concerning competition law. Consequently,

---

[70] Article V(1)(e) of the *New York Convention*; Article 36(1)(v) of the UNCITRAL Model Law.
[71] Article 34(2)(b)(ii) of the UNCITRAL Model Law; this standard was implemented in several states. It allows the court to set aside the arbitral award if it is *"in conflict with the public policy of this State."* On the other hand, not all states have adopted the standard.
[72] ECJ Judgment, Case C-126/97 of 1 June 1999 (*Eco Swiss China Time* v. *Benetton International N.V*), published in: ECR [1999] I-03055. The ECJ held that Article 81 of the TEC is a provision of *public policy*, in particular *Community public policy*, which is incorporated in the *public policy* of the individual Member States; from the perspective of a potential violation of Article 81 of the TEC, it is possible to apply the reservation regarding *public policy* to arbitral awards.

it cannot be ruled out that a Member State, or the ECJ in a future decision, would take account of the importance of consumer protection and deliver an identical decision in the case of consumer arbitration. This idea, however, must be considered erroneous. The *Directive*, or any other consumer protection legislation in the EU, as the case may be, leaves the question of whether to exclude consumer arbitration or not at the sole discretion of the Member States. It does not prohibit arbitration clauses, i.e. pre-dispute consumer contracts, either. Even arbitration clauses incorporated in the general terms and conditions do not conflict with the *Directive*.[73] Hence, it would be very controversial to claim that the prohibition of arbitrability of consumer disputes or the limitation of arbitration clauses (arbitration agreements) in consumer relations is a component of *European (EU) public policy*. Such a conclusion would not be correct.[74] The objective of EU law is to safeguard a minimum standard of consumer protection and the observance of certain fundamental principles. Moreover, while the protection of competition is considered a public law matter even under EU law, consumer contracts and consumer protection remain within the domain of private law, irrespective of the duties of the Member States relating to the preservation of certain minimum standards. Consequently, it is impossible to confuse the public law nature of laws regulating the protection of competition with the private law nature of consumer contracts, although the laws are mandatory in many respects. The mandatory nature of the laws regulating consumer contracts (or certain issues) does not shift this particular branch of law into the domain of public law and does not transform its rules into public law rules. Indeed, this has been confirmed, for instance, by the decision of the Austrian Supreme Court (OGH [AUT]).[75] To designate consumer protection as part of *European public policy* would be, irrespective of its importance, in conflict with its concept. Even if any such category as *European public policy* existed, which is rather doubtful, it is not possible to apply this category to consumer protection. Even though, it is not inconceivable that such an argument may well be raised and submitted for resolution, whether at the national level or at the level of the EU.

For more details, see *Bělohlávek, A.* Rozhodčí řízení, ordre public a trestní právo. [Title in translation: Arbitration, Ordre Public and Criminal Law]. Part I. Prague: C. H. Beck, 2008, marg. 584–587; *Bělohlávek, A.* Arbitration, Ordre Public and Criminal Law (bilingual title – in English and in Russian). Kiev [UKR]: Taxon, 2009, marg. 584–587 and many other authors.

[73] See Judgment of the BGH [DEU], Case No. III ZR 256/03 of 13 January 2005 annotated in detail in this book (in the part concerning consumer arbitration in Germany [DEU]).

[74] A perfectly correct decision (in the author's opinion) of the OGH [AUT], Case No. 3 Ob 144/09m of 22 July 2009, which is annotated in detail elsewhere in this book.

[75] Decision of the OGH [AUT], Case No. 3 Ob 144/09m of 22 July 2009. Published in: (i) 010/21 (Öhlberger) and in (ii) the Austrian Arbitration Association (ArbAut) Bulletin at: http://www.cm.arbitration-austria.at/newsletter_detail.php?archiv_id=44 [last access 3 July 2010]. This decision is analyzed in great detail elsewhere in this book.

666. Moreover, some EU Member States and especially non-Member States may argue that consumer protection laws are not even integrated into their *domestic (national) public policy*. As concerns non-Member States, we could point out, for instance, the decision of the Swiss Federal Supreme Court [CHE] in *Tensacciai* v. *Terra Armata* of 2006, in which the Court concluded that consumer protection is not a part of *public policy*, not even at the national level.[76]

(b) Arguments important for courts in proceedings which are connected with and follow arbitration

667. The courts are likely to debate and decide on the same arguments described in connection with the requests for arbitration. The reason for the absence of any repetition between these two phases can be related to the strict application of the *"Kompetenz-Kompetenz"* principle which forced the parties to prepare for arbitration as the primary proceedings. Another reason might inhere in the fact that one of the parties challenged the arbitrators' jurisdiction only after, and because, the arbitrators rendered an award unfavorable to the party.

668. In order to prevent this particular situation, many arbitration laws contain rules which stipulate that the parties may not plead lack of jurisdiction of the arbitral tribunal in the court proceedings after the arbitration is finished (especially in proceedings on annulment of the arbitral award) unless the plea was already raised before the arbitral tribunal. However, under the regime of EU law, the ECJ's ruling in *Mostaza Claro* v. *Centro Móvil* constitutes a specific exception to this rule in cases where consumer protection laws apply. Not only are consumers allowed to raise the defense as late as in the court proceedings following the arbitration, but the courts are even obliged to identify the consumer protection issue, if necessary, of their own motion. Indeed, the available case law of the ECJ in consumer disputes corroborates the opinion that the arbitrators must themselves and of their own motion identify any potential conflict with consumer protection laws. The reason is that if consumer arbitration in EU countries (in terms of the *Directive*) is to be conducted strictly according to valid and applicable law (i.e. no decision-making ex aequo et bono and no *amiable compositeur*), the mandatory nature of consumer protection means that the relevant issues ought to be identified and the applicable rules ought to be applied by the arbitrators themselves. If they conclude that the arbitration clause violates consumer protection law, they should terminate the proceedings of their own motion. However,

---

[76] Decision of the Swiss Federal Court of 8 March 2006 (in *Tensacciai* v. *Terra Armata*), annotated in: Rev. arb., 2006, p. 763 et seq.

the approach of an informed consumer[77] must be taken into account – and this applies to all stages of the proceedings (the trial itself, review proceedings within the meaning of proceedings on annulment of the arbitral award, exequatur, and enforcement proceedings).

V.4. Enforcement of arbitral awards rendered in consumer disputes

669. Most countries do not distinguish between national (domestic) and international (foreign) awards. Domestic arbitral awards are awards rendered in the state where the court is located, whereas foreign awards are rendered in a different state. But it is not the same difference as between domestic and international arbitration. A domestic arbitral award may be rendered both in a domestic and in an international dispute. The rules for the recognition and enforcement of domestic arbitral awards often differ from the rules for the recognition and enforcement of foreign arbitral awards.[78]

V.4.1. Jurisdiction

670. The court with jurisdiction over the recognition and enforcement of an arbitral award is a domestic court. The jurisdiction of a particular court is determined according to national laws. Dealings with the enforcement of an arbitral award may encounter consumer protection issues if any of the parties challenges the enforceability of the arbitral award on grounds of violation of consumer protection laws. In such case, the court must decide whether to grant the enforcement or not.

V.4.2. Laws applicable to the enforcement of arbitral awards

671. Every country enacts its own rules on the recognition and enforcement of arbitral awards. These rules are procedural rules, and the court which renders the decision applies its procedural law (*lex fori*). Depending on the applicable national concept, the rules on the recognition and enforcement of awards are either incorporated in a special law regulating arbitration and arbitral awards, or the court applies general procedural laws (sometimes containing special rules for arbitral awards).

672. The domestic laws on the enforcement of awards are often modeled on or inspired by the UNCITRAL Model Law.[79] The UNCITRAL Model Law is not a binding source of international origin; it is not an

---

[77] ECJ Judgment, Case C-243/08 of 4 June 2009 (*Pannon GSM Zrt v. Sustikné Győrfi Erzsébet* [*Pannon GSM*]), CELEX: 62008CA0243, the judgment was published in: ECR 2009, p. I-04713.
[78] See *Poudret, J. F., Besson, S. et Birti, S.* Comparative Law of International Arbitration. 2nd ed., London: Sweet & Maxwell, 2007, marg. 849.
[79] Amended in 2006. Available at: http://www.uncitral.org/pdf/english/texts/arbitration/ml-arb/MLARB-english_revised2006.pdf.

international treaty. It is a model solution presented as the expression of prevalent and substantially unified international practice. More than 50 countries have availed themselves of this possibility.[80] Chapter VIII of the UNCITRAL Model Law defines the rules for the recognition and enforcement of arbitral awards *"irrespective of the country in which* [the award] *was made."*[81]

673.   Apart from national laws, whether based on the UNCITRAL Model Law or not, national courts may also be faced with the obligation to abide by binding [on the courts] international treaties to which their state is a signatory. This is very frequent in international practice especially in connection with the enforcement of foreign arbitral awards. The oldest and most successful treaty relating to arbitration is the *New York Convention*,[82] ratified by 142 states,[83] which regulates the recognition of foreign arbitral awards in states which are bound by the *Convention*.

674.   Article V of the *New York Convention* contains an exhaustive list of alternative grounds justifying the refusal to recognize an arbitral award. The grounds listed in Article V(1) [of the *New York Convention*] may be applied only if invoked by the party against whom the enforcement is sought. They include: invalidity of the arbitration agreement (subparagraph (a)), breach of the right to present one's case (subparagraph (b)), decision ultra petita (subparagraph (c)), incorrect constitution of the arbitral tribunal (subparagraph (d)), and a situation where the arbitral award has not yet become binding (subparagraph (e)). The grounds specified in Article V(2) of the *New York Convention* may be applied by the national court of its own motion (*sua sponte*). They include lack of arbitrability of the dispute (subparagraph (a)) and violation of *public policy* (subparagraph (b)).

675.   In the countries which have adopted the *New York Convention* and whose lex arbitri is based on the UNCITRAL Model Law,[84] the *New York Convention* principally prevails, in compliance with the principle of precedence (preferential application) of the law of international origin (an international treaty). However, the structure of Article 36(1) of the UNCITRAL Model Law is identical to the structure of Article V of the *New York Convention* and lists the same grounds for which a national court may refuse recognition and enforcement of a foreign arbitral award.

---

[80] Available at:
http://www.uncitral.org/uncitral/en/uncitral_texts/arbitration/1985Model_ arbitration_status.html.
[81] UNCITRAL Model Law: Article 35(1).
[82] Available at: http://www.uncitral.org/pdf/english/texts/arbitration/NY-conv/XXII_1_e.pdf.
[83] Available at:
http://www.uncitral.org/uncitral/en/uncitral_texts/arbitration/NYConvention_ status.html.
[84] Naturally, this is not only in these countries. It is a broadly applied principle.

676. Another important treaty is the European Convention on International Commercial Arbitration of 1961 (the *"European Convention"*).[85] This *European Convention*, however, does not primarily focus on the enforcement of arbitral awards – the provisions of the *European Convention* regulating these matters are based on the *New York Convention*.[86] Nevertheless, it does not limit the grounds for the refusal to enforce an award by limiting the consequences of the annulment of the award in the country where it was made. The *European Convention* has been signed by 32 states, but the applicability of the *European Convention* in consumer matters is rather limited.

677. Subject to the specific conditions of consumer arbitration, the enforcement of arbitral awards may be refused on various grounds, including lack of arbitrability or invalidity of the arbitration agreement. Violation of *public policy* is another possible reason.[87]

678. As concerns the absence of arbitrability, the question is whether this reason could constitute grounds for a refusal to recognize and enforce an arbitral award which was rendered pursuant to a regime (laws) which provide(s) very extensive protection to the consumer, such as the laws of many European countries. For instance, disputes not exceeding 5,000 GBP cannot be submitted to arbitration in [GBR] – although it has been argued that these rules ought to be considered contrary to the *New York Convention* and therefore inapplicable in cases falling within the scope of the *New York Convention*.[88] In any case, consumer disputes are principally arbitrable under EU law (subject to the *Directive*),[89] as well as in certain non-Member States, for instance in Switzerland [CHE].[90] It is indeed very exceptional that the arbitrability of consumer disputes would be principally excluded. Usually the law only incorporates certain special and limiting rules for the purpose of protecting the consumer in the conclusion of arbitration agreements and, to a lesser extent, during the arbitration itself. Consequently, the **absence of arbitrability of a**

---

[85] European Convention on International Commercial Arbitration, concluded in Geneva on 21 April 1961.

[86] See *Fouchard, Gaillard, Goldman.* On International Commercial Arbitration, 1999, para. 1714–1715.

[87] However, as the developing practice in the individual countries shows, the approach of the states regarding the application of the reservation concerning *public policy* in consumer disputes is not homogenous. For instance, in its Decision Case No. 3 Ob 144/09m of 22 July 2009, the Austrian Supreme Court (OGH [AUT]) concluded that this particular reason for the refusal of recognition and enforcement of the award (here an arbitral award made in Denmark [DNK]) does not apply. Conversely, the Polish Supreme Court (SN [POL]) in its Decision Case No. No IV CSK 200/06 of 22 February 2007 refused to enforce the respective arbitral award (an arbitral award made in the U.S.).

[88] *Jarrosson, Ch.* Note on Cour d'appel de Paris, 7 December 1994. Rev. Arb. 1996, No. 2, p. 256.

[89] For a detailed commentary on EU law, see above.

[90] See *Favre-Bulle, X.* Arbitrage et Règlement alternative des litiges (ADR): une autre justice pour les consommateurs? In: *Théovenoz, L. et Reich, N.* (eds.) Droit de la consommation, Liber Amicorum Bernd Stauder, Genève: Schulthess, 2006, p. 97 et seq., here pp. 101–103.

consumer dispute in the country of recognition/enforcement does not usually constitute grounds for a refusal to enforce the arbitral award, providing the dispute is arbitrable according to the law applicable to the arbitration agreement and, subsidiarily, according to the law of the seat of arbitration. Similarly, it is not possible to refuse recognition/enforcement of a foreign arbitral award in consumer disputes, or any other disputes, on grounds of invalidity of the arbitration agreement under the law of the country of recognition/enforcement if the arbitration agreement is valid under the law applicable to the arbitration agreement. Such a situation is easily conceivable in practice – many countries require the fulfillment of specific criteria regarding the form of the arbitration agreement in consumer disputes on pain of invalidity.[91]

679.   As concerns the validity of the arbitration agreement, the *New York Convention* stipulates that enforcement may be refused if any of the parties proves that the [arbitration] agreement is not valid under the law which governs the agreement (Article V(1)(a) of the *New York Convention*). If the agreement is subject to a law which generally allows arbitration in consumer disputes, such as the U.S., the arbitration agreement may still be found invalid on other grounds. These grounds are usually stipulated by, or at least based on, general legal principles or provisions of contract law.

680.   Take for instance a situation where a contract concluded online between a Belgian consumer and a U.S. professional contains a prearbitration clause governed by California law. The *New York Convention* does not allow Belgian courts to refuse enforcement on grounds of validity of the arbitration agreement unless the agreement is invalid under California law.

681.   The exclusion of arbitration in consumer disputes or the submission of such disputes to the exclusive jurisdiction of courts may influence the validity of the arbitration agreement but may in some countries be considered contrary to *public policy*. However, as repeatedly emphasized in this work, at least as concerns Article V(2)(b) of the *New York Convention*, what is being referred to is *international public policy*. These issues are reiterated elsewhere in this book. When deciding on the compliance of the award with *public policy*, the courts do not assess the award itself; they assess its effects under their national legal system. As concerns consumers residing in the country where the enforcement is sought, arbitral awards rendered in consumer disputes may conflict with

---

[91] Cf. *Moller, H.* Schiedsverfahrensnovelle und Volstreckung ausländischer Schiedssprüche. NZG, 1999, pp. 143–146, here p. 145 and Note No. 34; demonstrated by *Moller* in the example of Section 1032(5) of the ZPO [DEU] in conjunction with the application of the *New York Convention*.

the rules which prescribe the exclusive jurisdiction of a particular authority for consumer disputes (such as Sections 21–22 of the Court Jurisdiction Act [CHE]).[92] Arbitral awards rendered in consumer disputes may also be viewed as decisions conflicting with *public policy* as a result of the fact that prearbitration clauses are excluded from consumer contracts. However, it needs to be emphasized again that this conclusion cannot be considered generally (universally) applicable, and, as Austrian case law indicates, the courts may arrive at the conclusion that it is not a case of a violation of *public policy* under the meaning of Article V(2)(b) of the *New York Convention*. This is not the case of a breach of *public policy* under the meaning of this provision of the *New York Convention*, but a broader unification of international practice might be a fairly long-term process.

682.   As already mentioned above, in matters concerning EU law, the courts of the Member States are obliged to consider *EU public policy* when making decisions on the enforceability of awards. Certain doubts regarding the concept itself, i.e. *EU public policy* have been intentionally left aside in this study. But even the ECJ itself has not yet ruled that consumer protection would be a component of *EU public policy*; the decision in *Mostaza Claro* v. *Centro Móvil* only refers to a special *public interest* in consumer protection. *Public interest* is by no means the same category as *public policy* (for more details, see Chapter II of this book), especially not the specific *public policy* enshrined in Article V(2)(b) of the *New York Convention*. The fact that *public policy* and *public interest* are two completely different categories is corroborated, for instance, by the concept of the overriding mandatory provisions employed by the EU conflict of laws (European private international law). However, overriding mandatory provisions are a category completely different from *public policy*. *Public interest* may influence the classification of a particular provision as an overriding mandatory provision which neutralizes the application of applicable (substantive) law (standards) and applies to the extent of the obligation it mandates, instead of the provision of applicable substantive law. Conversely, *public policy*, as a component of the fundamental pillars of the legal system, has negative effects; it (*substantive public policy*[93]) does not contain any specific rule but eliminates the effects of the application of foreign law, without stipulating its own substantive standard to be applied.

---

[92] The Swiss Federal Act on Court Jurisdiction in Civil Matters of 24 March 2000, RS 272.
[93] *Substantive public policy* must be distinguished from *procedural public policy*. The latter eliminates the effects of a foreign decision if a fundamental procedural standard was breached during the making of the decision. Cf. *Bělohlávek, A.* Výhrada veřejného pořádku hmotněprávního a procesního ve vztazích s mezinárodním prvkem [Title in translation – Ordre Public Exclusion in a Substantive and Procedural Sense in Relations with an International Dimension]. Právník [Lawyer], 2006, Vol. 145, No. 11 et al.

683. Apart from that, the courts of the EU Member States may also apply the *Recommendation*. Any award rendered in proceedings which does not comply with the principles stipulated in the *Recommendation* may be considered contrary to *public policy*. These principles include:

► **Independence** of the decision-making body is considered. If the arbitral institution is perceived as an institution with a too close relationship to one of the parties,[94] especially the professional, it may constitute grounds for a refusal to enforce the award rendered by the institution.

► The observance of the **adversarial** principle is largely comparable to the grounds for a refusal pursuant to Article V(1)(b) of the *New York Convention* regarding the right to present one's case. Specifically, consumer disputes require that the arbitrators take care to provide a sufficient opportunity to the consumer to exercise his or her rights. Consequently, it must be kept in mind that the consumer might not approach the proceedings as professionally as the professional.

► The principle which stipulates that the arbitral award must not deprive the consumer of the protection provided to him or her by the mandatory provisions of the state in the territory of which the decision-making authority exercises its jurisdiction is another.

► The prohibition of pre-arbitral clauses is also considered. It has to be pointed out, specifically with reference to this point that the *Recommendation* is not binding. Not all Member States prohibit arbitration clauses (pre-arbitral clauses) in consumer disputes.

684. For example, in the same arbitration agreement concluded between a Belgian consumer and a professional from the U.S. with a pre-arbitral clause governed by California law, the *New York Convention* would allow the Belgian courts to refuse enforcement if they concluded that the arbitral award is contrary to *public policy*. According to other EU provisions, such a court decision would subsequently be enforceable in the EU Member States.

685. It is also necessary to point out that the laws in the individual countries may stipulate different levels of consumer protection standards, and consequently different limits for arbitration, for different industries and areas. As concerns *public policy* and questions connected with the enforcement of an arbitral award, *public policy* may have a different intensity in different sectors; the intensity attributed to consumer protection may differ as well. For example, the protection of consumers in medical care would probably enjoy greater importance (intensity) than the sale of consumer goods.

---

[94] This is probably the case with the National Arbitration Forum (NAF) in the United States. At the time of drafting this memorandum, the NAF was being sued by San Francisco for its decisions in consumer credits, the overwhelming majority of which favored the professionals. See Wall Street Journal Law Blog, 7 April, 2008. Also available at: http://blogs.wsj.com/law/.

V.4.3. Enforcement of arbitral awards rendered in states with a lower degree of consumer protection

686. The Internet has expanded consumers' possibilities and allowed them to enter into contracts away from their habitual residence. In doing so, they may (intentionally or not) enter into arbitration agreements governed by the law of foreign countries. As mentioned above, the individual legal systems exhibit major differences in their approach to consumer arbitration.

687. For instance, if we look at the U.S. as one of the leading representatives of the Internet economy, it is by no means exceptional that consumers accept contractual terms containing arbitration clauses in contracts (contract terms and conditions) offered by overseas merchants. These arbitration clauses, as described in the excursus into U.S. law and the practices of the U.S. federal government and the individual U.S. states, are usually valid and enforceable in the U.S.[95] However, such arbitration clauses anticipate that the arbitration will take place in the U.S., with or even without the consumer's attendance. The arbitration clause is usually held valid in the place of the proceedings and under the law applicable to the arbitration agreement. As concerns the form of these arbitration agreements and their validity, it is a valid term, and it is hardly conceivable that enforcement of such an arbitral award would be refused on grounds such as failure to meet formal requirements.[96] Nonetheless, enforcement of the award could in many countries be refused, because, for instance, the arbitration clause would de facto constitute an obstacle to consumer protection in terms of an effective right to oppose the claim.[97]

688. The cases described in the preceding paragraph are situations in which the arbitral tribunals are faced with the question of whether to consider the risk of unenforceability of the future arbitral award or not. If the arbitral tribunal arrives at a negative conclusion (i.e. the risk of unenforceability exists), the tribunal ought to refuse its jurisdiction. This especially applies to consumer disputes which entail a high probability that the enforcement of the arbitral award (where the operative part of the award imposes an obligation on the consumer) will be sought in the country of the consumer's habitual residence unless the professional discovers that the consumer has assets in a different country, too.

---

[95] Recently, however, purchases by consumers via websites of merchants established in Asian countries have become just as common.

[96] Cf. *Moller, H.* Schiedsverfahrensnovelle und Volstreckung ausländischer Schiedssprüche. NZG, 1999, pp. 143–146, here p. 145 and Note No. 34; demonstrated by *Moller* on the example of Section 1032(5) of the ZPO [DEU] in conjunction with the application of the *New York Convention.*

[97] Cf. the decision of the Polish Supreme Court (SN [POL]), Case No. No IV CSK 200/06 of 22 February 2007, whereby the enforcement of an arbitral award made in the U.S. was refused. The cited Polish decision is annotated elsewhere in this book – see this section regarding the enforcement of foreign arbitral awards.

However, it should be emphasized that recommending arbitral tribunals take into account the potential unenforceability of their awards in the country where enforcement might be sought, is by no means prevalent, and the opinions voiced in international practice generally deny that the arbitral tribunals would be bound by any such obligation. Undeniably, opinions which reject any such obligation on the part of the arbitral tribunals are persuasive. Nonetheless, consumer disputes (and similarly, for instance, employment disputes) are special types of disputes in which any possible refusal of enforcement in the country where enforcement might *potentially* be sought should be taken into consideration by the arbitrators.

689.   Consumer disputes are typically disputes which require individual assessment and evaluation primarily at the law-finding stage of the [arbitral] proceedings. This often minimizes the potential for any generalization of the case law relating to these disputes in broader interpretation practice and, consequently, the potential for any generalization at the international level. The potential for broader generalization is diminished despite the fact that use of consumer contracts and the resolution of their related consumer disputes moved long ago beyond state borders. Indeed, a similar conclusion can be made with respect to employment disputes and some other types of disputes.[98] On the other hand, there exists a significantly large and, as yet, untapped potential in the comparison of the approach adopted by foreign courts in the exercise of their duty of supervision over arbitration or in the enforcement and recognition of arbitral awards. Such a comparison could especially be made in those countries which mandatorily draw on the same legal basis for consumer protection, such as the EU Member States bound by EU law and its consumer protection standards.

V.4.4.   Decision of the Austrian Supreme Court (OGH [AUT]), Case No. 3 Ob 144/09m of 22 July 2009: Breach of consumer protection laws does not form part of international or *EU public policy*

(a)   Importance of the decision

690.   The question of whether or not a breach of consumer protection laws in the country where the arbitral award was made constitutes grounds for a refusal to recognize and enforce the arbitral award in a different country has probably been most rigorously analyzed by the Austrian Supreme Court. The Austrian Supreme Court (OGH [AUT]) in its Decision 3 Ob

---

[98] Cf. the decision of the U.S. Court of Appeals, First Circuit, of 8 July 1997 (in Exxon Corporation v. Esso Worker's Union, Inc.); 118 F.3d 841. This decision is undoubtedly the benchmark for the resolution of employment disputes in the national regime [USA] and is often referred to; however, it can hardly be attributed any broader (international) importance.

144/09m of 22 July 2009[99] basically concluded that consumer protection is not a component of *international public policy* or *EU public policy*. The Court thus confirmed the conclusions reached by the ECJ in *Asturcom*, i.e. that consumer protection under EU standards does not extend into the international arena with respect to the enforcement and recognition of foreign arbitral awards. This is probably the first and, as yet, only decision which deals with consumer protection issues and the limitation of arbitrability under the law of the state where recognition and enforcement are sought, as concerns foreign arbitral awards and with respect to the *New York Convention*. Moreover, it is a decision which has analyzed all the relevant issues in great detail.[100] Indeed, such an approach is typical for Austrian decisions which are well-known for their clarity and high erudition.

(b) Facts of the case

691. A Danish enterprise [DNK] and an Austrian company (a limited liability company) [the "Austrian company"] entered into a franchise agreement. The agreement contained an arbitration clause referring to the Rules of the Danish Institute of Arbitration (Copenhagen Arbitration). The franchise agreement was acceded to by the Executive of the Austrian company and another natural person.[101] The accession statement stipulated that the acceders are direct, or indirect, as the case may be, owners of the franchise and as such guarantee the performance of all [and any] obligations of the franchisee under the agreement, including the payment of any recourse claims against the franchisee.

692. The Austrian company, as well as the natural persons, were ordered under the arbitral award pronounced by the Danish Institute of Arbitration to pay approximately 150,000 EUR. In the course of the arbitral proceedings, the respondents pleaded the inapplicability of the arbitration agreement to natural persons. However, they did not make that plea in the statement of defense but only later in the arbitral proceedings. The arbitral tribunal dismissed the plea as belated.

693. In the enforcement proceedings initiated in Austria [AUT], the two natural persons (the first and the second respondent) specifically argued

---

[99] Decision of the OGH [AUT], Case No. 3 Ob 144/09m of 22 July 2009. Published in: (i) SZ 010/21 (Öhlberger) and in: (ii) the Austrian Arbitration Association (ArbAut) Bulletin at: http://www.cm.arbitration-austria.at/newsletter_detail.php?archiv_id=44 [last access 3 July 2010].

[100] This is certainly an indisputable advantage of Austrian law and case law. Conversely, it is definitely a pity that, for instance, the reasons elaborated by French courts in their decisions are very brief. Moreover, Austrian case law and Austrian laws are easily accessible online and the publicly available databases are very well-organized. From a global perspective, this perfectly structured organizational system and public accessibility are unique.

[101] The published part of the decision does not clearly indicate the relationship of the person to the Austrian company – we may assume that he or she was a partner (member) of the company.[102] Cited reference above appears elsewhere in this book.

that there was no valid arbitration agreement, and, consequently, there were grounds to refuse enforcement of the arbitral award pursuant to Article V(1)(a) of the *New York Convention*. Besides, the respondents argued that the arbitration agreement between the natural persons on the one side and the Danish company on the other side was contrary to consumer protection laws, especially Section 617 of the ZPO [AUT];[102] referring to this argument, the parties claimed that the arbitral award was contrary to (*substantive*) *public policy (ordre public)* and, as a result thereof, enforcement ought to be refused pursuant to Article V(2)(b) of the *New York Convention*.

(c) Conclusions of the Austrian court

694.   The Austrian Supreme Court (OGH [AUT]) held that the loss of right to invoke the validity of an arbitration agreement cannot be subsequently remedied in a different country (the country of enforcement) by a refusal to recognize and enforce the arbitral award for a breach of *public policy*. According to this decision, an arbitration clause in business-to-consumer contracts does not automatically violate *Austrian public policy* despite the fact that Austrian laws do not allow arbitration clauses and only allow post-dispute arbitration agreements. This automatically implies that a breach of consumer protection laws does not violate *EU public policy*, let alone *international public policy*.

695.   The loss (extinguishment) of the right to invoke the invalidity of the arbitration agreement is valid; arbitration agreements in consumer relations do not per se constitute a breach of (substantive) *public policy* (*ordre public*).

(d) Reasons for the decision

696.   Any defects of the arbitration agreement must be pleaded in the arbitral proceedings. Failure to raise the plea validates the defect; see also Article V of the European Convention on International Commercial Arbitration (the *European Convention* which must also be applied).[103] The Danish Institute of Arbitration concluded that the plea was belated under applicable procedural law (and therefore the right to make the plea was extinguished). This may still certainly be subject to review in the proceedings on the recognition of the arbitral award (exequatur). The national laws (national lex arbitri) limiting arbitration agreements in consumer disputes cannot be applied to the recognition and enforcement of foreign arbitral awards. For the sake of completeness, it

---

[102] Cited reference above appears elsewhere in this book.

[103] The OGH [AUT] invokes its former case law, in particular Decision Case No. 3 Ob 221/04b, published in: (i) SZ 2005/9, (ii) IPrax, 2006, p. 496 et seq. Besides, the existing commentaries share this opinion.

is necessary to point out that the Austrian lex arbitri (ZPO [AUT]) contains explicit rules on the territorial scope of its application (Section 577 of the ZPO [AUT][104]). According to Section 577 of the ZPO [AUT];[105] provisions limiting the arbitrability of consumer disputes do not have any exterritorial effects. Such effects would neither exist in the present case (recognition and enforcement of foreign arbitral awards) in relation to persons with their place of residence/registered office in Austria until the place of proceedings is determined (unless, for instance, the seat of the arbitration is agreed in the arbitration agreement or by reference to procedural rules).[106] Besides, even if domestic laws (lex arbitri) allowed consideration of consumer protection laws in exequatur or in enforcement proceedings,[107] such laws could not be used in those cases to which the *New York Convention* applies. Domestic law would conflict with the *New York Convention*, the application of which takes precedence.

697. The Austrian Supreme Court (OGH [AUT]) explicitly stated that a domestic law limiting consumer arbitration does not apply to foreign arbitral awards.[108] A conflict with consumer protection laws may, in principle, breach *substantive public policy*.[109] In relation to Article V(2)(b)[110] of the *New York Convention*, however, such conclusion must be rejected. These agreements are also permissible in business-to-consumer contracts (Point 7 of Section 6(2) of the KSchG [AUT][111]),

---

[104] An approximate translation is provided below in the footnotes to this part of the book.
[105] An approximate translation is provided below in the footnotes to this part of the book.
[106] The proceedings were clearly domiciled in Denmark as the arbitration agreement contained an explicit reference to the Arbitration Rules of the Danish Institute of Arbitration (Copenhagen Arbitration).
[107] As the ECJ ruled in *Asturcom*, even EU laws leave this issue entirely at the discretion of the Member States. No EU imperative can be applied in this regard.
[108] Apart from Section 617, the OGH [AUT] explicitly invokes Section 577(2) of the ZPO [AUT].
[109] Cf. Article L 132-1 of the French Consumer Protection Act [FRA] implemented by Act No. 95-96 of 1 February 1995, Article 1, published in the Annex to JORF of 2 February 1995 and Regulation No. 2001-741 of 23 August 2001, Article 16, published in JORF of 25 August 2001. The approximate translation of the decision is provided in the excursus concerning France. It explicitly stipulates that the rules (unfair terms in consumer contracts) are a component of *public policy*.
[110] The Austrian decision explicitly invokes Article V(2)(a) of the *New York Convention*, which is, however, an obvious typing error.
[111] KSchG [AUT] (approximate translation, cit.): Section 6 – Unacceptable contractual terms – *"(1) The following is an indicative list of contractual terms which shall always be considered as inapplicable to consumers under the terms of Section 879 of the ABGB [AUT]: 1. the professional reserves an unreasonably long or insufficiently specific period for the acceptance or rejection of the consumer's offer to conclude the contract or an unreasonably long or insufficiently specific period during which the consumer is bound by the contract; 2. certain conduct by the consumer is considered tantamount to making or, as the case may be, not making a declaration [of the will to contract], unless the consumer was specifically informed about the importance of his or her acts at the beginning of the relevant period and had a reasonable opportunity to make his or her explicit declaration; 3. a representation by the professional which gives rise to legal consequences for the consumer is deemed delivered even if it was not delivered to the consumer; this does not apply to the effects of a statement*

although only on the basis of an individual contracting process. Section 14 of the KSchG [AUT],[112] which limits choice-of-court agreements, has

---

sent to the last address announced by the consumer if the consumer failed to inform the professional of a change in the consumer's address; 4. a notice or representation to be given by the consumer vis-à-vis the professional or a third party is made subject to more rigorous formal requirements than the written form, or it is to be delivered by special means; 5. remuneration payable for the professional's performance at the professional's request exceeds the amount stipulated at the conclusion of the contract unless the contract also anticipates a reduction of the remuneration subject to the agreed conditions, [and] providing the circumstances decisive for a modification of the remuneration are described in the contract and justified and [providing that] the modification is independent of the professional's will; 6. the consumer's right to deny performance pursuant to Section 1052 of the ABGB [AUT] until the other party's counter-performance is duly secured is limited or excluded in the event that the professional fails to provide his or her performance or if the provision thereof is jeopardized by the professional's unfavorable financial situation of which the consumer was not aware, and was not obliged to be aware, at the conclusion of the contract, for instance, because the right to deny performance is made dependent upon whether the professional acknowledges the defects of his or her performance; 7. the consumer's statutory right of retention is excluded or limited; 8. the consumer's right to discharge his or her obligation by way of offset is excluded or limited in the event that the professional becomes insolvent, or is excluded or limited with respect to the professional's counter-claims legally related to the consumer's obligations, to counter-claims whose existence has been confirmed by a court, or to counter-claims acknowledged by the professional; 9. the professional's obligation to compensate for personal injury is limited or excluded, or the professional's obligation to compensate for other damage is limited or excluded in the case of damage caused intentionally or due to gross negligence by the professional or by persons for whom the professional is responsible; 10. the professional or an authority or person under the professional's control are authorized to make binding decisions on behalf of the consumer on whether the performance provided by the professional to the consumer complies with their agreement; 11. the consumer is subject to a burden of proof which he or she would not otherwise have under the law; 12. the consumer's rights to an object taken over by the professional for further processing expire in an unreasonably short period of time; 13. the default interest payable by the consumer exceeds by more than five percentage points per year the interest rate agreed under the contract for a situation in which the payments are made in compliance with the contract; 14. the consumer's right to invoke a mistake or the absence or subsequent expiration of the reason to enter into the contract is limited or excluded in advance, for instance based on an agreement stipulating that the promises made by the professional do not apply to the main contractual performance or its essential qualities (Section 871(1) of the ABGB [AUT]); 15. [the consumer] undertakes to provide compensation for the costs of enforcement or collection of a due and outstanding performance unless the costs are specified separately and in itemized form or unless the costs are indispensable for a purposeful enforcement or collection of claims. (2) Unless the professional proves that [the respective terms] were individually negotiated, the same also applies to contractual terms according to which 1. the professional may cancel the contract without any legitimate reason; 2. the professional has the right to transfer his or her obligations or the entire contract to a third party who is not identified in the contract and the transfer absolves the professional from the obligation to provide the performance; 3. the professional may unilaterally change or deviate from the performance to be provided by the professional (unless the consumer may reasonably be expected to suffer the change of or the deviation from the performance, in particular because the change or deviation is negligible or justified as to its substance); 4. the professional is entitled to claim remuneration for the performance provided by the professional during the first two months following the conclusion of the contract which exceeds the originally agreed remuneration; 5. the professional's liability for compensation of damage caused to an object taken over by the professional for further processing is excluded; 6. the consumer's claims under Section 908 of the ABGB [AUT] are limited or excluded; 7. a dispute between the professional and the consumer is to be decided by one or more arbitrators. (3) An unclear or incomprehensible contractual term included in the general contractual terms and conditions or in contract forms is invalid."

[112] KSchG [AUT] (approximate translation, cit.): Section 14 – "(1) If the consumer has his or her residence or habitual residence in Austria or if he or she is employed in Austria, he or she can be sued

so far been applied to arbitration agreements *per analogiam*. The respondents (in the case) pleaded violation of this provision with reference to Section 617 of the ZPO [AUT].[113] However, the Austrian Supreme Court (OGH [AUT]) held that the plea was inadmissible primarily for the fact that the parties had initiated arbitration in the case.[114] The Supreme Court (OGH [AUT]) does not explicitly refer to the ECJ ruling in *Mostaza-Claro* v. *Centro Móvil*.[115] After all, in the context of the case, i.e. enforcement of a foreign decision, such reference would be unnecessary.[116] Such a reference could only be expected if the proceedings were concerned with the annulment of an arbitral award and/or the enforcement of a domestic (Austrian) arbitral award. However, enforcement of a foreign arbitral award subject to the *New York Convention* does not require application of the ECJ's case law. The arbitration agreement itself, though, is not contrary to the fundamental principles [*Grundwertungen*] of the Austrian law, i.e. the reservation concerning *public policy* does not apply. The fact that this is the legislator's view too is supported by the new wording (inapplicable in this case, as mentioned above) of Point 1 of Section 617(6) of the ZPO [AUT],[117] which would be superfluous if the mandatory consumer protection provisions were principally a component of *public policy* [*ordre public*], i.e. Point 8 of Section 611(2) of the ZPO [AUT].[118] The

---

pursuant to Sections 88, 89, 93(2) and Section 104(1) of the JN [Jurisdiktionsnorm /AUT/; Court Jurisdiction Act; author's note] *only in the court which has jurisdiction over the consumer's residence, habitual residence or place of employment; this does not apply to disputes which have already arisen. (2) Lack of jurisdiction of an Austrian court as well as lack of territorial jurisdiction (venue) are examined of the court's own motion at every stage of the proceedings; the court shall, however, apply the provisions regulating the subsequent validation of the lack of jurisdiction (subject-matter or territorial) of Austrian courts (Section 104(3) of the JN* [AUT]*). (3) Any contractual term which excludes the statutory jurisdiction of courts with respect to lawsuits filed by a consumer against a professional is inoperative vis-à-vis the consumer. (4) Subsections 1 through 3 or any parts thereof shall not apply if international law* [= international treaties, author's note] *or any special legislation explicitly stipulate otherwise."*

[113] Cited reference above appears elsewhere in this book.

[114] This conclusion could perhaps be contested under the ECJ ruling in *Mostaza-Claro*. However, in connection with the merits of the proceedings, any other conclusion on this particular issue would be irrelevant.

[115] ECJ Judgment, Case C-168/05 in *Elisa María Mostaza-Claro* v. *Centro Movil Milenium SL*, published in: ECR I 2006, p. 10437 et seq.

[116] The facts of the case are also significantly different from *Mostaza-Claro*.

[117] Cited reference above appears elsewhere in this book.

[118] ZPO [AUT] – Section 611 – "*(1) Recourse to a court against an arbitral award may be made only by means of an action for setting aside. This shall also apply to arbitral awards by which the arbitral tribunal has ruled on its jurisdiction. (2) An arbitral award shall be set aside if: 1. a valid arbitration agreement does not exist, or if the arbitral tribunal denies its jurisdiction despite the existence of a valid arbitration agreement, or if a party was under some incapacity under the law applicable to them to conclude a valid arbitration agreement; 2. a party was not given proper notice of the appointment of an arbitrator or of the arbitral proceedings or was for other reasons unable to present his case; 3. the award deals with a dispute not contemplated by or not falling within the terms of the arbitration agreement, or contains decisions on matters beyond the scope of the arbitration agreement or beyond the plea of the parties for legal protection, provided that, if the defect concerns only a part that can be*

documents available in this case did not permit the conclusion of a violation of *ordre public* pursuant to Article V(2)(a) of the *New York Convention* for any reason other than the reason alleged by the respondents (i.e. limitation of arbitrability of consumer disputes pursuant to Austrian law).

(e)   Commentary on the decision

698.   The Court (OGH [AUT]) concluded that Section 617 of the ZPO [AUT][119] does not apply if the seat of the arbitral tribunal (seat of arbitration) is abroad. In the reasons for its decision, the OGH [AUT] argues that Section 617 of the ZPO [AUT][120] does not belong to the category of provisions which, pursuant to Section 577(2) of the ZPO [AUT],[121] automatically apply if the seat of the arbitral tribunal (seat of the arbitration) is located outside Austria (refusal of the exterritorial scope of application, i.e. application independent of the place of

---

separated from the award, only that part of the award shall be set aside; 4. the composition of the arbitral tribunal was not in accordance with a provision of this section or with an admissible agreement of the parties; 5. the arbitral procedure was not carried out in accordance with the fundamentals of the Austrian legal system (ordre public). 6. the requirements have been met according to which a judgment of a court of law can be appealed by an action for revision under Article 530, paragraph (1), numbers 1 to 5 [ZPO/AUT/]; 7. the subject matter of the dispute is not capable of settlement by arbitration under the law of this state; 8. the award is in conflict with the fundamentals of the Austrian legal system (ordre public). (3) The reasons for setting aside stipulated in paragraph (2), numbers 7 and 8 are also to be examined by the court ex officio. (4) The action for setting aside must be made within three months. The time period shall begin with the day on which the claimant received the award or the additional award. (5) An application made in accordance with Article 610 paragraph (1) numbers 1 or 2 [of the ZPO /AUT/] shall not extend this time period. In the case of paragraph (2), number 6, the time period within which the action for setting aside must be brought, shall be determined in accordance with the provisions on the action for revision. (6) The setting aside of an arbitral award has no influence on the effectiveness of the underlying arbitration agreement. When an arbitral award on the same subject matter has already been finally set aside twice and when a further arbitral award in the same subject matter is to be set aside, upon application of a party, the court shall concurrently declare the arbitration agreement invalid with respect to that matter." (adopted from http://www.viac.eu/images/stories/documents/en/New_Code_of_Civil_Procedure.pdf [last access 12 April 2012]).

[119] This is the Austrian *lex arbitri* with respect to consumer contracts. Cited reference above appears elsewhere in this book, in connection with the excursus into Austrian law.

[120] Cited reference above appears elsewhere in this book.

[121] ZPO [AUT] (approximate translation, cit.): Section 577 – "(1) *The provisions of this Chapter apply if the place of arbitration is in Austria. (2) Sections 578, 580, 583, 584, 585, 593 paragraphs (3) to (6), Articles 602, 612 and 614* [of the ZPO/AUT/] *are also applicable if the place of arbitration is not within Austria or has not been determined. (3) As long as the place of arbitration has not yet been determined, the domestic jurisdiction shall apply for those judicial tasks as stipulated in the Third Title if one of the parties has its seat, domicile or ordinary residence within Austria. (4) The provisions of this Chapter shall not be applicable to institutions subject to the Austrian Associations and Societies Act (Vereinsgesetz) for the conciliation of disputes arising out of the circumstances of the association.* (Adopted from http://www.viac.eu/images/stories/documents/en/New_Code_of_Civil_Procedure. pdf [last access 12 April 2012]).

proceedings). The available commentaries consider the OGH's conclusions an obiter dictum under the applicable provisions.[122]

699. This means that according to the opinion of the OGH [AUT] (although the court did not explicitly say so), **a breach of those provisions which limit the arbitrability of consumer disputes** (Section 617(5) of the ZPO [AUT]), which limit the arbitrability of consumer disputes concerning the seat of the arbitral tribunal [seat of arbitration], **does not constitute a breach of the *ordre public* in terms of Article V(2)(b) of the *New York Convention*.**[123] The same commentaries criticize the fact that the decision does not invoke the limitation under Section 617(1) of the ZPO [AUT][124] prohibiting *ex ante* arbitration agreements, i.e. arbitration agreements entered into before the dispute arises.[125] Some experts argue that this constitutes a limitation of objective arbitrability.[126]

700. The Court neither invokes the limitation under Section 617(1) of the ZPO [AUT][127] prohibiting *ex ante* arbitration agreements, i.e. arbitration agreements entered into before the dispute between the professional and the consumer arises. The decision does not indicate whether the respondents in their defense also invoked the law applicable to the arbitration agreement, i.e. Danish law in the given case, in order to justify the invalidity of the arbitration agreement. This is surprising, because Article 7 of the Danish arbitration law [DNK] contains a prohibition on arbitration clauses (ex ante arbitration agreements) comparable to Section 617(1) of the ZPO [AUT] (Article 7(2) of the Danish arbitration laws).[128] In the case of a consumer contract, an arbitration agreement concluded before the dispute arose shall not be binding on the consumer.[129]

---

[122] Bulletin of the *Austrian Arbitration Association* (ArbAut) at: http://www.cm.arbitration-austria.at/newsletter_detail.php?archiv_id=44 [last access 3 July 2010].

[123] *Koller, Ch.* Schiedsvereinbarungen in Allgemeinen Geschäftsbedingungen. In: *Knyrim, R., Leitner, M., Perner, S. et Riss, O.* (eds.) Aktuelles AGB-Recht, Wien: Manz, 2008, p. 155. The reference is also contained in the commentary in: Bulletin of the Austrian Arbitration Association (ArbAut) at: http://www.cm.arbitration-austria.at/newsletter_detail.php?archiv_id=44 [last access 3 July 2010].

[124] Cited reference above appears elsewhere in this book.

[125] In certain legal systems, it is explicitly classified as a type of an arbitration agreement. Cf. Section 2(3)(a) of the ArbAct [CZE].

[126] *Koller, Ch.* Schiedsvereinbarungen in Allgemeinen Geschäftsbedingungen. In: *Knyrim, R., Leitner, M., Perner, S. et Riss, O.* (eds.) Aktuelles AGB-Recht, Wien: Manz, 2008, p. 188. The reference is also contained in the commentary in: Bulletin of the Austrian Arbitration Association (ArbAut) at: http://www.cm.arbitration-austria.at/newsletter_detail.php?archiv_id=44 [last access 3 July 2010].

[127] Cited reference above appears elsewhere in this book.

[128] The original German version of the material quotes the English mutation: In case of a consumer contract, an arbitration agreement concluded before the dispute arose shall not be binding on the consumer.

[129] This provision is also referred to and cited in the commentary on the respective decision of the OGH [AUT] in: Bulletin of the Austrian Arbitration Association (ArbAut) at: http://www.cm.arbitration-austria.at/newsletter_detail.php?archiv_id=44 [last access 3 July 2010].

V.5. Courts as *"juge d'appui"* in consumer disputes: Auxiliary role of courts with respect to arbitration

701. Most national arbitration laws (lex arbitri) provide that the court in the seat of the arbitration is obliged to assist the parties and the arbitrators in order to ensure that the arbitral proceedings proceed smoothly. The term used in international practice for judges providing such assistance is *"juge d'appui"* (literally *judges who support arbitration*, i.e. judges who perform auxiliary duties with respect to arbitration). The rights and duties of these courts may include appointment and replacement of arbitrators and the issue of interim measures.

V.6. Appointment of arbitrators

V.6.1. Appointment and replacement of arbitrators

702. All national arbitration laws are based on the principle of autonomy of the parties which allows them to appoint an arbitrator or agree on the method of his or her appointment.[130] Some parties may name the arbitrator in their arbitration agreement. If the arbitrator appointed in the arbitration agreement was simultaneously the drafter of the agreement, a Swiss court, for instance, would refuse enforcement of the award.[131]

703. If the parties do not opt for arbitration before a *permanent arbitral institution* and do not entrust a third party with the appointment of arbitrators, only the court may assist with the constitution of the arbitral tribunal.[132] All national arbitration laws allow the parties to address the court with a request for appointment of arbitrators.

704. There are many situations which require the replacement of an arbitrator, such as his or her death, removal by the parties, challenge of the arbitrator, and release of the arbitrator from his or her office by a court decision or resignation.

---

[130] See the UNCITRAL Model Law, Section 11(2).

[131] Decision of the trial court in Switzerland [CHE] of 19 May 1994; annotated in: ASA Bull., 1997, No. 2, p. 262. No other identification of the decision is available. These are typically situations in which the legal counsel who drafted the contract for the person presenting the contract offer is identified as the arbitrator. Such situations are naturally unacceptable and violate the fundamental principles of arbitration, namely the principle of independence and impartiality of the arbitrator. This solution is unacceptable both in consumer disputes and in arbitration generally, i.e. with respect to any disputes at all.

[132] At the national level, they exist in exceptional cases primarily with respect to special disputes. Special rules also apply in cases to which the *European Convention* which anticipates the existence of a special appointing authority in each contracting state. The duties of these authorities are usually discharged by national economic chambers (chambers of commerce and industry). The authority for the Czech Republic is the Chairman of the Economic Chamber of the Czech Republic. However, the importance of the *European Convention* for consumer arbitration is only marginal.

V.6.2. Challenging arbitrators

705. The arbitrator must not be connected with any of the parties and must not have any interest in the outcome of the dispute. The definition of independence varies under various national doctrines, legal systems, and their case law. These approaches also influence the interpretation of the grounds for challenging the arbitrator which in various legal systems allow for removal of the arbitrator or justify annulment of the arbitral award. The legal systems of most countries either refer to independence or impartiality,[133] lack of bias,[134] or all of these grounds.[135] Moreover, issues relating to consumer arbitration may be subject to the rules specified in the *Recommendation*.

706. As mentioned above, arbitrators in consumer disputes are sometimes connected with the professional (business) who is a party to the dispute. The position of arbitrator as a repeated participant might, under many national legal systems, be interpreted as affecting his or her independence or impartiality. The IBA Guidelines on Conflict of Interests in International Arbitration[136] stipulate that it is legitimate to question the independence and impartiality (lack of bias) of the arbitrator if the arbitrator has within the past three years been appointed as arbitrator on two or more occasions by one of the parties. Some *permanent arbitral institutions* (for instance, the ICC Court) also take into consideration, if necessary, whether the arbitrator was appointed in more disputes by one and the same law firm, and other factors. However, such limitations may not be applicable eo ipso in typical consumer disputes at the national level. This applies, for instance, to the Czech Republic [CZE] where the estimate (no precise statistics are available) is that arbitrators decide approximately 100,000 – 150,000 (!) disputes each year, the overwhelming majority of these being, naturally, disputes arising from consumer contracts. Moreover, it is certainly better if disputes are resolved by experts with the relevant expertise. A consistent (rigorous) application of certain, otherwise internationally recognized, principles (for instance, repeated appointments of the arbitrator by a particular party or law firm) would in many cases render the entire system of resolution of consumer disputes non-functional.

707. Conversely, if the consumer (a party to the dispute) is not well aware of his or her rights, it is necessary to ask whether arbitrators are obliged to advise the consumer. If they provide such advice, they may face a bias challenge. However, if they fail to do so, they increase the likelihood of

---

[133] For instance, Switzerland [CHE].
[134] For instance, France [FRA].
[135] For instance, France [FRA].
[136] These rules were approved on 22 May 2004; available online at: www.ibanet.org/Document/...
[last access 15 August 2011].

annulment of the arbitral award due to the fact that they failed to offer effective protection of the consumer's rights. Speaking of EU law, let us look at the ECJ's ruling in *Mostaza Claro* v. *Centro Movil*; the ECJ held that if the obligation to raise the issue is imposed on the courts, we cannot expect the arbitral tribunals to do so. As concerns other legal systems, especially the laws of non-Member States of the EU, Swiss law, for instance, does not require that the arbitrator rule on his or her jurisdiction, or raise doubts regarding his or her jurisdiction, of his or her own motion; if his or her jurisdiction is challenged by the parties, the arbitral tribunal is obliged to assess all relevant circumstances.[137] However, the arbitrator should take into account situations which could result in, for instance, lack of arbitrability of the dispute, potential unenforceability of the arbitral award, etc. This conclusion applies especially in specific types of disputes such as consumer disputes. Swiss case law is certainly important for international arbitration. But, arguably, it cannot serve as the benchmark for consumer disputes at the international level. The same also applies to other legal systems which have traditionally more experience with dispute resolution. Consumer disputes are a category of disputes in connection with which any attempts at transnational generalizations may lead to misleading conclusions.

708.   An interesting decision was rendered by the German Federal Court of Justice (BGH [DEU]) in connection with the constitution of an arbitral tribunal.[138] The court held that the appointment of a particular arbitrator in a consumer contract might not have been correct but that fact did not render the arbitration agreement invalid. The reason is that German law provides (just like most legal systems) that the party who challenges the arbitrator (the constitution of the arbitral tribunal/panel) may address the court with a motion to disqualify the arbitrator and replace him or her with another person. Indeed, Germany [DEU], just like Austria [AUT] and other countries adhering to traditional, continental *civil law* doctrine, has long exhibited an inclination to intensify its support for arbitration in basically all respects. It is true that the multi-layered judicial system in these countries which is connected with or follows arbitration may be seen as a setback, but the case law of the courts is, conversely, very rich, which indicates an arbitration-friendly approach, and (as opposed to many other countries which have sometimes been labeled as traditional supporters of arbitration) provides consistent case law without any unexpected or surprising variations.

---

[137] See the decision of the Swiss Federal Supreme Court of 16 October 2001 (in P. v. O.), annotated in: ASA. Bull., 2002, p. 97; the author has no precise identification of the decision at his disposal (adopted).
[138] Judgment of the BGH [DEU], Case No. III ZR 164/06 of 1 March 2007. This judgment is annotated in detail in the excursus into German consumer arbitration law.

V.7. Applications for interim measures, including anti-arbitration injunctions

709.   There are several reasons why it is important that the competent court has the jurisdiction to issue interim measures supporting arbitration. First of all, the appointment of the arbitral tribunal may, under certain national regimes, take a considerable period of time and an interim intervention is often necessary. Second, the operative part of the arbitral award may only apply to the parties to particular arbitral proceedings (inter partes effect). The law in certain countries provides that an interim measure may impose obligations on a third party as well.

710.   The measures adopted by the court could include an injunction to preserve the status quo or prevent impairment of the debtor's assets, interrogation of witnesses, or preservation of property or evidence.

711.   Courts in certain countries are endowed with the power to issue decisions prohibiting arbitral tribunals from continuing with pending arbitration proceedings or prohibiting the parties from initiating arbitration in the first place (*anti-arbitration injunctions*[139]). Such decisions prohibiting arbitration are usually rendered only in *common law* countries.[140] However, in the international arena, this concept is questionable, and the decisions are usually not enforceable except in the state in which they were made.

712.   The power to issue decisions prohibiting arbitration is significantly limited under EU law. It is basically the domain of English law. Most EU Member States reject this option. Switzerland [CHE], as a non-Member State, has also ruled that Swiss law does not recognize anti-arbitration injunctions.[141] One may therefore conclude that (i) anti-arbitration injunctions made by courts abroad are not enforceable in most countries and that (ii) most courts in other countries cannot render such anti-

---

[139] As the opposite to *anti-suit injunctions*, i.e. prohibitions issued by courts in *common law* countries in which the proceedings are to be domiciled under the applicable arbitration agreement; the injunction prohibits a contracting party from commencing or continuing currently pending litigation due to the existence of an arbitration agreement.

[140] These countries are also familiar with *anti-suit injunctions* prohibiting the parties from filing a claim with a court or continuing in pending litigation if the subject matter of the dispute is covered by an arbitration agreement. Most civil law countries severely criticize this concept, or they even hold the instrument contrary to the fundamental principles of law. From the perspective of international public law, lawyers in many countries argue that this measure interferes with the judicial sovereignty of another country, i.e. the other country's sovereignty.

Recently, however, most *anti-arbitration injunctions* have probably been made in India. For example, from the disputes submitted to the ICC International Court of Arbitration (ICC Court) where one of the parties (usually a respondent from India) requested the injunction, only one case has been reported in which an Indian Court refused to issue such an injunction.

[141] The decision of the trial court in Geneva [CHE], Case No. C/1043/2005-15 SP of 2 May 2005.

arbitration injunctions. The possibility that, in the future, such measures adopted by courts in connection with consumer disputes may arise cannot be excluded. However, these measures usually do not have any extraterritorial effects and are not capable of having any effects in many other countries.

713.   Courts as *juge d'appui* must take into consideration the requirements of consumer arbitration. The issue of costs may also be an important factor in the selection of arbitrators.

BIBLIOGRAPHY

I. Monographs

I.A. Literature directly related to the topic

Agostinelli, P., Garofalo, L. (ed.), *Mannino, P., L., Moscati, E. et Vecchi, P., M.* Commentario alla disciplina della vendita di beni di consumo Garofalo, Padova: CEDAM, 2003.

Allotti, V. La clausole arbitrali nei contratti con i consumatori: l'esperienza ingles. Rivista dell' arbitrato, 1998, Vol. 8, p. 360 et seq.

Alpa, G. Il diritto dei consumatori, Roma / Bari: Editori Laterza, 1999.

Alpa, G. L'expérience en Italie. The "Unfair Terms" Directive, Five Years On, Evaluation and Future Perspectives. In: Materials from a conference the organization of which was initiated by the European Commission 1 – 3 July 1999 in Brussels (B), Brussels: European Publishers, 2000, p. 53 et seq.

Alpa, G., De Nova, G., Capilli, G., Colantuoni, L., Leo, C., Maniaci, A. et Putti, P., M. L'acquisto di beni di consumo, collana a cura di De Nova, Milano: IPSOA, 2002, sub art. 1519septies, p. 62 et seq.

Amato, C. Per un diritto europeo dei contratti con i consumatori, Milan: Giuffré, 2003.

Anderson, M. G. Arbitration Clauses in Retainer Agreements: A Lawyer's License to Exploit the Client. J. Disp. Res., 1992, p. 341 et seq.

Añoveros, B. Los contratos de consumo intracomunitarios: problemas de Derecho aplicable, Madrid / Barcelona: Marcial Pons, 2003.

Arsic, J. International Commercial Arbitration on the Internet – Has the Future Come Too Early? JIA, 1997, Vol. 14, p. 209 et seq.

Audit, B. Droit international privé, 4th ed., Paris: Économica, 2006.

Bachand, F. L'intervention du juge canadien avant et durant un arbitrage commercial international. Cowansville, Qué.: Yvon Blais, 2005.

Barnert, T. Die formelle Vertragsethik des BGB im Spannungsverhältnis zum Sonderprivatrecht und zur Judikativen Kompensation der Vertragsdisparität, Baden-Baden: Nomos, 2001.

Baudouin, J.-L. Les obligations, 3rd ed., Cowansville, Qué.: Yvon Blais, 1989.

Baumert, A. Europäischer ordre public und Sonderanknüpfung zur Durchsetzung von EG-Recht unter besonderer Berücksichtigung der sogenannten unmittelbaren horizontalen Wirkung von EG-Richtlinienbestimmungen, Frankfurt a. M.: Peter Lang, 1994.

Béguin, J. L'arbitrage commercial international. Montréal: Quebec Research Centre of Private & Comparative Law, 1987.

Bělohlávek, A. et Hótová, R. Znalci v mezinárodním prostředí (v soudním řízení civilním a trestním, v rozhodčím řízení a v investičních sporech). [Title in translation: Experts in the International Environment (in Civil and Criminal Court Proceedings, in Arbitration and in Investment Disputes)]. Prague: C. H. Beck, 2011.

Bělohlávek, A. et Rozehnalová, N. CYArb – Czech (& Central European) Yearbook of Arbitration: The Relationship between Constitutional Values, Human Rights and Arbitration, Huntington (New York): JurisNet, 2011, Vol. 1.

Bělohlávek, A. et Rozehnalová, N. CYArb – Czech (& Central European) Yearbook of Arbitration: The Relationship between Constitutional Values, Human Rights and Arbitration, Huntington (New York): JurisNet, 2012, Vol. 2.

Bělohlávek, A. et Rozehnalová, N. CYIL – Czech Yearbook of International Law, Huntington (New York): JurisPublishing Inc., 2010, Vol. 1.

Bělohlávek, A. et Rozehnalová, N. CYIL – Czech Yearbook of International Law, Huntington (New York): JurisPublishing Inc., 2011, Vol. 2.

Bělohlávek, A. et Rozehnalová, N. CYIL – Czech Yearbook of International Law, Huntington (New York): JurisPublishing Inc., 2011, Vol. 3.

Bělohlávek, A. Rozhodčí řízení, ordre public a trestní právo. [Title in translation: Arbitration, Ordre Public and Criminal Law]. Part I and II, Prague: C. H. Beck, 2008.

Bělohlávek, A. Zákon o rozhodčím řízení a o výkonu rozhodčích nálezů. Komentář [Title in translation: Act on Arbitration and the Enforcement of Arbitral Awards. Commentary], Prague: C. H. Beck, 2004.

Benno, J. Consumer Purchases through Telecommunications in Europe: Application of Private International Law to Cross-border Contractual Disputes, Oslo: Tanro, 1993.

Bianca, M. et Grundmann, S. EU Sales Directive: Commentary, Oxford: Intersentia, 2002.

Bin, M. Le garanzie nella vendita dei beni di consumo. In. *Galgano, F.* Trattato di diritto commerciale e di diritto pubblico dell'economia, diretto da Galgano, XXXI, Padova: CEDAM, 2003.

Bitterich, K. Die Neuregelung des Internationalen Verbrauchervertragsrechts in Art. 29a EGBGB, Frankfurt a. M.: Peter Lang, 2003.

Blaschek, B., Enthofer-Stoisser, R., Medwed, D., Perz, H., Pirker-Hörmann, B. et Reiffenstein, M. (eds.) Konsumentenpolitik im Spannungsfeld von

Liberalisierung und sozialer Verantwortung. In: Festschrift für Gottfried Mayer, Wien: Springer, 2004.

Blaurock, U. (ed.) Gerichtsverfahren zwischen Gerechtigkeit und Ökonomie: Referate des 11. Deutsch-französischen Juristentreffens am 10. und 11. Juni 2004 in Prais. Rechtsvergleichung und Rechtsvereinheitlichung, Part I, Tübingen: Mohr Siebeck, 2005.

Boele-Woelki, K. et Lazic, V. Where Do We Stand on the Rome I Regulation? In: *Boele-Woelki, K. et Grosheide, W.* (eds.) The Future of European Contract Law, Den Haag: KLI, 2007, pp. 19–41.

Boelke-Woelki, K. Internet, consument en ipr : een verkenning. In: *van Buren-Dee, J.-M.* (ed.) Consument zonder grenzen, Consument en recht, Deventer: Kluwer, 1996, pp. 301-313.

Boisséson de, M. Le droit français de l'arbitrage interne et international, Paris: Gide Loyrette Nouel, 1990.

Born, G., B. International Arbitration and Forum Selection Agreements: Drafting and Enforcing, 2nd ed., Den Haag: KLI, 2006.

Bouchard, M. L'autorisation d'exercer le recours collectif. C. de D., 1980, Vol. 21, p. 855 et seq.

Bröcker, M. Verbraucherschutz im europäischen Kollisionsrecht, Frankfurt a. M.: Lang, 1998.

Bruin, R. Consumer Trust in Electronic Commerce: Time for Best Practice, Den Haag / London / Boston: KLI, 2002.

Brulard, Y. et Demolin, P. Les transactions commerciales avec les consommateurs sur Internet. In: *Montero, E.* (ed.) Internet face au droit. Cahier du centre de recherche Informatique et Droit, Brussels: Story-Scientia, 1997, pp. 2-64.

Cabeçadas, I. M. Le centre d'arbitrage des litiges de la consommation de Lisbonne. Revue Européenne de Droit de la Consommation, 1999, p. 391 et seq.

Calais-Auloy, J. et Steinmetz, F. Droit de la consommation, 5th ed., Paris: Dalloz, 2000.

Calliess, G.-P. Grenzüberschreitende Verbrauchervertäge, Tübingen: Mohr Siebeck, 2006.

Capilli, G. In: *De Nova, G.* (ed.) L'acquisto di beni di consumo, collana a cura di De Nova, G., Milano: IPSOA, 2002, sub art. 1519sexies, p. 54 et seq.

Cartwright, P. et al. Consumer Protection in Financial Services, Den Haag / London / Boston: KLI, 1999.

Collins, L. (ed.) Dicey, Morris and Collins on the Conflict of Laws, Part 1, 14th ed. London: Sweet & Maxwell, 2006.

Coteanu, C. Cyber Consumer Law and Unfair Trading Practices, Hampshire / Burlington: Ashgate Publishing, 2006.

Cross, R., G. Revenue Management: Hard-core Tactics for Market Domination, New York: Broadway Books, 1997.

Dalla Massara, T. In: *Garofalo, L.* (ed.), *Mannino, P., L., Moscati, E. et Vecchi, P., M.* Commentario alla disciplina della vendita di beni di consumo Garofalo, Padova: CEDAM, 2003, sub art. 1519nonies, p. 711 et seq.

De Cristofaro, G. Difetto di conformità al contratto e diritti del consumatore. L'ordinamento italiano e la direttiva 99/44/CE sulla vendita e le garanzie dei beni di consumo, Padova: CEDAM, 2000.

De Nova, G. In: *Alpa, G., De Nova, G., Capilli, G., Colantuoni, L., Leo, C., Maniaci, A. et Putti, P. M.* L'acquisto di beni di consumo, collana a cura di De Nova, Milano: IPSOA, 2002, sub art. 1519bis, p. 16 et seq.

Deixler-Hübner, A. Konsumentenschutz, Wien: LexisNexis, 1997.

Dickie, J. Producers and Consumers in EU E-Commerce Law, Oxford: Hart Publishing, 2005.

Dohrn, T. Die Generalklausel der Richtlinie über unlautere Geschäftspraktiken, Köln a. R.: Carl Heymanns Verlag / Wolters Kluwer Deutschland, 2008.

Drahozal, C. et Friel, R., A. A Comparative View of Consumer Arbitration. Arbitration, 2005, Vol. 2, p. 133 et seq.

Eccher, B., Nemeth, K. et Tangl, A. (eds.) Verbraucherschutz in Europa: Festgabe für em. o. Univ.-Prof. Dr. Heinrich Mayrhofer, Wien: Verlag Österreich, 2002.

Emanuelli, C. Droit international privé québécois. 2nd ed., Montréal: Wilson & Lafleur, 2006.

Fadda, R. Il risarcimento dei danni, in Le garanzie nella vendita di beni di consumo, in Trattato di diritto commerciale e di diritto pubblico dell'economia, diretto da Galgano, Padova: Cedam, 2003.

Feil, E. Konsumentenschutzgesetz, Wien: Linde, 2002.

Fiala, J., Hurdík, J. et Selucká, M. Současné aktuální otázky spotřebitelského práva. [Title in translation: Current Consumer Law Issues]. Brno: MU, 2008.

Fischer, G. Das Kollisionsrecht der Verbraucherverträge jenseits von Art. 5 EVÜ. In: *Hübner, U.* (ed.) Festschrift für Bernhard Großfeld zum 65. Geburtstag, Heidelberg: Recht und Wirtschaft, 1999, p. 277 et seq.

Fouchard, Ph. Clause abusives en matière d'arbitrage. Rev. arb., 1995, p. 149 et seq.

Frąckowiak, J. et Stefanicki, R. Ochrona konsumenta w prawie polskim na tle koncepcji EFFET UTILE. Wrocław: Uniwersytet Wrocławski, 2011.

Gaillard, E. et Savage, J. Fouchard, Gaillard, Goldman on International Commercial Arbitration. Den Haag: Kluwer Law International, 1999.

Ganssauge, N. Internationale Zuständigkeit und anwendbares Recht bei Verbraucherverträgen im Internet, Tübingen: Mohr Siebeck, 2004, p. 185 et seq.

Gołaczyński, J. (ed.) Kolizyjne aspekty zobowiązań elektronicznych, Warszawa: Oficyna a Wolters Kluwer business, 2007.

Gołaczyński, J. Kolizyjne aspekty umów zawieranych z udziałem konsumentów. In: *Gniewek, E.* (ed.) Zawieranie i wykonywanie umów. Wybrane zagadnienia, Acta Universitatis Wratislaviensis, Series – Prawo, Wrocław: Wyd. Uniwersytetu Wrocławskiego, 2004.

Gołaczyński, J. Umowy elektroniczne w prawie prywatnym międzynarodowym, Warszawa / Kraków: Oficyna Wolters Kluwer Business, 2007.

Greatorex, P. et Falkowski, D. Anti-Social Behaviour Law, Bristol: Jordan Publishing, 2006.

Guillemard, S. Le droit international privé face au contrat de vente cyberspatial. Cowansville, Qué.: Yvon Blais, 2006.

Haydock, R., S. et Henderson, J., D. Arbitration and Judicial Civil Justice: An American Historical Review and a Proposal for a Private Arbitral and Public/Judicial Partnership. Pepperdine Dispute Resolution Law Journal, 2002, Vol. 2, p. 141 et seq.

Heiderhoff, B. et Zmij, G. (eds.) Law of E-Commerce in Poland and Germany, München: Sellier European Law Publishers, 2005.

Hein, J. et von Hinden, M. (eds.) Die richtige Ordnung: Festschrift für Jan Kropholler zum 70. Geburtstag, Tübingen: Mohr Siebeck, 2008.

Hill, J. Cross-Border Consumer Contracts, Oxford: OUP, 2008.

Hill, J. The Exercise of Jurisdiction in Private International Law. In: *Capps, P., Evans, M. et Konstadinidis, S.* (eds.) Asserting Jurisdiction: International and European Legal Perspectives. Oxford: Hart Publishing, 2003.

Horová, O. Ochrana spotřebitele [Title in translation: Consumer Protection], Prague: Vysoká škola ekonomická [University of Economics], 2002.

Howells, G. et Wilhelmsson, T. EC Consumer Law, Aldershot: Ashgate, 1997.

Hulva, T. Ochrana spotřebitele. [Title in translation: Consumer Protection]. Prague: Aspi, 2004.

Hurdík, J. Osoba a její soukromoprávní postavení v měnícím se světe [Title in translation: Persons and Their Private-Law Status in a Changing World], Brno: Masarykova univerzita [Masaryk University], 2004.

IA. Das Recht der Europäischen Union: Kommentar, Sekundärrecht. A, Verbraucher- und Datenschutzrecht, Vol. 3, München: C. H. Beck, 2003.

IA. Kupní smlouva mezi podnikateli a její dopad na spotřebitele [Title in translation: Purchase Contract Between Professionals and Its Implications for the Consumer], Prague: Sdružení obrany spotřebitelů České Republiky [Consumer Protection Association of the Czech Republic], 2009.

IA. Ochrana spotřebitele při prodeji v obchodě v ČSSR a ve Finsku [Title in translation: Consumer Protection in Retail Sales in the Czechoslovak Socialist Republic and in Finland], Prague: Univerzita Karlova [Charles University], 1990.

IA. Oprava a úprava věci (smlouva o dílo) [Title in translation: Repairs and Adjustments of Objects (Contract for Work)], Prague: Sdružení obrany spotřebitelů České Republiky [Consumer Protection Association of the Czech Republic], 2009.

IA. The Advertising Association (eds.) Marketing Pocket Book 1993, Henley-on-Thames: NTC Publications, 1992.

IA. Zákon o ochraně spotřebitele s komentářem [Title in translation: Consumer Protection Act Annotated], Prague: Sdružení obrany spotřebitelů České Republiky [Consumer Protection Association of the Czech Republic], 2008.

Imhof-Sheier, A.-C. Protection du consommateur et contrats internationaux, Etudes suisses de droit international/Schweizer Studien zum internationalen Recht, Genève: Libraire de l'Université Georg & Cie, 1981.

Isherwood, B. C. et Douglas, M. The World of Foods: Towards an Anthropology of Consumption, New York: Routledge, 1996.

Jehlička, O., Švestka, J., Škárová, M. et al. Občanský zákoník. Komentář [Title in translation: Civil Code. Commentary], 6th ed., Prague: C. H. Beck, 2001, p. 315 et seq.

Jobin, P.-G. (ed.) Baudouin et Jobin: Les obligations, 6th ed. Cowansville, Qué.: Yvon Blais, 2005.

Jordans, R. Consumer Protection in Arbitration in Several National Legislations: A Comparative Study, Wellington: Victoria University Wellington / Victoria University Press, 2002.

Jordans, R. Schiedsgerichte bei Termingeschäften und Anlegerschutz, Marburg: Tectum-Verlag, 2007.

Joustra, C. Jurisdiction in consumer disputes under the Brussels Convention. In: *Boele- Woelki* (ed.), Comparability and Evaluation; Essays on Comparative Law, Private International Law and International Commercial Arbitration, 1994.

Karimi, A. Les clauses abusives et l'abus de droit. Paris: LGDJ, 2001.

Kaufmann-Kohler, G. et Schultz, T. Online Dispute Resolution: Challenges for Contemporary Justice. KLI, 2004.

Kerans, R. P. Standards of Review Employed by Appellate Courts. Edmonton: Juriliber, 1994.

Klabusayová, N. Principy a trendy ochrany spotřebitele [Title in translation: Principles and Trends in Consumer Protection], Ostrava: VŠB, Technická univerzita [University of Mining, Technical University], 2005.

Klauer, S. Das europäische Kollisionsrecht der Verbraucherverträge zwischen Römer EVÜ und EG- Richtlinien, Studien zum ausländischen und internationalen Privatrecht – Vol. 99, Tübingen: Mohr Siebeck / Max Planck Institut für ausländisches und internationales Privatrecht, 2002.

Knoepfler, F. Arbitrage On-Line. In: *Bieber, R.* Mélanges en l'honneur de Bernard Dutoit, Series: Comparativa 73, Genève: Droz, 2002, pp. 154-162.

Kocher, E. Funktionen der Rechtsprechung. Konfliktlösung im deutschen und englischen Verbraucherprozessrecht, Beiträge zum ausländischen und internationalen Privatrecht 86, Tübingen: Mohr Siebeck, 2007.

Kosesnik-Wehrle, H., Lehofer, H., P. et Mayer, G. Konsumentenschutzgesetz (KSchG) : mit den geänderten Bestimmungen des ABGB und den EU-Richtlinien : Kurzkommentar, Wien: Manz, 1997.

Kroeger, H. Der Schutz der "marktwchwächeren" Partei im internationalen Vertragsrecht, Frankfurt a. M.: Mentzner, 1984.

Krohn, L. Consumer Protection and the Law: A Dictionary, Calif: ABC-CLIO, 1995.

Kučera, Z. et Tichý, L. Zákon o mezinárodním právu soukromém a procesním. Komentář. [Title in translation: Act on Private International Law and Procedure. Commentary]. Prague: Panorama, Prague, 1989.

Kučera, Z. Mezinárodní právo soukromé [Title in translation: Private International Law], 7th ed., Prague/Plzeň: Doplněk, 2009, pp. 337–341.

Kučerová, A., Bartík, V., Peca, J., Neuwirth, K. et Nejedlý, J. Zákon o ochraně osobních údajů [Title in translation: Personal Data Protection Act], Prague: C. H. Beck, 2003.

Leible, S. Kollisionsrechtlicher Verbraucherschutz im EVÜ und in den EG-Richtlinien. In: *Schulte-Nölke, H. et Schulze, R.* (eds.) Europäische

Rechtsangleichung und nationales Privatrecht, Baden-Baden: Nomos, 1999, p. 353 et seq.

Łętowska, E. Europejskie prawo umów konsumenckich, Warszawa: C. H. Beck, 2004.

Libánský, V. et al. Spotřebitelská legislativa EU a její implementace do práva členského a kandidátského státu [Title in translation: EU Consumer Legislation and Its Implementation in the Law of the Member and Candidate State], Prague: CEFRES, 2001.

Lluelles, D. et Benoît, M. Droit des obligations. Montréal: Thémis, 2006.

Lonbay, J. (ed) Enhancing the Position of the European Consumer, London: British Institute of International and Comparative Law, 1997.

López Sánchez, M-A. et Orero Núñez, M. Le système espagnol d'arbitrage des litiges de consommation. Revue Européenne de Droit de la Consommation, 1996, p. 120 et seq.

Loquin, É. Compétence arbitrale, Juris-classeur Procédure civile, fasc. 1034. France: Éditions Techniques, 1975.

Loussouarn, Y., Bourel, P. et de Vareilles-Sommières, P. Droit international privé, 8th ed., Paris: Dalloz, 2004.

Lowe, R. et Woodroffe, G. Consumer Law and Practice, 6th ed., London: Sweet & Maxwell, 2004.

Lüderitz, A. Anknüpfung im Parteiinteresse. In: Festschrift für Gerhard Kegel, Frankfurt a. M.: Metzner, 1987, p. 31 et seq.

Lühring, A. Missbrauchliche Klauseln in Verbraucherverträgen, Hamburg: Verlag Dr. Kovac, 2000.

Lurger, B. et Augenhofer, S. Österreichisces und Europäisches Konsumentenschutzrecht. 2nd ed., Wien / New York: Springer, 2008.

Lurger, B. Vertragliche Solidarität, Entwicklungschancen für das allgemeine Vertragsrecht in Österreich und in der Europäischen Union, Baden Baden: Nomos, 1998.

Lurger, B. Zur Umsetzung der Kollisionsnormen von Verbraucherschutzrichtlinien. Die internationale Dimension des Rechts. In: *Terlitza, I., Schwarzenegger, P. et Boric, T.* Festschrift für Willibald Posch zum 50 Geburtstag, Wien: Österreichische Staatsdruckerei, 1996, p. 179 et seq.

Mackay, H. (ed.) Consumption and Everyday Life (Culture, Media and Identities series), Thousand Oaks: Sage Publications, 1997.

Makarov, A. N. Sources. In: Lipstein, K. (ed.) International Encyclopedia of Comparative Law, Vol. III, Private International Law. New York: Oceana, 1972.

Marquis, L. Le droit français et le droit québécois de l'arbitrage conventionnel. In: *Glenn, H., P.* (ed.) Droit québécois et droit français: communauté, autonomie, concordance. Cowansville, Qué.: Yvon Blais, 1993, p. 447 et seq.

Martin, J. et Turnaer, Ch. Consumer Law, London: Hodder Arnold, 2005.

Martinek, M. "Systematische Überregulierung und kontra-intentionale Effekte im Europäischen Verbraucherschutzrecht," in: *Grundmann S.* (ed.) Systembildung und Systemlücken in Kerngebieten des Europäischen Privatrechts, Tübingen: Mohr Siebeck, 1999, p. 511 et seq.

Meškić, Z. Europäisches Verbraucherrecht: Gemeinschaftsrechtliche Vorgaben und europäische Perspektiven. *Reichelt, G.* (ed.) Schriftenreihe des Ludwig Boltzmann Institutes für Europarecht, Vol. 18, Wien: Manz, 2008.

Micklitz, H. W. Directive 93/13 In Action: A Report on a Research Project on Unfair Terms in Consumer Sales Contracts. In: *Willet, Ch.* (ed) Aspects of Fairness in Contract, London: Blackstone Press, 1996, p. 75 et seq.

Micklitz, H. W. German Unfair Contract Terms Act and the EC Directive 93/13. In: *Lonbay, J.* (ed) Enhancing the Position of the European Consumer, London: British Institute of International and Comparative Law, 1997, p. 173 et seq.

Michalski, L. Verbaucherschutzrecht, Köln a.R.: Carl Heymanns Verlag, 2002.

Mikroulea, A. Verbandsklage auf Schadensersatz im griechischen Verbraucherschutzgesetz. In: *Hopt, K. J. et Tzouganatos, D.* (eds.) Europäisierung des Handels- und Wirtschaftsrechts. Gemeinsame oder unterschiedliche Probleme für das deutsche und griechische Recht? Beiträge zum ausländischen und internationalen Privatrecht 82, Tübingen: Mohr Siebeck, 2006.

Mortelmans, K. et Watson, S. The Notion of Consumer in Community Law: A Lottery? In: *Lonbay, J.* (ed) Enhancing the Legal Position of the European Consumer, London: British Institute of International and Comparative Law, 1996, p. 36 et seq.

Mothejzíková, J., Steiner, V. et al. Zákon o rozhodčím řízení a o výkonu rozhodčích nálezů s přílohami. [Title in translation: Act on Arbitration and Enforcement of Arbitral Awards with Annexes]. Prague: C. H. Beck, 1996.

Nebbia, P. et Askham, T. EU Consumer Law, Richmond: Richmond Law & Tax, 2004.

Nebbia, P. Unfair Contract Terms in European Law. A Study in Comparative and EC Law, Oxford: Hart Publishing, 2007.

Niddam, L. A. Unilateral Arbitration Clauses in Commercial Arbitration. Arbitration Dispute Resolution Law Journal, 1996, Vol. 5, p. 147 et seq.

North, P. et Fawcett, J., J. Cheshire and North's Private International Law. 13th ed., London: Butterworths, 1999.

Odams de Zylva, M. Effective Means of Resolving Distance Selling Disputes. European Workshop on Business Process Models and Technical Requirements for Online Dispute Resolution, 2001, p. 10.

Oppenheim, S. C., Weston, G. E., Maggs, P. B. et Schester, R. E. 1986 Supplement to Unfair Trade Practices and Consumer Protection – Cases and Comments, St. Paul: West Publishing Co., 1986.

Osajda, K. et Łętowska, E. Nieuczciwe klauzule w prawie umów konsumenckich, 2nd ed., Warszawa: C. H. Beck, 2005.

Oughton, D. et Lowry, J. Textbook on Consumer Law, London: Blackstone Press, 1997.

Parisien, S. La protection accordée aux consommateurs et le commerce électronique. In: Poulin, P. et al. (eds.) Guide juridique du commerçant électronique. Montréal: Thémis, 2003, p. 175 et seq.

Pauknerová, M. Evropské mezinárodní právo soukromé [Title in translation: European Private International Law], Prague: C. H. Beck, 2009, pp. 276-277.

Phuong, C. The International Protection of Internally Displaced Persons, Cambridge / New York: Cambridge University Press, 2005.

Pizzio, J. P. Code de la consommation, Paris: Montchrestien, 1995.

Pokorná, J. Subjekty obchodního práva [Title in translation: Commercial Law Entities], Brno: Masarykova univerzita [Masaryk University], 1997.

Pokorný, M. Zákon o mezinárodním právu soukromém a procesním [Title in translation: Act on Private International Law and Procedure], Prague: C. H. Beck, 1998.

Pokorný, M. Zákon o mezinárodním právu soukromém a procesním. Komentář [Title in translation: Act on Private International Law and Procedure. Commentary], 2nd ed., Prague: C. H. Beck, 2004.

Poullet, Y. Transactions via Internet et protection des consommateurs. Verkoop op afstand en telematica, Anvers: Kluwer Rechtswetenschappen, 1997, pp. 127-164.

Quebec. Civil Code Revision Office. Report on the Québec Civil Code, Vol. I, Draft Civil Code. Québec: Éditeur officiel, 1978.

Quebec. Civil Code Revision Office. Report on the Québec Civil Code, Vol. II, Commentaries. Québec: Éditeur officiel, 1978.

Quebec. Ministère de la Justice. Comité de révision de la procédure civile. Document de consultation. La révision de la procédure civile. Sainte-Foy, Qué.: Le Comité, 2000.

Quebec. Ministère de la Justice. Commentaires du ministre de la Justice — Le Code civil du Québec: Un mouvement de société, t. I et II. Québec: Publications du Québec, 1993.

Quebec. Ministère de la Justice. Projet de loi 125: Code civil du Québec, Commentaires détaillés sur les dispositions du projet, Livre X: Du droit international privé et disposition finale (Art. 3053 à 3144). Québec: Le Ministère, 1991.

Reich, N. A European Concept of Consumer Rights. In: *Ziegel, J., S.* (ed.) New Developments in International Consumer and Commercial Law, Oxford: Hart Publ., 1998, p. 431 et seq.

Reich, N. Zur Wirksamkeit von Schiedsklauseln bei grenzüberschreitenden Börsentermingeschäften, Entscheidung des Court of Appeal vom 12. Juli 1996 un des Oberlandesgerichts Düsseldorf vom 8. März, 1996. Zeitschrift für europäisches Privatrecht, 1998, p. 981 et seq.

Reinhart, G. Zur Auslegung des Begriffs "Verbraucher" im Kollisionsrecht. Lebendiges Recht: von den Sumerern bis zur Gegenwart. In: *Trinkner, R., von Westphalen, F., G. et Sandrock, O.* Festschrift für Reinhold Trinkner zum 65. Geburtstag, Heidelberg: Recht und Wirtschaft, 1995, p. 657 et seq.

republiky, 2005.

Rieg, A. La lutte contre les clauses abusives des contrats (Esquisse comparative des solutions allemande et française). In: *Rodière, R.* Etudes offertes à René Rodière, Paris: Dalloz, 1981, pp. 221-245.

Rozehnalová, N. et Týč, V. Evropský justiční prostor [Title in translation: European Justice Area], Brno: Masarykova univerzita [Masaryk University], 2006.

Rozehnalová, N., Týč, V. et Novotná, M. Evropské mezinárodní právo soukromé [Title in translation: European Private International Law], Spisy Právnické fakulty MU Brno, řada teoretická [Collection of Papers, Faculty of Law, Masaryk University in Brno, Academic Series], Vol. 206, Brno, 2000.

Rudisch, B. Das "Heininger"-Urteil des EuGH vom 13. 12. 2001, Rs C-481/99: Meilenstein oder Stolperstein für den Verbraucherschutz bei Realkrediten? In: *Eccher, B., Nemeth, K. et Tangl, A.* (eds.) Verbraucherschutz in Europa: Festgabe für em. o. Univ.-Prof. Dr. Heinrich Mayrhofer, Wien: Verlag Österreich, 2002, pp. 189-205.

Rudisch, B. Grenzüberschreitender Verbraucherschutz im Gefüge von internationalem Privatrecht und internationalem Verfahrensrecht. In: *Schnyder, K., A., Heiss, H. et Rudisch, B.* (eds.) Internationales Verbraucherschutzrecht, Tübingen: Mohr Siebeck, 1995, pp. 191-228.

Rutherford, M. Documents-Only Arbitration in Consumer Disputes. In: *Bernstein, R. et al.* Handbook of Arbitration Practice, London: Sweet & Maxwell, 1998.

Růžička, K. Rozhodčí řízení před rozhodčím soudem při Hospodářské komoře České republiky a Agrární komoře České republiky. [Title in translation: Arbitration in the Arbitration Court Attached to the Economic Chamber of the Czech Republic and Agricultural Chamber of the Czech Republic]. Dobrá Voda: Aleš Čeněk, 2003.

Selucká, M. Ochrana spotřebitele v soukromém právu. [Title in translation: Consumer Protection in Private Law]. Prague: C. H. Beck, 2009.

Senff, T. Wer ist Verbraucher im internationalen Zivilprozeß? Frankfurt a. M.: P. Lang Verlag, 2001.

Schäfer, H.-B. (eds.) Effiziente Verhaltenssteuerung und Kooperation im Zivilrecht, Tübingen: Mohr Siebeck, 1997, pp. 77-107.

Schelle, K. et Schelleová, I. Rozhodčí řízení: historie, současnost a perspektivy. [Title in translation: Arbitration: Past, Present and Perspectives]. Prague: Eurolex Bohemia, 2002.

Schiavetta, S. Does the Internet Occasion New Directions in Consumer Arbitration in the EU? Journal of Information, Law and Technology, University of Warwick, 2004, No. 3, p. 3.

Schnyder, K., A., Heiss, H. et Rudisch, B. (eds.) Internationales Verbraucherschutzrecht, Tübingen: Mohr Siebeck, 1995.

Schuhmacher, W. Verbraucherschutz in Österreich und in der EG, Wien: Orac, 1992.

Schütze, R. A. et al. Institutionelle Schiedsgerichtsbarkeit, Köln/R.: Carl Heymanns, 2006

Schwartz, D. S., Enforcing Small Print to Protect Big Business: Employee and Consumer Rights Claims in an Age of Compelled Arbitration. Wisc. L. Rev., 1997, p. 33 et seq.

Schwarz, E. H. Schutzkollisionen im internationalen Verbraucherschutz: dargestellt an der Neuregelung des Rechts der Allgemeinen Geschäftsbedingungen in Portugal, Heidelberg: Winter, 1991.

Silberstein, S. Consumer Law, 4th ed., London: Sweet & Maxwell, 2004.

Skory, M. Klauzule abuzywne w polskim prawie ochrony konsumenta, Krakow: Kantor Wydawniczy Zakamycze, 2005.

Srbinova, D. Principt za zaščita na ikonomičeski po-slabata strana kato ograničitel na avtonomija na voljata pri potrebitelskite dogovori. In: Avtonomija na voljata v meždunarodnoto častno pravo, [Title in translation: The Principle of Protecting the Weaker Economic Party as a Factor Limiting the Autonomy of Will in Consumer Contracts. In: Autonomy of Will in Private International Law], Sofia: Sibi, 2008 [Title in original: *Сърбинова, Д.* Принципът за защита на икономически по-слабата страна като ограничител на автономия на волята при потребителските договори. В: Автономия на волята в международното частно право, София: Сиби, 2008].

Stuyek, J., Terryn, E., Colaert, V., Van Dyck, T., Peretz, N., Hoekx, N. et Tereszkiewicz, P. (eds.) An analysis and evaluation of alternative means of consumer redress other than redress through ordinary judicial proceedings – Final Report: A Study for the European Commission, Health and Consumer Protection Directorate-General Directorate B – Consumer Affairs, Leuven: The Study Centre for Consumer Law / Centre for European Economic Law Katholieke Universiteit Leuven, 2007.

Sullivan, R. Sullivan and Driedger on the Construction of Statutes. 4th ed., Markham, Ont.: Butterworths, 2002.

Švestka, J., Jehlička, O. et Kratochvíl, M. Právní ochrana spotřebitele v ČR [Title in translation: Consumer Protection under Czech Law], Prague: C. H. Beck, 1999.

Talpis, J. A. et Castel, J. G. Interpreting the rules of private international law. In: Reform of the Civil Code, Vol. 5B: Private International Law. Translation – Altschul, S. Material drafted for: Barreau du Québec and the Chambre des notaires du Québec. Montréal: Barreau du Québec, 1993.

Tauss, J. (ed.) Deutschlands Weg in die Informationsgesellschaft: Herausforderungen und Perspektiven für Wirtschaft, Wissenschaft, Recht und Politik, Baden-Baden: Nomos, 1996.

Tetley, W. International Conflict of Laws: Common, Civil and Maritime. Montréal: Yvon Blais, 1994.

Thévenoz, L. et Reich, N. (eds.) Consumer Law: Liber Amicorum Bernd Stauder, Genèva: Schulthess, 2006.

Thuilleaux, S. L'arbitrage commercial au Québec: Droit interne — Droit international privé. Cowansville, Qué.: Yvon Blais, 1991.

Tichý, L. Evropské právo [Title in translation: European Law], Prague: Linde, 1999.

Toggenburg, G. N. (ed.) Minority Protection and the Enlarged European Union: The Way Forward, Budapest: Open Society Institute, 2004.

Ulmer, P., Brandner, H. E., Hensen, H.-D. et Schmidt, H. AGB-Gesetz: Kommentar zum Gesetz zur Regelung des Rechts der Allgemeinen Geschäftsbedingungen, 6th ed., Köln a. R.: O. Schmidt, 1990.

Van Boom, W. et Loos, M. (eds.) Collective Enforcement of Consumer Law: Securing Compliance in Europe through Private Group Action and Public Authority Intervention, Groningen: Europa Law Publishing, 2007.

Vigoritti, V. Note su arbitrato e tutela di interessi minori nell'esperienza italiana e comparativa. Rivista dell' arbitrato, 1998, Vol. 8, p. 445 et seq.

Vischer, F. Connecting Factors. In: Lipstein, K. (ed.) International Encyclopedia of Comparative Law, Vol. III: Private International Law. New York: Oceana, 1999.

Vranken, J. B. M. Over partijautonomie, contractsvrijheid en de grondslag van gebondenheid in het verbintenissenrecht. In: *Barendrecht, J., M., Chao-Duivis, M., A., B. et Vermeulen, H., A., W.* (eds.) Beginselen van contractenrecht: Opstellen aangeboden aan B. W. M. Nieskens-Isphording, Deventer: W.E.J. Tjeenk Willink, 2000, pp. 145-155.

Walker, J. Castel & Walker: Canadian Conflict of Laws. Vol. 1. Markham, Ont.: LexisNexis / Butterworths, 2005 (card index, here after updating in 2007, edition 7).

Wegrzynowski, L. Niedozwolone postanowienia umowne jako srodek ochrony slabszej strony umowy obligacyjnej, Warszawa: C. H. Beck, 2006.

Weston, G. E., Maggs, P. B. et Schechter, R., E. Unfair Trade Practices and Consumer Protection: Cases and Comments, 5th ed., St. Paul: West Publishing, 1992.

Wilhelmsson, T. et al. Consumer Law in the Information Society, Den Haag / London / Boston: KLI, 2001.

Willet, Ch. (ed) Aspects of Fairness in Contract, London: Blackstone Press, 1996.

Wohland, P. E-Commerce-Geschäftsmodelle im deutschen Tourismusmarkt, Series: Schriften zum europäischen Management, Berlin: Gabler / Roland Berger / Springer, 2008.

Wyler, É. et Papaux, P. Extranéité de valeurs et de systèmes en droit international privé et en droit international public. In: *Wyler, É. et Papaux, A.* (eds.) L'extranéité ou le dépassement de l'ordre juridique étatique. Paris: Éditions A. Pédone, 1999, p. 239 et seq.

Zheng, Sophia Tang Electronic Consumer Contracts in the Conflict of Laws. Oxford / Portland (Oregon): Hard Publishing, 2009.

I.B. Literature closely related to the topic

Agénor, P. R. The Economics of Adjustment and Growth, 2nd ed., Cambridge: Harvard University Press, 2004.

Anurov, V. N. Tretejskoje soglashenije. Moscow: Prospekt, 2009.

Arp, B. International Norms and Standards for the Protection of National Minorities, Leiden: Brill Academic Publishers, 2008.

Atiyah, P. S. An Introduction to the Law of Contract, 5th ed., Oxford: Clarendon Press, 1995.

Bach, P. Vorvertragliche Informationspflichten des Versicherers nach der VAG-Novelle. In: *Wandt, M.* (ed.) Festschrift für Egon Lorenz, Recht und Ökonomie der Versicherung, Karlsruhe: Verlag Versicherungswirtschaft, 1994, p. 45 et seq.

Bauerreis, J. Das französische Rechtsinstitut der action directe und seine Bedeutung in internationalen Vertragsketten, Berlin: Duncker & Humblot, 2001.

Beatson, J. et Friedmann, D. (eds.) Good Faith and Fault in Contract Law, Oxford: Oxford University Press, 1995, p. 99 et seq.

Becker, Ch. Theorie und Praxis der Sonderanknüpfung im internationalen Privatrecht, Aachen: Shaker, 1995.

Bělohlávek, A. Mezinárodní právo soukromé evropských zemí. [Title in translation: Private International Law of European Countries]. Prague: C. H. Beck, 2010.

Bělohlávek, A. Římská úmluva / Nařízení Řím I. Komentář. [Title in translation: Rome Convention / Rome I Regulation. Commentary]. Prague: C. H. Beck, Part I and II, Prague: C. H. Beck, 2009 (especially the commentary on Articles 6, 8, and 9 of the Rome I Regulation).

Berger, K. Internationale Wirtschaftsschiedsgerichtsbarkeit, Verfahrens-und materiellrechtliche Grundprobleme im Spiegel moderner Schiedsgesetze und Schiedspraxis, Berlin/New York: De Gruyter, 1992.

Binder, P. International Commercial Arbitration and Conciliation in UNCITRAL Model Law Jurisdictions, 2nd ed., London: Sweet & Maxwell, 2005.

Bourdieu, P. Distinction, New York: Routledge, 1979.

Bourdieu, P. Distinction: A Social Critique of the Judgement of Taste, London: Lincoln, 1984.

Brauer, W. et Mück, T.(eds.) Informatik 2001 – Wirtschaft und Wissenschaft in der Network Economy – Visionen und Wirklichkeit, Wien: Springer, 2001, pp. 1002–1009.

Brierley, J. E. C. et Macdonald, R.,A. Quebec Civil Law: An Introduction to Quebec Private Law, Toronto: Edmond Montgomery, 1993.

Buchner, B. Kläger- und Beklagtenschutz im Recht der internationalen Zuständigkeit, Tübingen: Mohr Siebeck Verlag, 1998.

Casey, J. B. et Mills, J. Arbitration Law of Canada: Practice and Procedure. Huntington, N.Y.: JurisPublishing, 2005.

Castel, J. -G. Canadian Conflict of Laws, 4th ed. Toronto: Butterworths, 1997.

Collier, J. G. Conflict of Laws, 3rd ed., Cambridge, U.K.: CUP, 2001.

Cornu, G. (ed.) Vocabulaire juridique, 8th ed., Paris: Presses universitaires de France, 2000.

Côté, P.-A. et Jutras, D. Le droit transitoire civil: Sources annotées. Cowansville, Qué.: Yvon Blais, 1994.

Côté, P.-A. The Interpretation of Legislation in Canada. 3rd ed., Scarborough, Ont.: Carswell, 2000.

Delimatsis, P. International Trade in Services and Domestic Regulations: Necessity, Transparency, and Regulatory Diversity, Oxford: Oxford University Press, Inc., 2007.

Dobiáš, P. Mezinárodní pojistné právo se zřetelem k řešení pojistných sporů v rozhodčím řízení (Vybrané kapitoly). [Title in translation: International Insurance Law with Respect to the Resolution of Insurance Disputes in Arbitration (Selected Chapters)]. Prague: Leges, 2011.

Drahozal, Chr. R. Commercial Norms, Commercial Codes, and International Commercial Arbitration. Vanderbilt Journal of Transnational Law, 2000, Vol. 33, p. 79 et seq.

Drasch, W. Das Herkunftslandprinzip im IPR, Baden-Baden: Nomos, 1997.

Gautrais, V. Know your law: Guide respecting the management of technology-based documents. Québec: Fondation du Barreau du Québec, 2005.

Goldstein, G. et Groffier, E. Droit international privé, t. I, Théorie générale, et II, Règles spécifiques. Cowansville, Qué.: Yvon Blais, 2003.

Hajn, P. Soutěžní chování a právo proti nekalé soutěži [Title in translation: Competitive Conduct and Unfair Competition Law], Brno: Doplněk, 2000.

Hennis, M. Globalization and European Integration: The Changing Role of Farmers in the Common Agricultural Policy, Lanham / Boulder / New York / Toronto / Oxford: Rowman and Littlefield Publishers, 2005.

Jacquet, J.-M. Sociabilité et droit du commerce international. In: *de Chazournes, L., B. Gowlland-Debbas, V. et al.* Liber Amicorum Georges Abi-Saab, Den Haag / Boston: Martinus Nijhoff, 2001, pp. 251-265.

Jarosson, Ch. La notion d'arbitrage. Paris: LGDJ, 1987.

Jeloschek, Ch. Examination and Notification Duties in Consumer Sales Law: How far should we go in protecting the consumer? München: Sellier European Law Publishers, 2006.

Joustra, C. Consumer Law. In: *Hartkamp et al.* (eds) Towards a European Civil Code, 2nd ed., Nijmegen / The Hague / Boston: Ars Aequi Libri / Bo KLI, 1998, p. 133 et seq.

Kohte, W. et al. Das neue Schuldrecht, Kompaktkommentar, München: Luchterhand, 2003.

Kolodziej, A. Konsumenckie prawo odstapienia od umowy sprzedazy rzeczy, Warszawa: LexisNexis, 2006.

Kötz, H. Welche gesetzgeberischen Maßnahmen empfehlen sich zum Schutze des Endverbrauchers gegenüber Allgemeinen Geschäftsbedingungen und Formularverträgen? Gutachten zum 50. Deutschen Juristentag, München: Beck, 1974.

Krejci, H. (ed.) Handbuch zum Konsumentenschutzgesetz, Wien: Orac, 1981.

Luminoso, M. et Bin, M. Le garanzie nella vendita dei beni di consumo, Padova: CEDAM, 2003.

Mates, P. et Neuwirth, K. Právní úprava ochrany osobních údajů v ČR [Title in translation: Personal Data Protection Law in the Czech Republic], 2nd ed., Prague: IFEC, 2001.

Mates, P. Ochrana osobních údajů [Title in translation: Personal Data Protection], Prague: Karolinum Publishing, 2002.

Matoušová, M. et Hejlík, L. Osobní údaje a jejich ochrana [Title in translation: Personal Data and Protection Thereof], Prague: ASPI, 2003.

Matoušová, M. Ochrana osobních údajů v otázkách a odpovědích [Title in translation: Questions and Answers on Personal Data Protection], Prague: ASPI, 2004.

Meier, I. J., Schnyder, K. A., Einhorn, T. et Gisberger, D. (eds) Private Law in the International Arena. Liber Amicorum Kurt Siehr, Den Haag: TMC Asser Press, 2000, p. 155 et seq.

Micklitz, H., Stuyck, J., Rott, P. et Howells, G. La protection des consommateurs acheteurs à distance, Bruxelles: Bruylant, 1999.

Miller, C. J. et al. Consumer and Trading Law: Text, Cases and Materials, Oxford: Oxford University Press, 1998.

Miller, C. J. et Goldberg, R. S. Product Liability, 2nd ed., Oxford: Oxford University Press, 2004.

Miller, D. A Theory of Shopping. Ithaca / New York: Cornell University Press, 1998.

Nemeth, K. Kollisionsrechtlicher Verbraucherschutz in Europa: Art 5 EVÜ und die einschlägigen Verbraucherschutzrichtlinien, Wien: Manz, 2000.

Neumayer, K. Les Contrats d'adhésion dans les pays industrialisés. Lausanne: Droz / Université de Lausanne – Département de droit, Series: Comparativa, Vol. 66, 1999.

Nielsen, R. et Szyszczak, E. The Social Dimension of the European Union, Copenhagen: Copenhagen Business School Press, 1997.

O'Hara, E. A. et Ribstein, L., E. The Law Market, New York: Oxford University Press, 2009, pp. 133-160.

Padovec, V. Ochrana spotřebitelů v obchodě [Title in translation: Protection of Consumers in Commerce], Prague: Merkur, 1971.

Payne, C. Are International Institutions Doing Their Job? Int. Arb., 1996, Vol. 90, p. 244 et seq.

Pouliadis, A. K. Die Bedeutung des Verbraucherschutzrechts im Kontext der Entwicklung eines europäischen Vertragsrechts: Das Beispiel der Kaufrechtsrichtlinie. In: *Hopt, K., J. et Tzouganatos, D.* (eds.) Europäisierung des Handels- und Wirtschaftsrechts. Gemeinsame oder unterschiedliche Probleme für das deutsche und griechische Recht? Beiträge zum ausländischen und internationalen Privatrecht 82, Tübingen: Mohr Siebeck, 2006.

Poulin, D. Guide juridique du commerçant électronique. Montréal: Thémis, 2001.

Prechal, S. Directives in EC law, 2nd ed., Oxford: Oxford University Press, 2006.

Rammeloo, S. Das neue EG-Vertragskollisionsrecht – Die Artt 4, 5 und 6 des Übereinkommens über das auf vertragliche Schuldverhältnisse anzuwendende Recht vom 19. 6. 1980 – eine rechtsvergleichende Analyse objektiver Vertragsanknüpfungen, Köln a.R.: Heymanns, 1992.

Reich, N. The rights of consumers enshrined in the Treaty. In: *IA.* Report of the Proceedings of the Dublin Forum on Consumer Policy and the Amsterdam

Treaty, Dublin: Irish Dept. of Trade, Enterprise and Employment, 1998, p. 16 et seq.

Riepl, G. Europäischer Verbraucherschutz in der Informationsgesellschaft. Neue Juristische Monographien, Vol. 14, Wien: NWV, 2002.

Rozehnalová, N. Právo mezinárodního obchodu [Title in translation: Law of International Commerce], Brno: Masarykova univerzita [Masaryk University], 2004.

Rudisch, B. Produktvielfalt und Produktdifferenzierung auf einem verbraucherorientierten Kapitalmarkt. In: *Marxer, B., Reichert-Facilides, F. et Schnyder, A., K.* (eds.) Gegenwartsfragen des liechtensteinischen Privat- und Wirtschaftsrechts, Tübingen: Mohr Siebeck, 1998, pp. 99-132.

Rymarz, W. Międzynarodowe prawo drogi morskiej, Gdańsk: Wydawn. Morskie, 1985.

Sári, C. EU Legislation on Consumer Protection, with Special Regard to the Directive 1999/44/EC (Sale of Consumer Goods and Associated Guarantees), Zurich: Consulegis, 2005.

Saria, G. (ed.) Reise ins Ungewisse: Reiserecht in einem geänderten Umfeld, Wien: NWV, 2005.

Schaub, M. European Legal Aspects of E-commerce, Groningen: Europa Law Publishing, 2004.

Schulte-Nölke, H. EC Consumer Law Compendium – Comparative Analysis, Bielefeld: Universität Bielefeld, 2006.

Schulte-Nölke, H., Twigg-Flessner, Ch. et Ebers, M. EC Consumer Law Compendium: The Consumer Acquis and Its Transposition in the Member State, München: Sellier European Law Publishers, 2008.

Schwander, I. Lois d'application immédiate, Sonderanknüpfung, IPR-Sachnormen und andere Ausnahmen von der gewähnlichen Anknüpfung im internationalen Privatrecht, Zürich: Schulthess, 1975.

Slater, D. Consumer Culture and Modernity, Cambridge: Polity Press, 1997.

Smejkal, V. et al. Právo informačních a telekomunikačních systémů [Title in translation: Law of Information and Telecommunication Systems], 2nd ed., Prague: C. H. Beck, 2004.

Spickhoff, A. Die Produkthaftung im Europäischen Kollisions- und Zivilverfahrensrecht. In: *Baetge, D., Hein, J. et Hinden, M.* (eds.) Die richtige Ordnung: Festschrift für Jan Kropholler zum 70. Geburtstag, Tübingen: Mohr Siebeck, 2008, p. 671 et seq.

Spindler, G. et Borner, F. E-Commerce Law in Europe and the USA, Berlin / Heidelberg / New York: Springer, 2002.

Stefanicki, R. Ochrona konsumenta w swietle ustawy o szczególnych warunkach sprzedazy konsumenkiej, Warszawa: Wolters Kluwer Polska, 2006.

Valdhans, J. Právní úprava mimosmluvních závazků s mezinárodním prvkem. [Title in translation: Laws Regulating Non-Contractual Obligations with an International Dimension]. Prague: C. H. Beck, 2012.

Van Gerven, W. The European Union: A Policy of States and Peoples, Stanford: Stanford University Press, 2005.

van Meenen, I. Lauterkeitsrecht und Verbraucherschutz im IPR – eine Untersuchung des vertrags- und deliktkollisionsrechtlichen Schutzes gegen verbraucherfeindliche Rechtswahlvereinbarungen, Frankfurt a. M.: Peter Lang, 1995.

Vékás, L. Vertragsfreiheit versus Verbrauchervertragsrecht und Gleichbehandlungsgrundsatz. Aus der Sicht einer nationalen Privatrechtskodifikation. In: *Baetge, D., von Hein, J. et von Hinden, M.* (eds.) Die richtige Ordnung: Festschrift für Jan Kropholler zum 70. Geburtstag, Tübingen: Mohr Siebeck, 2008, pp. 517-530.

Voland, T. Verbraucherschutz und Welthandelsrecht. Müncher Universitätsschriften. Reihe der Juristischen Fakultät, Vol. 210. München: C. H. Beck, 2007.

Völker, S. Preisangabenrecht. Reihe: Gelbe Erläuterungsbücher, München: C.H.Beck, 2002.

von Staudinger, J., Kessal-Wulf, S., Köhler, H. et Martinek, M. Kommentar zum Bürgerlichen Gesetzbuch mit Einführungsgesetz und Nebengesetzen, Verbraucherkreditgesetz, Haustürwiderrufsgesetz, Paragraph 13a UWG, Teilzeit-Wohnrechtegesetz, Berlin: de Gruyter, 2001.

von Westphalen, F., Volker, E. et von Rottenburg, F. Verbraucherkreditgesetz, Haustürwiderrufsgesetz, Fernabsatzgesetz, 3rd ed., Köln a.R.: Otto Schmidt Verlag, 2002.

Werro, F. La péremption dans la loi sur la responsabilité du fait des produits: Une limitation des droits du lésé par rapport au droit commun de la responsabilité du fabricant. In: *Thévenoz, L. et Reich, N.* (eds.) Consumer Law: Liber Amicorum Bernd Stauder, Genèva: Schulthess, 2006.

Woelki, K. (ed) Comparability and Evaluation: Essays on Comparative Law, Private International Law and International Commercial Arbitration, Dordrecht / Boston / Norwell: M. Nijhoff Publishers / Distributors for the U.S. and Canada, Kluwer Academic Publishers, 1994, p. 233 et seq.

Wouters, J. (eds.) Europees Gemeenschapsrecht en Internationaal Privaatrecht, Series: Praadvizen, Mededelingen van de Nederlandse Vereiniging voor Internationaal Recht – Vol. 113, Deventer / Den Haag: Kluwer / Nederlandse Vereiniging voor Internationaal Recht, 1996. pp. 49-142.

Zweigert, K. Einige Auswirkungen des Gemeinsamen Marktes auf das Internationale Privatrecht der Mitgliedstaaten. In: *von Caemmerer, E., Schlochauer, H.-J. et Steindorff, E.* (eds.) Probleme des europäischen Rechts. In: Festschrift für Walter Hallstein zu seinem 65. Geburtstag, Frankfurt a. M.: Vittorio Klostermann, 1966, pp. 555-569.

Zweigert, K. et Kötz, H. An Introduction to Comparative Law, 3rd ed., Oxford: Clarendon Press, 1997.

II. Articles in Periodicals and Anthologies

II.A. Literature directly related to the topic

Adams, J. E. Basis of the Contract Clauses and the Consumer. The Journal of Business Law, 2000, p. 203 et seq.

Alderman, R. Pre-Dispute Mandatory Arbitration in Consumer Contracts: A Call for Reform. Houston Law Review, 2001, Vol. 38, pp. 1237-1268.

Alderman, R. M. Consumer Arbitration in the United States: A System in Need of Reform. Revista Latinoamericana de Mediación y Arbitraje, 2002, Vol. 3, p. 118 et seq.

Alexandridou, E. Implementation of the EC directive on unfair contract terms in Greece. ERPL, 1997, Vol. 2, p. 173 et seq.

Alexandridou, E. Neue Entwicklungen in der griechischen Verbraucherschutzgesetzgebung. VuR, 1995, p. 387 et seq.

Alexandridou, E. The Greek Consumer Protection Act of 1994. GRUR Int., 1996, p. 200 et seq.

Alpa, G. The implementation of the EC directive on unfair contract terms in Italy. ERPL, 1997, Vol. 2, p. 181 et seq.

Arenas, R. Tratamiento jurisprudencial del ámbito de aplicación de los foros de protección en materia de contratos de consumidores del Convenio de Bruselas de 1968. REDI, 1996, Vol. 1, p. 39 et seq.

Babjáková, G. Smlouvy uzavírané se spotřebitelem. [Title in translation: Consumer Contracts]. Právní fórum, 2011, Vol. 8, No. 7, pp. 334-339.

Bachand, F. Does Article 8 of the Model Law Call for Full or Prima Facie Review of the Arbitral Tribunal's Jurisdiction? Arb. Int., 2006, Vol. 22, p. 463 et seq..

Balate, E. La mis en oeuvre de la directive 93/13 ce concernant les clauses abusives dans les contrats conclus avec les consommateurs en droit belge. ERPL, 1997, p. 143 et seq.

Bardač, R. Ochrana spotrebiteľa pred exekúciou vykonanou na základe rozhodcovského rozsudku. [Title in translation: Protecting the Consumer from Enforcement Proceedings Based on Arbitral Awards]. In: *Blaho, P. et Švecová, A.* (eds.) Právo v euroópskej perspektíve [Title in translation: Law from the European Perspective], Part II, Trnava: Právnická fakulta, Trnavská univerzita v Trnave [Faculty of Law, Trnava University in Trnava], pp. 729-739.

Bates, D. A Consumer's Dream or Pandora's Box: Is Arbitration a Viable Option for Cross-Border Consumer Disputes? Fordham International Law Journal, 2004, Vol. 27, p. 823 et seq.

Beauchard, J. Poznámky ke spotřebitelskému zákoníku. [Title in translation: Notes on the Consumer Code]. Právní praxe, 1996, No. 10, p. 651 et seq.

Bejček, J. Obchodní podmínky v kupní smlouvě. [Title in translation: Business Terms in a Purchase Contract]. Daňová a hospodářská kartotéka (DHK), 1996, No. 12.

Bejček, J. Princip rovnosti a ochrana slabšího. [Title in translation: Principle of Equality and Protection of the Weaker Party]. In: Sborník vědecké konference "Princip rovnosti a princip ochrany slabšího" v Brně 18. 12. 2003 [Collection of Papers from the Academic Conference "The Principle of Equality and The Principle of Protecting the Weaker Party," held in Brno on 18 December 2003], Brno: Masarykova univerzita [Masaryk University], 2003, pp. 3-6.

Bělohlávek, A. Rozhodčí řízení ad hoc vs. řízení před stálými rozhodčími soudy a postavení tzv. rozhodčích center. [Title in translation: Ad Hoc Arbitration v. Proceedings before Permanent Arbitral Institutions and the Status of the So-Called Arbitral Centres]. Bulletin advokacie, 2005, No. 10, p. 54

Bělohlávek, A. Arbitrabilita sporů. [Title in translation: Arbitrability of Disputes]. Právní zpravodaj, 2003, No. 3, p. 6 et seq.

Bělohlávek, A. Arbitration from the Perspective of the Right to Legal Protection and the Right to Court Proceedings (the Right to Have One's Case Dealt with by a Court): Significance of Autonomy and Scope of the Right to a Fair Trial. In: *Bělohlávek, A. et Rozehnalová, N.* CYArb – Czech (& Central European) Yearbook of Arbitration: The Relationship Between Constitutional Values, Human Rights and Arbitration, Huntington (New York): JurisNet, 2011, Vol. I, pp. 47-70.

Bělohlávek, A. Confidentiality and Publicity in Investment Arbitration, Public Interest and the Scope of Powers Vested in Arbitral Tribunals. In: *Bělohlávek, A. et Rozehnalová, N.* CYArb – Czech (& Central European) Yearbook of Arbitration, Huntington (New York): JurisNet, 2011, Vol. 1, pp. 23-47.

Bělohlávek, A. et Kalla, P. Náhradní způsoby řešení sporů [Title in translation: Alternative Dispute Resolution]. Vybrané aspekty české ekonomiky – Sborník vydaný u příležitosti 65. narozenin prof. Ing. Jiřího Kerna, CSc. [Selected Aspects of the Czech Economy – Collection of Papers Published on the Occasion of the 65th Birthday of Prof. Ing. Jiří Kern, CSc.], Ostrava: Ekonomická fakulta VŠB – Technická univerzita [Faculty of Economics, University of Mining – Technical University], 2004, pp. 9-16.

Bělohlávek, A. et Pezl, T. Mezinárodní a tuzemské rozhodčí řízení z pohledu čl. 36 listiny základních práv a svobod a pravomocí soudů a ústavou garantovaných práv (Institut zrušení rozhodčího nálezu v souvislosti se zákazem revision au fond). [Title in translation: International and Domestic Arbitration from the Perspective of Article 36 of the Charter of Fundamental Rights and Freedoms and the Powers of the Courts and the Rights Guaranteed under the Constitution (Annulment of Arbitral Awards in Connection with the Prohibition of Revision au Fond)]. Právník, 2006, Vol. 146, No. 7, pp. 768-802.

Bělohlávek, A. et Pezl, T. Postavení rozhodčího řízení v systému ochrany práv a ústavního pořádku České republiky a dalších zemí. [Title in translation: Status of Arbitration in the System of the Protection of Rights and Constitutional Laws of the Czech Republic and Other Countries]. Právní rozhledy, 2004, No. 7, pp. 256–261.

Bělohlávek, A. et Profeldová, T. Amendment of the Slovak Arbitration Act of 9 March 2010 Has Not Been Signed by the President of the Slovak Republic. In: *Bělohlávek, A. et Rozehnalová, N.* (eds.) CYArb – Czech (& Central European) Yearbook of Arbitration, Huntington (New York): JurisNet, 2011, Vol. I, pp. 445-448.

Bělohlávek, A. et Profeldová, T. Arbitration in the Case Law of the Constitutional Court of the Czech Republic with regard to the Nature and Purpose of Arbitration. In: *Bělohlávek, A. et Rozehnalová, N.* CYArb – Czech (& Central European) Yearbook of Arbitration: The Relationship between Constitutional Values, Human Rights and Arbitration, Huntington (New York): JurisNet, 2011, Vol. 1, pp. 343-361.

Bělohlávek, A. Franšíza z pohledu tuzemského, evropského a mezinárodního práva soukromého (franšíza jako zvláštní smluvní koncepce a kolizní úprava Nařízení Řím I – Nařízení EP a Rady /ES/ č. 593/2008). [Title in translation: Franchise from the Perspective of Domestic, European and Private International Law (Franchise as a Specific Contractual Concept and the Conflict-of-Law Rules in the Rome I Regulation – Regulation of the EP and of the Council /EC/ No. 593/2008)]. Obchodní právo, 2009, Vol. 18, No. 3, pp. 2-39.

Bělohlávek, A. Místo konání rozhodčího řízení. [Title in translation: Seat of Arbitration]. Právní zpravodaj, 2004, No. 3, pp. 13–15.

Bělohlávek, A. Ochrana spotřebitele a spotřebitelská smlouva. [Title in translation: Consumer Protection and Consumer Contracts]. Právní rádce. 2001, No. 6, pp. 37–38.

Bělohlávek, A. Rozhodčí řízení v tzv. smluvních vztazích spotřebitelského typu. [Title in translation: Arbitration in So-Called Consumer Contractual Relationships]. PrFo, 2010, Vol. 7, No. 3, pp. 89-99.

Bělohlávek, A. Smlouva o obchodním zastoupení a obchodní zástupce. [Title in translation: Agency Contracts and Commercial Agents]. Právní rádce, 2002, No. 5, pp. 34 – 35.

Bělohlávek, A. Spotřebitelská smlouva z pohledu mezinárodního práva soukromého. [Title in translation: Consumer Contracts from the Perspective of Private International Law]. Právní rádce, 2005, Vol. 13, No. 8, p. 4 et seq.

Bělohlávek, A. Ústavní soud České republiky opustil striktní smluvní výklad koncepce rozhodčího řízení: Nález ÚS ČR z 8. března 2011, sp. zn. I ÚS 3227/07 (komentář a rozbor k nálezu ústavního soudu). [Title in translation: The Constitutional Court of the Czech Republic Has Abandoned the Strict Contractual Interpretation of the Concept of Arbitration: Judgment of the Constitutional Court of the Czech Republic of 8 March 2011, Case No. I ÚS 3227/07 (Commentary on and Analysis of the Constitutional Court Ruling)]. Bulletin advokacie, 2011, No. 12, pp. 40-44.

Bělohlávek, A. Volba práva v závazkových vztazích s mezinárodním prvkem. [Title in translation: Choice of Law in Obligations with an International Dimension]. Právní fórum, 2006, No. 3, p. 82 et seq.

Bělohlávek, A. Vznik rozhodčí smlouvy a oprávnění rozhodců. [Title in translation: Formation of the Arbitration Agreement and Powers of the Arbitrators]. Právní zpravodaj, 2005, Vol. 6, pp. 11-13.

Bělohlávek, A. Zavedení tzv. exequatur do českého právního řádu. [Title in translation: Introduction of the So-Called Exequatur into Czech Law]. Právní zpravodaj, 2004, No. 5, pp. 16-17.

Bělohlávek, A. Alternativní způsoby řešení civilních a obchodních sporů (tzv. ADR) v evropském kontextu. [Title in translation: Alternative Methods of Resolution of Civil and Commercial Disputes (the So-Called "ADR") in the European Context]. Právní rozhledy (Annex – Evropské právo), 2003, No. 6, pp. 8-11.

Berger, C. Gerichtspflicht infolge Internetpräsenz nach der neuen Verordnung über die gerichtliche Zuständigkeit und die Anerkennung und Vollstreckung von Entscheidungen in Zivil- und Handelssachen (EuGVVO)? – Zugleich Plädoyer für einen Gerichtsstand der virtuellen Niederlassung." In: *Bauknecht, K., Berger, K., P.* Schiedsgerichtsbarkeit und

Finanztermingeschäfte: Der „Schutz" der Anlager vor der Schiedsgerichtsbarkeit durch § 37h WpHG. ZBB, 2003, pp. 77 – 93.

Berger-Walliser, G. Mißbräuchliche Klauseln in Verbraucherverträgen nach Inkrafttreten des Code de la consommation und Umsetzung der EG-Richtlinie 93/13 in Frankreich. RIW, 1996, pp. 459-463.

Bernitz, U. Swedish standard contracts law and the EEC Directive on contract terms. ERPL, 1997, Vol. 2, p. 213 et seq.

Bianca, C. M. Consegna di aliud pro alio e decadenza dai rimedi per omessa denunzia nella direttiva 1999/44/CE. Contratto e impresa-Europa, 2001, p. 16 et seq.

Bienvenu, P. The Enforcement of International Arbitration Agreements and Referral Applications in the NAFTA Region. R. du B., 1999, Vol. 59, p. 705 et seq.

Bland, F. P. Hearings on Mandatory Binding Arbitration: Are They Fair to Consumers? Testimony Given to the United States House of Representatives Judiciary Committeee on 12 June 2007.

Bončková, H. et Žondra, M. Aplikace práva EU českými soudy v soukromoprávních věcech v letech 2004-2008: Část III. Směrnice. [Title in translation: Application of EU Law by Czech Courts in Private-Law Matters in 2004-2008: Part III of the Directive]. Právní fórum, 2011, Vol. 8, No. 4, pp. 145-160.[1]

Boré, L. L'Action en représentation conjointe: class action française ou action mort-née? Rec. Dalloz, 1995, p. 267 et seq.

Bourgoignie, T. Droit et politique communautaures de la consommation: de Rome à Amsterdam. Revue Européenne de Droit de la Consommation, 1997, Vol. 3, p. 197 et seq.

Bourgoignie, T., Domont-Naert, F., Gomard, B., De Lamberterie, I., Wallaert, Ch., Voulgaris, J., Phillips, J., Bessone, M., Hoffmann, C., Steenhoff, G., J., W., Rieg A., Salvat, O. et Tallon, D. Le Contrôle des clauses abusives dans l'intérêt du consommateur dans les pays de la C.E.E. Rev. int. dr. comp., 1982, Vol. 34, pp. 505-1113.

Brierley, J. E. C. Arbitration Agreements: Articles 2638-2643. In: Reform of the Civil Code, Vol. 3B: Marine Insurance, Carriage by Water, Affreightment, Deposit, Loan, Suretyship, Gaming and Wagering, Transaction, Arbitration Agreements, Insurance and Annuities. Translation: *Altschul, S.* Document drafted for: Barreau du Québec and the Chambre des notaires du Québec. Montréal: Barreau du Québec, 1993.

---

[1] See especially the chapter: Directive on unfair terms in consumer contracts, pp. 146-153.

Brierley, J. E. C. Quebec's New (1986) Arbitration Law. Canadian Business Law Journal, 1987-1988, Vol. 13, p. 58 et seq.

Brodec, J. Spotřebitelské smlouvy. [Title in translation: Consumer Contracts]. Právník, 2004, No. 9, pp. 907-919.

Brundschuh, K. D. Die Rechtsprechung des Bundesgerichtshofes zum Börsenterminhandel. WM, 1986, p. 725 et seq.

Budnitz, M. E. Arbitration of Disputes between Customers and Financial Institutions: A Serious Threat to Consumer Protection. Ohio St.Y. Disp. Res., 1995, Vol. 10, p. 267 et seq.

Burian, J. et Horská, J. Rozhodčí doložka ve spotřebitelských smlouvách ve světle aktuální judikatury českých soudů a ESD. [Title in translation: Arbitration Clause in Consumer Disputes in Light of the Current Case Law of Czech Courts and the ECJ]. Bulletin advokacie, 2010, No. 4, p. 22 et seq.

Canada. Industry Canada. Office of Consumer Affairs. Your Internet Business: Earning Consumer Trust. A guide to consumer protection for on-line merchants. Ottawa: The Department, 1999.

Carrington, P. Regulating Dispute Resolution Provisions in Adhesion Contracts. Harvard Journal on Legislation, 1998, Vol. 35, pp. 225-231.

Ciearin, C. The Protection of the Weak Contractual Party in Italy vs. the United States "Doctrine of Unconscionability." Global Jurist Advances, 2003, Vol. 3, No. 3.

Craswell, R. Passing on the Costs of Legal Rules: Efficiency and Distribution in Buyer-Seller Relationships. Stanford Law Review, 1991, Vol. 43, p. 361 et seq.

Dauer, E. Judicial Policing of Consumer Arbitration. Pepperdine Disp. Res. L. J., 2000, Vol. 91, No. 1, p. 3 et seq.

Dauner-Lieb, B. Europäisches Verbraucherschutzrecht als Motor der Veränderung des deutschen Privatrechts – Schuldrecht im Spannungsverhältnis zwischen Privatautonomie und Verbraucherschutz. In: *Baetge, D., von Davies, I.* Posted workers: Single market or protection of national labour systems? CMLR, 1997, p. 571 et seq.

David, M. K povaze rozhodčí smlouvy podruhé a jinak. [Title in translation: Another, Different Article on the Nature of Arbitration Agreements]. Bulletin advokacie, 2011, No. 10, pp. 27-29.

Davo, H. Clauses abusives: bref aperçu de la loi du 1er février 1995 transposant la directive 93/13/CEERR. Revue européenne de droit de la consommation, 1995, pp. 215-221.

Davo, H. Clauses abusives: loi du février 1995 transposant la directive 93/13/CEE en droit français. ERPL, 1997, Vol. 2, p. 157.

De Cristofaro, G. Promesse di vincite" transfrontaliere e Convenzione di Bruxelles: dai "contratti" ai "contatti" con i consumatori? Corriere giuridico, 2003, pp. 70-74.

de la Hosseraye, J. et de Witt, N. Commerce électronique: Juridiction compétente et loi applicable. Bulletin européen et international, 2000, No. 2, pp. 2-4.

De Nayer, B. Acheter et vendre sur l'Internet: réflexions sur le cadre juridique belge. Consumentenrecht, 1997, pp. 5-22.

Dean, M. Defining Unfair Terms in Consumer Contracts – Crystal Ball Gazing? Director General of Fair Trading v First National Bank plc. The Modern Law Review, 2002, Vol. 65, pp. 773-781.

Debussere, F. International Jurisdiction over E-Consumer Contracts in the European Union: Quid Novi Sub Sole? International Journal of Law and Information Technology, 2002, Vol. 10, No. 3, pp. 344-366.

Delogu, L. T. I patti modificativi della responsabilità del venditore: la direttiva 1999/44/CE, l'odierno diritto italiano e le prospettive di riforma. Contratto e impresa-Europa, 2000, p. 489 et seq.

Demaine, L. J. et Hensler, D. R. "Volunteering" to Arbitrate through Predispute Arbitration Clauses: The Average Consumer's Experience. Law & Contemp. Problems, 2004, Vol. 67, p. 55 et seq.

Dettling, D. Vom individuellen zum kollektiven Vebraucherschutz. GPR, 2005, No. 3, p. 122 et seq.

Doležalová, M. Nová směrnice Evropského parlamentu a Rady 2008/122/ES o ochraně spotřebitele. [Title in translation: The New Directive 2008/122/EC of the European Parliament and of the Council on the Protection of Consumers]. Bulletin advokacie, 2009, No. 5, pp. 56-57.

Drahozal, Chr. et Friel, R. A Comparative View of Consumer Arbitration. Arbitration, 2005, Vol. 71, pp. 131-139.

Drahozal, Chr. R. et Zyontz, S. An Empirical Study of AAA Consumer Arbitration. Ohio St. J. on Disp. Resol., 2010, Vol. 25, p. 843 et seq.

Drahozal, Chr. R. Unfair Arbitration Clauses. U. Ill. L. Rev., 2001, p. 695 et seq.

Dreher, M. Der Verbraucher – Das Phantom in den opera des europäischen und deutschen Rechts? Juristenzeitung, 1997, pp. 167–178.

Drobnig, U. Neue rechtliche Konzepte für den europäischen Verbraucherschutz. Notarius International, 1998, pp. 98-106.

Dulaková Jakúbeková, D. Spotrebiteľská zmluva nanovo a inak. [Title in translation: Consumer Contract – Anew and Differently.] Justičná revue, 2008, Vol. 60, Nos. 6-7, pp. 936-946.

Dutta,   A.   Kolidierende   Rechtswahlklauseln   in   allgemeinen Geschäftsbedingungen: Ein   Beitrag   zur   Bestimmung   des Rechtswahlstatuts. Zeitschrift für vergleichende Rechtswissenschaft, 2005, p. 461 et seq.

Eilmannsberger, T., Schoißwohl, B. et Tremmel, E. Rechtssprechungsübersicht Europäischer Gerichtshof April 2000 bis September 2000. Ecolex, 2000, p. 917 et seq.

Eisenberg, T., Miller, G. et Sherwin, E. Arbitration's Summer Soldiers: An Empirical Study of Arbitration Clauses in Consumer and Nonconsumer Contracts. U. Mich. J. L. Reform, 2008, Vol. 41, p. 871 et seq.

Elischer, D. Koupě na zkoušku v mezinárodním srovnání: Návrat do civilního korpusu aneb východiska a možnosti českého zákonodárce *de lege ferenda*. [Title in translation: Trial Purchase in International Comparison: Return to the Civil Corpus a.k.a. Premises and Possibilities of the Czech Legislator *De Lege Ferenda*]. Právní fórum, 2008, Vol. 3, No. 6, p. 257 et seq.

Esplugues Mota, C. A. Noción de consumidor. Delimitación de la misma en el artículo 13 del Convenio de Bruselas de 1968 sobre competencia judicial internacional, reconocimiento y ejecución de resoluciones judiciales en material civil y mercantil. Comunidad Europea Aranzadi, 1993, p. 33 et seq.

Fabre-Magan, M. Duties of Disclosure and French Contract Law: Contribution to an Economic Analysis. In: *Fadda, R.* Il contenuto della direttiva 99/44/CE: una panoramica. Contratto e impresa-Europa, 2000, p. 410 et seq.

Fallon, M. et Francq, S. Towards Internationally Mandatory Directives for Consumer Contracts? In: *Basedow J., Meier I., Girsberger D., Schnyder A. K. et Einhorn T.* (eds.), Private Law in the International Arena, Liber Amicorum Kurt Siehr, The Hague, T.M.C. Asser Press, 2000.

Fallon, M. Le droit applicable aux clauses abusives après la transposition de la directive n° 93/13 du 5 avril 1993. Revue Européenne de Droit de la Consommation, 1996, Vol. 1, p. 3 et seq.

Favre-Bulle, X. Arbitrage et Règlement alternative des litiges (ADR): une autre justice pour les consommateurs? In: *Thévenoz, L. et Reich, N.* (eds.) Droit de la consommation, Liber Amicorum Bernd Stauder, Genève: Schulthess, 2006, p. 97 et seq.

Ferri, G. B. Divagazioni intorno alla direttiva N°44 del 1999 su taluni aspetti della vendita e delle garanzie dei beni di consumo. Contratto e impresa-Europa, 2001, p. 63 et seq.

Fiala, J. Novela občanského zákoníku po schválení Poslaneckou sněmovnou. [Title in translation: Amendment to the Civil Code after Approval by the House of Representatives]. Právní zpravodaj, 2000, No. 8, p. 1 et seq.

Fiala, J. Novela občanského zákoníku zvyšuje ochranu spotřebitele. [Title in translation: Amendment to the Civil Code Enhances Consumer Protection]. Právní zpravodaj, 2002, No. 3.

Fiala, J. Senát k novele občanského zákoníku. [Title in translation: The Senate on the Amendment to the Civil Code]. Právní zpravodaj, 2000, No. 8, p. 3.

Fortier, L. Y. Delimiting the Spheres of Judicial and Arbitral Power: "Beware, My Lord, of Jealousy." Can. Bar Rev, 2001, Vol. 80, p. 143.

Fumagalli, L. Le clausole abusive nei contratti con i consumatori tra diritto comunitario e diritto internazionale privato. Riv.dir.int.pr.proc, 1994, p. 15 et seq.

Gansfort, G. Wirksame Einbeziehung der Allgemeinen Beförderungs-bedingungen der Luftfahrtunternehmen in den Pauschalflugreise-Vertrag. TranspR, 1989, pp. 131-139.

Garofalo, L. et Rodeghiero, A. In: *Mannino, P., L., Moscati, E. et Vecchi, P., M.* Commentario alla disciplina della vendita di beni di consumo Garofalo, Padova: CEDAM, 2003, sub art. 1519nonies, p. 711 et seq.

Garofalo, L. In: *Garofalo, L.* (ed.), *Mannino, P., L., Moscati, E. et Vecchi, P., M.* Commentario alla disciplina della vendita di beni di consumo Garofalo, Padova: CEDAM, 2003, sub art 1519quater, p. 354 et seq.

Garofalo, L. In: *Garofalo, L.* (ed.), *Mannino, P., L., Moscati, E. et Vecchi, P., M.* Commentario alla disciplina della vendita di beni di consumo Garofalo, Padova: CEDAM, 2003, sub art. 2 d. lgs. 2 febbraio 2002 n°24, p. 797 et seq.

Gojová, J. Rozhodčí doložka ve spotřebitelské smlouvě a její ústavněprávní limity. [Title in translation: Arbitration Clause in a Consumer Contract and Its Limits under Constitutional Law]. Právní fórum, 2012, Vol. 9, No. 1, pp. 46-48.

Gołaczyński, J. Wybór prawa właściwego dla zobowiązań z umów elektronicznych. Prawo Teleinformatyczne, 2006, No. 2.

Grundmann, S. Europäisches Vertragsrechtsübereinkommen, EWG-Vertrag und § 12 AGBG. IPRax, 1992, p. 1 et seq.

Guzmán Zapater, M. La Prórroga de la competencia en los contratos de venta internacional concluidos por consumidores. REDI, 1987, Vol. 39, p. 447 et seq.

Habersack, M., Kleindiek, D. et Wiedenmann, K.-U. Die EG-Richtlinie über mißbräuchliche Klauseln in Verbraucherverträgen und das künftige AGB-Gesetz. ZIP, 1993, pp. 1670-1675.

Halfmeier, A. Widersprüchliches Verhalten als opt-out aus dem Europäischen Verbraucherschutzrecht? GPR, 2005, No. 4, p. 184 et seq.

Hanefeld, I. et Wittinghofer, M., A. Schiedsklauseln in Allgemeinen Geschäftsbedingen SchiedsVZ, 2005, Vol. 3, No. 5, pp. 217-229.

Hau, W. Vorgaben de sEuGH zur Klausel-Richtlinie – (zu EuGH 27.6.2000 – verb Rs C-240/98 bis C-244/98 – Océano Grupo Editorial/Rocio Murciano Quintero). IPRax, 2001, p. 96 et seq.

Havel, B. Poznámky k ustanovení § 53 odstavec 8 občanského zákoníku (induktivni náhled). [Title in translation: Notes on Section 53(8) of the Civil Code (Inductive View)]. Právník, 2004, No. 1, pp. 68-81.

Hazan, M. Attuata la direttiva 99/44/CE: si rafforza la tutela del consumatore. Contratti, 2002, p. 399 et seq.

Heiskanen, V. Dispute Resolution in International Electronic Commerce. JIA, 1999, Vol. 16, p. 29 et seq.

Henry, X. Clauses abusives : où va la jurisprudence accessible ? L'appréciation du rapport direct avec l'activité, 2003, Vol. 37, p. 2557 et seq.

Hesselink, W. M. European Contract Law: A Matter of Consumer Protection, Citizenship, or Justice? European Review of Private Law, 2007, No. 3, pp. 323-348.

Hill, R. The Internet, Electronic Commerce and Dispute Resolution: Comments. JIA, 1997, Vol. 14, p. 103 et seq.

Hlaváč, A. Aktuální vývoj v otázce platnosti rozhodčích doložek ve spotřebitelských smlouvách. [Title in translation: Current Developments Concerning the Validity of Arbitration Clauses in Consumer Contracts]. Právní rádce, 2010, Vol. 18, No. 12, pp. 12-15.

Honoatieu, B. L'arbitrabilité. Recueil des Cours de l'Académie de Droit International, 2003, p. 97 et seq.

Hörnle, J. Legal controls on the use of arbitration clauses in B2C e-commerce contracts. Masaryk University Journal of Law & Technology, 2008, Vol. 2, No. 23, p. 29 et seq.[2]

Huet, A. Chronique de jurisprudence du Tribunal et de la Cour de Justice des Communautés Européennes. Journal du droit international, 2003, pp. 651-659. (Notes on the ECJ ruling in C-96/00).

Huet, J. JCP E Semaine Juridique Commerce électronique: loi applicable et règlement des litiges. Propositions des grandes entreprises (GBDe), édition entreprise, 1999, No. 41, pp. 1601-1602.

---

[2] Also available online at: http://mujlt.law.muni.cz/storage/1234798613_sb_03_hornle.pdf [last access 14 August 2011].

Hülle, T. Mandatory and Directory Provisions of the Current Civil Code in the Europeanization of National Law, The Lisbon Treaty and Some Other Legal Issues (CD ROM), Brno: Tribun EU, 2008.

Hülle, T. Nekalá soutěž na scestí aneb kudy cesta nevede po reformě B2C vztahů. [Title in translation: Unfair Competition Has Gone Astray a.k.a. Blind Alley after the Reform of B2C Relationships]. In: Dny práva – 2008 – Days of Law, Brno: Tribun EU, 2008.

Hülle, T. Skutečně může čas otupit i právo na ochranu soutěžní tvořivosti? [Title in translation: Can Time Really Dull the Right to the Protection of Competitive Creativity?] Právní rozhledy, 2008, No. 20.

Hülle, T. Směrnice 2005/29/ES na ochranu proti nekalým obchodním praktikám vůči spotřebitelům, její transpozice a projevy v českém právu [Title in translation: Directive 2005/29/EC Concerning Unfair Business-To-Consumer Commercial Practices, the Transposition and Manifestations Thereof in Czech Law] in Nové jevy v hospodářské a finanční kriminalitě – Vnitrostátní a evropské aspekty [New Phenomena in Economic and Financial Crimes – National and European Aspects], Brno: Tribun EU, 2008.

Hulmák, M. et Tomančáková, B. Rozhodčí řízení jako vhodný prostředek řešení sporů mezi dodavatelem a spotřebitelem. [Title in translation: Arbitration as a Suitable Mechanism for the Resolution of Disputes Between Suppliers and Consumers]. Obchodněprávní revue, 2010, Vol. 2, Part I: No. 6, p. 168 et seq., Part II: No. 7, p. 189 et seq.

Hulva, T. Ochrana spotřebitele při prodeji v obchodě. [Title in translation: The Protection of Consumers in Retail Sales]. Bulletin advokacie, 2005, No. 1, pp. 32-40.

Hulva, T. Ochrana spotřebitele v komunitárním evropském právu. [Title in translation: Consumer Protection in European Community Law]. Bulletin advokacie, 2004, Nos. 7-8, p. 16 et seq.

Janovec, M. Zrušení rozhodčího nálezu soudem. [Title in translation: Annulment of Arbitral Awards by Court]. Právní fórum, 2010, No. 4, p. 181 et seq.

Jordans, R. Application of consumer protection provisions as foreign mandatory laws in international arbitration. ADRJ, 2004, Vol. 15, No. 3, p. 194 et seq.

Jordans, R. Außergerichtliche Streitbeilegung – ein Überblick. VuR, 2004, p. 92 et seq.

Jordans, R. Der rechtliche Charakter von Ombudsman-Systemen und ihren Entscheidungen. VuR, 2003, p. 253 et seq.

Jordans, R. et Felke, K. Case Note to the Judgment of the European Court of Justice C-27/02, Petra Engler v. Janus Versand GmbH. ERPL, 2006, p. 130 et seq.

Jordans, R. et Felke, K. EWS-Kommentar zum Urteil des EuGH vom 20.1.2005, Rs. C-27/02.

Jordans, R. Ist Mediation regulierungsbedürftig? Teil I: Begriffe und Gesetze. Forum Mediation, 2003, p. 17 et seq.

Jordans, R. Note to the Judgment of the European Court of Justice, Case C-168/05. SIAR, 2007, No. 1, pp. 48-50.

Jordans, R. Note to the Judgment of the German Federal Supreme Court (BGH), Case II ZR 65/03. SIAR, 2005, No. 2.

Junker, A. Vom Citoyen zum Consommateur – Entwicklungen des internationalen Verbraucherschutzrechts. IPRax, 1998, p. 65 et seq.

Favre-Bulle, X. Arbitrage et Règlement alternative des litiges (ADR): une autre justice pour les consommateurs? In: Théovenoz, L. et Reich, N. *(eds.) Droit de la consommation,* Liber Amicorum Bernd Stauder, Genève: Schulthess, 2006, p. 97 et seq.

Kanda, A. et Matějka, J. Spotřebitelské smlouvy a jejich význam v informační společnosti. [Title in translation: Consumer Contracts and Their Importance in the Information Society]. In: *Dvořák, J. et Kapoor, A. et Klindt, T.* "New Legislative Framework" im EU-Produktsicherheitsrecht – Neue Marktüberwachung in Europa? EuZW, 2008, Vol. 19, No. 21, pp. 649-654.

Kaplinsky, A. S. et Levin, M. J. Is JAMS in a Jam over Its Policy regarding Class Action Waivers in Consumer Arbitration Agreements? Bus. Law., 2006, Vol. 61, p. 923 et seq.

Katsh, E., Rifkin, J. et Gaitenby, A. E-Commerce, E-Dispute, and E-Dispute Resolution: In the Shadow of "eBay Law." Ohio State Journal of Dispute Resolution, 2000, Vol. 15, p. 705 et seq.

Kaufmann-Kohler, G. et Peter, H. Formula One Racing and Arbitration: The FIA Tailor-Made System for Fast Track Dispute Resolution. Arb. Int., 2001, Vol. 17, p. 173 et seq.

Kaufmann-Kohler, G. Arbitration agreements in online business transactions. In: *Briner, R., Fortier, L. Y., Berger, K. P. et Bredow, J. (eds.)* Law of International Business and Dispute Settlement in the 21st Century. Liber Amicorum Karl-Heinz Böckstiegel. Köln a. R.: Heymanns, 2001, p. 358 et seq.

Kessedjian, C. L'Action en justice des assotiations de consommateurs et d'autres organisations représentatives d'intérêts collectifs en Europe. Riv. dir. int. priv. proc., 1997, Vol. 2, p. 282 et seq.

Kierstead, S. Referral to Arbitration under Article 8 of the UNCITRAL Model Law: The Canadian Approach. Can. Bus. L. J., 1999, Vol. 31, p. 98 et seq.

Kiesel, K., Buschena, D. et Smith, V. Do Voluntary Biotechnology Labels Matter to the Consumer? Evidence from the Fluid Milk Market. American Journal of Agricultural Economics, 2005, Vol. 87, No. 2, pp. 378-392.

Kirry, A. Arbitrability: Current Trends in Europe. Arb. Int., 1996, p. 377 et seq.

Klima, P. Frankreich: Mißbräuchliche Klauseln in Verträgen. RIW, 1992, pp. 98-102.

Knoblochová, V. Rozsudky Soudního dvora dotýkající se právních vztahů v oblasti ochrany spotřebitele. [Title in translation: Judgments of the Court of Justice Affecting Legal Relationships in the Field of Consumer Protection]. EMP, 2001, No. 4, p. 15 et seq.

Král, R. K přesahující transpozici Směrnic ES. [Title in translation: Concerning the Transcending Transposition of EC Directives]. Právník, 2001, No. 9, pp. 903-912.

Krampera, J. Neplatnost nepřiměřených ujednání ve spotřebitelských smlouvách. [Title in translation: Invalidity of Unfair Terms in Consumer Contracts]. Bulletin advokacie, 2009, Nos. 1-2, pp. 44-46.

Kronke, H. Electronic Commerce und Europäisches Verbrauchervertrags-IPR. RIW, 1996, pp. 985-993.

Kühn, Z. Teoretické problémy aplikace komunitárního práva v nových členských státech. [Title in translation: Theoretical Problems with the Application of Community Law in the New Member States]. Právní fórum, 2005, No. 9, p. 14 et seq.

Kulhavý, F. Pojetí obchodní kupní smlouvy. [Title in translation: The Concept of a Commercial Purchase Contract]. Právo a podnikání, 1996, No. 6, p. 21 et seq.

Kusák, V. et Piltz, A. Odpovědnost za škody způsobené vadou výrobku ve Spojených státech amerických a český výrobce. [Title in translation: Liability for Damage and Losses Caused by Defective Products in the United States of America and the Czech Manufacturer]. Právní rozhledy, 1999, No. 10, p. 532 et seq.

Lavický, P. Spotřebitelské smlouvy. [Title in translation: Consumer Contracts]. Časopis pro právní vědu a praxi, 2001, No. 2, pp. 200-208.

Law Commission (UK/EN). Law Commissions' Joint Consultation Paper: Unfair Terms in Contracts. Law Commission, 2002, Document No. 16.

Law Commission (UK/EN). Law Commissions' Joint Report: Unfair Terms in Contracts. Law Commission, 2005, Document No. 292.

Lefebvre, B. Le contrat d'adhésion. R. du N., 2003, Vol. 105, p. 439 et seq.

Lehmann, M. A Plea for a Transnational Approach to Arbitrability in Arbitral Practice, Colum. J. Transnat'l L., 2003-2004, Vol. 42, p. 753 et seq.

Leible, S. Gerichtsstandsklauseln und EG-Klauselrichtlinie. RIW, 2001, p. 422 et seq.

Leible, S. Gewinnbestätigung aus Luxemburg: Zur internationalen Zuständigkeit bei Gewinnmitteilungen aus dem Ausland. IPRax (Praxis des internationalen Privat- und Verfahrensrechts), 2003, pp. 28-34.

Libánský, V. Spotřebitelská legislativa Evropské unie a její implementace do práva ČR. [Title in translation: Consumer Legislation of the European Union and its Implementation in Czech Law]. Právní rozhledy, 1999, No. 9, p. 2 et seq.

Lisse, L. K právnímu postavení arbitrážních center. [Title in translation: Regarding the Legal Status of Arbitral Centres]. Bulletin advokacie, 2006, No. 1, p. 40

Lisse, L. Rozhodčí doložka ve spotřebitelských smlouvách a judikatura ESD. [Title in translation: Arbitration Clauses in Consumer Contracts and the Case Law of the ECJ]. Právní fórum, 2010, No. 12, p. 581 et seq.

Lorenz, E. Internationale Zuständigkeit deutscher Gerichte und Anwendbarkeit von § 661a BGB bei Gewinnmitteilungen aus dem Ausland: Erweiterungen des Verbrauchergerichtsstands durch die "Brüssel I-Verordnung." IPRax 2002, p. 192 et seq.

Luminoso, M. Appunti per l'attuazione della direttiva 1999/44/CE e per la revisione della garanzia per vizi nella vendita. Contratto e impresa-Europa, 2001, p. 89 et seq.

Luminoso, M. Chiose in chiaroscuro in margine al d.lgs. n°24 del 2002: problemi e dilemmi. In: *Luminoso, M. et Luminoso, M.* Proposta di modificazione del codice civile per l'attuazione della direttiva 1999/44/CE. Contratto e impresa-Europa, 2001, p. 133 et seq.

Macdonald, E. Scope and Fairness of the Unfair Terms in Consumer Contracts Regulations: Director General of Fair Trading v First National Bank. The Modern Law Review, 2002, Vol. 65, pp. 763-773.

Maglio, V. Il rapporto tra direttive comunitarie e diritto internazionale privato in materia di tutela dei consumatori. Contratto e impresa/Europa, 1996, p. 705 et seq.

Maisonneuve, M. Le droit américain de l'arbitrage et la théorie de l'unconscionability. Rev. arb., 2005, p. 101

Manicini, T. L'abusivita della clausola compromissoria per arbitrato irrituale nei contratti noc il consumatore. Banca borsa tit. cred., 2008, No. 2 (II), p. 111 et seq.

Mankowski, P. Verbraucherkreditverträge und europäisches IPR: Internationale Zuständigkeit und Eingriffsrecht: Entscheidung der französischen Cour de Cassation vom 23. Mai 2006. ZEuP, 2008, No. 4.

Markward, K. Inhaltskontrolle von AGB-Klauseln durch den EuGH – Zugleich Besprechung EuGH, Urt. v. 1.4.2004 – Rs C-237/02. ZIP, 2005, pp. 152-157.

Marotta-Wurgler, F. "Unfair" Dispute Resolution Clauses: Much Ado about Nothing?. In: *Ben-Shahar, O.* (ed.) Boilerplate: The Foundation of Market Contracts, 2007, p. 45 et seq.

Marquis, L. La compétence arbitrale: une place au soleil ou à l'ombre du pouvoir judiciaire. R.D.U.S., 1990, Vol. 21, p. 303 et seq.

Marquis, L. La notion d'arbitrage commercial international en droit québécois. McGill L. J. 1991-1992, Vol. 37, p. 448.

Martin, L. S. Keep it online: The Hague Convention and the need for online alternative dispute resolution in international business-to-consumer e-commerce. Boston University International Law Journal, 2002, Vol. 20, p. 125 et seq.

Matejka, J. Úprava spotřebitelských smluv v právním řádu ČR se zvláštním zřetelem k tzv. distančním smlouvám. [Title in translation: Czech Rules on Consumer Contracts with Special Regard to So-Called Distance Contracts]. Právník, 2002, No. 9, pp. 946-980.

Matthews, J. M. Consumer Arbitration: Is It Working Now and Will It Work in the Future? Fla. Bar J., 2005, Vol. 79, p. 1 et seq.

Meese, A. J. Economic theory, trader freedom, and consumer welfare: State Oil. Co. v. Khan and the continuing incoherence of antitrust doctrine. Cornell Law Review, Vol. 84, pp. 763-797.

Metzger, A. Europäischer Verbraucherschutz, Effektivitätsgrundsatz und nationale Ausschlussfristen. ZEuP, 2004, p. 153 et seq.

Meyer-Hauser, B. Consumer Transactions in Cyberspace: On-line Contracting. International Sales Quarterly, 1997, No. 3, pp. 5-8.

Micklits, H. W. et Weatherill, S. Consumer Policy in the European Community: Before and After Maastricht. Journal of Consumer Policy, 1993, p. 287 et seq.

Micklitz, H. W. et Reich, N. Europäisches Verbraucherrecht – Quo vadis? Verbraucher und Recht, 2007, p. 121 et seq.

Micklitz, H. W. Verbraucherschutz im Vertrag über die EU. EuZW, 1993, p. 593 et seq.

Mitchell, C. Leading a Life of its Own? The Roles of Reasonable Expectation in Contract Law. Oxford Journal of Legal Studies, 2003, Vol. 23, No. 4, pp. 639-665.

Mogilnicki, E. J. et Jensen, K. D. Arbitration and Unconscionability. Ga. St. U. L. Rev., 2003, Vol. 19, p. 761 et seq.

Moller, H. Schiedsverfahrensnovelle und Volstreckung ausländischer Schiedssprüche. NZG, 1999, pp. 143-146

Moorman, Ch. D. R. et Mela, C. F. The Effect of Standardized Information on Firm Survival and Marketing Strategies. Marketing Science, 2005, Vol. 24, No. 2, 263-274.

Müller, W. et Keilmann, A. Beteiligung am Schiedsverfahren wider Willen? SchiedsVZ, 2007, p. 113 et seq.

Mustill, M. J. Arbitration: History and Background. J. Int. Arb., J. Int'l Arb., 1989, Vol. 6, p. 43 et seq.

Němeček, P. Zamyšlení nad § 652 odst. 2 ObchZ a § 55 odst. 2 ObcZ. [Title in translation: Essay on Section 652(2) of the Commercial Code and Section 55(2) of the Civil Code]. Právní rozhledy, 2005, No. 12, pp. 442-446.

Němečková, O. Absurdita protikladnosti principu rovnosti a principu ochrany slabšího. [Title in translation: Absurd Contradiction Between the Principle of Equality and the Principle of Protection of the Weaker Party]. In: Sborník vědecké konference „Princip rovnosti a princip ochrany slabšího" [Collection of Papers from the Academic Conference "The Principle of Equality and The Principle of Protecting the Weaker Party"]. Brno 18 December 2003, Brno: Masarykova univerzita [Masaryk University], 2003.

Normand, J. et Balate, E. Relations transfrontalieres et consomation: quels (s) Juge(s) et quelle(s) loi(s)? Cahiers de Droit Européen, 1990, p. 272 et seq.

Nový, Z. Spotřebitelské úvěry a rozhodčí řízení. [Title in translation: Consumer Credits and Arbitration]. Jurisprudence, 2010, No. 8, p. 22 et seq.

Nowaczyk, P. Comment: The Condition of Polish Commercial Mediation. World Arbitration & Mediation Review, 2010, Vol. 4, No. 1, pp. 87-94.

O'Connor, K. Civil Justice Reform and Prospects for Change. Brooklyn Law Review, Vol. 59, p. 917 et seq.

Parker, Ch. Restorative Justice in Business Regulation? The Australian Competition and Consumer Commission's Use of Enforceable Undertakings. The Modern Law Review, 2004, Vol. 67, pp. 209-246.

Patalano, J. E. Contracting for Judicial Review of Arbitration Agreements: Sidestepping the FAA Weakens Arbitration Viability. Suffolk J. Trial & App. Advoc., 2003, Vol. 8, p. 81 et seq.

Pauknerová, M. Czech Republic – Jurisdiction over Consumer Contracts under Article 15(1)(B) of the Brussels I Regulation, and the Definition of the Concept of "Consumer's" Domicile. Yearbook of Private International Law, 2007, Vol. 9, pp. 495-502.

Paulsson, J. Arbitration Unbound: Award Detached from the Law of Its Country of Origin. ICLQ, 1981, Vol. 30, p. 358 et seq.

Pavelka, M. Rozhodčí řízení před tzv. rozhodčími centry. [Title in translation: Arbitration in So-Called Arbitral Centres]. Bulletin advokacie, 2005, Nos. 7-8, p. 58

Pecha, R. K právní povaze rozhodčích nálezů. [Title in translation: Concerning the Legal Nature of Arbitral Awards]. Bulletin advokacie, 2003, No. 5, pp. 41–45.

Pelikánová, I. České právo, Evropa a rozhodčí doložky. [Title in translation: Czech Law, Europe and Arbitration Clauses]. Bulletin advokacie, 2011, No. 10, pp. 17-26.

Pipková, H. K postupné implementaci směrnic ES o ochraně spotřebitele do občanského zákoníku: Základní práva spotřebitele. [Title in translation: Regarding the Gradual Implementation of EC Consumer Protection Directives in the Civil Code: Fundamental Rights of the Consumer]. Právní rádce, 2001, No. 7.

Pipková, H. Ochrana spotřebitele ve vztahu ke komunitárnímu právu. [Title in translation: Consumer Protection in Relation to Community Law]. PrRa, 2005, No. 8.

Plíva, S. Smlouvy uzavírané podnikatelem. [Title in translation: Contracts Concluded by Professionals]. Právo a podnikání, 1995, No. 7, p. 2 et seq.

Pocar, F. La protection de la partie faible en droit international privé. RC, 1984, IV, p. 341 et seq.

Posh, W. The implementation of the EC Directive on Unfair Contract Terms into Austrian Law. ERPL, 1997, Vol. 2, p. 135 et seq.

Price, R. D. When Is a Consumer Not a Consumer? The Modern Law Review,1989, Vol. 52, No. 2, pp. 245-251.

Québec. Assemblée nationale. Journal des débats, vol. 29, n° 46, 1re sess., 33e lég., 16 juin 1986, p. 2975.

Québec. Assemblée nationale. Journal des débats, vol. 29, n° 55, 1re sess., 33e lég., 30 octobre 1986, p. 3672.

Québec. Assemblée nationale. Journal des débats, vol. 30, n° 134, 2e sess., 33e lég., 21 juin 1989, pp. 6941 et 6970.

Raban, P. Autorizovaní rozhodci nebo adjudikátoři? Je efektivně zajištěna spravedlnost ve spotřebitelských vztazích? [Title in translation: Authorized Arbitrators or Adjudicators? Is Justice in Consumer Relations Effectively Safeguarded?] Bulletin advokacie, 2010, No. 6, pp. 15–21.

Raban, P. Drobní dlužníci a zakázaná smluvní ujednání. [Title in translation: Small Debtors and Prohibited Contractual Terms]. Právní rádce, 2009, Vol. 17, No. 11, p. 20 et seq.

Raban, P. Je efektivně zajištěna spravedlnost ve spotřebitelských vztazích? [Title in translation: Is Justice in Consumer Relations Effectively Safeguarded?] PrRa, 2010, Vol.18, No. 2, pp. 46-52.

Raban, P. K odpovědnosti rozhodce a rozhodčího soudu. [Title in translation: Concerning the Liability of Arbitrators and Arbitral Tribunals]. Bulletin advokacie, 2003, No. 1, pp. 25–34.

Raban, P. Soukromé rozhodčí soudy a stanné rozhodčí řízení. [Title in translation: Private Arbitral Tribunals and Arbitration By Default]. Právní rádce, 2005, No. 11, p. 4 et seq.

Rabl, T. EuGH: Absolute Nichtigkeit von unfairen Verbraucherverträgen? ecolex, 2000, p. 783 et seq.

Radeideh, M. Fair Trading in EC Law, Information and Consumer Choice in the Internal Market, Groningen: Europa Law Publishing, 2005.

Raiser, L. Das Recht der Allgemeinen Geschäftsbedingungen, Hamburg: Hanseatische Verlagsanstalt, 1935.

Rammeloo, S. Die Auslegung von Art. 4 Abs. 2 und Abs. 5 EVÜ: Eine niederländische Perspektive. IPRax, 1994, p. 243 et seq.

Ramsay, I. Consumer Law and Structures of Thought: A Comment. Journal of Consumer Policy, 1993, Vol. 16, pp. 79-94.

Randall, S. Judicial Attitudes toward Arbitration and the Resurgence of Unconscionability. Buff. L. Rev., 2004, Vol. 52, p. 185 et seq.

Reed, P. Delocalization of International Commercial Arbitration: Its Relevance in the New Millenium. The American Review of International Arbitration, 1999, No. 10, pp. 179–180.

Reich, N. The implementation of Directive 93/13/EEC on unfair terms in consumer contracts in Germany. ERPL, 1997, Vol. 2, p. 165 et seq.

Reich, N. Verbraucherpolitik und Verbraucherschutz im Vertrag von Amsterdam. VuR, 1999, p. 3 et seq.

Reinking, K. Die Beweislast und ihre Umkehr. Deutsches Autorrecht, 2004, No. 9, p. 550 et seq.

Riedler, A. Änderungen des KSchG durch das ZRÄG 2004. RZ, 2003, p. 266 et seq.

Rochette, S. Commentaire sur la décision United European Bank and Trust Nassau Ltd. c. Duchesneau — Le tribunal québécois doit-il examiner le caractère abusif d'une clause d'élection de for incluse dans un contrat d'adhésion?," Droit civil en ligne, Repères, Bulletin de droit civil, Éditions Yvon Blais Inc, 2006.

Roth, H. Beweislastumkehr beim Verbrauchsgüterkauf. Zeitschrift für Wirtschaftsrecht, 2004, No. 43, p. 2025 et seq.

Rott, T. Effektiver Rechtsschutz vor missbräuchlichen AGB. EuZW, 2003, p. 6 et seq.

Rozehnalová, N. et Havlíček, J. Rozhodčí smlouva a rozhodci ve světle některých rozhodnutí... aneb quo vadis...? [Title in translation – Arbitration Agreement and Arbitrators in Light of Several Judgments ... Or Quo Vadis ...?] Právní fórum, 2010, No. 3, p. 114 et seq.

Rozehnalová, N. Určení fóra a jeho význam pro spory s mezinárodním prvkem. [Title in translation: Determination of the Forum and Its Importance for Disputes with an International Dimension]. Bulletin advokacie. 2005, I: No. 4, pp. 16–23 and II: No. 5, pp. 12–16.

Růžička, K. K otázce právní povahy rozhodčího řízení. [Title in translation: Concerning the Legal Nature of Aribitration]. Bulletin advokacie, 2003, No. 5, pp. 32–40.

Růžička, K. Odvolání v rozhodčím řízení? [Title in translation: Appeal in Arbitration?] Právní praxe v podnikání, 2000, No. 4.

Růžička, K. Volba práva. [Title in translation: Choice of law]. Právo a podnikání, 1996, Vol. 5, No. 1, pp. 11-15.

Říhová, K. et Valdhans, J. Judikatura ESD v oblasti evropského justičního prostoru ve věcech civilních, část VIII. [Title in translation: Case Law of the ECJ in the European Judicial Area in Civil Matters, Part VIII]. Právní fórum, 2007, Vol. 4, No. 9, pp. 305-316.

Salač, J. K povaze Evropského práva na ochranu spotřebitele. [Title in translation: Concerning the Nature of European Consumer Protection Law]. Právní rozhledy, Evropské právo, 2000, No. 6.

Salmon, K. T. The Enforcement of Adjudicators' Awards under the Housing Grants Construction and Regeneration Act 1996: Part 26. Arbitration, 2008, Vol. 74, No. 1, pp. 87-94.

Saumier, G. Les objections à la compétence internationale des tribunaux québécois: nature et procédure. R. du B., 1998, Vol. 58, p. 145.

Scottish Law Commission. Scottish Law Commissions' Joint Report: Unfair Terms in Contracts. Scottish Law Commission, 2005, Document No. 199.

Selucká, M. Ochrana spotřebitele v případu Verein für Konsumenteninforrnation v. Karl Heinz Henkel. [Title in translation: Protection of the Consumer in Verein für Konsumenteninforrnation v. Karl Heinz Henkel]. Jurisprudence, 2005, Vol. 14, No. 2, pp. 44-46.

Selucká, M. Ochrana spotřebitele? Nenápadná změna se zásadními dopady. [Title in translation: Consumer Protection? An Inconspicuous Amendment with Major Implications]. Právní rozhledy, 2010, Vol. 18, No. 14, p. 513 et seq.

Seraglini, Ch. Les parties faibles face à l'arbitrage international: à la recherche de l'équilibre. Gaz. Pal., Cah. de l'arbitrage, 2007, No. 4, p. 5 et seq.

Schmidt, J. P. Schiedsgerichtsbarkeit und Mediation in Deutschland und Braislien – Jahrestagung der Deutsch-Brasilianischen Juristenvereinigung e.V. SchiedsVZ, 2011, pp. 101-104.

Schmitz, P. Schiedsvereinbarungen in der notariellen Praxis. Theinische Notar-Zeitschrift, 2003, No. 12, pp. 591-612

Skýpala, R. Rozhodčí doložky a "jiné problémy ochrany práv slabší strany." [Title in translation: Arbitration Clauses and "Other Problems with the Protection of the Weaker Party's Rights"]. Právní rozhledy, 2011, Vol. 19, No. 11, pp. 49-50.

Slováček, D. Arbitrabilita spotřebitelských sporů. [Title in translation: Arbitrability of Consumer Disputes]. Právní rozhledy, 2011, Vol. 19, No. 10, pp. 364-366.

Slováček, D. Ochrana spotřebitele a rozhodčí doložky. [Title in translation: Consumer Protection and Arbitration Clauses]. Bulletin advokacie, 2009, Nos. 7-8, p. 47 et seq.

Slováček, D. Rozhodčí řízení a směrnice o nepřiměřených podmínkách ve spotřebitelských smlouvách. [Title in translation: Arbitration and the Directive on Unfair Terms in Consumer Contracts]. Právní rozhledy, 2010, Vol. 18, No. 9, pp. 331-334.

Smit, H. May an Arbitration Agreement Calling for Institutional Arbitration be Denied Enforcement Because of the Costs Involved? American Review of International Arbitration, 1997, Vol. 8, p. 167 et seq.

Sokol, T. K aktuálním problémům rozhodčího řízení [Title in translation: Regarding Contemporary Problems in Arbitration]. Právní rádce, 2011, Vol. 19, No. 9, pp. 4-14.[3].

---

[3] Special chapter on the "Resolution of Disputes from Consumer Contracts," see pp. 13-14.

Sorkin, D. E. Judicial Review of ICANN Domain Name Dispute Decisions. Computer & High Tech. Law Journal, 2001, Vol. 18, p. 35 et seq.

Speidel, R. E. Consumer Arbitration of Statutory Claims: Has Predispute (Mandatory) Arbitration Outlived Its Welcome? 40 Ariz. L. Rev., 1998, Vol. 40, p. 106 et seq.

Spindler, G. Internationales Verbraucherschutzrecht im Internet. MMR, 2000, pp. 18–25.

Spitzer, H. EuGH zum Verhältnis zwischen Verbraucherkreditrichtlinie und Haustürgeschäfte-Richtlinie. Ecolex, 2002, p. 398 et seq.

Staudinger, A. Gewinnzusagen aus dem Ausland und die Frage der Zuständigkeitskonzentration im Europäischen Zivilprozessrecht. Zeitschrift für europäisches Privatrecht, 2004, pp. 767-782.

Sternlight, J. Panacea or Corporate Tool?: Debunking the Supreme Court's Preference for Binding Arbitration. Washington University Law Quarterly, 1996, Vol. 74, pp. 637-712.

Sternlight, R. Consumer Arbitration. In: *Brunet, E. et al.* (eds.) Arbitration Law in America: A Critical Assessment, 2006, p. 174 et seq.

Sternlight, R. Is the U.S. Out on a Limb? Comparing the U.S. Approach to Mandatory Consumer and Employment Arbitration to that of the Rest of the World. U. Miami L. Rev., 2002, Vol. 56, p. 831 et seq.

Stuyck, J. European Consumer Law after the Treaty of Amsterdam: Consumer Policy in or Beyond the Internal Market. CMLR, 2000, p. 357 et seq.

Svoboda, K. Pohled české soudní praxe na rozhodčí nález týkající se práv ze spotřebitelské smlouvy. [Title in translation: Arbitral Awards Concerning Rights from Consumer Contracts from the Perspective of Czech Judicial Practice]. Obchodní právo, 2010, Vol. 19, No. 11, pp. 2-7.

Šmehlíková, R. Princip rovnosti a ochrany slabšího v současné právní úpravě čs. civilního procesu. [Title in translation: The Principle of Equality and Protection of the Weaker Party in the Contemporary Czech Law of Civil Procedure]. Právní fórum, 2005, No. 3, p. 113 et seq.

Talpis, J. A. et Goldstein, G. Analyse critique de l'avant-projet de loi du Québec en droit international privé," R. du N., 1989, Vol. 91, p. 456 et seq.

Talpis, J. A. et Goldstein, G. Analyse critique de l'avant-projet de loi du Québec en droit international privé. R. du N., 1988, Vol. 91, p. 606 et seq.

Talpis, J. A. Choice of Law and Forum Selection Clauses under the New Civil Code of Quebec. R. du N., 1994, Vol. 96, p. 183 et seq.

Tamm, M. Das Grünbuchder Kommission zum Verbraucher-Acquis und das Modell der Vollharmonisierung – eine kritische Analyse. Europäische Zeitschrift für Wirtschaftsrecht, 2007, p. 756 et seq.

Taylor, S. The Harmonisation of European Product Liability Rules: French and English Law. ICLQ, 1999, Vol. 48, No. 2, pp. 419–430.

Tenreiro, M. Les clauses abusives dans les contrats avec les consommateurs (Directive no 903/13//CEE du Conseil du 5 avril 1993). Europe, 1993, No. 5, pp. 1-4.

Thuilleaux, S. et Proctor, D. M. L'application des conventions d'arbitrage au Canada: une difficile coexistence entre les compétences judiciaire et arbitrale. McGill L. J. 1992, Vol. 37, p. 470 et seq.

Tomášek, M. Princip minimální harmonizace při transpozici směrnic v oblasti ochrany spotřebitele. [Title in translation: Principle of Minimum Harmonization in the Transposition of Consumer Protection Directives]. Právní fórum, 2004, Vol. 1, No. 1, pp. 14-19.

Tomsa, M. K problematice právní úpravy rozhodčího řízení. [Title in translation: Regarding Arbitration Laws]. Obchodněprávní revue, 2011, Vol. 3, No. 9, pp. 267-270.

Tomsa, M. Nepřiměřenost rozhodčí doložky ve spotřebitelských smlouvách. [Title in translation: Unfairness of Arbitration Clauses in Consumer Contracts]. Obchodní právo, 2011, Vol. 20, No. 6, pp. 2-8.

Trapl, V. K otázce zřizování stálých rozhodčích soudů [Title in translation: Regarding the Issue of the Formation of Permanent Arbitral Institutions], Právní praxe v podnikání, 1999, Vol. 8, No. 7, p. 19

Trejo, R. C. et Vestweber, U. Time-Sharing in Spanien. RIW, 1999, p. 516 et seq.

Tremblay, R. La nature du différend et la fonction de l'arbitre consensuel. R. du N., 1988, Vol. 91, p. 246 et seq.

Tröder, J. Die Einbeziehung von Schiedsabreden in notarielle Urkunden. Mitteilungen der Rheinischen Notarkammer, 2000, pp. 379-383.

Uda, G. M. Integrazione del contratto, solidarietà sociale e corrispettività delle prestazioni. Rivista del diritto commerciale, 1990, p. 301 et seq.

Ulmer, P. Zur Anpassung des AGB-Gesetzes an die EG-Richtlinie über mißbräuchliche Klauseln in Verbraucherverträgen. EuZW, 1993, pp. 337-347.

Unberath, H. et Johnston, A. The double-headed approach of the ECJ concerning consumer protection. CMLR, 2007, Vol. 44, No. 5, pp. 1237-1284.

Valdhans, J. Kolizní problematika odpovědnosti za výrobek, nekalosoutěžního jednání a odpovědnosti za výrobek. [Title in translation: Conflict-of-Law

Issues Regarding Liability for Products, Unfair Competition and Liability for Products]. In: Collection of Papers from the VIIIth Annual International Conference Organized by the Faculty of Economics, University of Mining – Technical University Ostrava 2006, Ostrava: University of Mining – Technical University Ostrava, 2006, p. 193 et seq.

Valencia, F. Parties faibles et accès à la justice en matière d'arbitrage. Rev. arb., 2007, p. 45 et seq.

Valoušková, Z. O neplatnosti rozhodčích doložek ve prospěch soukromých rozhodčích soudů. [Title in translation: Regarding the Invalidity of Arbitration Clauses Vesting Jurisdiction in Private Arbitral Tribunals]. Bulletin advokacie, 2010, No. 5, p. 35 et seq.

van den Bergh, R. Wer schützt die europäischen Verbraucher vor dem Brüsseler Verbraucherschutz? Zu den möglichen adversen Effekten der europäischen Richtlinien zum Schutze des Verbrauchers. In: *von Claus, O. et Bernard, N.* Discrimination and Free Movement in EC Law. ICLQ, 1996, Vol. 45, pp. 81-108.

van Vogel, A. Verbraucherprivatrecht im Privatrechtssystem – Zur systematischen Stellung verbrauchervertraglicher Vorschriften im Recht der Europäischen Gemeinschaft und ihrer Mitgliedstaaten. GPR, 2005, No. 4, p. 164 et seq.

Varvařovský, P. Rozhodčí řízení v judikatuře Ústavního soudu. [Title in translation: Arbitration in the Case Law of the Constitutional Court]. Právní fórum, 2010, No. 3, p. 143 et seq.

Vermeys, N. W. Commentaire sur la décision Dell Computer Corporation c. Union des consommateurs — Quand 'browsewrap' rime avec 'arbitrabilité.' Droit civil en ligne, Repères, 2005.

Vlas, P. Supreme Court, 21 June 2002, Spray Network NV (Amsterdam) v. Telenor Venture AS (Oslo, Norway). NJ 2002, 563, p. 118 et seq.

Vojčík, P. Spotrebiteľská zmluva (ochrana spotrebiteľa). [Title in translation: Consumer Contract (Protection of the Consumer)]. Bulletin slovenskej advokácie, 2008, Vol. 14, No. 12, pp. 15-21.

Volmer, M. Klauselkontrolle am Beispiel der MaBV-Bürgschaft. ZflR, 2004, 460-462.

von Hippel, E. Der Schutz des Verbrauchers vor unlauteren Geschäftsbedingungen in den EG-Staaten. RabelsZ, 1977, Vol. 41, pp. 237-280.

von Hoffmann, B. Über den Schutz des Schwächeren bei internationalen Schuldverträgen. RabelsZ, 1974, Vol. 38, pp. 396-420.

von Wilmowsky, P. Der internationale Verbrauchervertrag im EG-Binnenmarkt. ZEuP, 1995, p. 735 et seq.

Waldenberger, A. Grenzen des Verbraucherschutzes beim Abschluß von Verträgen im Internet. BB, 1996, pp. 2365-2371.

Ware, S. J. Arbitration and Unconscionability After Doctor's Associates, Inc. v. Casarotto. Wake Forest L. Rev., 1996, Vol. 31, p. 1001 et seq.

Ware, S. J. Default Rules from Mandatory Rules: Privatizing Law Through Arbitration. Minnesota Law Review, 1999, Vol. 83, p. 703 et seq.

Ware, S. J. The Case for Enforcing Adhesive Arbitration Agreements – with Particular Consideration of Class Actions and Arbitration Fees. J. Am. Arb., 2006, Vol. 5, p. 251 et seq.

Weil, D., Fung, A., Graham, M. et Fagotto, E. The effectiveness of regulatory disclosure policies. Journal of Policy Analysis and Management, 2008, Vol. 25, No. 1, pp. 155-181.

Wicke, H. Anmerkungen zu einem allgemeinen Teil des europäischen Verbrauchervertragsrechts. GPR, 2005, No. 3, p. 106 et seq.

Wiebecke, M. ... und es gibt sie doch – Schiedsgerichtsbarkeit in Finanz- und Kapitalmarkttransaktionen. SchiedsVZ, 2008, pp. 34-39.

Wiesemann, H. P. et Falletti, E. Internet Auctions and Harmonization: A Comparison between Italy and Germany. ERPL, 2006, Vol. 14, No. 1, pp. 3-22.

Wilhelmsson, T. Control of Unfair Contract Terms and Social Values: EC and Nordic Approaches. JConsPol, 1993, pp. 435-453.

Wilhelmsson, T. The implementation of the EC directive on unfair contracts terms in Finland. ERPL, 1997, Vol. 2, p. 151 et seq.

Willet, C. The Directive on Unfair Terms in Consumer Contracts and its Implementation in the United Kingdom. ERPL, 1997, Vol. 2, p. 223 et seq.

Wittwer, A. Verbrauchergerichtsstand für grenzüberschreitende Gewinnzusagen. European Law Reporter, 2002 pp. 393-394.

Wouters, J. Europees en nationaal conflictenrecht en de interne markt voor financiele diensten. In: *de Ly, F. et Zaradkiewicz, K.* Ochrona nabywców timesharing'u w prawie polskim. Edukacja Prawnicza, 2001, No. 1, p. 13.

Zoulík, F. Soukromoprávni ochrana slabší smluvní strany. [Title in translation: Protection of the Weaker Contracting Party in Private Law]. Právní rozhledy, 2002, No. 3, p. 109 et seq.

II.B. Literature closely related to the topic

Ackermann, T. Warenverkehsfreiheit und "Verkaufsmodalitäten." RIW, 1994, pp. 189-194.

Adomeit, K. Das Günstigkeitsprinzip – jetzt auch beim Kaufvertrag. JZ, 2003, No. 21, p. 1054 et seq.

Arnokouros, G. I. The Transposition of the Consumer Sales Directive into the Greek Legal System. ERPL, 2001, Vol. 9, pp. 259-277.

Arnold, A. et Dötsch, W. Verschärfte Verbraucherhaftung beim Widerruf? NJW, 2003, p. 187 et seq.

Arnold, R. Nová směrnice ES o spotřebitelské koupi zboží – nový krok v oblasti ochrany spotřebitele. [Title in translation: The New EC Directive on the Consumer Purchase of Goods – A New Step in Consumer Protection]. Evropské právo, 1999, No. 9, pp. 16-22.

Bales, R. A. The Employment Due Process Protocol at Ten: Twenty Unresolved Issues and a Focus on Conflict of Interest. Ohio St. J. on Disp. Resol., 2005, Vol. 21, p. 165 et seq.

Bandúrová, M. Zájezd jako stěžejní právní pojem v podnikání v cestovním ruchu. [Title in translation: "Tour" as the Crucial Legal Concept for Professionals in Tourism]. Bulletin advokacie, 2008, No. 6, pp. 38-40.

Beale, H. et Howells, G. EC Harmonisation of Consumer Sales Law: A Missed Opportunity? Contract Law Journal, 1997, Vol. 12, pp. 21-46.

Bělohlávek, A. Posuzování právní subjektivity některých druhů zahraničních obchodních společností osobního typu v řízeních před tuzemskými soudy a v jiných řízeních II. [Title in translation: Classification of the Legal Personality of Certain Types of Foreign Personal Corporations in Domestic Court Proceedings and Other Proceedings II]. Soudce, 2007, No. 9, pp. 18-23.

Bernreuther, F. Der Ort der Rechtsdurchsetzung des Herkunftlandsrechtes nach Art. 3 Abs. 2 EC-RiL und das Grundgesetz. WRP, 2001, pp. 513–525.

Bridwell, P. The Philosophical Dimensions of the Doctrine of Unconscionability. The University of Chicago Law Review, 2003, Vol. 70, No. 4, pp. 1513-1531.

Brzobohatý, T. Povaha cenných papírů jako předmětu soukromoprávního vztahu. [Title in translation: The Nature of Securities as the Subject of Private-Law Relationships]. Právní praxe v podnikání, 1998, No. 7, p. 51 et seq.

Buchberger, D. Die Entscheidung des EuGH in der Rs „Océano/Quintero." ÖJZ, 2001, p. 128 et seq.

Calvo, R. L'attuazione della direttiva n° 44 del 1999: una chance per la revisione in senso unitario della disciplina sulle garanzie e i rimedi nella vendita. Contratto e impresa-Europa, 2000, p. 463 et seq.

Canada-Bartoli, L. A propos de l'art. 6.2 de la directive. ERPL, 1995, p. 347 et seq.

Ciatti, A. L'ambito di applicazione della direttiva comunitaria sulla vendita e le garanzie dei beni di consumo. Contratto e impresa-Europa, 2000, p. 433 et seq.

Clausnitzer, J. et Woopen, H. Internationale Vertragsgestaltung – Die neue EG – Verordnung für grenzüberschreitende Verträge (Verordnung). BB, 2008, p. 1798 et seq.

Colvin, A. J. S. An Empirical Study of Employment Arbitration: Case Outcomes and Processes. J. Empirical Legal Stud., 2011, Vol. 8, p. 1 et seq.

Crépeau, P.-A. Une certaine conception de la recodification. In: Du Code civil du Québec: Contribution à l'histoire immédiate d'une recodification réussie. Montréal: Thémis, 2005, p. 23 et seq.

Cromwell, T. A. Aspects of Constitutional Judicial Review in Canada. S.C. L. Rev., 1995, Vol. 46, p. 1027 et seq.

De Nova, G. La ricezione della Direttiva sulle garanzie nella vendita di beni di consumo. Riv. dir. priv., 2001, p. 759 et seq.

Di Majo, A. Garanzia e inadempimento nella vendita di beni di consumo. Europa e diritto privato, 2001, p. 4 et seq.

Eilmannsberger, T. Zur Direktwirkung von Richtlinien über Private. JBl, 2004, No. 5, p. 283 et seq.

Emanuele, C. F. Sui contratti conclusi dai consumatori nella Convenzione di Roma del 1980 sulla legge applicabile alle obbligazioni contrattuali. Giust. civ., 1996, No. 2, p. 19 et seq.

Ferrante, E. L'attuazione della direttiva comunitaria sulle garanzie nelle vendite di beni di consumo: la legge austriaca e il progetto tedesco. Contratto e impresa-Europa, 2001, p. 423 et seq.

Feuchtmeyer, E. EuGH in Sachen Gabriel und weiter? Neues zur gerichtlichen Zuständigkeit bei § 661 a BGB. NJW, 2002, pp. 3598-3599.

Fiala, J. Důsledky zákona č. 136/2002 Sb. pro určení odpovědnosti za vady věci při prodeji v obchodě. [Title in translation: The Consequences of Act No. 136/2002 Coll. for the Determination of Liability for Defective Retail Products]. Právní zpravodaj, 2003, No. 1, p. 4 et seq.

Franzen, M. "Heininger" und die Folgen: Ein Lehrstück zum Gemeinschaftsprivatrecht. JZ, 2003, p. 321 et seq.

Gallo, P. Le garanzie nella vendita di beni di consumo. Prospettive di riformaalla luce della direttiva 1999/44/CE. Contratto e impresa-Europa, 2001, p. 78 et seq.

García Gutiérrez, L. Rudolf Gabriel. Revista española de Derecho Internacional, 2002, pp. 871-876 Notes on the ECJ ruling in C-96/00).

Garcimartin Alférez, F. J. The Rome I Regulation: Exceptions to the Rule in Consumer Contracts and Financial Instruments. Journal of Private International Law, 2009, Vol. 5, No. 1, pp. 85-104.

Gaudemet-Tallon, H. Note to the case *Bruno v Soc. Citibank*, Ct. App. Versailles, 1991. Rev. crit. dr. int. priv., 1992, p. 333 et seq.

Gautier, P.-Y. Les aspects internationaux de Internet. Travaux du comité français de droit international privé, 1997, p. 245.

Glenn, H. P. Droit international privé. In: La réforme du Code civil, t. 3, Priorités et hypothèques, preuve et prescription, publicité des droits, droit international privé, dispositions transitoires. Textes réunis par le Barreau du Québec et la Chambre des notaires du Québec. Sainte-Foy, Qué.: Presses de l'Université Laval, 1993, p. 669 et seq.

Gołaczyński, J. Przeniesienie własności nieruchomości na zabezpieczenie. Rejent, 1994, No. 5, pp. 38-53.

Gołaczyński, J. Timesharing-zagadnienia kolizyjnoprawne. Rejent, 2001, Nos. 7-8, pp. 60-81.

Gołaczyński, J. Wzorce i niedozwolone klauzule umowne w praktyce bankowej po wejściu w życie ustawy z dnia 2 marca 2000r. o ochronie niektórych praw konsumentów oraz odpowiedzialności za szkodę wyrządzona przez produkt niebezpieczny. Przegląd Sądowy, 2001, Nos. 11-12, pp. 78-93.

Gołaczyński, J. Zasada państwa pochodzenia w prawie handlu elektronicznego. Prawo Teleinformatyczne, 2007, No. 1.

Grether, D. M., Schwarz, A. et Wilde, L. The Irrelevance of Information Overload: An Analysis of Search and Disclosure. Southern California Law Review, 1986, Vol. 59, pp. 277-303.

Guillemard, S. et Prujiner, A. La codification internationale du droit international privé: un échec? C. de D., 2005, Vol. 46, p. 175 et seq.

Harding, M. M. The Limits of Due Process Protocols. Ohio St. J. of Disp. Resol., 2004, Vol. 19, p. 369 et seq.

Hill, J. Choice of Law in Contract under the Rome Convention: The Approach of the UK Courts. ICLQ, 2004, Vol. 53, p. 325 et seq.

Holub, M. Time-Sharing podle českého práva, aneb zase jedna harmonizace – několik poznámek. [Title in translation: Time-Sharing under Czech Law,

Yet Another Harmonization – A Few Notes]. Bulletin advokacie, 2003, Nos. 11 – 12, p. 67 et seq.

Hradilová, V. Problematika pravomoci soudů v americké doktríně mezinárodního práva soukromého. [Title in translation: Jurisdiction of Courts under the U.S. Conflict of Laws Doctrine]. Jurisprudence, 2007, No. 2, pp. 41-43.

Hülle, T. Directive 2005/29/EC and its Meaning for Current Protection Against Unfair Competition in the European Union. Biuletyn Wydziału prawa, 2007, No. 12.

Husták, Z. Investiční služby – veřejnoprávní a soukromoprávní sankce. [Title in translation: Investment Services – Sanctions under Public Law and Private Law]. In: Dny práva 2009 [2009 Days of Law], p. 1411 et seq.

IA. Cross-Border Contracts: Rome I Consultation – Consumer law issues. Consumer Law Today, 2008, No. 5, pp. 8-12.

Idot, L. Consommateurs. Europe 2002 Octobre Comm. n° 353, 2002, p. 28 et seq.

Idot, L. Rudolf Gabriel: Consommateurs. Europe 2002 Octobre Comm. n° 353, s. 28 et seq. (Notes on the ECJ ruling in C-96/00).

Jordans, R. et Felke, K. Der Referentenentwurf für die Umsetzung der Fernabsatzrichtlinie für Finanzdienstleistungen. WM, 2004, p. 166 et seq.

Jordans, R. et Felke, K. Internationalrechtliche Fragen von Gewinnzusagen. IPRax, 2004, p. 409 et seq.

Jordans, R. et Felke, K. The Implementation of the EU Directive concerning the distance marketing of consumer financial services in Germany and the United Kingdom. JIBLR, 2004, Vol. 19, No. 5, p. 188 et seq.

Jordans, R. Recent ECJ decisions on "doorstep deal" cancellation rights: A comment from a German perspective. Butterworth's Journal of International Banking and Financial Law, 2006, p. 75 et seq.

Jordans, R. Zur rechtlichen Einordnung von Gewinnzusagen. IPRax, 2006, s. 602 et seq. (And a commentary on the Judgment of the BGH, Case No. III ZR 191/03 of 1 December 2005).

Jud B. Neue Dimensionen privatautonomer Rechtswahl: die Wahl nichtstaatlichen Rechts im Entwurf der Rom I.-Verordnung. JBL, 2006, p. 695 et seq.

Juenger, F., K. Parteiautonomie und objektive Anknüpfung im EG-Übereinkommen zum Internationalen Vertragsrecht. Eine Kritik aus amerikanischer Sicht. RabelsZ, 1982, p. 57 et seq.

Kanda, A. Nové trendy ve vývoji smluvního práva v oblasti soukromého práva. [Title in translation: New Trends in the Development of Contract Law within the Domain of Private Law]. Právník, 2003, No. 7, pp. 649-664.

Karsten, T. Verbraucherschutz bei Verträgen im Fernabsatz. IPRax, 1999, pp. 1-9.

Kawecka-Pysz, J. Kolizyjnoprawne aspekty nabywania nieruchomości położonych w Polsce przez cudzoziemców. Rejent, 1999, No. 20, p. 106 et seq.

Kincl, M. Spotřebitelské smlouvy. [Title in translation: Consumer Contracts]. Daňová a hospodářská kartotéka (DHK), 2003, No. 11, p. 95 et seq.

Kocher, E. Informationspflichten des europäischen Verbrauchervertragsrechts in der deutschen Rechtsgeschäftslehre: What you see is what you get? Zeitschrift für Europäisches Privatrecht, 2006, No. 4, pp. 785-806.

Kopp, S. et Kemp, E. Consumer Awareness of the Legal Obligations of Funeral Providers. Journal of Consumer Affairs, 2008, Vol. 41, No. 2, pp. 326-340.

Krebber, S. Die volle Wirksamkeit von Richtlinien in länderübergreifenden Sachverhalten. ZVglRWiss, 1998, p. 97 et seq.

Kronman, A. T. Mistake, Disclosure and the Law of Contracts. Journal of Legal Studies, 1978, Vol. 7, p. 1 et seq.

Kučera, Z. K výkladu vůle stran při sjednávání rozhodčí doložky. [Title in translation: Concerning the Interpretation of the Parties' Will in Negotiating an Arbitration Clause]. Právní zpravodaj, 1962, No. 6.

Loos, M. B. M. The Influence of European Consumer Law on General Contract Law and the Need for Spontaneous Harmonization. European Review of Private Law, 2007, No. 3, pp. 515-531.

Lopez-Tarruella Martinez, A. International consumer contracts in the new Rome I Regulation: How much does the regulation change? European Journal of Consumer Law, 2007-2008, No. 3, p. 348 et seq.

Lorenz, E. Die Rechtswahlfreiheit im internationalen Schuldvertragsrecht. RIW, 1987, p. 569 et seq.

Lorenz, S. Sachmangel und Beweislastumkehr im Verbrauchs-güterkauf – Zur Reichweite der Vermutungsregelung in § 476 BGB. NJWft, 2004, No. 42, p. 3020 et seq.

Ludovic, M. et Gonzales, A. Lamy Un point sur les règles applicables à l'Internet et au commerce en ligne. Lamy Droit de l'informatique, 1999, pp. 6-15.

Luminoso, M. Riparazione e sostituzione della cosa e garanzia per vizi nella vendita dal codice civile alla direttiva 1999/44/CE. Contratto e impresa-Europa, 2001, p. 842 et seq.

Mankowski, P. Art. 5 des Vorschlags fur eine Rom I-Verordnung – Revolution im Internationalen Verbrauchervertragsrecht? ZVglRWiss, 2006, Vol. 105, No. 2, pp. 120-163.

Mankowski, P. Rudolf Gabriel: Entscheidungen zum Wirtschaftsrecht, 2002, pp. 873-874. (Notes on the ECJ ruling in C-96/00).

Marek, K. Smlouva o úvěru. [Title in translation: Credit Contract]. Časopis pro pravní vědu a praxi, 2006, No. 1, pp. 53-58.

Mark, W. et Weidemaier, C. The Arbitration Clause in Context: How Contract Terms Do (and Do Not) Define the Process. Creighton L. Rev., 2007, Vol. 40, p. 655 et seq.

Mates, P. Úprava odpovědnosti v zákoně o ochraně spotřebitele. [Title in translation: Liability Rules in the Consumer Protection Act]. Obchodní právo, 1995, No. 10, p. 12 et seq.

Mayer, P. Actualité du contrat international. Les Petites Affiches, 2000, pp. 55-61.

Meinhof, A. Neuerungen im modernisierten Verbrauchervertragsrechtdurch OLG-Vertretungsänderungsgesetz – Heininger und die Folgen. NJW, 2002, p. 2373 et seq.

Melzer, F. K diskuzi o úpravě ochrany spotřebitele ve vládním návrhu občanského zákoníku. [Title in translation: Concerning the Discussion about Consumer Protection in the New Civil Code (Cabinet Bill)]. Právní rozhledy, 2009, No. 21, pp. 771-776.

Micklitz, H. W. Verbraucherschutz in den Grundregeln des Europäischen Vertragsrechts. ZVrglRWiss, 2004, Vol. 103, No. 1, pp. 88-102.

Morse, C. G. J. Consumer Contracts, Employment Contracts and the Rome Convention. ICLQ, 1992, Vol. 41, No. 1, p. 21 et seq.

Pelikánová, I. Podnikatel a podnikání podle obchodního zákoníku. [Title in translation: Businessmen and Business under the Commercial Code]. Právo a podnikání, 1994, No. 3, p. 15 et seq.

Polčák, R. Nekalá soutěž na internetu. [Title in translation: Unfair Competition on the Internet]. Obchodní právo, 2005, No. 5, pp. 2-8.

Polčák, R. Nekalá soutežní agrese na internetu. [Title in translation: Unfair Competitive Aggression on the Internet]. Právní rozhledy, 2005, No. 13, pp. 473-477.

Quaisser, W. Východní rozšíření Evropské unie: důsledky pro blahobyt a zaměstnanost v Evropě. [Title in translation: Eastern Enlargement of the European Union: Consequences for Prosperity and the Employment Rate in Europe]. Mezinárodní vztahy, 2000, Vol. 35, No. 3, pp. 59-66.

Racine, J.-B. Cour de cassation, 1re, ch. civ of 19 October 1999. JDI, 2000, pp. 329-341.

Riefa, C. Article 5 of the Rome Convention on the Law Applicable to Contractual Obligations of 19 June 1980 and consumer e-contracts: The need for reform. I&CTL, 2004, Vol. 13, No. 1, pp. 59-73.

Romy, I. Le "for du consommateur" et les contrats de services financiers à la limière de la jurisprudence récente du Tribunal fédéral. SZZP, 2009, Vol. 5, No. 3, pp. 317-332.

Rossbach, O. et Merkt, H. Das "Übereinkommen über das auf bestimmte Rechte in Bezug auf bei einem Zwischenverwahrer sammelverwahrte Effekten anzuwendende Recht" der Haager Konferenz für Internationales Privatrecht. ZVglRWiss, 2003, Vol. 102, No. 1, pp. 33-52.

Rüssel, U. Das Gesetz zur Förderung der außergerichtlichen Streitbeilegung – der Weg zu einer neuen Streitkultur? NJW, 2000, pp. 2800-2802.

Salač, J. K aktuálním otázkám volby práva ve smlouvách v mezinárodním obchodním styku. [Title in translation: Concerning Current Issues Relating to the Choice of Law in Contracts Negotiated in International Commerce]. Právní rozhledy, Annex: Evropské právo, 2003, No. 5, p. 1 et seq.

Selucká, M. In: *Eliáš, K.* (ed.) Občanský zákoník. Velký akademický komentář. [Title in translation: Civil Code. Grand Academic Commentary]. Vol. 1, Prague: Linde, 2008, pp. 300-321.

Selucká, M. Smlouva o poskytování přepravních služeb a její chápání v rámci Směrnice 9717/ES. [Title in translation: Contract of Carriage and the Interpretation Thereof under Directive 9717/EC]. Jurisprudence, 2006, Vol. 15, No. 1, pp. 44-48.

Schindler, S. Der Verbrauchsgüterkauf. Juristische Arbeitsblätter, 2004, No. 11, p. 837 et seq.

Schinkels, B. Zu den Auswirkungen des Vollharmonisierungskonzepts der Richtlinie über den Fernabsatz von Finanzdienstleistungen auf nationale Umsetzungsspielräume. GPR, 2005, No. 3, p. 109 et seq.

Sonnenberger, H. J. Das französische Recht der Allgemeinen Geschäftsbedingungen (conditions générales). RIW, 1990, pp. 165-174.

Staudinger, A. Rom, Brüssel, Berlin und Amsterdam – Chiffren eines Europäischen Kollisionsrechts für Verbraucherverträge. ZfRV, 2000, pp. 93-105.

Steyn, Lord, J. Contract Law: Fulfilling the Reasonable Expectations of Honest Men. LQR, 1997, Vol. 113, p. 433 et seq.

Stuyck, J. et Wytinck, P. Comment on Case C-106/89 Marleasing. CMLR, 1991, No. 28.

Tillman, C. The Relationship between Party Autonomy and the Mandatory Rules in the Rome Convention. JBL, 2002, p. 45 et seq.

Verkuil, P.,R. Privatizing Due Process. Admin. L. Rev., 2005, Vol. 57, p. 963 et seq.

von Hein, J. Günstigkeitsprinzip oder Rosinentheorie? Erwiderung auf Lorenz, NJW, 1999, 2215. NJW, 1999, p. 3174 et seq.

Wagner, R. Neue kollisionsrechtliche Vorschriften für Beförderungsverträge in der Rom I – Verordnung. Transportrecht, 2008, Vol. 31, No. 6, pp. 221- 224.

Whitford, W. The Function of Disclosure Regulation in Consumer Transactions. Wisconsin Law Review, 1973, Vol. 68, pp. 400-470.

Wilderspin, M. Rudolf Gabriel. Revue européenne de droit de la consommation, 2004, pp. 63-66 (Notes on the ECJ ruling in C-96/00).

Zerres, T. et Twigg-Flesner, Ch. Bedeutung und Funktion des Art. 6 VerbrKfRL und Verbrauchergarantien – eine rechtsvergleichende theoriegeleitete Betrachtung. ZVglRWiss, 2006, Vol. 105, No. 1, pp. 19-54.

III. Literature Available Online[4]

Alderman, R. M. Pre-dispute mandatory arbitration in consumer contracts: A call for reform.[5]

Arnaudo, L. L'abuso di informazioni nel gruppo creditizio. Electronic Law Journal, 1996, Vol. 2, Ref. No. of the article in the volume: 2.[6]

Bělohlávek, A. Evropský exekuční titul. [Title in translation: European Enforcement Order]. Právní rádce.[7]

Bělohlávek, A. Rozhodčí řízení a komunitární právo. [Title in translation: Arbitration and Community Law].[8]

Bruni, A. Mediation in Italy. Part. I, 2011.[9]

Collins, B. S. J. Report on the practical implementation of Directive 93/13/EEC in the United Kingdom and Ireland.[10]

---

[4] Irrespective of the language or the place of issue.
[5] Available online at: http://www.houstonlawreview.org/archive/downloads/38-4_pdf/HLR38P1237.pdf [last access 7 November 2011].
[6] Available online at: http://www.jus.unitn.it/cardozo/Review/home.html [last access 20 February 2009].
[7] Available online at: http://pravniradce.ihned.cz/c4-10078260-18321110-F00000_d-evropsky-exekucni-titul [last access 5 September 2008].
[8] Available online at: http://ipravnik.cz/proces/rozhodci021204.thml.
[9] Available online at: http://www.mediate.com/articles/BruniA1.cfm [last access 9 January 2012].
[10] Available online at: http://ec.europa.eu/consumers/cons_int/safe_shop/unf_cont_terms/event 29_03.pdf [last access 7 September 2007].

COTIF 7 CIM 1999 – Übereinkommen über den internationalen Eisenbahnverkehr vom 9. Mai 1980 in der Fassung des Änderungsprotokolls vom 3. Juni 1999.[11]

Davis, E. et Millar, S. United Kingdom: Recent Developments in Finance Litigation: Bank Charges. Mondaq, 6 August 2008.[12]

Drahozal, Chr. R. et Zyontz, S. Private Regulation of Consumer Arbitration, University of Kansas School of Law Working Paper No. 2011-4, 3 August 2011.[13]

Dyer, P. Report on the practical implementation of Directive 93/13/EEC in Sweden.[14]

Elgr, M. Kdy je podnikatel spotřebitelem? [Title in translation: When is the Professional in the Position of Consumer?][15]

European Consumer Centre of Estonia Alternative Dispute Resolution.[16]

Fernandez, P. Notion de consommateru: une précision intéressante.[17]

Fisher, D. Supreme Court Stuffs Challenge To Consumer Arbitration. Forbes, 27 April 2011.[18]

Friedman, D. J., Markley, J. E., Locke, A. A. et Holm, K. J. United States: Supreme Court Holds that Consumer Arbitration Agreements Can Bar Class Action Relief. Mondaq, 5 May 2011.[19]

Gillies, L. A Review of the New Jurisdiction Rules for Electronic Consumer Contracts within the European Union. The Journal of Information, Law and Technology, 2001, No. 1.[20]

---

[11] Available online at: http://cit-rail.org/de/home.html.
[12] Available online at: http://www.mondaq.com/article.asp?articleid=64464 [last access 6 September 2008].
[13] Available online at: http://ssrn.com/abstract=1904545 [last access 27 December 2011].
[14] Available online at: http://ec.europa.eu/consumers/cons_int/safe_shop/unf_cont_terms/event 29_03.pdf [last access 7 September 2007].
[15] Available online at: http://business.center.cz/ business/pravo/ochrana_spotrebitele/podnikatel_spotrebitelem.aspx [last access 2 December 2007].
[16] Available online at the website of ECC of Estonia at: http://www.consumer.ee/alternative-dispute-resolution-2/ [last access 9 January 2012].
[17] Available online at: http://www.legipme.com/actualite/droit-commercial-economique/notion-consommateur.html [last access 31 May 2009].
[18] Available online at: http://www.forbes.com/sites/danielfisher/2011/04/27/supreme-court-stuffs-challenge-to-consumer-arbitration/ [last access 27 December 2011]. Concerns, inter alia, the decision in Concepcion v. AT&T, annotated in this book.
[19] Available online at: http://www.mondaq.com/unitedstates/x/131316/Arbitration+Dispute+Resolution/Supreme+Court+Holds+That+Consumer+Arbitration+Agreements+Can+Bar+Class+Action+Relief [last access 27 December 2011].
[20] Available online at: http://elj.warwicick.ac.uk/jilt/01-1/gillies.html.

Guillemard, S. Liberté contractuelle et rattachement juridictionnel: le droit québécois face aux droits français et européen. E.J.C.L., vol. 8., 2 June 2004.[21]

Gutiérrez de Cabiedes, H. P. Group Litigation in Spain.[22]

Hamre, C. Class Actions, Group Litigation & Other Forms of Collective Litigation in the Norwegian Courts.[23]

Havlíček, J. Ochrana spotřebitele v rozhodčím řízení. [Title in translation: Consumer Protection in Arbitration].[24]

Henkel, A. Inhaltskontrolle von Finanzprodukten nach der Richtlinie 93/13/EWG des Rates über mißbräuchliche Klauseln in Verbraucherverträgen, Juristische Reihe Tenea, Vol. 76, Berlin: Tenea Verlag für Medien, 2004.[25]

Hondius, E. et Mom, A. Die Durchsetzung von Verbraucherrechten in den Niederlanden: Zwischen alternativer Konfliktlösung, Verbandsklage und „Polder-class-action."[26]

Hörnle, J. Legal controls on the use of arbitration clauses in B2C e-commerce contracts. Masaryk University Journal of Law & Technology, 2008, Vol. 2, No. 23, p. 29 et seq.[27]

Horváth, E. Neprijateľná rozhodcovská doložka [Title in translation: Unfair Arbitration Clause], najpravo.sk, 24 March 2011.[28]

Hülle, T. Co nového nám přináší směrnice 2005/29/ES o nekalých obchodních praktikách vůči spotřebitelům na vnitřním trhu do úpravy nekalé soutěže v ČR? [Title in translation: Novelties Introduced into Czech Unfair Competition Law by Directive 2005/29/EC Concerning Unfair Business-to-Consumer Commercial Practices in the Internal Market]. iPrávník, 28 May 2008.[29]

---

[21] Available online at: http://www.ejcl.org/82/abs82-1.html [last access 12 September 2007].

[22] Available online at: http://www.law.stanford.edu/display/images/dynamic/events_media/spain_national_report.pdf [last access 29 November 2011].

[23] Available online at: http://www.law.stanford.edu/display/images/dynamic/events_media/Norway_National_Report.pdf [last access 29 November 2011].

[24] Available online at: http://www.pravnik.cz/a/300/ochrana-spotrebitele-v-rozhodcim-rizeni.html

[25] Available online at: www.jurawelt.com/sunrise/media/mediafiles/13769/tenea_juraweltbd76_henkel.pdf [last access 31 December 2008].

[26] Available online at: http://www.bmelv-.de/cln_044/nn_749972/SharedDocs/downloads/02-Verbraucherschutz/Markt/Verbraucherrechtstage/24-Hondius-Mom.html__nnn=true [last access 29 November 2011].

[27] Also available online at: http://mujlt.law.muni.cz/storage/1234798613_sb_03_hornle.pdf [last access 14 August 2011].

[28] Available online at: http://www.najpravo.sk/judikatura/obcianske-pravo/spotrebitelske-zmluvy/neprijatelna-rozhodcovska-dolozka.html?print=1 [last access 2 January 2012].

[29] Available online at: http://www.ipravnik.cz [last access 31 December 2008].

IA. 2010 International Arbitration Survey: Choices in International Arbitration. Queen Mary University of London / School of International Arbitration.[30]

IA. Consumer welfare, innovation and competition, Innsbruck, 2009.[31]

IA. Commission of the EC, Bericht der Kommission über die Anwendung der Richtlinie 93/13/EWG des Rates vom 5. April 1993 über Missbräuchliche Klauseln in Verbraucherverträgen, Luxemburg: Amt für Amtliche Veröffentlichug der EG, 2000.[32]

IA. Commission of the EC, Workshops – Preliminary documents and final reports to Directive 93/13.[33]

IA. Commission of the EC, Study on the application of schemes for out-of-court resolution of consumer disputes in the individual EU Member States, including information on additional schemes about which the *Commission* was not informed of, 2009.[34]

IA. MiFID: průvodce spotřebitele – Investování do finančních produktů [Title in translation: Consumers Guide – Investments in Financial Products], Paris: CESR – The Committee of European Securities Regulators, 2008 (February).[35]

IA. Regular Report from the European Commission on the Czech Republic's Progress towards Accession, 2000.[36]

IA. Will consumers benefit from the full harmonization of rules concerning retail financial services? Current Issues in Consumer Law, 2007, No. 6.[37]

Knoblochová, V. Vývoj oblasti ochrany spotřebitele v EU. [Title in translation: The Development of Consumer Protection in the EU].[38]

Kolba, P. Report on the practical implementation of Directive 93/13/EEC in Austria.[39]

---

[30] A study executed with the support of many international corporations and law firms. It follows preceding studies executed in 2006 and 2008. Available at: http://www.arbitrationonline.org/research/2010/index.html [last access 5 August 2011] and elsewhere. Language: English.

[31] Available online at: http://www.linexlegal.com/transit.php?content_id=83208 – 29k (English version; last access 11 April 2009].

[32] Available online at: http://ec.europa.eu/consumers/cons_int/safe_shop/unf_cont_terms/uct03_de.pdf [last access 7 September 2007].

[33] Available online at: http://www.eur-lex.europa.eu.

[34] Available online at: http://ec.europa.eu/consumers/redress_cons/adr_study.pdf [last access 9 January 2012].

[35] Available online at: http://www.cnb.cz/cs/dohled_fin_trh/dohled_kapitalovy_trh/download/MiFID_CZ.pdf [last access 7 May 2009].

[36] Available online at: http://eur-lex.europa.eu [last access 7 September 2007].

[37] Available online at: http://www.kuluttajavirasto.fi/en-GB/040607_eng/ [last access 31 May 2009].

[38] Available online at: http://www.mpo.czlzprava7587.html.

[39] Available online at: http://ec.europa.eu/consumers/cons_int/safe_shop/unf_cont_terms/event29_03.pdf [last access 7 September 2007].

Koroloev, S. Towards the Non-arbitrability of Consumer Disputes in Ukraine.[40]

Kropáček, P. Rozhodnutí soudu v evropském (komunitárním) prostředí. [Title in translation: Court Decisions in the European (Community) Dimension]. Thesis, Law and Legal Science, Faculty of Law MU Brno. This thesis was successfully defended on 10 May 2006.[41]

Kuner, Ch. Legal Obstacles to ADR in European Business-to-Consumer Electronic Commerce.[42]

Langer, D. Arbitration and Consumer Law in Europe and the United States: Convergences and Divergences, Latin American Journal of Mediation and Arbitration, 2002.[43]

Lener, G. La nuova disciplina delle clausole vessatorie nei contratti dei consumatori. Obiter dictum: Electronic Law Journal, 1996, Vol. 2, Ref. No. of the article in the volume: 15.[44]

Líbal, B. 60721. Malé zamyšlení nad použitím rozhodčích doložek. [Title in translation: Short Essay on the Application of Arbitration Clauses]. epravo.cz. 23 March 2010.[45]

Latvia – Consumer Rights Protection Center.[46]

MacQueen, H. L. et Wortley, S. Fairness of Bank Charges: An English Decision. Scots Law News, Edinburgh: The University of Edinburgh / School of Law, 2008.[47]

Maštálka, I. Uzavírání rozhodčí doložky/smlouvy na internetu. [Title in translation: Negotiating Arbitration Clauses/Agreements on the Internet].[48]

Matějka, J. Malá poznámka k první úpravě spotřebitelských smluv, zejména pak k výkladu § 53 odst. 8 ObcZ. [Title in translation: Short Note on the First Rules of Consumer Contracts, Primarily the Interpretation of Section 53(8) of the CivC].[49]

---

[40] Available online at the website of the CIS Arbitration Forum, 2010, at: http://cisarbitration. com/2011/03/06/towards-non-arbitrability-of-consumer-disputes-in-ukraine/#more-426 [last access 11 January 2012].

[41] Available online at: http://is.muni.cz/th/60945/pravf_m/. (Library / Archives – Faculty of Law, Masaryk University in Brno).

[42] Available online at: http://www.kuner.com/data/pay/adr.html.

[43] Available at: http://www.med-arb.net [last access 17 October 2010].

[44] Available online at: http://www.jus.unitn.it/cardozo/Review/home.html. [last access 20 February 2009].

[45] Available online at: http://www.epravo.cz/top/clanky/male-zamysleni-nad-pouzitim-rozhodcich-dolozek-60721.html [last access 26 August 2011].

[46] Website at: http:// www.ptac.gov.lv. The website at: http://www.ptac.gov.lv/page/271 offers an English version of the Latvian Consumer Rights Protection Act [last access 9 January 2012].

[47] Available online at: http://www.law.ed.ac.uk/sln/blogentry.aspx?blogentryref=7483. [last access 6 September 2008].

[48] Available online at: www.itpravo.cz.

[49] Available online at: www.itpravo.cz.

Matějka, J. Většina českých i-shopů porušuje zákon – pro informovaného spotřebitele to ale může být velká výhoda! [Title in translation: Most Czech E-Shops Breach the Law – A Major Advantage for an Informed Consumer!][50]

Micklitz, H. W. Report on the practical implementation of Directive 93/13/EEC in Germany.[51]

Mirone, M. V. Unconscionability and Unfair Terms. Obiter dictum: Electronic Law Journal, 1996, Vol. 2, Ref. No. of the article in the volume: 18.[52]

Montrealer Übereinkommen 1999.[53]

Myšáková, P. Římská úmluva o právu použitelném pro závazky ze smluv (4) – Omezení autonomie vůle stran. [Title in translation: Rome Convention on the Law Applicable to Contractual Obligations (4) – Limitation of the Parties' Autonomy of Will]. E-Polis, online politological journal, Plzeň: AS CPSSU Plzeň, 8 June 2006.[54]

Nemeth, K. et Ortner, H. The Proposal for a New Directive Concerning Credit for Consumers. German Law Journal, 2003, Vol. 4, No. 8.[55]

OFT. OFT's Unfair Contract Terms Guidance, 2001, February.[56]

Palla, T. 55269. Rozhodčí doložky ve spotřebitelských smlouvách – ANO či NE? [Title in translation: Arbitration Clauses in Consumer Contracts – YES or NO?] epravo.cz. 23 October 2008.[57]

Palla, T. 55498. Spotřebitelské úvěry a nová směrnice – záchrana z EU? [Title in translation: Consumer Credits and the New Directive – Rescue from the EU?] epravo.cz. 28 January 2009.[58]

---

[50] Available online at: www.itpravo.cz.

[51] Available online at: http://ec.europa.eu/consumers/cons_int/safe_shop/unf_cont_terms/event29_03.pdf [last access 7 September 2007].

[52] Available online at: http://www.jus.unitn.it/cardozo/Review/home.html [last access 20 February 2009].

[53] Available online at: http://www.luftrecht-online.de/regelwerke/pdf/montreal-D.pdf http://www.icao.int/icao/en/leb/mtl99.pdf Übereinkommen vom 28. Mai 1999 zur Vereinheitlichung bestimmter Vorschriften über die Beförderung im internationalen Luftverkehr (Montrealer Übereinkommen 1999).

[54] Available online at: http://www.e-polis.cz/mezinarodni-pravo/154-rimska-umluva-o-pravu-pouzitelnem-pro-zavazky-ze-smluv-4-omezeni-autonomie-vule-smluvnich-stran.html [last access 1 June 2008].

[55] Available online at: http://www.germanlawjournal.com/article.php?id=300#_edn4. [last access 6 June 2009].

[56] Available online at: http://www.oft.gov.uk/.

[57] Available online at: http://www.epravo.cz/top/clanky/rozhodci-dolozky-ve-spotrebitelskych-smlouvach-ano-ci-ne-55269.html [last access 5 January 2012].

[58] Available online at: http://www.epravo.cz/top/clanky/spotrebitelske-uvery-a-nova-smernice-zachrana-z-eu-55498.html?print [last access 26 August 2011].

Palla, T. 63811. Právnická osoba jako spotřebitel? Už ne. [Title in translation: Legal Person in the Position of Consumer? Not Any More]. epravo.cz. 16 July 2010.[59]

Palla, T. Prostory obvyklé k podnikání dodavatele (ve smyslu § 57 Občanského zákoníku s přihlédnutím ke komunitárnímu původu tohoto pojmu). [Title in translation: Premises Commonly Used for Conducting the Supplier's Business (in Terms of Section 57 of the Civil Code, Considering the Community Origin of the Term)]. Published on ePravo.cz as Document No. 54970.[60]

Palla, T. Zneužívání rozhodčích doložek – stále nevyřešený problém. [Title in translation: Abuse of Arbitration Clauses – An Unresolved Problem].[61]

Pelikán, T. Spotřebitelská smlouva v bankovnictví. [Title in translation: Consumer Contract in Banking].[62]

Pelikán, T. Obecné otázky ochrany spotřebitele. [Title in translation: General Consumer Protection Issues]. *Spotřebitel* [Consumer], 10 February 2004.[63]

Plattner, L. I contratti di distribuzione in Italia, in Italiano e English: Distribution contracts in Italy. Obiter dictum: Electronic Law Journal, 1996, Vol. 2, Ref. No. of the article in the volume: 22.[64]

Polčák, R. et Štědroň, B. K některým otázkám e-kontraktace. [Title in translation: Selected Issues of E-Contracting].[65]

Preininger, M. Implementace evropského spotřebního práva v České republice [Title in translation: The Implementation of European Consumer Protection Law in the Czech Republic].[66]

Pulgram, L. F. United States: U.S. Supreme Court Enforces Class Action Waivers In Consumer Arbitration Agreements. Mondaq, 3 May 2011.[67]

---

[59] Available online at: http://www.epravo.cz/top/clanky/pravnicka-osoba-jako-spotrebitel-uz-ne-63811.html [last access 26 August 2011].

[60] Available online at: http://www.epravo.cz/top/clanky/prostory-obvykle-k-podnikani-dodavatele-ve-smyslu-57-obcanskeho-zakoniku-s-prihlednutim-ke-komunitarnimu-puvodu-tohoto-pojmu-54970.html. [last access 12 January 2008].

[61] Available online at: http://www.epravo.cz/top/clanky/rozhodci-dolozky-ves-spotrebitelskych-smlouvach-ano-ci-ne-55269.html

[62] Available online at: http://www.epravo.cz/top/clanky/spotrebitelska-smlouva-v-bankovnictvi-37494.html#_ftn4 [last access 2 May 2009].

[63] Available online at: http://www.spotrebitel.cz/index.php?option=com_content&view=article&id=101228&catid=78&Itemid=225 [last access 15 May 2011].

[64] Available online at: http://www.jus.unitn.it/cardozo/Review/home.html [last access 20 February 2009; this paper can be accessed at the above-mentioned website in both Italian and English).

[65] Available online at: http://www.itpravo.cz.

[66] Available online at: http://www.kod.ef.jcu.cz/wwwtajcucz/katedra/konference/cdrom05d/prispevky/s2-05-preininger.doc [last access 2 May 2009].

Raban, P. Drobní dlužníci a zakázaná smluvní ujednání. [Title in translation: *Small Debtors and Prohibited Contractual Terms].* Online text. Available online at: http://www.premyslraban.cz/drobni-dluznici.html [last access 10 August 2011].

Regaldo, F. EC Directive on Timesharing: One More Reason to Invest in Italy. Obiter dictum: Electronic Law Journal, 1996, Vol. 2, Ref. No. of the article in the volume: 24.[68]

Reich, N. The Consumer as Citizen – The Citizen as Consumer – Reflections on the Present State of the Theory of Consumer Law in the EU.[69]

Sarles, J. W. Solving the arbitral confidentiality conundrum in international arbitration, 2010.[70]

Schulte-Nölke, H., Twigg-Flessner, C. et Ebers, M. (eds.) EC Consumer Law Compendium.[71]

Schultz, T. Online Arbitration: Binding or Non-binding? ADR Online Monthly (November 2002).[72]

Sousa, A. H. *Class Action, Group Litigation & Other Forms of Collective Litigation.*[73]

Stern, W. L. et McGuire. United States: Consumer Arbitration Update. Mondaq, 21 July 2005.[74]

Šuster, M. Pozor na rozhodčí doložky ve smlouvách o úvěrech. [Title in translation: Beware of Arbitration Clauses in Credit Agreements].[75]

Tager, E. M., Parasharami, Archis, A. et Ranlett, K. S. United States: National Arbitration Forum to Cease Administering Consumer Arbitrations: Many Consumer Arbitration Provisions May Need Revision. Mondaq, 31 July 2009.

---

[67] Available online at: http://www.mondaq.com/unitedstates/x/131064/Arbitration+Dispute+Resolution/US+Supreme+Court+Enforces+Class+Action+Waivers+In+Consumer+Arbitration+Agreements [last access 27 December 2011].

[68] Available online at: http://www.jus.unitn.it/cardozo/Review/home.html [last access 20 February 2009].

[69] Available online at: www.iaclaw.org/Research_papers/melangescalais2ok.pdf [last access 10 May 2009].

[70] Available online at: http://www.appellate.net/articles/Confidentiality.pdf [last access 11 September 2010]. Language: English.

[71] Available online at: http://ec.europa.eu/consumers/cons_int/safe_shop/acquis/comp_analysis_en.pdf.

[72] Available online at: http://www.ombuds.org/center/adr2002-11-schultz.html [last access 13 August 2011].

[73] Available online at: http://www.law.stanford.edu-/display/images/dynamic/events_media/Portugal_National_Report.pdf [last access 29 November 2011].

[74] Available online at: http://www.mondaq.com/unitedstates/article.asp?articleid=33859 [last access 27 December 2011].

[75] Available online at: http://www.penize.cz/18995-pozor-na-rozhodci-dolozky-ve-smlouvach-o-uverech

Tager, E. M., Parasharami, Archis, A. et Ranlett, K. S. United States: Illinois Supreme Court Rules that Arbitrtion Agreement is Unenforceable Because It Selects the National Arbitration Forum, Which No Longer Handles Consumer Arbitrations. Mondaq, 10 February 2011.[76]

Terradas, B. A. Restrictions on Jurisdiction Clauses in Consumer Contracts within the European Union. Oxford University Comparative Law Forum, 2003, No. 1.[77]

Thiry-Duarte, M. O. Report on the practical implementation of Directive 93/13/EEC in France.[78]

Thornthwaite, M. United States: Court Finds Arbitration Clauses Dealing with CROA Disputes are Permissible but Stays Case Pending Supreme Court Review. Mondaq, 16 November 2011.[79]

Tonner, K. et Haupstock, A. Air Passenger Contract: IATA Recommendation 1724 and Standard Terms Control by National Regulations, Paper presented at the 15th IFTTA Conference in Monaco, 6 June 2003.[80]

Traverso / Coppola / Luzatto / Silvestri, E. Consumers' Collective Actions: An Update on Italian Draft Legislation.[81]

Uhlíř, A. Rozhodčí řízení v pracovněprávních vztazích, aneb konec práva na spravedlivý proces. [Title in translation: Arbitration in Employment Relations, the End of the Right to a Fair Trial]. Britské listy [British Papers]. 31 March 2011.[82]

Vitanen, K. Collective Litigation in Finland.[83]

Vitásek, J. Směrnice o právech spotřebitele rozděluje europoslance. [Title in translation: The Consumer's Rights Directive Divides Members of the European Parliament]. Euractiv, 29 June 2010.[84]

Vlasák, M. Pravomoc soudů členských států evropských společenství ve sporech ve věcech občanských a obchodních (dle Nařízení Brusel I). [Title

---

[76] Available online at: http://www.mondaq.com/unitedstates/article.asp?articleid=122638 [last access 27 December 2011].

[77] Available online at: http://ouclf.iuscomp.org/articles/anoveros.shtml.

[78] Available online at: http://ec.europa.eu/consumers/cons_int/safe_shop/unf_cont_terms/event 29_03.pdf [last access 7 September 2007].

[79] Available online at: http://www.mondaq.com/unitedstates/x/153766/Consumer+Credit/Court+Finds+Arbitration+Clauses+Dealing+With+CROA+Disputes+Are+Permissible+But+Stays+Case+Pending+Supreme+Court+Review [last access 27 December 2011].

[80] Available online at: http://www.estig.ipbeja.pt/~ac_direito/Tonner.pdf [last access 25 April 2009].

[81] Available online at: http://www.law.stanford.edu/display/-images/dynamic/events_media/Italian_National_Report_supplementary.pdf [last access 29 November 2011].

[82] Available online at: http://blisty.cz/art/57999.html [last access 26 August 2011].

[83] Available online at; http://www.law.stanford.edu-/display/images/dynamic/events_media/Finland_Legislation.pdf [last access 29 November 2011].

[84] Available online at: http://www.euractiv.cz/evropske-pravo/clanek/smernice-o-pravech-spotrebitele-rozdeluje-europoslance-007670 [last access 5 August 2011]. Language: Czech.

in translation: Jurisdiction of Courts of the Member States of the European Communities in Disputes Relating to Civil and Commercial Matters (pursuant to the Brussels I Regulation)]. Thesis (unpublished), Faculty of Law of the Masaryk University in Brno, Department of International and European Law, school (academic) year 2006/2007. Available in the information system of the archive and library service of the Faculty of Law, MU (CZ). [85]

Warschaer Abkommen 1955 [86] Abkommen zur Vereinheitlichunv von Regeln über die Beförderung im internationalen Luftverkehr in der Fassung des Haager Zusatzprotokolls vom 28. September 1955.

Werlauff, E. Class actions in Denmark – from 2008.[87]

Wright, I. Spotřebitelské smlouvy. [Title in translation: Consumer Contracts].[88]

IV. Master's, Doctoral, and Dissertation Theses as well as Other Qualification, Scientific, and Scientific-Pedagogical Papers

Böhm, B. Verbraucherschutz im internationalen Privatrecht – die Reichweite Art. 29 EGBGB an Hand ausgesuchter Fälle. Dissertation thesis successfully defended at Bayreuth University [DEU], 1993.

Čapková, M. Kolizní norma jako prostředek ochrany spotřebitele. [Title in translation: Conflict-of-Law Rules as the Means of Consumer Protection]. Undergraduate thesis successfully defended at the Faculty of Law of the Masaryk University in Brno, Department of International and European Law, academic year 2005/2006. Available in the information system of the archive and library service of the Faculty of Law, MU.[89]

Kelbl, J. Ochrana spotřebitele z pohledu mezinárodního práva soukromého a procesního. [Title in translation: Consumer Protection from the Perspective of Private and Procedural International Law]. Master's thesis (unpublished), Brno: Faculty of Law of Masaryk University, Department of International and European Law. Successfully defended in the (academic)

---

[85] Available online at: http://is.muni.cz/th/77158/pravf_m/Diplomova_prace.doc [last access 5 September 2008].
[86] Available online at: http://www.luftrecht-online.de/regelwerke/uebersicht-read/aenderungen_warschaer_abkommen.htm.
[87] Available online at: http://www.law.stanford.edu/display/images/dynamic-/events_media/ Denmark_Legislation.pdf [last access 29 November 2011].
[88] Available online at: http://obcanskepravo.juristic.cz/69897/ [last access 2 May 2009].
[89] Available online at: http://is.muni.cz/th/108395/pravf_b/bakalarska_prace_Capkova.pdf?info =1;zpet=%2Fvyhledavani%2F%3Fsearch%3D%C4%8Capkov%C3%A1,%20M.%20Kolizn%C3%AD%20 norma%20jako%20prost%C5%99edek%20ochrany%20spot%C5%99ebitele.%26start%3D1 [last access 29 December 2011].

school year 2007/2008. Available in the information system of the archive and library service of the Faculty of Law, MU.[90]

Müller, R. Orgány ochrany veřejného zájmu (Nejvyšší kontrolní úřad a Úřad pro zastupování státu ve věcech majetkových). [Title in translation: Authorities for the Protection of Public Interest (Supreme Audit Office and Office for Government Representation in Property Affairs)]. Thesis successfully defended at the Department of Administrative Studies, Administrative Law and Financial Law, Faculty of Law, Masaryk University 2009/2010, available in the information system of the archive and library service of the Faculty of Law, MU.[91]

Osička, T. Ochrana spotřebitele při koupi spotřebního zboží (rozbor a srovnání vybraných ustanovení německé a české právní úpravy). [Title in translation: Protection of Consumers in the Purchase of Consumer Goods (Selected Provisions of German and Czech Law Analyzed and Compared)]. Dissertation thesis successfully defended at the Department of Civil Law, Faculty of Law of Masaryk University in Brno on 25 September 2006.

Pavelka, D. Smernica 1999/44/ES a jej implementácia do súkromného práva ČR (ochrana spotrebiteľa). [Title in translation: Directive 1999/44/EC and its Implementation in Czech Private Law (Consumer Protection)]. Thesis successfully defended at the Department of Civil Law, Faculty of Law of Masaryk University in Brno on 10 September 2008. Available in the information system of the archive and library service of the Faculty of Law, MU.[92]

Rozehnal, T. Rozhodčí smlouva jako základ pro založení pravomoci/příslušnosti rozhodců. [Title in translation: Arbitration Agreement as the Basis for the Arbitrators' Jurisdiction]. Thesis successfully defended at the Department of Civil Law, Faculty of Law of Masaryk University in Brno in the academic year 2006/2007.[93]

Tomečková, V. Spotřebitel při obchodech uzavřených mimo provozovnu. [Title in translation: Position of the Consumer in Transactions Negotiated Away from Business Premises]. Thesis successfully defended at the Department of Civil Law, Faculty of Law of Masaryk University in Brno in the academic

---

[90] Available online at: http://is.muni.cz/th/107972/pravf_m?info=1;zpet=%2Fvyhledavani%2F%3F search%3DOchrana%20spot%C5%99ebitele%20z%20pohledu%20mezin%C3%A1rodn%C3%ADho%2 0pr%C3%A1va%20soukrom%C3%A9ho%20a%20procesn%C3%ADho%26start%3D1 [last access 29 December 2011].
[91] Available online at: http://is.muni.cz/th/134899/pravf_m/Diplomova_prace__Roman_Muller.pdf [last access 14 January 2011].
[92] Available online at: http://is.muni.cz/th/107937/pravf_m/diplomova_praca.pdf?info=1;zpet=%2 Fvyhledavani%2F%3Fsearch%3DPavelka,%20D.%20Smernica%201999%2F44%2FES%20a%20jej%20i mplement%C3%A1cia%20do%20s%C3%BAkromn%C3%A9ho%20pr%C3%A1va%20%C4%8CR%26sta rt%3D1 [last access 29 December 2011].
[93] Available online at: http://is.muni.cz/th/61238/pravf_m/diplomova_prace_Tomas_Rozehnal.txt [last access 14 January 2012].

year 2007/2008. Available in the information system of the archive and library service of the Faculty of Law, MU.[94]

Vallová, M. Ochrana spotřebitele: ČR a EU. [Title in translation: Consumer Protection: The Czech Republic and the EU]. Dissertation thesis successfully defended at the Faculty of Law of Masaryk University in Brno, Department of International and European Law, academic year 2006/2007. Available in the information system of the archive and library service of the Faculty of Law, MU.[95]

Vašicová, H. Odpovědnostní vztahy při ochraně spotřebitele. [Title in translation: Liability Relationships in Consumer Protection]. Thesis successfully defended at the Department of Environmental and Land Law, Faculty of Law of Masaryk University in Brno in the academic year 2006/2007. Available in the information system of the archive and library service of the Faculty of Law, MU.[96]

---

[94] Available online at: http://is.muni.cz/th/124225/pravf_m?info=1;zpet=%2Fvyhledavani%2F%3Fs earch%3DTome%C4%8Dkov%C3%A1,%20V.%20Spot%C5%99ebitel%20p%C5%99i%20obchodech%2 0uzav%C5%99en%C3%BDch%20mimo%20provozovnu.%26start%3D1 [last access 29 December 2011].
[95] Available online at: http://is.muni.cz/th/61243/pravf_r?info=1;zpet=%2Fvyhledavani%2F%3F search%3DVallov%C3%A1,%20Mark%C3%A9ta%26start%3D1 [last access 29 December 2011].
[96] Available online at http://is.muni.cz/th/97864/pravf_m/Odpovednostni_vztahy_pri_ochrane_ spotrebitele.pdf?info=1;zpet=%2Fvyhledavani%2F%3Fsearch%3DVa%C5%A1icov%C3%A1,%20H.%2 0Odpov%C4%9Bdnostn%C3%AD%20vztahy%20p%C5%99i%20ochran%C4%9B%20spot%C5%99ebite le.%26start%3D1 [last access 29 December 2011].

INDEX - REGISTERS

I. Introductory Notes to the Index

o Unless explicitly provided otherwise or unless the context indicates otherwise, the singular includes the plural and vice versa. The individual terms are in most cases arranged in the singular. Exceptions are usually justified by terminology, the usual use of the term or similar reasons.

o The individual terms are ordered alphabetically (or alphanumerically).

o Composite terms usually require that the reader look up the main heading (noun) and then the modifying subheadings (adjectives).

o Numbers always refer to paragraphs (paragraphs are numbered on the side).

o Bold paragraph numbers mean that the respective term is analyzed in detail in the relevant segment and, as the case may be, also in the immediately following paragraphs.

II. Keyword Index

III. Table of Cited Rules (Normative Acts and Other Sources)

III.1 Rules of national origin

III.2. Rules of international (other than national) origin, including EU rules and rules of international (supranational) courts

III.3. Internationally applied / recognized rules of other than state (public) origin

IV. Table of References to Decisions Rendered in Arbitration or Litigation (Overview According to Parties, *Fora*, Designation, and Date of Decision)

IV.1. Decisions of national courts and constitutional courts arranged by individual state

IV.2. Table of cases – Decisions rendered by international *fora* (courts, tribunals) arranged by individual institution

ECtHR
(a) According to case number

IV.3.   Decisions arranged by designation of parties (alphabetically)

Travel Vac SL v. Manuel José
   Antelm Sanchis   97
Tree Financial Corp. v. Randolph
                      553, 660
Trinidad Lake Petroleum Co. – see
   United States Asphalt Refining
   Co. v. Trinidad Lake Petroleum
   Co.
Trizec Properties, Inc. v. Superior
   Court   588
Trujillo – see Jose Trujillo et al. v.
   Apple Computer, Inc. et AT&T
   Mobility, LLC
Trustees of Cal. State University &
   Colleges – see Tiernan v.
   Trustees of Cal. State University
   & Colleges
Turco – see Sweden et Maurizio
   Turco v. Council of the EU
Unectef – see Union nationale des
   entraîneurs et cadres techniques
   professionnels du football
   (Unectef) v. Georges Heylens
   et al.
Union des Consommateurs et
   Olivier Dumoulin – see Dell v.
   Union des Consommateurs et
   Olivier Dumoulin
Union nationale des entraîneurs et
   cadres techniques professionnels
   du football (Unectef) v. Georges
   Heylens et al.   36
United Kingdom – see Bryan v.
   United Kingdom
United States Asphalt Refining Co.
   v. Trinidad Lake Petroleum Co.
                         580
V2000 – see Meglio v. V2000
V2000 – see Renault v. V2000
van der Weerd – see J. van der
   Weerd et al., H. de Rooy Sr. et H.
   de Rooy Jr., Maatschap H. et J.
   van 't Oever et al. B. J. van

Middendorp v. Minister van
   Landbouw, Natuur en
   Voedselkwaliteit
van Duyn – see Yvonne van Duyn v.
   Home Office
van Veen – see Jeroen van Schijndel
   et Johannes Nicolaas Cornelis
   van Veen v. Stichting
   Pensioenfonds voor
   Fysiotherapeuten
VB Pénzügyi Lízing Zrt. v. Ferenc
   Schneider   198, 299
Victoria v. Superior Court   584
Vincent Concepcion et al. v. AT&T
   Mobility LLC   603
Volksbank Filder eG. – see Annelore
   Hamilton v. Volksbank Filder eG.
Volt Info. Sciences v. Leland
   Stanford Jr.   584
von Colson – see Sabine von Colson
   et Elisabeth Kamann v. Land
   Nordrhein-Westfalen
Warrior & Gulf Nav. Co – see
   Steelworkers v. Warrior & Gulf
   Nav. Co
Westminster Building Company
   Limited v. Beckingham
                466, 504 et seq., 639
Williams – see ShowMeTheMoney
   v. Williams
Wind SpA – see Rosalba Alassini
   et Filomena Califano v. Wind
   SpA
X v. Austria (dec. Commission)   78
Yvonne van Duyn v. Home Office
                         35 et seq.
Zealander & Zealander v. Laing
   Homes Limited   466, 503, 505
Zellner – see Richard Zellner v.
   Phillip Alexandre Securities and
   Futures Ltd.

V. Table of References to States